ESSENTIALS OF BUSINESS
RESEARCH METHODS

JOSEPH F. HAIR, JR.
Louisiana State University

BARRY BABIN
University of Southern Mississippi

ARTHUR H. MONEY
Henley Management College, U.K.

PHILLIP SAMOUEL
Kingston University, U.K.

WILEY

www.wiley.com/college/hair

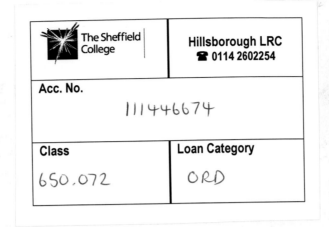
Acquisitions Editor *Jeff Marshall*
Marketing Manager *Charity Robey*
Production Manager *Lari Bishop*
Designer *Shoshanna Turek*
Illustration Editor *Jaye Joseph*
Copy Editor *Karen Thompson*
Indexer *Melody Englund*
Cover Design *Jennifer Fisher*
Cover Images *Globe image and newspaper and glasses image: © Corbis.*
   All other images © PhotoDisc, Inc.

This book was set in Minion and printed and bound by Malloy, Inc. The cover was printed by
The Lehigh Press, Inc.

This book is printed on acid free paper.∞

ISBN 0-471-27136-5

Printed in the United States of America

10 9 8 7 6 5 4 3 2 1

To my loving and supportive wife Dale, and to my son Joe III, and his wife Kerrie.
Joseph F. Hair, Jr.

For my family (living and deceased), especially Amie and James, for providing
support, inspiration, and motivation.
Barry Babin

To my wife Gillian, my children John, Kevin, and Arthur, and to Karen,
my mother; and in memory of my father and brother Stanford.
Arthur H. Money

To my wife Maria, my children Paul, Clare, James, and Irene, and to my mother
and the memory of my late father.
Phillip Samouel

Brief Contents

Contents

Part II
BEGINNING THE RESEARCH PROCESS   47

Chapter 2

■ FUNDAMENTALS OF RESEARCH DESIGN   49

Chapter 8

■ SAMPLING APPROACHES AND CONSIDERATIONS   207

Part IV
DATA ANALYSIS AND PRESENTATION   223

Chapter 9
■ UNDERSTANDING AND PRESENTING DATA   225

Chapter 14

ADVANCED ANALYSIS AND PRESENTATION APPROACHES   391

Preface

Business research in the new millennium presents many challenges for managers. Businesses are challenged to be more decisive and offer higher quality products and services, and they must do so with fewer people at lower costs. This means modern business managers must make more decisions in a shorter period of time, and those decisions must be better. Fortunately, the tools and technologies available to business professionals have expanded dramatically. Computing power, accessibility, and expertise no longer represent significant barriers to processing information. The speed and memory of PC's has been doubling every eighteen months while prices drop. Windows-based and other user-friendly interfaces have brought sophisticated statistical software packages into the "click-and-point" era, greatly reducing the need for specialized computer skills to access electronic data processing capability. Now, even "unsophisticated" users can analyze large quantities of complex data with relative ease. The intelligence that emerges from application of these new tools and technologies contributes to better decision making.

Better business intelligence is essential to better decision making. This book is about making better decisions by using a type of intelligence that only research can create. Research turns mere information into intelligence. This book places minimal emphasis on statistical theory and maximum effort in providing basic skills that cover a wide range of potential business research applications. By doing so, we believe the reader will be better able to cope with the fast-paced decision-making environment that is business today and tomorrow.

MANAGERS NEED BUSINESS RESEARCH SKILLS

Fortunately, the amount of information available to the decision makers has exploded in recent years, and will continue to do so in the future. Until recently, much information just disappeared. It either was not collected or was discarded, often because there was no cost-effective way of keeping it. Today this detailed information is collected and stored in data warehouses, and it is available to be "mined" for improved decision-making. Sometimes the information can be analyzed and understood with simple statistics. Other times turning it into business intelligence requires more complex tools. In this book, we cover both the simple and the more complex tools in an easy to understand manner. Managers and entrepreneurs who lack business research knowledge and resources simply cannot benefit from the intelligence emerging from this expanded database of information.

Most business research texts are quite long and take an encyclopedic approach. This book covers all important topics in a concise manner and focuses on the essentials of business research for managers. It includes coverage of the increasing role of knowledge management, as well as how to conduct information-gathering activities more effectively in a rapidly changing business environment. The fundamentals of business research, such as research design, sampling, and measurement and scaling, are presented in a highly readable format. Illustrations are used in conjunction with many practical examples to highlight significant points.

A "Research in Action" feature provides applied examples of real research problems and current issues throughout all chapters. Some Research in Action examples summarize actual research studies, such as focus group results for Chrysler's PT Cruiser and the Gallup Organization's survey covering the twelve dimensions of a great workplace. Others describe Web sites that help you to design better survey questionnaires or provide an overview of secondary data sources. Case studies involving applications of research approaches also are included, as well as instructions on how to use statistical software to analyze data. With more than seventy "Research in Action" boxes, the text material is truly brought to life!

The book is entirely based on the need for managers to make better decisions. Thus, research is couched within the greater decision-making context. Because managers increasingly must make decisions based on almost unlimited information in data warehouses, we provide more coverage of data analysis techniques in this book than do other texts. We recognize that most business students will not be data analysts. But an understanding of data analysis techniques will help them to better utilize the increasing amounts of information they will be expected to apply in decision-making. Our straightforward, hands-on approach will make the book particularly successful with advanced undergraduates in all business disciplines and graduate business students, both in traditional and executive programs. The book also will serve as an effective reference guide for advanced users, including basic researchers and beginning doctoral students.

Changes in the business environment have created opportunities as well as uncertainty, and they make the role of business research even more important in improving decision-making. For example, information technology has made more accurate financial forecasting possible, has improved employee productivity, and enables more information to be collected and stored at a reasonable price. Knowledge is power, but managers must convert the increasing amount of information into knowledge before they can use this power. Businesses that are best able to harness this power will be the ones who are successful in the long run. Hence, a main focus of the text is the collection, evaluation, understanding, and use of information from the manager's perspective.

EXCELLENT PEDAGOGY

Our pedagogy has been developed from many years of conducting and teaching business research. To bring the concepts to life and make the text more interesting, we focus on a single case throughout the book. Phil Samouel is a restaurant entrepreneur in New York. His Greek restaurant competes with Gino's Italian Ristorante. Phil hires a business research consultant to help him and the case study is used to illustrate the principles of business research throughout the text. The consultant has recommended two surveys—one of customers and the other of Phil's employees. Both questionnaires are included in the text and two databases from the results of the surveys are used to demonstrate the data analysis techniques. A sample report of the surveys' initial findings is included as an appendix to the reporting chapter. Exercises at the end of the chapters provide an opportunity for students to further examine the findings of the two surveys and to use them in preparing a more comprehensive report on the restaurant case study. Electronic copies of the questionnaires and databases are available on our Web site.

The Samouel's restaurant case provides a running example, which saves the reader time in gaining familiarity with different cases from chapter to chapter. We refer to the case when we discuss research design alternatives, as well as when we evaluate different sampling approaches. The thinking behind the employee questionnaire is provided in the measurement and scaling chapter and the rationale for the customer survey questionnaire is reviewed in the questionnaire design chapter. In all of the data analysis chapters we use the case study data to illustrate SPSS and the various statistical techniques. A copy of the research proposal given to Phil Samouel is provided in Appendix 1-A, and a summary of the research report is included in the appendix to Chapter 12. The focus on a single case study throughout the text enables the reader to more easily understand the benefits and pitfalls of using research to improve business decision making.

ORGANIZATION OF THE BOOK

The text and all major supplements are organized around the learning objectives shown at the beginning of the chapters. Instead of a single summary of the chapter, there are summaries by each learning objective. This organizational approach makes the book very readable for students and easy to teach for instructors. In short, it delivers value for both students and teachers.

The organization of the book follows the logic of the business research process. It is organized into five parts. Part 1, the introduction, provides an overview of the scope of business research and the research process. It also includes an appendix on preparing research proposals, as well as others on the Samouel's and Gino's case study, how to use SPSS, and how to use Excel. Part 2 provides an overview of research design, creative decision-making, and ethics. Part 3 covers data collection, measurement and scaling, questionnaire design, and sampling. In Part 4 we examine data analysis and presentation, including correlation and regression and writing and presenting research reports. In Part 5 we discuss advanced topics in business research, such as multivariate data analysis and perceptual mapping that are increasingly being used for data mining tasks.

COMPREHENSIVE INSTRUCTOR AND STUDENT RESOURCES

The text has an extensive set of resources for instructors and students. For instructors, there is a test bank providing a wide variety of questions on all the major concepts in the book. The instructor's manual includes lecture outlines, answers to end-of-chapter questions, and teaching notes for the Internet exercises. Each chapter has thirty to forty PowerPoint slides to summarize and illustrate the key concepts. Two datasets for the restaurant case in both SPSS and Excel format are provided for instructors to use in teaching, and students to use in learning. Additional end-of-chapter assignments give the user an opportunity to experience a wide range of analytical applications using the datasets. This eliminates the need for instructors and/or students to hunt for data demonstrating business research concepts and techniques. We make it available to the user.

The text's Web site (www.wiley.com/college/hair) includes a wide array of supplementary materials for instructors to use to facilitate their teaching. In addition to electronic copies of all instructors' teaching support materials, the book has copies of sample questionnaires used in research projects, answers to frequently asked questions on business research provided by the text's authors, and copies of the datasets. In short, we believe it is one of the most comprehensive Web sites of any business research text.

ACKNOWLEDGEMENTS

We would like to thank the reviewers for their valuable comments on the earlier drafts of the book. Their useful suggestions helped to make the book much better. We give our thanks and appreciation to: J. Bandyopdhyay, Central Michigan University; Gerry Work, Nova Southeastern University; Michael P. Bumler, Illinois State University; Nell Tabor Hartley, Robert Morris University; Robert Hurt, California State Polytechnic University–Pomona; Jud Faurer, Metro State College of Denver; Burt Kaliski, New Hampshire College; Lloyd W. Shell, Nicholls State University; and Kelly D. Wason, Tarleton State University.

There are many people to thank at Leyh Publishing and John Wiley & Sons. We thank Rick Leyh first for encouraging us to write the book, and then for his support throughout the completion of the book. Jana Pitts also was very helpful, as well as Jeff Marshall. Michele Chancellor provided many helpful production suggestions.

Finally, we owe a debt of gratitude to our past students who inspired us to write this book. Their questions and comments helped us to know what and how to cover the many important topics. We also thank those special teachers who inspired us to a life-long mission of learning and sharing knowledge. Moreover, we hope that future students, by using this book, will enjoy a much easier pathway to learning business research and statistics than was typical for us.

Joe Hair, Louisiana State University, USA
Barry Babin, University of Southern Mississippi, USA
Arthur Money, Henley Management College, UK
Phillip Samouel, Kingston Business School, UK

About the Authors

Joe F. Hair, Jr. is Alvin C. Copeland Endowed Professor of Entrepreneurship, Ourso College of Business Administration, Louisiana State University. He was a United States Steel Foundation Fellow at the University of Florida,–Gainesville, where he earned his Ph.D. in Economics and Business Administration. He is the author of twenty-six books and more than seventy articles on a variety of topics. He has been retained as a consultant for firms in the food, lodging, healthcare, transportation, banking, utilities, and electronics industries, as well as by the U.S. Department of Agriculture and the U.S. Department of Interior. He has presented executive development and management training programs for numerous companies in a wide variety of industries, and served as an expert witness in several litigation matters.

Barry Babin holds a Ph.D. in Business Administration. He is author of over fifty research articles covering a wide range of topics and appearing in marketing, retailing, psychological, and management oriented journals. Currently, he is Associate Editor of the *Journal of Business Research* and Professor of Marketing and Consumer Research at the University of Southern Mississippi. Prior experience includes engineering, managerial, and marketing related experience in numerous industries including defense, specialty retailing, and consumer products. He is former President of the Society for Marketing Advances and his research has been recognized with several national and international awards. He performs consulting and executive education in the areas of creative decision making and business research.

Arthur H. Money is Professor of Management and Chairman of the faculty of Information Systems, Project and Operations Management at Henley Management College, Henley on Thames, England. Prior to joining Henley Management College he was Professor of Business Administration in the Graduate School of Business of the University of Cape Town. Professor Money received his Ph.D. degree (1972) in Mathematical Statistics from the University of Cape Town. Currently he is a member of the Executive of the European Doctoral Programs Association of Management and Business Administration (EDAMBA) and on the Steering Committee of the European Doctoral School of Knowledge and Management (EUDOKMA). He has authored more than one hundred journal articles, working papers, and book chapters, and is the co-author of five books and co-editor of two books. Professor Money focuses his research on statistics, management science, and applications in the areas of information systems, finance, and marketing.

Phillip Samouel was educated in the UK gaining a BA First Class Honors in Social Science and two masters, one in Economics and the other in Management Science, from the London School of Economics and Imperial College, respectively. He earned his Doctorate in Business Administration from Henley Management College/Brunel University in 1995 and most recently received an Honorary Ph.D. from the Academy for the National Economy, Moscow. His career has included successful endeavors both in academia and the commercial world. Between 1974 and 1984 he built Sammy George Fashion Ltd, a garment manufacturer in London with its own label—London Lady. Since 1984 he has been running a successful Farming Enterprise. Ladyland Farm–The Living Classroom, which also is an Education Centre delivering aspects of the UK Science National Curriculum to over thirty-five thousand children a year. He is currently on the faculty of Kingston University, UK, where he has been Head of Department–Business Strategy and Operations, Director of the Business School, and most recently Dean of Faculty and a member of the University's Executive until 2002.

Introduction

1

Business Research for the 21st Century

Learning Objectives

1. Provide an orientation to modern-day business research.

2. Define business research and the people who use it.

3. Discuss recent business trends and how they affect business research.

4. Examine research-related technologies.

5. Introduce the text case analysis.

INTRODUCTION

Research is a discerning pursuit of the truth. Those who do research are looking for answers. In our everyday lives, we all play the role of researcher. A trip to the movies is rarely undertaken without some period of discernment. During this process, prospective movie patrons first determine what type of movie would best fill their present desire. They may form a preliminary opinion of several movies based on previous knowledge of the actors and producers involved, then move on to discuss a specific film. *"Is The Mystery of the Blue Dog Café worth seeing?"* Media sources, previews, and input from personal acquaintances often provide information to answer this question. Then, if they are confident about their conclusion, they make a decision. This simple illustration contains the basic elements of business research. Good decision-making depends upon accurately predicting whether you will enjoy *The Mystery of the Blue Dog Café*.

Although formal research training is relatively new to the business world, business research is perhaps as old as commerce itself. International commerce expanded rapidly with the rise of Phoenician traders during the Early Classical period, about 500 B.C.[1] Investors in trading expeditions soon realized it was too risky to simply load ships with surplus goods and sail from port to port until a buyer was found. So, they began to gather information about how goods might be altered to appeal to specific markets. With this information, merchants made strategic decisions involving product differentiation and market segmentation. Merchants discovered the existence of price and quality segments. Wine from the countries of Thaos and Chios was highly sought after by some markets. Thasian and Chiot wine sold for as much as one drachma per liter compared to a quarter-drachma per liter for other wines. Wine makers from southern Italy performed "research" while peddling their own goods on the seas. Thus, they too attempted to capitalize on the new intelligence. While they were unable to match the quality of Thasian or Chiot wines, they appealed to these markets by making imitations of higher quality wines. Thus, research may have led to the first product "knock-offs."[2]

Research also proved a key to success in selling fineware (dinnerware or china). Corinthians lost out to the Athenians in serving the early Etruscan market for fineware. The Athenians produced a style known as Tyrrhenian. Tyrrhenian fineware more closely matched Etruscan taste. It was "cheap and gaudy ... and often carried mock inscriptions, presumably to impress Etruscans who would not have been able to read."[3] Perhaps this fineware was the pink flamingo of its day. There seems to be little doubt, therefore, that the product was produced with a specific market in mind based upon information gathered from the market.

The general rise in literacy, the industrial revolution, further advances in transportation, the advent of the computer, and the general expansion of commerce worldwide have changed the way research is done. Frederick Taylor used early motion picture technology to film workers and show them how to improve their productivity. Similarly, General Electric was among the first companies to use consumer research to design new products.

Today, there are literally thousands of firms whose primary business involves providing research services that help businesses answer key strategic, tactical and operational questions. Business research has become much more formalized and technical, but the end is much the same as that of the Phoenician merchant. How do I find the answers to improve my performance and make life better for customers, employees, and owners? Business research can do much to meet this challenge.

BUSINESS RESEARCH DEFINED

A TRUTH-SEEKING FUNCTION

We opened the book with a simple definition of science as a truth-seeking function. Science seeks to explain the *world that really is*. "Real-world," or physical, scientists seek the truth about the world's physical realities. Chemists deal with chemical phenomena, biologists with biological phenomena, and so forth. Social scientists, such as psychologists and sociologists, seek to describe the realities of individual human behavior and the interactions of humans within a society. Business researchers generally fall more in line with social scientists because in reality business is about people.

Like the scientists described above, business researchers pursue the "truth" about business phenomena. The essence of business is people serving people through participation in a value-creating process with exchange at its core. This includes all the support systems necessary to facilitate this process. Business research seeks to predict and explain all phenomena that taken together comprise the ever-changing business environment. Thus, **business research** is a truth-seeking function that gathers, analyzes, interprets, and reports information so that business decision makers become more effective.

ELEMENTS OF BUSINESS RESEARCH

The scope of business research is broad and the types of phenomena business researchers study is expanding rapidly. Time and motion studies are relatively infrequent today, although they were essential in the development of scientific business management. Instead, we may study employee productivity as a function of a communication channel's bandwidth or how purchasing patterns have changed because of the Internet. Thus, business research is truly dynamic in that researchers are constantly studying new issues with new tools. Below is a list of key elements of business research that help provide a clearer picture of what is involved.

1. Business research is broad. It involves the study of a countless range of phenomena and focuses on:
    a. Studying people including employees, consumers, supervisors, managers, and policy makers.
    b. Understanding systems or groups of people including strategic business units, offices, labor forces in factories, management groups, boards of directors, CEOs, market segments, cultures, subcultures, corporate cultures, communities, companies, and industries.
    c. Examining the interaction of people with systems including auditing/accounting systems, legal systems, management practices, compensation systems, manufacturing systems, production processes, and financial systems.
2. Business research can be formal. Researchers can undertake a systematic and sometimes exhaustive project aimed at answering a very specific decision question. Toyota is interested in knowing the effects "one-price" retailing might have on auto purchases. One-price retailing means car prices are not subject to negotiation. They are testing the idea in several North American markets. Customers

in Montreal for example, generally prefer the one-price system by about two to one.[4] The effect of one-price retailing may extend beyond customers. Toyota also should research the effect this will have on their dealer network and employees. Thus, this single issue results in a fairly comprehensive study. This is a good example of a one-shot research project. **One-shot research projects** are performed to address a single issue at a specific point in time.

3. Business research can be informal. Restaurant owners and/or managers often spend a portion of each night circulating through the dining room. They will stop at each table and ask, "is everything alright?" The information they receive in return helps identify patterns that will aid decision making and enhance the restaurant experience for their customers. While this sort of research is easy for small entrepreneurial ventures, it's more of a challenge for larger firms. New technologies are creating ways, however, in which informal feedback can be input electronically so that regularities can be identified, perhaps through data mining or some expert system, and the appropriate actions can be taken. Informal research is often **ongoing.** This means that it is performed constantly and not directed toward any specific issue.

4. Good research is replicable. A goal of scientific research is that it be as objective as possible. That is, scientists are more or less play-by-play announcers who describe events as they see them ("I call 'em like I see 'em"). When research is objective, it is generally **replicable,** meaning that another researcher could produce the same results using the identical procedures employed by the original researcher. Coke's research into a better tasting product was motivated in part by the Pepsi Challenge. The Pepsi Challenge was a promotion in which consumers were intercepted in a supermarket, allowed to taste two unidentified colas, and given a six-pack of the one they preferred. Pepsi routinely televised these on live television. More people chose Pepsi in the Pepsi Challenge. Coke, questioning the authenticity of this research, conducted their own taste challenges, but kept them out of the public eye. Coke's research confirmed the Pepsi Challenge results. When consumers didn't know what they were drinking, they preferred the taste of Pepsi. Thus, the Pepsi Challenge research was replicable.

5. Good research should provide more benefit than it costs. Ultimately, this is of primary importance in determining if the research was any good. Management shouldn't commission a $300,000 research project on a $30,000 decision. Many decisions are made with little or no research because they don't involve a lot of risk. Other times, research is done in a perfunctory manner in an effort to limit the cost relative to the potential benefits of the decision.

Business research is scientific inquiry. But the terminology of business research differs depending upon what motivates a particular study. **Applied business research** is motivated by an attempt to solve a particular problem faced by a particular organization. For example, Coke may want to know why Pepsi is gaining market share in New York City. **Basic business research** is motivated by a desire to better understand some business-related phenomena as it applies to all of an industry or all of business in general—for example, why people are drinking more bottled water and less cola. Applied business research helps decision makers make specific decisions bound by time and an organization. Basic research helps develop theory that attempts to describe and predict business events, so that all business decision makers can benefit. Exhibit 1-1 compares applied and basic business research.

EXHIBIT 1-1	EXAMPLES OF APPLIED AND BASIC BUSINESS RESEARCH

Applied Research Issues	Basic Research Issues
What is the effect of digital audio and photo managing on Samsung's DVD market share?	How does technological turbulence affect business performance?
How will the acquisition of new vineyard property affect profitability of Martinelli Winery?	What factors relate to consumer perceptions of a wine's overall quality?
How would imposing a salary-based pay system affect customer satisfaction at Bernard's Acura?	Are consumers more satisfied with car dealerships whose salespeople are compensated with a straight salary than they are with dealerships whose salespeople are compensated with sales commission?
Can prospective employee psychological profiles be used to reduce turnover at Sacred Heart Hospital?	Does job stress affect the job performance and satisfaction of male and female service providers equally?

SOURCE: *Business Wire*. 2002. Samsung Selects Planetweb's Digital Entertainment Software to Power New Line of Interactive DVD Players. (7 January), accessed via Lexis-Nexis, March 7, 2002.

WHAT DOES BUSINESS RESEARCH STUDY?

The boundaries of business research today are virtually limitless. Business research is intended to result in better decision making. Business decisions often involve all aspects of business. Therefore, it should be no surprise that business research involves all aspects and all functions of business.

Marketing managers often are interested in the behavior of the firm, brand image, customer satisfaction, and brand and product positioning, among other things. We can all recall times when we have responded to some type of consumer satisfaction study. The Baldridge awards for product quality are typical for marketing research studies. Marketing information is vital in strategic decisions. Which strategic orientation should the firm take? Should it diversify or stay entrenched as a specialist within a niche market? Business researchers contribute significantly to marketing decisions by conducting business research studies.

For *manufacturing firms,* efficient and effective production processes are essential if customers are to realize product quality and satisfaction. Business research often is tasked with identifying processes that create the optimal amount of product and/or service quality. Further, since employees are ultimately responsible for quality production, a great deal of research is directed at understanding employee behavior by focusing on important variables including job satisfaction, employee performance, and employee turnover (quitting intentions). In the U.K., research indicates firms incur 3,933 GBP per year in additional costs (approximately $7,000 U.S.) for every employee quitting their job.[5] Similarly, U.S. firms estimate average turnover costs at $10,000 or more for each employee that leaves.[6] Thus, turnover receives a great deal of attention from researchers and decision makers.

Strategic and tactical decisions often involve capital investment. Online grocers have not enjoyed the early success many experts predicted. Many may have underestimated the capital intensity required in such a venture. One of the keys to their eventual survival is selecting the best way to obtain this capital.[7] Business research on financing alternatives could help answer this question. Exhibit 1-2 illustrates some of the business research implications that might be involved in an entrepreneurial venture in the online grocery industry.

Accounting rules also present a need for research. Different accounting procedures bring with them different financial implications. It is clear that Arthur Andersen should have more closely examined the accounting procedures used at Enron. So, decisions must be researched for potential tax implications as well as their impact on product and SBU (Strategic Business Unit) financial performance.

Industries change, but the research process itself remains much the same. Research continues to be an investigation searching for truthful explanations and accurate predictions. The tools researchers use, however, have and will continue to change. Information businesses are those that exchange information or information-related services such as distribution and storage, for some type of fee. As "information-only" products become an ever-increasing part of the economy, it will be interesting to see what new tools may be needed, if any. Information-only businesses are a major portion of e-commerce. They include relatively small companies that, for example, might provide service instructions for restaurant refrigerator technicians. But they also include large companies such as Yahoo! and AOL TimeWarner as well as specialized firms such as Pricescan.com (www.pricescan.com), which provides price information on thousands of products at the click of a mouse.

Several aspects of information-only businesses present a challenge for business researchers. For example, how will researchers identify important "attributes" of information-only products? "Stickiness" is a term that has been used to describe an important attribute of information products. Stickiness is how much it costs to transfer a given unit of information to an information seeker.[8] Does this cost affect the end-user, or only channel members? Further, what is the best way to determine the price of information-only

EXHIBIT 1-2	BUSINESS RESEARCH APPLICATIONS FOR A START-UP VENTURE IN ONLINE GROCERY SALES		
Decision Involved	**Research Topic**	**Implications**	
What type of capital resources should be used?	Identify the financial and risk implications associated with the various options.	Online grocers are highly capital intensive. The result is cash starvation during the early months of operation.	
What markets should we serve?	Identify the potential profitability of potential markets.	Online grocers must identify markets with high volume potential relative to a small service area.	
What product assortments should be emphasized?	Identify the shopping value associated with product acquisition of various types.	Online grocers must determine the products for which customers believe physical product interaction is a value added process.	
What type of personnel should be involved in operations?	What is the impact of outsourcing on perceived service quality?	Online grocers may find it more cost effective to outsource certain operational components including product delivery.	
How should customers be	What is the potential response rate from the different options for inducing trial?	Customer acquisition costs are extremely high for online retailers. Therefore, successful online grocers will likely enjoy relative efficiency in enticing customers.	

products since the cost to transfer information-only products is practically zero? Should price, therefore, be determined by a buyer's willingness to pay instead of being based on cost?[9] This clearly has implications for the way pricing studies are conducted. With information-only products, greater emphasis also is placed on protecting the intellectual property rights. This means researchers must help define the boundaries of infringement to provide legal protection for information-only companies.

What types of businesses benefit from research? All types of businesses can benefit from research. Large and small businesses can answer key questions about markets and about their own internal work environments.[10] Many low-technology firms use research. For example, hotels and restaurants frequently collect information on satisfaction and on lodging and dining out patterns to enable them to better serve their customers. The new ever-growing class of highly skilled, highly educated entrepreneurs also understand the key to success is being able to identify new ways to provide customers with enduring and more satisfying bundles of benefits.[11] Clearly, research has played a key role in technological development as it addresses various aspects related to the adoption of new technologies.

Business research is no longer confined to for-profit businesses. Nonprofit institutions such as the Catholic Church have found research useful in addressing questions related to recruiting clergy and increasing fund-raising activities without sacrificing spirituality.[12] Thus, far from being exclusive to a small set of large companies, all types of businesses can benefit from research. See the "Research in Action" box to learn more about how religious organizations utilize business research.

TRENDS IMPACTING BUSINESS RESEARCH

Recent business trends have affected business research in many ways. They have helped shape the types of research performed, the way research is conducted and the phenomena that are studied, as well as the importance of research in business decision-making. Among the more important trends impacting business research are expanding market freedom, internationalization, relationship marketing, and, particularly, the information revolution.

EXPANDING MARKET FREEDOM

Since President Reagan's famous "tear down this wall" speech in 1987, free markets have emerged in many formerly closed markets. Most managers in the former Soviet Union, for example, were not motivated to develop or acquire research capabilities.[13] Soviet consumers represented a captive audience except for the black market. There was little job mobility so there was little incentive to study the internal, organizational workings of the firm. Little advantage could be gained through the added intelligence that research could bring.

As free and competitive markets emerged, companies became motivated to answer questions about the types of products and services consumers wanted. One result has been a greater emphasis on product quality requiring input from both customers and employees. The Volga, perhaps the best-known Russian automobile, has a long and infamous history as a symbol of the poor product quality that epitomized Soviet industry. More recently, Gaz, the Russian manufacturer of the Volga, used research input to expand their product line and market share. Gaz assessed market trends, then entered the mini-van market with the Gazelle and has penetrated markets in Iraq, Hungary, and even the United States![14]

RESEARCH IN ACTION
RESEARCHERS ARE KEEPING THE FAITH

A major company such as Target or Old Navy wouldn't dream of opening a store in a new market without first researching and establishing a viable need in that market, so why should it be any different for churches? That's the question that Percept, a firm based in Costa Mesa, California, asked and answered when it was founded in 1987. Percept (www.perceptnet.com) supplies demographic information to churches by integrating data about religious attitudes, preferences, and behavior of the American people based on its block-by-block "ethographics"—the company's religious equivalent to psychographics.

Percept's approach is similar to National Decision Systems, a firm that specializes in psychographics and breaks the U.S. population into fifty lifestyle segments. It then determines which group is most prevalent in each Zip Code + 4 area, usually about ten to fifteen households. Businesses use this data to determine marketing strategies such as whether consumers respond to hard-sell or soft-sell messages or if there's a market for a new product. In contrast, Percept's customers are religious organizations.

Percept has taken these fifty lifestyle segments, and through a series of polls and secondary information culled from the U.S. Census Bureau, Claritas, The WEFA Group, and its own proprietary national Ethos Survey Series, has established the church-going preferences—the "ethos"—of each group. One of Percept's segments, "The Rising Potential Professional" for example, has a median household income and a per capita income that is considerably higher than the national average. When asked by Percept to identify specific programs or characteristics they look for in a church, the segment "Rising Potential Professionals" is interested in "Sports/Camping, Cultural Programs, Spiritual Retreats, Adult Theological Discussion Groups, Intellectual Worship and Community-Focused Missions." People who fall into the group "Suburban Mid-Life Families" however, are more concerned with "Divorce Recovery Programs, Marriage Enrichment Opportunities, Parent Training Programs and Participatory Music" from their churches. Information like this is useful in designing liturgy and spiritual development programs that provide the most value to the customer.

While some may argue that slick business and marketing strategy techniques have no place in religion, many churches, parishes, and denominational agencies across the U.S. are purchasing this demographic information in hopes of better understanding their congregations' needs and identifying potential churchgoers in their regions. As churches try to find ways to reach their target audience, they are employing the same business research methods as more traditional businesses in hopes of gaining similar results.

SOURCE: Felten, Eric. 2000. Data Divining; Mainline Churches Put Their Faith in Demographic Marketing. *The Wall Street Journal.* (28 April), p. W17; www.perceptnet.com.; and communication with Tom Hoyt, VP, Marketing Communications, Percept.

Russian managers also must learn to deal with free labor markets. Job satisfaction in Russia remains low. In fact, many skilled Russian workers have been attracted to the United States by better working conditions in American companies.[15] Since Russian labor markets traditionally have been understudied,[16] business research may provide gains to managers that are even greater than those resulting from similar studies in developed economies. As firms benefit from exercising decision making, research becomes an essential part of effective decision making.

INTERNATIONAL RESEARCH

Business research today is truly an international endeavor. Firms around the world now perform business research to improve their decision making. This research influences decisions often involving unfamiliar cultures. For example, foreign acquisition decisions can be made with much more certainty when the competitive and economic market structures are known. Similar to Gaz, Skoda was the Communist nationalized automotive producer from the Czech Republic. Skoda also had an infamous reputation for quality. After its initial introduction to the U.K. market in 2000, 98 percent of British consumers rated it as a "low-quality, low-end product." Since Volkswagen acquired Skoda, however, business research has been used to improve product quality and design promotional campaigns that use humor to counter the negative image. By careful consumer profiling, Skoda targets consumers who are highly rational in their decision making rather than emotional. The result was a dramatically increased response to direct marketing appeals and a sales increase of over 23 percent in 2001.[17]

Internationalization means business research also must take an international focus.[18] Difficult managerial decisions involving consumers and employees in a foreign culture are made even more difficult by an array of communication barriers, both verbal and nonverbal. These decisions require research regarding cultural differences including the ability to translate meaning from one language into the same meaning in another language.

The Internet means many businesses now consider the world their market. But to do so, the company's Web site must be offered in multiple languages. In such cases, translational equivalence becomes essential. **Translational equivalence** means text can be translated from one language to another, then back to the original language with no distortion in meaning. See Exhibit 1-3 for examples of translational inequivalence.

Beyond mere translational equivalence,[19] researchers must investigate Internet usage patterns as well as the technical details of browsers and computers. Different languages are accompanied by different alphabets. Many computer system configurations are unable to properly translate these characters. Without the proper hardware and software, for instance, a Russian Web page can easily end up looking like Chinese!

Issues such as these are sure to arise as businesses cross international boundaries. Research designed to understand the cultural dimensions of doing business is more cost effective than a mistake that creates an undesirable or ambiguous meaning.

EXHIBIT 1-3	RESEARCH COULD PREVENT ERRORS LIKE THESE

Description of Situation	Intended Meaning (Product Name/Slogan)	Interpreted Meaning
English name of a U.S. product and its German interpretation.	Clairol Mist Stick	Piece of Manure
English name of a U.S. product and its Spanish interpretation.	Matador (AMC auto)	Killer Auto
Japanese interpretation of English name.	Guess Jeans	Vulgar/Low-Class/Ugly Jeans
German interpretation of product term.	Credit Card	Guilt Card
Japanese interpreter's translation from Japanese into English to be sold in China.	Ready to Eat Pancakes	Strawberry Crap Dessert

SOURCES: Semon, Thomas T. 2001. Cutting Corners in Language Risky Business. *Marketing News* 35 (23 April), 9. Cohen, Andy. 1998. What You Didn't Learn in Marketing 101. *Sales and Marketing Management* 150 (February), 22–25. Steinmetz, Greg. 1997. Germans Finally Open Their Wallets to Credit Cards But Aren't Hooked Yet. *The Wall Street Journal*. (6 April), A14. Reese, Shelly. 1998. Culture Shock. *Marketing Tools* 5 (May), 44–49.

RELATIONSHIP MARKETING

Business has entered the *relationship marketing* era. Relationship marketing emphasizes long-term interactions between a business and its stakeholders. It seeks to identify mutually beneficial exchanges where both the firm and the stakeholder maximize value. The emergence of relationship marketing is changing research in terms of who and what is studied.

A principal component of relationship marketing is the realization a firm cannot be everything to everybody. That is, the firm recognizes that not every customer, not every employee and not every shareholder provide a good match for a long-term relationship. Frederick Rheichheld encourages firms to be "picky" and choose relationship partners carefully.[20] Otherwise, limited resources will be spent on unprofitable customers.

Successful companies have loyal customers, loyal employees and loyal stakeholders.[21] Relationship marketing has placed an increased emphasis on the study of loyalty-related factors. Employee loyalty issues such as turnover and organizational commitment have been studied often because of their relationship to firm performance.[22] Turnover represents the average tenure of an employee and suggests a replacement rate needed to maintain production. Organizational commitment is the degree to which an employee identifies with the goals and values of a firm.[23] When employees are highly committed they exhibit high loyalty. Knowledge of turnover and commitment factors increases the likelihood of organizational success.

Researchers now extend the idea of loyalty to customer and shareholder populations. New concepts such as customer share and customer churn increasingly are studied. Customer share is the proportion of resources a customer spends with one firm in a given competitor set.[24] For example, a customer that goes to McDonald's five out of ten times when they eat fast food would have a customer share of about fifty. Customer churn is the annual turnover rate of customers. Wireless phone companies are using research to reduce customer churn because it averages about 30 percent annually and is very costly. Businesses also are researching customer commitment—the degree to which customers identify with the values of a firm. They have learned that like loyal employees, customers are willing to sacrifice to maintain valuable relationships.[25] None of these areas was researched as recently as twenty years ago.

Similarly, companies have placed greater emphasis on relationships with employees. The dramatic increase in dual-income families has placed greater stress on employees as their free time becomes more constricted. Thus, employers have to pay attention to life outside of the workplace in an effort to maintain a cohesive workplace. Research such as this has led to a number of innovative programs designed to help employees deal with routine aspects of everyday life. Childcare support is far from the least of the innovative workplace characteristics stemming from this work.

INFORMATION REVOLUTION

The information age has facilitated many research processes. Technological advances in computing and electronic storage have dramatically increased research efficiency. This has all happened in a very short period of time. For example, most readers of this book were born before the widespread diffusion of desktop personal computers. Likewise, most readers of this book have never even heard of a "card reader." A card reader enabled an analyst to feed data into a computer using elongated cardboard index cards. By punching patterns of holes in the card, different values could be represented. Thus, it wasn't unusual for a researcher to carry around stacks of literally thousands of cards. One stack contained data, another stack contained a computer program that would hopefully analyze the data, assuming no errors in the pattern of holes existed. The researcher typically would place the cards in a card reader and then go to lunch. It might take hours for the mainframe computer to process the program. Upon returning from lunch, the analyst would fetch a printout that either contained results or more commonly for first-time runs, an error message.

Cards had to be guarded with great care. A dropped stack of cards caused more than a few broken hearts for researchers. Now, the data contained in the thousands of cards can be stored on a single computer disk. Moreover, it is likely placed into a file in "real-time," programs that analyze the data likely are never seen by the researcher who simply "points and clicks," and the computer takes only a fraction of a second to run even the most advanced statistical programs.

Almost as certainly as the card reader is now obsolete, more new technologies will emerge that will make our current methods of data input, storage and analysis obsolete. The following are several information technology developments having a great impact on business decision making and research.

Electronic Communication

Email has replaced the telephone and traditional "snail-mail" for many types of business communications, including many matters directly related to research. Questionnaires are now routinely administered either through email directly or by providing access to a hosted Web site. Chapter 5 contains a more complete description of the technological advances in data collection. Electronic communication also is impacting the developments discussed below.

Networking

Networking refers technically to systems of computers that are connected to each other through various servers. The Internet connects your computer to nearly every other computer in the world. From a business perspective, networking allows greater communication and data transfer between interested parties. In some cases, networking allows for "real time" (instantaneous) information transfer from markets to the analyst. Fedex's package tracking system provides an example of real-time information transfer. Firms are increasingly adopting intranets as well. An **intranet** is an Internet-like network that links computers internally within an organization. A researcher who needs sales and profit data for the last twenty quarters, for example, can tap into a company's financial records directly and retrieve the desired information. No paper work is necessary, and there's no delay waiting for the accounting department to process the request!

A company can expand its intranet network so that suppliers and vendors also have access to the network. This capability allows for automated purchase systems and increased manufacturing flexibility. Intranet technology has been advantageous to Delicato, Inc., a family-owned California wine maker. It has automated research reports on product line profitability that previously required formal requests to the information technology department. The automated research results are then input into a system that adjusts grape purchasing and vineyard production in an effort to focus on those grape varietals that are producing the most profitable wines.[26]

Data Warehouses

Company information is now stored and cataloged in an electronic format. Twenty years ago, data may have been stored on computer cards or magnetic tape and most commonly, it would have been accessed through paper reports generated by a computer program. Today, these electronic data warehouses replace other more costly approaches to storing data. Electronic data warehousing clearly has changed the way analysts and decision makers do their jobs.

The availability of **off-the-shelf data** has made some research tasks infinitely easier. Off-the-shelf data is readily available information compiled and sold by companies. For example, an analyst researching several different locations for a new branch office within the U.S. can likely access all the needed statistical data without ever leaving the office. All public U.S. census data is cataloged electronically and is accessible in numerous formats through its Web site.[27] Previously, the researcher would have had to go to one of the U.S. Census Depository libraries, find the correct volumes, then find the correct tables, then manually transfer the numbers into some usable format. A laborious process that may have taken days or weeks is now reduced to hours. Likewise, retail site location research projects that would have taken weeks previously are now nearly automated through the use of Geographic Information Systems (GIS). GIS systems can create, within a few minutes, numerous maps that overlay information from census data inventories on top of satellite photo imagery. For example, it may identify the location of households with income profiles between $75,000 and $125,000 and two teenage children at home.

Further, numerous industry statistics are now available electronically. In the past, for example, consumer products sales personnel anxiously awaited the monthly reports on market share such as the SAMI (Sales and Marketing Index). Now, subscribers have 24/7 access to many indices like the SAMI via a notebook computer or palm pilot.[28] Chapter 3 contains a list of off-the-shelf electronic data sources.

Organizational Learning

Motivated by the low cost of electronically storing information and a desire to better understand multiple relationships, many organizations have developed formal systems aimed at recording all important events in a database. The resulting database is an electronic representation of **organizational memory.** Some input into these systems is automated. Information from routine financial and market reports, for instance, is fed automatically into a database. Other information, such as a list of effective employee motivational tools, must be input through a special report. The result is an internal data warehouse. **Organizational learning** can be defined as the internalization of both external and internal information to be used as an input to decision making. Within a few short years, organizational learning has taken on a central role in the selection of business strategies aimed at improved firm performance.[29]

One relatively new organizational learning tool is **data mining.** Data mining electronically mines data warehouses for information that identifies ways to improve organizational performance. Data mining is not performed with a pick or a shovel. Rather, the analyst's tool is an algorithm (a lists of steps in the form of computer commands) that automatically analyzes potential relationships between events stored in the electronic warehouse.

Data mining represents "knowledge discovery in databases" or KDD.[30] The KDD process involves the following steps:

1. Establishing access to relevant data
2. Selecting the set of events (data) to be analyzed
3. Cleaning this data so it is understood by the algorithm
4. Developing and using rules for selecting interesting relationships
5. Developing a report of relationships that may affect firm performance

Data mining began with the early advent of significant computing power in the 1960s. Researchers developed Automatic Interaction Detection (AID) software that considered possible relationships between all possible pairs of quantified data within a data set.[31] During the 1960s, a mainframe computer could analyze all potential relationships between literally *dozens* of variables in a *few hours*. A data set with twenty-four variables would require 16,777,216 (2^{24}) computations. Today, sophisticated data mining tools use more powerful multivariate procedures such as cluster analysis, which is discussed in detail later in the book. Tools like this allow variables to be analyzed more than two at a time and in greater number. If we analyzed twenty-four variables in all possible three-way comparisons, 282,429,536,481 computations are required. We won't even attempt to demonstrate what would be required with more variables and more combinations! But, modern computing power allows even these types of analyses to be performed with a personal or laptop computer in seconds! Thus, the researcher has much greater power to find information that will improve business performance.

An interesting, perhaps infamous, example of data mining is provided by the U.S. Internal Revenue Service (IRS). The IRS oversees federal tax collection. Data mining is used by the IRS to analyze combinations of events described on U.S. taxpayers' tax forms to identify candidates with high potential for unreported (and therefore untaxed) income.[32] Similarly, companies can use data mining research to identify profitable customers, more effective employees and attractive investments, among other things. More recently, researchers are combining data mining with traditional research tools, including survey research, to further improve the value of database technology in decision making.[33] The "Research in Action" box shows how Harrah's Casinos is successfully using data mining.

Satellite Technology

Business research even extends beyond the Earth. Many companies are gathering and analyzing information obtained from **GPS,** or Global Positioning Satellite devices. GPS allows real-time tracking of movement. For example, delivery companies can equip trucks with a GPS system. Every move the truck makes is monitored by a signal sent from a GPS device on the truck, back to a satellite, and then back to a company computer. Researchers can then analyze these patterns to increase the efficiency of the delivery system.[34] Similarly, car rental companies are placing GPS devices on their cars. With this, customers enjoy the benefits of electronic directions. In return, the companies now know exactly how rental customers use their cars. This may enable better services and pricing alternatives. In the future, customers may be asked to do their shopping while carrying around a pocket-sized GPS. This would allow researchers to examine mall and store traffic patterns precisely. Information like this could be very useful in answering questions about how much rent a potential retail location could fetch. The "Research in Action" box discusses GPS applications further.

The information age has transformed modern economies. Researchers are expected and able to be more productive than they were a generation ago. Likewise, decision

RESEARCH IN ACTION
HARRAH'S CASINOS IS STACKING THE ODDS IN THEIR FAVOR.

It's true. By using sophisticated technology and hiring a team of business research experts, the company has dramatically improved the odds that Harrah's will win the jackpot in the high-stakes competition for share-of-customer.

The company discovered the power of business research in the early 1990s when company officials were struggling to defend their market share against larger, ritzier competitors. In one of its first experiments with business research, Harrah's learned through testing that $60 in free chips was a much less expensive but far more effective incentive than the industry's standard free hotel, steak dinner, and $30 of free chips offer. Similarly, the company stopped offering bonus points to spend in the casino gift shops and restaurants when research showed most avid gamblers were not motivated by these offers. Today, no marketing program is launched without being tested first.

Here's how Harrah's plays the game.

When a customer arrives at one of the company's twenty-five casinos anywhere in the country, they are encouraged to register for the company's Total Rewards program to earn freebies such as trips, meals, and hotel rooms. At this point in the game, the casino learns at least the customer's name, address, phone number, and age. Customers can provide additional information if they are inclined. With this knowledge, the company can already guess the profitability of the customer. For instance, their research has shown that the most profitable customers are 62-year-old women who live within thirty minutes of a Harrah's casino because they generally have a large disposable income and can easily visit the casino regularly. Conversely, a 32-year-old male who lives four hundred miles from the nearest Harrah's casino is not going to be a profitable customer to the company. Using this information, Harrah's can determine whether a customer is worth pursuing with marketing dollars, and, if so, whether they are more likely to respond to the offer of a free hotel room, a free meal, or cash.

But Harrah's doesn't stop here. Instead, they use a sophisticated computer network to track the customer's time and activities while visiting their casinos. Now they know what games the customer prefers, the amount of their average bets, how many bets the customer places, and how much time they spend gambling. At this point, Harrah's has a much better picture of the customer and can place them in one of ninety customer segmentations the company has developed for determining and testing the best marketing approach to use. For example, Harrah's now knows which customers enjoy participating in slot tournaments and can make sure to notify them whenever a tournament is scheduled. Customer responses to marketing efforts also are recorded, enabling the company to further fine-tune their effectiveness. For instance, by monitoring the customer's response, the company may learn that the customer is only interested in slot tournaments with a potential of winning more than $100,000.

As a result of the new focus on business research and data mining, Harrah's now knows that 80 percent of company revenues and almost 100 percent of company profits come from the 30 percent of their customers who spend between $100 and $500 per visit. Therefore, those are the customers on which the company focuses it marketing efforts. Today, Harrah's estimates they have increased their share of customer profit from 36 cents of every dollar the customer spends in casinos to 42 cents. This increase translates into a $100 million revenue increase in the first two years since the Total Rewards program was implemented and record earnings of $3.7 billion in 2001, an 11 percent increase from 2000. Finally, more than half of the revenues from Harrah's three Las Vegas casinos now come from loyal Harrah's customers.

SOURCES: Brinkley, Christina. 2000. Lucky Numbers. *The Wall Street Journal.* (4 May), A1. Del Jones. 2001. Client Data Means Little Without Good Analysis. *USA Today.* (24 December), B4. Nickell, Joe Ashbrook. 2002. Welcome to Harrah's. *Business 2.0.* (April), 48–54.

```
RESEARCH IN ACTION
GLOBAL BIG BROTHER SYSTEM?
```

Are there ethical dimensions to GPS as a research tool? Acme Rent-A-Car of New Haven, Connecticut placed GPS units on all it rental cars. Thus, the rent-a-car company knows *everyplace* a customer goes. Not only do they know where you stop, but how fast you drive on the way there. Acme began sending their customers speeding tickets based on GPS tracking. Eventually, a customer sued, alleging that Acme was violating a driver's privacy. Thus far, the courts have ruled in the customer's favor.

Insurance companies also are using GPS technology. Not only can they research driving behavior much better than in the past, but they are able to address issues related to pricing. GPS systems used by Progressive insurance in Texas have resulted in drastically reduced rates for some customers, and increased rates for others. Drive less, as shown by the GPS, and you pay less. Drive within the speed limit, and you pay less. Some consumer advocates argue that this is also a violation of their right to privacy.

SOURCES: Cardwell, Annette. 2002. Building a Better Speed Trap. *Smartbusiness.com* 14 (December/January), 28. Carnahan, Ira. 2000. Insurance by the Minute. *Forbes* 166 (11 December), 86.

makers have more relevant information available to use as input to strategic and tactical decision making. Exhibit 1-4 summarizes several implications of the information age and business research.

Interestingly, some individuals are asking whether or not technology has advanced further than our desire and ability to take advantage of it. How many people really need 2.5 Gigahertz of processing speed? This may be part of the reason for the technology industry's recent performance slump.[35] Exhibit 1-5 lets you test your technology IQ and see how you are adapting to the technology explosion.

THE MANAGER-RESEARCHER RELATIONSHIP

Effective decision making requires that both managers (decision makers) and researchers perform their respective roles responsibly and ethically. Ethics in the researcher-manager relationship means both parties treat each other honestly and fairly. In addition, the researcher should realize that a breech in professional ethics harms the entire research industry. Conflict between the decision maker and the researcher (even when they are one in the same person) is inevitable. The decision maker wants to spend minimal money, utilize minimal human resources, and wants the answer immediately and without error. The researcher realizes that implementing research designs can be expensive, involves substantial time and labor resources, can be time consuming, and is never error free. Somewhere in between, there needs to be a reasonable compromise.

WHO PERFORMS BUSINESS RESEARCH?

The business researcher becomes formally involved in the decision-making process once a decision maker, who may be either an entrepreneur or a manager, recognizes a need for new information. The researcher's role is to fill this need. Decision makers use researchers who are either (1) employed by the same firm or (2) part of an external consulting

EXHIBIT 1-4	HOW THE INFORMATION AGE IS AFFECTING RESEARCHERS AND DECISION MAKERS

1. **Matter matters less.** Company value is increasingly found in intangible or "soft" assets. In the new economy, knowledge is the key to success. Information-only products account for a significant portion of the economy. Therefore, researchers are required to process more and produce better information and intelligence

2. **Distance matters less.** Many employees can perform their work from remote locations beyond the traditional workplace. Customers can shop from anywhere, including an airplane, their office, and, believe it or not, their car! Researchers can conduct Delphi interviews (a type of expert opinion polling) with top executives from every continent in the world simultaneously.

3. **Time matters more.** Given the new world of 24-hour-a-day instantaneous connections, the pressure to react quickly has increased enormously. Business customers are demanding reduced cycle times. Cycle time is the amount of time consumed between the point when an order is placed with a supplying company and the time when the benefits are realized. Thus, those companies that can reduce response time will benefit greatly. Researchers must continuously trade off the demand for quick results with the desire for meaningful results.

4. **Customization matters more.** Research, including database technologies, makes it easier for companies to customize products. This is especially true for information-only products. Therefore, the ability of companies to have a better and deeper understanding of their customers means more than ever.

5. **People matter more.** Convenient worldwide communication has continued to shift the power away from the top of the organizational chart. Purchasers can compare prices for products among hundreds of competing sellers with the click of a mouse. Employees can offer their skills to hundreds of potential employers in a similar manner. Traders have similar access to worldwide investment opportunities. Therefore, businesses that treat customers, employees, and shareholders with true empathy and respect will maintain a unique and sustainable point of differentiation. Again, this increases the need for research into the processes by which these stakeholders receive value from their relationships. High tech solutions should also be "high touch," meaning the human element is their most important feature.

SOURCE: Hair, Joseph F. and Barry J. Babin. 2002. Technology and the New Economy: Implications for Higher Education and the Marketing Discipline, *Advances in Marketing and Purchasing,* Arch Woodside and Ellen Moore, editors, Elsevier Science, Ltd., London: Volume 11 pp. 57–68

agency. Research decisions involve varying degrees of complexity and internal complications. From time to time, therefore, even firms that have **in-house research** departments may out-source a research project to an external firm. The following describes several situations that make hiring an outside consultant advantageous over doing the research "in-house."

1. The research firm may have special expertise or capabilities within a specific area of research. For example, a German firm wishing to begin operations and marketing in the United States might hire an American research firm to investigate potential locations, employee behaviors, and market receptivity. Similarly, would you like to find out about some aspect of the business environment in Japan? Tamtam.com provides an electronic brokering service. Tamtam.com will quickly put you in touch with a firm specializing in Japanese business research. The research firm may even be able to do the project quicker and/or cheaper when they have the corresponding degree of specialized skills and technology.

EXHIBIT 1-5	TEST YOUR TECHNOLOGY IQ

Can you match the acronyms and terms on the left with the descriptions on the right? All of these may have a significant impact on business research processes.

Acronym	Definition	Implication
1. PUSH	**a.** Allows real-time voice, video and data transfer by continuously reallocating unused bandwidth.	Improved and faster electronic communication
2. SMART	**b.** Monitors software usage among all computers on network.	Usage patterns can be tracked and product improvements can be made with increased efficiency.
3. ATM	**c.** A technology which automatically delivers customized information to a person via a browser interface	Researchers have greater access to more relevant information in less time.
4. ASP	**d.** A document transfer and preparation system which allows the user to focus on the logical structure of a message rather than the format codes.	More efficient information processing
5. LATEX	**e.** A technology in which a microprocessor resides on a personalized card (the size of a credit card). Information can be exchanged with computer interfaces by reading the card.	Researchers can track behavior more closely and accurately enabling decision makers to better customize solutions.
6. Crypto Rage	**f.** The anger associated with computer hackers' attempts to breech computer security and/or infect systems with computer viruses (not a new age rock group).	System security should be a high priority.
7. PATROL	**g.** Secure, remote hosting of complex database software that enables more companies affordable access to sophisticated tracking and information gathering.	Better access to information for researchers and decision makers in a wider variety of firms.

ANSWERS: 1-c, 2-e, 3-a (Asynchronous Transfer Mode), 4-g (Application Service Provider), 5-d (Lamport, Tex),* 6-f, 7-b. *
www.technology.com/encyclopedia, accessed February 24, 2002.

2. An **outside research** firm can conduct and interpret research more objectively. The outside firm is not influenced by the corporate culture or worldview. Therefore, when a decision is likely to evoke intense emotions among different factions of the company, an outside firm may be a good idea. Otherwise, the in-house researcher must present results that will anger somebody, and this same researcher has to continue to work with this person. In some cases, the researcher may present research that suggests some manager's brainchild project is a bad idea. This is necessary despite the fact the manager may have invested many months in developing the project. The outside consultant can present the results and then return to the safety of a different company.

3. The outside firm may provide fresh insight into a problem. Particularly when employees within the firm have been unsuccessful in studying the problem previously, an outside firm may offer fresh insight and new approaches.

Likewise, there are reasons why internal researchers may be advantageous.

1. Generally, in-house researchers can provide information more quickly than an outside agency. One reason is that since they are part of the same corporate culture, less time is needed to gain an understanding of the decision issue. They already possess a great deal of the knowledge that an outside researcher would have to acquire through interviews.

2. Other employees can more easily collaborate with in-house researchers. A member of a consulting team may be viewed as an outsider and thus a threat. In contrast, many employees with whom the researcher must collaborate may know him/her quite well. Thus, there is a certain amount of trust in the relationship that is difficult for an outside agency to duplicate.

3. The in-house researchers can often do the research for less money. External consultants can be very expensive. Consultants may charge hourly rates in excess of $150 an hour or more for research work. The one exception to this is when the research requires a specialized skill or access that a consulting firm may already possess, and which would be expensive to obtain otherwise.

4. The in-house researchers may be better able to follow up on a research project. One project often spawns the need for others. If a small follow-up study is needed, the in-house firm can begin the work right away. The outside consulting agent can also do the follow-up study, but at the very least, a new contract often has to be written and agreed upon.

As we discuss the obligations of researchers and decision makers further in Chapter 4, the information generally pertains to both in-house researchers and consultants.

SUMMARY

Provide an Orientation to Modern Day Business Research

Businesspeople have been doing research for several millennia. It's as old as international trade itself. Relatively speaking, the formal study of business research is young. The need for business research is increased as firms face more opportunity, in the form of increased trade, or more potential competition. These conditions create an environment in which a business stands a better chance of benefiting from its decisions if it uses research.

Define Business Research and the People Who Use It

As researchers in general go about trying to find the truth, business researchers go about trying to find the truth about business-related things. Business research is a truth-seeking function responsible for gathering, analyzing, interpreting, and reporting information so that business decision makers become more effective. There are few limits to what a business researcher might be asked to study. The work could involve any business discipline and it could affect tactical and/or strategic business decisions. All organizations—both profit and nonprofit, big or small—who manage employees, study systems, or market to customers are potential users of business research.

CASE STUDY

SAMOUEL'S AND GINO'S RESTAURANTS

To help illustrate business research principles and concepts, we have prepared a case study that will be used throughout all the chapters in the book. The case study is about two restaurants in New York City that are competitors. One of the restaurants is Samouel's Greek Cuisine. The other restaurant is Gino's Ristorante, a southern Italian restaurant located about a block away. Both restaurants cater to the upscale crowd for lunch and dinner. Phil Samouel, owner of the Greek restaurant, came to New York about twenty-five years ago and has owned several other businesses. This is his first restaurant venture. He opened the restaurant about four years ago and his major competitor is Gino's. Gino's Ristorante has been in business about ten years and is owned and managed by Gino. Gino and his mother emigrated from Sicily and brought many family recipes. His mother runs the kitchen and makes sure the food is properly prepared.

We will refer to the case study as we discuss the various research topics. For example, Phil Samouel hired a research company to conduct exit interviews with both his customers and Gino's customers. Results of the survey will help him better understand what customers think about the two restaurants so he can prepare an effective business plan. In Chapter 12 we provide a copy of a **research proposal** given to Phil so he could decide if the value of the research project justified its cost. When we discuss sampling in Chapter 5, we evaluate different sampling approaches and point out why the research company recommended exit interviews. Similarly, we provide copies of the actual questionnaires in Chapters 6 and 7 to illustrate survey concepts and enable students to collect similar data on local restaurants to compare with our case study results. In all the data analysis chapters, we use the case study data to illustrate **SPSS** and the various statistical techniques. Finally, a summary of the research report provided to Phil Samouel is presented in Chapter 12. The focus on a single case study of a typical business research problem will enable you to more easily understand the benefits and pitfalls of using research to improve business decision making.

Discuss Recent Business Trends and How They Affect Business Research

Several trends are affecting business research. These include relationship marketing, which has brought new concepts and a greater need to integrate research studies across multiple stakeholder groups; the internationalization of business, which requires researchers to study previously unfamiliar cultures; and the information revolution, which enables researchers easier access to greater volumes of data. These trends are increasing the importance of business research.

Examine Research-Related Technologies

Technologies were also discussed in this chapter. Data warehousing provides the researcher with off-the-shelf data saving weeks of time and avoiding expensive data collection in many situations. Researchers ability to network via the Internet and intranets has allowed information to be shared more readily. These tools have made the researcher more productive.

KEY TERMS

applied business research	intranet	outside research
basic business research	networking	replicable research
business research	off-the-shelf data	research
data mining	one-shot research project	research proposal
data warehouse	ongoing research	SPSS
GPS	organizational learning	translational equivalence
in-house research	organizational memory	

ETHICAL DILEMMA

NRG, an online music retailer, places a cookie on its customers' computers in order to identify the customer whenever they log onto the company Web site. The cookie allows NRG to maintain a database of information about their customers including name, address, email address, purchase history, and credit card information. The technology even allows NRG to track their customers' movement to other Web sites. NRG analyses this information internally to make product, inventory, and promotional decisions.

After a favorable article about NRG runs in a leading business publication, the marketing director of a clothing company who is interested in targeting NRG's customer base contacts NRG. Instead of paying a marketing research firm to help them identify the online shopping habits of its target audience, the company wants to know if NRG would be willing to sell its information. What do you think NRG should do?

REVIEW QUESTIONS

1. How did research tie to early business strategy in the Early Classical period over 2,500 years ago?
2. What is research?
3. What is business research?
4. List and briefly describe trends affecting business research.
5. What is a data warehouse?
6. What is the difference between the Internet and an intranet?
7. Describe the manager–researcher relationship?

DISCUSSION AND APPLICATION ACTIVITIES

1. How do you think the emergence of the computer since 1945 has affected the field of business research?
2. Explain how a company like Marriot might be able to use data mining.
3. Suppose you wished to start and entrepreneurial venture involving the manufacture of portable fax machines in Turkey for export to the U.K. List at least five areas in which business research may provide information that will allow for better decision making as you begin this venture.
4. Suppose a company wished to do a research project that tested whether or not a level of management could be removed from the entire organization without any

serious negative consequences. Should this project be conducted by in-house researchers or by outsiders?

INTERNET ACTIVITIES

1. Use the Web search engines Google, Yahoo!, and Lycos. Search using the key words *business research*. Prepare a brief report telling what you found and how it differed.

2. The Roper Center at the University of Connecticut has one of the largest collections of public opinion data in the world. Their Web site, located at www .ropercenter.uconn.edu has an online magazine and the results of many surveys. Identify two articles or studies related to this chapter and prepare a report on what you learned.

3. Go to www.autonomy.com. Surf the Web site and prepare a report on the types of business research support available on that site.

NOTES

1. Nevett, Terence R. and Lisa Nevett. 1994. The Origins of Marketing: Evidence from Classical and Early Hellenistic Greece (500-30 B.C.). *Research in Marketing* 6: 3–12.
2. Grace, V. R. 1961. Amphoras and the Ancient Wine Trade. Princeton, N.J.: American School of Classical Studies at Athens.
3. Nevett and Nevett. 1994. p. 9.
4. Gibbens, Robert. 2002. Toyota Extends One-Price Retailing: Montreal Now, Vancouver and Toronto to Follow. *National Post,* 22 January.
5. Roberts, Zoe. 2001. UK Businesses Sustain Their Highest Labour Turnover Costs. *People Management* 7 (October 11): 11.
6. CFO. 1998. Please Don't Go. 14 (May): 23.
7. Sacirbey, Omar. 2000. Online Grocers Restock Capital. *IPO Reporter* 24 (29 May): 10.
8. E. Von Hippel. 1998. Economics of Product Development by Users: the Impact of 'Sticky' Local Information. *Management Science* 44 (5): 629B644.
9. Nezleck, George S. and Gezzinus J. Hidding. 2001. An Investigation into the Differences in the Business Practices of Information Industries. *Human Systems Management* 20 (2): 71–82.
10. Lingard, Helen. 2001. The Effect of First Aid Training on Objective Safety Behaviour in Australian Small Business Construction Firms. *Construction Management and Economics* 19 (October): 611–619.
11. Sahlman, William A. 1999. The New Economy is Stronger than You Think! *Harvard Business Review* 77 (Nov./Dec.): 99–107.
12. FRM. 1995. Keep Faith First, Fund-Raising Will Follow. *Fund Raising Management* 26 (November): 48.
13. Papmehl, Anne. 2001. Russia Has Emerged as an Enticing Business Market. *CMA Management* 75 (November): 50–51.
14. *Eastern Economist Daily*. 2000. Russia Begins Selling Cars in the U.S. (October 12): Global News Wire. MTI Econews. 2000. GAZ to Open Office in Hungary. (30 March): MTI Hungarian News Agency.
15. Glantz, William. 2001. Gorbachev Touts Russian Workers. *The Washington Times,* 25 April: B8.
16. Griffin, Mitch, Barry J. Babin, and Doan Modianos. 2000. Shopping Values of Russian Consumers: The Impact of Habituation in a Developing Economy. *The Journal of Retailing* 76 (Spring): 20–53.
17. James, Diana. 2002. Skoda is Taken from Trash to Treasure. *Marketing News* 36 (18 February): 4–5.
18. Hall, Ernest. 1999. Broadening the View of Corporate Diversification: an International Perspective. *International Journal of Organizational Analysis* 7 (January): 25–54.
19. Singh, Jagdip. 1995. Measurement Issues in Cross-National Research. *Journal of International Business* 26 (3): 597–619; Steenkamp, Jan-Benedict E.M. and Hans Baumgartner. 1998. Assessing Measurement Invariance in Cross-National Research. *Journal of Consumer Research* 25 (June): 78–90.

20. Reichheld, Frederick F. 2001. Lead for Loyalty. *Harvard Business Review* 79 (July/August): 76–84.

21. Ibid.

22. Mathieu, J. E. and D. M. Zajac. 1990. A Review and Meta-Analysis of the Antecedents, and Consequences of Organizational Commitment. *Psychological Bulletin* 108 (September): 171–195.

23. Reichers, Arnon E. 1985. A Review and Reconceptualization of Organizational Commitment. *Academy of Management Review* 10 (3): 465–475.

24. Babin, Barry J. and Jill P. Attaway. 2000. Atmospheric Affect as a Tool for Creating Value and Gaining Share of Customer. *Journal of Business Research* 49 (August): 91–101.

25. Gilliland, David I. and Daniel C. Bello. 2002. Two Sides to Attitudinal Commitment: The Effect of Calculative and Loyalty Commitment on Enforcement Mechanisms in Distribution Channels. *Journal of the Academy of Marketing Science* 30 (Winter): 24–43.

26. Duvall, Mel. 1998. Winery Juices Up Database Link. *Inter@ctive Week* 5 (22 November): 43.

27. www.census.gov

28. Sales and Marketing Index.

29. Hooley, Graham, Gordon Greenley, John Fahy and John Cadogan. 2001. Market-focused Resources, Competitive Positioning and Firm Performance. *Journal of Marketing Management* 17: 503–520; Menon, Anil, Sundar G. Bharadwaj, Phani Tej Adidam and Steven W. Edison. 1999. Antecedents and Consequences of Marketing Strategy Making: A Model and Test. *Journal of Marketing* 63 (April): 18–40; Minor, Anne S., Paula Bassoff and Christine Moorman. 2001. Organizational Improvisation and Learning: A Field Study. *Administrative Science Quarterly* 46 (June): 304–337.

30. Rigdon, Edward. 1997. Data Mining Gains New Respectability. *Marketing News* 6 (6 January): 8.

31. O'Brien, Terrence E. and Paul E. Durfee. 1994. Classification Tree Software. *Marketing Research* 6 (Summer): 36–40.

32. Rigdon, Edward.

33. Morgan, Michael S. 2000. Research Boosts Database's Power. *Marketing News* 9 (8 October): 16.

34. Security for Buyers of Products, Systems and Services. 1998. Customer Tracking Pays Off. 35 (August): 79.

35. informationweek.com, "Intel's Got The Speed; Do Customers Need It?" www.informationweek.com, accessed 20 February 2002.

Appendix 1-A: Research Proposals

Before conducting a research project, the business researcher must clearly understand the problem to be investigated. Once the problem is defined, a plan of action is developed to investigate and make recommendations on how to solve the problem. A research proposal is a formal document summarizing what the problem is, how it will be investigated, how much it will cost, and how long the research will take to complete. If accepted, it typically represents a contract between the researcher and the client (the one requesting the research be conducted).

The research proposal plays a critical role in any research project. It identifies and defines the problem to be investigated, it outlines the approach and methods the researcher will use, it specifies the deliverables from the project (what the client will actually get from the project), and it includes a budget and timeframe for completion. A formal written proposal is the result of interactions between the client and the researcher through which the client's concerns (problems) are translated into research problems, and a proposed approach to solve the problem(s) is agreed upon.

Researchers benefit from preparing written proposals. The first benefit is that proposal preparation clarifies that the problem to be investigated is the one the client requested. Business research helps managers improve their decisions. If the problem as defined in the research proposal does not facilitate improved decision making, then the problem must be redefined or the research should not be undertaken. Once the proposal is accepted, it provides a direction and a plan for the researcher. By following the plan, the researcher can assess progress on completion of the project and make adjustments as needed. Finally, the written proposal documents the agreement between the researcher and the client and minimizes the possibility of later misunderstandings. Clients know what information they will receive and researchers know what information they must provide.

Clients also benefit from a written research proposal. First, when the client reviews the proposal they can verify the researcher truly understands the problem to be investigated. If changes are needed, they can be made before the project is begun. Once the project is underway, the client can use the proposal as a means of ensuring the project's deliverables are what they expected, and that the project is executed as promised. Finally, a written proposal enables the client to evaluate the quality and value of a proposed project. If several proposals have been solicited, the client can compare the scope, methods, and proposed budget. This helps to ensure that high quality research that provides value for its cost will be delivered as expected. Exhibit A-1 provides an example of a proposal that was submitted to a healthcare organization to update their strategic plan.

EXHIBIT A-1	RESEARCH PROPOSAL FOR CHILDREN'S HEALTH FOUNDATION

I. INTRODUCTION AND OBJECTIVES

Children's Health Foundation has progressed significantly since our initial strategic planning engagement in 1998. At that time, management was in transition, Children's had no clear strategy, and Regional Health System, a full-service competitor, was applying steady pressure through the board and medical staff to absorb Children's into their system. Much has occurred since that time. Internally, the organization of Children's has matured significantly—the management team has coalesced, programs have been assessed and improved, costs have been reduced, and facilities developed. Externally, the payor environment has changed radically, with managed care spreading and freedom of choice for patients and physicians being reduced. In this new age of healthcare, Children's must establish a strategic direction.

We believe Children's must rethink all aspects of its strategy. The current plan has been updated periodically over the past five years, but the core directions have remained heavily hospital-focused and facility-program oriented. These are no longer sufficient strategic foundations for the future. The new plan must be "next generation," concentrating on a healthcare market dominated by managed care, physician-hospital integration, a broader service area, and affiliations with other systems. In short, the strategic plan must be redeveloped from the ground up.

The objectives of the proposed planning process for developing this new strategic plan are as follows:

1. Develop and agree upon a new forecast for the healthcare market served by Children's Health Foundation, fully understanding the revised geography, demand, competition, and trends.

2. Identify and agree upon Children's positioning in the market.

3. Identify the best strategy for Children's to achieve its mission, serve its communities, and prosper in the new environment.

4. Achieve a common understanding of these requirements between the board, management, and the physician leadership of the organization.

Following is a proposed work plan and schedule for achieving these objectives.

II. SCOPE OF WORK AND PROCESSES

We recommend developing the plan in four phases of work, beginning in January 2003 and finishing in May 2003, with an interim leadership retreat in April. Following is an overview of the key tasks and expected timeframes.

1. *Project Initiation.* Our major goal early in the project will be to define the type of database, analysis, and findings framework that provides good system-wide evaluations. Major tasks include, but are not limited to: agree upon information needed to support discussion, request and obtain data, develop interview lists, meeting dates, and preliminary agendas, and agree upon an initial list of issues to focus on. This should be completed by mid-February.

2. *Situation and Objectives.* The basic goal of this group of tasks is to develop a shared understanding of the expected market, and of Children's position in this market. This will provide the baseline for identifying the critical objectives for the future. Major activities include: forecast the external market for healthcare in Children's market area; complete a demographic analysis and forecast; forecast outpatient, inpatient, and physician demand under the expected environment; model Children's expected and needed market share positions and volume implications under a range of scenarios; complete a SWOT (Strength, Weakness, Opportunity, Threat) assessment of Children's position; and identify critical success objectives for the hospital over the next five to ten years. These activities should be completed by mid-April.

3. *Strategy and Requirements.* Working from the objectives, short- and long-term strategies will be developed. Areas we expect to cover include, but are not limited to: assessment of the number of patients needed to support the system; payor interfaces needed to support alternate patient sources, including managed care, indemnity, Medicaid, etc.; medical staff and physician business development initiatives; internal organization and governance requirements to support strategic initiatives; and mission implications. We expect these areas to be initially addressed during the March–April period. At the retreat in late April, the board and management can review preliminary strategic directions and provide input as needed.

4. *Action Planning.* The intent of this final group of activities is to ensure priorities are set and the basis for implementation is outlined. This also will include submission of the database and project documentation to the Children's management team for subsequent use. Areas we anticipate covering

(continued)

EXHIBIT A-I	**RESEARCH PROPOSAL FOR CHILDREN'S HEALTH FOUNDATION (CONTINUED)**

include: prioritization and timeframes for key initiatives; resource requirements needed to support action steps; implementation process with key groups, including physicians, employees, board and community leaders; and final report submission. These tasks should be completed by late May.

The process we propose centers around regular meetings with a planning steering committee of eight to ten senior management and medical staff, supported by board presentations and perhaps medical staff briefings at key points. In addition, we expect to conduct approximately thirty-five individual interviews with a cross-section of physicians, board members, payors, potential affiliates, and management. Our proposed scope of process includes the following: five sessions with the steering committee, thirty-five individual interviews, presentation at April retreat, six 2-day on-site visits, and discussions with key individuals scheduled into the planned site visits.

III. CONSULTING TEAM AND PROPOSED BUDGET

Assuming the project can be authorized by late December, we are prepared to commit a very strong consulting team to Children's, and are holding open our schedules accordingly. John Frusha, Principal Investigator, will lead this engagement and participate in all aspects of the work. He directed the original plan in 1998 as well as all interim updates. He has a national experience base and is well versed in the issues confronting Children's Health Foundation. Buddy Chen, a Manager in our strategy services group, will coordinate the day-to-day activities. He has broad experience with projects and issues of the type proposed. Jana Reynolds will provide

staff consulting support. She has a strong healthcare background and will be the point person in developing and analyzing the database, as well as in conducting the interviews. Resumes for all three of these individuals are attached.

Our professional fee for conducting this project as proposed is estimated to be $106,000. This estimate is based on the levels of participation identified below:

> John Frusha—100 hours @ $300/hour = $30,000
>
> Buddy Chen—150 hours @ $250/hour = $37,500
>
> Jana Reynolds—220 hours @ $175/hour = $38,500

Direct out-of-pocket expenses including travel and lodging, secretarial support, overnight delivery, long distance telephone, and secretarial support are charged at cost in addition to above fees. Based on our past experience with Children's, this is a substantial quote. Two perspectives may be helpful in assessing this proposal. First, the current plan must be updated for the future. Other projects of similar scope typically run $130,000 to $150,000. Our past experience and familiarity with Children's situation has allowed us to complete this project on a budget that is 20–30 percent lower. Second, the budget for the previous plan was $70,000. Five years of inflation and the increased complexity of the current healthcare environment make the current bid very comparable, in our opinion. Also, our proposed team is more experienced than the previous one.

This team, quote, and timetable are good through the end of December 2002, after which time our changing availability may dictate revisions. Please accept this as a working draft, subject to additional discussion to ensure the scope of the project is in line with your needs.

STRUCTURE OF A RESEARCH PROPOSAL

Research proposals can take a variety of forms. Some proposals are quite long and detailed. For example, public domain proposals for federal, state, and local projects typically are the most detailed. Others are of moderate length, such as the one for Children's Health Foundation shown in Exhibit A-1. Finally, some are very short, perhaps as short as one page, such as the one shown in Exhibit A-2. No matter what the length or level of detail, virtually all proposals should include the following:

- Project Title
- Background Information—specifies events leading up to request for the proposal to be prepared and submitted
- Problem Statement and Research Objectives
- Research Strategy and Methods—data to be collected, how it will be collected and analyzed. This summarizes steps that will be taken to achieve the research objectives

- Nature of the Final Report to be submitted—specifies type and nature of report
- Schedule and Budget
- Qualifications of Project consultants and research firm

The structure of the proposal is dictated by the nature of the research project being proposed. Fundamentally, the proposal should have enough information to ensure that the proposed project will solve the problem, and the results will help the client to improve their decisions.

EXHIBIT A-2 | **LETTER PROPOSAL TO INITIATE BUSINESS-TO-BUSINESS SURVEY**

AdMark International, LLC
12538 N. Peachtree Blvd.
Atlanta, Georgia 30024

Engagement Memo

To: Suzanne Wagner, Senior Manager
Louisiana Specialty Chemicals, Inc.

From: Bill Black, Principal Investigator
AdMark International

Re: Project Contract/Engagement

B-T-B SURVEY

Date: February 26, 2003

Project Deliverables:

- Telephone interviews based on list provided by client (N = 50)
- Complete approximately 25–30 interviews (about 55–60 percent)
- Make ten callbacks to customer list over a three-week period
- Questionnaire same as previous survey
- Begin project first week in March; survey programming and data collection will take about four weeks. Report preparation will take approximately two weeks. Total project time about six to eight weeks.
- Open-ended questions to be taped and transcribed; client will be provided copy, but respondent identity will be kept confidential.
- PowerPoint Presentation Report provided to client
- Principal Investigator available for consultation regarding project

Budget:

- Cost of Project = $12,000
  - □ $6,000 due to initiate project.
  - □ $6,000 due upon submission of report.
- One day site visit to discuss findings (optional)
  - □ $1,500 plus travel expenses.

Accepted as proposed above: _____ _____

Suzanne Wagner   Date

Most business research proposals are moderate in their length and level of detail. Exhibit A-3 shows the research proposal that was submitted to Phil Samouel to help him improve his restaurant operations.

EXHIBIT A-3	**RESEARCH PROPOSAL FOR SAMOUEL'S GREEK CUISINE RESTAURANT**

STATEMENT OF PROBLEM

Phil Samouel, owner of Samouel's Greek Cuisine restaurant, believes his revenues and profits are not as high as they could be. He wants to find out how to attract more new customers, keep his current customers, and convince customers to spend more when they come and to come back more often. He also wants to ensure he is operating his restaurant as effectively and efficiently as possible.

Phil is a successful manager and businessman, but he is fairly new to the restaurant business. He, therefore, has decided the best way to improve his business is to hire a restaurant consultant. Through a contact at his advertising agency, Phil identified a business research firm called AdMark International. He contacted them and asked that they conduct a preliminary assessment of his restaurant operations and prepare a research proposal for him to review. The proposal is expected to include proposed projects, deliverables from the projects such as recommended strategies and action plans, as well as a schedule and budget. The outcome of this preliminary assessment is summarized as follows:

RESEARCH QUESTIONS

After discussions with Phil Samouel and several of his employees, the account manager from the research firm concluded that the primary questions facing Samouel's restaurant are:

- Are employees being managed to maximize their productivity as well as commitment to the success of the restaurant?
- What are the best approaches to attract new customers and to keep and grow existing customers?

RESEARCH APPROACH

To answer these questions, two separate but related research projects are recommended. The first project will evaluate current employees to determine their productivity, job satisfaction, and commitment. To do so, a survey of employees that has been used by a wide variety of organizations will be administered and tabulated. The second project will involve a survey of customers of Samouel's and his major competitor, Gino's Italian Ristorante.

Employee Assessment Project

The employee assessment project can be broken down into three researchable questions. They are:

ERQ-1: How do employees feel about the work environment at Samouel's?

ERQ-2: How committed are the employees to helping make the restaurant a success?

ERQ-3: Do different groups of employees have different feelings about working at Samouel's?

ERQ-1: The first research question concerns the work environment at Samouel's. Specific aspects of the work environment to be examined include: compensation, supervision, coworkers, and overall satisfaction with the work at Samouel's. Phil Samouel believes he has good employees, but knows there is always room for improvement. Moreover, he has never specifically asked his employees how they feel about working at his restaurant, and he has hired a lot of new young workers in the past year (twenty-six new workers between the ages of 18–34), many that are part-time.

ERQ-2: The second employee research question focuses on how committed the employees are to ensuring the success of Samouel's restaurant. From observing employees and listening to their comments, Phil believes the age and the length of time employees have worked at the restaurant may be related to commitment to the organization. Phil's consultant says that he has read some articles in trade publications suggesting this might be typical.

ERQ-3: The third employee research question focuses on whether there are any differences among the employees regarding how they feel about working at Samouel's. Phil's observations of employees suggest this is true and his consultant says his informal discussions with employees would support this.

Customer Assessment Project

The customer assessment project can be broken down into three researchable questions. They are:

CRQ-1: What is the level of satisfaction of Samouel's customers relative to the customers of its primary competitor, Gino's?

(continued)

CRQ-2: Do customers rate Gino's more favorably than they do Samouel's?

CRQ-3: What factors contribute to restaurant customer satisfaction?

CRQ-1: The first research question concerns the competitive positioning of Samouel's relative to Gino's. Phil Samouel's opinion is that Gino's has the advantage of being located in a more established residential area, and that its longer history than Samouel's has resulted in a larger, more loyal customer base. In addition, Mr. Samouel believes that Gino's is able to charge higher prices without sacrificing business. Since satisfied customers may be willing to reward the restaurant by paying higher prices, it is important to examine these issues.

CRQ-2: The second research question addresses whether customers evaluate Samouel's and Gino's differently. Customers will be asked to rate the two restaurants on twelve attributes. The question, then, is do the ratings of the two restaurants differ significantly in ways that might influence satisfaction and loyalty? If the perceptions differ on critical selection variables then action plans can be developed to overcome these problems.

CRQ-3: The third research question asks which factors determine customer satisfaction. Mr. Samouel has expressed belief that satisfaction is determined mostly by food quality and the service of his employees. This belief is supported by a search of existing basic research reported in trade and academic journals. It has been documented that customers evaluate service industries in general based on two classes of attributes. Core attributes represent those that most directly provide the primary benefit sought by most customers. In the case of a restaurant, food-related attributes would qualify as a core attribute. Relational attributes represent those that are less tangible and deal with human-human and human-environment interactions. Customer perceptions of the environment and employees fall into this category for restaurants.

Several articles in restaurant trade publications reported this breakdown. They discussed the importance of food quality, including the freshness and variety, and restaurant cleanliness as two key factors shaping customer's service quality perceptions.[1] Thus, when customer perceptions of food, employees, and atmosphere improve, their satisfaction with the restaurant also should improve. The results of this survey will be very important in assessing Samuel's restaurant to identify strategies for improvement.

METHODOLOGY

Samples

Data must be collected to examine the preceding issues. Exit interviews as patrons depart Gino's Italian Ristorante and Samouel's Greek Cuisine are proposed because this will be a good way to identify and interview Gino's customers. Interviews will be conducted between 12:00 and 2:00 P.M. and 7:00 to 10 P.M., Monday through Saturday, for a period of ten days. Interviews during these hours will enable comparisons between lunch and dinner patrons. Customers will be approached randomly and asked four screening questions. One, do they occasionally dine out in restaurants? Two, did they just dine in the restaurant? Three, is their annual household income $20,000 or more? And four, have they completed the questionnaire before? A yes for the first three questions and a no for the second will prompt a request to participate in the survey. If the customer agrees, they will be provided with a clipboard containing the study questionnaire, a comfortable place to complete it, and $5 for their participation. The goal will be to obtain at least one hundred interviews with customers of each restaurant. An employee survey also will be conducted. An attempt will be made to interview as many employees as possible, but not fewer than sixty.

Measures

Measures for the study will be developed following interviews with Phillip Samouel and his management team, as well as from consulting previous industry research. The employee survey will have been previously validated and its reliability assessed. The survey will include questions about the working conditions, compensation, co-workers, supervision, commitment to the organization, likelihood to search for another job, and classification variables such as age and gender. The customer survey will include perceptions of the food, atmosphere, prices, employees, and so forth. Classification questions such as age and gender, as well as relationship variables like satisfaction and future patronage, also will be included.

Data Analysis Approach

After the data is collected, it will be analyzed and summarized in an easy-to-understand format. The statistical software SPSS will be used to ensure the relevant issues are examined in a comprehensive and cost-effective manner. Both simple as well as advanced statistical techniques will

(continued)

| EXHIBIT A-3 | RESEARCH PROPOSAL FOR SAMOUEL'S GREEK CUISINE RESTAURANT (CONTINUED) |

be used where appropriate. Usage of the statistical techniques will be according to commonly accepted research assumptions and practices.

SCHEDULE AND BUDGET

Schedule

The two projects are quite extensive. The employee survey will take approximately thirty days to complete. This will entail obtaining interviews from as many employees as possible, but no fewer than 50 percent of the workforce at the restaurant, and representation from all management employees. The customer survey will take the longest time. It will take approximately eight weeks to design the questionnaire, collect data, and analyze and interpret the findings. Preliminary findings of the projects and updates will be given every two weeks. The final report, including recommendations, will be available ten weeks after the contract has been signed and the initial payment has been received.

Budget

The total cost for the two projects is shown below:

Employee Survey	$ 5,000
Customer Survey	$15,000
Total Cost	**$20,000**

Terms: 50 percent will be due to initiate the project, and the balance is to be paid when the final report is submitted.

Qualifications

The consultants assigned to this project have a combined thirty-five years of experience in the restaurant industry. The principal investigator has completed projects with over four hundred clients in the past fourteen years. The individual biographical sketches of the research team assigned to this project are attached for your review.

NOTES

1. Klara, Robert. 1999. Fast and Fancy. *Restaurant Business* 98 (June 1): 19–21; Stern, Jane and Michael Stern. 2000. Familiarity Usually Breeds Regular Restaurant Customers. *Nation's Restaurant News* 34 (November 20): 24–26.

Appendix 1-B: Case Study Databases

SAMOUEL'S AND GINO'S RESTAURANTS

Several of the chapters in this book illustrate how to use statistical techniques to analyze and understand data. Simple statistical techniques often are adequate, but at other times it may be helpful to use more complex techniques. The emphasis in this text is on how businesses can use business research and statistical techniques to make better decisions. To help students more easily understand the various research issues and statistical techniques, we use two survey research projects and their databases to examine the research problems discussed in the chapters. The databases are from the case study introduced in Chapter 1 on Samouel's Greek Cuisine restaurant and Gino's Italian Ristorante. Following is a description of the database variables, how they are measured, and how they are coded.

To help him compete more effectively with Gino's Italian Ristorante, Phil Samouel retained a business and strategy consultant. The consultant recommended that two surveys be completed. One was a survey of customers of the two restaurants. The other was a survey of Phil's employees. We provide an overview of the employee survey first and then the customer survey.

EMPLOYEE DATABASE

The database consists of sixty-three interviews with employees of Samouel's Greek Cuisine restaurant. (See SPSS file Employee Survey N = 63.sav.) There is another file that includes seven employee questionnaires with missing data (Employee Survey N = 71 with missing data.sav). The questionnaire included twenty-one measures the business consultant had used with other restaurants. Employees first were asked their feelings about the work environment at Samouel's. Employees were asked to evaluate twelve statements (Variables X_1–X_{12}) covering topics such as coworkers, supervision, compensation and overall feelings about their work. Next, employees were asked several questions designed to measure their level of commitment to Samouel's management and the organization. The commitment questions asked how they felt about working at Samouel's restaurant and about their likelihood of searching for another job in the next six months. Interviewers asked two more questions—age and work type (part-time vs. full-time)—and recorded the gender of the respondents without asking them. Finally, about a week after the survey was completed, the management team at Samouel's restaurant assigned a performance rating for all employees that participated in the survey and this was recorded in the database. The variables, sample questions, and their coding are shown as follows.

Work Environment Measures

The work environment opinions were measured as follows:
The following list is a series of statements that could be used to describe the work environment at Samouel's Greek Cuisine restaurant. Using a scale from 1 to 7, with 7 being "Strongly Agree" and 1 being "Strongly Disagree," to what extent do you agree or disagree that each statement describes your work environment at Samouel's?

X_1—I am paid fairly for the work I do.

X_2—I am doing the kind of work I want.

X_3—My supervisor gives credit and praise for work well done.

X_4—There is a lot of cooperation among the members of my work group.

X_5—My job allows me to learn new skills.

X_6—My supervisor recognizes my potential.

X_7—My work gives me a sense of accomplishment.

X_8—My immediate work group functions as a team.

X_9—My pay reflects the effort I put into doing my work.

X_{10}—My supervisor is friendly and helpful.

X_{11}—The members of my work group have the skills and/or training to do their job well.

X_{12}—The benefits I receive are reasonable.

For example, if a respondent chose a "7" on statement X_8, it would indicate he or she "Strongly Agrees" that his or her "work group functions as a team." On the other hand, if he or she chose a "1" for statement X_8 it would indicate this employee strongly disagrees and perceives that his or her work group does not function as a team.

Relationship Measures

Several measures of organizational commitment were included in the survey. They are listed as follows, along with their coding.

X_{13}—Loyalty: I have a sense of loyalty to Samouel's restaurant.

　　　　7 = Strongly Agree; 1 = Strongly Disagree

X_{14}—Effort: I am willing to put in a great deal of effort beyond that normally expected to help Samouel's restaurant to be successful.

　　　　7 = Strongly Agree; 1 = Strongly Disagree

X_{15}—Proud: I am proud to tell others that I work for Samouel's restaurant.

　　　　7 = Strongly Agree; 1 = Strongly Disagree

Classification Variables

X_{16}—Intention to Search:　　1 = Extremely Unlikely

　　　　　　　　　　　　　　2 = Very Unlikely

3 = Somewhat Unlikely

4 = Neither–about a 50-50 chance

5 = Somewhat Likely

6 = Very Likely

7 = Extremely Likely

X_{17}—Length of Time an Employee:

= Employee < One Year

= Employee 1–2 Years

= Employee > 2 Years

X_{18}—Work Type: Part-Time = 1; Full-Time = 0

X_{19}—Gender: Male = 0; Female = 1

X_{20}—Age:

1 = 18–25

2 = 26–34

3 = 35–49

4 = 50–59

5 = 60 and older

X_{21}—Performance:

1 = Very Low Performance

2 = Somewhat Lower Performance

3 = Average Performance

4 = Somewhat Higher Performance

5 = Very High Performance

CUSTOMER DATABASE

The customer survey database consists of two hundred interviews with customers of two restaurants in New York City. (See SPSS file Customer Survey N = 200.sav.) One of the restaurants is Samouel's Greek Cuisine. The other restaurant is Gino's Italian Ristorante, a southern Italian restaurant located about a block away. Both restaurants cater to the upscale crowd for lunch and dinner.

To help him better understand what customers think about the two restaurants, Phil Samouel hired a research company to conduct exit interviews with his customers and Gino's customers. A total of 230 interviews were completed, but thirty of them had missing data. He asked the research company to complete one hundred interviews with no missing data for customers from each restaurant. Thus, the total usable sample was two hundred interviews. A questionnaire consisting of twenty-five measures was developed, pretested, and finalized for use. Customers first were asked their perceptions of the two restaurants on twelve factors (Variables X_1–X_{12}). The perceptions questions were asked in a random sequence to avoid order bias. Respondents then were asked to rank four general restaurant selection factors in terms of their importance in selecting a restaurant where they wanted to eat (Variables X_{13}–X_{16}). The four factors were identified from a review of previous research and two focus groups as being the most widely used determinant attributes for selecting fine dining restaurants. Next, respondents were asked five relationship questions, including how satisfied they were with the restaurant, how likely they were to recommend it to a friend, how likely they are to come back in the future, how often they eat there, and how long they have been a customer of that particular restaurant (X_{17}–X_{21}). Interviewers asked two more questions, about age and income respectively, and recorded the gender of the respondents without asking them. The variables, examples of questions, and their coding are shown in the following paragraphs. The Competitor variable (X_{25}) indicates whether interviews were conducted with either Samouel's customers or Gino's customers.

Perceptions Measures

The perceptions were measured as follows: I am going to read a list of characteristics that could be used to describe Samouel's Greek Cuisine (or Gino's Ristorante). Using a scale from 1 to 7, with 7 being "Strongly Agree" and 1 being "Strongly Disagree," please indicate the extent to which you agree or disagree that _____ has:

X_1—Excellent Food Quality
X_2—Attractive Interior
X_3—Generous Portions
X_4—Excellent Food Taste
X_5—Good Value for the Money
X_6—Friendly Employees
X_7—Appears Clean and Neat
X_8—Fun Place to Go
X_9—Wide Variety of Menu Items
X_{10}—Reasonable Prices
X_{11}—Courteous Employees
X_{12}—Competent Employees

For example, if a respondent said a "7" on Excellent Food Quality, it would indicate he or she strongly agrees that _____ has Excellent Food Quality. On the other hand, if a respondent said a "1" for Generous Portions, it would indicate he or she strongly disagrees and perceives _____ to have portions that are too small.

Selection Factor Rankings

Data for the restaurant selection factors were collected as follows:

I am going to read a list of factors (reasons) many people use when selecting a restaurant where they want to dine. Think about your visits to fine dining restaurants in the last thirty days and please rank each reason from 1 to 4, with 4 being the most important reason for selecting the restaurant and 1 being the least important reason. There can be no ties, so make sure you rank each attribute with a different number.

The list of reasons was read in a random sequence to avoid order bias.

X_{13}—Food Quality

X_{14}—Atmosphere

X_{15}—Prices

X_{16}—Employees

Relationship Measures

Several measures of possible relationships with the restaurants were asked. They are listed as follows, along with their coding.

X_{17}—Satisfaction:

7 = Highly Satisfied; 1 = Not Very Satisfied

X_{18}—Likely to Return in Future:

7 = Definitely Will Return; 1 = Definitely Will Not Return

X_{19}—Recommend to Friend:

7 = Definitely Will Recommend; 1 = Definitely Will Not Recommend

X_{20}—Frequency of Patronage:

3 = Very Frequently (four or more times a month)

2 = Frequently (one to three times a month)

1 = Occasional (less than once a month)

X_{21}—Length of Time a Customer:

1 = Customer < One Year

2 = Customer 1–3 Years

3 = Customer > 3 Years

Classification Variables

Questions for the classification variables were asked at the end of the survey. Responses were coded as follows:

X_{22}—Gender: Male = 0; Female = 1

X_{23}—Age: 1 = 18–25

2 = 26–34

3 = 35–49

4 = 50–59

5 = 60 and older

X_{24}—Income 1 = $20,000–$35,000 annually

2 = $35,001–$50,000 annually

3 = $50,001–$75,000 annually

4 = $75,001–$100,000 annually

5 = > $100,000 annually

X_{25}—Competitor: Gino's Customer = 1 and Samouel's Customer = 0

Appendix 1-C: How to Use SPSS

The data analysis and presentation techniques you will learn in this book are all available in the popular software package SPSS. Many instructors request that a copy of the student version of this package be included with your book. This package is very user-friendly and enables you to easily learn the various statistical techniques without having to use formulas and calculate the results. The approach is a simple Windows-based "point-and-click" process.

When you run the SPSS software, you will see a screen like that in Exhibit C-1. Recall that copies of the case study databases are available from our Web site at www.wiley.com/college/hair or from your instructor. To load your copy of the restaurant employee database you must tell the program where to find your copy of the database—it is named Employee Survey N = 63.sav. We provide instructions for the employee survey database here, but everything is set up the same with the customer survey database if you would like to use it instead.

When you load SPSS, a screen labeled in the top left-hand corner Untitled—SPSS Data Editor should be visible in the background. In the foreground is a dialog box called SPSS for Windows Student Version. If you have never run SPSS, you will have to tell the program where to find data. If you have previously run the SPSS program you can simply highlight the location of the database and click on OK at the bottom of the screen. The SPSS Data Editor screen without the dialog box in the foreground is shown in Exhibit C-1.

Across the top of the screen is a toolbar with a series of pull-down menus. Each of these menus leads you to several functions. An overview of these menu functions follows.

MENUS

There are ten pull-down menus across the top of the screen. You can access most SPSS functions and commands by making selections from the menus on the main menu bar. Following are the major features accessed from each of the ten menus on the Student Version 11 of the SPSS software.

File = create new SPSS files; open existing files; save a file; print; and exit.

Edit = cut and/or copy text or graphics; find specific data; change default options such as size or type of font, fill patterns for charts, types of tables, display format for numerical variables, and so forth.

View = modify what and how information is displayed in the window.

EXHIBIT C-1   **SPSS DATA EDITOR WINDOW WITH NO DATA**

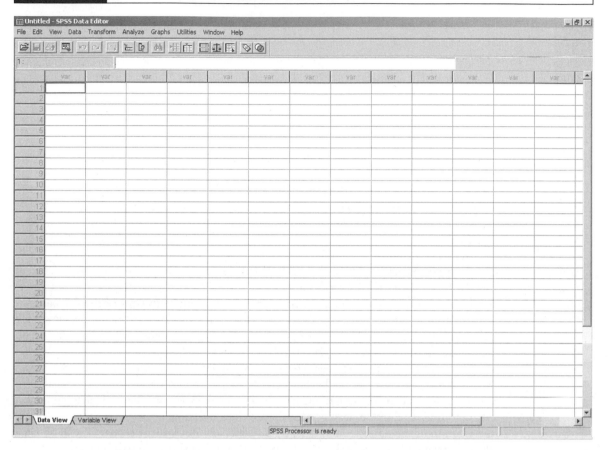

Data = make changes to SPSS data files; add variables and/or cases; change the order of the respondents; split your data file for analysis; and select specific respondents for analysis by themselves.

Transform = compute changes or combinations of data variables; create new variables from combinations of other variables; create random seed numbers; count occurrences of values within cases; recode existing variables; create categories for existing variables; replace missing variables; and so on.

Analyze = prepare reports; execute selected statistical techniques such as frequencies, correlation and regression, factor, cluster, and so on.

Graphs = prepare graphs and charts of data, such as bar, line, and pie charts; also boxplots, scatter diagrams, and histograms.

Utilities = information about variables such as missing values, column width, measurement level, and so on.

Window = minimize windows or move between windows.

Help = a brief tutorial of how to use SPSS; includes a link to the SPSS home page at www.spss.com.

ENTERING DATA

There are two ways you can enter data into SPSS files. One is to enter data directly into the Data Editor window. This can be done by creating an entirely new file or by bringing data in from another software package such as Excel. The other is to load data from a file that has been created in another SPSS application.

Let's begin with explaining how to enter data directly into the Data Editor window (see Exhibit C-1).

The process is similar to entering data into a spreadsheet. The first column is the name of the variable. You are only allowed to have an eight-character name. A more complete name is permitted for the Label column. We discuss this in more detail when we review the Variable View screen. You can also cut and paste data from another application. Simply open the Data Editor window and minimize it. Then go to your other application and select the desired data and click copy, return to the Data Editor window and paste the data in it, making sure you correctly align the columns for each of the variables.

Now let's talk about how to load a previously created SPSS file, such as those that come with your text. Load the SPSS software and you should see an Untitled SPSS Data Editor screen. Click on the Open File icon and you will get an Open File dialog box. Click on Look in to indicate where to look for your file. For example, look in the Compact Disc or 3 1/2" Diskette that accompanied this text. This will locate your SPSS files and you can click on either the employee survey data or the customer survey data. This will load the file and you will be ready to run analyses.

DATA VIEW

When you open your SPSS file it will show the Data View screen. Exhibit C-2 shows the Data View screen for the Samouel's employee survey. You will note the restaurant employee survey database is shown as already loaded into your SPSS software (these are the numbers in the columns on the screen). This screen is useful when running data analysis or building data files. The other view of the Data Editor is Variable View. The Variable View shows you information about the variables. To move between the two views go to the bottom left-hand corner of the screen and click on the view you want. We discuss the Variable View screen in the next section.

The employee survey database is set up in columns. The first column on the far left labeled "id" is a unique number for each of the sixty-three respondents in your database. The remaining columns are the original data from the interviews conducted with Samouel's employees. In the first twelve columns to the right of the id you have the values for the work environment variables (X_1–X_{12}). For example, employee respondent 1 gave Samouel's a "5" on the 7-point scale for the first variable (X_1). Similarly, that same respondent rated the restaurant a "5" on the second variable (X_2) and a "5" on the third one (X_3). As you scroll to the right you will see the data for all twenty-one variables.

VARIABLE VIEW

Exhibit C-3 shows the Variable View screen for the Samouel's employee survey. In this view, the variable names appear in the far left-hand column. Then each of the columns defines various attributes of the variables described below:

EXHIBIT C-2	DATA VIEW OF SAMOUEL'S EMPLOYEE SURVEY DATABASE

Employee Survey N = 63.sav - SPSS Data Editor   _|B|x|

File Edit View Data Transform Analyze Graphs Utilities Window Help

	Name	Type	Width	Decimals	Label	Values	Missing	Columns	Align	Me
1	id	Numeric	3	0	ID	None	None	8	Center	Nomi
2	x1	Numeric	4	0	X1 -- Paid Fairly	{1, Strongly Disagree}...	None	8	Center	Scale
3	x2	Numeric	4	0	X2 -- Work I Want	{1, Strongly Disagree}...	None	8	Center	Scale
4	x3	Numeric	4	0	X3 -- Supervisor Praises	{1, Strongly Disagree}...	None	8	Center	Scale
5	x4	Numeric	4	0	X4 -- Work Group Cooperation	{1, Strongly Disagree}...	None	8	Center	Scale
6	x5	Numeric	4	0	X5 -- Learn New Skills	{1, Strongly Disagree}...	None	8	Center	Scale
7	x6	Numeric	4	0	X6 -- Supervisor Recognizes Pot	{1, Strongly Disagree}...	None	8	Center	Scale
8	x7	Numeric	8	0	X7 -- Accomplishment	{1, Strongly Disagree}...	None	8	Center	Scale
9	x8	Numeric	4	0	X8 -- Work Group - Team	{1, Strongly Disagree}...	None	8	Center	Scale
10	x9	Numeric	4	0	X9 -- Pay Reflects Effort	{1, Strongly Disagree}...	None	8	Center	Scale
11	x10	Numeric	4	0	X10 -- Supervisor Friendly/Helpful	{1, Strongly Disagree}...	None	8	Center	Scale
12	x11	Numeric	4	0	X11 -- Work Group - Skills/Traini	{1, Strongly Disagree}...	None	8	Center	Scale
13	x12	Numeric	4	0	X12 -- Benefits Reasonable	{1, Strongly Disagree}...	None	8	Center	Scale
14	x13	Numeric	4	0	X13 -- Loyalty	{1, Definitely Disagree = 1}...	None	8	Center	Scale
15	x14	Numeric	4	0	X14 -- Effort	{1, Definitely Disagree = 1}...	None	7	Center	Scale
16	x15	Numeric	4	0	X15 -- Proud	{1, Definitely Disagree = 1}...	None	8	Center	Scale
17	x16	Numeric	4	0	X16 -- Intention to Search	{1, Extremely Unlikely}...	None	8	Center	Scale
18	x17	Numeric	4	0	X17 -- How Long an Employee	{1, Less than 1 year}...	None	8	Center	Ordin
19	x18	Numeric	4	0	X18 -- Work Type	{0, Full Time}...	None	8	Center	Nomi
20	x19	Numeric	4	0	X19 -- Gender	{0, Males}...	None	8	Center	Nomi
21	x20	Numeric	4	0	X20 -- Age	{1, 18 - 25}...	None	8	Center	Scale
22	x21	Numeric	4	0	X21 -- Performance	{1, Very Low Performance}...	None	8	Center	Scale
23										
24										
25										
26										
27										
28										
29										
30										
31										
32										

◄ ► \ Data View λ **Variable View** /   ◄ | ►

SPSS Processor is ready

Name = This is an eight-character abbreviated name for each variable.

Type = The default for this is numeric with two decimal places. This can be changed to express values as whole numbers or it can do other things such as specify the values as dates, dollar, custom currency, and so forth. To view the options, click first on the Numeric cell and then on the three shaded dots to the right of the cell.

Width = This defines the width of the data in the columns.

Decimals = This enables you to define the number of decimals to use with your data.

Label = In this column, you give a more descriptive title to your variable and it is not limited to eight characters. For example, with the Samouel's employee survey, variable X_1 is labeled as X_1—Paid Fairly and variable X_2 is labeled as X_2—Work I Want. When you have longer labels and want to be able to see all of them, you can go to the top of the file and click between the Label and Values cells and make the column wider.

Values = In the values column you can assign a label for each of the values of a variable. For example, with the Samouel's employee survey data variable X_1—Paid Fairly we have indicated that a 1 = Strongly Disagree and a 7 = Strongly Agree. To view the options, click first on the Values cell and then on the three shaded dots to the right of the cell. You can add new labels or change existing ones.

Missing = Missing values deserve attention when using SPSS. If you do not handle them properly, it may cause you to get incorrect results. Use this column to indicate values that are assigned to missing data. Data may be missing for numerous reasons. Most commonly, a respondent has simply failed to respond to an item. One simple way to treat a missing response is to leave the cell for that particular response blank. A blank numeric cell is designated as system-missing and a period (.) is placed in the cell. In the early days of data analysis, data entry was often confined to single digits. Common convention was to assign the digit "9" to represent a missing response. Thus, any digit can be assigned to represent missing data. To do so, you can record the values that will be considered as missing data in the appropriate window. These observations will not be included in data analyses. To use this option, click on the Missing cell and then on the three shaded dots to the right. You will get a dialog box that shows the default of no missing data. To indicate one or more values as missing click on Discrete missing values and place a value in one of the cells. You can record up to three separate values. If you want to specify a range of values, click on this option and indicate the range to be considered as missing.

Column = Click on the column cell to indicate the width of the column. The default is eight spaces but it can be increased or decreased.

Align = The default for alignment is initially left, but you can change to either center or right alignment.

Let's look at the Variable View screen for the employee survey database. It is shown in Exhibit C-3. To see the Variable View screen go to the bottom left-hand corner of the screen and click on Variable View. The name of the variable will be in the first column, but if you look at the fifth column it will tell you more about the variable. For example, variable X_1 is "paid fairly" while X_2 is "work I want." All of the remaining variables have a similar description. Also, if you look under the Values column it will tell you how the variable is coded; e.g., 1 = Strongly Disagree and 7 = Strongly Agree. If the variable label or description is too long to see, you simply left click on the menu bar on the line separating two columns at the top of the column (e.g., between Label and Values) and move the column line to the right to show all of the information.

RUNNING A PROGRAM

The two menus you will use most often are "Analyze" and "Graphs." Let's do a simple chart to show you how easy it is to use SPSS. Click on the Graphs pull-down menu first. When you do, select Bar and you will get a dialog box called Bar Charts. There are three options on the top left, but for now use "Simple" which is the default (already checked). We also use the default in the "Data in Chart are:" box. This default tells the program to create a bar chart showing the count of the number of responses in each of the categories of the 7-point scale for this question. Now click Define and use the default = N of cases. Your database variables are shown in a window to the left of the screen. Highlight variable X_1—Paid Fairly and then click on the arrow button to the left of the Category Axis box to move the variable into the box. Now click OK and you will get the bar chart shown in Exhibit C-4.

EXHIBIT C-3	VARIABLE VIEW OF THE SAMOUEL'S EMPLOYEE SURVEY DATA

Employee Survey N = 63.sav - SPSS Data Editor

File Edit View Data Transform Analyze Graphs Utilities Window Help

1 : id   1

	id	x1	x2	x3	x4	x5	x6	x7	x8	x9	x10	x11	x12
1	1	5	5	5	5	5	5	5	4	5	5	3	4
2	2	3	5	4	5	5	4	5	5	5	5	5	3
3	3	2	4	7	3	5	7	4	2	3	5	2	3
4	4	5	5	7	3	5	7	5	3	5	6	4	5
5	5	3	4	5	4	5	5	4	4	4	6	4	4
6	6	3	6	7	4	5	7	6	5	5	5	5	4
7	7	4	4	5	4	3	5	4	4	4	6	3	4
8	8	5	4	6	2	5	6	4	2	5	5	2	5
9	9	5	6	6	6	6	5	6	5	5	5	5	5
10	10	4	5	6	5	5	6	5	5	5	5	5	5
11	11	3	5	5	3	6	5	5	3	4	5	4	3
12	12	5	4	4	2	6	4	4	2	4	4	3	5
13	13	4	3	3	2	5	3	3	2	5	5	2	5
14	14	5	5	7	5	6	7	5	3	6	6	4	4
15	15	5	5	4	3	3	4	5	3	5	5	2	5
16	16	5	5	7	3	5	6	5	3	6	6	4	5
17	17	4	5	7	2	5	7	5	3	5	5	3	4
18	18	5	5	6	2	5	5	5	2	5	5	2	5
19	19	3	4	3	3	4	3	6	2	4	4	4	4
20	20	5	5	5	5	6	5	5	5	5	4	3	5
21	21	4	4	6	2	4	6	5	2	4	5	3	4
22	22	4	4	3	2	4	3	3	2	4	4	2	4
23	23	5	6	7	3	6	7	6	3	6	6	2	5
24	24	3	5	7	2	5	6	5	1	3	6	1	3
25	25	4	5	3	3	5	3	5	3	4	5	3	4
26	26	5	7	6	6	3	6	7	4	7	5	4	5
27	27	5	5	4	4	6	4	4	4	5	4	4	5
28	28	5	7	4	6	5	4	7	5	6	5	5	5
29	29	5	5	7	4	4	7	4	2	5	6	3	5
30	30	3	4	3	3	5	3	4	3	3	5	4	3
31	31	5	5	7	5	3	6	4	3	5	6	4	5

Data View \ Variable View

SPSS Processor is ready

There are several things we can learn about this variable from the bar chart. First, the highest rating on the 7-point scale is a 5 and the lowest rating is a 2 (7 = strongly agree and 1 = strongly disagree). Second, the rating given most often is a 5 and the one given least often is a 2. Recall the question for this variable read: Using a scale from 1 to 7, with 7 being "Strongly Agree" and 1 being "Strongly Disagree," to what extent do you agree or disagree that the statement "I am paid fairly for the work I do" describes your work environment? Based on how the respondents answered this question, the bar chart tells us that overall the respondents agree they are paid fairly. We recommend you explore some of the other pull-down menus at this point and take the tutorial to begin familiarizing yourself with the SPSS software. As you go through the chapters, Click-through sequences for different problems are provided. This will help you to easily apply the statistical techniques that are most often used in analyzing data for business research reports and managerial decision making.

There are several other comprehensive statistical programs available. In addition, many spreadsheets, like Excel, offer macros that will perform many analyses including ANOVA and regression. Familiarity with SPSS will allow one to learn how to use these alternative approaches quickly and easily.

EXHIBIT C-4 SPSS BAR CHART OF EMPLOYEE SURVEY VARIABLE X_1—PAID FAIRLY

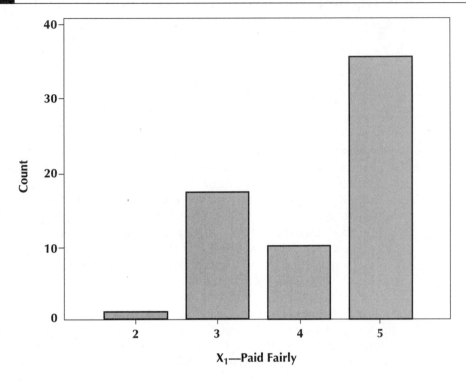

Appendix 1-D: How to Use EXCEL

Learning to use Microsoft Excel is fairly straightforward. When Excel is opened, a new file (database) is automatically started. You can enter your data into the file and it can be saved at any time under any specified name.

To begin a database, numbers must be entered into the cells. The rows in the spreadsheet are identified by numbers (1, 2, 3, …, up to 999), and columns are identified by letters (A, B, C, …, up to Z). Data can be typed in at any time on the spreadsheet, whether it is a title or a description of the numbers being listed. Text can also be used like numbers in a list, such as a list of employees interviewed or a "grocery list" of items purchased. The most common layout for a spreadsheet is to list the information in a particular column, as shown in Exhibit D-1.

The spreadsheet in Exhibit D-1 shows the interim and final grades for a class over the course of one semester. The grades for four students were recorded and the final grade was computed by Excel from a total of 320 possible points. Excel computed both the total and the final average. As you can see, both numbers and text were entered into the cells to produce a chart that is easily understandable. For the total and the final average, a formula was typed into the white text box at the top of the page on the toolbar. The white text box is long enough for you to type in certain formulas, as well as to delete and insert words and numbers that are incorrect or missing.

Do not try to insert text or numbers into a cell that already has data in it. If you try to insert text or numbers, the program will erase all of the existing information already present in the cell. Therefore, it is necessary to do any editing or inserting of numbers or text in the text box at the top of the page.

EXHIBIT D-1 | **EXAMPLE OF EXCEL SPREADSHEET**

	A	B	C	D	E
1		Class Grades			
2		Student A	Student B	Student C	Student D
3	Test 1	92	85	87	93
4	Test 2	88	90	96	92
5	Project	90	86	97	85
6	Quiz 1	10	8	8	9
7	Quiz 2	9	10	10	8
8	Total	289	279	298	287
9	Final Average	90.31	87.19	93.13	89.69

Sometimes the space provided by the cell is not wide enough to fit the desired text or numbers a user may need. The columns, identified by a letter, can be made larger by following a very simple procedure. Place the cursor on the right-hand edge of the box that contains the letter that identifies the column. When placed in the correct position, a double-sided arrow will appear in place of the traditional arrow. This signifies that Excel is ready to increase the size of the column and the cursor is in the correct position. Left-click the mouse and hold down the button while dragging the mouse to the right. This will increase the entire column to fit the text.

To make the column smaller, just repeat the procedure, except drag the mouse to the left after clicking on the edge of the box. This entire process will work to increase the size of the rows as well. Instead of dragging the mouse to the left and right, simply click on the bottom of the box containing the number that identifies the row. Then, drag the mouse up or down to adjust the row to the desired height.

FORMULAS

When producing a table it is sometimes desirable to execute functions with the numbers in the columns or rows, such as to add, subtract, multiply, divide, etc. To do this, a formula must be entered into the text box at the top of the page on the toolbar. To enter a formula, click on the text box and press the equal (=) key. When writing formulas, the equal (=) key must always be entered first. This tells the computer that the user desires to write a formula and that it will be calculating numbers. For example, in Exhibit D-1 the final average was the students' total points divided by 320. In the cells reserved for each student's final average, a formula was entered and the computer calculated the answer.

The procedure for entering a formula is as follows: (1) click on the text box, (2) press the equal (=) button, (3) enter the desired calculation (in our example of student grades, for Student A: (289/320)*100), (4) press enter, and the answer (90.31) automatically appears. This is the basic procedure for simple calculations.

CALCULATING CELL VALUES

Sometimes the Excel user wants to calculate the value of two or more cells that are not in the same column or the same row. In this case, the user must tell the program which particular cells he or she wishes to include in the calculation. For example, in Exhibit D-2 the chart shows a grocery list with a few items. At the bottom, the total cost has been separated into total food cost and total drink cost. The column with the

EXHIBIT D-2   **SAMPLE CALCULATION OF CELL VALUES**

	A	B
1	Chips	$ 2.50
2	Beer	$14.99
3	Bread	$ 1.29
4	Soft Drinks	$ 3.99
5	Cereal	$ 4.75
6	Apples	$ 2.29
7	**Total Cost of Food**	**$10.83**
8	**Total Cost of Drinks**	**$18.98**

list of items on the far left of the chart is the "A" column. The column with the prices is the "D" column. The list starts with "Chips" on Row 2 and ends with "Apples" on Row 7.

Exhibit D-2 shows the computation for total cost of food. The following steps were taken: (1) click on the text box on the toolbar to enter a formula, (2) press the equal (=) key, (3) press D2 + D4 + D6 + D7, because the Chips, Bread, Cereal, and Apples are all included and the prices for those items are in the listed cells, respectively, (4) press enter, and the total ($10.83) should appear. This means you told the computer to add $2.50 + $1.29 + $4.75 + $2.29. To compute the cost of the drinks, the same steps would be taken, except you would enter D3 + D5 to get your answer. This process is the same for scenarios where the user must use subtraction, multiplication, and division.

One last rule of thumb is that it is not necessary that you perform calculations on numbers only in the same column. You can tell the computer to compute numbers from any column, as long as the computational formula is entered properly. For example, in Exhibit D-1 you can calculate the average score on Test 1 for all four students.

MEAN, MEDIAN, MODE, STANDARD DEVIATION

Computing the mean, median, mode, and standard deviation is a process that takes very little time. After entering a set of numbers into a column, select a cell below the listed numbers. Go up to the top of the screen to the General Command Bar and select "Insert." Drag the cursor down the box and select "Function." A large box will pop-up on the screen that is titled "Insert Function." Go to the "Or select a category" box and click on the down arrow to bring up all of the different categories of functions. Scroll down until you have located the "Statistical" category and select it. Make sure that it comes up in the "Or select a category" box. Now, all statistical functions should come up in the large text box below the "Or select a category" box. Scroll down to find Median, Mode, or Standard Deviation, whichever is needed at the time. You will not find Mean on the list, because it is shown on this list as "Average" so to calculate the mean use the average function.

After selecting the function that is desired, press "OK" and another dialog box will appear. It is titled "Function Arguments" and only serves to let the user make sure that what they are doing is correct. Make sure that the cells listed in the text box highlighted in black are correct, and then simply press "OK" and the computer will begin to calculate the answer. In a very short time period, the computer will be finished and you will have your answer already placed in the desired cell.

Many other types of statistical analysis can be computed using Excel. Simply follow the Excel click-thru sequence of: Insert → Function → Or select a category → All. After the sequence is completed, scroll down the list of functions in the large text box, highlight the desired analysis, and follow the instructions. We provide specific instructions in the "Research in Action" boxes in the chapters for selected types of analysis.

Beginning the Research Process

2

Fundamentals of Research Design

Learning Objectives

1. Explain how a study is created based upon a description of the business decision involved.

2. Describe the role of theory and science in business research.

3. Describe the three basic business research designs.

4. Explain the roles of exploratory and confirmatory research.

5. Understand the difference between primary and secondary data.

6. Explain the roles of qualitative and quantitative research.

INTRODUCTION

Business students often struggle with starting a research project because they do not know how things like questionnaires and statistical analyses eventually produce results, or how to use survey findings to develop meaningful conclusions. But experienced researchers have the benefit of prior knowledge of the research issues as well as the statistical tools available to do the job. This chapter tries to answer the question, "Where do I start?" We begin with an overview of the basic business research process.

THE BUSINESS RESEARCH PROCESS

The **business research process** provides a roadmap with directions for conducting a business research project. Generally, three phases are involved. They are the formulation, execution, and analytical phases. Each is summarized in Exhibit 2-1. The more detailed elements are discussed throughout the chapter.

The *formulation* stage involves defining the substance and process of the research. This stage is very much like writing a recipe. The substance of the research provides the ingredients that will eventually produce the desired result. A step-by-step set of instructions is provided with any recipe, and this is the process by which the separate ingredients are made into something meaningful. With business research a similar process is followed.

After formulating the research, the *execution* phase begins. Here the researcher is actively gathering information from the appropriate sources. This information is then checked for errors, coded, and stored in a way that allows it to be analyzed quickly and conveniently.

The third phase is *analytical*. In this phase, the data are analyzed. Hypotheses are tested and either (a) supported, or (b) not supported, based upon comparing the actual study

---

EXHIBIT 2-1 | **THE BASIC BUSINESS RESEARCH PROCESS**

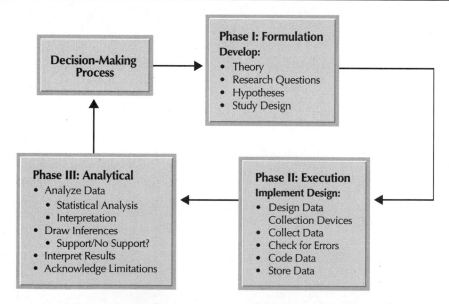

outcome with the outcome predicted in the formulation stage. Results are examined to provide answers to the key **research questions.** The decision-maker can then take actions based upon better knowledge of the situation.

THEORY AND SCIENCE IN BUSINESS RESEARCH

THEORY

Theory is a set of systematically related statements, including some **law-like generalizations** that can be tested empirically.[1] A specific theory is a proposed explanation for some event. Sometimes theories have been confirmed by past research. Other times they are proposed theories with either limited or no validation. Law-like generalizations are expectations of what will happen under specified circumstances that allow predictions of reality.

Competition is an example of a theory in business strategy. The theory of competition predicts that firms within an industry that are able to differentiate themselves over time gain a competitive advantage. A key law-like generalization of the theory of competition is that differentiation is a competitive advantage that enables firms to charge higher prices.[2] Basic business research still tests this generalization empirically and for the most part the notion is supported. Management strategy at Nordstrom's department store has led to a commitment to a relatively highly trained workforce. This point of difference makes customers more willing to pay a higher price than they might elsewhere. Therefore, we evaluate theories based on how well they predict outcomes.

Researchers develop theory based on the accumulated body of previous research. Thus, a researcher will search out previously reported studies that involve similar phenomena. Also, applied business researchers rely on the history of a particular company to help develop a set of expectations in a given research situation. Without theory, the formulation stage becomes more difficult because business researchers cannot set boundaries on the study situation.

The Fuel for Research

Theories provide key inputs into the research process. Business theories explain and predict business phenomena. Decision makers want to know the likelihood these explanations and predictions are accurate. Thus, theory helps shape the research questions and specific predictions are expressed in hypotheses. Research projects then validate or invalidate these predictions.

A problem arises because theories often are incomplete. Consider for example a theory of the relationship between advertising and sales. Given the key nature of this relationship to business success, and the variety of research questions that might be influenced by this theory, a great deal of research investigates this topic.

What do you think is the relationship between advertising and sales? Does advertising cause sales? There may be a good reason to expect it to do so. Thus, a theoretical explanation can be developed, as the following example shows.

> Increased advertising means more people will know about a business. Knowledge precedes desire and therefore, advertising will eventually increase sales.

To this day, however, the advertising-sales relationship is an unsettled issue despite many, many studies of this topic. Some researchers counter the logic of the previous example claiming that sales cause advertising:

> The theory is that before any firm can advertise they need resources.
> The resources are derived from sales. Therefore, firms that sell more can
> advertise more.

Since advertising is a critical business variable, many researchers attempt to develop a theory explaining how sales and advertising are interrelated. Like most theories, this one contains gaps in knowledge; for example, uncertainty over whether sales cause advertising or advertising causes sales. Such gaps motivate further research.

Normative business decision rules often are theory based. A **normative decision rule** explains what someone should do when faced with a situation described by a theory. For example, Phil Samouel, owner of Samouel's Greek Cuisine, may learn that Gino's Ristorante does more lunch business. He may discover that unlike Samouel's, Gino's lunch prices are lower than their dinner prices. After further study supporting the generalization that lower lunch prices lead to higher lunch-time volume, Samouel's restaurant may follow the normative rule that a restaurant's lunch prices should be lower than dinner prices. Normative rules can even end up in an automated expert system like those described in the next chapter.

Behavioral learning theory provides managers with normative decision rules about issues dealing with the amount and timing of employee compensation. However, behavioral learning theory contains many gaps. For example, it isn't always clear why behavioral patterns result from a conditioning effect. Has the employee gained new knowledge as the result of training, and does he or she use this knowledge to rationally perform the desired behavior? Or, are the changes more instinctively based, like the conditioned responses observed among animals? Do employees use some type of higher (cognitive) learning? If so, employees can be reasoned with cognitively, placing a greater emphasis on process training. If not, employee behavior would best be controlled by rewarding desired outcomes and providing disincentives (punishment) for undesirable outcomes. Researchers are motivated to close these gaps and to provide managers with better normative decision rules. Thus, theory provides fuel for research.

The Practicality of Theory

It has been said that: "nothing is more practical than a good theory."[3] But the opposing view is often voiced by business people—"Your explanation is too theoretical. Give us something we can use!" Obviously, there are differences of opinion on the benefits of theory. Let's look at the role theory plays in the decision-making and research process.

People who take their car into a mechanic often describe symptoms of some problem by trying to duplicate the sound the car is producing. When the car owner doesn't give a sound, the mechanic may ask: "What does it sound like?" Why is everyone so concerned with the sound? It's because sound enables the mechanic to develop a "theory" about the car. The mechanic does this by integrating the new information about the sound with previous automotive knowledge. Using this theory, the number of parts that must be checked can be narrowed down to a manageable number. Without some type of theory, the mechanic might as well begin checking parts in alphabetical order.

This analogy illustrates one of the key roles of theory. It points us in a direction that hopefully is more likely to produce valuable results quickly. This is important to Phase I of the research process because most of the research steps will follow naturally from the theory. In particular, theory is extremely valuable because it suggests what the researcher needs to measure to provide useful results.

A great deal of research is aimed at developing descriptive theories of business, the marketplace, and consumer practices. **Descriptive theory** simply describes the way things are. The theory of perfect competition in economics simply describes the effects that firms will experience when operating in an intensely competitive environment. At a micro level, a learning organization develops a better theory of itself. Specifically, learning (accumulated knowledge) is put to use acquiring resources that enable the organization to outperform others.[4] At a macro level, the overall quality of business practices within a nation often is tied directly to the quality of basic research produced there. Indeed, some say the United Kingdom's difficulties in effectively managing its railway and phone systems are a result of an inability to develop research-based theory.[5] See the "Research in Action" box to learn how theory is impacting the Internet.

Theory seeks to explain and predict. Researcher's goals are much the same. Both theory and practice are inseparable because businesses hope to use theory to do a better job of explaining and predicting. Rational decision-making is based upon explanation and prediction. Ultimately, good decisions are based on explanations and predictions that have high truth content. In other words, the theory, including its explanations and predictions, is valid.

Decisions can be made without the benefit of theory and research. But when this happens they are either wild guesses or decisions based upon pure intuition. Exhibit 2-2 contrasts the difference between **theory-based** and **intuition-based decisions.** Since businesses normally have a great deal at stake in their decision making, which is the best way to proceed?

Perhaps you've heard people try to explain their reasons for investing in certain stocks or their theory of the stock market. Did the theory encourage you to follow their advice? Exhibit 2-2 shows the benefits of using reality-based theory. Which set of decisions is likely to describe ways of winning more often? The intuition-based rules can be tested, just as the theory-based rules also can be tested. However, only the theory-based rules offer sound explanations. The explanations are derived from basic probabilities or expected values

---

RESEARCH IN ACTION

NERDS TO THE RESCUE: MATHEMATICAL THEORY IS USEFUL?

Students have been heard to say "I don't see the use of these math courses." Many might think there is nothing less practical than pure mathematical theory. However, new search technologies have taken advantage of mathematical theories. Google (www.google.com) is perhaps the most effective commercial search tool available to business. The secret to Google's effectiveness lies in an esoteric branch of mathematics known as graph theory. Graph theory defines the location of points in space mathematically. For example, graph theory seeks to explain edges, which are connections between multiple points. Using this theory, Tom Leighton and Daniel Lewin developed software that defined electronic searches in terms of mathematical edges. Thus, they drew the analogy of edges to connections between hyperlinks (the active text in a Web page that transports you to a new web location) to invent a more efficient way of searching. Perhaps you will be thankful for theory next time "Google" helps you find important information. For more on this story, see: A Better Web Through Higher Math, *Business Week Online* 2002, January 22, (www.businessweek.com, accessed March 12, 2002).

EXHIBIT 2-2	CONTRASTING THEORY- AND INTUITION-BASED DECISIONS

An Illustration based on a theory of playing the card game 21 or blackjack.

Theory-Based Decision Rules	Intuition-Based Decision Rules
Generally, stand (do not take another card) on more than 17	Always sit on an end seat at the blackjack table
Draw (ask for another card) when the dealer is showing a face card	Tuesdays are the best days to play blackjack
The decision to stand (not take another card) or draw depends on the cards that have been seen so far	Wear a green shirt whenever playing cards

given that the game is played with a finite number of cards with equal numbers of each particular card value. Chances are, the intuition-based decision rules do not have as compelling a rationale. Thus, while intuition does play a role in decision making, business people usually would like to know why a certain course should be taken and how likely is it to bring success. Theory helps provide answers to these why questions in the form of explanation and prediction.

SCIENCE: THE METHODOLOGY OF RESEARCH

The Scientific Method

Most students first study the scientific method in grade school. Students are usually able to associate the scientific method with testing a **hypothesis** through the use of experimentation. The scientific method used by business researchers is really no different than the one learned in grade school.

Science is what is known about some definable subject. It tries to describe reality truthfully. The **scientific method** is the method researchers use to gain this knowledge. So, it is much the same as the basic business research process shown earlier. The business research process seeks to describe the realities of business actions and interactions truthfully.

Exhibit 2-3 describes the scientific method. The top portion includes observation, discovery, and developing hypotheses. These three stages together describe the process of scientific discovery. There is no right way to discover ideas. Ideas can come from intuition, hunches, deductive or inductive reasoning. Once some order can be made of the observations, the ideas can be stated as a discovery. A review of previously conducted research on similar topics is often helpful in moving from pure observation toward some working discovery or idea. The researcher then begins a preliminary investigation to try and translate the discovery into a testable hypothesis or set of hypotheses.

A research question poses an issue of interest to the researcher and is related to the specific decision faced by the firm. A *hypothesis* is a formal statement of some unproven supposition that tentatively explains certain facts or phenomena. A hypothesis often describes some systematic (nonrandom) events that can be tested using data. Exhibit 2-4 provides some examples of potential business hypotheses. Generally, a hypothesis restates a research question in more specific terms. For example, a research question may imply the existence of some relationship, but the hypothesis typically goes further by stating the direction of the relationship.

Exhibit 2-5 illustrates how these different questions all work together with theory. Theory provides knowledge that helps make sense out of the entire decision-making situation. Current events and business problems are compared with existing knowledge and phrased as research questions with the help of theory. Here theory may suggest things that are related to each other. Further knowledge may result in stating the research questions very specifically and formally as hypotheses. The hypotheses can then be tested by collecting data

EXHIBIT 2-3	THE SCIENTIFIC METHOD CONTRIBUTES TO BUSINESS DECISION-MAKING THROUGH RESEARCH

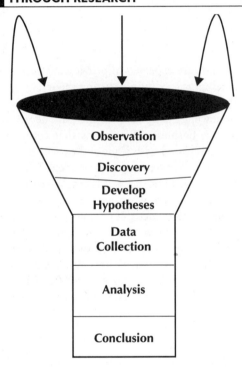

EXHIBIT 2-4	RESEARCH QUESTIONS LEAD TO HYPOTHESIS

Research Question	A Corresponding Hypothesis
Does advertising influence sales?	Advertising is positively related to sales.
Is sales territory size related to customer service ratings?	Sales territory size is negatively related to customer service ratings.
Do flexible schedules create increased labor efficiency?	Business units using flex-time have lower unit labor costs than do those using standard schedule procedures.
Does package color affect product quality ratings?	Consumers rate products with blue packages as higher in quality than products in orange packages.
Is region related to beverage consumption?	Southerners drink more beer per capita than do people from the north.
Is an employee's gender related to job satisfaction?	Female employees report higher job satisfaction than do male employees with the same job.

| EXHIBIT 2-5 | THE FLOW OF KNOWLEDGE BETWEEN KEY RESEARCH COMPONENTS |

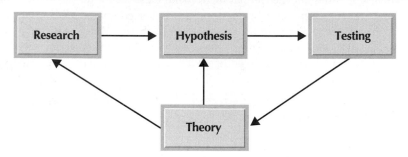

and analyzing the results. The results are expected to provide answers to the hypothesized relationships and end up reinforcing or modifying existing theory.

The ability to place research questions and hypotheses into words represents significant progress, as illustrated in the following example. Over the past decade, casual Friday has become commonplace in American business. This means that company dress codes are relaxed on Friday. Suits and ties are replaced with jeans and casual shirts. This decision was based upon the theory that more relaxed workers are better workers. The idea can be expressed as a research question by adding additional knowledge: "Is employee dress related to job performance?" Still more specificity allows the following hypothesis to be written: "Employees in casual clothing will show higher job performance than employees in business clothing." This could be tested by comparing performance between two dress groups. Ten years of studies of this type have not supported this hypothesis. In fact, business people are deciding that for many jobs, performance is actually harmed by casual dress. As a result, estimates indicate the number of firms offering casual Fridays dropped 6 percent in 2001.[6] This finding is causing a re-examination of the original theory. Perhaps relaxed workers are not always better!

Rigor of Science

Beyond hypothesis development, the scientific method moves on to the testing phase (the narrow part of Exhibit 2-3) where data are collected. Relevant **data** represent facts about hypothesized variables. This data is then examined using statistical analyses to determine if the findings either "support" or "do not support" hypotheses. If the findings match the pattern described in the hypothesis, then the hypothesis is supported. Thus, a conclusion can be drawn that hopefully will allow for more informed decision-making.

In the discovery phase of the scientific method, there are virtually no guidelines and, thus, no right or wrong ways to develop ideas or inferences. Testing is quite different. Indeed, it is the rigor of testing that distinguishes the scientific method. Testing is the way to get to the conclusion, and the conclusion allows an expansion of knowledge and more informed decision-making. Testing is highly critical and analytical. Ultimately, "good" science uses the scientific method and can be characterized by the following:

1. It is empirical—meaning that it is compared against reality.
2. It is replicable or objective—meaning that the researcher's opinion is independent of the results. Other researchers conducting the study would obtain the same results.

3. It is analytical—meaning that it follows the scientific method in breaking down and describing empirical facts.

4. It is theory driven—meaning that it relies on the previous body of knowledge.

5. It is logical—meaning that conclusions are drawn from the results based on logic.

6. It is rigorous—meaning that every effort is made to minimize error.

Pragmatics of Business

The rigor of science often is traded off against the pragmatics of business. Business people usually cannot get an answer too quickly. Thus, there is give and take between the desires of the business person and the desires of the researcher. For example, while the researcher may wish to use a sample representative of an entire population, this may take longer and cost more than the decision maker will invest. Researchers always sacrifice some rigor for expediency. While this may introduce error, as long as the decision maker is informed of this, and the results are qualified based on these shortcuts, the researcher should proceed with the project. Good research also follows the principle of **parsimony**. This means that a simpler solution is better than a complex solution. Parsimonious research means applying the simplest approach that will address the research questions satisfactorily.

BASIC RESEARCH DESIGNS

A research design provides the basic directions or "recipe" for carrying out the project. Following the principle of parsimony, the researcher should choose a design that (1) will provide relevant information on the research questions and (2) will do the job most efficiently. Once the researcher decides on a study design, the formulation phase of the basic research process is complete.

Many research designs can be used to study business problems. Fortunately, business research designs can be grouped into one of three categories. Researchers generally choose from among an (1) exploratory, (2) descriptive, or (3) causal design. An **exploratory research** project is useful when the research questions are vague or when there is little theory available to guide predictions. At times, decision makers and researchers may find it impossible to formulate a basic statement of the research problem. Exploratory research is used to develop a better understanding. **Descriptive research** describes some situation. Generally, things are described by providing measures of an event or activity. Often, descriptive research accomplishes this by using *descriptive statistics*. These include frequency counts (how many), measures of central tendency like the mean or mode, or a measure of variation such as the standard deviation. **Causal research** designs are often the most intricate. They are designed to test whether one event causes another. Does X cause Y? The three basic research designs are explained in greater detail below.

EXPLORATORY RESEARCH

Exploratory research is particularly useful when the decision maker has very little information. Put another way, exploratory designs are for the researcher who does not know much! It is discovery-oriented. Thus, it is the one design not intended to test specific research hypotheses.

Exploratory research is particularly useful within highly innovative industries. Microsoft, Siemens, IBM, and Dupont, for instance,[7] are companies that place a high priority on discovering new ideas from exploratory research. The research not only identifies new technologies, but just as importantly, it is aimed at discovering those technologies that address real business or consumer needs. Siemens, the German-based telecommunications firm, employs over forty thousand people in research-related positions. Their programmatic exploratory research program is aimed at discovering potential matches between needs and technologies one, two, or three decades in advance.

The importance of exploratory research in product innovation has been described by Swaddling and Zobel as follows:[8]

> When conducted well, *exploratory research* provides a window into consumer perceptions, behaviors, and needs. It enables companies to develop successful new products more consistently. This superior understanding of the consumer leads to effective decision-making and recognition of market opportunities, a distinct definition of the business in which your company competes, and a high probability of producing innovative new products that drive extraordinary profits (p. 21).

Exploratory research was instrumental in helping Chrysler realize many consumers, when driving their cars, needed to carry more than two people and more than a trunk full of cargo. Further, consumers wanted to do this in a very convenient way. Ford and General Motors believed the station wagon satisfied these needs. But Chrysler's exploratory research helped turn the minivan concept into something that consumers reacted to very favorably. Exploratory research later helped the minivan concept evolve into the SUV (Sport Utility Vehicle) craze. Similarly, exploratory research is useful in identifying innovative production and management practices. For example, it has been used to develop incentive compensation systems for divisional CEOs with the goal of increasing unit innovativeness.[9]

Exploratory research can take many forms. A thorough literature review can be very useful in providing a better understanding of some issue. *Literature reviews* are conducted by searching through company records, trade and academic journals, as well as other sources where research is reported. It is important to point out that a literature review may also be an early part of a descriptive or causal design too. Electronic search engines like Google or Lexis-Nexis have made the search process simpler. The researcher can enter key terms related to the research question and locate dozens, perhaps hundreds of potential sources containing related research. A few of the more widely used exploratory interview techniques are discussed below.

Focus Groups

Focus groups are one of the most widely used exploratory interview techniques. All types of for-profit as well as not-for-profit organizations use them to gather information. With focus groups, a small number of people (8–12) are brought together in a discussion format led by a trained moderator (interviewer). The moderator has a pre-determined list of topics to discuss but permits the participants to respond in their own words. Specific responses are followed up with probing questions such as "Does anything else come to mind?" Probing means that a researcher delves deeply into a response to identify possibly hidden reasons for a particular behavior. The "why, why, why" technique we discuss in Chapter 3 is one probing technique. For example, if a moderator is exploring reactions to a company's proposed new casual Friday policy and one participant says "I do not like the fact that we cannot wear open-collar shirts" the moderator might ask "Why?" or "How would you change it?" We discuss focus groups in much more detail in Chapter 5.

Depth Interviews

A depth, or in-depth interview, is a one-to-one discussion session between a trained interviewer and a respondent. Respondents usually are chosen carefully because they have some specialized insight. For example, a researcher exploring sexual harassment at a particular company would likely conduct depth interviews with employees. As with a focus group, the interviewer first prepares an outline that guides the interview. Also as in a focus group, the responses are unstructured. Indeed, a depth interview allows much deeper probing than does a focus group. Depth interviews also are covered in more detail in Chapter 5.

Delphi Technique

The *Delphi technique* is another exploratory interview approach. A Delphi interview seeks the input of some acknowledged expert, usually with respect to forecasting or predicting future events. It's a specific form of expert polling. Bill Gates might be an expert on software technologies. Donald Trump might be an expert on commercial real estate. Tiger Woods might be an expert on golf equipment. These interviews are usually less formal and shorter than focus groups or depth interviews. The normal approach is simply to ask an expert questions like: "What do you think the future holds for _____?" or "How do you explain _____?" Experts' time is very valuable so sometimes these opinions are sought in writing instead of in person.

Projective Techniques

Focus groups and depth interviews involve some type of interview process. Both the researcher and the respondent are actively engaged. When we conduct interviews there is always a risk the interview process itself will influence respondents. Perhaps respondent comments are not entirely accurate. The inaccuracy may be because of incomplete recall, a suppression of information because of social concerns or an unwillingness to provide an accurate response to the question. There are some things people simply will not tell an interviewer.

Projective data can be collected in an interview as well. In projective interviewing, the researcher presents the respondent with an ambiguous stimulus. For example, the interviewer may provide the respondent with a stick-man cartoon showing a grocery store employee eating an apple in the store. The respondent, a grocery store employee, is then asked to complete the picture in words and/or images. Since the respondent is describing another person and not him/herself, the researcher is more confident the explanation is true. For example, a respondent is more likely to mention whether or not the apple was purchased or pilfered. This picture completion type of exercise is known as *thematic apperception*. As with all projective approaches, the researcher will infer that the characteristics applied to the ambiguous figure actually reside within the respondent. Thus, projective approaches are a good way to discover hidden motivations. Other projective approaches include word association and ink blot tests. The "Research in Action" box describes a classic study that used the projective technique approach.

RESEARCH IN ACTION

ARE INSTANT COFFEE DRINKERS REALLY THAT BAD?

Suppose you found a grocery list that contained the following items: a loaf of bread, five lbs. of flour, an eight-ounce jar of Maxwell House Instant Coffee, two pounds of ground beef, a fifteen-ounce can of cling peaches. How would you describe this person? This projective approach was applied by a researcher studying the reasons people select instant versus ground coffee. A group of respondents was asked to respond to a list of this type. Another group responded to a list identical in all respects with the exception that instant coffee was replaced by ground coffee. The respondents were asked to describe the woman who purchased these groceries in as much detail as possible, based on nothing but the list. While the ground coffee purchaser generally received positive responses, the instant coffee buyer was often described as "lazy," "living alone," "a poor homemaker," "careless with her money" and even as "an old maid!" This led to the theory that the process of purchasing and making instant coffee was not as fulfilling as making coffee in a more traditional way. Keep in mind that this data was collected fifty years ago. Do you think things have changed?

SOURCE: Haire, Mason. 1950. Projective Techniques in Marketing Research, *The Journal of Marketing*, 14 (April), 649–656.

DESCRIPTIVE RESEARCH

Who is likely to be most satisfied? When should we maximize production? How much investment is required? Which brands are most preferred? What advertisements are most effective? How are experience and performance related? Where do people go on vacation? These are the types of questions that can be answered by descriptive research. Descriptive research designs are usually structured and specifically designed to measure the characteristics described in a research question. Hypotheses, derived from theory, usually serve to guide the process and provide a list of what needs to be measured.

Studies tracking seasonal trends are good examples of descriptive studies. A company like Frito Lay (potato chips and similar snack items) may benefit from seasonality information for numerous reasons. For example, more chips and snack items are sold in the summer so seasonality information would improve decisions regarding flexible production capacity. Exploratory research might reveal that consumers feel more like eating tortilla chips in certain types of weather. It might further suggest that chips are eaten with certain foods. A research question might ask whether or not chip consumption is seasonal. Further consideration may suggest hypotheses that tortilla chip sales are highest in the winter, while potato chip sales are highest in the summer. A descriptive study could track monthly sales of each product over a ten-year period. The results would describe the seasonality of chip consumption and directly address the research questions and hypotheses.

Descriptive studies usually involve all phase II (see Exhibit 2-1) activities. Data collection may involve some type of **structured interview** process. A questionnaire containing specific items that ask respondents to select from a fixed number of choices is often used. Sometimes, data may be collected on production processes or products. Bar codes can be scanned and provide information on the movement of goods for example, including purchase data. A descriptive study using scanner data would be able to compare weekly Tabasco sauce sales with and without a price promotion. Unlike exploratory studies, descriptive studies are often confirmatory. In other words, they are used to test hypotheses.

Cross-Sectional Studies

Descriptive studies can provide the user with a snapshot, or a description of business elements at a given point in time. These types of studies provide *cross-sectional* data. Data are collected at a single point in time and summarized statistically. As an example of a cross-sectional study, data could be collected in a nationwide survey to examine different attitudes of cross-sections of the American public toward senior executives who sell their stock in publicly traded companies shortly before the price of the stock falls. In such cases, it would appear that executives are making decisions based on insider information. Attitudes toward this behavior could be examined by cross sections of the population, such as age, gender, ethnic origin, income, rural versus suburban versus city, and so forth. This is a one-shot study or cross-sectional study to examine attitudes toward such actions. Most surveys fall into this category.

Surveys Sample surveys typify cross-sectional studies. Perhaps you have seen a civil engineer or surveyor examining a piece of land. They are surveying property to describe its characteristics. What are its boundaries and elevation and what are its distinguishing characteristics? Likewise, business researchers *survey* a sample of business elements in an effort to describe a population's characteristics. When surveying land, the surveyor peers through a transit to take measurements. Generally, business research takes measurements using a questionnaire or some other structured response form. The business elements could be strategic business units, retail units, hospitals, salespeople, production workers, brands, products or customers, among others. A key distinguishing feature of cross-sectional studies is that the elements are measured only once during the survey process.

Descriptive statistics based on sample measurements describe the population. Typical statistics include rankings (best to worst), simple frequency counts (how many), cross-classifications (contingent frequencies), group means, contingent means (means by groups) or correlations. Each of these is discussed in a later chapter.

Since population characteristics are being inferred from a sample, or subset of the population, cross-sectional descriptive studies must carefully consider how well this subset represents the larger population. Researchers work on the assumption that the sample characteristics equal those of the population. Error is introduced into the process to the extent that the sample and population are actually different. Thus, for the sake of convenience, a researcher may use MBA students to comprise a sample in a study of how managers evaluate subordinates. The MBA students would play the role of managers in the study. Error is introduced to the extent that MBA students are indeed different than practicing managers. Sampling approaches and ways to minimize error are discussed in Chapter 8.

Suppose a researcher wanted to study the effect of background music on service quality perceptions. A specific research question deals with whether or not men and women rate background music and service quality similarly. Questionnaires could be used to measure customers' perceptions of background music and service quality using a 7-point scale. A sample of eight hundred department store customers could be *surveyed* over the course of one week. Answers to their questions could then used to describe the population's beliefs. After data have been collected, results are tabulated and summarized statistically, and conclusions drawn.

EXHIBIT 2-6	DEPARTMENT STORE SHOPPER RATINGS OF BACKGROUND MUSIC AND SERVICE		
	n	Background Music: Mean[a]	Service Quality: Mean[a]
Women	500	5.07	6.04
Men	300	4.61	6.22
Overall	800	4.89	6.11

[a]A 7-point scale was used by shoppers to rate the music and service quality, with 1 = "Unfavorable" and 7 = "Very Favorable."

Exhibit 2-6 shows a table containing descriptive, cross-sectional results of this type. Several conclusions are possible from these results. For instance, men rate the department store's service quality higher but women like the background music more. Further analysis might show whether or not reactions to the music are related to service quality and perhaps even buying behavior. Conclusions derived from these results are valid to the extent that the eight hundred department store shoppers are representative of all department store shoppers. Studies of this type are fairly common and they exemplify cross-sectional data.[10]

Longitudinal Studies

Longitudinal studies also use a sample to describe business elements. Rather than describing them at a single point in time, however, longitudinal data describe events over time. Longitudinal studies are appropriate when research questions and hypotheses are affected by how things vary over time. Unlike cross-sectional studies, longitudinal studies require data to be collected from the same sample units at multiple points in time. The data represent a *time series* of observations. Longitudinal data allow tracking of business elements so that trends can be observed.

Time is critical to business. Organizations often track employee performance over time. This data may allow top managers to know how performance varies with time on the job. Similarly, many financial statistics are tracked including all well-known stock exchange indices. In most industrialized nations, including the United States, consumer confidence is also tracked. By analyzing these two trends together, we can see how closely the two indices correspond. Is this information useful for making investment decisions?[11] Product

RESEARCH IN ACTION
IS THERE A BAD TIME FOR A BEER?

Is beer seasonal? Time and beer are related. First, beer shows a fairly strong seasonal trend. Research shows that beer sales are about 15 percent higher during the summer months than they are during the rest of the year. But, it isn't quite that simple. There are spikes in beer sales around the winter holidays. Wintertime beer sales are concentrated around these times. However, time and beer go together in other ways too. Cyclical patterns in demand over long periods of time can be observed. Theoretically, these patterns are due to cyclical patterns in consumer choices for alcoholic beverages. If wine is in, beer is out. And there is even more. Forty percent of all weekly beer sales are sold in twelve hours, from 4 P.M. to 10 P.M. Friday and Saturday.

Both beer companies and retailers tie their promotional efforts to these promotional trends. During these times, co-promotions may be used. Research is conducted in a certain area to determine which foods are most often consumed with beer. Promotions might be run on these foods and beer simultaneously to try to make up for the usual drop in sales.

SOURCE: Kelly, Becky. 1999. Beer for All Seasons, *National Petroleum News*, 91 (August), 34–36.

TRENDS IN LONG-TERM ALCOHOL CONSUMPTION

U.S. Alcohol Consumption per Capita by Beverage

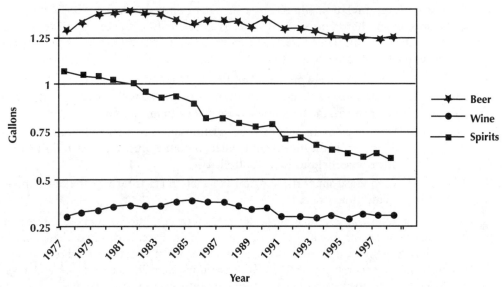

This chart tracks how much alcohol the average American consumes each year. To read this chart, keep in mind that each beverage is only partially alcohol. A typical wine for example is 10–13 percent alcohol, spirits (whiskey) are 40–50 percent alcohol and beer is about 4–6 percent alcohol. The chart shows a downturn in spirits consumption over the time period beginning in 1977. Beer consumption also shows a slight decrease, although the average American still consumed 1.25 gallons of alcohol by beer in 1998, which equates to 25 gallons per year. Alcohol consumption via wine displays a peak during the mid-1980s and perhaps the start of an upward trend toward the end of the 1990s. This data might be useful to beverage companies in identifying competitive and market pressures that affect sales and operations.

sales often are tracked since many products have seasonal demand meaning the amount consumed is not constant through time. See the "Research in Action" boxes to learn about seasonality in beer, wine, and alcohol consumption.

Longitudinal studies sometimes employ a panel. A **panel** is a fixed sample arranged for the purpose of collecting data. Although panels can contain any business element as a unit, they are generally comprised of human elements. In this case, the people involved agree to have repeated measurements taken over an extended period of time. Nielsen television ratings are derived from a panel of television viewers who agree to have their program selection automatically monitored. Nielsen provides each panel member a meter that is connected to their television. Periodically, the meter electronically records what channel the TV is tuned to. Some electronic meters also include a heat sensor to distinguish whether the room in which the TV is located has humans watching the TV or the family pet! Nielsen also provides a diary to each panel member. The diary is used to record demographics and other personal details about the household. We discuss panels as a method of collecting data in Chapter 5.

CAUSAL RESEARCH

Causality

Causal studies test whether or not some event causes another. Does X cause Y? More precisely, a **causal relationship** means a change in one event brings about a corresponding change in another event. *Causality* means a change in X (the cause) makes a change in Y (the effect) occur! There are four conditions researchers look for in testing cause and effect relationships:[12]

1. Time sequence—the cause must occur before the effect.
2. Covariance—a change in the cause is associated with a change in the effect. In other words, the two variables are related to one another.
3. Non-spurious association—the relationship is true and not really due to something else that just happens to affect both the cause and effect. This requires that other potential causes be controlled.
4. Theoretical support—a logical explanation exists for why the cause and effect relationship exists.

The following example illustrates these four conditions. Suppose a researcher were testing whether or not a change in compensation systems causes a change in employee turnover. First, the time sequence condition means the researcher need only study changes in turnover occurring after the compensation system is altered. Since a change cannot affect what happened in the past, it is illogical to suspect that a change in the compensation plan announced and instituted in July 2003 caused employees to quite their jobs in December 2002.

Second, the researcher would examine whether or not a change in compensation is systematically related to employee turnover rates. This is accomplished by comparing turnover rates before and after changes.

Third, even if a relationship is observed, is there something else going on at the same time that could explain any observed changes? For example, what if a competing firm opened a new facility at the same time data were collected? Would any changes in turnover be caused by the compensation system changes or by the increased demand for labor brought about by the competition?

Fourth, some theoretical explanation is needed. A change in compensation may affect how workers feel about their jobs, which will affect whether or not they are comfortable continuing employment with the company. Causality can be established to the extent that these conditions are met.

Decision makers are greatly aided by known cause and effect relationships. Knowing something enables them to predict what will happen if they effect some change. Causality is a powerful concept. Thus, causal designs require very precise execution. Moreover, they can be complex, often take a long time from planning to execution, and can be very expensive.

Experiments Causality is established through experimentation. An **experiment** is a causal design in which a researcher controls a potential "cause" and observes any corresponding change in hypothesized effects. *Control* is accomplished by experimentally manipulating the causal variable. A **manipulation** means the causal variable is altered over different levels or conditions. The manipulated variable is called an experimental treatment.

For example, if price is hypothesized to cause changes in sales, a price treatment might manipulate a product's price between two levels, $4 and $6, while observing sales at each price point. Or, price might be manipulated over three levels. The price might be set at $4, $5, and $6. Each level is referred to as a treatment level or condition.

BASIC EXPERIMENTAL DESIGN: LAB AND FIELD EXPERIMENTS

Business researchers choose between two experimental types. **Laboratory (lab) experiments** manipulate the hypothesized causal variable within an artificial setting. An artificial setting allows maximum control. Laboratory experiments are the most scientifically precise types of studies. Suppose the researcher wishes to test whether or not humor causes greater recall of product information for a new pain medication. The researcher could recruit one hundred participants from a relevant population. Participants could report to a testing facility where the experiment would take place. Fifty participants could be assigned to view a television program containing a humorous commercial for the painkiller. The remaining fifty would see the very same television program under the very same conditions. The only exception is that a serious commercial for the painkiller replaces the humorous commercial. Afterwards, each participant is asked to recall information about the painkiller. Since participants are free from outside influences, the researcher would have a great deal of confidence that any difference in the average recall between the groups is due to the type of appeal. Higher recall in the humor condition would support the original hypothesis. The high degree of control associated with lab experiments produces high internal validity. This means that any observed differences in the outcome are indeed a result of the experimental manipulation.

A **field experiment** represents the second approach. The primary difference is that a field experiment is conducted in a natural setting. A manipulation is implemented within the relevant business context. Suppose a researcher wished to investigate this hypothesis:

> Incentive-based compensation produces higher job satisfaction than does a salary-based compensation system.

Six different business units within an organization could be selected for a pilot study. Employees from these six units become the experimental subjects. Three of the units could be randomly selected to receive compensation for the next six months based solely on salary. The other three would receive the incentive-based compensation system. At the end of the trial, job satisfaction could be measured and a comparison made that would test the research hypothesis. Since a field experiment is conducted in a realistic setting, we say they provide high external validity. This means there is a greater chance the results found in a field experiment will be representative of the population.

Comparing Lab and Field Experiments

The advantages and disadvantages of each type of experiment generally arise from the choice between high internal or high external validity. The primary strength of field experiments is the natural or realistic setting. However, the real setting makes results susceptible to influence from other potential causes. Could any differences in job satisfaction be due to things other than the compensation system in the field experiment described above? Were the six physical settings identical? Were all supervisors equally well qualified and did they apply precisely the same approach to maximize performance? Answers to these questions are uncertain and could possibly lead to erroneous conclusions.

These questions do not arise with lab experiments. However, the same factors that create high internal validity tend to reduce external validity. In the humorous/serious advertising exposure lab experiment, participants viewed the commercial under circumstances that were different from their normal home setting. Can the results produced in this unnatural setting be duplicated when the environment is changed to viewing commercials at home? Perhaps the experiment participants were paying closer attention to the programming and advertisements than they would at home. If so, the results may not generalize to a natural setting. Unfortunately, it is impossible to recommend which experimental type is better. The best approach may vary from situation to situation. Exhibit 2-7 summarizes advantages and disadvantages of each approach.

Pilot tests and test markets are field experiments. In each case, they are very expensive and time consuming. A test market of a new product, for example, requires that a small production run be set up to produce the actual goods. This might involve shutting down an assembly line, making the necessary adjustments to produce the new product, and then actually producing enough for the test market. The product would then have to be promoted and monitored by a sales force. Price promotions, coupons, and advertising may be needed, some containing potential experimental treatments ($1 off versus $2 off). The goods have to be shipped to retailers, likely not through the usual channels. All of this adds up to a very expensive research design.

In addition, a field experiment reveals your hand to competitors. When a new food product is test marketed, for instance, some of the first purchases frequently are made by competitors. They may bring the product back to their labs where the recipe is broken down. No more secret recipe! Furthermore, competitors sometimes react to the test market and distort or sabotage the results. A mild competitor reaction might be to significantly increase promotion during the field experiment. Thus, sales of the new product may be lowered. In other cases, the competitor may send representatives from store to store to buy the entire supply of the new product. In this way, the company is denied the results that a

| EXHIBIT 2-7 | COMPARING THE BENEFITS OF FIELD AND LABORATORY EXPERIMENTS |

Goal/Benefit/Outcome	Best Experimental Approach	Comment
Maximize Internal Validity	Lab Experiment	Researcher has maximum control of external influences.
Maximize External Validity	Field Experiment	The natural setting is more realistic but subject to influences that cannot be controlled.
Most Believable Results	Field Experiment	Study seems less contrived.
Costs the Most	Field Experiment	Implementation in the field is more difficult than implementation in a lab. The scale of the project is larger.
More Flexible Design	Field Experiment	Changes can be made as the study progresses.
Relatively Timely (can be carried out in a shorter period of time)	Lab Experiment	Implementation in the lab is usually a small-scale project.

RESEARCH IN ACTION

FAT-FREE BUT NOT TROUBLE-FREE?

Frito Lay introduced Olestra Potato Chips in Omaha Nebraska as part of a test market. The test market was one of the early tests of the markets receptivity to the product. Although Lay's competitors did not attempt to sabotage the test market, a political health advocacy group did. They feared side effects such as severe diarrhea that could be associated with consumption of very large amounts of Olestra. The group launched a negative publicity campaign against Frito Lay and Olestra and implemented other in-store tactics to distort the test market results. These tactics had both negative and positive effects. While the group viciously attacked Frito Lay and Olestra, the "healthier" chips also received a great deal of free publicity. But, in no case were the market conditions normal.

SOURCE: *Omaha World Herald* (1996), "Test Markets Gauge What Sells in Omaha," September 1, 1M.

---

test market would provide. Clearly, this is a questionable approach, but it is sometimes carried out in a typical consumer good setting. Was the attempted sabotage of Olestra Potato Chips as described in the "Research in Action" box ethical? What is your opinion?

BASIC EXPERIMENTAL DESIGNS: BETWEEN AND WITHIN SUBJECTS FACTORIAL DESIGNS

Generally, human participants in research are called **respondents.** A respondent that participates in an experiment is called a **subject.** Have you ever been a guinea pig? This expression refers to the fact that guinea pigs are often used in medical experiments. Experimental medical products may be tested on real guinea pigs. Fortunately in business research, our manipulations are more benign than those received by a genuine guinea pig.

One other key design decision concerns how treatment levels should be assigned to experimental subjects. There are two approaches—between and within subjects. Exhibit 2-8 is helpful in illustrating these two approaches. In each experiment, the researcher asks subjects to rate the service quality of a simulated dining experience. The implicit theory is that service quality *depends* upon the two treatments (lights and music). Thus, it is referred to as a **dependent variable.**

A **between-subjects design** is one in which every research subject receives only one level of each experimental treatment. Thus, in a lab experiment examining the effect of lighting intensity (bright or soft) and music (Rock & Roll or Classical) on service quality ratings, each subject would perform the experimental task under one of the four possible lighting-music combinations (Groups A–D). Exhibit 2-8 shows that one hundred subjects could be randomly assigned a number from one to one hundred. Subjects 1–25 are designated group A, subjects 26–50 = group B, subjects 51–75 = group C, and subjects 76–100 = group D. Every subject in each group receives only one combination of effects. In the hypothetical results shown here, the twenty-five subjects from group D performed the rating task under soft lights with classical music, and they provided the highest ratings.

A **within-subjects** design is one in which each subject receives multiple combinations of experimental treatments. Now, each subject would perform the task under all four combinations. In Exhibit 2-8, only the twenty-five subjects in Group A are needed to produce one hundred observations. Each person in this group will perform the task under all four

EXHIBIT 2-8	TESTING THE EFFECT OF LIGHTS AND MUSIC ON SERVICE QUALITY RATINGS

Treat.1 (Lights)	Treat. 2 (Music)	Group	Between-subjects Assignment	Quality Rating	Within-subjects Assignment	Quality Rating
Bright	Rock & Roll	A	1-25	30	1-25	31
Soft	Rock & Roll	B	26-50	20	1-25	27
Bright	Classical	C	51-75	16	1-25	25
Soft	Classical	D	76-100	42	1-25	33

Note: Service quality was rated on a scale ranging from 1 = very poor to 50 = excellent.

possible treatment combinations. While within-subjects designs are more economical, because a single subject performs multiple trials, they are riskier because subjects may determine the researcher's intentions based upon the demands created by the experimental task. The degree to which the task allows the subject to determine the hypothesis is known as a **demand effect.** More simply, with a within-subjects design the subject has a much greater chance of being affected by the task than in a between-subjects design. Therefore, a within-subjects design may produce different results than a between-subjects design. Although within-subjects designs can be very useful, and they sometimes are required by a specific research question, business researchers use between-subjects designs more often to minimize problems with potential demand effects.

A **factorial design** is one that controls the levels of two or more experimental treatments at the same time. Thus, rather than conducting two separate experiments, one examining how music type (Rock & Roll or Classical) affects service quality ratings, and another examining how lighting intensity (bright or soft) affects service quality perceptions, the researcher can conduct one experiment that tests both effects. One advantage of factorial designs is efficiency. It is normally more economical cost-wise and time-wise to conduct one experiment than two.

A second advantage is that factorial designs permit the analysis of interactions. **Interaction** refers to the combined effects of multiple variables. So, perhaps the music and lighting together create an effect that is greater than either two experimental variables alone. For example, customers may perceive much higher service quality under soft lights with classical music rather than with rock and roll music. However, customers may perceive slightly higher quality under bright lights if rock and roll music is played. Thus, the proper decision is based not on a single variable, but on the combined effect of two variables.

Exhibit 2-9 shows a graphical depiction of these hypothetical experimental results. Results from factorial designs are often depicted in this manner. The chart can be interpreted as follows:

> First, the average height (position on the y axis) of the soft lights line is higher than the average height of the bright lights line. The average quality rating for soft lights (A = 31) higher than for bright lights is (B = 23). Thus, a main effect is observed for lights indicating that soft lights treatment produces higher quality ratings than the bright lights condition.

| EXHIBIT 2-9 | THE EFFECT OF LIGHTS AND MUSIC ON SERVICE QUALITY |

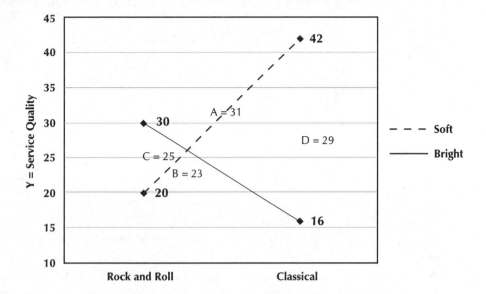

Second, the average height of the distance between the two mean rock & roll observations (C = 25) is less than the average height of the distance between the two mean classical music observations (D = 29). Thus, another main effect may suggest that classical music produces higher service quality ratings.

Third, the fact that the lines cross suggests an interaction. While bright lights produce higher quality with rock & roll music (30) than with classical music (16), soft lights produce higher quality with classical music (42) than with rock & roll (20). Lines that are approximately parallel result when no interaction is present.

Researchers generally use the term main effect to refer to the impact that any single experimental variable has on a response variable. In our example, music and lighting type are experimental variables. Likewise, service quality ratings are the response (outcome) variable. So, if the means differ either by music or lighting type, there is a main effect.

Sometimes, researchers will introduce a blocking factor into the design. A blocking variable is a grouping variable the researcher doesn't manipulate or control in any way. Gender is a common blocking variable. Its effect on the outcome variable also will be analyzed, but the researcher cannot manipulate the gender of an experimental subject! It can only be observed.

Experiments often are described with an $l \times m \times q$ description. L, m, and q refer to experimental or blocking variables. So, a $2 \times 2 \times 2$ between-subjects experimental design suggests two levels of the first experimental treatment, two levels of the second, and perhaps two levels of a blocking factor. In the experiment described previously, the first 2 could refer to the two levels of lighting (soft or bright), the second 2 could refer to the two

RESEARCH IN ACTION

WHAT HAPPENS WHEN STUDENTS GRADE THEIR OWN EXAMS?

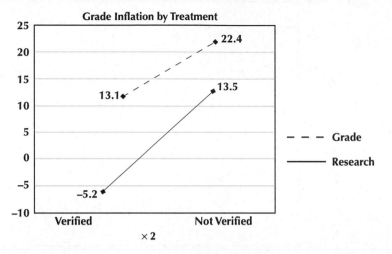

Should students grade their own tests? Managers have asked whether or not employees should provide their own performance assessments. After all, who knows the employee's work better? Researchers have examined this issue by testing the effect student self-evaluation would have on their grade. The researchers conducted a 2 × 2 between subjects lab experiment. The first experimental treatment manipulated the "Purpose" of the evaluation over two levels: Student-subjects were told that their self-evaluation would be used for (1) research purposes only (not affect his or her grade) or (2) for the purpose of determining his or her final grade. The second experimental treatment manipulated "Verification" and also had two levels: The first level informed the student that his or her self-evaluation would be compared against an instructor's objective evaluation, while the second level said that that no verification record existed. The key outcome was grade inflation, meaning how much better a student's self-grade was compared to the actual grade achieved by the student.

The results show that students do inflate their grades. This lab experiment suggests that both purpose and verification knowledge affect self-appraisals. Two main effects are found. Students gave themselves a higher grade than they deserved when they expected the appraisal was for actual grading purposes as opposed to for research purposes only. Also, students inflated their grade more when led to believe that their self-grade would not be evaluated.

The chart in the upper portion of this box shows the results graphically. Note that the grade line (dashed) is higher than the research line (solid) demonstrating the main effect of purpose. The main effect of verification is also displayed. Note that the average height between the points above the no verification label is higher than the average height between the points above the verification label. Thus, what would your decision be? Should student self-appraisals be allowed?

SOURCE: Farh, Jing-Lih and James D. Werbel. 1985. The Effects of Purpose of the Appraisal and Expectation of Validation on the Quality of Self-Appraisals, *Academy of Management Proceedings*, p. 260–263. Also, Farh, Jing-Lih and James D. Werbel, 1986. Effects of Purpose of the Appraisal and Expectation of Validation on Self-Appraisal Leniency. *Journal of Applied Psychology*, 71 (August): 527–530.

music levels (rock & roll and classical), and the final 2 could refer to two levels of gender (male and female). The "Research in Action" box on "What Happens When Students Grade Their Own Exams?" is a good example of a 2 × 2 design. If the researcher had also examined gender (blocking variable) it would have been a 2 × 2 × 2 design.

It's impossible to give complete coverage to the topic of experimental designs within a single chapter. There are many good texts on this topic alone.[13] We'll discuss analyzing experiments more in Chapter 10 when Analysis of Variance (ANOVA) is covered.

ETHICAL DIMENSIONS OF EXPERIMENTAL DESIGNS

Experimental designs often involve some type of deception. This presents the researcher with a special obligation to maintain the fair and moral treatment of participants. The ethical treatment of experimental subjects is discussed in detail in Chapter 4.

PLANNING AND IMPLEMENTING THE RESEARCH DESIGN

SELECTING THE BEST DESIGN

Selecting the right research design depends upon the research question. If the research question involves primarily discovery or clarification of some issue, an exploratory design is best. Research questions that emphasize the description of some quantity, the relative amounts of some variable or the extent to which some variables are related probably calls for a descriptive design. On the other hand, a research question that states cause and effect means a causal design will be used through an experiment. Beyond the design decision, researchers face other issues in planning a research design.

Observations to Data to Knowledge

Research projects often involve analysis of data. *Data* are simply information recorded with the intent of representing facts. The government maintains records with data that describe facts about each citizen. This information includes where you are employed, how old you are and how much money you make each year, among other things. In research, we are usually interested in data on more than one characteristic. The term *data set* refers to a collection of information describing multiple facts on multiple units of analysis. Often, researchers will investigate relationships among these characteristics. Once the data are analyzed successfully, and statistical results addressing specific research questions and/or hypotheses have been interpreted, knowledge results. This knowledge is used to make more effective business decisions.

Objective versus Subjective Data

Data can be characterized numerous ways. One important way is distinguishing objective from subjective data. **Objective data** are independent of any single person's opinion. Objective data provide numbers that are difficult to dispute. For example, if one were interested in describing the number of automobile deaths per one hundred thousand people by country, the data are published by the U.S. Congressional Services based on death certificate reports. The numbers show that in the United States from 1990 to 1995, this number ranged from 46.8 to 40.6 deaths per 100,000, a small decline. This can be compared to the 1990–1995 numbers for Russia that ranged from 98.6 to 108.3 deaths per 100,000. There seems to be little opinion involved in these data. Practically any researcher would accept these numbers and use them as reported without any further interpretation. Thus, these data are objective.

There are other ways to obtain objective data. Business people often may wish to study strategic business units, individual retail stores, advertisements or some other nonhuman, and thus non-subjective, unit of analysis. A researcher might be interested in describing the esprit-de-corps (perhaps as part of a study of the culture in each unit) among the workforces in its different factories. This number cannot simply be looked up. Instead, the number will have to be derived from reports provided by the people who work there. The more consistency among reports of esprit-de-corps within a unit, the more difficult it is to dispute the score. When multiple reports can be provided that show high consistency, the multiple reports can be aggregated to create a single objective score. Too much inconsistency would lead one to question whether an objective assessment is possible.

Subjective data are indeed an individual's opinion. When the business researcher collects data using individual employee esprit-de-corps measures they are subjective. They are one employee's opinion of this characteristic. When they are aggregated, they become relatively more objective because the score is not dependent solely on one person's opinion. All perceptual data are subjective. Thus, an employee's rating of job satisfaction, supervisor support or work involvement is subjective. Similarly, customer ratings of a hotel's service quality, their satisfaction with the hotel or their attitude toward the hotel's advertising also are subjective.

Another class of subjective data is researcher dependent. Some types of data collection require the opinion of the researcher to complete some measurement. Retail units often analyze email complaints. The hope is that the sources of complaints can be identified and rectified. A researcher will read the complaint and then score it by assigning numbers or by placing it in a category. These data are subjective and researcher dependent because the researcher ultimately assigns the number (score).

Primary versus Secondary Data Data also can be described as primary or secondary based upon its source. **Primary data** are collected for the purpose of completing the current research project. Thus, the researcher has been involved in every aspect of turning the data into knowledge. This includes designing the data collection device, collecting the data, coding it (phase II), checking it for errors and then analyzing and interpreting the data (phase III). Any research design that calls for a survey to be designed and implemented will result in primary data.

Secondary data are data that have been collected for some other research purpose. Secondary data may still address the research question at hand. So, researchers should always check for potential secondary data sources before collecting primary data. Secondary data are often free or can be purchased for much less than the cost of collecting primary data. Recent trends have increased the use of secondary data. Technology has made secondary data more readily accessible to greater numbers of decision makers. Obviously, secondary data can be obtained much more quickly. So, the two key advantages of secondary data are saving money and saving time.

These advantages have to be weighed against the disadvantages. One disadvantage is that secondary data seldom fit the purpose at hand precisely. This only stands to reason since they were collected for another purpose. The most serious lack of fit issue is that the measures contained in the secondary data may not match the hypotheses perfectly. For example, a researcher may be interested in testing the relationship between household size and miles driven per year. The U.S. Federal Highway Department maintains statistics on automobile ownership and usage for countries around the world. Likewise, statistics can be found that represent household size. However, the information might be based on different definitions of households or automobile usage. Data for some countries may consider a household as an extended family whereas others may measure the size of the nuclear family. Likewise, the automobile data may account for things such as leased automobiles, truck miles versus car miles or even rentals differently. That's not to mention the fact that units, such as automobile usage, may need be converted from English (miles) to metric (kilometers), or vice versa.

The second significant issue arising with secondary data is that its quality is more difficult to assess. Since researchers design the data collection for primary data, they know all the details. But with secondary data you must rely on the integrity of the original source for assurance the data are accurate. Measurement details and reliability estimates generally are available if you rely on the original source of secondary data. Secondary data must be held to equally as high a standard in judging its truth content as would be typical of primary data. In other words, just as researchers must verify the reliability and validity of data collected specifically for a current research purpose, they should verify the reliability and validity of secondary data. For this reason, caution should be applied in using data from an unknown or unfamiliar source.

Sources of Secondary Data There is virtually an endless list of potential sources for secondary data. The researcher may wish to begin by searching internal sources. Internal sources refer to data previously collected by or for the organization itself. This includes previous primary data collection efforts as well as routine record inventories. Useful data may be found in employee annual evaluation reports, salesperson itineraries, sales invoices, company financial reports and records, customer complaints, billing records, bank ledgers, and previous strategic planning documents.

After exhausting the potential internal secondary data sources, the researcher considers external data sources. There are countless volumes of secondary data available from both nonprofit and for-profit organizations. Fortunately, these sources can many times be accessed and searched with an electronic search engine. The key to a successful computer search is inputting useful key words into a search engine. Most libraries have access to several search

---

RESEARCH IN ACTION
DATA CAN BE FISHY!

Secondary data is abundant on-line. All one needs is a good search engine and a little imagination. Your local library has access to many search engines that charge a fee to use them. However, suppose you were interested in a statistical overview of aquaculture (fish farming) as part of an environmental analysis for a prospective entrepreneurial business venture.

Google.com can supply the bait! Go to www.google.com, enter fishing and statistics in the search window, and press search. Google will recommend several sites. One is http://www.fao.org/fi/statist/FISOFT/FISHPLUS.asp. There, you will find over a dozen downloadable data sets containing information on total and regional aqua culture production. Since the data is charted for over twenty years, this would be very useful in plotting and analyzing trends in the marketplace. Perhaps you might be surprised how easy it is to find volumes of information on even the most obscure topics.

---

engines that can identify potentially relevant research studies and/or data. Individuals and private companies may also subscribe to an online database vender for a fee. Some provide access to print articles from trade periodicals, academic journals and general business magazines. Others provide access primarily to statistical data. Exhibit 2-10 provides a list of some secondary data sources. Note that any list of this type is subject to change as companies change their URLs and Web page contents. So, if one doesn't provide the help you need, try another. The "Research in Action" box gives you an example of what you might find using an electronic search engine.

Quantitative versus Qualitative Data Many students fear a business research course because it is associated with math. They often also think of it as a statistical discipline. Business research is a discipline that uses statistics. These statistics often are performed on quantitative data collected from company financial records, sales records or questionnaires. **Quantitative data** are measurements in which numbers are used directly to represent the properties of something. Since they are recorded directly with numbers, they are in a form that lends itself to statistical analysis. Chapter 5 describes some methods for quantitative data collection.

Qualitative data represent descriptions of things that are made without assigning numbers directly. Qualitative data generally are collected using some type of **unstructured interview.** Focus groups and depth interviews are commonly applied qualitative research approaches. Rather than collecting information by assigning numbers, the data are collected by recording words and sometimes pictures. Researchers sometimes have respondents make a collage using pictures from magazines. The researcher then analyzes the collage for potential meaning.[14] Exhibit 2-11 compares and contrasts quantitative and qualitative data.

The research components that are strengths of a quantitative study, such as structure and representativeness, are not typical in qualitative research. Qualitative researchers prefer an unstructured interview as a way of probing deeply into an issue. Since respondents are free to choose their own words, the researcher cannot predict the specific direction of the interview. The lack of structure allows identification of issues that would not be revealed by a structured questionnaire. Similarly, the qualitative researcher often may prefer a respondent who is atypical in some way. Respondents highly involved in a situation are especially desirable since new discoveries are often relatively extreme.

Objectivity was stressed as an important component of science. Quantitative data help provide objectivity in that hypotheses are tested by applying statistical criteria to the measures. Since the observed units supplied the numbers, the researcher's opinion does not affect the hypothesis test. In contrast, qualitative data requires interpretation. For example, it is pretty obvious that "cool" clothing usually means the respondent likes it. However, if clothing is referred to as "funky" or "comfortable," is that desirable? These terms present the research with ambiguity when reading an interview transcript. Comfortable could mean clothing that is loose fitting possibly allowing freedom of movement, or it could mean the clothing makes consumers feel comfortable about their bodies.[15] Thus, the researcher's subjective opinion must be used to resolve the ambiguous meaning. Since a subjective opinion is involved, qualitative data are more difficult to replicate.

Does subjectivity make qualitative research unscientific and less useful? Absolutely not! Qualitative researchers sometimes assess inter-rater reliability. *Inter-rater* reliability means that multiple "raters" will evaluate a common qualitative data point. Reliable data

EXHIBIT 2-10	SOME USEFUL SOURCES FOR SECONDARY DATA

Source	Description
www.census.gov	The statistical repository for all U.S. Census data. This data is useful for research questions dealing with population broken down in various levels of detail. For example, population counts by state, county, or zip code are readily available. Some data are available for countries outside the U.S. General commerce statistics also are available. Statistics on employment by region and/or industry, payroll information, counts of businesses by industry, some consumption statistics and government spending information is available.
Global Interact Network Mailing List (GINLIST) ciber.bus.msu.edu/ginlist	Provides access to a wide variety of international business statistics including population data, industry and market analyses, import/export statistics, public data from the World Bank, as well as access to dozens of official international statistical profiles including the U.K., most of Europe, Australia, Hong Kong, and many others.
www.usatrade.gov/website/ccg.nsf	Contains access to hundreds of international business resources including statistical charts providing an overview of commerce in countries around the world. Labor and consumption statistics are available. These statistics are made available by the U.S. Department of Commerce's International Trade Administration.
www.usadata.com	Statistical profiles for the top sixty U.S. consumer markets including data on marketing activities, competitive intensity, advertising, and consumer behavior.
www.hoovers.com	Statistics on hundreds of public U.S. companies. Basic financial statistics and company profiles are included. Access to annual reports is available. Made available by Hoover's Business Press.
Standard & Poor's Corporate Records www.standardandpoors.com	Basic financial statistics, profiles, news releases are available for over 10,000 public companies.
ABI/Inform www.abiinform.com	An electronic database accessible through many libraries or on-line by subscription. Access to over 800 trade and academic journals. These journals contain research studies that may be useful in trying to address the research question at hand. These studies are also of great use in formalizing research questions and hypotheses. A public web site is currently under construction.
EBSCO www.ebscohost.com	An information service that provides full text access to thousands of periodicals covering the social sciences, business literature, the humanities and general science. Extremely useful in identifying previous research on a given topic. Widely available through libraries or by subscription. Check with your library for access.
General Social Survey www.icpsr.umich.edu	An annual survey of 35,000 U.S. households containing 2,500 questions that provide basic information of economic relevance including consumer confidence indices, spending patterns, and satisfaction data.
cyberatlas.internet.com /big_picture/demographics	Provides a basic view of internet usage around the world including who is using it and what they are doing. Contains results from the Baruch College-Harris poll commissioned by *Business Week*.
SIRS Knowledge Source www.sks11.sirs.com	Full text articles from newspapers, magazines, journals, and U.S. government publications exploring social, scientific, health, historic, and business issues around the world. Useful in identifying previous research on a given topic. Available by subscription and through libraries.
Lexis-Nexis Database www.lexisnexis.com	An excellent source for identifying current events within and outside the U.S. as reported in newspapers and business periodicals. Access to many government statistics also is provided. Some private statistical tables also are available. Available by subscription or through libraries.
www.stat-usa.gov	Daily economic reports on economic news, import and export data, and related statistics.

EXHIBIT 2-11	A COMPARISON OF QUALITATIVE AND QUANTITATIVE DATA	

Description	Quantitative Data	Qualitative Data
Purpose	More useful for testing.	More useful for discovering.
	Provides summary information on many characteristics.	Provides in-depth (deeper understanding) information on a few characteristics.
	Useful in tracking trends.	Discovering 'hidden' motivations and values.
Properties	More structured collection techniques and objective ratings.	More unstructured collection techniques requiring a subjective interpretation.
	High concern for representativeness.	Little concern for representativeness.
	Relatively short interviews (1 to 20 minutes).	Relatively long interviews (1/2 to many hours)
	Interviewer is passive.	Interviewer is active and should be highly skilled.
	Large samples (over 50).	Small samples (1-50).
	Results objective.	Results subjective.

exists when the raters agree on its meaning, and this provides an indication that the results can be replicated. However, this is not called for often since most qualitative research is conducted for purposes other than testing. It stops short of the testing phase of the scientific method. Since it is discovery oriented, the criticism of subjectivity isn't relevant. Subjectivity becomes a weakness only when researchers try to generalize conclusions based upon a single researcher's opinion. The focus group researchers for Pontiac interpreted the respondents' comments about its design positively. Further concept testingusing quantitative analyses may not have supported the hypotheses suggesting a positive influence of the car's design.

Some researchers debate the superiority of qualitative research over quantitative research or vice versa. However, this view is near-sighted. A comparison of the two approaches suggests that they complement each other very well. Qualitative techniques are more often part of an exploratory design. Thus, a very important alliance between the two is that qualitative studies may develop ideas that can be tested with some type of quantitative approach. Effective decision-making often requires input from both quantitative and qualitative data.

SUMMARY

Explain How a Study Is Created Based Upon a Description of the Business Decision Involved

This chapter introduces the basic research process. Three phases are involved. Phase I translates the overall research issues into research questions and hypotheses. Theory plays a key role in translating information about some business situation into a researchable idea. Theory, business practices and intuition enable the research questions to be translated into hypotheses. Phase II, the Execution phase, is concerned with the activities that collect data. Phase III, the Analytical phase, is where the data are interpreted relative to the hypotheses. Hypotheses are either supported or not supported based upon these results.

Describe the Role of Theory and Science in Business Research

The scientific method is discussed. In many ways, the basic business research process follows the same methodology as the scientific method. The process starts by considering all relevant input. This input is combined with current knowledge to produce research questions or hypotheses. These are then tested in an analytical way. It is important to note that no recommendation is provided for the most acceptable way to discover ideas. However, ideas can only be supported or found false through testing. The scientific method provides a process for discovering and testing ideas.

Describe the Three Basic Business Research Designs

A research design is selected based upon this process. If hypotheses cannot be developed based on the information provided and the theory available, then an exploratory design is the best approach. If the researcher is interested in frequencies, levels of some variables, or basic relationships, a descriptive design is probably called for. If the researcher is interested in testing whether one thing causes another, then a causal design should be used.

The chapter introduces focus groups and depth interviews. Both are important discovery-oriented exploratory research tools. Depth interviews are preferable when a respondent may be more open in a private setting as opposed to a group setting. Focus groups are preferable when the group dynamics will not hinder comment. In fact, there may be times when the group dynamics encourage discussion.

The basic elements of experimental design are discussed. Lab experiments are performed in a contrived (laboratory) setting. Field experiments are conducted in the field. Lab experiments maximize the chances of any differences in a response variable being due to the experimental variable. Realism is often sacrificed for this advantage. Field experiments enhance the chance that any findings from the study will transfer to the population concerned. The basics of factorial designs were discussed including definitions for main effects and interactions. Main effects are differences attributable to the causal variable itself. Interaction effects are due to the combined effect of multiple variables.

Explain the Roles of Exploratory and Confirmatory Research

The first half of the basic research business process is oriented toward discovery. There are few if any rules about discovery. The whole point is to develop some ideas worthy of testing. Testing is the second half of the research process. There is only one way to test ideas. The idea must be compared with reality or expectations. This is known as empirical testing.

Understand the Difference Between Primary and Secondary Data

Data also can be described as primary or secondary. Primary data are collected for the purpose of completing the current research project. Thus, the researcher has been involved in every aspect of turning the data into knowledge. This includes designing the data collection device, collecting the data, coding it (phase II), checking it for errors and then analyzing and interpreting the data (phase III). In contrast, *secondary data* are data that have been collected for some other research purpose. Secondary data may still address the research question at hand so researchers should always check for potential secondary data sources before collecting primary data. Secondary data are often free or can be purchased for much less than the cost of collecting primary data. Recent trends have increased the use of secondary data. Technology has made secondary data more readily accessible to greater numbers of decision makers and it can be obtained much more quickly.

Explain the Roles of Qualitative and Quantitative Research

Good research involves both qualitative and quantitative research. Qualitative data are collected without the direct use of numbers. Quantitative data are collected with numbers. Qualitative data tend to be subjective, meaning a researcher or decision maker must interpret the text (words) or pictures that represent research. Quantitative data are more objective since the statistical results do not depend upon the researcher's opinion. They are reliant only upon the researcher's skills as an analyst.

KEY TERMS

between-subjects design	focus groups	quantitative data
business research process	hypothesis	research questions
causal relationship	interaction	respondents
causal research	intuition-based decisions	secondary data
cross-sectional studies	laboratory experiments	science
data	law-like generalizations	scientific method
demand effect	longitudinal studies	structured interview
dependent variable	manipulation	subject
depth interviews	normative decision rule	subjective data
descriptive research	objective data	survey
descriptive theory	panel	theory
experiment	parsimony	theory-based decisions
exploratory research	primary data	unstructured interview
factorial design	projective technique	within-subjects
field experiment	qualitative data	

ETHICAL DILEMMA

Brian Webster is account manager for Reliable Research, Inc. He tells customers that the firm recommends to that they begin by conducting a survey to benchmark customer perceptions before conducting any experiments to determine how customers would react to any new business decisions. Brian's assistant is aware that Reliable already has the information about public perceptions of a client from a recent survey conducted on behalf of this client's major competitor. Therefore, he feels Reliable should present the results of the other survey as secondary research to save the client money. When he mentions his concern to Brian, Brian feels that it is not unethical to conduct a new survey even if they know the probable results. Instead, he believes it would be more unethical to disclose the results of work conducted on behalf of another client. Who do you agree with?

REVIEW QUESTIONS

1. What are the three phases of the basic business research process? Briefly explain each.
2. What role(s) does theory play in the basic business research process?
3. What is a hypothesis? How is a hypothesis created? How is a hypothesis tested?
4. What are the characteristics of good science?
5. What is parsimony?
6. What role does a moderator play in a focus group interview?
7. Describe the difference between a structured and an unstructured interview.
8. What does the term cross-sectional mean?
9. How is "control" implemented within an experimental design?
10. What is an interaction?

DISCUSSION AND APPLICATION ACTIVITIES

1. Suppose you work for a major consumer goods company. One of the products that you represent is a salad dressing. A competitor is beginning a test market involving a new spicy ranch flavor. Their salespeople are going from store to store placing it on the shelves. Your boss asks you to go to these stores and buy all the salad dressing. Why might he or she ask you to do this? What would be your reaction? Consider the ethical implications of this behavior.
2. What does "manipulation" refer to in the context of business research? Provide an example of manipulation.
3. What are normative decision rules? Are they theory?
4. Describe a basic experimental design that would examine the following research question: Does the time of day and temperature affect employee productivity?
5. Describe a basic experimental design that would examine the following research question: Does the time of day and temperature affect consumers' price sensitivity?

INTERNET EXERCISES

1. Use some Web-based search engines, such as those discussed in this chapter, to find the following pieces of information:
   a. The number of people employed in automobile manufacturing in the United States, the United Kingdom, Germany, and Japan.
   b. Basic demographic profiles for the following U.S. zip codes: 70814, 39402, 39401, and 70739.
2. Visit this Web site: www.advisorteam.com/. Follow the first time user instructions to take the Keirsey Temperament Sorter II. Which personality type do you belong to? Discuss the different types in class. What types of jobs would you recommend to someone with your personality type? What types of jobs would you not recommend to someone with your personality type?

NOTES

1. Hunt, Shelby. 1983. *Marketing Theory: The Philosophy of Marketing Science.* Irwin: Homewood, Ill..
2. Chamberlin, Olin. 1939. *The Theory of Monopolistic Competition.* Harvard University Press: Cambridge, Mass.
3. Lewin, Kurt. 1948. *Resolving Social Conflicts and Field Theory in Social Science.* Harper and Row: New York.
4. Dickson, Peter R. 1992. Toward a General Theory of Competitive Rationality. *Journal of Marketing* 56 (January): 69–83; Hunt, Shelby D. and Robert M. Morgan. 1996. The Resource-Advantage Theory of Competition: Dynamics, Path Dependencies, and Evolutionary Dimensions. *Journal of Marketing* 60 (October): 107, 114; Hunt, Shelby D. and Robert M. Morgan. 1997. Resource-Advantage Theory: A Snake Swallowing Its Tail or a General Theory of Competition. *Journal of Marketing* 61 (October) 74–83.
5. Caulkin, Simon. 2002. Management: A Mess in Theory, A Mess in Practice. *The Observer* (January 13): 9.
6. Remington, Lindsey. 2002. Arizona Firms Return to More Conservative Dress. *The Tribune,* Mesa, Ariz. (February 8), accessed through Lexis-Nexis, March 13, 2002.
7. Teresko, John. 1997. Research Renaissance. *Industry Week* 246 (9 June): 139–150.
8. Swaddling, Jeffrey D. and Mark W. Zobel. 1996. Beating the Odds. *Marketing Management* 4 (Spring/Winter): 20–34.
9. Holthausen, Robert and David F. Larcker. 1995. Business Unit Innovation and the Structure of Executive Compensation. *Journal of Accounting and Economics* 19 (May): 279–304.
10. For a review of similar studies, see: Chebat, Jean-Charles, Claire Gelinas Chebat and Domanique Vaillant. 2001. Environmental Background Music and In-Store Selling. *Journal of Business Research* 54 (November): 115–124.
11. See Pethokoukis, James M. 2002. That Old Blue-Sky Feeling Again. *U.S. News & World Report* 132 (1/14): 30 for an example of data tracking consumer confidence and various financial indices over time.
12. See Hunt, 1983.
13. Cochran, William G. and Gertrude M. Cox. 1992. *Experimental Designs.* Wiley: New York.
14. Rickard, Leah. 1994. Focus Groups Go to College. *Advertising Age* 65 (14 November): 39.
15. Letelier, Maria F. Flores, Charles Spinosa and Bobby J. Calder. 2000. Taking an Expanded View of Customers' Needs: Qualitative Research for Aiding Innovation *Marketing Research* 12 (Winter): 4–11.

Creative Decision Making and Research

Learning Objectives

1. Describe the role of research in helping businesspeople make decisions.

2. Present a creative and analytical business decision-making process.

3. Discuss the importance of writing actionable research questions.

4. Suggest techniques for being more creative.

5. Understand concepts related to evaluating alternatives and choice.

INTRODUCTION

In Chapter 2 we discussed the business research process. Here, we integrate the business research process into the more general decision-making process. Both processes involve decision making. Business researchers decide the type of research design, data, and statistical approach that will be used to address actionable **research questions.** An important outcome of this process is that it provides valuable knowledge to the decision maker. Decision makers then use the results of the research to enhance business operations. This chapter introduces this more general process of business decision making and describes how research plays a major role.

RESEARCH AND DECISION MAKING GO TOGETHER

It is all too easy for a student to concentrate solely on the specific material within a given chapter. Thus, while specific topics can be mastered, at least temporarily, the student may not realize how these topics fit within some larger scheme. Research can be like this. The student may master topics such as sampling and cross-tabulation, but may all too easily forget the "big picture." This chapter reminds the student of the overall purpose of all the specific material. That is, becoming a more effective decision maker.

Exhibit 3-1 visually displays the flow of activities within a creative, analytical decision-making process. The process includes creativity because business opportunities often are taken advantage of best by selecting a novel solution. At the same time, the process is analytical because it involves critical evaluation of alternative solutions. We'll refer to this process as the **CAB process** decision-making model (C for creative, A for analytical, and B for business). The process is very practical in that it maximizes the chances of a desirable outcome.

Research is essential to the success of this process. First, ongoing research feeds into the system and is the primary mechanism for gathering information used to form the research

EXHIBIT 3-1   **CREATIVE-ANALYTICAL BUSINESS DECISION-MAKING PROCESS**

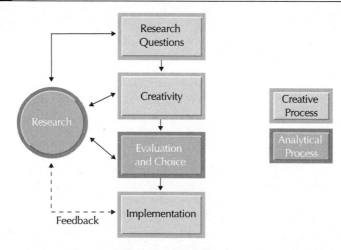

questions. Second, creative processes are needed to generate alternatives and to carry out research designs. Third, evaluation and choice occurs through a combination of intuition and critical evaluation. Critical evaluation often involves some type of **empirical test.** An empirical test is one in which data are gathered and analyzed to draw conclusions. Thus, research is needed in the evaluation phase. After an alternative is selected, an implementation plan must be developed. This may send the process back to the creativity phase and research may be needed to critically evaluate alternative implementation plans. Fourth, research plays a key role in monitoring and feedback. Data warehouses become repositories for ongoing research that may eventually be used by an **expert system** as discussed in Chapter 1. Thus, the study of business decision making includes research, since research is essential to improved decision making. Also, any study of business research should include a discussion of decision making, since it is often why research is necessary.

Creativity also plays a key role in shaping research. Often, the research may need creative input to help design a study. From time to time, creative processes are used to design effective exploratory studies. Thus, research designs and techniques are very much interdependent.

THE NATURE OF DECISION MAKING

What keeps businesspeople so busy? They make a lot of decisions. The word decide is derived from the Latin, *decidere,* meaning to cut off.[1] This Latin root emphasizes the point that in decision making, there is a time for seeking input from people involved, but at some point the decision maker must act. There comes a point in time when decisive action must be taken. As a decision maker, we would prefer to be well informed at this point.

Can a businessperson blindly make a decision? Practically speaking it is impossible because the mere ability to express the situation in thought or words activates an internal memory search. This memory search is an initial and inexpensive research project. Indeed, for routine decisions with low risk, this may be an adequate form of research. If the decision maker is less familiar with a problem, or if the risk associated with a bad decision is high, more information is used as an input to the decision, and thus more resources (time and money) are allocated to researchers. Exhibit 3-2 illustrates the relative amount of research typically performed across different types of decision situations. Notice that the largest amount of research is conducted when decision makers face unfamiliar, high-risk situations. In contrast, routine low-risk decision making involves very little research.

One of the worst experiences a chef faces is discovering an important ingredient is missing from the pantry only after deciding tonight's menu. In such situations, the key to implementation is improvisation. Good decision makers, like good chefs, make the best out of the ingredients at hand. If the initial survey of the pantry was thorough, the chef may be able to act quickly and use the available resources to create a different but equally delicious dish. If the initial survey was not comprehensive enough, the result may be tuna casserole!

Like the chef and the menu, research generally provides benefits beyond the original menu itself. President Eisenhower, reflecting on strategy development during World War II, drew the simple but eloquent conclusion. "A plan is nothing; planning is everything." Even though information and resources may not always be used precisely as decision makers envision, the very same preparation, information and resources enable better decision making among the people carrying out the plan. So information provided by research has value in two ways:

EXHIBIT 3-2	HOW MUCH RESEARCH IS DONE?

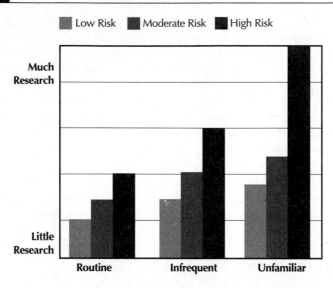

■ Low Risk ■ Moderate Risk ■ High Risk

1. providing a more informed answer to the questions that initially motivated the research and

2. increasing the knowledge of personnel and the firm overall so that more informed decisions can be made in general

Exhibit 3-3 provides some interesting leadership perspectives on decision making. These perspectives show that decision making is never done with perfect information. Information provided by research helps make sure, however, that the decision maker is informed. The leader then weighs the merits of this information against intuition in taking decisive action.

THE DECISION MAKING PROCESS

Opportunity truly does present itself every day. *Opportunity* is a situation (a particular point in time and/or place) that makes a potentially advantageous outcome possible. Opportunities are seized through good decision making.

Exhibit 3-1, introduced at the beginning of this chapter, displays the CAB business decision-making process. Sometimes this process may be followed formally. Other times the process may be informal. Research can play an important role in any phase of the decision-making process.

Problem solving involves a reactive process to overcome a potentially negative situation. Decision making occurs during problem solving, but decision making is a more general term. Decisions are not always evoked by a negative situation, as the word problem denotes. In other words, things don't have to be wrong in order for decision making to occur. Business decision making occurs whenever businesspeople select from among alternative courses of action, each of which will likely lead to a different outcome.

EXHIBIT 3-3	SOME LEADERSHIP PERSPECTIVES ON DECISIONS

"Nothing is more difficult, and therefore more precious, than to be able to decide."	Napoleon Bonaparte
"Indecision and delays are the parents of failure."	George Canning
"The risk of a wrong decision is preferable to the terror of indecision."	Maimonides
"A decision is the action an executive must take when he has information so incomplete that the answer does not suggest itself."	Admiral Arthur W. Radford
"Don't let adverse facts stand in the way of a good decision."	Colin Powell
"It's easy to make good decisions when there are no bad options."	Robert Half
"Be willing to make decisions. That's the most important quality in a good leader. Don't fall victim to what I call the 'ready-aim-aim-aim syndrome.' You must be willing to fire."	T. Boone Pickens
"A decision is what a man makes when he can't find anybody to serve on a committee."	Fletcher Knebel

SOURCE: *Journal of Business Strategy.* 2001. Decisions, Decisions, Decisions. 22 (5): 48.

RESEARCH QUESTIONS

Information is gathered constantly, both through formal and informal processes. Routine research reports, such as market share reports, sales data, employee productivity, etc., as well as qualitative assessments from employees and customers, including their complaints and suggestions, are important knowledge sources for organizations.

When is an opportunity or crisis spotted? Businesses undergo continuous and periodic **monitoring.** Constant monitoring can be performed by a *management (or marketing) information system* (MIS). An **MIS** generates reports using information fed routinely into the computer through automatic or manual mechanisms. Modern technology has automated this research activity. For example, when the checkout clerk scans your purchase, an electronic history of this event is stored. At the end of the day, managers can produce sales reports that allow them to compare daily performance against expectations. This information may be helpful in making many routine decisions involving labor hours scheduled and restocking. If the store is part of a chain, the information typically is sent to a central computer that automatically generates periodic financial and performance reports. These periodic reports may sound an alarm that something is abnormal. Perhaps sales or labor costs are too high or too low within certain regions. In this manner, opportunities can be spotted and crises avoided.

A **Decision Support System (DSS)** is a typical component of an MIS. A DSS consists of software that allows a manager to interact with the MIS to examine potential outcomes related to common decisions. The software uses information stored in the data warehouse, along with input by the manager, to generate forecasts or "'what if'" type responses. For example, the DSS may suggest a likely outcome of decisions to change production schedules, product assortments, pricing, financial allocations, or similar changes.

RESEARCH IN ACTION
DON'T TRASH THOSE TEE-TIMES!

GolfBC, a Vancouver, B.C., Canada-based golf management firm has developed an expert system that manages tee-time allocations across multiple Vancouver area courses. The system also develops promotional programs based on tee-time usage rates. These promotions encourage golfers to play at relatively unpopular golf times such as weekday mornings or late evenings. As part of the program, golfers swipe a card with each round of play and accumulate points that can be redeemed for free golf. This results in data used to make the adjustments. A weekend round at the Nicklaus North course in Whistler, B.C. might cost a member as much as four thousand points. But, a twilight time on a weeknight might be as little as 1,500 points. This system automates the entire decision-making process. Learn more about this innovative company at www.GolfBC.com.

SOURCE: Brown, Jennifer. 2002. Every Day's a Saturday. eBusiness Journal 4 (January): 14–16.

An *expert system* is another component of the DSS. An expert system is software that automates some decisions. Merrill Lynch uses an expert system to determine customer asset allocations. The system integrates survey research (customer responses to a questionnaire) with real-time risk and return information to determine how a customer's investment resources are allocated among mutual funds.[2] Likewise, expert systems use customer orders and peak usage times to adjust prices and promotions automatically. Have you ever wondered why airline prices can vary dramatically from passenger to passenger? It's likely that an expert system has automatically taken action based on information from routine inputs like ticket purchase information. The action may raise or lower prices based upon seat availability with the goal of optimizing the profit yield. Expert systems allow the entire decision-making process to take place automatically for many routine decisions. The "Research in Action" box explains how an expert system helps manage golf courses in Vancouver, Canada.

In the research question formulation phase of problem solving, available information is screened and used to devise a formal statement of actionable research questions. Answers to these research questions provide alternative courses of action for the organization. Often, both the researcher and the decision maker are involved in this process. The decision maker identifies issues and the researcher plays a key role in translating the issues into researchable questions.

Businesspeople make decisions either because they want to improve a situation or to avoid a catastrophe. In either case, *decision making* is motivated by the realization that there is a gap between the current or expected future state and a more desirable future state. The businessperson in this situation has either recognized a problem or identified an opportunity.

Not all decisions are equal. Sometimes, a decision-making situation occurs with little notice and great potential for negative implications. The manager is faced with **crisis management.** At other times, decision making is more proactive, designed to take advantage of potentially favorable conditions. Therefore, decision making takes place along a continuum between a state of crisis and pure opportunity, as depicted in Exhibit 3-4.[3]

The importance of this stage of the decision-making process cannot be overemphasized. Bad or poorly worded research questions are likely to produce useless answers. It is the infamous GIGO principal (garbage in–garbage out). Yet, this stage, along with the creativity phase, frequently is neglected. Identifying the right question often can be the most difficult part of

EXHIBIT 3-4	DECISIONS ARISE FROM AN OPPORTUNITY FOR IMPROVEMENT

Decision making can be depicted along a continuum between crisis management and pure opportunity, as follows:

CRISIS	PURE OPPORTUNITY
Immediate Response Needed	Response Can Be Timed (Long-Run Orientation)
Unplanned	Plan can be developed
Tactical	Strategic
Preprogrammed Solution Usually Used	Novel Solution Often Desired

the decision-making process. Exhibit 3-5 lists several reasons why identifying the right question is so difficult. Several of these reasons are discussed in more detail following.

Incorrect Assumptions

First, describing the situation accurately can be extremely difficult. How often is the first or most obvious question the best to pursue? You may have heard the expression thinking out of the box. It comes from the brainteaser in which a person is asked to connect all of nine dots using three straight lines. Some dots are provided below for your convenience. People are seldom asked to formally write this down as a research question before trying to solve the problem. The natural inclination is for one to define the situation as "How can I draw lines within the box that will connect all nine dots?" Perhaps you want to try this.

EXHIBIT 3-5	BARRIERS TO DEVELOPING EFFECTIVE PROBLEM IDENTIFICATION AND DEVELOPMENT OF ACTIONABLE RESEARCH QUESTIONS

Barrier	Result	Suggested Solution
1. Incorrect Assumptions	People tend to imply more assumptions than really exist.	List all assumptions and think about the situation as if each didn't exist.
2. Functional Fixedness	Learned rules are hard to undo.	Try to ask the same question several different ways. What, why, how, when, where, and who?
3. Expedience	People want to develop solutions right away. This encourages myopic thinking.	Allocate time for this stage of decision making.
4. Communication Difficulties	Inability to effectively state the desired result or information need (i.e. between manager and researcher).	Construct an effective research proposal including dummy tables.
5. "The" Solution	People tend to think there is only one solution to a problem, therefore there is only one question.	Phrase questions in ways that invite many solutions. In what ways can we, …?
6. Unclear Goals	Unsure of the true underlying issues.	Separate true issues from symptoms. Probing interviews. Asking why, why, why?

Is this possible? Do not try for too long. By overcoming natural inclinations, however, one might draw lines that are either much longer or wider than the box, and not parallel to the rows or columns. Once one realizes the implied assumption of working inside the box is false, the problem becomes much simpler. Our individual learning and experience, however, leads us to work with false assumptions, such as remaining within the box.

Functional Fixedness

It is also important to note that two different people or organizations may interpret the same information differently. Production people may view information showing a drop in market share as a marketing problem. But the marketing people may view a drop in market share as a production problem! Specialization and experience create a narrow worldview. **Functional fixedness** is a term that describes the fact that once one learns an effective rule or action, increased familiarity with the process makes it difficult to see other ways of doing the same thing, even if they are simpler. That is, it creates tunnel vision.

In the history of delivery, Federal Express is a relative newcomer. Many firms, including UPS (circa 1907), Roadway (circa 1930), Saia and the U.S. Postal Service were delivery specialists long before FedEx. However, they were unable to solve the problem of one-day delivery. Conventional wisdom suggests that a delivery, especially a speedy delivery, should be made over the shortest route. Their worldview was shaped very much by their experience. While experience is a useful asset in many ways, its one drawback is functional fixedness.

Although these firms certainly invested thousands of hours trying to solve the twenty-four-hour delivery problem, it was eventually solved in a student's term paper. That student, Fred Smith, was not an employee of any of these companies. Unclouded by the functional fixedness that comes with experience, his term paper proposed that all packages should be routed through a central facility rather than sent via the shortest route. From the central location, they could then be rerouted to their destinations. In less than thirty years, FedEx has grown to a company of over two hundred thousand employees! You can probably think of other entrepreneurs whose key to success was overcoming functional fixedness. Perhaps their lack of experience was a big advantage.

One way to make sure that you are not looking at a problem with tunnel vision is to ask a lot of questions. The answers help describe the situation and provide avenues for locating alternatives. **Interrogatories** are part of a technique that facilitates these questions. Interrogatories are conducted simply by stating different questions about some situation. When all the different interrogatory beginnings are used, it insures the problem has been examined from multiple points of view. Suppose a researcher interviews a vice president of a fast food franchise who describes a situation involving sagging breakfast sales. The following questions might result from interrogatories:

1. What are people doing in the morning?
2. Where are people eating breakfast?
3. Why do people skip breakfast?
4. When do people eat breakfast?
5. Who spends the most money on breakfast foods?
6. How do people eat breakfast?

RESEARCH IN ACTION

FUNCTIONAL FIXEDNESS LEFT BEHINDS—WHY ARE U.S. RAILS FOUR FEET EIGHT AND ONE-HALF INCHES APART?

The standard U.S. Rail Gauge is four feet eight and one-half inches. So, a train that weighs hundreds of tons is balanced on wheels that are less than an arm's length apart. Why is it that distance and how did it get that way? The following excerpt from Michael Michalko, a leading creativity expert, tells the rest of the story (http://www.creativethinking.net/, accessed 3/02):

"Why did the English people build them like that? Because the first rail lines were built by the same people who built the pre-railroad tramways, and that's the gauge they used. Why did "they" use that gauge then? Because the people who built the tramways used the same jigs and tools that they used for building wagons, which used that wheel spacing. Okay! Why did the wagons use that odd wheel spacing? Well, if they tried to use any other spacing the wagons would break on some of the old, long distance roads, because that's the spacing of the old wheel ruts.

So who built these old rutted roads? The first long distance roads in Europe were built by Imperial Rome for the benefit of their legions. The roads have been used ever since. And the ruts? The initial ruts, which everyone had to match for fear of destroying their wagons, were first made by Roman war chariots. Since the chariots were made for or by Imperial Rome they were all alike in the matter of wheel spacing. Thus, we have the answer to the original questions. The United States standard railroad gauge of 4 feet, 8.5 inches derives from the original specification for an Imperial Roman army war chariot, which was the width, at the time, of two horses' behinds."

By simply asking these questions and providing responses, the total solution space is expanded, which gives the decision maker a better chance of finding an actionable solution and gives the researcher a better chance of studying relevant phenomena. The "Research in Action" box tells how functional fixedness influenced the width of rail lines.

Effective Communication

Effective communication is essential because multiple people are usually involved in the decision-making process. The dialog among the people must be conducted in an open and effective manner. Moreover, everyone involved should be allowed to express their ideas freely and without fear of repercussion from superiors. This type of communication environment makes developing effective research questions more likely.

The research proposal plays a key role in effective communication between a decision maker and the researcher. A research proposal is a written document that states the purpose of the research, the budget for the research, a time frame in which the research will be conducted and the research tools that will be employed. A good proposal should document the specific research questions the proposed research will address. Weak proposals often lead to research projects that do not provide the information decision makers need.

Here is a simple way to help insure effective communication between a decision maker and a researcher. A key part of the research proposal should be a set of **dummy tables.** Dummy tables contain the proposed tables and corresponding discussion that likely will appear in the final report. The only exception is that any numerical results in a dummy table are made up. Thus, prior to signing off on the research, the manager must agree that the data resulting from the research project will help the organization make a better decision. In other words, when the manager signs off on the project, there is a high likelihood the researcher and manager are on the 'same page.'

Inviting Multiple Solutions

Earlier, we used the term expanding the solution space. All too often, we have a tendency to work on the most obvious question, or the first one that someone is able to put into words. Decision makers who follow this approach risk seeking solutions before they are ready to do so. Once the first possible solution is advanced, a group will launch into an evaluation of the idea. This may sound reasonable, but think about this. If Kate is trying to decide on a better way to improve employee morale, is she more likely to come up with a good idea if three or three hundred ideas are considered? It is only logical that those who come up with more ideas will have more good ideas. They may have more bad ideas, but the evaluation phase is there to screen these out. This is what we mean by expanding the solution space. A larger solution space, one that considers a much larger number of potential questions and solutions, will eventually lead to better research and better answers.

One way to help ensure a larger solution space is to write out all formal research questions. Try phrasing all questions in an active way that invites multiple solutions, because the way they are written is important. Begin with:[4]

"In what ways can we _____ to achieve _____[goal to be accomplished]?"

Kate may first express the thought as, "What should I do to improve morale?" But using IWWCW (In What Ways Can We), she can now express the idea much more productively as, "In what ways can we improve morale quickly so that we can improve our customer service rating?" Now, the expression invites multiple solutions (*ways* instead of *way*) and includes an explicit recognition of the state that needs to be achieved. It also may evoke other ways of achieving the desired goal.

Issues or Symptoms

Issues are not the same as **symptoms.** *Issues* are the things that if altered will close the gap between the actual and desired states. Like a medical doctor, the business professional will create a much better long-term outcome if the real issue is treated, not just symptoms. *Symptoms* are signals that some change may be needed to avoid further problems or take advantage of some opportunity. A runny nose and a sore throat are symptoms that could indicate some type of viral or bacterial infection. Likewise, decreased employee productivity could be symptomatic of some organizational management problem or of some problem with the physical workplace environment. These two issues would produce research questions involving entirely different variables. In either case, simply treating the symptom itself may simply make the problem worse.

Effective communication ensures that decision making and research is directed toward issues and not symptoms. Some preliminary research can be quite helpful in facilitating the communication task. Interviews using probing questions with representatives of all the actors in a situation can provide useful keys. A probing research technique is one that tries to reach beyond the obvious situation and identify the root causes of some state of affairs. A simple way to conduct a probing interview is to repeatedly ask the question why? Why, why, why is a probing technique based on the premise that by the time you ask someone to describe a problem to the third level, they have likely moved beyond mere symptoms.

Using the employee morale example from above, the following exchange may take place:

Researcher: Why do you think morale here has declined?

Employee: Because we don't feel as committed as we used to.

Researcher: Why do you think this is so?

Employee: It doesn't seem like hard work is rewarded as much as it used to be.

Researcher: Why do you think it is not rewarded?

Employee: Although our hourly wage increased, the incentives are now so hard to reach that most employees, whether they do good or bad work, end up making about the same amount.

So, this interchange might reveal pay policies as the real issue, for which a change can affect a desirable result. A program that had addressed morale directly may have had little or no result. Exhibit 3-6 gives more examples of issues and potential symptoms.

The research questions that result from the IWWCW process may be very specific or very broad. It may be necessary to break the questions down into components that are more specifically actionable. Also, more specific research questions are useful in writing more actionable research questions that include managerial variables. *Research questions* rephrase research issues into a form that is researchable. In other words, the variables are described in a way that provides helpful information to the decision maker. Examples of each are shown in Exhibit 3-6. The decision issues and research questions play a prominent role in both the research proposal and the final research report and presentation.

EXHIBIT 3-6 EXAMPLES OF ISSUES AND SYMPTOMS

Symptom	Potential Issues	Decision Issues	Research Questions
Low customer service ratings	Sales rep territories are too large.	Should we hire more sales reps so that territories are smaller?	Is sales territory size related to customer service ratings?
Stock-outs are reduced from last year.	Shelf space reduction has lowered retail inventories	Should we increase slotting allowances in an effort to gain more shelf space?	What is the relationship between shelf space and retail sales?
Initial sales are lower than expected.	Forecast techniques are inadequate.	How can we adjust our forecast techniques?	What variables are most predictive of a new product's sales?
Churn-rate is highest in the market.	Service provider may be unfriendly.	Should we change service management procedures?	Is service provider friendliness related to churn rate?
Labor costs are higher than the competition's.	Employee sick days are too high.	Should we create flex-time?	Do flexible schedules create increased labor efficiency (lower labor costs)?

CREATIVITY–GENERATING ALTERNATIVES

The creativity phase of the CAB decision-making process generates alternative answers to the research questions. Earlier, this example question was provided: "In what ways can we increase morale quickly so that we can improve our customer service rating?" The task now involves developing quantities of ideas that may achieve the desired result.

The creative phase is difficult for most business people. Formal education encourages us to be analytical. "Pick a single solution." Creative thinking involves an absence of convergence. Rather than converging on a single thought, the decision maker would like to consider many divergent thoughts. Novel solutions often involve combining things that are not generally thought of together. The material below describes why creative thinking can be so difficult.

Barriers to Creativity

Functional fixedness often inhibits good question formulation. But, it can be an even bigger problem in generating creative alternatives. Functional fixedness, along with other barriers to creativity, makes creativity a challenging phase of decision making. Some of these **creativity barriers** include:

1. Group Think—This is group functional fixedness. A group is often easily persuaded to focus on one or a few ideas. In fact, this frequently is a very natural way of thinking.

2. Emotional Inhibition—People don't like to feel dumb. But true creative breakthroughs like the fax machine, television, Post-It Notes™, and Velcro®, not to mention aircraft and spaceships, had to sound quite silly to those who lived prior to their widespread use. Chester Carlson invented xerography. He initially tried to sell the technology to Kodak in 1938. After hearing what we now know was an incredibly good idea, Kodak responded: "No one in their right mind would buy a copier when carbon paper is so cheap and easy to use."[5]

    Similarly, Thomas Edison proclaimed in 1880: "The phonograph is of no commercial value."[6]

Creative things, by their very nature, are unusual. So, Mr. Edison's statement could be excused. His statement is a little more striking, however, when one considers who invented the phonograph—Thomas Edison!

People naturally become attached to their own ideas. Therefore, we become defensive when others criticize our ideas. So, particularly in groups, people often will keep ideas to themselves. This is an effective way of avoiding possible criticism.

3. Expediency—Once someone takes ownership of a decision situation, there is a very natural tendency to get the decision made and move on. Therefore, as decision makers, we are very susceptible to giving initial ideas a great deal of credibility. Some companies, such as 3-M, deal with this problem by allocating a substantial portion of time for employees to work on any project of their own design.

Expediency causes premature judgment. It is very difficult to effectively develop and evaluate ideas at the same time. Some novel things that seem very bad at first turn out to be very good. Indeed, Post-It™ Notes resulted from glue that wasn't very sticky!

Improving Creativity

From a decision-making standpoint, *creativity* involves combining and synthesizing information into novel ideas. While most decision making is analytical, effective creativity is a divergent thinking exercise. This is clearly time for a divergence. Effective creativity means developing many possible alternatives, not just one! Again, a decision maker has much better odds when the decision space is maximized. So, if your career depended upon making the right strategic choice, would you rather have two alternatives to consider, or 202? Surely, there must be a good idea or two among the 202. How likely is it that the winner is among the two?

A number of leading creativity experts present rules for improving creativity.[7] The following list provides a synopsis of ideas aimed at overcoming barriers to creativity, and providing large numbers of potentially novel and useful ideas.

1. *Quantity creates quality.* There is a greater chance of finding a good idea among 202 ideas than there is among two.
2. *Defer judgment; all newborn ideas are equal.* There is a time for creating and a time for judging. Don't mix them up. Early judgment kills creativity.
3. *Craziness is encouraged.* Creative ideas are often strange. Funny things are often strange. Encourage people to come up with wild ideas. Not only might they be converted to good ideas, but the entertaining atmosphere improves creativity.
4. *Get away from the situation.* Sometimes a good cure for functional fixedness is just to get away from the issue. Changing one's environment also changes one's thoughts. Maybe there is a solution in that novel you've wanted to read!

RESEARCH IN ACTION
THINKING UPSIDE DOWN?

Upside down thinking works. Upside down thinking doesn't refer to standing on one's head and thinking. However useful that approach may be, upside down thinking refers to trying to think of ways to reach the opposite state of the one you are pursuing. It's simply reverse psychology applied to decision making. This approach makes an effective research tool by using it in interviews. When seeking innovative ideas, for example, a group leader may ask research respondents to think of the worst new product idea they can think of. For example, if you are thinking of innovative breakfast cereals, someone might shout out Weiner Crisp (a hot dog flavored cereal). After everyone has voiced his or her bad idea, a group discussion ensues. Here are some of the advantages to upside down thinking:

1. It's more fun than thinking of good ideas. People let their guard down and ideas flow more freely. A relaxed atmosphere is good for creativity and produces more novel responses.
2. Respondents become comfortable with each other and the process since there is no fear of seeming dumb.
3. Many people find this much easier than coming up with good ideas.
4. Successful ideas often are just a change or two away. After discussing the ideas, the group is challenged to identify those ideas that really will fail. They normally find this a harder task than you might think, because many of the ideas end up seeming good with a minor change.
5. What seems like a bad idea to one is sometimes a good idea to another.

SOURCE: DePaulo, Pete, Glenn Livingston and Sharon Livingston. 2002. Stinker Ideas Often Best Route to Most Creative Solutions. *Marketing News* 36 (March 4): 49.

In addition, by relaxing, your mind is freed and it gains access to thoughts it couldn't reach before.

5. *Run with your ideas*. Let thoughts flow freely. Try to piggy-back ideas. In a group setting, arrange people in a circle. Once an idea is put into words, each person takes turns adding their first impression to the idea. Usually, creative ideas may be some distance from the original.

Creativity Tools

It is true that businesspeople typically are not creative by nature. There is good news, however. Creativity can be learned. There are literally dozens of thinking techniques that force even the most uncreative mind into a creative orientation.[8] These techniques help produce an expanded solution space. Lists provide a very effective and simple way to enhance creativity. By listing at least ten responses to each separate interrogatory question, an expanded solution space is guaranteed.

Analogies also are very useful. For example, a decision maker might think about how some superhero might react to a tough business decision. When someone can see through things, is more powerful than a locomotive, and faster than a speeding bullet, they are bound to think of something more novel than a mild-mannered businessperson would.[9] Thus, Superman provides a tool to create an analogy.

Heuristic Ideation

Heuristic ideation is a very effective way of combining lists and forced combinations (or synthesis) to develop large numbers of ideas in a very short period of time. The technique was developed by a noted business researcher named Ed Tauber. Tauber served as a consultant to a consumer products company that was trying to find a way to make its new product developers more productive. In response, he developed the Heuristic Ideation Technique (HIT).[10]

HIT is initiated by describing some situation using the interrogatory terms introduced earlier in the chapter. Answers to two of the questions are considered in combination. One list of answers is written down the side of a page. The other list is written across the top. Exhibit 3-7 shows how a HIT matrix may look if a new product person

---

EXHIBIT 3-7 **A HIT MATRIX FOR NEW BREAKFAST FOODS**

What/How:	Fried	Boiled	Raw	Baked	Cold	MW	Toasted	Frozen	Grilled	w/Fruit
Bread	1	2	3	4	5	6	7	8	9	10
Cereal	11	12	13	14	15	16	17	18	19	20
Pancakes	21	22	23	24	25	26	27	28	29	30
Muffins	31	32	33	34	35	36	37	38	39	40
Scones	41	42	43	44	45	46	47	48	49	50
Bagels	51	52	53	54	55	56	57	58	59	60
Eggs	61	62	63	64	65	66	67	68	69	70
Bacon	71	72	73	74	75	76	77	78	79	80
Ham	81	82	83	84	85	86	87	88	89	90
Yogurt	91	92	93	94	95	96	97	98	99	100

were working to produce new breakfast food ideas. What do people eat for breakfast? Responses to this question are listed down the left-hand side. How are foods prepared? Responses to this question are listed across the top. Every combination of ideas represents an idea, or the beginnings of an idea. So, in less than five minutes, one hundred or more ideas can be produced. Perhaps the reader may find some of the ideas below to be ridiculous. Maybe idea 72, boil-in-a bag bacon, is one such idea. Now, don't fall prey to the tendency for quick judgment! Have you ever tried a toaster pastry, a slice and bake cookie, or a microwave pancake? Many common food products were discovered with this tool.

Researchers often make direct use of creativity. The last "Research in Action" example on "Thinking Upside Down?" demonstrated creativity in conducting research. Researchers often need creative ways of asking people questions—particularly when asking about things people would prefer not to talk about. In addition, experimentation in research designs often involves creativity. Identifying experimental treatments and how to manipulate them without revealing the research hypotheses can be tricky. The processes discussed here can directly aid the researcher in these tasks.

EVALUATION AND CHOICE

The best decision makers avoid any evaluation until a large set of alternatives has been developed. The goal of evaluation and choice is narrowing down the alternative course of actions to those most likely to produce a good outcome. Preliminary screening may be needed to reduce hundreds of ideas to a more manageable number. This could involve relatively informal processes. For example, an initial screening of all one hundred breakfast food ideas derived from HIT can be performed easily. Three product managers might rate each idea on key dimensions such as uniqueness, synergy with current production and marketability. The ideas that do best in the initial screening can then be evaluated more thoroughly.

Evaluative Criteria

Evaluative criteria are characteristics used to judge the merits of different alternatives. Each situation may call for a different set of evaluative criteria. A good problem statement should include specific mention of at least one key goal. Some alternatives may be judged against profit goals, others may be judged by job satisfaction standards, and so forth. Evaluative criteria are derived directly from the desired goals or outcomes. When decision makers, for example, are seeking ways to improve employee morale, researchers may be asked to measure progress using several specific indicators of morale, such as job satisfaction, absenteeism, worker involvement, and commitment.

Sometimes, however, evaluative criteria are more abstract and can be generalized over many decision-making situations. One such list is derived from the characteristics of successful innovations originated by Everett Rogers.[11] Good ideas generally possess high levels of some or all of these characteristics:

1. Advantageousness—They offer real advantage over the current state of affairs.
2. Trialability—The idea can be tried on a small scale prior to implementation.
3. Observability—The idea can be observed by concerned parties. Learning takes place more quickly as the information is transferred.

RESEARCH IN ACTION

A BEER WITH POOR TASTE?

Samuel Adams Beer is conducting a key test market as part of its market expansion strategy. Several different ads are being tested in different U.S. cities to examine their appeal to a younger market, aged 21–29 years. The ads vary in sensuality. One ad involves an exchange between a bar customer and a protective brother. After sharing a Sam Adams, the brother becomes less protective of his sister and encourages the two to get together. Another involves a man sharing secret videos of himself and his significant other after having a few Sam Adams beers. In addition to seeing which appeal is most effective, they are examining the effectiveness of the tagline, Mighty Tasty. The costs of production for each ad are the same as if it was to be run across their entire market because Sam Adams does not want the quality of the ads to influence customer reactions.

SOURCE: Vander Pool, Lisa. 2001. Boston Beer Unveils TV Blast in Test Markets. *Adweek Eastern Edition* 42 (17 D

---

4. Consistency—Alternatives that are consistent with current values and behaviors are better than ideas that lack consistency. Consistent ideas require little extracurricular change.

5. Simplicity—All things equal, simple alternatives are better than complex alternatives. They are more easily understood and accepted by people involved.

These general criteria often are particularly useful for initially screening large numbers of ideas. A good method to remember these evaluative criteria is to use the acronym **ATOCS,** each letter standing for its respective criterion. Good ideas come from ATOCS! The ideas that survive ATOCS can then be tested more specifically and rigorously, perhaps by carrying out a market experiment or some field testing.

Field Tests

More formal approaches are often used to evaluate from among a small number of good alternatives. A **test market** may be needed for some new consumer product. A pilot training program may be needed to examine a new employee productivity program.

A test market is an experiment that evaluates a new product or promotional campaign under real market conditions. The new product may be tested in different geographic markets using different designs. Perhaps it would be sold in three cities with three different package colors and three different prices. Therefore, the research can evaluate specific aspects of the new product.

Alternatively, many organizations may institute managerial change only after an initial pilot test. The pilot test is analogous to a test market in that it involves small-scale implementation of the idea being considered. If Daimler-Chrysler believed that ethics training was the key to better relationships with its sales personnel and an improved image, a pilot program might be implemented within twelve of its top one hundred U.S. sales districts. Within these districts, trainers would have to be hired, sales personnel would have to be compensated for time in training, materials would need to be purchased and outcomes monitored, just as if the program were being instituted across their entire dealership network.

Circuit City has recently lost market share to more specialized competitors like Gateway. As a result, it is currently faced with decisions involving, "In what ways can we regain and maintain market share to improve long-term profitability?" After generating numerous possibilities, they decided to focus on a strategy of improved image by coordinating changes in (1) employee compensation (commission) programs, (2) store atmospherics, and (3) advertising intensity. All Circuit City stores in the Chicago and Washington, D.C. areas are being used to test this strategy.[12] Some key tactical elements can be varied between these two locations. For example, the advertising intensity may be twice as high in Washington, D.C. as in Chicago. Likewise, different store designs can be implemented. The result is that these ideas are tested under real world conditions.

Test markets and pilot programs are expensive and time consuming. The Circuit City test market described above will take over a year to implement and cost well over one million dollars per store.[13] Many firms choose other less expensive evaluation techniques that can be completed in a shorter period of time. One alternative is to interview members of the targeted market about hypothetical changes. For example, price sensitivity analysis interviews potential consumers about the price of some goods or services. It involves asking respondents the following questions:[14]

1. At what price would you think the product is inexpensive but probably of acceptable quality?
2. At what price would you think the product is so inexpensive that the product is of very poor quality?
3. At what price would you think that the product is expensive, but that you would still purchase it?
4. At what price would you think that the product is too expensive to consider, although it is of very high quality?

Answers to these questions help business researchers advise decision makers on the appropriate course of action.

Researchers often play a key role in implementation. In fact, once the decision maker reaches this phase, the whole process may start over as it becomes necessary to generate creative alternatives for actually putting an idea into practice. Thus, implementation alternatives may be generated through creative processes and then evaluated as described above. The decision maker cannot ignore implementation. A great idea will almost certainly fail when improperly implemented.

The CAB decision-making process (Exhibit 3-1) shows a dashed line from implementation to research. This represents feedback from the decision-making process. The results of implementation become important information to be recorded for further use.

Monitoring involves assessing the extent to which a decision is accomplishing its stated objective. Is it working out as envisioned? The following example illustrates automatic monitoring. Is there a way to eliminate all the unsightly wires used to bring power to many urban homes? One way would be to generate electricity within the home using a self-contained fuel cell (essentially a large battery). An implementation of this idea is currently being tested in the Chicago area.[15] Undoubtedly, there are many goals associated with this implementation. Hopefully, the plan will lead to more efficient power generation for consumers. Also, it is hoped that marketing of fuel cells and related services will prove economical for consumers and profitable for the power companies. Each home with a fuel cell is hard-wired back to a real-time monitoring system. The system can track progress on these and other goals. The resulting information will help decide the ultimate fate of the residential fuel cell.

Creative decision making seeks to avoid failure. Business research itself exists to reduce the chances of failure. Innovative decision makers do not view failure in a literal sense. The feedback loop suggesting more information be gathered through more research is crucial in this view. As long as learning has taken place, has a venture really failed? Edison conducted hundreds of experiments trying to find the right material to build a filament for a light bulb. Hundreds failed. But Edison learned from each successive failure. In the process, he spun off dozens of other inventions, including the phonograph. He also moved a little closer with each step to identifying a substance that would carry a strong electric current without breaking. Thus, the decision support systems described above play a crucial role in making sure the feedback loop is supplying effective information to decision makers and expert systems.

SUMMARY

Describe the Role of Research in Helping Businesspeople Make Decisions

Research plays a key role in the CAB decision-making process. The researcher takes on the responsibility of providing the decision maker with knowledge that will lead to a better decision. Preliminary research plays a vital role in developing actionable research questions. Answers to the research questions should suggest a decision. Often, the research questions involve the evaluation of some proposed alternative with the hope of providing knowledge about the best choice.

Present a Creative and Analytical Business Decision-Making Process

The CAB process involves four key stages. In the research question phase, the information surrounding the current business situation is put into writing. This leads to a creative phase in which large quantities of potential solutions are identified. The third phase involves an analytical evaluation of any proposed alternatives. This may proceed with an initial screening of many ideas in order to choose a small number of alternatives that receive more formal evaluation. The fourth stage involves developing an implementation plan. In some ways, this starts the process over again. Many ideas for implementation may be devised and then evaluated. The results of the entire process are fed back into the research process and are often stored in a data warehouse. Here, the information may prove useful in future decisions. Business research can be involved in any phase of the CAB process. Knowledge of this process helps students understand the whole point of performing research.

Discuss the Importance of Writing Actionable Research Questions

The formal research questions resulting from the first stage of the CAB decision-making process eventually drives the rest of the process. Sometimes good ideas may be developed and tested, but the ideas address a poorly defined issue. What good is a good answer to the wrong question? The chapter discussed several barriers to writing good research questions, including functional fixedness and false assumptions. Functional fixedness and false assumptions both cause decision makers to describe problems and opportunities too narrowly. Approaches for overcoming these barriers also were provided. One very effective way is to write down many questions about the current situation. The questions should begin with *what, why, how, when, who,* and *where.* It is also important that symptoms be separated from the real issues that may be causing problems. Well-stated research problems are essential to the success of decision making.

Suggest Techniques for Enhancing Creativity

Creativity does not come naturally to many people. A set of rules for enhanced creativity was provided. Also, several creative tools were described. The rules are: quantity creates quality, defer judgment, encourage craziness, get away from the situation and run with your ideas. These included the direct application of analogies to some situation and the HIT technique. The HIT technique is effective in (1) developing forced combinations and (2) developing a large number of ideas very quickly.

Understand Concepts Related to Evaluation and Choice

Formal research often is involved in evaluating ideas. Prior to formal research, initial screening may be performed on a larger numbers of ideas. Test markets and pilot tests are formal research tools that identify which ideas are best from a small number of alternatives. These approaches are very expensive and often involve statistical analyses of study results. Thus, researchers frequently are asked to find more efficient alternatives. A combination of intuition and research results are used to make the final decision. The results of implementation should be fed back into the research system where it will become useful in answering future questions.

KEY TERMS

ATOCS	empirical test	monitoring
CAB process	evaluative criteria	opportunity
creativity barriers	expert system	research questions
crisis management	functional fixedness	symptoms
Decision Support System	interrogatories	test market
(DSS)	issues	
dummy tables	MIS	

ETHICAL DILEMMA

The board of directors for a growing healthcare organization is currently examining ways of reducing employee turnover through improved job satisfaction. One possibility involves improving the health benefits plan. However, they do not feel as though they have enough information on what plan options are available and what might be more desirable to employees. They request that Carmen Roberts, head of personnel, research benefit package options for the organization's employees and recommend an idea at the next board meeting. The board asks Carmen to survey other healthcare organizations about the packages they offer, poll employees about the benefits they want and collect options from area benefit providers.

Because of pressure to fill several unexpected employee openings that same month, Carmen only has time to check with their major competitor (a similar healthcare organization) and contact three local providers about their benefits packages. In addition, the only employee input she has gathered comes from the group of employees who eat lunch with her regularly. When the time for the meeting arrives, Carmen indicates that she has done the requested research herself. Based upon the results, she recommends that the firm adopt a plan similar to the one used by their major competitor. She presents only this idea and recommends that the board approve implementation. The next day an employee who has been offered a job in another industry shows Carmen the benefits package she was offered. It seems much more desirable and perhaps more economical than the package Carmen recommended to the board. What should Carmen do now? Where did Carmen go wrong?

REVIEW QUESTIONS

1. What stages are involved in the CAB decision-making process?
2. Describe the difference between crisis management and pure opportunity.
3. Describe at least four ways in which research and the CAB process go together.
4. Describe the barriers to effective problem identification and preparation of actionable research questions.
5. What is the difference between an issue and a symptom?
6. What is ATOCS?

DISCUSSION AND APPLICATION ACTIVITIES

1. Find a recent edition of *The Wall Street Journal*. Read a story about an organization that describes its current business situation. Identify symptoms and issues that describe the situation. From all of this, write formal actionable research questions using the approach discussed in the chapter.
2. Think about the current operating environment for your local university. Describe some of the issues it currently faces. Are these best described as crisis management or pure opportunity? Can you express them as formal, actionable research questions?
3. What assumptions are involved in the research questions you prepared in the previous questions? Try reversing the assumptions and developing lists of solutions considering the assumptions are reversed. Does the list contain any items that might lead to a creative solution?
4. What is the trade-off that is faced in the research/intuition ratio involved in decision making? In other words, as the decision maker relies more on research, what are the implications?

INTERNET ACTIVITIES

1. Go to the Web site for the Council of American Survey Research Organizations (CASRO). It can be found at www.casro.org. What is the mission of this organization and how does it benefit survey researchers?

2. Go to the Walker Information Web site located at www.walkerinfo.com and complete at least one of the three surveys. Prepare a report that tells what the three surveys are about, which survey you took and why, and what you learned on your visit to the Web site.

3. Go to the Monash Information Services Website at www.monash.com. Prepare a report describing what this Web site offers the user. Next click on The Spider's Apprentice link on the Monash home page. How does this guide help you to better use search engines?

4. Go to the Web site at www.mapblast.com. Click on the Business Solutions box and scroll down to the "Web:" dialog box. Look at the right side of the screen and click on "For more info …" Now click on the scrolling locator at the top of the screen to find the nearest Taco Bell restaurant. Explore the rest of this Web site. Prepare a report on how this site might be used by a business researcher.

NOTES

1. *Journal of Business Strategy.* 2001. Decisions, Decisions, Decisions. 22 (5): 48.

2. Labe, Russ and Raj Nigam. 1999. Management Science at Merrill Lynch Private Client Group. *Interfaces* 29 (March/April): 1–15.

3. Brightman, Harvey J. 1980. *Problem Solving: A Logical and Creative Approach.* GSU Publications: Atlanta, GA.

4. Couger, Daniel J. 1995. *Creative Problem Solving and Opportunity Finding.* Boyd and Fraser Pub. Co.: Hillsdale, Ill.

5. Ibid.

6. Hair, Joseph F. and Barry J. Babin. 2002. Technology and the New Economy: Implications for Higher Education and the Marketing Discipline, *Advances in Marketing and Purchasing,* Arch Woodside and Ellen Moore, editors, Elsevier Science, Ltd., London: Volume 11 pp. 57–68

7. Michalko, Michael. 1998. *Cracking Creativity: The Secrets of Creative Genius.* Ten Speed Press: Berkeley, Calif.; Michalko, Michael. 1991. *Thinkertoys: A Handbook of Business Creativity.* Ten Speed Press: Berkeley, Calif.; De Bono, Edward. 1999. *Six Thinking Hats.* Little, Brown and Company: New York; Couger. 1995.

8. Michalko (1991; 1998); Higgins, James M. 1994. *101 Creative Problem Solving Techniques.* New Management Publishing, Inc.

9. VanGundy, Arthur B. 1981. *Techniques of Structured Problem Solving.* Van Nostrand Reinhold Co.: New York.

10. VanGundy. 1981.

11. Rogers, Everett. 1983. *Diffusion of Innovations.* The Free Press: New York.

12. Heller, Laura. 2001. Circuit City Saves on New Look. *DSN Retailing Today* 40 (October 22): 20–23.

13. Vander Pool, Unveils TV Blast in Test Markets. *Adweek Eastern Edition* 42 (17 D

14. Winters, Lewis C. 1990. Pricing Research: Pre-Test-Market Alternatives. *Marketing Research* 2 (June): 73–75; Gabor, Andre, Clive W. Granger and Anthony Sowter. 1970. Real and Hypothetical Shopping Situations in Market Research. *Journal of Marketing Research* 7 (August): 355–359.

15. *Modern Power Systems.* 2001. 21 (June): 11.

CHAPTER

4

Ethics in Business Research

| **Learning Objectives** |

1. Define business ethics and discuss their relevance to research.

2. Provide an overview of the ethical obligations of business researchers.

3. Provide an overview of the ethical obligations of business decision makers.

4. Provide an overview of the ethical obligations of business research participants.

5. Describe the potential consequences of unethical actions.

INTRODUCTION

Business ethics is a growing field. Events such as the Enron scandal attract attention toward abuses of power and authority in the business world. The demand for more "ethical" businesspeople has created a greater emphasis on the formal study of business ethics.

Trust is an overriding issue in business ethics. If all parties involved in exchange could truly trust one another fully, there would be no need for any oversight of the exchange process. Where trust is lacking, some codified standards must be enforced. At a simple level, there are professional codes of ethics that govern behavior. For example, the American Marketing Association sponsors a program for a Professional Certification in Marketing Research. This certification requires that the participant agree to the code of ethics.

Stronger replacements for trust include rules, laws, and regulations. We would hope most employers could be trusted to take adequate measures to ensure employees' safety. However, the number and severity of worker injuries questioned this trust. As a result, the U.S. Congress passed the Occupational Safety and Health Act and created OSHA (Occupational Safety and Health Administration). OSHA monitors American workplaces. Although OSHA inspections are sometimes seen as a nuisance, they also help protect workers. If this trust had never been breeched, there would be no need for OSHA. Thus, this law takes the place of trust.

RESEARCH IN ACTION
ARE "THE BEST AND BRIGHTEST" THE RIGHTEST?

How ethical are college business students? Several studies of U.S. business ethics students have been conducted. One such study asked business students to rate themselves on a one hundred-point "ethical" scale with one hundred indicating a belief that he or she is completely ethical. The researchers go on to question the respondents about their ethical behavior as a student. Here are the results:

- The average ethical rating for students was 84 percent.
- 47 percent admit to cheating and lying.
- 5.2 percent report that they have not cheated as a college student.

Other researchers have examined the questions: What groups of businesspeople have the most ethical tolerance? What can be done to make businesspeople more ethical? This research is conducted by comparing responses to numerous questionable business practices (such as "An employee may need to lie to a coworker to protect the company"). These results show:

- College students report higher tolerance of unethical behavior than do experienced businesspeople.
- Male students report higher tolerance of unethical behavior than do female students.
- Taking an ethics course seemed not to affect respondents' ethical responses.

SOURCES: Greenman, Frederick E. and John F. Sherman III. 1999. Business School Ethics: An Overlooked Topic. *Business and Society Review* 104 (December) 171–178; Barbara C. Cole and Dennie L. Smith. 1995. Effects of Ethics Instruction on the Ethical Perceptions of College Business Students. *Journal of Education for Business* 70 (July/August), 351–357; Philip H. Varherr, Joseph A. Petrick, John F. Quinn, and Thomas J. Brady. 1995. The Impact of Gender and Major on Ethical Perceptions of Business Students: Management Implications for the Accounting Profession. *Journal of Academy of Business Administration* 1 (Spring 1995), 46–50.

Business ethics, as a field of study, addresses the application of moral principles and/or ethical standards to human actions within the exchange process. Moral principles imply responsibility. Thus, the judgment of right or wrong ethical business actions involves an evaluation of actions against the responsibilities that accompany a business position. Like other businesspeople, business researchers have social, market, legal, and ethical responsibilities.[1] Social responsibilities involve a concern for the way actions affect society or groups of people including employees, customers, and the community. Market responsibility means a concern for making sure that products are produced that consumers actually need and that the prices charged for these products are fair. Business researchers and business decision makers are concerned with all these responsibilities in the performance of their jobs.

RELEVANCE OF BUSINESS ETHICS

Business ethics are relevant to business researchers because ethical issues occur through many phases of the research process. **Ethical dilemmas** are situations when a person is faced with courses of actions that have differing ethical implications. For example, a business researcher may be placed in a situation in which both of two major competitors have asked for similar research projects. Several dilemmas occur. For example, the researcher could take both jobs and use proprietary information to help make recommendations for each company. Alternatively, the researcher could use research paid for by one client as a basis for the recommendations of another.

Ethical dilemmas arise from questions of fairness or justice, potential conflicts of interest, responsibility issues, power discrepancies, and honesty issues. All of these can occur in business research situations. Such dilemmas require sound ethical judgments. Ethical judgments ultimately involve an assessment of the fairness and justness of some course of action. Note that an ethical judgment is sometimes distinct from a contractual or legal obligation.[2]

Exhibit 4-1 helps demonstrate how various organizational, professional, and individual elements provide pressures and conflicts that produce ethical dilemmas. However, organizational, professional, and individual elements also provide checkpoints that counter motivations toward unethical actions. In the end, these three groups of elements help balance business decision making.

This balancing can be illustrated with a research example. An organization may be motivated to take advantage of a data collection opportunity. Perhaps this would involve collecting information in a way that violated the rights of research respondents (as discussed later). Or perhaps, they might ask a researcher to provide contact information from research respondents to be used as sales prospects. Neither would be ethical. Using strictly the organizational motivations for profit, these actions may be carried out. However, researchers are guided by a professional code of conduct that should stop them from willingly participating in an unethical data collection. Further, individual moral values may also come into play and help motivate a more ethical decision. A researcher's own personal value system may prohibit participation in unethical action.

ETHICAL OBLIGATIONS OF THE RESEARCHER

Business researchers are faced with ethical considerations and possible ethical dilemmas throughout a research project. They involve the researcher's dealings with management, respondents, and their own professional integrity. Here we focus on the ethical considerations

EXHIBIT 4-1	**ETHICAL BALANCE BETWEEN INDIVIDUAL, PROFESSIONAL, AND ORGANIZATIONAL VALUES**

SOURCE: Adapted from Anderson, Rolph. 1991. *Professional Personal Selling.* Englewood Cliffs, N.J.: Prentice Hall. 71.

between the person requesting the research (the manager or decision maker) and the person doing the research, before, during and after the project.

BEFORE THE RESEARCH PROJECT

The period just prior to the initiation of a research project is perhaps the most critical point in the entire research process. During this time, the researcher must interview key decision makers to gain a working knowledge of the situation. The researcher acquires an understanding of the project objectives during these interviews. The key here is to translate a decision issue into a researchable proposition. Once a study is envisioned, researchers need to honestly assess their capabilities, and if they lack the skills or resources to carry out the project, they should decline it. Also, if the researcher is unable to reach a consensus on the primary research questions, they should probe more or not accept the job.

The researcher must communicate exactly what the research will be able to do. This typically is referred to as the project deliverables. In other words, they must be certain the project will be able to address the research questions. The research project should begin only when they are confident in this regard. See the "Research in Action" box below for some general considerations a decision maker can use before giving the go-ahead for a research project.

Researchers are sometimes faced with potentially conflicting interests. For example, suppose a researcher completes an exhaustive study of book consumers' beliefs and sensitivities to various Web site characteristics for Barnes & Noble Book Stores. The project was very

---

RESEARCH IN ACTION

POINTS TO PONDER ON WHETHER TO DO RESEARCH

Decision makers and researchers both should realize that sometimes the best decision is not to do any research at all. The following questions can be useful in addressing this key issue. If several of these questions lack answers, perhaps the research should be postponed. Before beginning a research project, the decision maker should ask:

- What information do I need that is now unavailable?
- How could I use that information?
- What will it cost to get this information and how long will it take?
- Does the potential benefit exceed the cost?
- Do my competitors have the information?
- If my competitors have the information, how is this affecting their performance?
- What aspects of my current business situation do I not understand?

---

expensive and time consuming, but it allowed Barnes and Noble to effectively penetrate electronic retailing segments through a better electronic interface. After completing the study, the same researcher is approached by Amazon.com for a research project that would help them better design their Web site for online book consumers. Keep in mind that Barnes & Noble has paid the bill for this research and thus "owns" any data collected.

The researcher is presented with several choices. (1) Accept the job and use the data collected for Barnes & Noble (B&N) to help make recommendations based on "experience." (2) Accept the job and prepare a new report using the B&N data. (3) Accept the job and conduct a new study addressing the same research questions as in the B&N study using the same methodology. (4) Decline the job. Only the last choice completely avoids a conflict of interest. One and two are clearly unfair as the researcher would essentially be "stealing" information purchased by B&N to sell to Amazon.com at maximum benefit to the researcher. Option three presents a possibility. However, should either client find out about the other study, the researcher's credibility may be harmed.

DURING AND AFTER THE RESEARCH

Researcher-Decision Maker Relationship. The researcher has a moral obligation to have a thorough working knowledge of the analytical and statistical tools necessary to complete the project. Researchers should not apply a technique unless they can do so competently and confidently. Researchers sometimes are tempted to apply a more complex tool than is needed in an effort to seem more sophisticated or perhaps even to increase the perceived worth of the research. But only the right tool should be used. This is usually the simplest tool that will provide the necessary results.

The researcher is responsible for interpreting the results honestly and fully. Researchers may have an opinion about the research questions being examined, or they may have a good idea of the research outcome that management desires. But if the results disagree with a key decision maker's desires, the researcher faces a dilemma. In the late 1980s, R. J. Reynolds (RJR) invested over three hundred million dollars into Premier Cigarettes, an innovative "smokeless" tobacco.[3] At the time, F. Ross Johnson was RJR's CEO.

He was a tough, aggressive, no-nonsense leader who was very enthusiastic about Premier.[4] The initial concept test results were generally positive. Consumers, both smokers and non-smokers alike, were favorable toward the concept of a smokeless cigarette. Thus, RJR researchers enthusiastically presented these results. Further tests, using actual Premier cigarettes produced in small quantities, provided some good and some bad results. Among the discoveries was that a Premier cigarette emitted a *very familiar* but very undesirable odor when lit with a match. Couple this with the fact that one's taste is tied closely to their smell, and the recipe is disastrous for any product consumed by mouth. Researchers presented these smell and taste results with less enthusiasm than they did the fact that nonsmokers were favorable toward the idea of Premier Cigarettes. In the end, Premier cigarettes were introduced to the market despite these results. The point of this story is that the researcher is obligated to present the results fully and faithfully, even if the decision maker may not want to hear the results.

The researcher generally presents results both through a formal written report and a presentation. The presentation may be formal or informal. Chapter 12 discusses both the report and presentation in more detail. In presenting the findings, the researcher must present any limitations of the research. By the researcher's acknowledging and fully communicating any limitations, the decision maker has a more complete understanding of how much the results should affect the ultimate decision.

RESEARCHER OBLIGATIONS TO PARTICIPANTS

Researchers should serve as advocates for research participants. Without their participation, the researcher might well be without a job. The researcher should show respect to participants at all times. For example, the researcher should describe the nature and extent of participation required. If a survey requires knowledge about computer basics, the researcher should make this clear in the opening instructions. It is also essential that the researcher provide a fair estimate of the amount of time that will be required to complete the research task.

Researcher-Participant Relationship: Ethics and Technology

Many technological breakthroughs like those discussed in Chapter 1 benefit researchers tremendously. This benefit does not come without a cost. These new technologies also introduce new ethical dilemmas.

Technology increases the possibility that a research participant's privacy might be violated. Much of the information collected and stored in a data warehouse is done so with the promise that it will not be shared with others beyond those individuals directly involved with the research. Researchers have a duty to safeguard the privacy of this information. Personal data should not be shared with outside agencies in any form in which it could be traced back to an individual respondent. Research participant lists should not be sold to other companies to be mined for potential customers. Likewise, much employee and/or corporate financial data is equally sensitive. The appropriate safeguards such as electronic firewalls should be in place to prohibit unauthorized access to this information.

Additionally, technology gives us a better ability to monitor a research participant's behavior. The researcher must draw the line with respect to using such monitoring for purposes that would reach beyond the scope of the specific research project.

RESEARCH IN ACTION
"CLICK AND TELL?" PUBLIC OUTRAGE AT POTENTIAL INFORMATION PRODUCTS

Information has emerged as the hottest commodity on the Web. The more detailed it is, the more valuable it is to firms targeting a specific audience. This data can be cross-referenced with information from other businesses such as credit bureaus, retail stores, and insurers. The information bundle can then be sold. DoubleClick, the largest ad placement firm on the Internet, found itself in the midst of a privacy controversy. It planned to link Internet users' personal information to an offline direct marketing database without consumers' permission. Although the same type of data has been collected by individual businesses for decades, DoubleClick drew public criticism from every privacy organization, and it became the target of several privacy violation lawsuits.

Knowing your customers is of course, key in any business. But as a business researcher, you must also remember that consumer uneasiness about how gathered information is managed and sold is at an all-time high. According to one poll, 59 percent of online household heads "strongly distrust companies' ability or intention to keep personal information confidential, regardless of the policies the companies have in place." Therefore businesses need to be extremely cautious when predicting how consumers will react to potential invasions of privacy.

To avoid the privacy issues, online and off, businesses need to respect customers' private information. And before trying to collect data needed to target consumers, companies should first establish trust. DoubleClick learned this the hard way. Not only did the company suspend its efforts to link online and offline databases, it created a chief privacy officer position to monitor internal and external privacy and to help develop an industry-wide privacy standard.

SOURCE: Crane, Elizabeth. 2000. Double Trouble. *Ziff Davis Smart Business for the New Economy.* (October), 62.

Researcher-Participant Relationship: Ethical Dimensions of Experimental Designs

Researchers have an obligation to treat any participants in a research project ethically. As discussed in Chapter 2, causal designs and experiments involve manipulations. This makes an ethical dilemma more likely. The following ethical issues are always important, but they become especially relevant during lab experiments:

1. Coercing participation
2. Potential physical or psychological harm
3. Privacy
4. Informing subjects of the nature of the research

Coercion   Subjects should not be forced to participate in an experiment. Researchers often provide a modest incentive for participation. Should a potential subject choose not to participate, he or she would forego the incentive. Generally, this is relatively inconsequential. The small incentives involve money, merchandise, leave time, or a few points of credit, depending upon the type of person and research involved. Volunteer participants in the famous "Pepsi Challenge" received a free six-pack of the beverage they thought tasted the best. Researchers may feel obligated to find an appropriate compensation for the volunteer's time and effort. As in many areas of ethics, the line between incentive and **coercion** is not always clear. The incentive should never be of the type that a subject's current well being would be significantly damaged by choosing not to participate. For example, docking an employee's paycheck for not participating in some experiment is something beyond a mere incentive. Undue social pressure could represent coercion as well. Likewise, if a professor threatened to withhold a student's grade at the end of a semester due to refusal to participate in an experiment, the student would rightly feel coerced into participation.

In field experiments, it may be impractical to gain permission from participants. Practically every reader of this book has been a test market participant within the past few months without even knowing it. For example, test market participants are all consumers who enter a store where a new product test is being conducted. If you visit a grocery store, you have been subjected to a test market. In most of these cases, the experiment has such a trivial effect on any participant that there is very little possibility that someone's current well being has been harmed. In such cases, the obligation to ask permission is not needed.

Freedom from Harm   Experimental participants have a general right to be protected from undue physical or psychological harm. Subjects stand the potential to be harmed even in business research experiments. It might be rather obvious that potential harm may occur if a researcher studied job performance using three levels of nicotine or some other drug as an experimental variable. Unfortunately, the potential harm isn't always that clear.

For example, you might be surprised to learn that business researchers often study odors! A researcher may wish to perform an odor study that related scents or smells to employee alertness. This may be useful for understanding whether or not certain physical job environments should be impregnated with the scents artificially. An experiment could be conducted by manipulating the scent in a room in which a task will be accomplished. Is there potential for harm? Perhaps. It's possible that a subject may have a severe allergic reaction to one of the scents. So, before conducting such an experiment, the researcher should innocuously question subjects about potential allergies. The reason the questioning should be done innocuously is because if you first ask people about allergies to various scents (like flowers, peanuts, etc.), then they encounter the scent, they are very likely to guess the manipulation. The result is a demand characteristic that could invalidate any results.

Demand characteristics are experimental elements that may lead a subject to accurately guess the experimental hypotheses during their participation. This represents a critical threat to validity of the results. No longer is the researcher certain that the manipulation caused any effect since the subject's response may be biased by their knowledge.

It might also be possible to devise an experiment where a subject is put under undue stress. For example, if a researcher was asked to study the effect of stress on job performance, an experiment may likely result. The researcher may manipulate the time allowed for a task, and then observe the results in performance. However, another design may involve manipulating the punishment for a poor performance. Poor performance could be punished by informing subjects that the 15 percent lowest performers in the task would: a) have to work weekends for extra training, b) have their pay cut, or c) be fired. Even if the manipulation is only a ruse to conduct the study, do any of these levels exceed the threshold of acceptable stress?

Sometimes the harm isn't physical at all. For example, a researcher may wish to study the effect of confidence on ability to choose successful stocks. A research subject might be given a strategy with which to choose stocks and then subjected to a performance manipulation. For one group, the strategy would always work because the researcher would determine the outcome. For another group, the strategy would never work due to the opposing treatment level. Is the subject harmed?

Once again, there isn't always a clear line between the ethical and unethical. But, here are two questions that can serve as a useful guide:

■   Is it possible to restore the subject to his or her original condition?
■   Has the subject been subjected to unreasonable stress or risk without his or her knowledge?

If the answer to either of these questions is yes, the researcher should not proceed with this design. In the case of the fake stock market exercise, if the subject can be returned to his or her normal state before the experiment took place, then no ethical breech has occurred. However, if the subjects will leave the experiment with a false impression of their ability to play the stock market (in either direction), then they have been harmed.

Privacy   Research participants have a right to privacy. Any experimental results should be used only for the intended purpose. Individual responses should be held in strict confidence unless some other agreement is arranged. When possible, experimental subjects should be able to remain anonymous. Not only is this the more ethical approach, but it also protects the experiment from bias due to any socially desirable response patterns that might emerge.

Under no circumstances should a research project be used as a cover for some other purpose. On occasion, dishonest sellers may recruit research participants via the telephone, email or in person. Participation in the project is only a ploy used to try and close a sale at the end of the project or to add this customer to a prospect list. This practice is unethical from both a business and a research viewpoint. Research efforts should be clearly distinguished from direct marketing or selling and vice versa. Researchers should never act as sales agents in any capacity. If the client wishes to add a sales appeal, the researcher should refuse to do the project.

Similarly, **push polls** are sometimes used in political campaigns. Push polls are short phone calls used to spread negative, and often false, information about a candidate or issue under the guise of a poll.[5] The interview is usually less than one minute and does contain some opinion questions. However, the entire effort is designed to produce a known outcome through the information provided and the manner in which the questions are asked. Selling under the guise of research and push polling clearly represent blatant and avoidable dishonesty.

Fully Informing Subjects   Researchers usually have no reason to hide the research purpose in descriptive survey research. Thus, the instructions will generally provide a statement of the research's purpose. This statement is as specific as the respondent is able to understand it. Experiments however, present quite a different picture than standard survey research.

Experimental designs often involve deception by their very nature. Often, the researcher cannot disclose information about the experimental treatments. For example, in the hypothetical stock market experiment discussed previously, if the researcher revealed ahead of time that the manipulation will be carried out by providing false outcomes from hypothetical stock purchases, there would be little point in conducting the experiment. In other words, complete disclosure would spoil or confound the experimental results.

Most of you have probably heard of a placebo. A placebo is a false treatment. In a medical experiment testing a drug's effectiveness on weight loss, the drug might be administered intravenously in one of three ways: high dosage, low dosage, and no dosage (the placebo, which is often water). All participants, even the placebo group, get a shot. Quite often, the placebo group also will show some effect. In fact, research subjects (patients) being treated for depression with a placebo show improvement equal to or better than that experienced by subjects treated by the leading prescription anti-depressants.[6] Experimental subjects cannot be told that they are in a placebo condition, however, because then they would realize they were not actually receiving the experimental drug. As can be seen, the psychological effects can be strong and could confound any effect shown by the true treatment.

Thus, it may be impossible to fully inform a potential research subject prior to or during an actual experiment. They should be provided with a general description of the experimental events and provided enough information so they can make an informed decision about participation. However, in lab experiments subjects should be debriefed fully once their participation is complete. This allows subjects to be restored to their original condition.

Debriefing takes place after an experimental session is complete and involves revealing the true purpose of the experiment, the sponsor of the experiment, and generally a question and answer session. Not only are all questions answered, but the researcher normally uses this as an opportunity to assess demand characteristics. Thus, debriefing is not

---

RESEARCH IN ACTION
ELECTRIC SHOCK AND THE "RIGGED TRIAL"

Imagine you are watching a research subject taking part in an experiment examining the effect of punishment on learning. You observe a job "trainee" receiving specific instructions on how to perform a relatively simple job. Afterwards, the subject begins to perform the task. Each time the subject makes a mistake, a research assistant presses a button which gives the subject an electric shock, which you are told increases slightly each time, but which remains at a level that is safe, although perhaps uncomfortable. The trainee's job improvement initially improves. However, after about a dozen shocks, the trainee is obviously disturbed and greatly fears the possibility of another shock. His or her hand is trembling noticeably. Learning appears to be regressing not progressing.

Are there ethical implications with this research?

Now, suppose the researcher left the room and came to you, the observer, and offered you a chance to take the trainee's place. You are told that the previous person has become ineffective and a replacement is needed for the experiment to proceed. Would you help?

Or, suppose you were told that the researcher assistant had to leave the room and asks you to become "the teacher." Would you cooperate and shock the trainee for incorrect responses?

Would these changes affect the ethics of the experiment?

Finally, suppose you are told that the experiment is over and that, in reality, the trainee was only pretending to experience pain. In actuality, no shocks were administered. Indeed, the key dependent variable was your behavior. For example, did you agree to take the place of one of the participants? Or, how long did it take before you expressed concern for the poor trainee?

How does this change the ethics of the experiment?

For a more detailed description of this type of methodology, see Baron (1977), *Human Aggression.*

only an ethical thing to do, but it is very practical as well. Finally, subjects should be offered a summary of results should they so desire.

Human Resource Review Committee

Research organizations sometimes form a **human resources** (sometimes known as *human subjects*) **review committee.** This committee performs a review of research using human participants. The committee should check research procedures to make sure all participants are treated ethically. Research universities routinely perform such reviews prior to providing support for university-sponsored research.

A thorough human resource review is required for any research seeking U.S. government grant money. Recently, the federal government has acted to withhold money from John Hopkins University researchers based on what was perceived as a poorly contrived human resource review. This action was motivated by the death of a research subject participating voluntarily in university-sponsored research. The death resulted when a subject was given a medication that was not approved for use in humans. It caused a fatal toxic reaction in the victim's lungs. A government review ruled that even a cursory investigation of the drug would have revealed that it was: a) not approved and b) potentially dangerous.[7]

Although business research is often much safer than medical research, businesses should nonetheless have a high degree of concern for the welfare of participants. Research firms, and companies in general, should consider the benefits a human resource review committee in favorably balancing ethical dilemmas. Perhaps the role could be expanded beyond that of research participants to consider the ethical consequences of business decisions on customers and employees.

ETHICAL OBLIGATIONS OF THE DECISION MAKER

Ethics typically is not a one-way street, and the researcher-decision maker relationship is no exception. The decision maker has several important ethical obligations that if breeched diminish the quality and usefulness of the entire decision-making process.

BEFORE THE RESEARCH

The decision maker should participate fully and openly with the researcher. It is absolutely essential that the decision maker and researcher come to a consensus on the research objectives. Generally, when both parties agree on the research questions involved, consensus is reached. Consensus on research questions becomes a key part of the research proposal, as do the research objectives. If consensus cannot be reached, the research proposal should not be approved. Furthermore, if a researcher is denied access to some piece of information that is crucial in performing the research, the researcher's obligation is reduced.

The decision maker ultimately sets the time frame and budget for the project. But researchers generally make initial requests for time and money and the two meet somewhere in the middle. However, the researcher should communicate and the decision maker should accept the fact that limitations may reduce the quality of the research project correspondingly.

Additionally, the decision maker has an obligation to develop an understanding of the researcher and the research project. This understanding doesn't require that the decision maker become a researcher, but it does mean they should know enough about research to ask intelligent questions. If not, the decision maker should include someone else in the discussion that understands the nature of research projects.

DURING AND AFTER THE RESEARCH

The decision maker has an obligation to give genuine consideration to the research results. That is, the research shouldn't be commissioned simply to be able to show that it was done. If the decision maker has already truly made up her mind on the key issue prior to the research project, they should not request that the project be done. The researcher is placed in an awkward position when the results conflict with the decision maker's desires. It also is a waste of the researcher's time and the company's money.

Furthermore, there is an issue that is especially of interest to any potential researchers. The decision maker has an obligation to pay the researcher fully and on time. If the researcher successfully completes the project described in the research proposal, they should be paid regardless of the results. For instance, a real estate developer once requested a study of the traffic patterns and market potential for several different potential residential development sites. He agreed upon a proposal with a researcher who conducted the study and presented the results. However, the results did not indicate that the land had the value that the developer envisioned. The developer became quite upset and ended up paying the researcher only half of the agreed upon price and only after some months had passed. Likewise, an in-house researcher should not face repercussions if the results of a project are well thought out, but undesirable. Exhibit 4-2 summarizes some of the ethical dimensions of business research.

ETHICAL OBLIGATIONS OF THE RESEARCH PARTICIPANT

Participants in research also have obligations. Although it is difficult to control participation, the researcher should be aware of these issues. They include:

EXHIBIT 4-2	ETHICAL DIMENSIONS OF THE BUSINESS RESEARCHER-DECISION MAKER RELATIONSHIP

Researcher	Decision Maker
Maintain scientific rigor	Educate one's self (be able to understand researcher)
Confidentiality (not be involved in research with a competitor)	Establishes Budget
Search for truth (not to confirm desires)	Give due consideration to the results of the research
Arrive at a consensus "reason" for the research	Arrive at a consensus "reason" for the research
Admit research limitations including any resulting from budget and time constraints	Have realistic expectations
Present results understandably	Pay on time

WILLFUL PARTICIPATION

Research participants should decline the opportunity to participate if they have any doubt about whether they possess sufficient motivation to go through with the study. Most studies do not require a great deal of effort. After agreeing to participate, a respondent or subject should cooperate fully. This also means that participants should answer any **screening questions** honestly. Screening questions are preliminary questions that qualify participants as valid sample members. For example, a researcher studying aspects of retail employment may wish to develop a sample of people with recent retail experience. A participant may be tempted to make up some experience if he or she believes there is a desirable incentive for participation. This type of behavior will lead to response error since the participant lacks the necessary qualifications.

FAITHFUL PARTICIPATION

Participants should follow the research instructions to the best of their ability. On occasion, a participant may grow weary and begin responding without paying attention. Occasionally a response form may contain an unusual number of "neutral" responses or an unusually "back and forth" (or ping-pong) pattern. If mindless responses are more random, they may be difficult to detect and create more response error. The researcher is better off with no response than with a nonsense response.

    The participant should pay attention and follow instructions. These instructions may contain important information pertaining to the appropriate sequence of items or the point of view a respondent should take. Sometimes, the sequence is contingent upon a previous response. Also, the researcher may ask a respondent to respond with something other than his or her own view. In ethics research, a researcher may ask a sales manager participating in research how a typical salesperson would respond in a given ethical dilemma. Again, the failure to follow instructions could create error that could harm the results.

HONEST RESPONSES

It goes without saying that a participant should be honest. On occasion however, a respondent may have some ulterior motive. A participant may try to respond in a fashion that will produce a desirable outcome. For instance, an employer might commission an opinion survey asking unit managers whether or not small units should be closed. A manager might be torn between giving his or her honest responses about the viability of these units and a response that will help ensure that his or her job is not threatened. Participants should refuse to take part in research if they are hesitant to answer questions honestly.

PRIVACY

Researchers may sometimes request that a participant not discuss details of procedures with anyone else for a specified time. There could be many reasons for such a request. The researcher may have legitimate concerns about corporate espionage. If savvy competitors know what a company is studying, they may be able to make an educated guess about its strategy or tactics. In experiments, the researcher may not want an earlier subject to contaminate later subjects. A subject that reveals too much may increase demand characteristics, since the other subjects may be able to guess what factors are being manipulated. Therefore, experimental instructions or debriefing may often include a statement instructing those who have completed the task not to inform others about the details of the study.

IMPLICATIONS OF UNETHICAL ACTIONS

It's very easy for students of business to be lulled into a false sense of security derived from the belief that the ethical implications from business decisions are less serious than those associated with other disciplines such as medicine or engineering. However, this view is misguided. Businesses provide value. They provide value for customers, employees, and shareholders. A breech of responsibility by one party can very seriously affect the value equation in a way that harms others.

A breakdown in responsibility during the research process usually means that business decisions will be based on untrustworthy information. For example, a company president who commissions research investigating implications associated with three strategic acquisitions might request research simply to appease the Board of Directors. That is, the company president may already know which strategy will be implemented based on a strong personal preference. The actual research may strongly suggest that strategy A has the most positive effect on key business outcomes. Thus, it conflicts with the president's opinion. Worse yet, the president could ask the researcher to present results in a way that made choice C, the president's choice, seem most attractive. By enacting the strategy nonetheless, the president increases the likelihood that strategic decisions will not lead to the best outcome.

Such actions could be bad for customers, shareholders, and employees. The implications for customers might mean obtaining a less than most desirable product. This could have dire consequences in the case of potentially hazardous or health-related products. For shareholders, a lower long-term return might result. Employees may end up working in conditions that are not as good as they might have been had the research been followed. So, customers may be harmed, particularly for products with direct health and safety implications. Shareholders may have their portfolios become stagnant or decline. Employees may face long periods with no pay raises or even suspension from their regular job duties.

RESEARCH IN ACTION
MANAGING INTEGRITY IN DECISION MAKING

The U.S. FDA (Food and Drug Administration) has adopted standards for the use of research in decision making. The standards cover the entire research process and also emphasize the proper reporting and dissemination of results to insure that decisions are made with the maximum possible integrity. FDA officials refer to the standards as GCP, standing for Good Clinical Practices.

This measure was motivated by the realization that integrity in decision making is essential to avoid needless harm to consumers, employees and research participants. Misguided research contributes to factors such as inaccurate product labels and promotional materials and ultimately harms decision making by the agency, private companies and consumers. Ultimately, the FDA believes the standards will improve the integrity of decision making within the agency and within the industries it oversees. The result will be a reduction in the potential harm caused by unintended misuse of food and drugs.

SOURCE: FDA and the Quality and Integrity of Research. 2002. *FDA Consumer* 36 (January/February) 4–5.

The implications for each go beyond the direct. Business decision makers should be ever mindful that the lives of families of employees, customers, and shareholders are affected significantly by the quality of the decisions made. Likewise, since researchers provide input into these decisions, they share in this responsibility. Thus, ethics should be taken very seriously since unethical decisions usually cause harm to at least one of the parties involved in business exchange (see the "Research in Action" box).

Ethics in decision making does not always mean the company president in the previous example should act consistently with the research. However, it does mean, as mentioned in the obligations of decision makers, that the researcher should only ask for research that will provide information considered in the decision making process. Other issues may sometimes be more persuasive than the research, and these issues may include experience and intuition.

Researchers should also be mindful of protecting their own integrity, the moral image of their company and the image of their discipline. Recently, public perceptions of questionable behaviors committed by auditors overseeing the financial reporting of Enron, Inc. have seriously damaged the reputation of the individual auditors, their employer Arthur Andersen, and the accounting industry overall.[8] A decade ago, the image of the savings and loan industry was damaged similarly. Thus, unethical actions by a small number of researchers could severely damage the industry overall.

One simple guide for business researchers and decision makers who want to put integrity into practice is to always act as though your actions will be public. That is, your superiors, family, and friends will all know what you have done. This emphasizes the role played by one's conscience in shaping moral behavior.

An **ethics checklist** also can be useful. This is a list of questions that can be useful in guiding decision making. Researchers and decision makers may consider the following questions as useful in ensuring an ethical decision-making climate.

1. Will the actions taken harm this institution?
2. Will the actions taken harm individuals, including coworkers, clients, research participants or customers?
3. Will the information involved be misused by others?
4. Will the actions harm my discipline or industry?
5. Will the actions do harm to the personal integrity of researchers and/or decision makers?
6. Will the actions do harm to society at large?

SUMMARY

Define Business Ethics and Discuss Their Relevance to Research

Business ethics are defined as the application of moral principles and/or ethical standards to human actions within the exchange process. The ethical dimensions of the researcher-decision maker and researcher-participant relationships were discussed. All have important duties before, during, and after the research. Above all, researchers and decision makers should behave as professionals. Being professional means working with the knowledge that your actions affect other people's lives. Therefore, research should be done with great care and as much precision as the time and economic budget allow. Above all, effective communication is a key to minimizing conflict between researchers and decision makers.

Provide an Overview of the Ethical Obligations of Business Researchers

Business researchers have several important ethical obligations. They should strive to communicate effectively and develop a consensus reason for the research among all the key actors involved. Researchers should also use the right tool for job, which means avoiding overly complex research tools. Researchers should decline a job for which they lack expertise. They should also take great care to treat research participants fairly. The chapter discusses key aspects of this responsibility and includes a list of useful questions concerning the fair treatment of research participants. Human resource committees can provide useful reviews that insure the research addresses each question in an ethical way. Researchers should strive to communicate simply and clearly. Reports and presentations should be prepared with the level of sophistication of the audience in mind. Finally, researchers should clearly communicate all research limitations.

Provide an Overview of the Ethical Obligations of Business Decision Makers

Decision makers also have important ethical obligations. These also involve the treatment of researchers, other employees, consumers, and the public in general. Decision makers should also work to establish a consensus reason for doing research. They should not order research without due intention to consider it when making decisions. Decision makers should not hold the researcher responsible in any way for results that may be considered undesirable.

Provide an Overview of the Ethical Obligations of Business Research Participants

Research participants can also negatively influence business decision making. Unethical participant actions can lead to response error, which in turn, could lead to poor decision making. Research participants should participate willfully or decline the opportunity to participate. This means they should follow the research instructions faithfully and give the task the level of involvement required. Participants should provide honest responses and not seek to respond consistently with a manner that may affect any eventual decisions. Also, participants should respect the confidentiality of the research project if requested by the researcher.

Describe the Potential Consequences of Unethical Actions

Finally, researchers and decision makers should be mindful of the direct and indirect effects of unethical actions. The quality of decision making is affected by the integrity of the research. If decisions are made that serve to do something other than accomplish socially legitimate business goals, someone is likely to be harmed. Those potentially harmed include: employees, consumers, society, the institution, and the discipline or industry.

KEY TERMS

business ethics	ethical dilemmas	human resources review
coercion	ethics checklist	committee
debriefing		push polls

ETHICAL DILEMMA

Mr. Ralf Sanders owns a data imaging firm with over one hundred employees in the main office. Ralf commissions a study of the organizational culture within his company. The researcher suggests that employees may not respond accurately to a structured questionnaire because of the sensitivity of some of the topics. Instead, he suggests recording the conversations of employees in the company lunchroom using hidden microphones. The resulting conversations could be analyzed using content analysis. This would reveal key themes around which organizational culture may be structured. Should Mr. Sanders accept the offer? Why or why not? If not, what changes can be made to the proposed research design to make it more ethically acceptable to you?

REVIEW QUESTIONS

1. Define business ethics.
2. What things take the place of trust in the exchange process?
3. What is an ethical dilemma? List at least three ways one can occur in the business decision-making process.
4. What are four important considerations that should be given to research participants?
5. What is a human resource review committee? What benefits does it provide?
6. What does it mean for a decision maker to give "due consideration" to business research results?

DISCUSSION AND APPLICATION ACTIVITIES

1. Several recent studies raises questions about student integrity, such as discussed in the "Research in Action" box entitled "Are 'The Best and Brightest' the Rightest?" Do you believe that there is a relationship between the ethical behavior exhibited by a college student and the ethical behavior he or she will exhibit in the business world? Prepare a one-page position statement that either agrees or disagrees with the statement that "unethical college students will make unethical businesspeople."
2. How might the balancing act depicted in Exhibit 4-1 help ensure that human resources are not treated unfairly even if there are a few employees of questionable moral character involved in decision making?
3. Suppose a researcher was addressing the following research questions: Do experienced or inexperienced employees cope better with stress? Do employees cope better with stress before or after lunch? The researcher decides to implement a causal design, using an experiment. Subjects are randomly selected from the lists of two thousand experienced (three

years or more) and four hundred inexperienced (less than six months) employees provided by the decision maker. The subjects are not informed that they have been selected for the experiment.

The experimental design is implemented by having each subject's supervisor give each employee a task that should take no more than forty-five minutes to complete. The task requires the use of a computer. After only a few minutes of the task, the subject receives an urgent electronic message that a computer virus has infected his or her computer. In the "mild stress" condition, the virus message indicates that the subject has one hour to fix the computer or all email addresses will be wiped from the address book and all email files purged. In the "high stress" condition, the subject is told that unless the problem is fixed within one hour, all files will be permanently destroyed as will all the files on the computers of every user in the address book (including superiors). Several dependent variables are measured afterwards.

Evaluate this experimental design from a business research ethics perspective. Discuss the results in class. Is there a better way to design an experiment that would address these questions?

4. Find information on a current event that questions the ethics of some business. Did or could researchers have played a role in preventing this event?

5. What steps do you believe a researcher could take to ensure that research participants fulfill their ethical obligations in the research process?

INTERNET EXERCISES

1. Internet Exercise: Go to http://www.aapor.org/ethics/code.html. This presents the American Association of Public Opinion Research's code of ethics. Does it omit anything important? If you were considering a code of ethics for research at GM, what modifications would you make?

2. Internet Exercise: Go to http://www.rionethics.com/page4.html. Comment on the products offered. Do you believe that training in these areas will improve the quality of decision making? Can an individual employee be trained to have high moral character?

NOTES

1. Ferrell, O.C. and John Fraedrich. 1997. *Business Ethics*. Houghton Mifflin: Boston, Mass.
2. Robin, Donald P., Eric R. Reidenbach and Barry J. Babin. 1997. Ethical Judgements. *Psychological Review*.
3. McNath, Robert M. 2002. Smokeless Isn't Smoking. *American Demographics* 18 (October): 60.
4. Saporito, B. 1988. The Tough Cookie at RJR Nabisco. *Fortune* 118 (2): 32–41.
5. Bowers, Diane K. 1996. Tackling a Tacky Problem. *Marketing Research* 8 (Fall): 56–57.
6. For a summary of this research, see Vedantam, Shankar. 2002. Against Depression, A Sugar Pill is Hard to Beat. *Washington Post* May 7: A01.
7. Begley, Sharon, Donna Foote and Adam Rogers. 2001. Dying for Science. *Newsweek* 138 (7/30): 36.
8. Brown, Ken and Wiel Jonathon. 2002. When Enron Auditors Were on a Tear. *Wall Street Journal* 239 (3/21): C1.

Data Collection, Management, and Sampling

5

Data Collection Approaches

Learning Objectives

1. Understand data collection principles and practices.

2. Describe the differences between collecting qualitative and quantitative data.

3. Understand the differences between observation and survey methods.

4. Assess the use of questionnaires as instruments for data collection.

5. Appreciate the role of the various interviewing methods in obtaining data.

INTRODUCTION

Researchers, through measurement, describe phenomena that exist in the business world in terms of, for example, demographics, behavior, attitudes, beliefs, lifestyles and expectations of consumers and/or organizations. To describe phenomena, researchers must have data. Data are collected by means of one or more of the following: **observation, interviews** and/or **questionnaires.** Once data is obtained, it is then analyzed and becomes the basis for informed decision making, which in turn helps to reduce the risk of making costly errors.

Data collection requires considerable knowledge and skills in all aspects of survey methods and questionnaire design. These topics are discussed in this chapter.

DATA COLLECTION METHODS

The type and amount of data to be collected depends upon the nature of the study together with its research objectives. If the study is exploratory the researcher is likely to collect narrative data through the use of focus groups, **personal interviews,** or by observing behavior or events. This type of data can also be referred to as qualitative. Qualitative approaches to data collection typically are used at the exploratory stage of the research process. Their role is to identify and/or refine research problems that may help to formulate and test conceptual frameworks. Such studies normally involve the use of smaller samples or case studies.

If the study is descriptive or causal in nature, the researcher is likely to require a relatively large amount of quantitative data obtained through large-scale surveys or by accessing existing electronic databases. Quantitative data typically is obtained through the use of various numeric scales. Quantitative data collection approaches typically are used when the researcher is using well-defined theoretical models and research problems. Validation of the concepts and models usually involves the use of quantitative data obtained from large-scale questionnaire surveys.

Until recently, telephone surveys, mall intercepts, mail or fax surveys, and face-to-face interviews were the primary methods of data collection. Information technology is revolutionizing data collection in that large amounts of data, both qualitative and quantitative, can be obtained and integrated into databases relatively fast and at a very low cost when compared to the more traditional methods. These new methods include computerized questionnaires administered over the Internet, electronic capture of data at the point of sale, and electronic conversations or discussions both internally over an intranet and externally over the Internet. Indeed, Internet-based surveys alone now account for almost 10 percent of all data collection.

The various data collection approaches are depicted in Exhibit 5-1. Broadly speaking, these methods can be divided into two categories—observation and survey methods. Advantages and disadvantages of each approach will be discussed.

OBSERVATION

Observational data are collected by systematically recording observations of people, events, or objects.[1] Observational data can be obtained by use of human, mechanical, or electronic observation. An observational approach results in either narrative or numerical data. If narrative data is collected, it typically is in the form of written descriptions of behavior, or

EXHIBIT 5-1 DATA COLLECTION APPROACHES

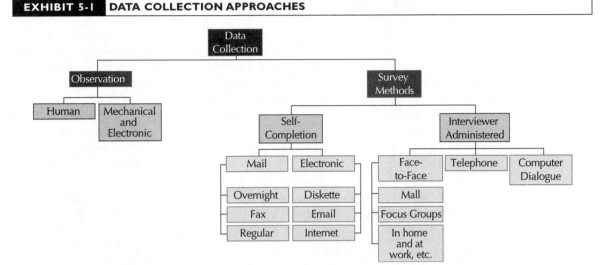

recorded on audio or videotape. If numerical data is involved, it would either involve a trained observer recording events using a structured questionnaire or a device that counts or tracks specific actions. For example, a researcher may study produce selection behavior in a supermarket by having an observer record the amount of time between the approach of the individual and the decision to purchase a particular item. This information could be recorded on a questionnaire along with purchase information. Similarly, Phil Samouel might evaluate the competence of the waiters in his restaurant on a number of predetermined criteria.

Today, however, probably the most widespread use of collecting observational data is either through scanning of purchases in supermarkets, drugstores, or other retail outlets, or over the Internet when companies observe an individual's click-through behavior. But what you may not realize is that when you phone a business and are informed the call may be recorded for quality control monitoring and training, what often happens is the recording is being used to collect observational data. Recording of such calls provides a rich source of qualitative data for assessing company procedures, employee performance, and customer comments.

A disadvantage of this approach is there is no opportunity to observe any unseen characteristics. For example, if behavior is being observed in a supermarket we do not know the vegetable or fruit, customer's attitude, hunger level or whether the purchase is for her or his own consumption. In contrast, a primary advantage of observational data is its *unobtrusive* approach. Unobtrusive means the respondent is unaware of his or her participation in a research project. Because individuals being observed have had no interaction with a researcher, such as instructions or a questionnaire, they cannot be influenced by any activities associated with collecting data. Thus, observational data collection avoids interview bias since no instructions, questions or interaction at all are involved.

Does this unobtrusive approach violate the research participant's right to privacy? Or is it possible the participant can be harmed in any way? If the behavior being observed is normally performed in public with the likelihood that others may notice, it is unlikely the person's privacy has been violated, or that they will be harmed. But observations of human behavior for research purposes should avoid recording the person's name. This is another way in which privacy is protected. On the other hand, private acts should not be observed. For example, retail store dressing rooms should not be used to collect observational data even though the data might be very useful in understanding why people buy clothes.

As a general rule, individuals do not know their behavior is being observed. But occasionally researchers may choose to request the participation of respondents in an observational study. As an example, mall shoppers may be given a GPS (Global Positioning System) transmitter that allows their behavior to be tracked throughout the mall. This provides researchers with useful information on shopping patterns. Researchers hope shoppers will forget they have the device so it will not influence their behavior. Similarly, GPS technology is being used to observe the location and driving patterns of commercial trucks, railroads, and school buses. In the United States, GPS technology is expected to be standard equipment on most new vehicles within five years.

Ethnographic research and **content analysis** are two special forms of the observational approach. We discuss both in the following paragraphs.

Ethnographic Research

Ethnographic research generally involves interperting behavior through observation of actual life experiences. Researchers typically will spend long periods of time with a respondent, and then write narratives that describe the respondent's behavior. For example, a researcher studying heavy beer consumption may actually spend days or weeks with a "heavy" beer consumer to try and discover all the needs addressed by beer consumption.[2] Similarly, a researcher may actually spend weeks or months as an employee in a workplace in an effort to understand the organization and the behavior of its employees.

More recently, ethnographic observational studies have paid consumers to place small video cameras in their homes or cars.[3] For example, 3M paid consumers to track their in-home movements via video in an effort to understand better how its Ergo hand-held electronic Internet appliance would be used. This eventually led to the belief that people would use it differently than they do the Internet via a computer. Similarly, Moen, one of the largest U.S. plumbing fixture manufacturers, went so far as to gain permission to videotape people in their showers! This enabled them to discover several aspects of shower behavior that people could not or would not voice. For example, they noticed that many women used a faucet handle for balance while shaving their legs. Findings like these enabled Moen to design shower fixtures that make for a better shower experience!

Content Analysis

Content analysis obtains data by observing and analyzing the content or message of written text. Examples of text where content analysis typically is used include reports, contracts, advertisements, letters, open-ended questions on surveys, and similar content. Through systematic analysis as well as observation, the researcher examines the frequency with which words and main themes occur and identifies information content and characteristics embedded in the text. The end result often is to quantify qualitative data.

The initial content analysis may count word or phrase frequency. For example, a researcher could analyze transcripts from employment interviews. The transcripts typically are analyzed by software that counts the frequency with which words and expressions occur. One successful application of content analysis has been in discovering expressions that indicate a dishonest response. A job candidate with a high count of short negative expressions such as

```
┌─────────────────────────────────────────────────────────────────┐
│                      RESEARCH IN ACTION                           │
├─────────────────────────────────────────────────────────────────┤
│        CONTENT ANALYSIS: SOFTWARE TO THE RESCUE!                  │
└─────────────────────────────────────────────────────────────────┘
```

Increasing use is being made of computer software to analyze data that is narrative in form. Such software is often known by the acronym CAQADS (Computer Assisted Qualitative Data Analysis Software). Two examples of such software are TextSmart and QSR NUD*IST.

TextSmart is a software package that was specifically developed to enable survey researchers to view, manipulate, and automate the coding or categorization of responses to open-ended questions. The ability to automate the examination and organization of narrative data is particularly helpful when a large scale survey is undertaken. The use of TextSmart is not restricted to analyzing responses to open-ended questions. It can be used to analyze any textual data. TextSmart output can be exported into SPSS for further analysis. For example, it is possible to perform a correspondence analysis on a contingency table resulting from a TextSmart analysis. SPSS provides technical support for the software.

For more information about TextSmart and related SPSS products visit the Web site www.spss.com.

QSR NUD*IST stands for Non-Numerical Unstructured Data Indexing and Theorizing. It is a popular computer software package used by researchers to analyze text from focus group or interview transcripts, literary documents, and so on. The software also can examine non-textual data such as photographs, tape recordings, films, and so on. It enables the user to index and link several documents in a structured way to produce categorical data in a form amenable to further analysis. A numerical summary of NUD*IST output can be exported to software programs such as SPSS and Excel.

"never" and "nothing," or a high number of qualifiers such as "kind of" or "I don't think," may end up classified as dishonest.[4] Moreover, "kind of" and "sort of" may both be interpreted as "hedging." An initial content analysis may reveal many words that have essentially the same meaning. If this occurs, categories of common meaning are developed.

Content analysis used to be a manual, time-consuming process. Today, there are several software packages that make the task much simpler. Two examples are described in the "Research in Action" box.

To use computer-aided content analysis software, the researcher needs an electronic copy of the narrative information. Initial applications of this type of software are mostly in academic or scholarly research. But as awareness of these software packages increases, use among applied business researchers will be more prevalent. An example of how a computer-aided content analysis package was used to examine and better understand qualitative interviews on organizational behavior and worker productivity is shown in Exhibit 5-2.

Researchers have used content analysis to discover the primary theme and purpose of business codes of ethics. Codes of ethics are available as secondary data for many large public firms. Content analyses of codes found in the *Fortune 500* database and *Business Review Weekly* database provide an interesting comparison among British, Australian, and American codes of ethics. For example, the themes that were identified suggested that codes are directed either toward owners, management or all employees of an organization. Themes emerging most often address employee conduct, community involvement, and customer treatment. Activities addressed most often include gift giving and receiving, conflicts of interest, and accurate record keeping. Relatively few passages described specific guidance on what is acceptable. The themes seem generally similar across the United Kingdom, Australia, and the United States. However, U.K. codes contained more community welfare references and Australian and U.S. codes contained more references to customer treatment and equal opportunity.[5]

| EXHIBIT 5-2 | AN APPLICATION OF COMPUTER-ASSISTED QUALITATIVE DATA ANALYSIS SOFTWARE |

Researchers interviewed sixteen sales managers to identify organizational variables considered important in the effective implementation of sales force automation systems (SFA). Responses were transcribed and submitted to computer-aided content analysis. The relative occurrence of key concepts and value-laden terms was tabulated, and categories of themes were developed for each question. A panel of experts then defined the categories by developing a list of key words that described each category. The software searched the entire text of the interviews and placed information into the categories. Then the panel of experts again examined the results to eliminate any information misplaced in a category due to contextual issues. The four questions asked, the categories developed, and the relative percentage of hits for each category in each question follows:

1. What employee behaviors should firms reward, support, and expect if they are interested in effectively implementing an SFA (Sales Force Automation) system?

Teamwork	28%
Computer Skills	35%
SFA Competence	37%

2. What kinds of information can SFA provide that would be valuable in terms of helping increase a firm's productivity?

Prospecting	34%
Account Development	32%
Buyer Profile	34%

3. Please describe the kind of organizational culture or shared values necessary to effectively implement an SFA system?

Information Sharing	41%
Teamwork	33%
SFA Commitment/Ownership	26%

4. Please describe issues that might limit or enhance the effectiveness of an SFA system?

| Resistance to Change | 61% |
| Insufficient Support for SFA | 39% |

As an example, for question 1, three categories were identified. Their relative importance was 28 percent for teamwork, 35 percent for computer skills, and 37 percent for SFA competence. The other questions are interpreted in a similar manner. Computer-aided content analysis software enables the business researcher to quickly and confidently analyze open-ended responses, and report the findings in an effective manner.

SOURCE: Pullig, Chris, Trey Maxham, T., and Joe Hair. 2002. Salesforce Automation Systems: An Exploratory Examination of Organizational Factors Associated with Effective Implementation and Saleforce Productivity. *Journal of Business Research* 55:5 (May) 401–16.

Content analysis is frequently used to interpret text interviews. It also is commonly used to discover themes and orientations of media programs and advertising. Given the visual nature of advertising, the content analyses may often involve identifying the frequency of themes expressed both in words and in pictures.[6] For example, television commercials directed at teenagers in the United States were recently analyzed using content analysis and it was determined that teens are exposed to over fourteen thousand ads a year containing sexual references. Similarly, news and other types of television programs are analyzed to determine the amount and type of violence included. Indeed, even video and computer games are examined to determine and classify their content. The "Research in Action" box describes a research opportunity that likely will require some careful thought regarding the best data collection method.

RESEARCH IN ACTION

WHEN WILL BUSINESS RESEARCH COME OUT OF THE CLOSET?

Twenty-one network and cable TV shows feature gay or lesbian characters in leading, supporting or recurring roles. Viacom's MTV networks and Showtime networks are developing a gay-targeted TV channel. The two leading gay magazines, *The Advocate* and *Out* have a circulation of 103,000 and 110,000 respectively. As alternative lifestyles are becoming more mainstream, companies are searching for research data to make well-informed conclusions about the growing gay, lesbian, bisexual, and transgender (GLBT) population.

Business research typically analyzes population demographics using the RAGE matrix—Race/ethnicity, Age, Gender, and Education. Income has recently being added as a fifth parameter. Now, with society's changing attitude toward diversity and the development of niche marketing, companies, marketers, and business researchers are questioning whether sexual orientation should now be added to the mix. Just as demographics such as age, gender, and ethnicity are widely accepted as helping to shape attitudes and spending patterns, sexual orientation is increasingly believed to have a similar influence over purchasing behavior.

Why the sudden interest in this segment? Until recently, there was little evidence to support the actual size of GLBT population. Then the Census Bureau released its Census 2000 figures showing impressive increases in the total number and geographic dispersion of GBLT households nationally over the past decade. The Census indicates 1.2 million adults are living with partners of the same sex in 99.3 percent of all U.S. counties, up from 290,000 in 52 percent of counties in 1990. Some researchers feel the population percentages are actually higher than what was reported because the census does not ask specific questions about sexual orientation—only household configurations—and does not include data on GLBTs who are single or not living together. Experts estimate that the GLBT segment makes up between 4 percent to 8 percent, or eleven million to twenty-three million, of the total U.S population. How does this segment compare to other more traditional demographics? The Asian American population is currently measured at twelve million or 4.2 percent of the total population. Some researchers also believe the GLBT segment is more lucrative than others. According to Packaged Facts (MarketResearch.com) total GLBT consumer discretionary spending is $340 billion, compared with Asian American spending estimated at $254 billion. In addition, the GLBT population is expected to grow significantly as more Americans feel comfortable in coming out.

No wonder companies such as American Express, Subaru of America, and Proctor & Gamble are trying to tap into this market. But without more research it's difficult for companies to make projections or comparisons with other demographic audiences. Some studies have been done but researchers feel that samples have not been representative of the total population. Internet surveys may lead the way in helping research firms collect data. New York-based Harris Interactive found that the anonymity of online questionnaires seem to garner more accurate results. For example, when the company utilized telephone surveys, only 2 percent of adult respondents identified themselves as "gay or lesbian," but 4 percent self-identified online. The company also found how the question is asked affects the response rates. When given the option to self-identify as "gay," "lesbian," "bi-sexual" or "trans-gendered," as opposed to "gay" or "lesbian," 6 percent responded. New York-based Simmons Market Research Bureau is also considering assigning sexual orientation as a standard demographic on its biannuall National Consumer Survey, a representative study that tracks the spending and media habits of thirty thousand Americans.

Now that data such as the Census is showing that the GLBT segment is a viable one, the demand for research should increase. As this happens, companies, marketers, and business researchers need to implement the same proven strategies used to measure other demographics.

SOURCES: Gardyn, Rebecca. 2001. A Market Kept in the Closet, *American Demographics* (November): 37–43; Halliday, Jean. Gay Ride, *Advertising Age* (February 25): 18; and Curry, Sheree R. 2002. TV Faces Obstacles, *Advertising Age* (February 25): 19, 21.

SURVEY METHODS

A survey is a procedure used to collect primary data from individuals. The data sought can range from beliefs, opinions, attitudes, and lifestyles to general background information on individuals such as gender, age, education, and income, as well as company characteristics like revenue and number of employees. Surveys are used when the research project involves collecting information from a large sample of individuals. The major difference between observation and surveys is that with surveys the respondent clearly knows information about their behavior and/or attitudes is being collected. Hence, the possibility always exists that this may influence their responses and create response bias.

Methods of collecting survey data fall into two broad categories: self-completion and interviewer-administered. Self-completion methods include **mail surveys** and **electronic surveys.** Interviewer-administered methods involve direct contact with the respondents through personal interviews, including face-to-face, telephone, and **computer dialogue.** Personal interviews, whether structured or unstructured, typically are used to obtain detailed qualitative information from a relatively small number of individuals. This approach sometimes is referred to as an in-depth survey. On the other hand, questionnaires are used to collect quantitative data from larger numbers of individuals in a relatively quick and convenient manner. Finding a company to assist in conducting a survey is a lot easier with the Internet as the "Research in Action" box on Quirks.com shows.

PANEL SURVEYS

A panel survey is a special type of survey method. Panel surveys collect data from the same group of respondents over a period of time. A large pool of panel members is recruited and when they are involved in a survey they record their responses in a diary. Information on panel members, such as demographic and household characteristics, is collected and used to determine which individuals are used for a particular survey. Panels can represent any group of individuals, from various types of consumer groups to business groups such as doctors, lawyers, CEOs, and so forth. Typically, the research company that maintains the panel will randomly select individuals as a representative sample to participate in a particular survey. Sometimes panel members are asked the same questions over time, in which case it is called a longitudinal panel study. Other times, the questions are only asked one time. Traditional methods of data collection have been by mail, telephone, personal interviews, and fax. But electronic data collection is rapidly increasing for panel surveys. Also, panel surveys can be either self-completion or interviewer assisted. An advantage of panel data is response rates are fast and substantially higher than other methods of data collection. See the "Research in Action" box to learn more about the emergence of electronic panel surveys.

QUESTIONNAIRES

A questionnaire is a predetermined set of questions designed to capture data from respondents. It is a scientifically developed instrument for measurement of key characteristics of individuals, companies, events, and other phenomena. Good survey research requires good questionnaires to ensure accuracy in the data.

In conducting a questionnaire-based study, there are a number of interrelated activities that must be considered. These include: the general design of the questionnaire, validation of the questionnaire by pre-testing, and the method by which the questionnaire is administered.

Questionnaire surveys generally are designed to obtain large quantities of data, usually in numerical form. A questionnaire consists of a standard set of questions with answers to the questions often limited to a few predetermined mutually exclusive and exhaustive outcomes. Mutually exclusive means each answer has a separate response category while

---

RESEARCH IN ACTION
QUIRKS.COM—YOUR ONLINE SOURCE FOR RESEARCH SERVICES

For over fifteen years Quirk's Research Review has been producing a monthly print magazine that reports on research trends and techniques in a simple and straightforward manner to promote the value of research. The company's Web site (www.quirks.com) is designed to encourage the use, understanding and value of research, while providing free access to as many research resources as possible. On the Web site, business researchers can search for and purchase over forty thousand research reports from more than 350 publishers.

The site also allows researchers access to archived articles from the magazine, including case histories on successful research projects, discussion of research techniques, the statistical use of data in marketing research and other topics relevant to the research industry. Some of the directories available online include the *Researcher SourceBook*™ which contains listings of more than 7,300 firms providing marketing research products and services; listings of worldwide focus group facilities; and listings of more than three hundred data processing and statistical analysis firms. After using the online directories to locate a firm, business researchers can then use the online Request for Proposal forms to send project parameters directly to a particular firm.

Another unique feature of the site is the Job Mart page that allows researchers to view or post research-related employment opportunities and view or post online resumes. From job postings and case studies to directories and a glossary of research terms, Quirks.com offers marketing and business research professionals the tools, information, and solutions to most any research questions they might face.

RESEARCH IN ACTION
DECISION ANALYST, INC. ENTERS INTERNET
PANEL SECTOR IN A BIG WAY!

Decision Analyst, Inc., located in Dallas, Texas, is a leader in using technology to collect data. President Jerry Thomas believes the future of marketing research belongs to the Internet. In the United States over 60 percent of adults currently have access to the Internet at home or work, and Internet users represent over 70 percent of total U.S. purchasing power and are rapidly becoming representative of the U.S. population. Many developed countries have or are quickly becoming similar in terms of Internet access and usage.

As a global leader in Internet-based research, Decision Analyst has conducted hundreds of online surveys via their worldwide Consumer Opinion Online panels of more than 3.5 million consumers in the United States, Canada, Europe, Latin America, and Asia, as well as their specialty panels of technology professionals, physicians, executives, and contractors. Based on its own experiences as well as observations from other professionals, Decision Analyst believes Internet-based surveys provide higher-quality data, and are faster and less costly than telephone surveys. For more information on this innovative company visit their Web site at: www.decisionanalyst.com.

exhaustive means a response category has been included for every possible answer. Questionnaire wording is very important to the accuracy of the information collected, and in Chapter 7 we give you guidelines on how to deal with this topic as well as other questionnaire design considerations.

Self-Completed Questionnaires

Questionnaires frequently are completed by the respondent without a researcher present. The assumption is respondents have the knowledge and motivation to complete them on their own. It does, however, mean the topic, design, and format must be sufficiently appealing that respondents actually complete and return the questionnaire. Examples of **self-completed questionnaires** include surveys given to theatre patrons either before or after the show, or perhaps at intermission, tabletop surveys at restaurants or in doctors' offices, and questionnaires sent by auto dealerships following service visits.

Self-completed questionnaires are delivered to respondents in several ways. Traditional approaches include mail and fax surveys. More recently, electronic delivery approaches are being utilized. A major problem with any kind of self-completion questionnaire is the loss of researcher control. You typically do not know whether the intended person completed the questionnaire, if respondents answer the questions in the sequence they are formatted in, or whether they asked for input from others. Any of these can introduce response bias. But perhaps the biggest problem with this type questionnaire is the very low response rate raising the question of whether those who responded are representative of the target population for the research project.

Mail Surveys

Surveys delivered to respondents via regular mail, fax, and overnight delivery typically are thought of as mail surveys. Some mail surveys are short, others are quite long, as many as five or six pages, and in some instances booklets requesting extensive information are used. With fax surveys the researcher has few options. The major limiting factor is that only individuals with fax machines can be surveyed. For business surveys this is not much of a problem, but few consumers have a fax machine at home.

With traditional mail and overnight delivery, however, decisions must be made on the envelope, cover letter, length, and incentive. All of these factors impact the response rate in some way. Attractive envelopes and stationery, well-written cover letters and questionnaires of reasonable length will all increase response rates. With longer surveys, an incentive will increase responses. While overnight delivery is a costly alternative, it often is used in business-to-business surveys if the budget permits. Prior agreement to participate generally is obtained over the phone. But actual delivery to the respondent is by overnight (Federal Express, Emery, etc.) because experience has shown that overnight packages are delivered to the respondent's desk and bypass traditional gatekeepers such as secretaries. If time is a factor, then traditional mail is not a good alternative. Generally speaking, researchers must allow at least three weeks for individuals to respond. But even then in most instances it will be necessary to send follow-up reminders to achieve a sufficient sample size, and this will take another two or three weeks. Some suggested approaches to increase mail survey response rates are summarized in the "Research in Action" box.

To conduct mail surveys you must have a list. If you are surveying your own customers or other individuals with whom you already have a relationship, a list will be available. If you are soliciting information from other individuals or organizations, however, it will be necessary to purchase a list. Several large companies sell lists. The "Research in Action" box describes one such list company.

Electronic Surveys

Three approaches are used to complete electronic, self-completion questionnaires. The traditional approach is to deliver a computer diskette to the respondents. The questionnaire is programmed on the diskette and respondents simply place the diskette in their computer, follow the instructions, and when completed return the diskette to the research company. Email and Web-hosted Internet are expected to replace this approach in the next few years.

Email surveys are popular, inexpensive, can be completed in a short period of time, and generally produce high quality data. But Web-hosted Internet surveys have more flexibility. To maintain anonymity of respondents and increase response rates, Web-hosted Internet surveys typically are created and hosted by an independent research company on their own server (computer). But companies sometimes host them on an in-house server. The greater flexibility of Internet surveys is due to the fact questionnaires located on in-house servers can

---

RESEARCH IN ACTION
HOW TO INCREASE MAIL SURVEY RESPONSE RATES

Below are some suggested ways to increase response rates in mail surveys:

Approach	Examples
Preliminary Contact	Letter, email or phone call ahead of time.
Personalization	Individually typed and addressed letter, personal signature, etc.
Response Deadline	Provide a due date in the letter.
Appeals	Convince respondent survey is important and has some social or other important value.
Sponsorship	Survey is sponsored by an important organization, such as a national trade organization or prestigious university.
Incentives	Nonmonetary gifts like summary of findings or a ballpoint pen; Monetary incentive like $1.00 to buy a cup of coffee
Questionnaire Length	Print on both sides of the paper and make no longer than four pages.
Type of Postage	Special commemorative stamp; Sending overnight delivery such as FedEx will bypass gatekeepers for business surveys, if the budget permits. Always include a postage-paid envelope to return the questionnaire.
Followups	Send follow-up reminders such as postcard. Sometimes respondents lose the questionnaire so sending a letter with a second copy can help.

SOURCE: Adapted from Conant, J. D. Smart and B. Walker. Mail Survey Facilitation Techniques: An Assessment and Proposal Regarding Reporting Practices, *Journal of Market Research Society* 32:4 : 569–580.

---

include manipulations not possible in email surveys in which the questionnaire is located on the client/respondent side (i.e., it is sent to the respondent and is completed on their own PC). Access to Web-hosted surveys is controlled by password to ensure only qualified respondents complete the survey according to specified instructions. Respondents are contacted and asked to participate, and then given a unique password. As with email surveys, Web-hosted surveys are quick and provide high quality data. But typically they are more expensive due to Web site programming costs.

A relatively recent innovation to Web-hosted surveys is the kiosk. A self-contained kiosk is located in a high traffic area and individuals sign on to obtain information and submit information. Drug stores use them to dispense medical information. Supermarkets use them to provide recipes and related information for food purchases. Conferences and trade shows use them to collect and disperse information, and rest stops on highways are beginning to use them. The main problem is the lack of control over who accesses them. But they do provide 24/7 access to information and ability to collect data.

INTERVIEWER-ADMINISTERED QUESTIONNAIRES

Interviewer-administered questionnaires are completed either face-to-face, over the telephone, or via computer dialogue. Face-to-face and **telephone interviews** are the most prevalent, but computer dialogue is the fastest growing. Computer dialogue approaches use digital technology and can quickly and easily obtain information from large groups of individuals.

Interviews

An interview is where the researcher "speaks" to the respondent directly, asking questions and recording answers. Interviews are particularly helpful in gathering data when dealing with complex and/or sensitive issues, and when open-ended questions are used to collect data. Interviews also enable the researcher to obtain feedback and to use visual aids if the interviews are face-to-face. For example, respondents might be shown a new corporate logo, a new corporate mission statement, building designs, automobile styles and colors, and so on, and asked to comment. Finally, interviews are flexible in where they can be conducted (at work, home, or in malls, etc.) and researchers can increase participation rates by explaining the project and its value.

To get the cooperation of the interviewee in a face-to-face interview, and thereby obtain quality information, the interviewer must make every effort to create a relaxed atmosphere within which to conduct the interview. Once this has been achieved, interviewers will ask the respondents to describe the situation or phenomenon of interest, followed by: Why? How? When? Where? and Who? questions. For example, if Phil Samouel wanted information about the food being served in his Greek restaurant, he might ask customers "What do you think about the quality of my food?" If their response is "We think it is very good," then he would follow-up by asking "Why do you say that?" as well as by asking them to give examples such as: "I really like the special of the day" or "The baklava is very good." In this way, Phil can really begin to understand what customers think about the food in his restaurant. In short, Phil can get actionable information for his business plan, not just general information that is of little value in taking corrective actions. In formulating questions for interviews, therefore, always ask yourself: "Will the answers I get to this question help me make a better decision about a particular business approach?" If not, do not ask them!

Interviews can vary from being highly unstructured to highly structured. Unstructured interviews are generally conducted in a very open manner. In contrast, the interviewer controls structured interviews in a consistent and orderly manner. Whether structured or unstructured, interviewing can take a variety of forms including face-to-face, telephone, or electronically via computer dialogue.

Structured Interviews   For structured interviews the interviewer uses an interview sequence with predetermined questions. For each interview, the interviewer is required to use the same interview sequence and to conduct the interview in exactly the same way to avoid biases that may result from inconsistent interviewing practices. Additionally, a standardized approach will ensure responses are comparable between interviews.

Each respondent is provided with an identical opportunity to respond to the questions. The interviewer may collect the responses in the form of notes or may tape record the interview. Taping should only be done with the permission of the interviewee. If the interview is not tape recorded, it is good practice to provide the interviewee with a copy of the interviewer's notes after they are completed as this will help ensure the interview is captured accurately.

Semi-structured Interviews   Sometimes a **semi-structured interview** approach is adopted. In this approach, the researcher is free to exercise his or her own initiative in following up an interviewee's answer to a question. The interviewer may want to ask related, unanticipated questions that were not originally included. This approach may result in unexpected and insightful information coming to light, thus enhancing the findings.

Semi-structured interviews have an overall structure and direction, but allow a lot of flexibility to include unstructured questioning. Perhaps the best-known semi-structured interview approach is the **focus group.** Focus groups are semi-structured interviews that use an exploratory research approach and are considered a type of qualitative research. Focus groups are structured in that the moderator has a list of topics and/or questions to cover. But they are *unstructured* because the moderator allows participants to answer questions in their own words and encourages them to elaborate on their responses.

Focus groups are relatively informal discussions among eight to twelve respondents. Respondents usually share something in common. They may all have the same job, work for the same company, be a customer of the same bank or do the same household chores.

This common ground is usually very much involved in the discussion. Unlike other survey approaches, a random sample is neither required nor desired.

Focus groups are guided by a *moderator* who encourages discussion and keeps the group on track, meaning they don't stray too far from the primary topic. A good moderator is a key to a successful focus group. Good moderators possess some or all of the following characteristics:[7]

1. Personality—the moderator should have good conversation and people skills. Focus group participants need to feel comfortable discussing the subject matter with this person. The moderator must be comfortable in encouraging comment from quiet respondents and suppressing comments from any dominant participants.

2. Attentive—focus groups usually last 60–120 minutes. The moderator has to pay close attention the entire time and allocate time so that all topics are covered.

3. Professional training—focus group moderators usually have a background in communications, psychology, advertising or marketing research.

4. Organization—the moderator should be prepared to lead the discussion in a logical sequence. A focus group outline is an essential part of this process. The outline is a discussion guide that lists all key discussion points that should be covered by the group. It is a good idea to get input from key decision makers in constructing this outline.

5. Objectivity—the moderator should not let his or her opinion interfere with the interview in any way. A moderator who has a very strong opinion on the subject matter may very well lead the discussion toward a personally desirable outcome. Sometimes, this effect is unintentional. This is why it is often advisable to have an outsider conduct the focus group interview. A good moderator may not even require a great deal of knowledge about the situation to be effective. It is difficult for moderators to be leading when they have no opinion.

6. Listening skills—generally, the less a moderator says the better the focus group. The key is getting the respondents to discuss the issues without having to individually ask each to answer every question. A quiet moderator is less likely to be leading.

The "Research in Action" box tells you what focus groups revealed as important reasons for selecting a family-style restaurant.

Focus groups are used across all business disciplines. For example, focus groups can be instrumental in developing ideas related to supervisory issues including compensation systems and flexible work scheduling.[8] Focus groups also have played a role in developing professional certification programs in finance and accounting.[9]

Politicians also use focus groups. Focus groups are useful in discovering potential issues that can reinforce or build a candidate's image. In the United States, focus groups are used as a rule in Presidential campaigns, in most campaigns for the U.S. Senate and in many statewide elections. They are particularly useful when the public's opinion is very diverse. President Clinton's administration relied on focus groups through his entire term.[10] Tag lines and phrases were developed from focus group sessions that communicated the intended messages effectively. American politicians are not the only ones using focus group research. Australian politicians successfully used input from focus groups to position candidates and policies based on tax issues.[11]

One of the authors was asked to conduct a series of focus groups in seven different metro areas in the United States. The client was a large chain of family-style restaurants that wanted to know what motivated customers to come to a particular restaurant. The information would help management better understand patronage behavior and be used in developing an advertising and promotion campaign. Eleven unique reasons were identified in the focus groups. They are listed as follows:

Reason	Percent of Time Mentioned
Quality of food	88%
Variety of menu items	51%
Expected cost of meal	39%
Convenient locations	34%
Friendly service	31%
Nutritious food	19%
Speed of service	17%
Competent, knowledgeable employees	17%
Atmosphere	15%
Portion size	14%
Special promotions, coupons, and discounts.	9%

Two focus groups were held in each market and a total of 137 individuals participated. How valid are these findings? How can they be used? Can they be generalized to the overall market for family-style restaurants?

In politics and out, however, making decisions based solely on focus group research is risky. Focus groups are discovery-oriented. The group size is very small, therefore the results are less likely to represent those of the population. Sometimes opinions are very dependent upon a particular group's chemistry. Researchers usually recommend two or three focus groups at a minimum to try and find consistent opinions. Therefore, conclusions drawn from focus groups are best tested using another more confirmatory approach. The "Research in Action" box describes two blunders that occurred because decisions were made based only on focus groups.

There are hundreds of research firms specializing in focus group research.[12] Focus group interviews generally require human and physical resources aside from a moderator. A support staff is needed to recruit participants, who are usually paid ($50–$150) for their time and participation. People are needed to coordinate the group and provide basic hospitality. Focus group interviews are usually recorded. A typical focus group room includes a two-way mirror and recording equipment. Focus group sponsors generally observe the interview through the mirror and the entire session is audio taped and/or videotaped. Respondents should be informed about the recording and given an option not to participate should they object. By now it should be no surprise that focus groups are expensive. A typical focus group session costs from $3,500 to $5,000 to conduct, including a fee for analysis and report preparation.

Technological developments are providing additional focus group opportunities. Electronic focus groups are conducted using password-protected Web site bulletin boards.

> **RESEARCH IN ACTION**
>
> **THE AZTEC AND THE CRUISER—A TALE OF TWO "BLUNDERS"**
>
> Businesses sometimes make decisions based solely on an exploratory design. However, this practice increases the risk. It usually occurs in a situation where the need for expediency takes priority over further confirmatory research. The story below illustrates risks associated with this approach.
>
> When a company introduces a new product, there are two ways to go wrong. One, the company can overestimate demand. Second, the company can underestimate demand. Both cause problems but certainly the latter situation is preferable to the former. The Chrysler PT Cruiser suffered from the latter problem. Focus group research suggested it was the kind of design that consumers would either love or hate. Thus, based on the proposition that the car did not have broad appeal, it entered into a niche car strategy. Chrysler developed production capacity for sixty thousand vehicles in the first model year. They took orders for 120,000 vehicles in the first year. Thus, many customers were disappointed in the wait or settled for another vehicle. They are now trying to double production capacity.
>
> Likewise, Pontiac conducted many focus groups discussing the Aztec. Consumers had a lot of positive things to say about the concept. Pontiac was enthused and developed production capacity for eighty thousand vehicles in the first model year. The focus groups failed, however, to fully communicate the product's design. During the first model year, Pontiac sold twenty thousand Aztecs. If you are looking for a deeply discounted vehicle, think Aztec! Research conducted afterwards trying to identify the source of the low sales volume suggests consumers think it is ugly, and not in a cute sort of way as some would say about the PT Cruiser.
>
> Could further confirmatory research have avoided these blunders? Perhaps. Has Chrysler put enough effort into studying the situation to warrant doubling production capacity? It is unclear. The success of this decision depends on new research questions, including, "Will the demand remain high when the novelty wears off or when me-too competitors make it not so novel?"
>
> SOURCE: Kobe, Gerry. 2001. How Focus Groups Failed Aztec, PT Cruiser. *Automotive Industries* 181 (February): 9.

A moderator posts a question and waits for participants to respond. If the group gets off course, or once enough discussion on a topic has been obtained, the moderator will post a new comment. Generally, this process will go on for a week to a month. Electronic focus groups are not seen as a replacement for traditional focus groups. While they are useful in obtaining large quantities of highly elaborate responses, they are even more expensive than a traditional focus group (about $12,000) and they are unable to capture the real-time face-to-face interactions of participants.[13]

Unstructured Interviews   An unstructured interview is conducted without the use of an interview sequence. This allows the researcher to elicit information by engaging the interviewee in free and open discussion on the topic of interest. A particular advantage of this approach is the researcher has the opportunity to explore in-depth issues raised during the interview.

Unstructured interviews are used when research is directed toward an area that is relatively unexplored. By obtaining a deeper understanding of the critical issues involved, the researcher is in a better position to not only better define the research problem, but also to develop a conceptual framework for the research. This will then form the basis for subsequent empirical research to test the ideas, concepts, and hypotheses that emerge.

All large accounting firms have a policy on shredding of documents. One would think such policies would be specific and well thought out. The recent Andersen/Enron situation indicates this is not necessarily true. A regional accounting firm retained one of the authors to conduct unstructured interviews with employees. The purpose of the interviews was to obtain information to assist in updating and improving its document shredding policy. The interviews were conducted individually and anonymity was guaranteed. In-depth interviews were used instead of focus groups because it was anticipated employees would be more open and honest with their comments if interviewed separately instead of in a focus group setting. Information was asked for on how the policy had been applied in the past, if it had worked well, were there situations in which they had any doubts about whether the policy was appropriately applied, how it could be improved, and so forth. Since more than forty individuals had to be interviewed and the responses tabulated, the process took several weeks and a substantial amount of time. But several gaps in the old policy were identified and management felt the outcome, a substantially improved policy, was worth the effort.

The "Research in Action" box provides an example of how a corporate policy on document shredding might be developed. An in-depth semi-structured interviewing approach was used instead of focus groups because it was believed employees would not be as open in their comments in a focus group setting.

Depth Interviews   A depth, or in-depth interview, is an unstructured one-to-one discussion session between a trained interviewer and a respondent. Respondents usually are chosen carefully because they have some specialized insight. For example, a researcher exploring employee turnover might conduct a depth interview with someone who has worked for five different restaurants in a period of two years. Like a focus group, the interviewer first prepares an outline that guides the interview (this is the structured part of an in-depth interview). Also like a focus group, the responses are unstructured. Indeed, a depth interview allows much deeper probing than does a focus group. Probing means that a researcher delves deeply into a response to identify possibly hidden reasons for a particular behavior. The "why, why, why" technique discussed in Chapter 3 is one probing technique.

Depth interview participants usually are more comfortable discussing potentially sensitive topics. For example, employees are far more likely to be candid in discussing their superiors' behaviors in a one-to-one setting than among a dozen coworkers. Some consumer issues also fall into the sensitive category. Consumers may discuss hygiene, financial or sexual preference issues more readily in a depth interview than in a focus group setting. Likewise, executives and top managers are more comfortable in a one-to-one setting. You might imagine that a focus group of product design engineers from Honda, Toyota, GM, Mercedes, and Ford might be a very quiet session.

Like focus groups, depth interviews can be very useful in clarifying concepts. Researchers need an operational definition for something before they can measure it. For example, what does a work climate of *trust and responsibility* mean? Depth interviews proved useful in identifying observable workplace events that employees identified with coworker responsibility. Depth interviews were used with restaurant employees to examine issues such as hiding tips to prevent them from being shared with coworkers and the effects of stress on workplace behavior including food preparation and wholesomeness. Depth interview participants indicated that the "CYA" principal (cover yourself) is associated with low trust in the workplace.

Depth interviews generally are more expensive than focus groups. Since the interviews are one-on-one as opposed to one-on-twelve, fees charged by the interviewer are multiplied. The interviewer may spend twelve hours with only six respondents. Further, since more text is generated, more analysis time is generally required. This adds up to a higher bill. Exhibit 5-3 compares and contrasts depth interviews and focus groups.

Personal versus Telephone Interviews   Personal interviews involve direct face-to-face contact with respondents. Telephone interviews are not face-to-face, but can still be very effective. Telephone interviewing generally is faster and less expensive than personal interviews, but lacks the ability to use visuals and generally respondents will not tolerate as long an interview as in a face-to-face situation. Telephone surveys do facilitate greater control, however, particularly when conducted from a central facility under a supervisor's monitoring.

The objectives of the research can impact the decision on which method of administering questionnaires is best. Exhibit 5-4 summarizes the advantages and disadvantages of the major methods of administering survey questionnaires.

Computer Dialogue   Computer dialogue involves the answering of questions online through the use of PCs. This could be in the form of online interviews or, in its simplest

---

| **EXHIBIT 5-3** | **A COMPARISON OF FOCUS GROUPS AND DEPTH INTERVIEWS** |

Benefits of Exploratory Research	Focus Groups	Depth Interviews
Helping to form hypotheses. Discussion provides clarity of thought aiding in expressing researchable propositions.	★★★★★	★★★★★
Identifying salient attributes of some situation. This might be some important product or job characteristic.	★★★★★	★★★★★
Aiding measurement in future studies by providing an operational definition of some concept.	★★★★★	★★★★★
Identifying usage patterns.	★★★★	★★★
Identifying key sources of difficulties for respondents.	★★★★	★★★★★
Identifying novel ideas.	★★★★★	★★★
Concept testing of new ideas. Present the idea for refining and guessing initial reactions.	★★★★★	★★
Discussing sensitive issues.	☹	★★★★★
Identifying personal problems of respondents.	☹	★★★
Effective in testing hypotheses.	☹	☹
An economical form of exploratory research	☹	☹

NOTE: The number of stars listed indicates how effective a technique is in producing the benefit listed. Five stars = highly effective; fewer stars = less effective. A frown indicates the technique is ineffective in producing a benefit.

form, an emailed questionnaire that facilitates discussion on a one-to-one basis or by a group. The interviewer initiates the contact and requests responses from participants. Individual responses can be identified, categorized, and compiled. Discussion can be carried on between an interviewer and participants either synchronously or asynchronously. Group Systems software such as Lotus Notes (see www.projectrak.com) and Group Vision (see www.groupvision.net) are able to facilitate synchronous discussion. Traditional email is an example of asynchronous capability. Technological advances in both hardware and software are popularizing this approach to obtaining data. It allows for instant data collection and analysis.

SUMMARY

Understand Data Collection Principles and Practices

The data collection method can influence the accuracy and reliability of survey data. Therefore, it is very important to select the correct method. Data collection can be divided into two types: *observation* and *survey methods*. Both methods can be used to capture narrative and/or numeric data using trained personnel and/or technology. Electronic data collection approaches are emerging as one of the most efficient and cost-effective means of collecting data. But traditional methods will continue to have their role long into the future.

EXHIBIT 5-4	ADVANTAGES AND DISADVANTAGES OF METHODS OF ADMINISTERING SURVEY QUESTIONS	
Methods of Administration	**Advantages**	**Disadvantages**
Through the Mail (post) This method involves mailing the questionnaire to predetermined respondents with a cover letter. Generally used when there is a large number of geographically dispersed respondents.	• Wider access and better coverage • Provides anonymity • Relatively low cost • Large sample size • Respondents complete questionnaire at own pace	• Questionnaire must be simple • Low response rate • Points of clarification are not possible • Follow-up of non-response is difficult
In Person This requires face-to-face contact with respondents. Generally, makes use of small samples to canvass opinions and when dealing with sensitive issues.	• Establish empathy and interest in the study • Can probe complex issues • Clarify respondents queries • High response rate	• Expensive in time and cost • May lead to interviewer bias • Difficult to obtain wide access • Relatively small sample size
Over the Telephone This is a form of personal interviewing which is used to obtain information quickly. Generally used to gain access to respondents that are geographically dispersed.	• Provides personal contact • Wide geographic coverage • Easy and quick access • Can be done with the aid of a computer	• Short interview time • Limited to telephone owners • Can be expensive
Electronic This is administered via the intranet and Internet through the use of email. It is becoming the most popular method for collecting data.	• Easy to administer • Low cost • Global reach • Fast capturing of data and analysis	• Loss of anonymity • Can be complex to design and program • Limited to computer users

Describe Differences between Qualitative and Quantitative Data Collection

Qualitative data is usually captured in narrative form and is used to describe human behavior or business phenomena. Quantitative data, on the other hand, is captured through the use of various numeric scales. Qualitative approaches to data collection are frequently used at the exploratory stage of the research process. Their role is to identify and/or refine research problems that may help to formulate and test conceptual frameworks. In contrast, quantitative approaches to data collection are often used when we have well defined research problems or theoretical models. Validation of these concepts and models usually involves the use of data obtained from large-scale questionnaire surveys.

Understand the Differences between Observation and Survey Methods

Data are obtained through observation and/or surveys. Observation data are collected through a systematic approach to recognizing and recording occurrences associated with people, events, and objects. Collection of such data can be achieved through trained observers or through mechanical means like videos, scanning or other electronic methods. Observation data can be both narrative and numeric.

A survey usually involves the collection of large amounts of data through the use of a *self-completion* or *interviewer-administered* questionnaires. Questionnaires can include both closed-ended and opened-ended questions, which yield numeric and narrative data, respectively. In cases where narrative data are obtained, they can be converted to numbers through coding techniques. An example of this is *content analysis.*

Assess the Use of Questionnaires as Instruments for Data Collection

A questionnaire is a means of obtaining data that are not already available in written or electronic form as secondary data, or cannot easily be obtained by observation. An example of data that cannot be obtained readily by observation is feelings or beliefs. Data generated by a questionnaire generally is referred to as primary data.

A questionnaire can be unstructured, semi-structured or highly structured. Irrespective of its structure, a questionnaire must produce accurate and reliable data amenable to statistical analysis using software packages such as SPSS. Key to achieving these objectives is the design and development of the questionnaire.

Appreciate the Role of the Various Interview Methods in Obtaining Data

An interview is the interaction between interviewer and interviewee through face-to-face, telephone or computer dialogue. Interviews are an appropriate means for gathering complex and sensitive information, or where a lot of elaboration is necessary to understand concepts. It is important that an interview be conducted in a relaxed and friendly atmosphere.

The nature of the interview can range from being highly unstructured to highly structured. Highly unstructured interviews do not require an interview schedule and this makes free and open dialogue between interviewer and interviewee possible. On the other hand, a highly structured interview requires an interview schedule of prepared questions to be followed when conducting the interview. In both types of interviews care must be taken to avoid biases and inconsistencies in the data collected.

Focus group interviews and depth interviews are both important discovery-oriented exploratory research tools. Depth interviews are preferable when a respondent may be more open in a private setting as opposed to a group setting. Focus groups are preferable when the group dynamics will not hinder comment. In fact, the group dynamics often encourage discussion.

KEY TERMS

computer dialogue	mail survey	self-completion
content analysis	observation	questionnaire
electronic survey	personal interview	semi-structured interview
ethnographic research	questionnaire	telephone interview
interview		

ETHICAL DILEMMA

Midway through a series of focus groups about the new mobile data package a regional telecommunications company is planning to offer, the research firm tells John Thompson, the product manager that customer response has been overwhelmingly positive. John reported the early feedback to his boss, who is excited because the company needs a new product that can help boost company sales before the end of the year if bonuses are to be paid. In anticipation, John decides to observe the final focus group himself. While observing, John begins to sense that the focus group facilitator is leading the subjects toward favorable responses. He fears the research is flawed but still believes the product will be popular with consumers. He is also aware that if he reschedules the focus groups with a new facilitator he will not have the data his boss needs to make the final decision about releasing the product until the first quarter of next year. If you were John, what would you do? Should John present the focus group findings to his boss without voicing his concerns? Did the researcher act unethically in disclosing the early but incomplete results?

REVIEW QUESTIONS

1. Why would a business researcher want to collect data?
2. What are the main data gathering methods? Comment on their strengths and weaknesses and illustrate their use with examples.
3. What are the advantages and disadvantages of conducting surveys on the Internet?
4. What is the difference between structured and unstructured interviews?
5. What are focus groups and when would the business researcher use them?

DISCUSSION AND APPLICATION ACTIVITIES

1. An organization is experiencing low morale among its employees. Why and how might survey research be used in this situation?

2. What are the main issues that need to be considered in selecting a method of data collection for a survey of opinions about diversity in the workplace?

3. What type of questions would one expect to find on a survey of opinions about business ethics? Illustrate with examples their purpose, wording, and coding. Would the topics in a business ethics survey differ from a survey of political ethics?

4. How would you go about creating a relaxed and friendly atmosphere during an interview? Give examples.

5. Go to the Web site for this book as www.wiley.com/college/hair. Click on the link to "Bar Soap Focus Groups" and review the list of bar soap purchase criteria that was identified in the focus groups. Rank the criteria from most important to least important in deciding which brand of soap to purchase. Now click on "Ranking Answer" to see if your answers are the same as the original sample. Can you think of any criteria that were not identified? If so, send an email to one of the authors of this book to see if they agree. Their email addresses are provided on the Home page of this Web site.

6. How have recent technology developments facilitated data collection?

7. "Bias in data collection cannot be avoided." Give your view on this statement and suggest ways to minimize bias.

8. Critique the following methods of data collection:

   a. A shopping mall places interviewers in the parking lot every Saturday to ask customers their zip code and the two or three stores they came to visit on this shopping trip.

   b. To evaluate the popularity of a new television series, NBC invited people to call a 900 number and vote yes, they would watch it again, or no, they would not watch it again. Each caller was charged $1.50.

   c. A supermarket recently completed a major renovation. To obtain customer reactions, the checkout personnel placed a short questionnaire into each customer's grocery bag while putting the groceries in.

INTERNET EXERCISES

1. Go to www.acnielsen.com and www.infores.com. Prepare a report on what these two companies are saying about their latest scanner-based technology.

2. Use an Internet Web browser such as Lycos, Yahoo, Dogpile, or Google. Conduct a search using the words "data collection." Prepare a report summarizing what you found.

3. Both scholarly and trade publications have documented that the quality of the food served at a restaurant is the major reason people choose to come in the first place, and it is certainly important in deciding to return. But what does "quality" mean? This concept is difficult to be actionable for the restaurant owner and manager because it can mean many things. You perhaps have some ideas about how it could become more

actionable. The results of a series of focus groups conducted by a major restaurant chain can be found on our Web site (www.wiley.com/college/hair). Find the excerpts from these focus groups, review them, and develop an actionable definition of food quality, one that could be used by the restaurant manager to develop strategies and action plans to compete more effectively.

4. Go to the Roper Center Web site, at www.ropercenter.uconn.edu. Identify two articles or studies related to this chapter and prepare a report on what you learned.

5. The U.S. Bureau of Labor Statistics conducts the National Longitudinal Surveys that reports on the current labor force and work history, status and so forth. Go to www.bls.gov and prepare a report summarizing the information available at this Web site and the methods used to collect the data.

6. The Web site for the Princeton University Survey Research Center is located at www.princeton.edu. Go to this Web site and prepare a report summarizing the types of information located on there and why it might be of interest to business researchers.

7. The U.S. Mint has a Web site at www.usmint.gov that includes a survey for visitors to the Web site to complete. Take the survey and prepare a report on the purpose of the survey and what you learned.

NOTES

1. Remenyi, Dan, Brian Williams, Arthur Money and Ethne Swartz. 1998. *Doing Research in Business and Management.* Sage: London.
2. Woodside, Arch G. and Elizabeth J. Wilson. 1995. Applying Long Interview in Direct Marketing Ressearch, *Journal of Direct Marketing Research,* 9(1), 37–65.
3. Khermouch, Gary. 2001. Consumers in the Mist. *Businessweek* 3721 (2/26): 92–93.
4. Hunt, William. 1995. Getting the Word on Deception. *Security Management* 39 (June): 26–27.
5. Robin, Donald P., M. FGialourakis, F. David and T.E. Moritz. 1989. A Different Look at Codes of Ethics, Business Horizons, 32 (1), 66–73; Farrell, Brian J. and Deirdre M. Cobin. 1996. A Content Analysis of Codes of Ethics in Australian Enterprises, Journal of Managerial Psychology, 11(1), 37–56.
6. Lawrence, Jennifer and Paul Berger. 1999. Let's Hold a Focus Group. *Direct Marketing* 61 (Dec.): 40–44. Greenbaum, Thomas L. 1993. *The Handbook of Focus Group Research.* Lexington: New York.
7. Maynard, Michael L. and Charles R. Taylor. 1999. Girlish Images Across Cultures: Analyzing Japanese versusU.S. Seventeen Magazine Ads, Journal of Advertising, 28 (Spring), 39–49.
8. Lussier, Robert N. 1995. Flexible Work Arrangement from Policy to Implementation. *Supervision* 56 (September): 10.
9. Internal Auditor. 1997. EAR Focus Groups Targer ISO 14000. 54 (June): 8.
10. Hunter, Pamela. 2000. Using Focus Groups In Campaigns: A Caution. *Campaigns and Elections* 21 (August): 38–41.
11. Walsh, Max. 1999. Focus Groups Set a New Agenda. *Bulletin with Newsweek* 117 (2/9): 7.
12. See *The Marketing News* 36 (March 4) for a directory of focus group firms and facilities. Also go to www.quirks.com.
13. James, Dana. 2002. This Bulletin Just In: Online Research Technique Proving Invaluable. *Marketing News* 36 (March 4): 45–46.

CHAPTER 6

Measurement and Scaling

Learning Objectives

- Understand the role of concepts in business research.
- Explain the notion of measurement.
- Provide an overview of the types of measurement scales.
- Distinguish between reliability and validity.

INTRODUCTION

Measurement is an important issue in business research. We must correctly measure the concepts we are examining. Otherwise, our interpretations and conclusions will not be accurate. To ensure the accuracy of our findings, we must consider how we measure as well as whether our measures are valid and reliable.

Measurement is a common occurrence for most people. College entrance examinations are measuring devices. So are employment tests. While we are in college, exams measure our achievement. Similarly, quarterly and annual reviews at work measure our progress. In a group setting, measurement is involved if we count the number of individuals, classify them as either male or female, or judge them as introverted or extroverted. Similarly, when we purchase auto insurance or take an exam to get a driver's license, measurement is involved. These are only a few examples of measurement in our everyday lives. In most instances we take the measurement process for granted. We seldom think about how we measure and the accuracy of the measurement. This chapter examines some of the more important issues we need to be aware of in measurement.

WHAT IS A CONCEPT?

A **concept** is a generic idea formed in the mind. The idea is a combination of a number of similar characteristics of the concept. The characteristics are the variables that collectively define the concept and make measurement of the concept possible. For example, the variables listed below were used to measure the concept of customer interaction.[1]

- This customer was easy to talk with.
- This customer genuinely enjoyed my helping her.
- This customer likes to talk to people.
- This customer was interested in socializing.
- This customer was friendly.
- This customer tried to establish a personal relationship.
- This customer seemed interested in me, not only as a salesperson, but also as a person.

By obtaining scores on each of the individual variables, you can measure the overall concept of customer interaction. The individual scores are then combined into a single score, according to a predefined set of rules. The resultant score is often referred to as a scale, an index or a summated rating. In the previous example of customer interaction, the individual variables were scored using a 5-point scale, with 1 = Strongly Disagree and 5 = Strongly Agree.

Suppose the research objective is to identify the concepts associated with a theory of restaurant satisfaction. The researcher is likely to review the literature on satisfaction, conduct both formal and informal interviews, and then draw on his or her own experiences to identify characteristics (variables) like quality of food, quality of service, and value for money as important components of a conceptual model of restaurant satisfaction. Logical integration of these characteristics then provides a theoretical framework and/or a conceptual model, which can facilitate empirical investigation of the concept of restaurant satisfaction.

MEASUREMENT IN BUSINESS RESEARCH

Measurement is fundamental to business research. To understand business research, or really any concept, we must be able to measure it. Without measurement, it is difficult, if not impossible, to comment on business behavior or business phenomena. This is because we subconsciously measure something when we say something about it. For example, if we buy an ice cream cone and say it tastes good, we are measuring. We are saying this tastes good compared to other flavors we have tasted previously. Similarly, if we say an employee is lazy, irresponsible, or uncooperative, we are measuring.

Managers are interested in measuring many aspects of business. Supervisors measure employee performance, motivation, turnover, and similar indices. Accountants measure profits and losses, assets and liabilities, depreciation, etc. Marketing managers measure awareness of a particular store or restaurant, favorable or unfavorable perceptions of various characteristics such as service quality, portion size or food taste, brand preference, and so on. The more effectively managers measure these business aspects, the better their decisions. The "Research in Action" box about the Gallup Organization provides an excellent example of how measurement has been used in American business.

MEASUREMENT DIFFICULTIES

When we think of measurement, most of us think in terms of our own experiences. How fast am I driving or how high is that airplane flying? Similarly, how much do I weigh or how tall am I? Measurement of things like this is easy because these things are not very complex. It is easy to use a ruler or set of scales to measure height or weight. In contrast, when we attempt to measure attitudes, opinions or perceptions it is much more difficult. Often we do not have precise definitions of concepts, such as satisfaction. Moreover, frequently we have to develop new scales (questions) to measure a concept because we do not have tools like rulers or speedometers to measure concepts precisely.

In business research we work with concepts that can range from being simple and concrete in nature to those that are extremely complex and abstract. Therefore, one of the first things we have to do is develop precise definitions of the concepts we examine in our research, thereby ensuring there is no ambiguity in their interpretation. In this book we use the terms concept and construct interchangeably. A concept is a mental abstraction or idea formed by the perception of some phenomena. Examples of concepts in business include job satisfaction, job commitment, brand awareness, brand loyalty, service quality, image, risk, channel conflict, empathy, and so on.

Consider concepts such as "age" and "income" as opposed to "satisfaction" and "competence of employees." For "age" and "income" there will, generally speaking, be agreement as to their definition. But for "satisfaction" and "competence of employees" there is unlikely to be a common interpretation of their meaning. The more complex and abstract the concept is, the more we need to provide an explicit definition.

Once we have defined the concepts, we still must be sure we measure them properly. The measurement process involves specifying the variables that serve as proxies for the concepts (constructs). A proxy is a variable that represents a single component of a larger

---

RESEARCH IN ACTION

BUSINESSES GET AN ATTITUDE ADJUSTMENT FROM GALLUP

For over seventy years, The Gallup Organization (www.gallup.com)——best known for its public opinion polling——has studied human nature and behavior and then converted its findings into integrated management solutions for companies around the world. Based on studies measuring how employee attitudes relate to performance, Gallup has observed that organizations with high performance levels also had high levels of employee engagement—workers who feel fully involved in their work. Engaged employees were more productive, made more money for the company, and stayed longer. The findings also demonstrated that customers who interacted with engaged employees returned more often, purchased more, were more loyal, and paid higher prices.

When Gallup began researching employee engagement, they analyzed psychometric, attitudinal, and financial data from more than 10,885 work units in 51 organizations and 23 industries. From the data gathered, Gallup identified twelve questions that measure employee engagement and link directly to critical performance outcomes, including productivity, employee retention, customer retention, safety, and profitability. These questions are now known as the Gallup Q12 (see following).

According to Gallup's data, the working population falls into three categories: people who are engaged (loyal *and* productive), those who are not engaged (just putting in time), and those who are actively disengaged (unhappy and spreading their discontent). Their research shows that the U.S. working population is 26 percent engaged, 55 percent not engaged, and 19 percent actively disengaged. The trick for an organization is to improve the ratio of engaged to actively disengaged workers. Gallup suggests that companies should survey their workforce with Q12 frequently (every six months) to find out which work units are engaged and which are not. Since individual workers are key to a more productive workplace, companies need to be vigilant about the quality of the employee's work life. Gallup found the most "engaged" workplaces (those in the top 25 percent of Q12 scores) were 50 percent more likely to have lower staff turnover, 56 percent more likely to have higher-than-average customer loyalty, 38 percent more likely to have above-average productivity, and 27 percent more likely to report higher profitability.

Q12: The Twelve Dimensions of a Great Workplace

Gallup defines a fully engaged employee as "one who can answer all the questions in the Gallup Q12 with a strong affirmative." The Q12 questions were identified through extensive research that correlates employee attitudes to five outcome measures: employee retention, productivity, customer satisfaction/engagement, safety, and profitability.

What is a great workplace?

- Item 1. I know what is expected of me at work.
- Item 2. I have the materials and equipment I need to do my work right.
- Item 3. At work, I have the opportunity to do what I do best every day.
- Item 4. In the last seven days, I have received recognition or praise for doing good work.
- Item 5. My supervisor, or someone at work, seems to care about me as a person.
- Item 6. There is someone at work who encourages my development.
- Item 7. At work, my opinions seem to count.
- Item 8. The mission or purpose of my company makes me feel my job is important.
- Item 9. My fellow employees are committed to doing quality work.
- Item 10. I have a best friend at work.
- Item 11. In the last six months, someone at work has talked to me about my progress.
- Item 12. This last year, I have had opportunities at work to learn and grow.

SOURCE: www.gallup.com; LaBarre, Polly. 2001. Marcus Buckingham Thinks Your Boss Has an Attitude Problem. *Fast Company* (August): 88.

concept and, taken together, several proxies are said to measure a concept. Proxies also are referred to in business research as indicator variables. Identification of proxy variables (indicators) is very important because the variables provide the numerical scores used to measure concepts in quantitative terms. The "Research in Action" box shows examples of the proxy variables for several concepts—source credibility, financial and performance risks, and pricing perceptions.

Variables that are relatively concrete in nature, such as gender, age, height, household income, food prices, and even social class, are easy to define and thus can be measured in an objective and fairly precise manner through observation, questioning or the use of a "calibrated" instrument, such as a ruler. The following examples illustrate how we might measure some of the more objective measures.

Gender

Suppose we need to know the gender of a customer. There is really no need for a definition of gender as people have a clear understanding of the concept. We determine the gender of a person either by observation or in a survey by including a question asking the respondent to state their gender. Thus, a simple concept like gender can be measured without error, assuming it is recorded correctly. The measurement involves assigning numerical scores to the outcome of the gender variable, such as 1 for male and 0 for female. Note the assignment of numbers is arbitrary and could just as easily be 1 for female and 0 for male.

Dining Out Expenditures

Now consider having to measure the average weekly eating out expenditures of a family. Again, the concept is easily understood and not in need of an explicit definition. To measure this concept, all we need to do is include a question in our survey that asks the respondent to state his or her family's average weekly expenditure on eating out. In this case, while the respondent will be clear as to what is being asked, he or she is likely to find it difficult to give a very precise answer. In this case measurement of the variable can be achieved by assigning a number on a continuum with a lower limit of 0. There still will be some error because the individual will be responding based on their recall of a previous period (assuming they did not keep a record of their expenditures). But ideally the error will be minimal because the concept is easily understood.

Total Family Wealth

Contrast the examples above on gender and dining out expenditures with the concept of "total family wealth." It is highly unlikely there is a common understanding of the concept of "total family wealth." The understanding will depend upon how well we define the concept. The definition can include *tangible variables* like cash, property, stocks and bonds, and even cars as well as *intangible variables* like education, health, and so on. In this case, a definition of the concept "total family wealth" will be complex, incorporating a combination of some or all of the variables considered as being manifestations or indicators of total family wealth. Further, measurement of the concept will involve the use of a series of questions to represent the variables that make up the concept. Then, from each participant in a survey, a numerical response to each of the questions is obtained. An overall measure of the concept usually is determined by combining the individual scores either by calculating

RESEARCH IN ACTION

EXAMPLES OF PROXY VARIABLES FOR CONCEPTS

Business researchers use proxy (indicator) variables to help them measure concepts or constructs for their research. The examples used here are typical of a wide variety of business research studies. Excerpts from the study are reported but the entire scale can be viewed in the original article.

Source Credibility Check

A six-item, seven-point scale was used. Respondents were asked to rate the spokesperson on each of the following:

- Trustworthy—Not Trustworthy
- Open-minded—Not Open-minded
- Good—Bad
- Expert—Not Expert
- Experienced—Not Experienced
- Trained—Untrained

Perceived Financial Risk

A three-item, seven-point scale was used. Respondents were asked:

- Considering the potential investment involved, for you to purchase the Hito VCR would be:
    Not risky at all—Very risky

- I think the purchase of the Hito brand VCR would lead to financial risk for me because of the possibility of such things as higher maintenance and/or repair costs:
    Improbable—Very probable

- Given the potential financial expenses associated with purchasing the Hito brand VCR, how much overall financial risk is associated with purchasing the Hito brand VCR?
    Very little risk—Substantial risk

Perceived Performance Risk

A three-item, seven-point scale was used. Respondents were asked:

- How confident are you that the Hito brand VCR will perform as described?
    Very confident—Not confident at all

- How certain are you that the Hito brand VCR will work satisfactorily?
    Certain—Uncertain

- Do you feel that the Hito brand VCR will perform the functions that were described in the advertisement?
    Do feel sure—Do not feel sure

Message Framing Check

Respondents were provided with an aided-recall question:

- How did the spokesperson in the advertisement rate most of the features of the Hito VCR?
            Hito rated superior to Toshiba ___
            Toshiba rated superior to Hito ___

(continued)

RESEARCH IN ACTION

EXAMPLES OF PROXY VARIABLES FOR CONCEPTS (CONTINUED)

Price Check

Respondents were asked the following using a seven-point scale.

- The price of the Hito VCR is:

    Very high—Very low

SOURCE: Grewal, D., J. Gotlieb, and H. Marmorstein. 1994. The Moderating Effects of Message Framing and Source Credibility on the Price-Perceived Risk Relationship. *Journal of Consumer Research* 21 (June): 145–153.

their sum or their average. The amount of error associated with this question will depend upon how precise the researcher was in defining the concept and its individual variables.

The above examples demonstrate the definitional and measurement problems confronting business researchers. Concepts such as gender and expenditure, for example, are easily defined and objectively measured in absolute terms. In contrast, concepts that are complex and abstract in nature, for example, "wealth," "satisfaction," "organizational commitment," and "image" are relatively difficult to define and measure objectively. To measure such concepts, researchers are likely to use subjective measures that include perceptions, attitudes, beliefs, opinions, and values. In the next section we describe how complex concepts like the above can be measured.

HOW WE MEASURE CONCEPTS

Measurement involves assigning numbers to a variable according to certain rules. The assigned numbers must reflect the characteristics of the phenomenon being measured. For example, if we are measuring how important food quality is in the selection of a restaurant we might say the number 5 represents very important and the number 0 represents not important at all. In this case, the "rule" is a higher number means something is relatively more important and a lower number means it is relatively unimportant.

There are four levels of measurement available to the researcher. The levels determine the sophistication of the measurement employed. The researcher must decide on the level of measurement to be used before the research is conducted. Such a decision also is influenced by the nature of the concept. For example, the respondent must be willing and able to provide information at the level sought. This may not be true if the researcher is asking questions about sensitive issues like sexual orientation, birth control use, medical condition, or even income. Similarly, if data is obtained by observation, the way the variable can be measured will depend on the situational context and the ability of the observer to accurately record the observed behavior. For example, if we are measuring purchases online this is very easy because all the information is collected from transactions online. Similarly, measurement of scanner data at a store checkout counter is easy because the information is automatically collected and stored in a computer database. On the other hand, if we watch people walk out of a movie theatre and try to observe whether or not they enjoyed the movie we have more difficulty. It is much more difficult to accurately measure a quality such as enjoyment via observation.

As you may recall, the business consultant hired by Phil Samouel recommended an employee survey as well as a customer survey. It would be very difficult, if not impossible, to interview Gino's employees because he would not permit it. Therefore, the employee survey is based on a sample of Samouel's employees. The employee survey questionnaire is shown in Exhibit 6-1 on page 152. We use the restaurant surveys to illustrate several points on measurement and questionnaire design in this chapter and in Chapter 7.

Measurement is achieved through the use of scales. A *scale* is a measurement tool that can be discrete or continuous. If it is discrete it can measure only the direction of the response. For example, a yes/no scale is discrete and only measures direction—either yes or no. Other examples of a discrete scale might measure whether an employee agrees or disagrees with a supervisor or company policy, or likes or dislikes a particular product or service. In contrast, when scales are continuous they not only measure direction, but intensity as well. For example, in addition to measuring agree/disagree, a continuous scale can measure the intensity of agreement, such as strongly agree or somewhat agree. Furthermore, the intensity of the scale can vary with a 3-point scale measuring little intensity while a 10-point scale provides the opportunity for measuring a great deal of respondent variation in intensity of feeling.

The four levels of measurement are represented by different types of scales: nominal, ordinal, interval, and ratio. Variables measured at the nominal or ordinal level are discrete and referred to as either categorical or nonmetric. Variables measured at the interval or ratio level are continuous and referred to as either quantitative or metric. In the following paragraphs we discuss the different measurement scales in more detail.

NOMINAL SCALE

A **nominal scale** uses numbers as labels to identify and classify objects, individuals. or events. For example, a basketball player is assigned a number and this is a nominal scale. When we use a nominal scale, each number is given to only one type of object (individual). Numbers used in this manner serve as a label to identify the basketball players. In business research, nominal scales are used to identify individuals, job titles or positions, brands, stores, and other objects. To illustrate this point consider the following example:

A survey of diners poses the following question:

Are you happy with the service at Samouel's Greek Cuisine?   Yes/No

In this case the restaurant is the *object* and the measured characteristic is *happiness with the service*. The *predetermined categories* are "happy" or "not happy" as reflected by the nominal scale with two discrete scale points—yes or no. In this case each respondent can be placed in one of the two categories—"yes I am happy" or "no I am not happy." The Samouel's employee survey shown in Exhibit 6-1 has two nominal questions—X_{18} and X_{19}—type of work and gender, respectively.

Nominal scales are not limited to just two categories. For example, we may characterize the restaurant according to ownership type—sole ownership, partnership or corporation. Similarly, we might measure occupation with a nominal scale using the categories teacher, banker, doctor, lawyer, and so forth. A requirement for a nominal scale is that its categories are mutually exclusive and exhaustive of all possibilities. This means each category must be different (no overlap) and all possible categories must be included.

To ensure all possible categories are considered, researchers typically use an "Other" category. But care must be taken to ensure that not too many respondents choose the "Other" category. More than 15 percent response to an "Other" category usually is considered too high. In such cases we must learn more about why individuals are choosing the "Other" category. For example, it is typical to indicate "Please Specify _____" beside the "Other"

EXHIBIT 6-1 **THE SAMOUEL'S EMPLOYEE QUESTIONNAIRE**

SCREENING AND RAPPORT QUESTIONS

Hello. My name is ____ and I work for AdMark International, a business research firm. As you know, Phil Samouel has hired my company to conduct a survey of his employees to better understand the work environment, and suggest improvements as needed. The survey will only take a few minutes and it will be very helpful to management in ensuring the work environment meets both employee and company needs. All of your answers will be kept strictly confidential. In fact, once the questionnaires are completed they will be taken to my office and kept there.

1. Are you currently an employee of Samouel's restaurant?   __ **Yes**   __ **No**
2. Do you have any questions before you take the survey?   __ **Yes**   __ **No**

    If they are currently employed by Samouel's restaurant and do not have any questions, hand them the survey and ask them to complete it. Tell them to ask you if there is any thing they do not understand.

WORK ENVIRONMENT SURVEY

Please read all questions carefully. If you do not understand a question, ask the interviewer to help you.

Section 1: Perceptions Measures

Listed below is a series of statements that could be used to describe Samouel's Greek Cuisine restaurant. Using a scale from 1 to 7, with 7 being "Strongly Agree" and 1 being "Strongly Disagree," to what extent do you agree or disagree that each statement describes your work environment at Samouel's:

	Strongly Disagree						Strongly Agree
1. I am paid fairly for the work I do.	1	2	3	4	5	6	7
2. I am doing the kind of work I want.	1	2	3	4	5	6	7
3. My supervisor gives credit and praise for work well done.	1	2	3	4	5	6	7
4. There is a lot of cooperation among the members of my work group.	1	2	3	4	5	6	7
5. My job allows me to learn new skills	1	2	3	4	5	6	7
6. My supervisor recognizes my potential.	1	2	3	4	5	6	7
7. My work gives me a sense of accomplishment.	1	2	3	4	5	6	7
8. My immediate work group functions as a team.	1	2	3	4	5	6	7
9. My pay reflects the effort I put into doing my work.	1	2	3	4	5	6	7
10. My supervisor is friendly and helpful.	1	2	3	4	5	6	7
11. The members of my work group have the skills and/or training to do their job well.	1	2	3	4	5	6	7
12. The benefits I receive are reasonable.	1	2	3	4	5	6	7

(continued)

---

category. We can then determine how individuals are responding and create another category to represent the responses that make up a large portion of the other responses.

Nominal scales are the lowest level of measurement and therefore provide data that is relatively low in precision. As a consequence, statistical analysis of the data is correspondingly low in sophistication. Data analysis is restricted, therefore, to counts of the number of responses in each category, calculation of the mode or percentage for a particular question, and use of the Chi-square statistic.

ORDINAL SCALE

An **ordinal scale** is a ranking scale. It places objects into a predetermined category that is rank-ordered according to some criterion such as preference, age, income group, importance,

EXHIBIT 6-1 THE SAMOUEL'S EMPLOYEE QUESTIONNAIRE (CONTINUED)

Section 2: Relationship Measures

Please indicate your view on each of the following questions:	Strongly Disagree						Strongly Agree
13. I have a sense of loyalty to Samouel's Restaurant.	1	2	3	4	5	6	7
14. I am willing to put in a great deal of effort beyond that normally expected to help Samouel's restaurant to be successful.	1	2	3	4	5	6	7
15. I am proud to tell others that I work for Samouel's restaurant.	1	2	3	4	5	6	7

16. How likely are you to search for another job in the next
six months

7 = Extremely Likely
6 = Very Likely
5 = Somewhat Likely
4 = Neither—about 50-50
3 = Somewhat Unlikely
2 = Very Unlikely
1 = Extremely Unlikely

17. How long have you been an employee of Samouel's restaurant?

1 = Less than one year
2 = One year to three years
3 = More than three years

Section 3: Classification Questions

Please indicate the number that classifies you best.

18. Your work type
   0 Full-Time
   1 Part-Time

19. Your gender
   0 Male
   1 Female

20. Your age in years
   1 18–25
   2 26–34
   3 35–49
   4 50–59
   5 60 and older

Note: Employee performance was done separately by Phil Samouel and recorded in database by the researcher. See Appendix 1-B

21. Your Performance
   1 Very low performance
   2 Somewhat low performance
   3 Average performance
   4 Somewhat high performance
   5 Very high performer

Thank you very much for your help. Please give your questionnaire to the interviewer.

---

etc. This scale enables the researcher to determine if an object has more or less of a characteristic than some other object. But it does not enable the researcher to determine how much more or less of the characteristic an object has. The following example illustrates this point.

A survey of diners poses the following question:

> Regarding your visits to restaurants in the last month, please rank the following attributes from 1 to 4, with 4 being the most important reason for selecting the restaurant and 1 being the least important. Please ensure no ties.

Food quality   [   ]
Atmosphere   [   ]
Prices   [   ]
Employees   [   ]

If we tabulated the results of the survey of restaurant selection factors and found that 40 percent of the respondents assigned a 4 to food quality, 30 percent a 4 to atmosphere, 20 percent a 4 to prices, and 10 percent a 4 to employees, then we would know that, relatively speaking, food quality is the most important reason, followed by atmosphere, prices, and employees. Thus, employees would be the least important reason for selecting a restaurant. This same question is used in the Samouel's and Gino's customer survey shown in Chapter 7.

The points on an ordinal scale do not indicate equal distance between the rankings. For example, the difference between a ranking of 3 and 4 is not necessarily the same as the difference between a ranking of 1 and 2. But we do know that a ranking of 4 is better than 3, just not how much better. In summary, ordinal scales allow entities to be placed into groups that are ordered.

A higher level of analysis is possible with ordinal data than is possible with nominal data. We can now calculate the median as well as percentages. We also can use Spearman rank-order correlation statistics.

INTERVAL SCALE

An **interval scale** uses numbers to rate objects or events so that the distances between the numbers are equal. Thus, with an interval scale, differences between points on the scale can be interpreted and compared meaningfully. The difference between a rating of 3 and 4 is the same as the difference between a rating of 1 and 2. An interval scale has all the qualities of nominal and ordinal scales, plus the differences between the scale points is considered to be equal. Therefore, in addition you can compare the differences between objects.

With an interval scale the location of the zero point is not fixed. Both the zero point and the units of measurement are arbitrary. The temperature scale is frequently mentioned as an example of an interval scale. For the Centigrade scale, a 1° C increase in temperature has the same meaning anywhere on the scale but it is not true to state that 2° C is twice as hot as 1° C. The explanation for not being able to state that 2° C is twice as hot as 1° C is that the origin or zero point for the centigrade scale is arbitrarily set at 0° C. When researchers use interval scales in business, they attempt to measure concepts such as attitudes, perceptions, feelings, opinions, and values through the use of so-called rating scales. Rating scales typically involve the use of statements on a questionnaire accompanied by pre-coded categories, one of which is selected by the respondent to indicate the extent of their agreement or disagreement with a given statement. To illustrate the use of rating scales, consider the following typical statement on a questionnaire:

> Please indicate the extent of your agreement or disagreement with the following statement by circling the appropriate number.

	Strongly Disagree	Disagree	Neither Agree nor Disagree	Agree	Strongly Agree
Samouel's restaurant is a fun place to go.	1	2	3	4	5

Strictly speaking, the above rating scale is an ordinal scale. It has become customary in business research, however, to treat the scale as if it were interval. Empirical evidence that people treat the intervals between points on such scales as being equal in magnitude provides justification for treating them as measures on an interval scale. To further illustrate this point, let's consider the following responses:

Response 1:

	Strongly Disagree	Disagree	Neither Agree nor Disagree	Agree	Strongly Agree
Samouel's restaurant is a fun place to go.	(1)	2	3	4	5

Response 2:

	Strongly Disagree	Disagree	Neither Agree nor Disagree	Agree	Strongly Agree
Samouel's restaurant is a fun place to go.	1	(2)	3	4	5

Response 3:

	Strongly Disagree	Disagree	Neither Agree nor Disagree	Agree	Strongly Agree
Samouel's restaurant is a fun place to go.	1	2	(3)	4	5

First, the responses can be ordered in terms of strength of agreement. Response 1 strongly disagrees, Response 2 disagrees, and Response 3 neither agrees nor disagrees. Second, we observe that respondent 1 is one unit away from respondent 2, who in turn is one unit away from respondent 3. Also, respondent 3 is two units away from respondent 1. Third, we cannot conclude the rating point 2 is twice the intensity of rating point 1 in terms of strength of agreement. Similarly we cannot conclude that the strength of agreement of respondent 3 is three times that of respondent 1. All we can conclude is that respondent 1 disagrees with the statement by two units more than respondent 3.

In summary, the numbers on an interval scale possess all the properties of nominal and ordinal scales and also allow for objects (respondents) to be compared in terms of their differences on the scale. When constructing rating scales, the researcher arbitrarily chooses the origin or anchor point of the scale. In the preceding example the scale ranged from 1 to 5. But it could just as easily have ranged from 0 to 4. Moreover, it was a 5-point scale but it also could have been a 7-point or 10-point scale.

The Samouel's employee survey questionnaire has several interval scales. First, all twelve statements that represent the work environment perceptions are measured using a 7-point Likert-type interval scale. Similarly, the questions that measure organizational commitment to Samouel's restaurant ($X_{13} - X_{15}$) are considered interval scales.

Interval scales include the properties of both nominal and ordinal scales. Therefore, data obtained using an interval scale are amenable to the same calculations as the earlier mentioned scales but also can handle more sophisticated calculations such as the mean, standard deviation, and Pearson's product-moment correlation coefficient.

RATIO SCALE

A **ratio scale** provides the highest level of measurement. A distinguishing characteristic of a ratio scale is that it possesses a unique origin or zero point, which makes it possible to compute ratios of points on the scale. The bathroom scale or other common weighing machines are examples of ratio scales because they have absolute zero points. When comparing one point to another, for example, you can say that a 200-pound person is twice as heavy as a 100-pound person. The following example is a ratio scale as it might be used in business research. Consider the question:

How many people are there in your household?

A response of 1 to the question can only be interpreted in one way. Namely, that there is only one person in the household. On the other hand, if we compare two responses, e.g., a response of 2 with a response of 4, we can conclude that the numbers in the household are 2 and 4, respectively. Further, we can state that the first household is smaller than the second household by two people. Finally, we can compute the ratio, $(4/2) = 2$, and conclude that the second household is twice the size of the first. Ratio scales possess all the properties of the other scales plus an absolute zero point. In terms of statistics, we can compute the coefficient of variation as well as the standard deviation and Pearson's product-moment correlation.

METRIC AND NONMETRIC SCALES

Broadly speaking, there are two types of scales—metric and nonmetric. **Metric scales** often are referred to as quantitative and nonmetric as qualitative. Nominal and ordinal scales are nonmetric and interval and ratio scales are metric. Business researchers use several types of metric and nonmetric scales. Exhibit 6-2 lists the various types of metric and nonmetric scales that are most frequently used in business research.

Metric Scales

We describe each of the types of metric scales and give examples in the following paragraphs.

Summated Ratings Scale   A **summated ratings scale** attempts to measure attitudes or opinions, typically using a 5-point or 7-point scale to assess the strength of agreement about a group of statements. For each point on the scale you develop a label to express the intensity of the respondent's feelings. There are several statements that typically all relate to a single concept, such as opinions about a company or product. When you sum the scales for all the statements, it is referred to as a summated ratings scale. When you use the scale individually, it is referred to as a **Likert scale.** An example of a Likert scale is:

When I hear about a new restaurant, I eat there to see what it is like.

Strongly Disagree	Disagree	Neither Agree nor Disagree	Agree	Strongly Agree
1	2	3	4	5

A 7-point Likert scale also can be used, as well as a 3-point scale. The more points you use, the more precision you get on the extent of the agreement or disagreement with a statement. An example of a 7-point scale is:

Gino's Italian Ristorante has a wide variety of menu choices.

Strongly Agree	Agree Somewhat	Agree Slightly	Neither Agree nor Disagree	Disagree Slightly	Disagree Somewhat	Strongly Disagree
1	2	3	4	5	6	7

Likert-type scales also are used to measure other concepts in business research such as importance or intentions. Examples of intentions and importance measures using Likert-type scales are shown below:

How likely are you to look for another job in the next six months?

Very Unlikely	Somewhat Unlikely	Neither Likely nor Unlikely	Somewhat Likely	Very Likely
1	2	3	4	5

How important are credit terms in selecting a vendor to do business with?

Very Unimportant	Somewhat Unimportant	Neither Important nor Unimportant	Somewhat Important	Very Important
1	2	3	4	5

Question X_{16} on the Samouel's employee questionnaire is an example of this type of scale, but it uses a 7-point scale instead of a 5-point scale.

EXHIBIT 6-2 TYPES OF METRIC AND NONMETRIC SCALES

Metric
• Summated Ratings (Likert)
• Numerical Scales
• Semantic Differential
• Graphic Ratings

Nonmetric
• Categorical
• Rank Order
• Sorting
• Constant Sum
• Paired Comparison

Numerical Scales   **Numerical scales** have numbers as response options rather than verbal descriptions. The numbers correspond with categories (response options). For example, if there are seven response positions the scale is called a 7-point numerical scale. This type of scale can be used to assess the level of agreement or disagreement. But it often is used to measure other concepts, such as important/unimportant, essential/not essential, likely/unlikely, satisfied/dissatisfied, and so on. An example follows of the phrasing with an important/not at all important question:

Using a 10-point scale, where 1 is not at all important and 10 is very important, how important is _____ in your decision to do business with a particular vendor?

You would fill in the blank with an attribute, such as reliable delivery, product quality, complaint resolution, competitive pricing, credit terms, and so forth.

Numerical scales frequently are used to measure behavioral intentions. Typical concepts examined with this type of scale include intention to buy, likelihood of seeking additional information, likelihood of seeking another job (turnover), likelihood of visiting a particular Web site, probability of investing in a particular stock, and so forth. Scales that measure behavioral components of an individual's attitudes ask about a respondent's likelihood or intention to perform some future action.

We noted earlier that Likert-type scales can be used to measure intentions and/or likelihood. A method other than Likert-type or numerical scores for measuring likelihood uses descriptive phrases such as the following examples:

Example 1:

How likely is it that you will pursue your MBA in the next three years?

__ I definitely will pursue my MBA in the next three years.
__ I probably will pursue my MBA in the next three years.
__ I might pursue my MBA in the next three years.
__ I probably will not pursue my MBA in the next three years.
__ I definitely will not pursue my MBA in the next three years.

Example 2:

How likely is it that you will look for another job in the next six months?

__ Extremely Likely
__ Very Likely
__ Somewhat Likely
__ Neither–about a 50–50 chance
__ Somewhat Unlikely
__ Very Unlikely
__ Extremely Unlikely

The choice of a particular method of measuring behavioral concepts depends upon the nature of the group being measured and the researchers preference. All of the approaches are considered acceptable. An example of how a numerical scale has been used in business research is reported in the "Research in Action" box.

Semantic Differential Scale   A **semantic differential scale** is another approach that measures attitudes. Both 5-point and 7-point scales are used depending on the level of precision desired and the education level of the targeted population. The distinguishing feature of semantic differential scales is the use of bipolar end points (or anchors) with the intermediate points typically numbered. The end points are chosen to describe individuals, objects or events with opposite adjectives or adverbs. Respondents are asked to check which space between a set of bipolar adjectives or phrases best describes their feelings toward the stimulus object. An example of how you might use the semantic differential to rate a supervisor follows.

Three researchers from Texas A&M University developed a model of service quality that has been used extensively in many industries. Its initial applications were in consumer studies but more recently it is being used in business-to-business studies. Examples follow of the approach these researchers suggested could be used to measure customer expectations using a telephone interviewing approach:

Instructions

Please think of the kind of company that would deliver excellent service quality—the kind of company with which customers would be pleased to do business. Please indicate the extent to which you think such a company would possess the characteristic described by each statement. If you feel a characteristic is "not at all essential" for an excellent company, then say the number 1 for the statement. If you feel a characteristic is "absolutely essential" for excellent companies, say 7. If your feelings are less strong, give me one of the numbers between 1 and 7. There are no right or wrong answers—all we are interested in is a number that truly reflects your feelings regarding companies that deliver excellent service quality to their customers.

1. When customers have a problem, an excellent company will show a sincere interest in solving it. Would you say this characteristic is not at all essential, absolutely essential, or somewhere in between? Remember, a 1 is not at all essential, a 7 is absolutely essential, or you could select a number anywhere in between 1 and 7 that you feel represents your feelings about excellent companies. ____
2. Employees of excellent companies will give prompt service to customers. ____
3. Excellent companies will have the customers' best interests at heart. ____
4. Employees of excellent companies will have the knowledge to answer customer questions. ____
5. Excellent companies will perform services right the first time. ____
6. Excellent companies will give customers individual attention. ____
7. Materials associated with products and services (such as pamphlets or statements) will be visually appealing in excellent companies. ____
8. Employees of excellent companies will never be too busy to respond to customer requests. ____

SOURCE: Parasuraman, A., V. Zeithaml, and L. Berry. 1985. A Conceptual Model of Service Quality and Its Implications for Future Research. *Journal of Marketing* (Fall): 44.

My supervisor is...

Courteous	__ __ __ __ __	Discourteous
Friendly	__ __ __ __ __	Unfriendly
Helpful	__ __ __ __ __	Unhelpful
Supportive	__ __ __ __ __	Hostile
Competent	__ __ __ __ __	Incompetent
Honest	__ __ __ __ __	Dishonest
Enthusiastic	__ __ __ __ __	Unenthusiastic

As another example, let's consider Phil Samouel's Greek Cuisine restaurant. Based on observing his customers, Phil Samouel believes a particular personality type patronizes his restaurant. To confirm this he identifies a number of personality characteristics that could describe restaurant customers. A semantic differential format is then used to collect data from his customers. For example:

Instructions

A number of personality characteristics that can be used to describe people are shown below. Notice that each feature has an opposite. Please look at each characteristic and then rate yourself according to whichever end of the scale you feel best applies. For example, if you think you are more modern you would place a mark on the modern end of the scale that most closely fits you. On the other hand, if you think you are more traditional then you would place a mark on this end of the scale. Please rate yourself on every feature and try to be as honest about yourself as possible.

Traditional	___ ___ ___ ___ ___	Modern
Self-confident	___ ___ ___ ___ ___	Not confident
Reserved	___ ___ ___ ___ ___	Sociable
Outgoing	___ ___ ___ ___ ___	Introverted
Liberal	___ ___ ___ ___ ___	Conservative
Sophisticated	___ ___ ___ ___ ___	Down-to-Earth

Semantic differential scales are easy to understand and considered a metric measure. The difficulty in using this type of scale is being able to come up with adjectives that are opposites. The "Research in Action" box provides an example of how the semantic differential scale was used to measure product complexity.

Graphic Ratings Scale   A **graphic ratings scale** is one that provides measurement on a continuum in the form of a line with anchors that are numbered and named. The respondent gives their opinion about a question by placing a mark on the line. Sometimes the midpoint is labeled and other times it is not. An example of how this scale might be used to assess restaurant perceptions follows:

On a scale from 0 to 10 how would you rate the atmosphere of Samouel's Greek Cuisine restaurant?

Poor	OK	Excellent
0	5	10

Graphic rating scales are used in other types of business research as well. An example of how this type of scale could be used to examine the concept of organizational commitment follows. Notice that the midpoint is not labeled and that numbers are not placed beside the scales. Respondents simply mark an X on the line at the appropriate place.

I talk about this company to my friends as a great place to work.

Strongly
Disagree   Strongly
                                                      Agree

RESEARCH IN ACTION
MEASURING PERCEIVED PRODUCT COMPLEXITY

An example of a concept that has been measured in business research using a 5-point semantic differential is the following:

Instructions

Using the rating scale shown below, please circle one number for each set of factors listed. The numbers have no specific values and are only designed to represent a continuous scale between the high and low definitions provided for each factor. Circle the number that reflects your opinion of where _____ falls on such a continuum (product goes in blank space).

Standardized Product	1	2	3	4	5	**Differentiated Product**
Technically Simple	1	2	3	4	5	Technically Complex
Easy to Install/Use	1	2	3	4	5	Specialized Installation/Use
No After Sales Service	1	2	3	4	5	Technical After Sales Service
Consequential Adjustment	1	2	3	4	5	Large Consequential Adjustment

SOURCE: McCabe, D. 1987. Group Structure: Constriction at the Top. *Journal of Marketing* 51 (October): 88–89.

I really care about the future of this company.

Strongly Disagree   Strongly Agree

For me, this is the best of all companies to work for.

Strongly Disagree   Strongly Agree

Nonmetric Scales

Nonmetric scales often are referred to as comparative scales. A distinguishing feature of a comparative scale is the responses to the questions are evaluated relative to each other rather than independently. These scales are considered ordinal measurement tools because objects are evaluated in a rank-ordered manner, often reflecting preference or importance. The following examples illustrate the variety of comparative scales.

Categorical Scale **Categorical scales** are nominally measured opinion scales that have two or more response categories. When there are more categories, the researcher can be more precise in measuring a particular concept. Categorical scales often are used to measure respondent characteristics such as gender, age or education level. But they also can be used to measure other concepts as follows.

How often is your supervisor courteous to you?
[ ] Never
[ ] Seldom
[ ] Sometimes
[ ] Often
[ ] Always

How interested are you in learning more about the benefits that are offered with this health plan?
[ ] Very Interested
[ ] Somewhat Interested
[ ] Not Very Interested

Rank Order Scale Individuals often place items or alternatives in a rank order. This typically is an ordinal scale that asks respondents to rank order a set of objects or characteristics in terms of preference, similarity, importance, or similar adjectives. An example of a **rank order scale** using importance follows.

Please rank the following five attributes on a scale from 1 (the most important) to 5 (the least important) in searching for a job.

Job Attributes	Ranking
Pay	
Benefits	
Co-workers	
Flexible Scheduling of Work Hours	
Working Conditions	

This scale measures only relative importance. That is, the importance of each job attribute relative to the other attributes. If pay is ranked highest in a sample survey we only know that relatively speaking it is higher. But we do not know how much higher.

Sorting **Sorting** scales ask respondents to indicate their beliefs or opinions by arranging objects (items) on the basis of perceived similarity or some other attribute. Sorting also can be used to rank order objects. It is particularly useful when there are a large number of objects. To use this scale, you prepare a card for each object and write the object on the card. Then give the cards to the respondent and ask them to arrange the cards in the order of their preference or importance. For example, let's say you wanted to rank order student's preferences for taking courses from different areas of study. There are many fields of study, including accounting, finance, management, information systems, psychology, marketing, education, law and so on. You would give respondents a stack of cards with the names of the fields of study you want them to compare and ask them to stack them in the order of their preference for each of the fields of study. The technique is particularly useful in ranking the importance of objects because it prevents respondents from giving all objects a high rating, as often happens when rating scales are used.

Constant Sum Scale   With a **constant sum scale,** respondents are asked to divide a constant sum over several categories to indicate, for example, the relative importance of the attributes. Suppose Federal Express wants to determine the importance of several attributes in the selection of an overnight delivery service. Respondents might be asked to allocate one hundred points across the following attributes to indicate their relative importance.

Attribute	Score
On-Time Delivery	_____
Price	_____
Tracking Capability	_____
Invoice Accuracy	_____
Sum	**100**

Generally speaking, the constant-sum scale can be used only with respondents who are well educated. When respondents follow instructions, the results approximate an interval scale. But the technique becomes increasingly difficult as the number of attributes increases. Unfortunately, the likelihood of the scores not adding up to one hundred can be a problem.

Another example of a constant sum scale follows. It demonstrates how data could be collected to determine the relative importance of components of a compensation package.

Suppose your monthly salary is $3,500. Think of an ideal compensation plan to meet your needs. How much would you like to allocate to each type of benefit? Please be sure that the points allocated among the benefits sum to one hundred.

Benefits	Score
Health Insurance	_____
Life Insurance	_____
Dental Insurance	_____
Salary	_____
Retirement	_____
Sum	**100**

The constant sum scale provides both a ranking and the magnitude of relative importance of each attribute. For the previous example, if salary is given a score of forty and health insurance is given a score of twenty, then we know salary is much more important than is health insurance. It should be noted that some analysts consider this scale to be metric while others consider it nonmetric.

Paired Comparison Scale   The **paired comparison scale** is a measurement method that involves presenting respondents with two attributes (or objects) and asking them to pick the preferred attribute (or object). Two or more attributes can be compared, but comparisons always are made in pairs. As the number of pairs increases, respondents may become tired and not make careful comparisons. Even a small number of objects can become a challenge. For example, with ten objects the number of paired comparisons is forty-five. We recommend no more than twenty comparisons, although the number of comparisons ultimately depends upon what other tasks the respondent is asked to complete. The following example illustrates how this technique could be used to determine the most important restaurant selection factor.

> Below you will find ten pairs of attributes that have been identified as being important when choosing a restaurant. For each pair mark the attribute you feel is more important to you in choosing a restaurant.

Pairs	Attribute 1	Attribute 2
Pair 1	Food Quality	Atmosphere
Pair 2	Food Quality	Prices
Pair 3	Food Quality	Service
Pair 4	Food Quality	Cleanliness
Pair 5	Atmosphere	Prices
Pair 6	Atmosphere	Service
Pair 7	Atmosphere	Cleanliness
Pair 8	Prices	Service
Pair 9	Prices	Cleanliness
Pair 10	Service	Cleanliness

As illustrated previously, a paired comparison scale consists of a set of attributes or characteristics that have been predetermined by the researcher and are presented to respondents in pairs. For each pair of attributes or characteristics, a respondent is then required to select the characteristic or attribute that is more important (or more highly preferred) within the pair. This approach also can be used to measure perceived similarity/dissimilarity of objects. For example, an individual could be asked to compare health insurance plans in terms of their benefits. The task would be to group the plans that are most similar (or dissimilar) on each of the attributes. The question might be phrased as follows:

> Which health plan is most similar to Blue Cross in terms of ...
> Amount of Deductible: Aetna *or* CIGNA HMO
> Prescription Drug Coverage: Aetna *or* CIGNA HMO
> Dental Coverage: Aetna *or* CIGNA HMO

PRACTICAL DECISIONS WHEN DEVELOPING SCALES

Several practical decisions are necessary when developing scales. They include: number of scale categories, odd or even number of categories, balanced or unbalanced scales, forced or non-forced choice, and category labels for scales.

NUMBER OF SCALE CATEGORIES

Should your scale have three, five, seven, or ten categories? From a research design perspective, the larger the number of categories the greater the precision of the measurement scale.

But, with more categories it is more difficult to discriminate between levels, and respondents face greater difficulty in processing information. Thus, the desire for a higher level of precision must be balanced with the demands placed on the respondent.

Respondents must be reasonably well educated to process the information associated with larger numbers of categories. For example, children probably can only use 3-point scales; with high school or comparable education a 5-point or 7-point scale is acceptable. College-educated individuals typically can respond to a 10-point scale. Likewise, individuals with experience in responding to scaling questions can respond to more categories of discrimination. But individuals exposed to scaling questions less often, for example, individuals from countries where interviewing is not commonplace, can more easily respond to scales with fewer categories. Generally speaking, from the researcher's perspective, you would prefer to use no fewer than five categories. This is because respondents frequently avoid the extremes and a 5-point scale, for example, may effectively become a 3-point scale.

NUMBER OF ITEMS TO MEASURE A CONCEPT

Concepts should be measured using scales with multiple items. When this is done the scales are referred to as **multi-item scales.** A multi-item scale consists of a number of closely related individual statements (items or indicators) whose responses are combined into a composite score or summated rating used to measure a concept. But is two items enough or should the researcher use ten or even twenty items to measure a concept? The general guideline is the statements need to be closely related, represent only a single construct, and must completely represent the construct to be measured with the multi-item scale. In the authors' experiences, a minimum of three items is necessary to achieve acceptable reliability but it is common to see at least five to seven items, and sometimes more.

ODD OR EVEN NUMBER OF CATEGORIES

The midpoint typically represents a neutral position when an odd number of categories are used in a scale. This type of scale is used when, based on the experience or judgment of the researcher, it is believed that some portion of the sample is likely to feel neutral about the issue being examined. On the other hand, if the researcher believes it is unlikely there will be many neutral respondents or wants to force a choice on a particular issue, then an even number of categories should be used.

BALANCED OR UNBALANCED SCALES

Scales can be either balanced or unbalanced. With a **balanced scale** the number of favorable and unfavorable categories is equal. With an **unbalanced scale** the number of favorable and unfavorable categories is unequal. Examples of balanced and unbalanced scales follow:

> To what extent do you consider TV shows with sex and violence to be acceptable for teenagers to view?

Balanced

___ Very Acceptable
___ Somewhat Acceptable
___ Neither Acceptable nor Unacceptable
___ Somewhat Unacceptable
___ Very Unacceptable

Unbalanced

___ Very Acceptable
___ Somewhat Acceptable
___ Unacceptable

Unbalanced scales are used when the researcher expects responses to be skewed toward one end of the scale. For example, in satisfaction studies it is common for respondents to give very favorable responses. Therefore, researchers may choose to use an unbalanced scale to the positive end to provide an opportunity for more options in the responses. This is an example of how the research problem should be considered in deciding whether to use a balanced or unbalanced number of scale categories. It should be noted, however, that unbalanced scales can create bias in the responses by giving more options toward one end of the scale. For example, in the previous unbalanced acceptable/unacceptable scale the two options for acceptable and one option for unacceptable would result in more acceptable responses than with a balanced scale.

FORCED OR NON-FORCED CHOICE

With a **forced choice** scale respondents are forced to make a choice. There is no midpoint that can be considered a neutral or no opinion category. If many respondents are likely to have not formed an opinion about a particular issue then a forced-choice scale will make them respond in one direction or another. It will, for example, make them respond either favorably or unfavorably, likely or unlikely, agree or disagree, aware or unaware, and so on. If a respondent selects the middle category when they have no opinion or are neutral this will cause error in the responses. In such cases it is better to use a forced choice scale and provide a no opinion option. No opinion response categories typically are placed at the far right end of the scale, as follows:

Very Unlikely					Very Likely	No Opinion
1	2	3	4	5	6	_____

CATEGORY LABELS FOR SCALES

The scales we discussed included three types of category labels—verbal labels, numerical labels and unlabeled choices. In such cases it is better to use a **non-forced choice** scale which provides a no option option. Using numerical labels gives some guidance to respondents on label interpretation, but less than verbal labels. Numerical labels are helpful because they tend to make responses more closely resemble interval data.

Numerical labels and unlabeled scales are used when researchers have difficulty in developing appropriate verbal descriptions for the middle categories. This typically occurs when the number of scale points exceeds seven. A compromise is to label the end points and the middle category if one uses an odd number of scale points. Examples of the three types of scale labeling follow:

Verbal Label

How important is the size of the hard drive in selecting a laptop PC to purchase?

Very Unimportant	Somewhat Unimportant	Neither Important nor Unimportant	Somewhat Important	Very Important
1	2	3	4	5

Numerical Label

How likely are you to purchase a laptop PC in the next six months?

Very Unlikely				Very Likely
1	2	3	4	5

Unlabeled

How important is the weight of the laptop PC in deciding which brand to purchase?

Very Important				Very Unimportant
___	___	___	___	___

CRITERIA FOR ASSESSING MEASUREMENT SCALES

Before using the scores from any concept (construct) for analysis, the researcher must ensure the variables (indicators) selected to represent and measure the concept do so in an accurate and consistent manner. *Accuracy* is associated with the term **validity** while *consistency* is associated with the term **reliability**. The most common criteria for assessing the accuracy and consistency of scales are displayed in Exhibit 6-3.

Our concern in selecting scales for questionnaires is on the quality of the measurement obtained. A scientific study must always address these two issues—reliability and validity. When these issues are addressed properly, measurement error is reduced. Measurement error occurs when the values obtained in a survey (observed values) are not the same as the true value. For example, if you ask a respondent to answer the following question:

Using a 10-point scale where 1 is poor and 10 is excellent, how does Samouel's Greek Cuisine restaurant rate on competitive prices?

EXHIBIT 6-3	CRITERIA FOR ASSESSING MEASUREMENT SCALES

Reliability
- Test-retest reliability
- Alternative forms reliability
- Internal consistency reliability

Validity
- Content validity
- Construct validity
  - Convergent validity
  - Discriminant validity
- Criterion validity
  - Concurrent validity
  - Predictive validity

You have measurement error if the response is 8, when in fact the true answer is 6. Measurement error is the result of: interviewer bias or errors, data input errors, respondent's misunderstanding or misrepresentation, and so forth. In conducting business research we always strive to reduce measurement error as much as possible. Measurement error is minimized when the observed numbers accurately represent the characteristics being measured and nothing else.

RELIABILITY

A survey instrument (questionnaire) is considered reliable if its repeated application results in consistent scores. This is contingent upon the definition of the concept(s) being unchanged from application to application. Reliability is concerned with the consistency of the research findings. Reliability is important no matter what form the question takes, but is most frequently associated with multi-item scales. Multi-item scales consist of multiple items (variables, indicators) representing a concept. An item is a single statement or question that respondents evaluate.

If the instrument is a multi-item scale, then for it to be reliable the scores (ratings) for the individual questions (items) that comprise the scale should be correlated. The stronger the correlations the higher the reliability of the scale will be. Similarly, the weaker the correlations the more unreliable the scale will be. Exhibit 6-4 is an example of a multi-item scale that was used to measure the construct "confirmation of expectations." To be reliable as a scale, the questions must be answered by respondents consistently, in a manner that is highly correlated. If they do not, it would not be reliable.

Test-Retest Reliability

Test-retest reliability is obtained through repeated measurement of the same respondent or group of respondents using the same measurement device and under similar conditions. Results are compared to determine how similar they are. If they are similar, typically measured by a correlation coefficient, we say they have high test-retest reliability.

Several factors cause problems with the use of test-retest reliability. The first time respondents take a test (survey) may influence their response the second time they take it. Also, situational factors such as how one feels on a particular day may influence how respondents answer the questions, and something may change in the time between repeated usage of the test. Finally, it often is very difficult and sometimes impossible to have the same respondents take a survey twice.

Alternative Forms Reliability

Alternative forms reliability can be used to reduce some of these problems. To assess this type of reliability the researcher develops two equivalent forms of the construct. The same

EXHIBIT 6-4	CONFIRMATION OF EXPECTATIONS OF A DISTRIBUTOR

Purpose:

Measures the extent to which a distributor rates the performance of a manufacturer as being up to expectations.

Instructions:

Following is a list of supplier (manufacturer) characteristics that might be important to your operations. Please indicate how well _____ has performed relative to the original level you expected them to perform at for each item listed. Circle the number that most accurately reflects your belief.

1 = Much worse than expected
2 = Somewhat worse than expected
3 = About as expected
4 = Somewhat better than expected
5 = Much better than expected

Product quality	1	2	3	4	5
Reliable delivery	1	2	3	4	5
Quality of advertising	1	2	3	4	5
Pricing	1	2	3	4	5
Technical support	1	2	3	4	5
Order processing speed	1	2	3	4	5
Credit terms	1	2	3	4	5
Problem resolution	1	2	3	4	5
Sales force call frequency	1	2	3	4	5
Responsiveness of sales force	1	2	3	4	5

Note: The name of the supplier is placed in the blank.

SOURCE: Excerpt adapted from: Cronin J. J., Jr., and M. H. Morris. 1989. Satisfying Customer Expectations: The Effect of Conflict and Repurchase Intentions in Industrial Marketing Channels. *Journal of the Academy of Marketing Science* 17 (Winter): 41–49.

respondents are measured at two different times using equivalent alternative constructs. The measure of reliability is the correlation between the responses to the two versions of the construct.

Internal Consistency Reliability

This type of reliability is used to assess a summated scale where several statements (items) are summed to form a total score for a construct. For example, one could assess the internal consistency reliability of a satisfaction construct with the following three items:

1. How satisfied are you with Samouel's Greek Cuisine restaurant?
2. How likely are you to return to Samouel's Greek Cuisine in the future?
3. How likely are you to recommend Samouel's Greek Cuisine to a friend?

Each of the above three statements measures some aspect of the satisfaction construct. Responses to the statements should be consistent in what they indicate about Samouel's restaurant. That is, a respondent who is very satisfied should be very likely to return in the future and very likely to recommend the restaurant to a friend. The "Research in Action" box shows how businesses are using multi-item scales to measure the satisfaction construct.

There are two types of internal consistency reliability. The simplest is *split-half reliability.* To determine split-half reliability, the researcher randomly divides the scale items in half and correlates the two sets of items. A high correlation between the two halves indicates high reliability. The second type of internal consistency reliability is *coefficient alpha,* also referred to as Cronbach's alpha. To obtain coefficient alpha you calculate the average of the coefficients from all possible combinations of split halves. Coefficient alpha ranges from 0 to 1. You can use the guidelines in Exhibit 6-5 as rules of thumb to interpret alpha values. Researchers generally consider an alpha of .7 as a minimum, although lower coefficients may be acceptable depending on the research objectives.

The "Research in Action" box (page 171) tells you how to use SPSS to calculate Cronbach's alpha for three of the perceptions variables on Samouel's and Gino's customer questionnaire. If you are not familiar with SPSS, we explain how to use it in Appendix 1-C of Chapter 1.

Words of Caution on Reliability

An acceptable level of reliability indicates respondents are answering the questions in a consistent manner. Good research requires acceptable reliability. The following guidelines can be used to ensure reliability in your scales:

1. The minimum number of items in a scale to measure a particular concept should be at least three.

2. The items included in the scale must be positively correlated. Where negative correlations arise between items:

   a. Check the wording of the questions and if a question is negatively worded then the scores for that question must be reverse coded. By "reverse coded" we mean that on a 5-point scale a 1 is recoded 5, a 2 is recoded as a 4 and so on. You can use the RECODE function in SPSS to do this.

   b. Should the negative wording check fail, then remove the offending item from the scale.

EXHIBIT 6-5 RULES OF THUMB ABOUT CRONBACH'S ALPHA COEFFICIENT SIZE*

Alpha Coefficient Range	Strength of Association
< .6	Poor
.6 to < .7	Moderate
.7 to < .8	Good
.8 to < .9	Very Good
.9	Excellent

* If alpha > .95, items should be inspected to ensure they measure different aspects of the concept.

RESEARCH IN ACTION

MULTI-ITEM CONCEPTS ARE WIDELY USED IN BUSINESS RESEARCH

If you think only academic researchers use multi-item concepts, think again. Burke Incorporated, one of the largest business research firms in the world, developed the "Secure Customer Index" to use in customer satisfaction and retention projects. The index is a three-item scale that asks respondents about satisfaction, likelihood to purchase or return in the future, and likelihood of recommending a particular business to others. The three items (indicators) are measured using a 5-point Likert-type scale. Secure customers are those respondents who choose a five on all three items. Burke has had good success using this approach on satisfaction studies with their clients.

The Secure Customer Index

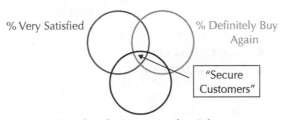

% Very Satisfied   % Definitely Buy Again

"Secure Customers"

% Definitely Recommend to Others

Copyright 2002, Burke, Incorporated. For more information on Burke, Incorporated and their services, go to www.burke.com.

RESEARCH IN ACTION

USING SPSS TO CALCULATE CRONBACH'S ALPHA

We can use SPSS to calculate Cronbach's alpha for the variables in the customer database. Questions X_6 on employee friendliness, X_{11} on employee courteousness, and X_{12} on employee competence are characteristics that reflect different aspects of employee quality. Cronbach's alpha can be used to determine whether the three items, combined into a single index, capture in a consistent manner the quality of employees. To perform a Cronbach's alpha analysis using SPSS, the click-through sequence is as follows: ANALYZE → SCALE → RELIABILTY ANALYSIS. Scroll down and highlight X_6—Friendly Employees, click on the arrow box to move it into the Items box. Repeat this procedure for X_{11}—Courteous Employees and X_{12}—Competent Employees. Next click on "OK" to run the program. The resulting output follows:

Reliability Analysis Scale (Alpha)

> Reliability Coefficients
> N of Cases = 200.0
> N of Items = 3
> Alpha = .8176

The Alpha value of 0.82 is "Very Good." Thus, we conclude that the three items can be combined to measure the quality of restaurant employees in a consistent manner.

3. Items in a scale that are correlated with other items in the scale at a level lower than .3 should be evaluated for removal from the scale.

VALIDITY

Validity is the extent to which a construct measures what it is supposed to measure. For example, if you want to know a family's disposable income, this is different from total household income. You may start with questions about total family income to arrive at disposable income, but total family income by itself is not a valid indicator of disposable income. A construct with perfect validity contains no measurement error. An easy measure of validity would be to compare observed measurements with the true measurement. The problem is we very seldom know the true measure. To assess measurement validity we use one or more of the following approaches:

- content validity
- construct validity
- criterion validity

Content Validity

Establishing the **content** or **face validity** of a scale involves a systematic but subjective assessment of a scale's ability to measure what it is supposed to measure. Validation, in general, involves consulting a small sample of typical respondents and/or experts to pass judgment on the suitability of the items (indicators) chosen to represent the construct. This is a commonly used validation method in business research. Generally speaking, content validity is not considered an adequate measure of validity, and business researchers typically go on to assess either construct or criterion validity.

To illustrate content validity, let's consider the construct of job satisfaction. A scale designed to measure job satisfaction should include items on compensation, working conditions, communication, relationship with coworkers, supervisory style, empowerment, opportunities for advancement, and so on. If any one of these major areas does not have items to measure it, then the scale would not have content validity.

Construct Validity

Construct validity assesses what the construct (concept) or scale is, in fact, measuring. To assess construct validity you must understand the theoretical rationale underlying the measurements you obtain. The theory is used to explain why the scale works and how the results of its application can be interpreted.

To assess construct validity, two checks have to be performed. The checks are convergent and discriminant validity. Convergent validity is the extent to which the construct is positively correlated with other measures of the same construct. Discriminant validity is the extent to which the construct does not correlate with other measures (constructs) that are different from it. These are objective tests, based on numerical scores, of how well the construct conforms to theoretical expectations.

Convergent Validity   Establishing convergent validity of a scale requires that the following be done:

Step 1. Based on theory and experience, identify another established construct that is claimed to measure the same concept as the one being validated.

Step 2. Obtain scores on both constructs.

Step 3. Compute the correlation between the scores.

If the scores are highly correlated, then it is concluded that convergent validity is evident.

Discriminant Validity   Establishing the discriminant validity of a construct requires a similar set of steps:

Step 1. Based on theory and experience, identify a construct that is claimed to be different from the concept being validated.

Step 2. Specify the manner in which the two scales representing the constructs are expected to differ. It is expected that the scores resulting from administering the scales on the same respondents will be uncorrelated.

Step 3. Obtain scores on both scales

Step 4. Compute the correlation between the scores.

If the correlation is low, then we conclude the construct exhibits discriminant validity.

Criterion Validity

Criterion validity assesses whether a construct performs as expected relative to other variables identified as meaningful criteria. For example, theory suggests employees who are highly committed to a company would exhibit high job satisfaction. Thus, correlations between measures of employee commitment and job satisfaction should be positive and significant. If this is so, then we have established criterion validity for our construct. Similarly, when we measure the construct of customer loyalty, a criterion for validating it would be the construct satisfaction. Very loyal customers should be highly satisfied with the business.

To establish criterion validity, we need to show that the scores obtained from the application of the scale being validated are able to predict scores obtained on a theoretically identified dependent variable, referred to as the criterion variable. One or both of two types of criterion validity checks can be performed. These checks are referred to as concurrent and predictive validity.

Concurrent Validity   To demonstrate **concurrent validity** of a construct some pre-specified association must be established between the scores on the construct being validated and the scores on a dependent variable as determined by theory. The scores of both variables are obtained at approximately the same point in time and should be highly correlated. For example, Samouel's highly satisfied customers also should be frequent patrons of his restaurant.

Predictive Validity   **Predictive validity** assesses the ability of a construct measured at one point in time to predict another criterion variable at a future point in time. The criterion variable can be either another individual variable or a multi-item scale. Thus, for a construct to have predictive validity it must be possible to predict future values of a dependent variable from scores obtained on the construct being tested. So, predictive validity differs from concurrent validity in that the scores on the dependent variable are obtained some time after the scores for the construct that is being validated. Validity is established if the scores are highly correlated. An example of predictive validity would be assessing whether the Graduate Management Admissions Test (GMAT) is a valid predictor of performance in graduate school in business.

How to Develop a Scale

In developing a scaling approach, we must consider the underlying theory as well as the reliability and validity of the scale. We also must consider the level of measurement (nominal, ordinal, interval, and ratio), any problems that might arise administering the scale, and the respondent's knowledge of the research issues. Our research objective is that the scale will be theoretically valid, reliable, and include the highest level of measurement possible. Moreover, respondents must be able and willing to respond to questions accurately and must not have negative attitudes regarding a particular issue being examined.

Consider the following problem that may concern our restaurant owner. Phil Samouel is interested in determining the image of his restaurant. A prerequisite to doing this is the development of a scale to measure the concept "image." The process of developing a scale involves a number of steps:

1. Definition of the concept or concepts to be measured
2. Identification of the components of the concept
3. Specification of a sample of observable and measurable items (indicators or proxy variables) that represent the components of the concept
4. Selection of the appropriate scales to measure the items
5. Combination of the items into a composite scale which in turn serves as a means of measuring the concept
6. Administer the instrument (scale) to a sample and assess respondent understanding
7. Assess reliability and validity
8. Revise instrument as needed

The instrument obtains perceptions of different components of the concept being measured. For example, components of the concept "restaurant image" might include assessments of the employees, food, atmosphere, and so on. Each of these components should have several indicators to measure them. A rule of thumb is each component should have a minimum of three items to be adequately measured. For example, measuring the image of a restaurant involves acquiring perceptions on such characteristics as the friendliness of the staff, parking facilities, the physical layout of the restaurant, the prices and so on. Similarly, measuring the concept of satisfaction with the restaurant involves several components. Possible components of the satisfaction concept are illustrated in Exhibit 6-6.

In developing an instrument to measure a concept, we generally look for previously developed scales. This is because scale development is difficult and time consuming. Fortunately, in the last twenty-five or thirty years many excellent scales have been developed and published. Several sources of scales are described in the "Research in Action" box.

EXHIBIT 6-6	POTENTIAL COMPONENTS OF THE CONCEPT "RESTAURANT SATISFACTION"

Concept:		Satisfaction	
Components:	**Quality of Food**	**Quality of Service**	**Price of Meals**
Items/Questions:	1. The food served must be of the highest quality.	1. When I visit a restaurant I expect its employees to be courteous.	1. When I visit a restaurant for a special occasion price is not important to me.
	2. The food served must be fresh.	2. I expect prompt service from a restaurant.	2. I am prepared to pay more for specialty dishes.
	3. The menu should offer a wide range of choices.	3. I expect the restaurant staff to be knowledgeable about the menu offerings.	3. When taking the family out to a restaurant price is important to me.

RESEARCH IN ACTION
WHERE TO FIND SCALES TO MEASURE RESEARCH CONCEPTS

Researchers like to use previously published scales in their research. This saves them a lot of time and effort in their own research. Sometimes these scales are used exactly as they were previously developed. Other times small modifications are made to the original instrument to more closely fit the needs of the specific research objectives. Several valuable sources of previously used scales follow. References are organized by the relevant discipline.

Organizational Behavior and Management

- Price, James L. 1997. Handbook of Organizational Measurement. *International Journal of Manpower* 18 (4, 5, 6). www.mcb.co.uk

This is a reference handbook and research tool that focuses on constructs to measure organizational behavior. It includes twenty-eight separate chapters reporting on constructs that measure a wide variety of work behaviors. Examples of constructs include: absenteeism, commitment, communications, innovation, involvement, compensation, power, productivity, technology, turnover, and others.

Management Information Systems (MIS)

Two Web sites provide measures of constructs associated with user reactions to computer systems.

- www.ucalgary.ca/~newsted/surveys.html. This Web site provides listings of constructs and attributes relevant to information systems research. All measures in the database were published in research journals.
- www.misq.org/archivist/home.html. This Web site is affiliated with MIS Quarterly and includes data and measures from articles published in the journal.

Marketing

- Bearden, William O. and Richard Netemeyer. 1998. "Handbook of Marketing Scales." 2nd edition. Sage Publications: Thousand Oaks, California.

(continued)

This book has information on over 130 scales, including a definition of the scale, type of scale and number of scale points, how the scale was developed, including the sample, and evidence of validity and reliability. It includes the following types of scales: individual traits such as opinion leadership and innovativeness, values such as social responsibility and materialism, involvement and information processing, reactions to advertising stimuli, performance of business firms, social agencies, and the marketplace, including ethical issues, sales management, and inter-intrafirm issues.

■ Bruner, Gordon Paul Hensel, 1992, *Marketing Scales Handbook.* American Marketing Association: Chicago, IL

This handbook includes scales in three primary areas: consumer behavior, advertising and organizational, sales force, and general. Specific examples include assertiveness, aggressiveness, arousal, brand switching, brand loyalty, complaining behavior, convenience, curiosity, information seeker, innovativeness, opinion leadership, risk, satisfaction, store image, novelty, source credibility, acceptance of coworkers, alienation from work, channel conflict, customer orientation, and so on. It reports scale name, origin, reliability, and validity for almost six hundred scales.

Psychological Measures

This is a Web site that provides assistance in finding psychological measures.

■ http://www.muhlenberg.edu/depts/psychology/cwolfe/Measures.html

General

■ Robinson, John P., Phillip R. Shaver and Lawrence S. Wrightsman, 1991, *Measures of Personal and Social Psychological Attitudes.* Academic Press: San Diego, CA.

This book contains published scales in eleven different areas: response bias, subjective well-being, self-esteem, social anxiety and shyness, depression and loneliness, alienation and anomie, trust and human nature, authoritarianism, sex roles, and values. Over 150 scales are reviewed and summarized.

■ Buros Institute of Mental Measurements Web site, which allows the user to search, locate, and obtain reviews of published tests and measurements. www.unl.edu/buros.

SUMMARY

Understand the Role of Concepts in Business Research

In business research we examine concepts of varying degrees of complexity. These concepts describe business phenomena that we must understand and explain to make effective decisions. Successful research requires clearly delineated definitions of concepts to avoid ambiguity in measuring them. In defining concepts, the researcher will draw upon established theory, literature, and business experience.

Explain the Notion of Measurement

Measurement involves quantifying the outcomes of variables by assigning numbers to the outcomes according to some preset rules. Managers measure many aspects of business, including employee performance and satisfaction, motivation, turnover, and profits. The measurement process involves specifying the variables (indicators) that serve as proxies for the concepts. Variables that are relatively concrete in nature, such as gender and age, are easy to define and measure. But many concepts are much less precise and more difficult to accurately measure.

Provide an Overview of the Different Types of Measurement Scales

To measure business phenomena we use four types of scales: nominal, ordinal, interval, and ratio. Nominal and ordinal scales are nonmetric variables. Interval and ratio scales are metric measurement tools.

Data analysis for nonmetric variables is limited. For nominal data-only counts, percentages and the mode can be computed. For ordinal data, we can compute the percentiles, median, and range. Data analysis is much more extensive for metric variables. In addition to the above, it is possible to compute means, standard deviations and other statistics.

When measuring a complex concept, we typically use multi-item scales where the individual items of the scale collectively capture different aspects of the concept. The multi-item scale index is a composite derived from the scores on its individual questions or statements.

Distinguish between Reliability and Validity

Before using a multi-item scale, the researcher must perform certain essential checks to ensure that the items selected to represent and measure a concept do so in an accurate and consistent manner. *Accuracy* is associated with the term *validity* while *consistency* is associated with the term *reliability*.

KEY TERMS

balanced scale	interval scale	predictive validity
categorical scale	Likert scale	rank order scale
concept	measurement	ratio scale
concurrent validity	metric scale	reliability
constant sum scale	multi-item scale	semantic differential scale
construct validity	nominal scale	sorting
content validity	non-forced choice	summated ratings scale
criterion validity	non-metric scales	unbalanced scale
face validity	numerical scale	validity
forced choice	ordinal scale	
graphic ratings scale	paired comparison scale	

ETHICAL DILEMMAS

Betamax

Two years ago, when a new CEO was hired, a business research firm conducted an organizational climate survey for Betamax. Since that time the new CEO has reorganized departments and tightened budgets. As a result company performance has improved and shareholders are happy. Richard Johnson, Betamax's human resources director, believes employees are also feeling better about their work environment. To measure the changes, Richard decides to conduct another organizational climate survey. However, in order to save money, Richard decides to conduct the survey himself using the questionnaire and scale that was used in the previous survey without consulting the original research firm. Is this unethical?

Nutrix

Nutrix, the maker of dietary healthcare supplements, has recently launched a new marketing campaign for Slender, an herbal supplement to increase weight loss. According to the product marketing materials, in an experiment conducted by Nutrix, people using Slender lost 5 percent more weight than those using a placebo. In addition, the people using Slender reported none of the side effects such as increased heart rate commonly reported to be caused by other weight loss products. As the product has gained popularity, critics have begun to attack the company's claims, arguing that Nutrix's research is not comprehensive enough because it fails to measure the long-term effects of Slender. In fact, according to critics, most people who use the product report that they are unable to maintain the weight loss after they quit taking Slender. Many also report experiencing withdrawal symptoms such as migraine headaches. Nutrix stands by their research, which shows the product is a safe weight-loss alternative, arguing that since patents are not available on herbal supplements the company cannot afford expensive, long-term studies. What do you think? Is the short-term measurement of effects adequate? Or should Nutrix be required to conduct long-term experiments before releasing its products?

REVIEW QUESTIONS

1. What is a *concept* in business research?
2. How do we measure concepts?
3. What is the difference between metric and nonmetric scales? Give an example of each.
4. What is reliability? How does it differ from validity?
5. What are the steps to follow in developing a scale?

DISCUSSION AND APPLICATION ACTIVITIES

1. Why would a business researcher want to measure concepts?
2. What key issues need to be considered by the business researcher in defining a concept? Illustrate this through a concept that you are familiar with.
3. What considerations need to be taken into account in determining the level of measurement of variables?

4. Make a list of concepts that college students might want to learn more about. Prepare a list of indicators (statements) for each concept. Decide on the type of measurement scale you will use and justify your selection.

5. If we tabulated the results of a survey of restaurant selection factors (4 = most imporant) and found that 40 percent of the respondents assigned a 4 to food quality, 30 percent a 4 to atmosphere, 20 percent a 4 to prices, and 10 percent a 4 to employees, then we would know that, relatively speaking, food quality is the most important reason, followed by atmosphere, prices, and employees. Discuss whether the results imply that food quality is twice as important as prices.

6. SPSS Application: We are interested in measuring a concept labeled "work environment." From the list of variables in the Samouel's employee database, select those you believe will collectively capture restaurant work environment. Assess the reliability of your chosen items in measuring this concept. (See "Research In Action" box in page 171.)

7. SPSS Application: Identify the work environment variables from the Samouel's employee survey. Select the six statements covering coworkers and supervision and calculate their reliability using SPSS. What did you find? (See "Research In Action" box in page 171.)

8. The Samouel's employee questionnaire has twelve indicators of job satisfaction. Develop a more comprehensive measure of job satisfaction covering areas not included in that questionnaire.

INTERNET EXERCISES

1. Complete a survey at one of the following Web sites and prepare a report on your experience.
   a. www.users.interport.net/~zang/personality.html
   b. www.utne.com/lens/bms/9bmseq.html
   c. http://future.sri.com/vals/valshome.html

2. Go to www.icpsr.umich.edu/gss. Find the General Social Survey and prepare a report telling what it is. How does it compare to the Yankelovich MONITOR that can be found at www.yankelovich.com?

3. VALS is a Values, Attitudes and Lifestyles survey that has been conducted for many years by SRI International. The VALS approach is well known and respected as a profiling approach that groups Americans based on questions about their values and lifestyles. Go the their website at http://future.sri.com, click on VALS and complete the survey for yourself. Prepare a brief report on what you found.

4. Go to the Web site at www.muhlenberg.edu/depts/psychology/cwolfe/Measures.html. The name of this Web site is "Finding Psychological Measures" and it states that the Web site is intended as a resource for undergraduate students and others to find psychological measures. Scroll down the Web site and, under the heading of General Resources, there are links to several Web sources of scales such as the American Psychological Association. Select the two sources you are most interested in and click through to the Web site. Prepare a brief report summarizing what you found and how it is useful to business researchers.

NOTES

1.   Williams, K. C., and R. L. Spiro. 1985. Communication Style in the Salesperson-Customer Dyad. *Journal of Marketing Research* 12 (November): 434–442.

7

Questionnaire Design

Learning Objectives

1. Understand that questionnaire design is difficult, and understand why.

2. Explain the steps involved in designing an effective questionnaire.

3. Recognize how the method of data collection influences questionnaire design.

4. Understand the types of questions and how they are used.

5. Understand the three major sections of AdMark International, a business research firm questionnaire and how they relate to each other.

INTRODUCTION

Few managers dispute the value of accurate information in improving decision making. The purpose of business research is to provide managers with accurate information, often from surveys. But information from surveys is accurate only if the questionnaire is properly designed. Many individuals believe questionnaires are easy to design. But those with experience in designing questionnaires know this is not true. Indeed, experienced researchers can easily make mistakes in **questionnaire design** if they overlook essential steps, such as pretesting.

This chapter describes the importance of careful questionnaire design and suggests an approach for developing good questionnaires. Specific guidelines to be followed at each stage in the design process are provided. But, unfortunately, few of the guidelines hold in all situations. Indeed, many individuals believe questionnaire design is much more of an art than a science.

QUESTIONNAIRE DESIGN

Questionnaire design is only one phase of several business research steps that are all interrelated. But it is a very important phase because data collected with questionnaires is used to improve decision making. A questionnaire is a prepared set of questions (or measures) to which respondents or interviewers record answers. In designing a questionnaire researchers must realize that there will be only one opportunity to interact with respondents, since a reasonable interval of time is necessary before the same respondent can be contacted again, and then it generally should involve either another topic or a different approach to the same topic. We review the essentials of questionnaire design in this chapter, but entire books have been written on the topic. For those who wish to review more extensive coverage of questionnaire design we refer you to the "Research in Action" box for additional sources of information on this topic.

The final outcome of a well-constructed questionnaire is reliable and valid data, if the related phases of the research are executed well. To achieve this you must follow a systematic process, such as that shown in Exhibit 7-1.

We discuss each of the steps in this chapter. Where possible, specific guidelines are given on the best approach to designing questionnaires. Similarly, examples of specific types of questions are provided. Finally, the questionnaire used for the customer survey in the Samouel and Gino case study is shown in Exhibit 7-2. We will use it to illustrate many of the issues.

STEP 1: INITIAL CONSIDERATIONS

Before developing a questionnaire, the researcher must be clear as to exactly what is being studied and what is expected from the study. This means the research problem must be clearly defined, project objectives must be clarified, and research questions agreed upon. If these tasks are completed properly, it is much more likely the research questions will be accurately answered. Once these are in place the questionnaire can be designed.

RESEARCH IN ACTION
THE ART AND SCIENCE OF QUESTIONNAIRE DESIGN

Is questionnaire design an art or a science? We say it is both. We refer you to the following source list for more detailed treatment of this important topic. The sources are organized into practical and theoretical categories.

Practically Oriented Books

Berdie, Douglas, and John Anderson. 1974. *Questionnaires: Design and Use.* Scarecrow Press: Metuchen, N.J.

Fink, Arlene. 1995. *How To Ask Survey Questions.* Sage Publications: Thousand Oaks, Calif.

Patten, Mildred. 1998. *Questionnaire Research.* Pyrczak Publishing: Los Angeles, Calif.

Payne, Stanley. 1951. *The Art of Asking Questions.* Princeton University Press: Princeton, N.J.

Peterson, Robert. 2000. *Constructing Effective Questionnaires.* Sage Publications: Thousand Oaks, Calif.

Theoretically Oriented Books

Belson, William. 1981. *The Design and Understanding of Survey Questions.* Gower: London.

Schuman, Howard, and Stanley Presser. 1981. *Questions and Answers in Attitude Surveys.* Academic Press: New York.

Sudman, Seymour, and Norman Bradburn. 1982. *Asking Questions.* Jossey-Bass: San Francisco, Calif.

EXHIBIT 7-1 STEPS TO BE FOLLOWED IN THE DESIGN OF A QUESTIONNAIRE

Step 1: Initial Considerations
- Clarify the nature of the research problem and objectives.
- Develop research questions to meet research objectives.
- Define target population and sampling frame (identify potential respondents).
- Determine sampling approach, sample size, and expected response rate.
- Make a preliminary decision about the method of data collection.

Step 2: Clarification of Concepts
- Ensure the concept(s) can be clearly defined.
- Select the variables/indicators to represent the concepts.
- Determine the level of measurement.

Step 3: Typology of a Questionnaire
- Determine the types of questions to include and their order.
- Check the wording and coding of questions.
- Decide on the grouping of the questions and the overall length of the questionnaire.
- Determine the structure and layout of the questionnaire.

Step 4: Pretesting a Questionnaire
- Determine the nature of the pretest for the preliminary questionnaire.
- Analyze initial data to identify limitations of the preliminary questionnaire.
- Refine the questionnaire as needed.
- Revisit some or all of the above steps, if necessary.

Step 5: Administering a Questionnaire
- Identify the best practice for administering the type of questionnaire utilized.
- Train and audit field workers, if required.
- Ensure a process is in place to handle completed questionnaires.
- Determine the deadline and follow-up methods.

EXHIBIT 7-2	THE SAMOUEL AND GINO CUSTOMER QUESTIONNAIRE

SCREENING AND RAPPORT QUESTIONS

Hello. My name is _____ and I work for AdMark International, a business research firm. We are talking to individuals today/tonight about dining out habits.

1. Do you occasionally dine out in restaurants?	__ Yes __ No
2. Did you just eat at Samouel's/Gino's?	__ Yes __ No
3. Is your gross annual household income $20,000 or more?	__ Yes __ No
4. Have you completed a restaurant questionnaire for our company before?	__ Yes __ No

If person answers "Yes" to the first three questions and "No" to the fourth question, then say: We would like you to answer a few questions about your experience today/tonight at Samouel's/Gino's restaurant, and we hope you will be willing to give us your opinions. The survey will only take a few minutes and it will be very helpful to management in better serving its customers. We will pay you $5.00 for completing the questionnaire.

If person says yes, give them a clipboard with the questionnaire on it, briefly explain the questionnaire, and show them where to complete the survey.

DINING OUT SURVEY

Please read all questions carefully. If you do not understand a question, ask the interviewer to help you.

Section 1: Perceptions Measures

Following is a set of characteristics that could be used to describe Samouel's Greek Cuisine/Gino's Ristorante. Using a scale from 1 to 7, with 7 being "Strongly Agree" and 1 being "Strongly Disagree," to what extent do you agree or disagree that Samouel's/Gino's has:

		Strongly Disagree						Strongly Agree
1.	Excellent Food Quality	1	2	3	4	5	6	7
2.	Attractive Interior	1	2	3	4	5	6	7
3.	Generous Portions	1	2	3	4	5	6	7
4.	Excellent Food Taste	1	2	3	4	5	6	7
5.	Good Value for the Money	1	2	3	4	5	6	7
6.	Friendly Employees	1	2	3	4	5	6	7
7.	Appears Clean and Neat	1	2	3	4	5	6	7
8.	Fun Place to Go	1	2	3	4	5	6	7
9.	Wide Variety of Menu Items	1	2	3	4	5	6	7
10.	Reasonable Prices	1	2	3	4	5	6	7
11.	Courteous Employees	1	2	3	4	5	6	7
12.	Competent Employees	1	2	3	4	5	6	7

Section 2: Selection Factors

Following are some factors (reasons) many people use in selecting a restaurant where they want to dine. Think about your visits to fine dining restaurants in the last thirty days and please rank each attribute from 1 to 4, with 4 being the most important reason for selecting the restaurant and 1 being the least important reason. There can be no ties, so make sure you rank each attribute with a different number.

Attribute	Ranking
13. Food Quality	4 3 2 1
14. Atmosphere	4 3 2 1
15. Prices	4 3 2 1
16. Employees	4 3 2 1

(continued)

EXHIBIT 7-2	**THE SAMOUEL AND GINO CUSTOMER QUESTIONNAIRE (CONTINUED)**

Section 3: Relationship Measures

Please indicate your view on each of the following questions:

17. How satisfied are you with Samouel's restaurant?

    Not at all Satisfied 1 2 3 4 5 6 7 **Very Satisfied**

18. How likely are you to return to Samouel's restaurant in the future?

    Definitely Will Not Return 1 2 3 4 5 6 7 **Definitely Will Return**

19. How likely are you to recommend Samouel's restaurant to a friend?

    Definitely Will Not Recommend 1 2 3 4 5 6 7 **Definitely Will Recommend**

20. How often do you patronize Samouel's restaurant?

    1 = Occasionally (Less than once a month)

    2 = Frequently (1–3 times a month)

    3 = Very Frequently (4 or more times a month)

21. How long have you been a customer of Samouel's restaurant?

    1 = Less than one year

    2 = One to three years

    3 = More than three years

Section 4: Classification questions

Please indicate the answer that classifies you best.

22. Your Gender   Male
                     Female

23. Your Age in Years   18–25
                         26–34
                         35–49
                         50–59
                         60 and older

24. Your Gross Income per Annum $20,000–$35,000

                                        $35,001–$50,000

                                        $50,001–$75,000

                                          $75,001–$100,000

                                          More than $100,000

INTERVIEWER RECORD

25. Samouel's = 0; Gino's = 1

Thank you very much for your help. Please give your questionnaire to the interviewer and you will be given your $5.00. Note: There were two forms of the questionnaire. One had questions that referred to Samouel's and the other referred to Gino's.

Developing research questions is one of the critical early tasks in questionnaire design. When an initial list of research questions is developed, they must be evaluated to determine if answers to these questions will provide the information needed to make a decision, understand a problem, or test a theory. The more specific the questions the easier they are to evaluate. For example, several possible research questions follow.

- Is sexual harassment a problem in this organization?
- Do employees in this organization support diversity in the workplace?
- Does religious affiliation influence support for human cloning?

- What are the most important factors influencing the purchase of a laptop computer?
- What are the good and bad issues of President Bush's policies on eliminating terrorism?

The preceding questions provide an initial start for the researcher, but a final evaluation requires them to be stated even more specifically. As an example, with the sexual harassment question the researcher would want to clarify what kinds of sexual harassment problems exist, how often they occur, if employees understand what harassment means, and so forth. This level of specificity is necessary if training is to be implemented to resolve any potential problems.

When the preliminary list of questions to be included in the questionnaire has been agreed upon, the researcher must evaluate them from the respondent's perspective. First, can the respondents understand the questions? This is particularly important when respondents are children, are less familiar with a particular research topic, or if the study examines technical issues. Along with understanding the questions, one must consider whether the potential respondents have the knowledge to answer the questions. If the research is designed to understand the purchase decision process for software in an organization, then those who will be asked to respond to the questions must be knowledgeable about this process. Finally, respondents must be willing to answer the questions. If the questions focus on sensitive topics, or if answering the questions might reveal an organization's competitive advantage, it is likely to be difficult if not impossible to obtain answers. Evaluation of questions in terms of respondents' ability and willingness to answer questions is an important early step in questionnaire design.

To enable the researcher to evaluate questions from the respondents' perspective, the target population for the study must be specified. If the target population is not precisely defined, the researcher cannot effectively evaluate the questions. It is at this point that the researcher considers to what extent respondents can be contacted and convinced to respond. If the survey must obtain information from a group of CEOs of *Fortune* 100 companies, or from physicians or even school children, this may be very difficult to accomplish. It also can influence the method of data collection and **questionnaire administration.** For example, to determine children's preferences for various shapes and tastes of cookies shaped like animals, one company chose to observe which cookies children ate and in which order rather than to ask them questions. Similarly, because different methods of questionnaire administration (e.g., telephone vs. personal) can influence the nature of responses, the method used must be carefully considered, particularly when questionnaires include attitude and behavior questions.

In addition to respondent capabilities, the researcher needs to consider whether the questions can be answered using a self-completion approach or if an interviewer-assisted approach is necessary. To some extent this is related to the potential respondents because some may be able to successfully answer self-completion questionnaires while others may not. For example, educational background, language capabilities such as vocabulary level, prior experience in completing questionnaires, age of respondents, and cultural issues related to responding can be important, particularly when these are different from the researcher's.

Researchers must be concerned not only with whether respondents will answer a particular question, but whether they will respond accurately. Potential respondents may refuse to answer questions on sensitive issues, or because they consider the question an invasion of their privacy. But what is sensitive or an invasion of privacy to one group may not be the same with another group. For example, in a recent survey of U.S. teenagers they willingly answered questions regarding personal experiences with various types of sexual practices, whereas older individuals are very reluctant to answer such questions. With questions of such a sensitive nature, however, all groups of respondents are likely to under-report their personal experiences.

Respondents may not answer a question because it is perceived to be too long or too difficult to answer. In contrast, respondents may willingly respond but do so in a manner they perceive to be socially responsible. For example, if asked about alcohol consumption an individual who drinks daily will almost always identify herself as an occasional drinker, if she answers the question at all. Finally, respondents may answer by guessing a response simply because they want to be helpful. Close consideration of all these issues is very important in minimizing error in data collected with questionnaires.

STEP 2: CLARIFICATION OF CONCEPTS

In designing the content, structure and appearance of a questionnaire, a number of aspects need to be taken into account. First, the concepts (constructs) to be measured must be identified, clearly defined, and then a method of measurement found. Second, decisions on other questions to include, such as classification and outcome information (e.g., intention to search for a job or likelihood to visit a particular Web site), types and wording of questions, questionnaire sequence and general layout must be made by the researcher. As a general rule, only questions relevant to the research objectives should be included. When done properly, these decisions will result in a questionnaire with a high response rate and minimal error. They also will ensure the necessary kind of data analysis can be used.

If the questionnaire requires attitudinal or opinion questions about a particular concept, the indicators and the level of measurement must be determined. For example, if management wants to better understand employee turnover, it would include questions related to the work environment, pay, benefits, coworkers, job expectations, role clarity, supervisory style, and so forth. Information on each of these topics could help clarify issues impacting employee turnover. Moreover, the target population must be considered in determining how to measure the indicators. At the end of Step 2, the researcher should have a list of potential questions to address the research objectives.

The Samouel's employee survey addressed some of these issues associated with job satisfaction and employee turnover. Recall from Chapter 6 that the first section of the questionnaire asked questions about the work environment. Four topics were included: supervisor, compensation, co-workers and overall satisfaction. Three indicators (statements) were included for each of these topics. Indicators of organizational commitment and likelihood to search for another job also were included. Thus, several concepts were measured in the Samouel's employee questionnaire.

STEP 3: TYPOLOGY OF A QUESTIONNAIRE

To achieve a high response rates and high quality responses, the researcher must pay particular attention to the length of the questionnaire as well as the manner in which the questions are structured, sequenced, and coded. This also will facilitate data collection and statistical analysis.

Typically, in gathering information through questionnaires we make use of different types of questions. The form of these questions and the order in which they appear in the questionnaire is very important. The types of questions and their order in the questionnaire depend upon the nature of the topic, how the questionnaire is administered, the target population's ability and willingness to respond, the type of statistical analysis, and similar factors. We now describe what we believe to be the most important considerations.

Close-Ended versus Open-Ended Questions

In broad terms, two forms of questions are used in questionnaires. The two types are known as close-ended and open-ended questions. With **close-ended questions** the respondent is given the option of choosing from a number of predetermined answers. An **open-ended question** places no constraints on respondents who are free to answer in their own words. Examples of open and close-ended questions follow:

Open-Ended Questions

- What do you think about your health insurance plan?
- Which mutual funds have you been investing in for the past year?
- How are the funds you are investing in performing?
- What do you think of airport security?

Close-Ended Questions

- Did you check your email this morning? __ Yes __ No
- Do you believe Enron senior executives should be put in jail? __ Yes __ No
- Should the United Kingdom adopt the Euro or keep the pound?
  - ☐ Adopt the Euro __
  - ☐ Keep the pound __
- Which countries in Europe have you traveled to in the last six months?
  - ☐ Belgium __
  - ☐ Germany __
  - ☐ France __
  - ☐ Holland __
  - ☐ Italy __
  - ☐ Switzerland __
  - ☐ Spain __
  - ☐ Other (please specify) _____
- How often do you eat at Samouel's Greek Cuisine restaurant?
  - ☐ Never __
  - ☐ 1–4 times per year __
  - ☐ 5–8 times per year __

☐ 9–12 times per year __
☐ More than 12 times per year __

Open-ended questions are relatively easy to develop because the researcher does not have to specify the answer alternatives ahead of time. Indeed, in instances where the researcher does not know the answer alternatives, such as in exploratory research, open-ended questions are the only possibility. Open-ended questions also are useful when the researcher believes the alternatives may influence the answer, or for "unaided recall" and "top-of-mind" awareness questions. For example, to determine unaided recall or awareness the researcher might ask: "When you think of banks in your area, which one comes to mind first?" Open-ended questions often follow an initial question, whether that question is open-ended or close-ended. In response to the earlier question about banks, when a bank is mentioned, the researcher might follow up with the question, "And is there a second bank that comes to mind?" Similarly, an open-ended question might follow a close-ended question like the following:

On a scale from 1 to 10, where 1 is *not at all customer oriented* and 10 is *very customer oriented,* how customer-oriented do you consider General Motors to be?

Following the response to this question, the interviewer would then follow-up with the question:

Why do you say that?

Open-ended questions provide rich information and often insight into responses. But, respondents need to be articulate and willing to spend time giving a full answer. The main drawback to open-ended questions is that it takes a great deal more time and effort to understand the responses. In self-completion questionnaires, open-ended questions should be used sparingly.

The design of close-ended questions is more difficult and time consuming than that of open-ended questions. This means close-ended questions typically are more expensive to design. But close-ended questions can be pre-coded, making data collection, data input and computer analysis relatively easy and less expensive. Close-ended questions typically are used in quantitative studies employing large-scale surveys.

All the questions in the Samouel's and Gino's customer and employee surveys are close-ended. This makes it easy for the answers to be placed in a data file and analyzed. Note also that the process of creating the data file has been greatly simplified because all of the answers have been pre-coded.

QUESTIONNAIRE SECTIONS

After the researcher decides the types of questions to ask, the preliminary questionnaire structure must be determined. The structure follows a three-part sequence. The initial questions are referred to as opening questions. The middle section has questions directed specifically at the topics addressed by the research objectives. The final section includes the **classification questions** that help the researcher to better understand the results. The "Research in Action" box shows a typical example of the three questionnaire sections as used in the hospitality industry.

RESEARCH IN ACTION

SERVICE QUALITY DRIVES COMPETITIVE STRATEGIES IN THE HOSPITALITY INDUSTRY

Almost all types of businesses in the hospitality industry, from hotels to restaurants and entertainment facilities, are realizing the importance of service quality as a competitive strategy. To improve service quality, businesses must have data for decision making. To obtain that data, they rely on customer surveys. The following is a typical example of the type of questionnaire a hotel might use to collect this type of data.

GUEST SATISFACTION SURVEY

Thank you for your recent stay at _____. Because we value your business, we would like your opinion as to how well we meet our goal of delivering excellent service to you every time you visit. A postage-paid envelope has been included for you to return your completed questionnaire.
   Sincerely

Jens E. Jorgensen, Senior Vice President, Customer Relations

Please check the boxes as requested.

1. Were you a recent guest at _____ in _____ city? __ Yes __ No
2. Was this your first visit to this particular hotel? __ Yes __ No
3. Was this your first visit to any of our hotels? __ Yes __ No
4. What was the primary reason for your stay?

   __ Business
   __ Pleasure
   __ Both business and pleasure

Please think of your stay at this hotel when completing the following questions:

5. How did you make your reservation?

   __ 800 number (Continue with Q. 6)
   __ Called hotel directly (Continue with Q. 6)
   __ Travel agent (Skip to Q. 7)
   __ Web site (Skip to Q. 7)
   __ Someone else made my reservation (Skip to Q. 7)
   __ Did not have a reservation (Skip to Q. 7)

6. If you made an advanced reservation, please rate the person you spoke with using a report card grade, where "A" is "Excellent" and "F" is "Poor." Circle the correct response.

	Excellent				Poor
How quickly was the call answered?	A	B	C	D	F
How courteous was the person you talked to?	A	B	C	D	F
How knowledgeable was the person you talked to?	A	B	C	D	F

7. Was the type of room you requested available? __ Yes __ No

(continued)

RESEARCH IN ACTION
SERVICE QUALITY DRIVES COMPETITIVE STRATEGIES IN THE HOSPITALITY INDUSTRY (CONTINUED)

For the following questions, please rate your satisfaction with the hotel you stayed at using a report card grade where "A" is "Excellent" and "F" is "Poor." Circle the correct response. If a question is not applicable to your stay, please circle the NA response.

	Excellent				Poor	
8. Check-In						
Exterior appearance of hotel	A	B	C	D	F	NA
Appearance of lobby	A	B	C	D	F	NA
Speed of check-in	A	B	C	D	F	NA
Courtesy of front desk staff	A	B	C	D	F	NA
Knowledge of front desk staff	A	B	C	D	F	NA
9. Hotel Staff						
Knowledgeable hotel staff	A	B	C	D	F	NA
Helpful housekeeping staff	A	B	C	D	F	NA
On-time wake up call	A	B	C	D	F	NA
Courtesy of hotel staff	A	B	C	D	F	NA
10. Guest Room						
Cleanliness of room	A	B	C	D	F	NA
Cleanliness of bathroom	A	B	C	D	F	NA
Cleanliness of carpet	A	B	C	D	F	NA
Cleanliness of bed linens	A	B	C	D	F	NA
Comfort of the bed	A	B	C	D	F	NA
Quietness of room	A	B	C	D	F	NA
Bathroom supplies sufficient	A	B	C	D	F	NA
Adequacy of phone equipment	A	B	C	D	F	NA
Working order of TV, radio, etc.	A	B	C	D	F	NA
Working order of heating and AC	A	B	C	D	F	NA
11. Other Facilities						
Condition of pool/spa	A	B	C	D	F	NA
Cleanliness of pool/spa	A	B	C	D	F	NA
Cleanliness of exercise facility	A	B	C	D	F	NA
Variety of exercise machines	A	B	C	D	F	NA
Convenience of business center	A	B	C	D	F	NA
Usefulness of business center	A	B	C	D	F	NA

12. What one thing could we have done to make your stay more satisfactory?

_____

_____

(continued)

13. Thinking of your overall experience at this hotel, how would you rate each of the following using a report card grade where "A" is "Excellent" and "F" is "Poor." Circle the correct response.

	Excellent				Poor
Overall condition/appearance of hotel	A	B	C	D	F
Overall staff service	A	B	C	D	F
Overall stay	A	B	C	D	F

14. If you were to return to this area, how likely would you be to stay at this hotel using a report card grade where "A" is "Very Likely" and "F" is "Very Unlikely." Circle the correct response.

Very Likely			Very Unlikely	
A	B	C	D	F

15. If a friend were planning a trip to this area, how likely would you be to recommend this hotel using a report card grade where "A" is "Very Likely" and "F" is "Very Unlikely." Circle the correct response.

Very Likely			Very Unlikely	
A	B	C	D	F

Classification Information

16. How many nights during the last year did you stay at a hotel? ____

17. What is your gender? __ Male __ Female

18. What is your age?

__ Under 25

__ 25–34

__ 35–49

__ 50–64

__ 65 and over

19. Which category best describes your total annual household income before taxes?

__ Under $30,000

__ $30,000–$45,000

__ $45,001–$60,000

__ $60,001–$90,000

__ $90,001–$150,000

__ $150,001 and over

If you have additional comments, please use a separate sheet of paper and mail them with your survey. Your comments are important to us. Upon receipt off the completed questionnaire, we will send you a coupon for a free nights stay.

Thank you for your cooperation.

Opening Questions

The first questions on a questionnaire are referred to as opening questions. Usually the first couple of opening questions are designed to establish rapport with the respondent by gaining their attention and stimulating their interest in the topic. It is typical to ask the respondent to express an opinion on an issue that is likely to be considered important, but still relevant to the study. Opening questions should be simple and nonthreatening, such as the ones following:

- Have you gone to a movie in the last month?
- What is your favorite seafood restaurant?

While rapport questions must be simple and easy to answer, they still must be relevant to the topic being researched.

Screening questions, sometimes referred to as filtering questions, are another type of opening question. They are used to ensure that respondents included in the study are those that meet the predetermined criteria of the target population. They may also be in the form of *skipping questions* that direct respondents to the appropriate section of the questionnaire. This ensures the respondent will not be required to answer irrelevant questions. An example of a screening question for a financial services telephone survey follows. It was used to ensure that the most knowledgeable individual in the household responds to the survey.

> Tonight we are talking with individuals who are eighteen years of age or older
> and have 50 percent or more of the responsibility for banking decisions in
> your household. Are you that person? __ Yes __ No

If the person says yes, they continue with the survey. If they say no, then the interviewer asks for the person who meets those criteria.

To summarize, the main objective of the opening questions is to include relevant participants and to create an atmosphere conducive to participation. Under no circumstances should the opening questions be of a sensitive nature. Note that the Samouel's and Gino's customer survey opening questions were easy to answer, relevant, and made sure the respondents had eaten at the restaurant and had not previously completed a questionnaire.

Research Topic Questions

The second group of questions includes those designed to provide information on the topic being researched This series of questions typically asks about such things as attitudes, beliefs, opinions, behaviors and so on. These questions usually are grouped into sections by topic, because respondents then find it easier to respond, and it helps maintain interest and avoid confusion. Moreover, since early questions can influence responses to later questions, the nature of question sequencing is to ask general questions early and more specific ones later. Moving from general to specific questions is referred to as a **funnel approach.** Note that with the Samouel's and Gino's customer questionnaire, the questions were organized by logical sections, starting with opinions about the restaurant. People like to give their opinions, so it will be easy to get them to answer these questions. The ranking of selection factors requires more thought so these questions were placed second. The ranking questions also were placed here because it minimizes the likelihood of the perceptions questions influencing answers to the relationship measures. Finally, the classification questions were at the end of the questionnaire, with the income question being the very last one.

Branching Questions

Branching questions are used to direct respondents to answer the right questions as well as questions in the proper sequence. Branching questions enable respondents to skip irrelevant questions or to more specifically explain a particular response. An example of a branching question follows:

- Have you heard or seen any advertisements for wireless telephone service in the past thirty days?
- If no, go to question #10.
- If yes, were the advertisements on TV or radio or both?
- If the advertisements were on TV or both, go to question #6.
- If the advertisements were on radio go to question #8.
- For both questions #6 and #8, the next question would be:
  - □ Were any of the advertisements for Sprint PCS?
- If yes for Sprint PCS, then ask:
  - □ What did the advertisement say?
- If no, go to question #10.

The main disadvantage of funnel questions is the possibility that respondents will become confused when the questionnaire is self-completion. For this reason, they work best with interviewer-administered questionnaires. This is particularly true with computer-assisted interviewing, where funnel questions can easily be used with both open-ended and closed-ended questions.

Classification Questions

With the exception of screening questions, demographic and socioeconomic type questions used for classification of respondents should be placed at the end of the questionnaire. The reason for placement at the end is these questions invariably seek information of a more personal nature, for example age and income, and if asked early on may affect the nature of responses to subsequent questions or even result in non-participation. Being at the end does not mean classification questions are less important. Putting them there simply is an effort to increase response and reduce error.

Because many classification questions are considered sensitive or an invasion of privacy, researchers have found that a funnel approach can be used to increase the response rate. Following is an example of how a funnel approach might be used with the income question:

- Is your total annual household income above or below $50,000?
- If the answer is below $50,000, then the next question might be: Is your total annual household income above or below $40,000?

This process can continue until the answer is as precise as the researcher would like it to be. In the preceding example, however, it would probably stop at this point if the response were "above," because knowing the annual household income is between $40,000 and $50,000 is generally as precise as the researcher needs.

PREPARING AND PRESENTING GOOD QUESTIONS

Converting research objectives into questions that will be understood and correctly answered by respondents is not an easy task. As noted earlier, entire books have been written on this topic. To assist you in preparing good questions, we suggest you observe the following guidelines.

Use Simple Words

Questions must be in a language familiar to the respondent. Avoid using jargon or technical terms unless absolutely necessary. In situations where technical terms must be used it is "good practice" to provide definitions for all words where misunderstandings could occur. The "Research in Action" box provides an example of why questionnaire wording is important yet so difficult.

Be Brief

Questions should be short and to the point, and if possible not exceed one line. The longer a question is, the more likely it will be misunderstood by respondents. Long questions have higher non-response rates and produce more error in responses. The higher error is a result of respondents tending to answer long questions before fully reading them because they are in a hurry to complete the questionnaire.

RESEARCH IN ACTION

SO YOU THINK YOUR RESPONDENTS UNDERSTAND YOUR QUESTIONS?

Recently a survey was conducted by the United Nations using a sample from several different countries. The question asked was:

Would you please give your opinion about the food shortage in the rest of the world?

The survey was a huge failure. Why?

- In Africa they did not know what *food* meant.
- In Western Europe, they did not know what *shortage* meant.
- In Eastern Europe they did not know what *opinion* meant.
- In South America they did not know what *please* meant.
- And in the United States they did not know what *the rest of the world* meant.

Note: The authors do not know the source or authenticity of this question. A former student sent the example to them. We included it because we believe it makes an important point in a humorous way.

Avoid Ambiguity

Wording should be clear, concise, and avoid vagueness and ambiguity. Questions are ambiguous when they contain words that are unfamiliar to respondents or the words can have more than one meaning. These include words such as: often, frequently, sometimes, occasionally, generally, normally, good, bad, fair, poor and so forth. An example of a poorly worded, ambiguous question follows:

How often do you consider your supervisor to be fair with all her/his subordinates?

___ Never
___ Occasionally
___ Quite Often
___ All the Time

The words *consider* and *fair* both can be interpreted very differently. Moreover, the response alternatives can mean different things to different respondents. Finally, to eliminate ambiguity, researchers often quantify vague alternatives. For example, if a researcher is investigating church attendance the question could be worded:

How often do you attend church?

___ Regularly
___ Often
___ Occasionally
___ Never

But this wording is clearly ambiguous. Three of the four frequency of attendance alternatives could mean different things to different respondents (never is the only clear one). A much better way to word this question is:

How often do you attend church?

___ Every Week
___ 1–3 times a month
___ Once a month
___ Between 2 and 12 times a year
___ Never

Open-ended questions typically are more ambiguous than close-ended questions. For example, consider the following question:

Do you like orange juice?

If a parent answered this question with a simple "Yes" and the interviewer does not follow with a probing question like, "Why?" there are at least two possible interpretations to the Yes answer. One is the parent personally likes orange juice. But another possibility is the parent likes orange juice because he or she believes it is healthy for his or her children to drink.

With open-ended questions, it sometimes can be useful to provide respondents with some help in answering questions. An *aided* question is one that provides the respondent with a stimulus that jogs the memory. Such information should be neutral in nature to avoid biasing the response. For example, a researcher may aid the respondent by asking for a recall on the most recent visit to a restaurant. Instead of just saying, "Where did you last eat out?", which is referred to as an unaided question, the researcher might say: "When you ate out the last time, did you go to Samouel's Greek Cuisine, Gino's Ristorante, Juban's Creole Restaurant, Mike Anderson's Seafood, or somewhere else?" The latter question phrasing is called an aided-response question.

Avoid Leading Questions

Leading questions imply that a particular answer is correct or lead a respondent to a socially desirable answer. This sometimes is referred to as "framing" the question to encourage a particular response. The "Research in Action" box provides an example of how framing can bias responses.

Avoid Double-Barreled Questions

Double-barreled questions include two or more issues and make interpretation difficult, or often impossible. For example, it is not uncommon to see questions like the following on a survey:

To what extent do you agree or disagree with the following statements:

- Harrod's employees are friendly and helpful.
- Harrod's employees are courteous and knowledgeable.

When questions like the above are used, it is impossible to know which of the two adjectives a respondent is reacting to. Moreover, respondents do not know how to answer if they have a different opinion about the two descriptors.

Be Careful About Question Order and Context Effects

Questions should be asked in a logical order organized by topics. Early questions should be general in nature and later ones more specific to minimize **position bias** introduced by the order of the questions. Examples of position bias and how to eliminate it follow:

Position Bias

Q-1 How important are flexible hours in evaluating job alternatives?

Q-2 What factors are important in evaluating job alternatives?

No Position Bias

Q-1 What factors are important in evaluating job alternatives?

Q-2 How important are flexible hours in evaluating job alternatives?

Position bias occurs above because asking the specific question about flexible hours before the more general question will cause the respondent to be more likely to include a reference to flexible hours in the general question.

An order bias also is possible on questions like the perceptions measures on the Samouel's and Gino's customer survey. Answers to early questions often influence how

---

RESEARCH IN ACTION

FRAMING YOUR QUESTIONS CAN INTRODUCE BIAS!

On a Saturday morning one spring day, one of the authors of this book was out working in the yard. A group of young folks got out of a van and began knocking on doors to solicit participation in a survey of exercise-related topics. They were students from a local college doing a class project for a local health club. The students were pleasant and polite in soliciting participation, and upon my agreement to participate, they began asking me the questions on the survey. About half of the way through the survey, they said the following:

When people were asked this question in the past, 90 percent said "Yes." Do you think belonging to a health club motivates people to exercise? Yes or No.

The author refused to answer the question and proceeded to inform the student interviewers that they did not ask if he believed belonging to a health club motivates people to exercise. They, in essence, asked: "How willing are you to give a response that differs from 90% of the others who have responded to this question in the past?" The young folks were shocked, but courteous. The author then informed them if they would like to learn how to design valid questionnaires they should take his research methods course at the local state university.

---

respondents answer the later questions. For example, the first question is on food quality at Samouel's/Gino's. If a respondent "Strongly Agrees" with the first (or early) question, then all later questions in that section are likely to be nearer the "Strongly Agree" end of the scale. Similarly, if early opinions toward a question are "Strongly Disagree," then later ones are more likely to be toward the disagree end of the scale. To avoid this type of order bias, researchers generally rotate the sequence in which respondents are asked a particular question. This is easy to do with telephone or Internet surveys. But with self-completed surveys, like mail surveys or the self-read and complete ones used with the Samouel's and Gino's case study, the only way to overcome this is to have two or more versions of the questionnaire with a different sequence of the questions in a particular section.

A **context effect** occurs when the position of a question relative to other questions influences the response. Marsh and Yeung[1] reported contextual effects when they studied "global self-esteem" as measured by questions like, "I feel good about myself" or "Overall, I have a lot to be proud of." They noted that if the question "I feel good about myself" is positioned on the questionnaire where the other statements refer to academic situations, then respondents will respond in terms of how they feel about themselves academically. But if the same question is positioned near other statements that refer to an individual's physical condition, they are more likely to answer the "I feel good about myself" relative to how they feel about themselves physically.

Check Questionnaire Layout

Presentation, spacing and layout of the questions can influence responses. This is particularly true with mail, Internet or other self-completion questionnaires. In Exhibit 7-2 shown previously, note that the questions on the Samouel's and Gino's questionnaire have been grouped into sections. Each section has a clearly marked heading and, where required, specific instructions on how to answer the questions. Finally, care was taken to avoid splitting a question over two pages.

Prepare Clear Instructions

Almost all questionnaires have instructions of some sort. Self-completion and **interviewer-assisted questionnaires** are likely to include instructions in the following areas:

Self-Completion Instructions

- Introducing and explaining how to answer a series of questions on a particular topic.
- Transition statements from one section (topic) of the questionnaire to another.
- Which question to go to next.
- How many answers are acceptable, e.g., "Check only one response." or "Check as many as apply."
- Whether respondents are supposed to answer the question by themselves, or can consult another person or reference materials.
- What to do when the questionnaire is completed, e.g., "When finished, place this in the postage paid envelope and mail it."

Interviewer-Assisted Instructions

- How to increase respondent participation.
- How to screen out respondents that are not wanted and still keep them happy.
- What to say when respondents ask how to answer a particular question.
- When concepts may not be easily understood, how to define them.
- When answer alternatives are to be read to respondents (aided response) or not to be read (unaided response).
- How to follow branching or skip patterns.
- When and how to probe.
- How to end the interview.

Whether instructions are used in self-completion or interviewer-assisted questionnaires, they always must be clear, concise and consistent throughout the questionnaire. Researchers often make instructions bold, italicized or all capital letters to distinguish them from questions and to increase the likelihood they will be easily understood.

With the growth of the Internet, several online support facilities have emerged to assist researchers in designing questionnaires. The Web site addresses of several vendors are given in the "Research in Action" box. Many of these Web sites are very good, particularly in the mechanical aspects of questionnaire design. But none of them can replace the knowledge and judgment of a researcher experienced in questionnaire design.

STEP 4: PRETESTING A QUESTIONNAIRE

No questionnaire should be administered before the researcher has evaluated the likely accuracy and consistency of the responses. This is achieved by pretesting the questionnaire using a small sample of respondents with characteristics similar to the target population. Respondents should complete the questionnaire in a setting similar to the actual research project. Moreover, they should be asked probing questions about each part of the questionnaire, from instructions to scaling to formatting to wording, to ensure each question is relevant, clearly worded and unambiguous. Asking questions such as these is relatively easy with consumer surveys because generally there is a large number to question. But with employee surveys there often is a small number of individuals to choose from and you do not want to include too many in the **pretest.** In such cases, researchers may choose to have the questionnaire evaluated by other experts or by individuals as similar to the employees as possible.

The pretesting approach depends upon several factors. When a research topic is new to a researcher the questionnaire should always be pretested. But even if the researcher has extensive experience with a topic, if the questionnaire will be used with a different group of respondents it must be pretested. Clearly, if a researcher has used a questionnaire in the United States and is asked to use it in England, it must be pretested. And of course, if the questionnaire were translated into French for use in France it must be extensively pretested. But even a questionnaire used in one geographic location of the United States, such as California, would need to be pretested if it were to be used in a Southern state such as Mississippi. Finally, longer questionnaires are more likely to need more extensive pretesting and pretesting always is required if the mode of administration has changed, such as using an Internet approach to administration instead of the telephone.

How large should the sample size be in a pretest? The smallest number would likely be four to five individuals and the largest number no more than about thirty. In the authors' experiences pretest sample sizes larger than thirty typically do not provide substantial incremental information to use in revising the questionnaire.

Based on feedback from the pretest, including the coding and analysis of the responses to individual questions, the questionnaire may require some refinement. The pretest may have to be undertaken several times, using a different set of respondents, depending upon the nature and extent of revisions suggested, before the researcher feels confident to proceed with the main survey. In cases where multi-items scales are used to measure concepts, this process at minimum provides a check of face validity.

STEP 5: ADMINISTERING A QUESTIONNAIRE

There are five major ways of administering a questionnaire. These include:

1. Through the mail, including overnight delivery.
2. Via fax.
3. In person.
4. Over the telephone.
5. Electronically via diskette, email or hosted Internet Web site.

For each of these approaches, there is an accepted "best practice" to increase the likelihood of higher response rates and quality responses to the questions. Each of these alternatives was discussed in Chapter 5. But the final decision on how to administer the questionnaire cannot be made until the final form of the questionnaire has been pretested and agreed upon.

RESEARCH IN ACTION

ONLINE SOFTWARE REVOLUTIONIZES QUESTIONNAIRE DEVELOPMENT

Need some help to develop a questionnaire? Researchers increasingly are turning to resources on the Internet. Below are some of the better Web sites providing help in the design of questionnaires and the collection of data online.

Decision Analyst www.decisionanalyst.com	A research firm located in Dallas, Texas, they have an Internet-based panel of over 3 million individuals, plus several specialty panels of physicians, attorneys, etc. They provide online assistance in questionnaire development.
Perseus Development www.perseusdevelopment.com	Their SurveySolutions XP Standard is an easy and cost effective way to gather information on the Web. It handles multiple choice, ranking, and scaling questions as well as open-ended ones. Its questionnaire design wizard provides good flexibility for skip patterns and randomization.
SPSS www.spss.com	SPSS Data Entry Builder enables you to create and deploy customized surveys on the Web, phone or paper, and save data to a central file accessible by password.
Socratic Technologies www.sotech.com	The Socratic Web SurveySM system operates on a CATI-like platform. It allows for quota controls and skip patterns as well as randomization of lists and attributes. Other features make it very flexible and comprehensive, including a system for handling multiple languages on international surveys.
Survey Builder www.surveybuilder.com	A survey design Web site that enables you to develop customized Web-based surveys. User-friendly and offers free trial.
SurveyPro.com www.surveypro.com	This site claims their breakthrough technology creates "on the fly" email surveys and forms in less than five minutes. Their format includes radio buttons, check boxes and data entry fields. Students and faculty are offered free access to use this site for surveys.
The Survey System www.surveysystem.com	A comprehensive software package that is simple enough for occasional users but powerful and flexible enough for business research professionals. Written in a modular format so the researcher can purchase only those modules needed.
Websurveyor www.websurveyor.com	This online survey software enables you to create professional questionnaires and have immediate and ongoing access to your results. You can analyze, filter export and report data online.

SUMMARY

Understand That Questionnaire Design Is Difficult, and Understand Why

Few managers dispute the value of accurate information in improving decision making. The purpose of business research is to provide managers with accurate information, often from surveys. But information from a survey is accurate only if the questionnaire is properly designed. Many individuals believe questionnaires are easy to design. But those with experience in designing questionnaires know this is not true. Indeed, experienced researchers can easily make mistakes in questionnaire design if they overlook essential steps, such as pretesting. In designing a questionnaire, researchers must realize there will be only one opportunity to interact with respondents, since a reasonable interval of time is necessary before the same respondent can be contacted again, and then it generally should involve either another topic or a different approach to the same topic. For this reason, a great deal of care must be taken to ensure the questionnaire will produce reliable and valid data.

Explain the Steps Involved in Designing an Effective Questionnaire

In developing a questionnaire, careful planning and a systematic approach are necessary to ensure the data collected are accurate. Clear definitions of concepts and how they might be communicated and measured are prerequisites for the design of a good questionnaire. Consideration must be given to the readability, presentation, structure and length of a questionnaire, because evidence has shown that these affect both the response quality and response rate. Finally, researchers also must be cautious about the type of questions used, their wording, and the coding of the responses.

Recognize How the Method of Data Collection Influences Questionnaire Design

There are five major ways of administering the questionnaire: mail, fax, person, telephone, and electronic (Internet or diskette). Each of the approaches has an accepted best practice. The method chosen must be appropriate for the study and yield an acceptable response rate and accurate data.

Understand the Types of Questions and How They Are Used

Typically, in gathering information through questionnaires, we make use of different types of questions. The form of these questions and the order in which they appear in the questionnaire is very important. The types of questions and their order in the questionnaire depend upon the nature of the topic, how the questionnaire is administered, the target population's ability and willingness to respond, the type of statistical analysis, and similar factors. Sometimes open-ended questions are best, while other times close-ended questions best achieve the research objectives. Similarly, rating scales are used sometimes while other times dichotomous questions are better.

Understand the Three Major Sections of a Questionnaire and How They Relate

After the researcher decides the type of questions to ask, the preliminary questionnaire structure must be determined. The structure follows a three-part sequence. The initial questions are referred to as opening questions. The middle section has questions directed specifically at the topics addressed by the research objectives. The final section includes the classification questions which help the researcher better understand the results.

KEY TERMS

branching question

classification question

close-ended question

context effect

double-barreled question

funnel approach

interviewer-assisted

    questionnaire

leading question

open-ended question

position bias

pretest

questionnaire

    administration

questionnaire design

ETHICAL DILEMMA

Shelly Appleby graduated from college in May and has just started working for a business research firm. She has been doing a great job, and as a reward her supervisor asks her to write the survey questions for a telephone survey of customer perceptions about local grocery store chains. She turns in her questions and is told by her supervisor that they looked good and only required minor editing. One month later, Shelly is included in the meeting to present the results to the grocery store that commissioned the survey. During the meeting, Shelly notices that the survey questions had been altered and, in her opinion, slanted to produce positive results about the client's stores. When she mentions her thoughts to her supervisor, her supervisor explains that while objectivity is fine in the academic world, in the real world, the most important thing is to make the client happy. Shelly disagrees with her supervisor. What should she do?

REVIEW QUESTIONS

1. What are the steps to follow in questionnaire design?
2. What is the difference between close-ended and open-ended questions? Give an example of each.
3. What is an opening question and why would a business researcher use one?
4. What is a classification question?
5. What are the guidelines for preparing good questions?
6. Why do you pre-test a questionnaire?

DISCUSSION AND APPLICATION ACTIVITIES

1. How does the researcher know which questions should be included in a questionnaire?
2. Design an open-ended questionnaire to obtain college students' opinions about diversity on campus.
3. Design a close-ended questionnaire to obtain college students' opinions about binge drinking on campus. Include questions to determine whether respondents themselves are binge drinkers.
4. Pretest the binge drinking questionnaire prepared in question 3 on eight to ten students. Prepare a report on your findings.
5. How can questionnaire design help to minimize error in research data?
6. Go to the Web site for this book (www.wiley.com/college/hair). Click on the link for the survey of Public Houses and Brewers in London. Could this questionnaire be used in the United States? If yes, how would it have to be changed, if at all? What is your opinion of the structure, layout and wording of the questionnaire?

7. Go to the Web site for this book (www.wiley.com/college/hair). Click on the link to the restaurant "Neighborhood Survey." Would you complete and return this survey? Why or why not? Are there questions that should have been asked that were not included on the survey? Identify any questions you feel were unnecessary and could be deleted? Prepare a report on your conclusions about this survey.

8. Go to the Web site for this book (www.wiley.com/college/hair). Click on the link to the "Binge Drinking" survey questionnaire. Evaluate the questionnaire in terms of wording, question sequence, layout and scales. Pay particular attention to the definition of binge drinking and comment on its validity and possible influence on answers to the questions.

9. SPSS Application: We are interested in measuring a concept labeled "restaurant atmosphere." From the list of variables in the Samouel's and Gino's customer survey database, select those you believe will collectively capture restaurant atmosphere. Assess the reliability of your chosen items in measuring this concept.

INTERNET EXERCISES

1. Go to the Surveypro.com Web site. Use the software to design a questionnaire to obtain student evaluations of college professors. See www.surveypro.com.

2. Go to www.google.com. Type in the phrase "questionnaire design" and conduct a search. What did you find? Try this with www.yahoo.com. How did it differ?

3. Go to www.raosoft.com/raosoft and surf the Web site. How does the company's software help you to distribute questionnaires over the Internet?

4. Complete a survey on one of the following Web sites and prepare a report on the differences and similarities.

   www.survey.net

   www.cc.gatech.edu/gvu/user_surveys/

   www.dssresearch.com/mainsite/surveys.htm

   www.hermes.bus.umich.edu/cgi-gin/spsurvey/questi.pl

5. Go to the Web site located at www.customersat.com. Prepare a report on what you learned about customer satisfaction surveys.

6. Go to the Web site located at www.strategos.com/survey/. Prepare a report that summarizes what you found on the Strategos Institute Web site. Include a critique of the questionnaire located on this Web site.

NOTES

1. Marsh, Herbert W. and Alexander S. Yeung. 1999. The Labiality of Psychological Ratings: The Chameleon Effect in Global Self-Esteem. *Personality and Social Psychology Bulletin* 25: 49–64.

CHAPTER 8

Sampling Approaches and Considerations

Learning Objectives

1. Understand the key principles in sampling.

2. Appreciate the difference between the target population and the sampling frame.

3. Recognize the difference between probability and non-probability sampling.

4. Describe different sampling methods.

5. Determine the appropriate sample size.

INTRODUCTION

A **census** involves collecting data from all members of a **population.** In most situations a census is not feasible. Therefore, a **sample** representative of the population is drawn.

A sample is a relatively small subset of the population. It is drawn using either probability or non-probability procedures. If a sufficiently large probability sample is drawn, then generalizations and statistical inferences can be made about the population. But careful consideration of **sampling** design issues is necessary to ensure that a **representative sample** is drawn.

Non-probability sampling typically is used in the exploratory phase of a study. The objective in such situations is to collect data quickly and inexpensively. Researchers usually are not interested in generalizing the findings to the population. Also, non-probability designs are widely used in selecting individuals for focus groups and pre-tests of survey questionnaires.

Sample size is an important consideration in sample design. With **probability sampling,** the choice of sampling method and the use of a sample of appropriate size are critical to be able to generalize the findings from the sample to the population.

In this chapter we discuss the basics of sampling. This includes what sampling is, the different probability and non-probability sampling designs, and the determination of sample size. Examples are given to illustrate their use in practice.

SAMPLING

Sampling design is part of the basic business research process. The sampling design process involves answering the following questions: (1) Should a sample or a census be used? (2) If a sample, then which sampling approach is best? and (3) How large a sample is necessary? In answering these questions, the researcher must always consider ways to minimize error that might occur due to the sampling process.

Business research involves collecting information to improve decision making. Collecting information involves contacting people who are knowledgeable about a particular topic. We refer to the group of knowledgeable people as a population or **universe.** A population, therefore, is the total of all the **elements** that share some common set of characteristics. The elements in a population can be people, drugstores, supermarkets, churches, hospitals, and so on. But all the elements must share a set of characteristics that ties them together. A census investigates all the elements in the population. In contrast, a sample investigates a small subset of the population to derive conclusions about the characteristics of the population.

While it may be possible to conduct a complete census of the population, business researchers seldom do. Contacting the entire population generally would be costly and time consuming. It often is difficult if not impossible to locate all the elements (people, objects, businesses, etc.). Also, use of the elements may destroy them. For example, quality control tests of products such as medicine, lubricants, chemicals, etc. always use sampling because the testing destroys the product.

Properly selected samples provide information that is sufficiently accurate to be used in business decision making. With probability sampling, business researchers at minimum are able to calculate the error associated with a particular sampling design and can make decisions with this knowledge in hand. With non-probability sampling, researchers are not able to calculate the error but have made informed judgments in an effort to obtain usable sample information. In the case study for this book, Phil Samouel had to make sampling decisions for his survey of customers. Before conducting the survey, Phil had to define his research problem. His Greek restaurant is reasonably successful, but not as successful as he initially expected. Gino's Italian Ristorante, his major competitor, is doing much better in attracting and retaining customers. Phil would like to know why. To fully understand the situation, he must know both customer and employee perceptions. He decided to conduct a survey of customers of both restaurants, as well as a survey of his employees. The customer surveys used exit interviews and the employee survey consisted of completing interviews with as many employees as possible within the pre-specified period of time.

Phil Samouel concluded that taking a census by collecting information from every element (individual) in the target population would be impossible. In the case of the customer survey, it would require getting information from all potential restaurant customers in New York City. But since New York City has a population of over ten million, a census is not realistic. A census is feasible if the population is small and relatively easy to contact in a short period of time. For example, many business-to-business populations are small (e.g., CEOs of chemical companies or purchasing agents for paper companies). But with consumer studies, in most instances the population is large and some form of sampling is necessary.

A sample must be representative of the population from which it is drawn. In other words, the sample should mirror characteristics of the population, thereby minimizing the errors associated with sampling. Use of an appropriate sampling design should achieve this objective.

SAMPLING PROCESS

Representative samples are generally obtained by following a set of well-defined procedures. These include the following steps:

1. Defining the target population.
2. Choosing the sampling frame.
3. Selecting the sampling method.
4. Determining the sample size.
5. Implementing the sampling plan.

We discuss each of these steps in the following paragraphs.

Business researchers must assist their clients in making decisions on each of these steps. But a lot of help is available from companies that specialize in working with researchers to obtain a representative sample. One of the most well known sampling companies in the United States is described in the "Research in Action" box.

Defining the Target Population

The research objectives and scope of the study are critical in defining the **target population** that will be studied. The target population is the complete group of objects or elements relevant to the research project. They are relevant because they possess the information the research project is designed to collect. Other practical factors may influence the definition of the *target population*. These include knowledge of the topic of interest, access to elements (individuals, companies, etc.), availability of elements and time frame. Elements or objects

RESEARCH IN ACTION
SURVEY SAMPLING GOES ONLINE

For over twenty-four years, Survey Sampling Inc. (SSI) has provided business researchers, marketers, pollsters and survey organizations with samples. Realizing the research possibilities available through the Internet, SSI (www.surveysampling.com) now utilizes web surveys, as well as the more traditional methods of contacting respondents such as telephone, mail, or personal interviews. To successfully conduct web surveys, SSI has learned that many factors, including hardware, software, questionnaire design and appropriate sampling have to be taken into consideration. With this in mind, SSI has filled the need for email samples (eSamples) with two types of eSampling services, SurveySpot™ Panel and SSI-LITe eSamples (Low Incidence Targeted Sampling).

SSI's SurveySpot™ Panel provides researchers with access to a multi-sourced Internet panel of people interested in participating in online research. Because SurveySpot™ records come from many sources, including banner ads, online recruitment methods and RDD (Random Digit Dialing) telephone recruitment, this service can deliver higher response rates than can be obtained using other sources. SurveySpot™ panelists can be targeted by education, ethnic group, gender, income, occupation, and race—and family members living in the same household can be targeted by age and gender.

SSI-LITe eSamples are designed to allow researchers to conduct directional research, particularly when low-incidence segments of the population are being targeted. Panelists can be targeted by hundreds of lifestyle categories including advertising, education, family, health, hobbies, Internet and travel.

Both SurveySpot™ and SSI-LITe records come from many sources and panelists are recruited through a variety of permission-based techniques. Files are created from self-reported, respondent-specific information, which gives researchers the advantage of reaching the exact targets they are after because the respondent has reported their particular interest. Further, since the panelists have agreed to being contacted with email messages concerning specific areas of interest, they are never "spammed" when receiving an eSample survey invitation.

The process for SSI's eSampling is quite simple. When a researcher secures SSI services, SSI will invite panelists, selected according to pre-qualifying requirements, via email to participate in a survey located on the researcher's Web site. SSI does not collect the data, since the company works within a non-competing position in the marketing research process. All data is collected at the researcher's own Web site. SSI can handle the infrastructure, servers, hardware, software and timing of the study. SSI also is equipped to handle random selection of prizewinners and administration of monetary rewards.

With the addition of web surveys, SSI is continuing its mission to provide quality samples for research projects. Through eSamples, SSI offers researchers a low cost per completed interview with national and international samples targeted by demographics, lifestyles and topics of interests.

---

available for selection during the sampling process are known as the **sampling unit.** Sampling units can be people, households, census tracts, businesses, or any logical unit relevant to the study's objective. When the sampling plan is executed, sampling units are drawn from the target population to use in making estimates of population characteristics. Exhibit 8-1 defines a target population for a survey of employees of a regional bank who participate in an incentive plan.

EXHIBIT 8-1	**A TARGET POPULATION FOR EMPLOYEES WITH INCENTIVE PAY**

Element	Employees with incentive pay
Sampling Unit	Customer service representatives and branch managers
Extent	All branch locations in state of Texas
Time	March, 2003

Choosing the Sampling Frame

The sampling frame provides a working definition of the target population. A **sampling frame** is a comprehensive list of the elements from which the sample is drawn. Examples of sampling frames are the Yellow Pages listing of restaurants, the telephone directory listing of individuals, a company's internal database listing its employees and/or customers, electronic directories available on CD-ROM or on the Internet, and even university registration lists. A sampling frame, therefore, is as complete a list as possible of all the elements in the population from which the sample is drawn.

Ideally, a sampling frame is an accurate, complete listing of all the elements in the population targeted by the research. In reality, a sampling frame often is flawed in a number of ways:

- It may not be up to date.
- It may include elements that do not belong to the target population.
- It may not include elements that do belong to the target population.
- It may have been compiled from multiple lists and contain duplicate elements as a result of the manner in which the list was constructed.

Before drawing a sample from the sampling frame list, the researcher therefore must confirm the list's accuracy irrespective of its origin. This will be discussed further in the next section dealing with sampling design issues.

Selecting the Sampling Method

Selection of the sampling method to use in a study depends on a number of related theoretical and practical issues. These include considering the nature of the study, the objectives of the study, and the time and budget available.

Traditional sampling methods can be divided into two broad categories: probability and non-probability. Probability methods are based on the premise that each element of the target population has a known, but not necessarily equal, probability of being selected in a sample. In probability sampling, sampling elements are selected randomly and the probability of being selected is determined ahead of time by the researcher. If done properly, probability sampling ensures that the sample is representative.

With non-probability sampling, the inclusion or exclusion of elements in a sample is left to the discretion of the researcher. In other words, not every element of the target population has a chance of being selected into the sample. Despite this, a skilful selection process can result in a reasonably representative sample. By "representative" we mean it represents the researcher's judgment of what she or he wants but is not based on chance.

The most common types of sampling methods are shown in Exhibit 8-2.

EXHIBIT 8-2	TYPES OF SAMPLING METHODS

Probability	Non-Probability
Simple Random	Convenience
Systematic	Judgment
Stratified	Snowball/Referral
Cluster	Quota
Multi-Stage	

Probability Sampling

In drawing a probability sample, the selection of elements is based on some random procedure that gives elements a known and non-zero chance of being selected, thereby minimizing selection bias. Probability sampling usually involves taking large samples considered to be representative of the target population from which they are drawn. Findings based on a probability sample can be generalized to the target population with a specified level of confidence. The most commonly employed probability sampling techniques are described as follows:

Simple Random Sampling   This is a straightforward method of sampling that assigns each element of the target population an equal probability of being selected. Drawing names from a hat or selecting the winning ticket from a container in a raffle are examples of simple random sampling. It is easy to draw names or numbers from a hat when you draw a sample from a small population. But when the target population is large, other approaches are necessary.

One popular method of **simple random sampling** is random digit dialing with telephone surveys. This technique is used because it overcomes the bias introduced when telephone directories do not include recent listings or unpublished numbers. Unfortunately, it has the disadvantage of creating non-working numbers as well as the problem of refusals to answer a phone. Indeed, telemarketing has created a huge refusal rate problem in the United States. Ten years ago, business researchers were able to complete telephone interviews using a sample to completion ratio of 4 to 1 (completion ratio = start with a total sample of 2000 listings to complete a sample of 500; i.e., 1500 refused, would not answer phone, etc.). Today, this ratio is often 10 to 1 (start with 5000 listings to complete 500 interviews). Part of the problem is certainly that potential respondents are not at home, or there may be lack of time or interest in the topic. But technology such as caller ID and other issues such as simply not wanting to be bothered are having a substantial impact on survey completion rates.

The procedure for drawing large samples involves the following steps:

1. Sequentially assign a unique identification number to each element in the sampling.
2. Use a random number generator to identify the appropriate elements to be selected into the sample.
3. Ensure that no element is selected more than once.

Software packages like SPSS will execute the above steps for you. If the determined sample size is sufficiently large, and the sampling design is properly executed, the resulting sample will be representative of the target population. In Exhibit 8-3, we illustrate the SPSS click-through sequence to draw a random sample of fifty cases from the one hundred Samouel's customers in our restaurant database. If you are not familiar with SPSS, go to Appendix 1-C where we provide a more detailed explanation of how to use the software.

Systematic Sampling   Systematic sampling is a process that involves randomly selecting an initial starting point on a list, and thereafter every n^{th} element in the sampling frame is selected. For example, suppose you have a list of ten thousand students who attend a particular university, and you want a sample of five hundred students. Your sampling objective is a representative cross-section of the student body. To draw the sample you must determine the sample size and then calculate the sampling interval—the number of population elements between each unit selected for your sample. In this case, the sampling interval is twenty (10,000 students / sample of 500 = 20). To draw the sample, you randomly select a number between one and twenty as a starting point. For example, say you randomly choose seven, then the sample would be the sampling elements numbered 7, 27, 47, 67, and

EXHIBIT 8-3	USING SPSS TO SELECT A RANDOM SAMPLE

Our sampling objective is to draw a random sample of fifty customers of Samouel's Greek Cuisine who were interviewed in the survey. Each of the one hundred interviews represents a sampling unit. The sampling frame is the list of one hundred customers of Samouel's included in the restaurant database. The SPSS click-through sequence to select the random sample is: DATA→SELECT→CASES→RANDOM→SAMPLE→OF→CASES→SAMPLE→EXACTLY→"50" CASES→FROM THE FIRST "100" CASES→CONTINUE→OK. In the preceding sequence you must click on each of the options and place 50 in the cases box and 100 in the from the first ___ cases box. The interviews (cases) not included in the random sample are indicated by the "/" through the case "ID" number on the left side of your computer screen.

Any data analysis done with the random sample will be based only on the random sample of fifty customers of Samouel's restaurant. For example, the table below shows the number and percentage of occasional, somewhat frequent and very frequent patrons of Samouel's restaurant that were included in the sample. Data in the frequency column indicates we selected twenty-seven occasional patrons, ten somewhat frequent patrons, and thirteen very frequent patrons, for a total of fifty customers. This table is an example of what you get when you use the SPSS software. We provide an introduction of how to use this software in Appendix 1-C of this book.

X_{18}—Frequency of Patronage

	Frequency	Percent	Cumulative Percent
Occasional Patron	27	54.0	54.0
Somewhat Frequent Patron	10	20.0	74.0
Very Frequent Patron	13	26.0	100.0
Total	50	100.0	

EXHIBIT 8-4	SELECTING A SYSTEMATIC RANDOM SAMPLE OF CUSTOMERS OF SAMOUEL'S GREEK CUISINE RESTAURANT

Over the past four years, Phil Samouel has compiled a listing of 1030 customers arranged in alphabetical order. A systematic sample of one hundred customers' opinions is his research objective. Having decided upon a sample size of one hundred to be selected from the sampling frame of 1030 customers, Phil calculates the size of the interval between successive elements of the sample by computing 1030 / 100. The size of the interval is determined by dividing the target population (sampling frame) size by the desired sample size (1030 / 100 = 10.3). In situations like this, where we end up with a decimal instead of a round number, you round to the nearest integer. Thus, we have effectively partitioned the sampling frame into one hundred intervals of size ten. From the numbers in the interval of 1 to 10, we then must randomly select a number to identify the first element for the systematic sample. If, for example, that number is 4, then we begin with the fourth element in the sampling frame and every tenth element thereafter is chosen. The initial starting point is the fourth element and the remaining elements selected for the sample are the fourteenth, twenty-fourth, thirty-fourth, and so on until the final element chosen is the 1024th. This will result in a sample of 103 customers to be interviewed in the survey.

so on. Similarly, in Exhibit 8-4 we tell you how to develop a systematic sampling procedure to survey Samouel's restaurant customers.

Systematic sampling produces representative data if executed properly. To work properly, the sampling interval must divide the sampling frame into relatively homogeneous groups. If there is a cyclical sequence to the sampling frame instead of a random sequence, systematic sampling will not work. For example, alphabetical listings are considered random and not cyclical. In contrast, if we wanted to do weekly interviews with Samouel's customers and our interval was seven, the sample would produce biased information because we would always interview on the same day of the week. To be truly random, we must conduct interviews across at least several different days of the week. Similarly, if our list of 1030 Samouel's customers is arranged according to frequency of dining and the first one hundred names on the list eat at Samouel's at least once a week and the remaining 930 eat at Samouel's an average of four times a year, we would have a problem using systematic sampling. If the sampling interval is 10 and our sample size is 103, then our sample would underrepresent the frequent customers (only ten frequent customers) and overrepresent the less frequent customers (ninety-three non-frequent customers). Thus, we must know ahead of time if there are underlying systematic patterns in the data so we can account for them in our sampling plan.

Stratified Sampling   This approach to drawing a sample from the target population requires the researcher to partition the target population into relatively homogeneous subgroups that are distinct and non-overlapping, called strata. The researcher usually does the stratification on the basis of some predetermined criteria that may be the result of his or her past experience, or could even be specified by the client. For example, in his survey Phil Samouel may wish to stratify his customers on the basis of a characteristic such as age, marital status, family size, income levels, frequency of patronage, levels of satisfaction or some combination of these.

The researcher determines the total sample size as well as the required sample sizes for each of the individual strata. For example, the total sample size might be four hundred and the four individual strata might each have a sample size of one hundred. The **stratified sample** is the composite of the samples taken from the strata. Elements for the stratified sample usually are selected either by drawing simple random or systematic samples of the specified size from the strata of the target population. With stratified sampling, elements must be selected from all the subpopulations (strata) of the target population. When done properly, stratified sampling increases the accuracy of the sample information but does not necessarily increase the cost. In practice a stratified sample is selected in one of two ways–proportionately stratified sampling or disproportionately stratified sampling. Descriptions of these two approaches follow:

In **proportionately stratified sampling,** the overall sample size will be the total of all the elements from each of the strata. The number of elements chosen from each strata is proportionate to the size of a particular strata relative to the overall sample size. So if we have a stratum that is 25 percent of the target population, then the size of the sample for that stratum will be 25 percent of the total sample. For example, if we use proportionally stratified sampling to select a sample of males and females at a university with ten thousand students, and six thousand students are females and four thousand students are males, then the sample would include 60 percent females and 40 percent males.

In **disproportionately stratified sampling,** the sample elements are chosen in one of two ways. One approach involves choosing the elements from each stratum according to its relative importance. Relative importance is usually based on practical considerations such as the economic importance of the various strata. For example, if Samouel's restaurant is located in an area dominated by older individuals who dine out less frequently, then sampling a higher proportion of younger customers that dine out more often would be viewed as more important to him. This is illustrated in the far right column of information shown in Exhibit 8-5.

EXHIBIT 8-5	WHICH IS BETTER? PROPORTIONATE OR DISPROPORTIONATELY STRATIFIED SAMPLES

Phil Samouel, owner of Samouel's Greek Cuisine restaurant, has a list of three thousand potential customers broken down by age. His business consultant has determined through the use of a statistical formula that a proportionately stratified sample of two hundred will produce information that is sufficiently accurate for decision making. The number of elements to be chosen from each stratum using a proportionate sample is shown in the fourth column of the table. But, if the consultant believes it is necessary that the sample size in each stratum be relative to its economic importance, and the 18 to 49 year age group are the most frequent diners and spend the most when dining out, then the number of selected elements would be disproportionate to stratum size as illustrated in the fifth column. The numbers in the disproportionate column would be determined based on the researcher's judgment of each stratum's economic importance.

Age Group (1)	Number of Elements in Stratum (2)	% of Elements in Stratum (3)	Number of Elements Selected for the Sample	
			Proportionate Sample Size (4)	Disproportionate Sample Size (5)
18–25	600	20	40 = 20%	50 = 25%
26–34	900	30	60 = 30%	50 = 25%
35–49	270	9	18 = 18%	50 = 25%
50–59	1020	34	68 = 34%	30 = 15%
60 and Older	210	7	14 = 7%	20 = 10%
Total	3000	100	200	200

With disproportionately stratified sampling based on economic or other reasons, the sample size from each stratum is determined independently without considering the size of the stratum relative to the overall sample size. The more important a particular stratum is considered, the higher will be the proportion of the sample elements selected from the stratum.

Another approach to selecting a disproportionately stratified sample considers the variability of the data within each stratum. Elements from each stratum are selected based on the relative variability of the elements. Strata with high relative variability will contribute a higher proportion of elements to the total (composite) sample. Similarly, the lower the variability of a stratum the lower will be its proportional representation in the composite sample. For example, assume our university with ten thousand students has 50 percent male students and 50 percent female students. We know that almost all the males drink beer and there is wide variation in beer drinking habits, with some drinking beer every day and a very small number who do not drink beer at all. On the other hand, only a small proportion of the female students even drink beer and not very often (the female students prefer wine), so there is not much variation in their beer consumption patterns. In this example, we would sample a larger number of male students in our survey so we could more accurately represent male beer consumption patterns. Since female students do not vary much in their beer consumption habits, the smaller sample of females should still accurately represent their behavior.

Cluster Sampling   In **cluster sampling** the target population is viewed as made up of groups called clusters. The clusters are naturally formed, relatively homogeneous groups, and any one of them can be viewed as a population or subpopulation in its own right. Thus, within each cluster the sampling elements should be heterogeneous and can be considered to be representative of the target population. In contrast to stratified sampling, where all strata must be sampled, with cluster sampling the individual clusters (subpopulations) where sampling occurs are chosen randomly and therefore not all clusters are sampled. Once the clusters are randomly selected, then, depending on the size of the clusters, information is collected from a random sample of elements if the size of the cluster is large, or from all elements if the size is small. Examples of clusters are ethnic groups, subsidiaries of a company, functional areas within a company, business units or geographic areas.

The most frequently used type of cluster sampling is geographic area sampling. For example, assume you want to interview managers of drugstores on the south side of Houston, Texas. No list of drugstores or managers is available. The researcher could obtain a list of zip code areas or census tracts each of which would be a cluster. The clusters to be sampled would be randomly selected and then all managers or a random sample of managers of drugstores would be interviewed in each selected cluster. This process generally works well and produces representative data but the clusters must be relatively homogeneous. For example, if the attitudes and experiences within a particular cluster are too similar, as they often are in geographic neighborhoods within a city, then the researcher must choose a larger number of clusters to sample and try to use clusters that have diverse characteristics.

The procedure for taking a cluster sample is as follows:

1. Define the cluster characteristics in a way that ensures the clusters are unambiguously identified in the target population. In this manner, the total number of clusters in the population will be known ahead of time.
2. Decide on how many clusters to sample.
3. Choose the cluster(s) in a random manner.
4. Obtain a sampling frame for the chosen clusters.
5. Decide whether to conduct a census on the chosen cluster(s) or whether to take a probability sample from the cluster(s).
6. If a probability sample is desired, determine the total sample size. If more than one cluster will be used then the sample size should be allocated appropriately. This generally is done on a proportionate sampling basis.

Exhibit 8-6 explains how Phil Samouel might use a cluster sampling process to identify the relevant customers to interview.

EXHIBIT 8-6   CLUSTER SAMPLING OF RESTAURANT CUSTOMERS

Phil Samouel would like to know the perceptions of his weekend customers because the average amount they spend on meals (for all customers on a particular check) is $124.00. This contrasts with an average check size of only $68.00 during the week. For this research project a cluster is defined as customers who dine at the restaurant on weekends. This will result in 52 clusters (one for each week) from which a random sample of clusters (weekends) can be drawn. There are two possible options now. All customers from the sampled clusters can be interviewed, in which case a census is conducted. Alternatively, elements (customers) can be drawn from the sample of clusters by one of the probability sampling methods discussed in the text, or by one of the nonprobability approaches discussed in the text.

Multi-stage Cluster Sampling What we previously discussed was single-stage cluster sampling. It involved dividing the population into clusters, randomly selecting a pre-specified number of clusters, and then either collecting information from all the elements in each of the clusters, or from a random sample. **Multi-stage cluster sampling** involves a sequence of stages. The first stage requires random selection of clusters (primary sampling units). In the second stage, a random selection of clusters is drawn from a second set of smaller clusters (secondary sampling units). When the process stops here it is referred to a two-stage cluster sampling. But more complex designs involving three or more stages are possible.

Non-Probability Sampling

In non-probability sampling the selection of elements for the sample is not necessarily made with the aim of being statistically representative of the population. Rather, the researcher uses subjective methods such as personal experience, convenience, expert judgment and so on to select the elements in the sample. As a result, the probability of any element of the population being chosen is not known. Moreover, there are no statistical methods for measuring the sampling error for a non-probability sample. Thus, the researcher cannot generalize the findings to the target population with any measured degree of confidence, which is possible with probability samples. This does not mean non-probability samples should not be used. Indeed, in some situations they may be the preferred alternative. The most frequently used non-probability sampling methods are now described.

Convenience Sampling A **convenience sample** involves selecting sample elements that are most readily available to participate in the study and who can provide the information required. For example, when exit interviews are used with restaurant customers they are chosen on the basis of having just finished a meal at the restaurant. Similarly, when a college professor interviews students at his university they represent a convenience sample. Convenience samples are used because they enable the researcher to complete a large number of interviews quickly and cost effectively. But they suffer from selection bias because the individuals interviewed are often different from the target population. Thus, it is difficult and dangerous to generalize to the target population when a convenience sample is used.

Judgment Sampling A **judgment sample,** sometimes referred to as a *purposive* sample, involves selecting elements in the sample for a specific purpose. It is a form of convenience sample in which the researcher's judgment is used to select the sample elements. Sample elements are chosen because the researcher believes they represent the target population, but they are not necessarily representative. An example of a judgment sample might be a group of experts with knowledge about a particular problem or issue; i.e., physicians who specialize in treating diabetes might be interviewed in a survey to learn about the most effective ways to convince diabetics to adopt good diets and exercise properly. The advantages of judgment samples are their convenience, speed and low cost.

Quota Sampling **Quota sampling** is similar to stratified random sampling. The objective is for the total sample to have proportional representation of the strata of the target population. Quota sampling differs from stratified sampling in that the selection of elements is done on a convenience basis.

In quota sampling the researcher defines the strata of the target population, determines the total sample size, and sets a quota for the sample elements from each stratum. In addition, the researcher specifies the characteristics of the elements to be selected, but leaves the actual choice of elements to the discretion of the person collecting the information. Thus, while quota sampling ensures proportionate representation of each stratum in the total sample, the findings from the sample cannot be generalized because the choice of elements is not done using a probability sampling method. As with judgment sampling, the advantages of quota samples are their convenience, speed and low cost.

Snowball Sampling   A **snowball sample,** also called a *referral* sample, is one where the initial respondents typically are chosen using probability methods. Then the researcher uses the initial respondents to help identify the other respondents in the target population. This process is continued until the required sample size is reached. Snowball sampling uses referrals to facilitate the location of rare populations or those where a list does not exist. For example, a wintertime phenomenon is the "snowbirds" from northern, colder U.S. states that come south, often to seaside locations, for the warmer weather. Because they are temporary residents, there are few lists and phone numbers, and property owner lists are not helpful. Thus, an effective approach might be to locate a few snowbirds in a community and ask them for referrals to other individuals or groups of individuals that have come south for the winter. This is a particularly good approach when the target is narrow, such as female snowbirds that play golf at least once a week.

Determine Sample Size

Efficient sample sizes can be drawn from either large (infinite) populations or small (finite) populations. Below, we discuss the determination of the sample size for both cases.

Sampling from a Large Population   Researchers often need to estimate characteristics of large populations. To achieve this in an efficient manner, it is necessary to determine the appropriate sample size prior to data collection.

Determination of the sample size is complex because of the many factors that need to be taken into account simultaneously. The challenge is to obtain an acceptable balance between several of these factors. These include the variability of elements in the target population, the type of sample required, time available, budget, required estimation precision, and whether the findings are to be generalized and, if so, with what degree of confidence.

Formulas based on statistical theory can be used to compute the sample size. For pragmatic reasons, such as budget and time constraints, alternative *ad hoc* methods often are used. Examples of these are: sample sizes based on rules of thumb, previous similar studies, one's own experience or simply dictated by what is affordable. Irrespective of how the sample size is determined it is essential that it should be of a sufficient size and quality to yield results that are seen to be credible in terms of their accuracy and consistency.

When statistical formulas are used to determine the sample size, three decisions must be made: (1) the degree of confidence (often 95 percent), (2) the specified level of precision (amount of acceptable error), and (3) the amount of variability (population homogeneity). The degree of confidence (confidence level) typically is based on management or researcher judgment. Historically a 95 percent confidence level (<.05 chance of estimated population parameter being incorrect) has been used, but a lower confidence level is acceptable where less risk is involved. Managerial and/or researcher judgment also is

EXHIBIT 8-7	ESTIMATING THE SAMPLE SIZE OF A MEAN

Case 1: Using a Rating Scale

Phil Samouel asked his research consultant to estimate the appropriate sample size considering the questions that will be asked on his survey of restaurant customers. The researcher must determine the sample size that will estimate the true perceived mean score for the characteristics of the restaurants (e.g., food quality, reasonable prices, etc.) to a desired level of precision and to a specified level of confidence. To do so, the researcher must consider all three elements in the sample size formula—the degree of variability in the population as measured by the standard deviation, the acceptable level of precision, and the specified level of confidence. The researcher is likely to proceed as follows:

The first element of the sample size formula that must be decided upon is the variability present in the responses to the question, for example, on food quality. Generally speaking, the true variability as measured by the standard deviation is not known. In most cases, therefore, it will have to be estimated either through the use of a pilot test sample or by some subjective method, such as the researcher estimating based on past experiences with similar types of questions.

It also is necessary to make some assumptions about the properties of the distribution of responses to the question on food quality. In general, it is assumed that the measure for the characteristic to be estimated follows a normal distribution. In our study, perceived food quality is measured with a 1 to 7 rating scale. This gives a range of 6 units (7 – 1 = 6). Once we know the range, we estimate the standard deviation (variability) of the rating scale by dividing the range by 4 (6 / 4 = 1.5). The division by 4 is based on the assumption that the distribution of the responses to the food quality question is normal. When we have a normal distribution, business researchers typically use a confidence interval of plus or minus 2 standard errors (95 percent), and we divide the range of responses by 4 to get the estimated standard deviation.

In consultation with the client, the researcher generally determines the acceptable level of precision and the desired level of confidence. Suppose that the precision is specified as 1/3 of a unit on the rating scale. This means the sample estimate should be accurate within 1/3 of a unit. A confidence level of 95 percent is desired.

We now have sufficient information to calculate our sample size using the formula:

Sample Size = [(degree of confidence required × variability) / (desired precision)]^2

Sample Size = [(2 x 1.5) / (.33)]^2 = 82.6

Thus, 83 is the minimum sample size the researcher should aim for in order to meet the specified precision and confidence goals.

Case 2: Using a Ratio Scale

Consider the case where we wish to estimate the average monthly expenditure on eating out. Although the true standard deviation (variability) is unknown, a pilot test study of thirty customers provides an estimate of the unknown standard deviation of $14. We want to be 95 percent confident that our estimate of the mean monthly expenditure on eating out is within $2 of the true population mean. Assuming the distribution of expenditures follows a normal distribution then the sample size is determined as follows:

Sample size = [(degree of confidence required × variability) / (desired precision)]^2

Sample size = [(2 × 14) / (2)]^2 = 196

We should aim for a sample of at least 196 to meet our pre-set criteria of an efficient sample size.

---

involved in determining the level of precision. The level of precision is the maximum acceptable difference between the estimated sample value and the true population value.

The third decision relates to the variability, or homogeneity, of the population. The variability of the population is measured by the population standard deviation. If the population is homogeneous, it has a small standard deviation. For example, the standard deviation in the age of college students is small and therefore requires a relatively small sample size. But if the population is heterogeneous, such as people attending a National Football League game, then a relatively large sample is necessary because the standard deviation in the age of this population is larger. In practice, it is unlikely the true standard deviation is known. Thus, the researcher typically uses an estimate of the standard deviation based on previous similar studies or a pilot study.

If you have information on these three factors, the sample size can be calculated as follows:

$$\text{Sample size (SS)} = (DC \times V / DP)^2$$

Where:

DC (Degree of Confidence) = the number of standard errors for the degree of confidence specified for the research results.

V (Variability) = the standard deviation of the population.

DP (Desired Precision) = the acceptable difference between the sample estimate and the population value.

Application of the above formula is presented in Exhibit 8-7. Also, note that the above formula does not include the population size. This is because, except with finite populations, the size of the population has no impact on the determination of the sample size. Specifically, a sample size of five hundred is equally useful in understanding the opinions of a target population of fifteen million as it is for one of one hundred thousand. This is always true for large populations. When working with small populations (e.g., 300–400, or smaller), the standard sample size formulas may lead to an unnecessarily large sample size. If, for example, the sample size as determined by the previous formula is larger than five percent of the population then the calculated sample size must be adjusted by the finite population correction factor.

Implement the Sampling Plan

The researcher implements the sampling plan after all the details of the sampling design have been agreed upon. The target population has been defined, the sampling frame has been chosen, the sampling method has been selected, and the appropriate sample size determined. If the sampling unit is companies, then the types of companies must be specified as well as the titles and perhaps names of the individuals that will be interviewed. Many details must be decided on before a final sample plan is accepted and implemented because once the data is collected it is too late to change the sampling design.

SUMMARY
Understand the Key Principles in Sampling

The key issues in sampling are to identify the target population, the sampling frame, and the method of sampling. Generally, a researcher seeks to draw a representative sample from the target population using either probabilistic or non-probabilistic procedures. Access to and participation of respondents whether they are companies or individuals is therefore an important consideration to ensure that the sample size is credible, efficient and representative.

Appreciate the Difference between the Target Population and the Sampling Frame

Before beginning sampling it is necessary for us to identify all of the elements of interest to our study. These elements could be individuals, or objects such as companies or even events. These elements are the target population. In practice there may not be an exhaustive list of these elements, so we make use of one or more lists that provide a good proxy for the population. It is this proxy that forms the sampling frame from which we draw the sample.

Recognize the Difference between Probability and Non-probability Sampling

The difference between the two sampling approaches is simple. For probability sampling methods the chances of selection of elements into a sample are known. In contrast, for non-probability sampling methods the chances of selection are not known. Also, to infer from a sample to a population, probability sampling must be used.

Describe Different Sampling Methods

Probability sampling, generally used in large-scale surveys, is based on a random procedure for selecting elements from the target population. If the sample size is sufficiently large, the sample selected should be representative. Probability sampling approaches include: simple random sampling, systematic sampling, stratified sampling, cluster sampling and multi-stage sampling. Each one of these sampling designs has advantages and disadvantages that must be considered before selecting a particular approach. If executed properly probability sampling enables you to make generalizations about the population with a specified degree of confidence.

Non probability sampling, generally used in exploratory research, involves selecting elements into the sample based on convenience, judgement, referral or quotas, without attaching probabilities to the elements in the target population. For such samples it is difficult to ensure they are representative, and thus the findings cannot be generalized to the population with a specified degree of confidence.

Determine the Appropriate Sample Size

To determine the sample size three pieces of information are needed. These are: the degree of confidence necessary to estimate the true value, the precision of the estimate, and the amount of true variability present in the data. In practice the researcher and client discuss and agree upon the desired level of confidence and the precision of the estimate. Further, since the true variability is unlikely to be known, it typically is estimated based on judgment or through a pilot study.

KEY TERMS

census	non-probability sampling	sampling frame
cluster sampling	population	sampling unit
convenience sampling	probability sampling	simple random sampling
disproportionately stratified sampling	proportionately stratified sampling	snowball sampling
elements	quota sampling	stratified sampling
judgment sampling	representative sample	systematic sampling
multi-stage cluster sampling	sample sampling	target population universe

ETHICAL DILEMMA

Mark Stephenson is an account manager for a business research firm. At the request of a local hospital's marketing director, he submits a proposal to conduct a patient satisfaction survey. His opinion is the sample should be random and collected either by phone or the Internet. After his presentation to the marketing director and the hospital president, the marketing director asks Mark to use exit interviews to collect the data instead. She explains that her boss feels exit interviews are just as valid and will save the hospital money. What should Mark do?

REVIEW QUESTIONS

1. What is sampling and why do we use it?
2. What are the steps in the sampling process?
3. What is the difference between probability and non-probability sampling?
4. What is the difference between proportionately and disproportionately stratified sampling?
5. How do you determine the appropriate sample size?

DISCUSSION AND APPLICATION ACTIVITIES

1. Discuss the difficulties that you may face in defining the target population and its associated sampling frame. Comment with examples on how you would overcome these.
2. In which situations is non-probability sampling preferred to probability sampling? Comment with examples.
3. For each of the probabilistic sampling designs illustrate their use with examples.
4. What considerations need to be taken into account when determining the appropriate efficient sample size?
5. Would you prefer to use a sample of twenty thousand voters or two thousand voters to describe voting behavior in national elections? Explain with reasons justifying your choice.

INTERNET EXERCISES

1. Go to the Google search engine and type in the words *population sampling*. Prepare a brief summary of what you get.
2. Go to the following Web sites: www.surveysystem.com/sscalc.htm and www.svys.com. Use the functions on the Web sites. Prepare a brief report of what is on the Web site do and how it works. Include comments as to how useful this Web site would be to business researchers.
3. Go to the following Web site: http://random.mat.sbg.ac.at/links. Use the functions on the Web site. Prepare a brief report of what the Web sites do and how they work. Include your comments as to how useful these Web sites would be to business researchers.
4. Go to the Web site: www.surveysystem.com/sscale.htm. On this Web site Creative Research Systems has placed a sample size calculator and some basic information about sampling and sample size. Prepare a brief report of what the Web site offers the user. Include comments on how useful this Web site would be to business researchers.

Data Analysis and Presentation

CHAPTER

9

Understanding and Presenting Data

Learning Objectives

1. Understand the importance of and approaches to data preparation.

2. Explain the benefits of charts and graphs for understanding data.

3. Explain measures of central tendency.

4. Understand how measures of dispersion differ from those of central tendency.

5. Explain how to identify and deal with outliers.

6. Discuss diagnostic tools used to better understand data.

INTRODUCTION

Business researchers typically have lots of data to help managers improve their decision making. One of their primary tasks is to convert data into knowledge. There are some basic approaches you can use to better understand your data and its underlying relationships. These approaches are helpful because in most situations today there are "too many numbers" to look at and identify patterns that might be useful. Most every data set needs some summary information developed, therefore, to summarize and describe the numbers it contains. The basic statistics and descriptive analysis covered in this chapter were developed for this purpose. In later chapters we show you more sophisticated methods to use when the simple approaches cannot explain the data relationships.

The easiest way to learn how statistics helps us to understand data relationships is to actually use the techniques. This means you must have some data to analyze. To help you we have prepared two databases that can be analyzed with the statistical techniques covered in this book. Once you have familiarized yourself with the databases you can apply all the statistical techniques to the data. We provide instructions throughout the chapters on how to use the SPSS software package. But the same types of analysis can be accomplished with SAS or other similar software packages. Descriptions of the variables and their **coding** are contained in Appendix 1-B of Chapter 1. An electronic copy of the data also is available on our Web site at www.wiley.com/college/hair. Learn more about SPSS from the "Research in Action" box.

The chapter initially provides an explanation of how to handle **data preparation** before you analyze your data. We then show you how to graphically display data so decision makers can better understand it. For example, if you conducted a survey of McDonald's customers, you would be able to most effectively show which survey respondents are the most frequent customers compared to the least frequent customers, and perhaps why.

RESEARCH IN ACTION
SPSS ANALYZES THE WORLD!

Globally, information is increasing exponentially. Organizations, both for-profit and not-for-profit, are collecting information in data warehouses to analyze and use to improve their decision making. To help people and organizations cope with information overload, a new management philosophy has emerged which is referred to as "knowledge management." Experts in this field say that probably 70 percent of the information decision makers need is already available. The problem is most organizations are not able to locate, retrieve, and analyze the information quickly.

Information technology experts build the infrastructure to locate and retrieve the information. But it still must be analyzed to identify the "pearls of wisdom" that are hidden in the mountains of data. This is where SPSS and other software companies come into the picture. Data analysis software packages have been available for over thirty years, but only recently have been adapted for user-friendly, Windows-based applications. Today, organizations have desktop access to very powerful data analysis techniques and one of the most popular is marketed by SPSS.

SPSS, Inc. (www.spss.com) claims their "solutions and products enable organizations to manage the future by learning from the past, understanding the present, as well as predicting potential problems and opportunities." Their "major strength and key differentiator is [their] breadth and depth of technology and expertise in data mining and statistical analysis—the technologies that make predictive analytics possible." SPSS delivers analytical tools and solutions to organizations around the world. For more information on SPSS, go to their Web site at www.spss.com.

For ease in learning, we often refer to the Samouel's and Gino's case and databases. But with access to the Internet, business researchers have a lot of online information and databases available to them. Several of the better Web sites are described in the "Research in Action" box.

DATA PREPARATION

After data has been collected and before it is analyzed, the researcher must examine it to ensure its validity. Blank responses, referred to as **missing data,** must be dealt with in some way. If the questions were pre-coded, then they can simply be input into a database. If they were not pre-coded, then a system must be developed so they can be input into the database. The typical tasks involved are **data editing,** which deals with missing data, coding, transformation, and entering data. We will discuss each of these.

DATA EDITING

Before questionnaire data can be used it must be edited. This means it must be inspected for completeness and consistency. Some inconsistencies may be able to be corrected at this point. For example, a respondent may have not answered the question on marriage. But in other questions she responded that she had been married ten years and had three children all under the age of eighteen. In such cases the researcher may choose to fill in the unanswered marriage question. Of course, this has some risk because the individual may have recently been divorced, or in some instances individuals choose to have children but not be married. If this is true, the researcher would be introducing bias in the data if he or she chose to mark the married category. Thus, if possible it is always best to contact individuals to complete missing responses.

Editing also involves checking to see if respondents understood the question or followed a particular sequence they were supposed to in a branching question. For example, assume the researcher is using an experimental design with two treatments. One treatment is designed to be a supportive work environment and the other treatment a much less supportive environment. To verify that a respondent interpreted the treatment properly, the researcher may do what is called a **manipulation check.** That is, after a respondent has answered the questions, he or she is asked to comment on how supportive both of the work environments were. If the respondent indicates both work environments are equally supportive it means he or she did not respond appropriately to the treatment. In such situations, the researcher may choose to remove that particular respondent from the data analysis because they did not see the difference in the two work environments.

Finally, editing may result in the elimination of questionnaires. For example, if there is a large proportion of missing data, then the entire questionnaire my have to be removed from the database. Similarly, a screening question may indicate you want to interview only persons who own their own home. But the response on a completed questionnaire may say a particular respondent is a renter. In such cases, the questionnaire must not be included in the data analysis. We talk about how to deal with missing data in the next section.

RESEARCH IN ACTION
ONLINE INFORMATION AND DATABASES

1. INFORMATION SERVICE	DIALOG
	Conducting searches and displaying title lists of search results is free, $3.45 per article.
Database	**Type of data**
ABI/INFORM	Citations and summaries of articles appearing in professional publications, academic journals, and trade magazines published worldwide. Information on company histories, competitive intelligence, and new product development.
Public Opinion Online (POLL)	Full text collection of public opinion surveys conducted in the United States.
Marketsearch: International Directory of Published Market Research	Directory of over 20,000 published market research studies on worldwide markets.
Business Dateline	Full text of articles from 550 regional business publications in the United States and Canada.
PTSP Prompt	Contains 1,100 active international trade and business publications, plus archive sources.
2. INFORMATION SERVICE	DOW JONES NEWS RETRIEVAL (DOW JONES AND COMPANY)
	$69 for a yearly subscription, plus $2.95 per article.
Database	**Type of data**
Business Newsstand	Articles from leading newspapers and business magazines, including *The Wall Street Journal, The New York Times, The Washington Post,* and *Los Angeles Times, Barron's, Business Week, Fortune,* and *Forbes.*
Company & Industry Center	Financial profiles, company screening reports, comparison reports, industry reports, and more than fifty full text market research reports.
Historical Market Data Center	More than twenty-five years' worth of historical price quotes on stocks, bonds, mutual funds, market indexes, and options.
The Wall Street Journal Interactive Edition	Business news including current stock and fund quotes and fund quotes and in-depth briefing books on more than 10,000 companies.
Company/Industry Quick Search	Company financial profiles, contact information, business descriptions, corporate performances, stock performance, press releases, and trade articles.
3. INFORMATION SERVICE	EBSCO
	Free access through participating universities and library systems.
Database	**Type of data**
EBSCOMasterFILE Premier	Full text for 1,880 periodicals covering nearly all subjects including general reference, business, and health.
Academic Search Elite	Full text for over 1,530 journals covering the social sciences, humanities, general science, multicultural studies, and education.

(continued)

Business Source Premier	Full text for 2,280 scholarly business journals covering management, economics, finance, accounting, and international business.
Business Wire News	Full text newswire database incorporating business wires from around the world.

4. INFORMATION SERVICE   **GALE GROUP DATABASES**
Free access through participating universities and library systems.

Database	Type of data
Business and Company	Company and industry news and information,
Resource Center	profiles, brand information, rankings, investment reports, company histories, chronologies, and periodicals.
General BusinessFile ASAP 1980–Present	Broker research reports, trade publications, newspapers journals, and company directory listings with full text and images available.
General Reference Center Gold	Many full text articles from newspapers, 1980–present reference books, and periodicals on current events, popular culture, business and industry coverage, the arts and sciences, sports, hobbies, etc.
National Newspaper Index 1997–Present	Indexes from *The New York Times, The Wall Street Journal, The Christian Science Monitor, Los Angeles Times,* and *The Washington Post.*

5. INFORMATION SERVICE   **SIRS KNOWLEDGE SOURCE**
Prices vary based on which products and how many you purchase.

Database	Type of data
SIRS Researcher	Full text articles from newspapers, magazines, journals, and U.S. government publications exploring social, scientific, health, historic, economic, business, political, and global issues.
SIRS Government Reporter	Full text documents concerning health, science, economics, environment, politics, foreign affairs, workplace issues, business and industry. Includes government documents, U.S. Supreme Court decisions, and information about federal departments, agencies, and elected officials.
SIRS Renaissance	Current information on music, literature, film, performing arts, culture, architecture, philosophy, religion, and visual arts.

MISSING DATA

Business researchers almost always have missing data, whether from surveys or internal sources such as data warehouses. Missing data can impact the validity of the researcher's findings and therefore must be identified and the problems resolved. Missing data typically arise because of data collection or **data entry** problems. The business researcher must assess how widespread the missing data problem is and whether or not it is systematic or random. If the problem is of limited scope, the typical solution is to simply eliminate respondents and/or questions with missing data. When missing data is more widespread the researcher must deal with it differently, because by removing respondents with missing data the sample size may become too small to provide meaningful results. In our restaurant survey, we collected a total of seventy-one employee surveys. But seven of them had missing data on one or more of the questions. In this case, we chose to simply remove the seven surveys with missing data and work with the remaining sixty-three interviews.

We will cover two approaches to deal with missing data, although other alternatives are possible.[1] The first approach is to identify the respondents and variables that have a large number of missing data points. These respondents and/or variables are then eliminated from the analysis. The second approach is to estimate the missing values by substituting the **mean.** Unfortunately this is only appropriate for metrically measured variables. When non-metric variables have missing data the respondent/question must be eliminated from analysis in most situations. If you are using the SPSS software, it has a procedure for substituting the mean before any data analysis. If you wish to do so, go to the Transform pull down menu, scroll down, and click on Replace Missing Values. Highlight and move variables with missing data into the box. Several methods of replacement are possible but we recommend you use the default that is Series mean and then click OK. For those who do not wish to replace missing data ahead of time, three techniques—regression, discriminant, and factor analysis—have options for excluding observations with missing data or replacing values with the mean.

CODING AND DATA ENTRY

Responses must be coded either before or after the data are collected. If at all possible, it is best to code them ahead of time. Coding means assigning a number to a particular response so the answer can be entered into a database. For example, if you are using a 5-point Agree–Disagree scale then you must decide if Strongly Agree will be coded with a 5 or a 1. Most researchers will assign the largest number to Strongly Agree and the smallest to Strongly Disagree; e.g., a 5 = Strongly Agree and a 1 = Strongly Disagree, with the points in between being assigned 2, 3, or 4. A special situation arises when the researcher has a two-category variable like gender. Some researchers use a coding approach that assigns a 1 = male and a 2 = female. But we recommend that in such instances a coding approach be used that assigns a 1 to one of the categories and a 0 to the other category. This enables greater flexibility in data analysis and is referred to as using dummy variable coding. We discuss this approach in a later chapter.

When interviews are completed using a computer-assisted approach, the responses are entered directly into the database. When self-completed questionnaires are used, it is good to use a scanner sheet because then responses can be directly scanned into the database. In other instances, however, the raw data must be manually keyed into the database using a PC. Most popular software, for example SPSS, includes a data editor that looks like a spreadsheet (see Appendix 1-C) that can be used to enter, edit, and view the contents of the database. Missing values typically are represented by a dot (.) in a cell so they must be coded in a special way as was indicated earlier.

Human errors can occur when completing the questionnaire, when coding it, or during data entry. Therefore, at least 10 percent of the coded questionnaires, as well as the actual database typically are checked for possible coding or data entry errors. Questionnaires to be checked usually are selected by a systematic, random sampling process.

DATA TRANSFORMATION

Data transformation is the process of changing the original form of data to a new format. This is typically done to more easily understand the data or achieve some other research objective. For example, with measurement scales we often have both negatively and positively worded statements. In such cases, the researcher typically will reverse code the questions that are negatively worded so a summated scale can be calculated to interpret the results. That is, if a 5-point scale is used, a 5 will be transformed to a 1 and a 4 to a 2; a 3 does not have to be changed. Another situation that might require transformation is when data is collected on the respondent's age. Generally, less response bias is associated when respondents are asked what year they were born in rather than how old they are. In such cases, the researcher would simply transform the birth year into the age of the respondent.

Researchers may also choose to collapse or combine adjacent categories of a variable in a way that reduces the number of categories. For example, a 7-point Agree–Disagree scale may be reduced to a 3-point scale by combining the 5, 6, and 7 responses and the 1, 2, and 3 responses. The 4 responses would remain the middle or neutral category.

Another important data transformation involves creating new variables by re-specifying the data with logical transformations. For example, we may choose to combine Likert scales into a summated rating. This would involve combining the scores (raw data) for several attitudinal statements into a single summated score. The summated score for a three-statement attitude scale is calculated as follows:

Summated score = variable 1 + variable 2 + variable 3

Another approach the researcher could use is to calculate the average summated score. This involves calculating the summated score and then dividing it by the number of variables. When this approach is used, the new, transformed, composite variable is comparable in scaling to the original scale. For example, if we had three 5-point statements the summated score might be 4 + 4 + 5 = 13. But if we used the average summated score the result would be 4 + 4 + 5 = 13 / 3 = 4.3.

USING CHARTS AND GRAPHICS TO BETTER UNDERSTAND DATA

Graphics and charts help you to more easily understand your data. They also more effectively communicate complex issues and make your business research reports more visually appealing. In this chapter we illustrate the value of frequency distributions, **bar charts, pie charts,** and line charts. We also review visuals that help us evaluate the quality of our data, such as stem-and-leaf and box-and-whisker plots.

FREQUENCY DISTRIBUTION

Business researchers often answer research questions based on a single variable. For example, the researcher may need to answer questions such as the following:

1. How likely is it that the employees of a particular business will search for another job? For example, are they very likely, somewhat likely, or not likely at all to search for a new job in the next six months?

> **RESEARCH IN ACTION**
>
> **USING SPSS TO CALCULATE SUMMATED AND AVERAGE SUMMATED SCORES**
>
> The work environment statements on the Samouel's employee survey include three measures related to the supervisor. They are variables X_3, X_6, and X_{10}. To calculate the summated score, load the employee survey data (Employee Survey N = 63.sav). The click-through sequence is: TRANSFORM → COMPUTE. First type a variable name in the Target Variable box. In this case we are calculating a summated score for the supervisory statements, so let's use the abbreviation SUMSUP for Summated Supervisor. Next click on the Numeric Expression box to move the cursor there. Look below at the buttons and click on the parenthesis to place it in the Numeric Expression box. Now highlight variable X_3 and click on the arrow box to move it into the parentheses. Go to the buttons below and click on the plus (+) sign. Go back and highlight variable X_6 and click on the arrow box to move it into the parentheses. Again click on the plus (+) sign. Finally, go back and highlight variable X_{10} and click on the arrow box to move it into the parentheses.
>
> Next click on "OK" and you will get the summated score for the three variables. You can find it as a new variable at the far right-hand side of your data editor screen.
>
> To calculate the average summated score you follow the same procedure as before. This time you must type a different Target Variable name than used before. Let's use the abbreviation ASUMSUP to indicate average summated supervisor rating. After you have moved all three variables into the parentheses and before you click on OK, you click the cursor to place it after the parentheses. Next go to the buttons below the Numeric Expression box and click on the slash sign (/ = the division sign) to place it after the parenthesis. Now again go to the buttons below the Numeric Expression box and click on 3. You click on 3 because you are calculating the average of the three variables. Next click on OK and you will get the average summated score for the three variables. You can find it as a new variable at the far right-hand side of your data editor screen.

---

2. What percentage of the patrons of a restaurant should be classified as very frequent, somewhat frequent, or infrequent users? For example, if you interview a sample of individuals as they leave Burger King, what percentage of them come there frequently versus infrequently?

3. What is the geographic location of customers? For example, are there more owners of Mercedes in Germany than in the USA?

Questions like these can be answered by examining a table that describes the data. The table is called a frequency distribution. Frequency distributions examine the data one variable at a time and provide counts of the different responses for the various values of the variable. The objective of a frequency distribution is to display the number of responses associated with each value of a variable. Typically, a frequency distribution shows the variable name and description, the frequency counts for each value of the variable, and the cumulative percentages for each value associated with a variable.

Let's use our Samouel's employee survey database to illustrate a frequency distribution. Exhibit 9-1 shows the three questions we use from the employee survey in many of the examples in this chapter. Note that employees were asked to indicate their feelings about working at Samouel's restaurant by responding to a 7-point Agree/Disagree scale. In the examples, question 13 is labeled "Loyalty," 14 is labeled "Effort," and 15 is labeled "Proud."

The frequency distribution for variable X_{15}—Proud is shown in Exhibit 9-2. In the frequency distribution table, the first column with numbers in it shows the various responses

EXHIBIT 9-1	EMPLOYEE SURVEY QUESTIONS USED AS EXAMPLES

Please indicate your view on each of the following questions:

	Strongly Disagree						Strongly Agree
13. I have a sense of loyalty to Samouel's Restaurant.	1	2	3	4	5	6	7
14. I am willing to put in a great deal of effort beyond that normally expected to help Samouel's restaurant to be successful.	1	2	3	4	5	6	7
15. I am proud to tell others that I work for Samouel's restaurant.	1	2	3	4	5	6	7

(ratings) to the question. For example, responses to this question were on a 7-point scale, but the lowest rating was a 4 and the highest was a 7. The second column, labeled Frequency, is the count of the number of times a particular rating was given by respondents. In this example, a rating of 5 was given by twenty-eight respondents. The third column, Percent, shows the percent of all respondents (N = 71) selecting the value for this variable. For example, 39.4 percent of the respondents gave a rating of 5 on this question (28/71 = 39.4%). The fourth column, Valid Percent, displays the percent of valid responses (N = 69). In other words, the percentage of "responses," not the percent of "respondents." For the survey there were eight respondents that had missing data on one or more of the questions. But, for this question (X_{15}) there were only two respondents (2.8%) with missing data. If there is no missing data the percentages in the Percent and Valid Percent columns will be the same. Cumulative Percent, the last column, is the cumulative percentage from the top to the bottom based on the valid response column. The cumulative percentage is simply the sum of the Valid Percents. In this survey, 55.1 percent of the respondents gave a rating of 5 or below.

Frequency distributions have many uses in business research. Frequency distributions are used to describe the responses to a particular variable by displaying the counts and percentages both before and after adjustment for non-responses (missing data). A frequency

EXHIBIT 9-2	FREQUENCY DISTRIBUTION FOR VARIABLE X_{15}—PROUD FROM THE EMPLOYEE SURVEY WITH MISSING DATA

X_{15}—Proud

Valid Responses	Frequency	Percent	Valid Percent	Cumulative Percent
4	10	14.1	14.5	14.5
5	28	39.4	40.6	55.1
6	21	29.6	30.4	85.5
Definitely Agree = 7	10	14.1	14.5	100.0
Total	69	97.2	100.0	
Missing	2	2.8		
Total	71	100.0		

RESEARCH IN ACTION
USING SPSS TO PREPARE A FREQUENCY DISTRIBUTION TABLE AND HISTOGRAM

It is easy to use SPSS to calculate the frequency distribution table in Exhibit 9-2. Set up your SPSS software and load the employee survey database with missing data (Employee Survey_N = 71 with Missing Data.sav). The click-through sequence is: ANALYZE → DESCRIPTIVE STATISTICS → FREQUENCIES. Scroll down and highlight X_{15}—Proud and click on the arrow box to move it into the Variables box. Click on Charts and then under Chart Type, click on Histograms and right below it With Normal Curve and finally Continue. Next click on OK to execute the program. The result will be the frequency chart and histogram shown in Exhibits 9-2 and 9-3.

distribution can be used to perform an "eyeball" check of the data, and to easily determine the amount of non-response, if any. If a rating appears in the frequency distribution that is not a valid response, the researcher also can determine when there are data inaccuracies. For example, seeing a zero on the frequency distribution in Exhibit 9-2 (where a 1–7 scale was used) would indicate a problem with the data since that rating was not possible given the coding of this variable. Cases in which ratings are out of range would be investigated and corrective actions taken. The researcher also can examine the data for each variable to see if there are any **outliers**—cases with extreme values that may distort the total picture. For example, an individual who eats at McDonald's more than ten times each week would be likely to be so unusual the person may be considered an outlier.

Histograms

A frequency distribution also provides evidence of the shape of the distribution for the variable. Are most of the responses on the high or low end of the response values? A vertical bar chart, or **histogram,** can be constructed from the information in the frequency distribution, and the shape of the actual data as presented in the histogram can be compared to the expected shape. Exhibit 9-3 is a histogram for the proud variable (X_{15}). It shows that

EXHIBIT 9-3 **HISTOGRAM FOR EMPLOYEE "PROUD" VARIABLE WITH MISSING DATA**

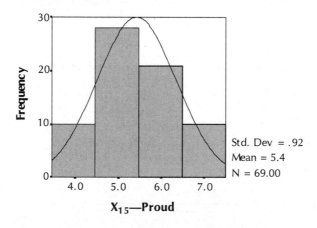

Std. Dev = .92
Mean = 5.4
N = 69.00

most employees of Samouel's restaurant are moderately proud to be working there. That is, most of the employees gave a "Proud" rating of 5, 6, or 7. A normal curve (bell-shaped) is superimposed over the histogram to facilitate comparison of the actual distribution with the normal curve. The distribution in this example conforms reasonably well to a normal curve. At the lower right hand corner of the graph, the mean, **standard deviation,** and sample size are indicated. Note the sample size is 69. This indicates there is missing data on this variable for two respondents.

The results shown previously would be of interest to Phil Samouel, owner of Samouel's Greek Cuisine. But a comparison of the satisfaction of his customers with those of Gino's also would be of interest to him. By making this comparison he could determine if there are differences in the satisfaction levels of the customers of the two restaurants. The question used to measure satisfaction on the Samouel's and Gino's customer surveys is shown in Exhibit 9-4.

The frequency tables in Exhibit 9-5 show the customer satisfaction ratings for the two restaurants. Note that you can now compare the satisfaction ratings for the two restaurants. First go to the Frequency column and look at the Total for both Samouel's and Gino's. You will see that each total is one hundred—the number of customers interviewed at each restaurant that had no missing data on their questionnaires. Now let's look at how the two customer groups responded to this question. To the far right is a column labeled Cumulative Percent. If you look at the third from the top number in this column you will see the number 68.0 percent for Samouel's. This is the percent of satisfaction ratings of 5.0 or lower. But when you look at Gino's you see that only 35 percent of his customers gave a satisfaction rating of 5 or below. These numbers tell us that Gino's customers are more satisfied than are Samouel's customers. How do we know this? It is based on the fact that

---

EXHIBIT 9-4   **CUSTOMER SURVEY QUESTION MEASURING SATISFACTION**

	Not Satisfied at All	1	2	3	4	5	6	7	Very Satisfied
17. How satisfied are you with Samouel's restaurant?									

EXHIBIT 9-5   **FREQUENCY TABLE COMPARING SAMOUEL'S AND GINO'S**

X_{17}—Satisfaction

X_{25}—Competitor			Frequency	Percent	Valid Percent	Cumulative Percent
Samouel's	Valid	3	10	10.0	10.0	10.0
		4	42	42.0	42.0	52.0
		5	16	16.0	16.0	68.0
		6	24	24.0	24.0	92.0
		Highly Satisfied = 7	8	8.0	8.0	100.0
		Total	100	100.0	100.0	
Gino's	Valid	4	7	7.0	7.0	7.0
		5	28	28.0	28.0	35.0
		6	27	27.0	27.0	62.0
		Highly Satisfied = 7	38	38.0	38.0	100.0
		Total	100	100.0	100.0	

RESEARCH IN ACTION

USING SPSS TO COMPARE SAMOUEL'S AND GINO'S ON CUSTOMER SATISFACTION

To compare the two restaurants on customer satisfaction, first load the customer database into your SPSS software—Customer Survey_N = 200.sav. Then, you first must go to your SPSS software and click on the pull-down menu labeled "Data." Scroll down and click on Split File, then on Compare Groups. Now scroll down and highlight variable X_{25}—Competitor and move it into the box labeled "Groups based on:", and click OK.

Now you can compare the two restaurants. The click-through sequence is: ANALYZE → DESCRIPTIVE STATISTICS → FREQUENCIES. Highlight X_{17}—Satisfaction and click on the arrow box to move it into the Variables box. Click on Charts and then under Chart Type click on Histograms, and right below it With Normal Curve and finally Continue. Next click on OK to run the program. The results will be the same as shown in Exhibits 9-5 and 9-6.

Gino's customers give higher ratings on the satisfaction variable (X_{17}) than do Samouel's customers. For example, as noted earlier, 68 percent of Samouel's customers rate his restaurant a 5 or below, while only 35 percent of Gino's customers rate his restaurant 5 or below. Information such as this can be very useful to business researchers, owners, and managers.

Visual comparisons using a histogram of the satisfaction ratings of the two restaurants make it even easier to compare the ratings. A histogram simply takes the information in a frequency table and displays it in a chart. We quickly see from Exhibit 9-6 that Samouel's has very few ratings of 7 (Highly Satisfied) and Gino's has many. Moreover, Samouel's has many ratings of 4 while Gino's has very few ratings of 4. Thus, it is easy to see that Gino's customers are more highly satisfied than are Samouel's.

Bar Charts

Bar charts show the data in the form of bars that can be displayed either horizontally or vertically (the only difference between a bar chart and a histogram is that there is no space

---

EXHIBIT 9-6   **HISTOGRAMS COMPARING SAMOUEL'S AND GINO'S**

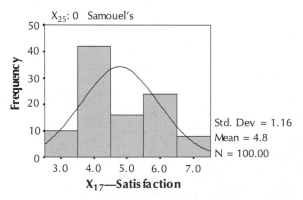

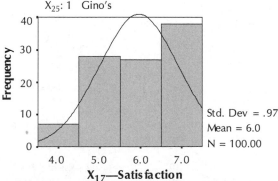

RESEARCH IN ACTION

FLORENCE NIGHTINGALE AND THE PIE CHART

Florence Nightingale is best remembered as the mother of modern nursing. Few realize, however, that she also occupies a place in history for her use of graphical methods to convey complex statistical information.

After witnessing deplorable sanitary conditions in the Crimea, she wrote *Notes on Matters Affecting the Health, Efficiency and Hospital Administration of the British Army* (1858), which included colorful polar-area diagrams where statistics being represented were proportional to the area of a wedge in a circular diagram. These charts visually illustrated that far more deaths were attributable to non-battle causes such as unsanitary conditions, than to battle-related causes.

With this information, Nightingale helped to promote the idea that social phenomena could be objectively measured and subjected to mathematical analysis. And, through this statistical approach, Nightingale convinced military authorities, Parliament, and Queen Victoria to carry out her proposed hospital reforms—which resulted in a decline in the mortality rate for soldiers.

As Nightingale demonstrated, statistics provided an organized way of learning and led to improvements in medical and surgical practices. She also developed a Model Hospital Statistical Form that could be used to collect and generate consistent data and statistics. She became a Fellow of the Royal Statistical Society in 1858, an honorary member of the American Statistical Association in 1874, and has been acknowledged as a "prophetess" in the development of applied statistics.

SOURCE: www.math.yorku.ca/SCS/Gallery/flo.html

---

between the bars in a histogram). Bar charts are very useful for showing both absolute and relative magnitudes, and for comparing differences. Exhibit 9-7 is an example of a vertical bar chart for the distribution of responses to a question in the Samouel's employee survey (X_{15}—Proud). The question asked how proud an employee is that she or he worked at Samouel's restaurant. Respondents rated the question using a 7-point scale where 7 = Definitely Agree and 1 = Definitely Disagree. For example, the frequency (10) for the value of Definitely Agree = 7 is the vertical bar on the right side of the chart. This chart shows that a moderately high proportion of Samouel's employees are proud to work there (a high proportion of employees responded with a 5, 6, or 7 on the 7-point scale). Note that none of the responses were lower than a four on the 7-point scale.

Pie Charts

Pie charts display relative proportions of the responses. Each section of the pie is the relative proportion. That is, the pie sections are shown as a percent of the total area of the pie. In Exhibit 9-8 there is a pie chart for variable X_{15}—Proud in the Samouel's employee survey. Generally, six or seven sections in a pie chart are considered the maximum possible, and three to four is ideal.

The pie chart is another way to present data visually. The proportion of Samouel's employees that indicated they were very proud to work there (responded with a 5, 6, or 7) was very high—over 80 percent. Check out the "Research in Action" box for an interesting historical perspective on the pie chart.

The numbers and percentages in our restaurant examples show how customers and employees rate various aspects of the restaurant operations. Because numbers were involved, frequency distributions, bar charts and pie charts all can be used to calculate

---
RESEARCH IN ACTION

USING SPSS TO CREATE BAR CHARTS AND PIE CHARTS

You can use your SPSS software to create the bar chart in exhibit 9-7. Load the employee database. The click-through sequence to prepare a bar chart for variable X_{15}—Proud is: ANALYZE → DESCRIPTIVE STATISTICS → FREQUENCIES. Highlight X_{15} and click on the arrow box to move it into the Variables box. Click on Charts and Bar Charts, and then Continue. Next click on OK to execute the program. You should now see the same bar chart as in Exhibit 9-7.

You also can use your SPSS software to create pie charts. The click-through sequence is: ANALYZE → DESCRIPTIVE STATISTICS → FREQUENCIES. Highlight X_{15}—Proud and click on the arrow box to move it into the Variables box. Click on Charts and Pie Charts, and then Continue. Next click on OK to run the program. The pie chart is shown in Exhibit 9-8.

---

descriptive statistics. We next discuss the normal curve and then measures of **central tendency** and dispersion.

THE NORMAL DISTRIBUTION

One of the most useful distributions for business researchers is the **normal distribution,** also called the normal curve. The normal distribution describes the expected distribution of sample means as well as many other chance occurrences. The normal curve is symmetrical, bell shaped, and almost all (99 percent) of its values are within plus/minus

EXHIBIT 9-7	**BAR CHART AND FREQUENCY TABLE FOR VARIABLE X_{15}—PROUD TO WORK AT SAMOUEL'S**

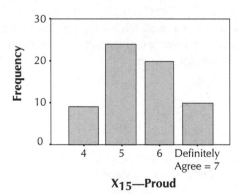

Response	Frequency	Percent	Valid Percent	Cumulative Percent
4	9	14.3	14.3	
5	24	38.1	38.1	14.3
6	20	31.7	31.7	52.4
Definitely Agree = 7	10	15.9	15.9	84.1
Total	**63**	**100.0**	**100.0**	**100.0**

EXHIBIT 9-8	PIE CHART OF VARIABLE X_{15}—PROUD

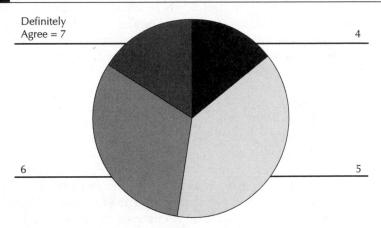

three standard deviations from its mean. An example of a normal curve is shown in Exhibit 9-9. Note that when you have a normal distribution 68 percent of the values are within plus or minus one standard deviation and 95 percent are within plus or minus two standard deviations. The normal distribution is particularly important because it provides the underlying basis for many of the inferences made by business researchers.

MEASURES OF CENTRAL TENDENCY

Frequency distribution tables are easy to read and provide a great deal of basic information about your data. Many times, however, researchers need to summarize and condense information to better understand it. Measures of central tendency can be used to do this. The mean, median, and mode are measures of central tendency. Measures of central tendency locate the center of the distribution as well as other useful information.

Mean

The **mean** is the arithmetic average, and is one of the most commonly used measures of central tendency. For example, if you are interested in knowing the daily consumption of soft drinks, you can calculate the mean (average) number soft drinks an individual drinks each day. The mean can be used when your data is measured with either an interval or a ratio scale (also called metric). The data typically shows some degree of central tendency with most of the responses distributed close to the average, or mean value.

EXHIBIT 9-9	THE NORMAL CURVE

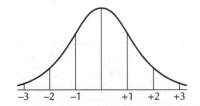

In most instances the mean is not sensitive to data values being added or deleted. For this reason, statisticians say it is a "robust" measure of central tendency. If extreme values (referred to as outliers) occur in the distribution, however, the mean can misrepresent the true characteristics of the data. For example, suppose you ask four individuals how many Cokes they drink in a single day. Respondent answers are as follows: Respondent A = 1 Coke; Respondent B = 10; Respondent C = 5; and Respondent D = 6. In addition, you have observed that respondents A and B are females and respondents C and D are males. With this knowledge, you now can compare consumption of Cokes between males and females. Looking at the females first (Respondents A and B) we calculate the mean number of Cokes to be 5.5 (1 + 10 = 11 / 2 = 5.5). Similarly, looking at the males next (Respondents C and D) we calculate the mean number of Cokes to be 5.5 (5 + 6 = 11 / 2 = 5.5). We could conclude there are no differences in the consumption patterns of males and females if we consider only the mean number of Cokes consumed per day. But if we consider the underlying distribution, it is obvious there are some differences. The two females are at the extremes while both males are in the middle of the distribution. Drawing conclusions based only on the mean can distort our understanding of the Coke consumption patterns of males and females in situations like the preceding example. Of course, we must also consider that in this example we were referring to a small sample and as the sample size increases the ability to accurately infer to the larger population improves. So sample size must be considered as well in drawing conclusions about distributions and their characteristics, such as means.

The mean is most often used with interval or ratio data (metric). But as noted above, when extreme values occur within the data the mean can distort the results. In those situations, the median and the mode should be considered.

Median

The next measure of central tendency, the **median,** is the value that is in the middle of the distribution. In other words, the median is the value below (and above) which half the values in the sample distribution fall. For this reason, it is sometimes referred to as the 50th percentile. For example, let's assume you interviewed a sample of individuals about the number of soft drinks they drink in a typical week. You might find the median number of soft drinks consumed is 10, with the number of soft drinks consumed above and below this number being the same (the median number is the exact middle of the distribution). If you have an even number of data observations, the median is the average of the two middle values. If you have an odd number of observations, the median is the middle value. The median is the appropriate measure of central tendency for ordinal data.

Mode

The **mode** is the measure of central tendency that identifies the value that occurs most often in the sample distribution. For example, the typical individual may drink an average of three Cokes per day, but the number of Cokes that most people drink is only two (the mode). The mode is the value that represents the highest peak in the distribution's graph. The mode is the appropriate measure of central tendency for data that is nominal (categorical).

Example of Measures of Central Tendency

The statistics table in Exhibit 9-10 contains the measures of central tendency for the 63 employee surveys with no missing data. Note that the mean is 5.49, the median is 5.0, the mode is 5 and there is no missing data. Since this variable is measured on a 7-point scale, with

---

RESEARCH IN ACTION

USING EXCEL TO COMPUTE MEASURES OF CENTRAL TENDENCY

You can use Excel to compute the measures of central tendency. First, highlight the numbers included in the calculation (e.g., column or row of numbers). To do this, click on the column desired and it will highlight all the data in the column. Next, go to the bottom of the column and click on the first open cell at the bottom of the column. Then follow the sequence below.

The Excel click-through sequence is: Insert → Function → Or select a category → All. After the sequence is completed, scroll down the list of functions in the large text box and highlight MEAN (Average), MEDIAN, or MODE, whichever is desired. Select OK and the "Function Arguments" box will appear. This box lets the user make sure that the correct column(s) have been selected. Select OK again and the computer will begin its calculation. The answer will appear in the cell selected at the bottom of the column.

To calculate the mean for variable X_{15} on the employee survey, highlight column P (that is the one that has the data for X_{15}), and then go to the bottom of the column and click on the first open cell. Follow the above sequence of steps and select average, and then click on OK twice. The results will be the same as in Exhibit 9-10. A similar process is followed to calculate the median and the mode.

---

1 = Definitely Disagree and 7 = Definitely Agree, this shows that employees feel very proud to work at Samouel's (the middle of the 7-point scale = 4).

Next look at the histogram in Exhibit 9-11. We have imposed a normal curve on the chart to enable you to compare the responses to it. The chart visually shows you the lowest point on the 7-point scale for X_{15}—Proud is 4 and the highest is 7. It also shows the distribution is fairly normal and does not present a problem.

MEASURES OF DISPERSION

Measures of central tendency seldom give a complete picture of a sample distribution. For example, if McDonald's collects data about customers' attitudes toward a new steak sandwich, you could calculate the mean, median, and mode of the distribution of answers. But you also might want to know if there is much variability in the respondent's opinions about the steak sandwich. For example, recall our discussion of the mean and Coke consumption where males and females averaged the same consumption, but females were very high and very low in the distribution and males were in the middle. If McDonald's survey of attitudes toward the new steak sandwich is very consistent (little variation) and on the positive end of the scale, they would likely be pleased. On the other hand, if the responses varied from the very low extreme (negative) to the very high extreme (positive) they would want to investigate the new sandwich more before adding it to their menu. Specifically, they would want to know why there are negative responses (very low extreme) and what could be done to eliminate or minimize them. You can learn more about this problem by examining the measures of **dispersion** associated with the distribution of sample responses on the customer survey.

EXHIBIT 9-10	MEASURES OF CENTRAL

Statistics
X_{15}—Proud

N	Valid	63
	Missing	0
Mean		5.49
Median		5.00
Mode		5

RESEARCH IN ACTION

USING SPSS TO CALCULATE MEASURES OF CENTRAL TENDENCY

You can calculate the measures of central tendency with the SPSS software. The SPSS click-through sequence is: ANALYZE → DESCRIPTIVE STATISTICS → FREQUENCIES. Let's again examine X_{15}—Proud from the employee survey (Employee Survey N = 63.sav). Click on X_{15} to highlight it and then on the arrow button for the Variables box to use it in your analysis. Next open the Statistics box and click on Mean, Median, and Mode, and then Continue. Next click on Charts, Histogram and then right below it With Normal Curve and Continue. We will use the defaults for the Format box, so click on OK to run the program. The results will be the same as shown in Exhibits 9-10 and 9-11.

Measures of dispersion describe the tendency for sample responses to depart from the central tendency. Calculating the dispersion of the data, or how the responses vary from the mean, is another means of summarizing the data. Typical measures of dispersion used to describe the variability in a distribution of numbers include the **range,** the **variance,** the standard deviation, **skewness,** and **kurtosis.**

Range

The range is the simplest measure of dispersion. It defines the spread of the data and is the distance between the largest and the smallest values of a sample frequency distribution. We also can define the range by saying it identifies the end-points of the sample distribution. For example, if our McDonald's survey of opinions about a new steak sandwich asked the likelihood of purchasing the sandwich using a 10-point scale and the highest likelihood rating is 8 and the lowest rating is 1, the range is seven (8 − 1 = 7).

Variance

To determine how far away a respondent is from the mean we can calculate individual deviation scores for each respondent. If the deviation scores are large, we will find that the distribution has a wide spread or variability. The problem with deviation scores is that when

---

EXHIBIT 9-11   **HISTOGRAM WITH NORMAL CURVE FOR X_{15}—PROUD**

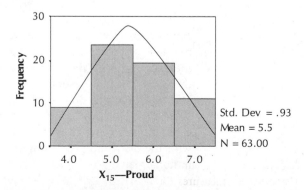

Std. Dev = .93
Mean = 5.5
N = 63.00

X_{15}—Proud

we try to calculate an average deviation for all respondents the positive deviation scores always cancel out the negative ones, thus leaving an average deviation value of zero. To eliminate this problem we can square the deviation scores and then calculate the average. The result is a measure called the variance. It is useful to describe the variability of the distribution and is a very good index of the degree of dispersion. The variance is equal to zero if each and every respondent in the distribution is the same as the mean. The variance becomes larger as the observations tend to differ increasingly from each other and from the mean.

Standard Deviation

The variance is often used in statistics. But it does have a major drawback. The variance is a unit of measurement that has been squared. For example, if we measure the number of Cokes consumed in a day and wish to calculate an average for the sample of respondents, the mean will be the average number of Cokes and the variance will be in squared numbers. To overcome the problem of having the measure of dispersion in squared units instead of the original measurement units, we use the square root of the variance, which is called the standard deviation. The standard deviation describes the spread or variability of the sample distribution values from the mean, and is perhaps the most valuable index of dispersion.

To obtain the squared deviation we square the individual deviation scores before adding them (squaring a negative number produces a positive result). Once the sum of the squared deviations is determined, it is divided by the number of respondents minus 1. The number 1 is subtracted from the number of respondents to help produce an unbiased estimate of the standard deviation. If the estimated standard deviation is large, the responses in a sample distribution of numbers do not fall very close to the mean of the distribution. If the estimated standard deviation is small, you know that the distribution values are close to the mean.

Another way to think about the estimated standard deviation is that its size tells us something about the level of agreement among the respondents when they answered a particular question. For example, in Samouel's employee survey, respondents were asked to indicate their loyalty and pride about working at Samouel's (X_{13} and X_{15}) using a 7-point scale. If the estimated standard deviation of these two variables is small (< 1.0) it means the respondents were very consistent in their opinions about working at Samouel's. In contrast, if the estimated standard deviation of these two variables is large (> 3.0), then there is a lot of variability in their opinions.

One final concept to be clarified is the standard error of the mean. The standard deviation of the sampling distribution of the mean is referred to as the standard error of the mean. When we have information on the population we can determine the standard deviation. Since we seldom have population information we typically draw a sample and estimate the standard deviation. When we draw only one sample we refer to this as the estimated standard deviation. When we draw many samples from the same population, we have a sampling distribution of all the possible values of the sample means. The standard deviation of this distribution of means is the standard error of the mean.

Skewness and Kurtosis

We often are interested in the shape of our distribution. Two measures we typically look at are skewness and kurtosis. Skewness measures the departure from a symmetrical (or balanced)

RESEARCH IN ACTION

USING EXCEL TO COMPUTE THE STANDARD DEVIATION

You can use Excel to compute the standard deviation. First, highlight all of the numbers included in the calculation (a column or row of data). To do this, click on the column (or row) desired. Next, go to the bottom of the column (or somewhere on the Excel spreadsheet) and click on the first open cell. Then follow the sequence below.

The Excel click-through sequence is: Insert → Function → Or select a category → All. After the sequence is completed, scroll down the list of functions in the large text box and highlight STDEV, which stands for standard deviation. Select OK and the Function Arguments box will appear. This box lets the user make sure that the correct column(s) or rows(s) have been selected. Select OK again and the computer will begin its calculation. The answer will appear in the cell selected.

To calculate the standard deviation for variable X_{15} on the employee survey, highlight column P (that is the one that has the data for X_{15}), and then go to the bottom of the column and click on the first open cell. Follow the above sequence of steps and select STDEV, and then click on OK twice. The results will be the same as in Exhibit 9-12. Remember that if you have already calculated the mean for variable X_{15} on the employee survey then you must delete the calculated mean from the cell before computing the standard deviation.

---

distribution. In a symmetrical distribution the mean, median, and mode are in the same location. A distribution that has respondents stretching toward one tail or the other is called skewed. When the tail stretches to the left (smaller values) it is negatively skewed. When the tail stretches to the right (larger values) it is skewed positively. When a distribution is symmetrical the skewness is zero, and the larger the number the larger the skewness. With a positive skew we get a positive number and with a negative skew we get a negative number. When skewness values are larger than +1 or smaller than −1 this indicates a substantially skewed distribution.

Kurtosis is a measure of a distribution's peakedness (or flatness). Distributions where responses cluster heavily in the center are peaked. Distributions with scores more widely distributed and tails further apart are considered flat. For a normal curve the value of kurtosis is zero. A large positive value means the distribution is too peaked while a large negative value means the distribution is too flat. A curve is too peaked when the kurtosis exceeds +3 and is too flat when it is below −3.

Measures of central tendency and dispersion can reveal a lot about the distribution of a set of numbers from a survey. Business researchers often are interested, however, in solving research problems involving more than one variable at a time. We will explain how to do this in later chapters.

Example of Measures of Dispersion

The measures of dispersion for X_{15}—Proud on Samouel's employee survey are shown in Exhibit 9-12. The highest response on the 7-point scale is a 7 (maximum) and the lowest response is a 4 (minimum). None of the respondents gave a 1, 2, or 3 on this question. The range is calculated as the distance between the smallest and the largest values in the set of responses and is three ($7 - 4 = 3$). The standard deviation is .931 and the variance is .867. A standard deviation of .931 on a 7-point scale is relatively small and indicates the responses are reasonably close to the sample mean of 5.49.

EXHIBIT 9-12	MEASURES OF DISPERSION

Statistics
X_{15}—Proud

Valid N	63
Missing	0
Std. Deviation	.931
Variance	.867
Skewness	.086
Std. Error of Skewness	.302
Kurtosis	–.809
Std. Error of Kurtosis	.595
Range	3
Minimum	4
Maximum	7

OUTLIERS

An outlier is a respondent (observation) that has one or more values that are distinctly different from the values of other respondents. Like missing data, outliers can impact the validity of the researcher's findings and therefore must be identified and dealt with as well. Outliers may result from data collection or data entry errors. This type typically is identified and corrected in the data-cleaning phase of the research project. A second type of outlier may be an accurate observation that represents the true characteristics of the population, but still distorts the findings. For example, if we calculated the average net worth of the households located in the neighborhood where Bill Gates of Microsoft lives, the resulting average would be much higher with Gates included as opposed to being eliminated, because his extremely high net worth makes him an outlier. Certainly Gates's neighbors are wealthy, but they have a far smaller net worth than he does. In this situation, the question would be "Is the average net worth of households in Bill Gates's neighborhood more representative with him included or excluded?" The answer here is it depends upon the research objectives. The true average would include Bill Gates. But removing him would be much more representative of the typical net worth in the neighborhood.

The third type of outlier is a respondent(s) that has one or more values that are unique, but there is no apparent reason (with the Bill Gates example we knew the reason, here we do not). In cases like this, if the researcher cannot determine the outlier represents a valid segment of the population it must be removed. For more information on the nature of outliers and how to deal with them see Hair, et al. 2003, *Multivariate Data Analysis: With Readings.* Prentice-Hall, 6th edition.

OTHER DIAGNOSTIC MEASURES

We will discuss two other useful diagnostic tools to better understand your data. The first is **box and whiskers plots** and the second is **stem and leaf plots**.

RESEARCH IN ACTION
USING SPSS TO CALCULATE MEASURES OF DISPERSION

We will illustrate the measures of dispersion using the X_{15}—Proud variable from Samouel's employee survey and the SPSS software. The SPSS click-through sequence is: ANALYZE → DESCRIPTIVE STATISTICS → FREQUENCIES. To do so, highlight X_{15} and then click on the arrow button to move it into the Variables box. Next click on Statistics and go to the Dispersion box. Click on Standard deviation, Variance, Range, Minimum and Maximum, Skewness and Kurtosis, and then Continue. If you would like to create Charts, click on this box and choose from your options of Bar, Pie, and Histogram. We will use the defaults for the Format box so click on OK to run the program. The results will be the same as in Exhibit 9-12.

BOX AND WHISKER PLOTS

A valuable tool for examining your data is the box and whisker plot. It visually displays the distribution's location, spread, shape, tail length, and outliers. Boxplots are visual representations of the median, upper and lower quartiles, and the largest and smallest respondent values. A rectangular box is in the middle and includes 50 percent of the data values (two inner quartiles). A centerline in the box marks the median value. The top whisker and bottom whisker extend as straight lines to the largest and smallest values from the box, and include the remaining data, with the exception of outliers (extreme values). Across the end of the whisker is a hinge. The hinge is located so as to encompass all the values within 1.5 times the interquartile range from either edge of the box. Any value outside plus or minus 1.5 times the interquartile range is considered an outlier. Boxplots are an excellent diagnostic tool for business researchers. They visually represent the shape (symmetry) of the data, the skewness, the spread, and show outliers, if any. Exhibit 9-13 shows a box and whiskers plot for the Samouel's employee survey variable X_{13}—Loyalty. The hinges show the highest rating for this variable is 7 and the lowest is 4, while the median value is 6. The two inner quartiles are not the same size. The lower quartile is larger, indicating there are more respondents in this quartile than in the upper quartile. There are no outliers for this question since there are no observations outside of the hinges.

Exhibit 9-14 shows a box and whiskers plot for the Samouel's employee survey variable X_{14}—Effort. The median is 5 and the entire inner quartile is either at or above the median. This means 25 percent of the responses are either a 3 or a 4. Note that this plot has identified an outlier response of 3 at the low end of the scale. It shows that respondent 58 is more than 1.5 times the interquartile range from the box, and that the hinge is located 1.5 times the width of the box away from the bottom of the box and respondent 58 is further away. The distribution is not symmetrical but skewed somewhat to the top, which is the higher end of the scale. The spread that includes 99 percent of the values (plus/minus three standard deviations) goes from 4 to 7.

EXHIBIT 9-13	BOX AND WHISKERS PLOT FOR EMPLOYEE SURVEY VARIABLE

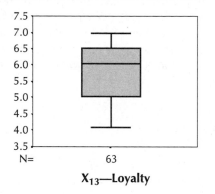

N= 63

X_{13}—Loyalty

RESEARCH IN ACTION

USING SPSS TO DERIVE A BOXPLOT

You can derive a boxplot using SPSS. The SPSS click-through sequence is: ANALYZE → DESCRIPTIVE STATISTICS → EXPLORE. Highlight variable X_{14}—Effort and then click on the arrow box for the Dependent List box to use it in your analysis. Keep the Default in the Display box, open the Statistics box and click on Outliers and Continue, then go to Plots and unclick Stem and Leaf because we discuss this in the next section, and then on Continue. For the Options box we will use the defaults so click on OK to execute the program. The boxplot for variable X_{14} is shown in Exhibit 9-14. SPSS identifies outliers by showing the respondent number.

EXHIBIT 9-14 BOX AND WHISKERS PLOT AND HISTOGRAM FOR EMPLOYEE SURVEY

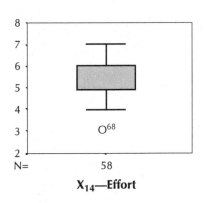

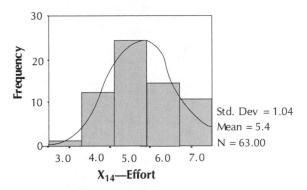

Std. Dev = 1.04
Mean = 5.4
N = 63.00

STEM AND LEAF DISPLAYS

Stem and leaf displays are a diagnostic tool closely related to histograms. But unlike histograms, they do not group data values into intervals and thereby lose information. Stem and leaf displays show actual data values that can be inspected directly without the use of enclosed bars. This feature displays the distribution of values within the interval and preserves their rank order for finding the median, mode, and other summary statistics. The range of values is easily visualized and both shape and spread impressions are immediate. Patterns in the data are easily observed, such as gaps where no values exist, areas where values are clustered, and outliers that differ from the main data.

Exhibit 9-15 shows the stem and leaf plot for variable X_{14}—Effort. The column to the far left is the frequency of a particular response. The value of a response is listed under the Stem column and respondents are plotted under the Leaf with zeros. For example, for the value four (Stem) the frequency on the left indicates twelve and on the right under the Leaf column there are twelve zeros to indicate twelve responses. With small sample sizes each zero represents one response in that particular category of a leaf. But with larger samples each leaf (0) may represent two or more respondents (cases). In sum, this is a form of horizontal bar chart created with zeros. At the top of the chart it notes that there is one extreme value (outlier) that is equal to or less than 3.

SUMMARY

Understand the Importance of and Approaches to Data Preparation

After data has been collected, and before it is analyzed, the researcher must examine it to ensure its validity. Blank responses, referred to as missing data, must be dealt with in some way. If the questions were pre-coded then they can simply be input into a database. If they were not pre-coded then a system must be developed so they can be input into the database. The typical tasks involved are editing, dealing with missing data, coding, transformation, and entering data.

EXHIBIT 9-15	STEM AND LEAF PLOT FOR EMPLOYEE SURVEY VARIABLE X_{14}—EFFORT

X_{14}—Effort Stem and Leaf Plot

Frequency	Stem and Leaf
1.00 Extremes	(=<3.0)
12.00	4 . 000000000000
.00	4 .
24.00	5 . 000000000000000000000000
.00	5 .
15.00	6 . 000000000000000
.00	6 .
11.00	7 . 00000000000
Stem width:	1
Each leaf:	1 case(s)

Explain the Benefits of Charts and Graphs for Understanding Data

Graphics and charts help you to more easily understand your data. They not only add clarity but also impact on research reports. The most often used charts and graphs include frequency distributions, bar charts, pie charts, and line charts. We also use visuals that help us determine whether we have missing data and outliers, such as stem and leaf graphs and box and whisker plots.

Explain Measures of Central Tendency

Measures of central tendency enable researchers to summarize and condense information to better understand it. The mean, median, and mode are measures of central tendency. Measures of central tendency locate the center of the distribution as well as other useful information.

Understand How Measures of Dispersion Differ from Those of Central Tendency

Measures of dispersion describe the tendency for responses to depart from the central tendency (mean, median, and mode). Calculating the dispersion of the data, or how the

RESEARCH IN ACTION
USING SPSS TO DERIVE A STEM AND LEAF PLOT

You can derive a stem and leaf plot using SPSS. The SPSS click-through sequence is: ANALYZE → DESCRIPTIVE STATISTICS → EXPLORE. Highlight variable X_{14}—Effort and then click on the arrow box for the Dependent List box to use it in your analysis. Keep the Default in the Display box, open the Statistics box, and click on Outliers and Continue. For the Plots and Options boxes we use the defaults so click on OK to execute the program. The result will be the same as the stem-and-leaf plot in Exhibit 9-15.

responses vary from the mean, is another means of summarizing the data. Typical measures of dispersion used to describe the variability in a distribution of numbers include the range, the variance, the standard deviation, skewness, and kurtosis.

Explain How to Identify and Deal with Outliers

When you have outliers, as well as observations with missing data, you must decide whether to retain or eliminate them. The most conservative approach is to eliminate them to avoid distorting or misrepresenting your findings. If you retain them, you must have a valid reason for doing so. This is also true if you decide to replace the missing data with an estimate of the value and then retain them in your analysis. Retaining observations with missing or replaced data is risky and must be done cautiously.

Discuss Other Diagnostic Tools Used to Better Understand Data

Two diagnostic tools that help us to better understand our data are box and whisker plots and stem and leaf displays. Box and whiskers plots are a visual representation of the range and variation of the distribution. They also are useful for identifying outliers. Stem and leaf displays show actual data values and quickly illustrate outliers that differ from the main data distribution or gaps in data where no values exist or where values are clustered.

KEY TERMS

bar chart	dispersion	normal distribution
box and whiskers plot	frequency distribution	outliers
central tendency	histogram	pie chart
coding	kurtosis	range
data editing	mean	skewness
data entry	median	standard deviation
data preparation	missing data	stem and leaf displays
data transformation	mode	variance

ETHICAL DILEMMA

Ann Webster is a sales analyst for a large grocery company. The company is planning its annual meeting and Ann's boss has asked her to prepare visuals for the company's performance presentation. The company president is planning to downplay the fact that the company's overall sales are slipping by focusing on the performance of the company's top five stores. Therefore, Ann is asked to prepare separate bar charts for each of the top stores listing the sales periods in ascending order and to prepare a bar chart of the overall sales figures with sales period in descending order. Although the data will be factual, Ann realizes that the graphics will mislead board members. What should she do?

REVIEW QUESTIONS

1. What are some useful online databases? Tell why each is useful.

2. Why is it necessary to prepare data before analyzing it?

3. How can frequency distributions help us better understand our data?

4. How do measures of central tendency differ from measures of dispersion?

5. What is an outlier?

6. What are the box and whiskers and stem and leaf displays used for?

DISCUSSION AND APPLICATION ACTIVITIES

1. Why would the business researcher want to use charts and graphs?

2. What is the value of measures of central tendency and dispersion?

3. Why are missing data and outliers a problem?

4. SPSS Application: Examine all the variables in the employee database using histograms, skewness, range, and box and whiskers to determine if you have any problems with the data.

INTERNET ACTIVITIES

1. The SPSS statistical software package has a home page at www.spss.com. Go to their Web site and identify and summarize the statistical techniques that can be used with the activities in this chapter.

2. The home page for the American Statistical Association is www.amstat.org. Go to their Web site and identify and summarize the career options that one might have if they are interested in statistics.

3. Go to www.yankelovich.com. Prepare a report summarizing the MONITOR. How can business researchers use the data from this research?

4. Go to www.acop.com. Prepare a report summarizing the Web site and the types of surveys being completed.

5. Go to www.raosoft.com. Prepare a report summarizing the functions and value of this Web site to business researchers.

NOTES

1.   Hair, Joseph F., William C. Black, Rolph Anderson and Ronald Tatham. 2003. *Multivariate Data Analysis: With Readings.* Prentice-Hall, 6th edition.

CHAPTER 10

Basic Data Analysis Methods

Learning Objectives

- Discuss hypothesis testing and why we use it.
- Explain the concept of statistical significance.
- Understand how to choose the appropriate statistical technique.
- Explain the difference between sample statistics and population parameters.
- Explain the differences between the t-test, ANOVA, and Chi-square.

INTRODUCTION

Data becomes knowledge only after analysis has identified a set of descriptions, relationships, and differences that are of use in decision making. Data is collected in business research for two broad purposes—discovery and hypothesis testing. When the purpose is discovery the researcher uses descriptive statistics such as those discussed in the preceding chapter. When the purpose is hypothesis testing the researcher uses inferential statistics. Descriptive statistics are used to describe and characterize the sample being examined. In contrast, inferential statistics enable the business researcher to draw conclusions about a population from a sample.

In this chapter, we first describe hypothesis testing. Next, we review and explain the relationship between **sample statistics** and **population parameters.** Finally, we cover several univariate and bivariate statistics that can be used to test hypotheses. Throughout this book we use the statistical software package SPSS. The "Research in Action" box describes a less expensive, but still reasonably comprehensive, statistical software package called XLSTAT.

WHAT IS A HYPOTHESIS?

Measures of central tendency and dispersion are useful tools for business researchers. Often, researchers will have some preliminary ideas regarding data relationships based on

---

RESEARCH IN ACTION
XLSTAT OFFERS AFFORDABLE STATISTICAL ANALYSIS

There are many high quality statistical analysis software packages available for business researchers that provide broad analysis and investigation capabilities. But these packages, such as SPSS, STATISTICA, and SAS, are quite sophisticated and often too pricey for students, the occasional analyst, and small businesses. Fortunately, there is a user-friendly and cost-effective alternative—XLSTAT.

In 1993, French statistician Thierry Fahmy developed an easy-to-use Excel add-on for basic statistical analysis and data analysis. XLSTAT was designed to help users gain time by eliminating the complicated and risky data transfers between applications for data analysis. Since its inception, XLSTAT has been expanded to incorporate the following procedures: Data Management, Data Analysis, Models, Excel Utilities, and Test and Confidence.

XLSTAT offers over forty different functions to enhance Excel that make it an everyday statistical solutions package for small businesses. Not only can the package perform simple techniques like Box Plots, Frequencies, and other descriptive statistics, it also provides fairly extensive data analysis procedures, including the following: Clustering 1 and 2; Correlations/Principal Components Analysis (PCA); Correspondence Analysis (CA); Descriptive Statistics; Discriminant Analysis; Factor Analysis; Histograms; Multidimensional Scaling (MDS); Multiple Correspondence Analysis; and Odds Ratio.

Because XLSTAT is quick, easy-to-use, reliable, and, best of all, affordable, the software is used by many businesses and universities in over seventy countries throughout the world. An XLSTAT demo can be downloaded through the Web site (www.xlstat.com), which can be used twenty times before expiring. Both electronic and CD-Rom versions of the XLSTAT package also can be purchased online. In addition, the company offers a low cost version of XLSTAT (approximately $50) for students and "NGOs, Third World countries or disabled people," so that everyone has access to the tools needed for effective statistical analysis.

SOURCES: www.xlstat.com; Ken Deal. 2001. Statistical Analysis When You Don't Need the Big Guns. *Marketing Research: A Magazine of Management and Applications* (Summer): 48.

the research objectives. These ideas are derived from previous research, theory, and/or the current business situation, and typically are called hypotheses. In statistics, a hypothesis is an unproven supposition or proposition that tentatively explains certain facts or phenomena. A hypothesis also may be thought of as an assumption about the nature of a particular situation. Statistical techniques enable us to determine whether the proposed hypotheses can be confirmed by the empirical evidence. An example of a hypothesis would be "The number of Cokes consumed by an individual on a hot day will be greater than on a cooler day." We begin this chapter with a discussion of developing hypotheses and then move on to how to test them.

HOW TO DEVELOP HYPOTHESES

Hypotheses are developed prior to data collection, generally as a part of the research plan. Hypotheses enable researchers to explain and test proposed facts or phenomena. For example, Phil Samouel may want to test the proposition that 70 percent of his employees are "proud" to be working at his restaurant. Similarly, he may wish to compare two or more groups of individuals and determine if there are differences between the groups. For example, he might want to use the results of his employee survey to test the proposition that part-time employees are more likely to search for another job than are full-time employees.

There are many hypotheses that can be developed from our restaurant surveys. For example, say we find that of the two hundred restaurant customers surveyed, 15 percent say they visit these two restaurants at least two times per month. But in a survey conducted last year, 12 percent said they visited these restaurants at least two times per month. The question is whether or not the difference in the percentages is useful information for Phil in developing his business plan. In other words, "Are significantly more people eating at the restaurants two times per month this year compared to last year?" or is this finding a result of sampling error?

There is a difference in the percentages that visit the restaurants at least two times per month. We have previously noted, however, that sampling error could distort the results enough so there may not be any statistical differences between this year's and last year's percentages. If the difference between the percentages were quite large, the analyst would be more confident there is, in fact, a true difference between the groups. Some uncertainty would still exist, however, as to whether the observed difference is meaningful. In this instance we have intuitively considered the amount of difference between the means. But we have not considered the size of the sample used to calculate the means and we have not considered the sample variances.

Null and Alternate Hypotheses

The **null hypothesis** is that there is no difference in the group means. It is based on the notion that any change from the past is due entirely to random error. In this case, the null hypothesis would be that there is no difference between the 12 percent visiting the restaurant an average of two times a month last year and the 15 percent found this year. Statisticians and business researchers always test the null hypothesis. Another hypothesis, called the **alternative hypothesis,** states the opposite of the null hypothesis. The alternative hypothesis is that there is a difference between the group means. If the null hypothesis is accepted, we do not have a change in the status quo. But if the null hypothesis is rejected and the alternative hypothesis accepted, the conclusion is there has been a change in behavior, attitudes, or some similar measure.

Directional and Nondirectional Hypotheses

Hypotheses can be stated as directional or nondirectional. If you use terms like more than, less than, positive, or negative in stating the relationship between two groups or two variables, then these hypotheses are directional. An example of a directional hypothesis would be: "The greater the stress experienced on the job, the more likely an employee is to search for another job." Another way of stating a directional hypothesis is the "If—Then" approach: "If employees are given more safety training, then they will have fewer accidents."

Nondirectional hypotheses postulate a difference or relationship, but do not indicate a direction for the differences or relationship. That is, we may postulate a significant relationship between two groups or two variables, but we are not able to say whether the relationship is positive or negative. An example of a nondirectional hypothesis would be: "There is a relationship between stress experienced on the job and the likelihood an employee will search for another job." Another example of a nondirectional hypothesis is: "There is a relationship between job commitment and likelihood to search for another job."

SAMPLE STATISTICS VERSUS POPULATION PARAMETERS

Inferential statistics helps us make judgments about the population from a sample. A sample is a small subset of the total number of respondents in a population. We use different terminology to refer to characteristics of the sample than we do to refer to characteristics of the population. Sample statistics are summary values of the sample and are computed using all the observations in the sample. Population parameters are summary values of the population but they are seldom known. This is the reason we use sample statistics to infer population parameters. A null hypothesis refers to a population parameter, not a sample statistic. Based on the sample data, the business researcher can reject the null hypothesis or accept the alternative hypothesis—e.g., there is a meaningful difference between the groups, or there is no meaningful difference. In the latter case, the researcher would not be able to detect any significant differences between the groups. It is important to understand that while the null hypothesis may not be rejected, it is not necessarily accepted as true.

In business research, the null hypothesis typically is developed so that its rejection leads to an acceptance of the desired situation. That is, the alternative hypothesis represents what we think may be correct. Using our soft drink consumption example, the null hypothesis is

---

RESEARCH IN ACTION
STEPS IN HYPOTHESIS DEVELOPMENT AND TESTING

1. State the null and alternative hypotheses.
2. Make a judgment about the sampling distribution of the population and then select the appropriate statistical test based upon whether you believe the data are parametric or nonparametric.
3. Decide upon the desired level of significance (p = .05, .01, or something else).
4. Collect data from a sample and compute the statistical test to see if the level of significance is met.
5. Accept or reject the null hypothesis. That is, determine whether the deviation of the sample value from the expected value would have occurred by chance alone (e.g., five times out of one hundred).

---

there is no difference between the soft drink consumption by males and females. The alternative hypothesis is that soft drink consumption differs between males and females. In statistical terminology, the null hypothesis is notated as H_0 and the alternative hypothesis is notated as H_1. If the null hypothesis H_0 is rejected, then the alternative hypothesis H_1 is accepted. The alternative hypothesis is always the one you must prove.

TYPE I AND TYPE II ERRORS

There always is a risk the inference a researcher draws about a population may be incorrect. Thus, in business research, error can never be completely avoided and statistical tests the researcher performs to accept or reject the null hypothesis may be incorrect. Researchers, therefore, need to be aware of two types of errors associated with hypothesis testing. The first type of error is termed **Type I error.** Type I error, referred to as alpha (α), occurs when the sample results lead to rejection of the null hypothesis when it is true. In our restaurant database, a Type I error would occur if we concluded, based on the sample data, that satisfaction with Samouel's and Gino's is different when in fact it is the same. The probability of this type of error (α), also referred to as the level of significance, is the amount of risk regarding the accuracy of the test the researcher is willing to accept. Thus, the level of significance is the probability of making an error by rejecting the null hypothesis.

Depending on the research objectives and situation, business researchers typically consider either $< .05$ or $< .01$ an acceptable level of significance. The researcher is willing, therefore, to accept some risk they will incorrectly reject the null hypothesis, but that level of risk is specified before the research project is carried out. If the research situation involves testing relationships where the risk of making a mistake is high, the researcher would specify a higher level of significance, e.g., $< .01$. For example, in examining the relationship between two chemicals that might explode, or the failure rate of an expensive piece of equipment, the researcher would not be willing to take very much risk. On the other hand, when examining behavioral relationships or when the risk is less costly, then the researcher is willing to take more risk. In some situations, the researcher may even accept a 0.10 level of significance.

The second type of error is referred to as **Type II error.** Type II error occurs when, based on the sample results, the null hypothesis is not rejected when it is, in fact, false. Type II error generally is referred to as beta (β) error. Usually, the researcher specifies the alpha error ahead of time, but the beta error is based on the population parameter (mean or proportion) and/or the sample size.

A third important concept in testing hypotheses for statistical significance is the statistical power of the test. The power of a test is the ability to reject the null hypothesis when in fact the null hypothesis is false. The statistical power of a test can be described as $(1 - \beta)$, the probability of correctly rejecting the null. The probability of a Type II error is unknown, but it is related to the probability of a Type I error. Extremely low levels of α will result in a high level of β error, thus it is necessary to reach an acceptable compromise between the two types of error. Sample size can help control Type I and Type II errors. Generally, the researcher will select the α and the sample size in order to increase the power of the test and to minimize α and β.

TESTING AND ANALYZING RELATIONSHIPS

After the researcher has developed the hypotheses and selected an acceptable level of risk (statistical significance), the next step is to test the hypotheses. In this section we discuss the statistics used to actually test hypotheses. First we tell you how to select the appropriate statistical technique to test the hypotheses. We then discuss the use of the **t-test, Chi-square,** and **ANOVA** to test hypotheses.

CHOOSING THE APPROPRIATE STATISTICAL TECHNIQUE

When we test hypotheses we are converting data to knowledge. A number of statistical techniques can be used to test hypotheses. The choice of a particular technique considers (1) the number of variables and (2) the **scale** of measurement. Other considerations could be samples size and the distribution properties of the variables.

Number of Variables

The number of variables examined together is a major consideration in the selection of the appropriate statistical technique. Univariate statistics uses only one variable at a time to generalize about a population from a sample. For example, if the researcher wants to examine the average number of cups of Starbucks coffee college students drink during finals, only a single variable is used and univariate statistics is appropriate. If the business researcher is interested in the relationship between the average number of cups of Starbucks coffee college students drink during finals and the number of hours spent studying for finals, two variables are involved and a bivariate statistical technique is required. Often business researchers will need to examine many variables at the same time to represent the real world and fully explain relationships in the data. In such cases, multivariate statistical techniques are required. We examine univariate and bivariate statistics in this chapter and multivariate statistical techniques in later chapters. There are many Web sites that can help you learn more about statistics and data. The "Research in Action" box describes a few of the better Web sites we have used.

Scale of Measurement

Measurement and scaling were discussed in Chapter 6. We use that information here to show which statistical techniques are used with a particular type of scale. Exhibit 10-1 provides an overview of the types of scales used in different situations. Suppose the researcher has a nominal scale like Starbucks® coffee drinkers versus Maxwell House® coffee drinkers. The mode would be the only appropriate measure of central tendency. A Chi-square test could be used to test whether the observed number of Starbucks coffee drinkers is what one would expect it to be. For example, if a sample survey showed that 24 percent of college students at your university drink Starbucks coffee, and you expected it to be 30 percent

EXHIBIT 10-1	**TYPE OF SCALE AND APPROPRIATE STATISTIC**

Type of Scale	Measure of Central Tendency	Measure of Dispersion	Statistic
Nominal	Mode	None	Chi-Square
Ordinal	Median	Percentile	Chi-Square
Interval or Ratio	Mean	Standard Deviation	t-Test, ANOVA

RESEARCH IN ACTION
STATISTICS ON THE WORLD WIDE WEB

Want to learn more about statistics? Just turn on your computer. The following sites offer data sources, materials, real-life examples, and interactive statistics lessons for students.

Chance

The goal of Chance's Web site is to make students more informed, critical readers of current news stories that use probability and statistics. One section of the site adds current chance news items to a traditional statistics course. Another section uses case studies concentrating on certain major issues that occur regularly in the news such as the U.S. census, statistics issues in the courts, medical trials, and statistics in sports. A third section follows the news as it happens. In all these courses, Chance uses activities, computer simulations, data sets, and videos to help students understand issues that may not be found in a standard statistics text.

http://www.dartmouth.edu/~chance/teaching_aids/data.html

Data and Story Library

Data and Story Library (DASL) is an online library of stories and data files that uses real-life examples to illustrate the basic statistics methods. Each story applies a particular statistical method to a set of data. Each data file has one or more associated stories. The data can be downloaded as a space- or tab-delimited table of text, easily read by most statistics programs. Stories are classified according to statistical methods and major topics of interest.

http://lib.stat.cmu.edu/DASL/

Documents Center at UM

Documents Center, created by the University of Michigan, offers a comprehensive set of links to datasets of all types, from agriculture to weather. For example, students can access demographic statistics from Census 2000 in a pdf report for each state with single table for state, counties, cities and townships. This data includes gender, ages in 5-year age groups, number over age 65 by gender, seventeen races, household relationships and household types.

http://www.lib.umich.edu/govdocs/stats.html

Electronic Encyclopedia of Statistical Exercises and Examples

A related link on the DASL site is the Electronic Encyclopedia of Statistical Exercises and Examples (EESEE). This site is geared toward students of statistics and contains data files along with related questions and answers that guide students through an examination of basic statistical techniques. EESEE is being used as a supplement to the introductory statistics classes being taught at Ohio State University. As well as containing data files with questions and answers, EESEE also contains homework problems and solutions, longer paper suggestions and real data examples in a user-friendly interface.

http://lib.stat.cmu.edu/DASL/Reference/eesee.html

FEDSTATS

FEDSTATS offers a full range of official statistical information available to the public from the Federal Government on agencies reporting expenditures of at least $500,000 per year in one or more statistical activities such as statistical surveys, data analysis, collection and processing of data. Use the site's linking and searching capabilities to track economic and population trends, health care costs, aviation safety, foreign trade, energy use, farm production, and more. Students can access official statistics collected and published by more than seventy Federal agencies without having to know in advance which agency produced them.

http://www.fedstats.gov/

(continued)

RESEARCH IN ACTION

STATISTICS ON THE WORLD WIDE WEB (CONTINUED)

Journal of Statistics Education

The *Journal of Statistics Education* is designed to provide statistics education to all levels, including elementary, secondary, post-secondary, post-graduate, continuing, and workplace education. The site features articles on statistical and probabilistic reasoning research. The site also features departments called "Teaching Bits: A Resource for Teachers of Statistics" and "Datasets and Stories." "Teaching Bits" summarizes interesting current events and research that can be used as examples in the statistics classroom, as well as relevant items from education texts. The "Datasets and Stories" department identifies interesting datasets and describes their useful educational features and can be downloaded for further analysis.

http://www.amstat.org/publications/jse/

Statistics.com

Comprehensive directory of links to online statistics sources, by subject for quick reference. For example, when a student searches this site's index for Advertising, links to *Advertising Age's* marketing data on national advertisers, expenditures in newspapers, and top one hundred U.S. markets are provided.

http://www.berinsteinresearch.com/stats.htm

StatLib

StatLib offers a system of distributing statistical software, datasets, and information by electronic mail, FTP, and World Wide Web. For example, students searching the dataset archive for body fat could access lists of estimates of the percentage of body fat determined by underwater weighing and various body circumference measurements for 252 men. Site also hosts StatLib Forum, a collection of bulletin boards for students to post, answer, and discuss questions of other people about software and datasets in StatLib.

http://lib.stat.cmu.edu/

StatWeb

The Statistical Science Web is designed to provide an all-in-one guide to statistical science resources, with special attention to Australian resources. The site provides a comprehensive directory of links to online statistics sources including Statistical Associations, Teaching Resources and Data Sets, Statistical Computing, and General Computing.

http://www.statsci.org/

WebStat

Created by the University of South Carolina, WebStat offers students access to basic data analysis procedures. WebStat software and its full range of basic data analysis procedures runs through a browser so students don't have to download and install it on a computer. Software includes: data analysis tools for introductory statistics; easy to use, step-by-step guidance through data analysis procedures; a wide range of methods for importing data, including over the World Wide Web; graphics, including pie charts, histograms, box plots, and scatter plots; numerics, including t-tests, regression, and ANOVA. Results can be saved and printed from Web browser.

http://www.stat.sc.edu/webstat/

based on a national survey, you could use Chi-square to determine if the differences were statistically significant.

With ordinal data you can use the median, percentile, and Chi-square, plus anything you can use with nominal data. For example, if we have ranking data for two factors that are thought to be important in the selection of a coffee house, we would use the median, percentile, and Chi-square. If the two ranking factors are coffee taste and atmosphere, we could use the Chi-square statistic to determine whether customers of Starbucks and customers of CC's ranked these factors differently. Finally, if we have the actual count of the number of cups of coffee the typical customer of Starbucks and CC's drank each time they were there we have ratio data and could calculate the standard deviation and determine if there are differences in the mean number of cups consumed using the t-test or ANOVA.

PARAMETRIC VERSUS NONPARAMETRIC HYPOTHESIS TESTS

There are two major groups of statistical procedures. The groups are referred to as **parametric** and **nonparametric.** The major difference in these two groups of statistics lies in the underlying assumptions about the data. In general, when the data are measured using an interval or ratio scale and the sample size is large, parametric statistics are appropriate. It is also assumed the sample data are collected from populations with normal (bell-shaped) distributions. When the assumption of a normal distribution is not possible, the researcher must use nonparametric statistics. When data are measured using an ordinal or nominal scale it is generally not appropriate to make the assumption that the distribution is normal and therefore nonparametric or distribution-free statistics should be used. In this chapter we discuss the nonparametric statistic Chi-square and the parametric statistics t-test and ANOVA.

SAMPLE STATISTICS VERSUS POPULATION PARAMETERS

We previously defined a population as the total of all the elements that share some common set of characteristics. For example, the population could be all the students at a university, it could be all the persons who live in a particular state or country, or it could be all the customers of Samouel's and Gino's restaurants. In contrast, a sample is a small subset or some part of all the elements in the population. For example, if we wanted to determine the average number of glasses of wine consumed with dinner at Samouel's restaurant, we would not interview all the customers. This would be expensive, take a long time, and likely be impossible because of the difficulty of finding all the customers. Instead, a sample of one hundred customers (out of a total of one thousand customers) might be considered large enough by Phil to provide accurate information about the average number of glasses of wine consumed.

We use sample statistics to estimate population parameters. A population parameter is a characteristic of the entire population. Sample statistics are based on the data in the sample. An example of a sample statistic would be the number of glasses of wine Samouel's customers say they drink obtained from the sample of one hundred. Similarly, it might be the number of cups of coffee consumed by a sample of students in a survey at a particular university, or the percentage of individuals in a sample who say they prefer Coke® over Pepsi.® The sample statistic is based on the sample data but is used to estimate the population parameter. The actual population parameters seldom are known since the cost to perform a census of the population is prohibitively high. An exception to this is the U.S. census that is conducted every ten years.

There are three approaches for statistically analyzing sample data. We can use univariate, bivariate, or multivariate statistics. Univariate means we statistically analyze only one variable at a time. Bivariate analyzes two variables while multivariate examines many variables simultaneously. We begin with univariate but will discuss all three approaches in this book.

Univariate Tests of Significance

Testing hypotheses using statistical tests involves much more than the tabulations included in a frequency distribution or the calculation of measures of central tendency or dispersion. Researchers not only describe data using means or percentages. They provide tests of the likelihood the sample numbers correctly or incorrectly estimate the population characteristics. The simplest types of tests are **univariate tests** of significance. Univariate tests of significance are used to test hypotheses when the researcher wishes to test a proposition about a sample characteristic against a known or given standard. The following are some examples of propositions:

- Employee satisfaction at Microsoft is at least 5.5 on a 7-point scale.
- The new product will be preferred by 90 percent of our current customers.
- The average monthly electric bill in Atlanta, Georgia exceeds $300.00.
- The market share for Community Coffee in south Louisiana is at least 70 percent.
- More than 50 percent of current Diet Coke customers will prefer the new Diet Coke that includes lemon taste.

We can translate these propositions into null hypotheses and test them. In the following paragraphs we provide an example from our restaurant database of a univariate hypothesis test.

Univariate Hypothesis Testing

Phil Samouel would like to know if his customers think his prices are reasonable. He also would like to know how Gino's customers perceive that restaurant's prices (see "Research In Action"). Survey respondents indicated their perceptions of prices using a 7-point scale on which 1 = "Strongly Disagree" the restaurant has reasonable prices, and 7 = "Strongly Agree." Phil's business consultant has told him the question is an interval scale, and previous research has shown the responses are approximately normally distributed.

To examine Phil's question about pricing, we first must develop the hypothesis and agree upon the level of significance for rejecting or accepting the hypothesis. Phil thinks customers consider the prices of menu items to be somewhat reasonable. After talking with his consultant, they have agreed that a rating of 5 on a 7-point scale would represent somewhat reasonable prices. Therefore, they would expect the responses to the question on reasonable prices to have a mean of 5.0. The null hypothesis is the population mean will not be different from 5.0. The alternative hypothesis is the sample mean of the answers to X_7—Reasonable Prices will be different from 5.0.

Recall that researchers often consider <.05 (5%) as the most risk they want to take in rejecting the null hypothesis. In this case, however, Phil has decided he only needs to be 90 percent certain the mean is not 5.0. That is, he is willing to assume a 10 percent risk in examining the pricing issue. Using this significance level means that if the survey of customers were conducted many times, the probability of incorrectly rejecting the null hypothesis when it is actually true would occur ten or fewer times out of one hundred (.10).

The null hypothesis that the mean of the perceptions of pricing is not different from 5.0 can be tested using the one sample t-test. The results of using this test are shown in Exhibit 10-2. The first table labeled One-Sample Statistics displays the mean and standard deviation for X_{10}—Reasonable Prices. Samouel's customers give him a mean of 4.14 and Gino's 3.97. The respective standard deviations are .932 and .937. The One-Sample Test table shows the results of the t-test for the null hypothesis that the mean response to X_{10}—Reasonable Prices is 5.0. The t-test statistic for Samouel's is −9.225, and the significance level is .000. Similarly, the t-test statistic for Gino's is −10.993, and the significance level is .000. This means that the null hypothesis for both restaurants can be rejected and the alternative hypothesis accepted

RESEARCH IN ACTION
USING SPSS TO CALCULATE A ONE-SAMPLE T-TEST

Since Phil would like to know customers' opinions on pricing for both his restaurant and for Gino's, before testing the hypotheses we must split the sample into Samouel's customers and Gino's customers. Recall that this involves going to the Data pull-down menu and doing the following: Data → Split File and then click on Compare groups. Next highlight X_{25}—Competitor and click on the arrow button to move it in the Groups Based on: box. Now click OK and you will be back to the SPSS Data Editor screen. All data analysis now will be comparing customers from the two restaurants.

The click-through sequence to run the one-sample t-test is: ANALYZE → COMPARE MEANS → ONE-SAMPLE T-TEST. Click on X_{10}—Reasonable Prices to highlight it and then on the arrow box to move X_{10} into the Test Variables box. In the box labeled Test Value, enter the number 5.0. This is the number you want to compare the respondents' answers against. When you click on the Options box, note that 95 is the default in the confidence interval box. This is the same as setting the significance level at .05. Since Phil has decided to accept more risk we must change this number. The level of risk Phil will accept is 10 percent (.10) so change the 95 in the Confidence Interval box to 90. Then, click on the Continue button and OK to execute the program. The results are shown in Exhibit 10-2.

EXHIBIT 10-2 ONE-SAMPLE T-TEST OF SAMOUEL'S AND GINO'S PRICES

One-Sample Statistics

X_{25}—Competitor		N	Mean	Std. Deviation
Samouel's	X_{10}—Reasonable Prices	100	4.14	.932
Gino's	X_{10}—Reasonable Prices	100	3.97	.937

One-Sample Test

Test Value = 5.0

X_{25}—Competitor		t	df	Sig. (2-tailed)	Mean Difference
Samouel's	X_{10}—Reasonable Prices	−9.225	99	.000	−.86
Gino's	X_{10}—Reasonable Prices	−10.993	99	.000	−1.03

with a high level of confidence. The level of significance of .000 means there are no chances in ten thousand that rejecting the null hypothesis would be incorrect.

From a practical standpoint, the results of the univariate hypothesis test indicate that customers from both restaurants felt the prices of the menu items were not very reasonable, instead of moderately reasonable as Phil thought. From Phil's point of view, this means his customers believe his prices are not as reasonable as he thought. Of course, Gino's customers think his are not very reasonable either so Phil does not have a competitive advantage here even though perceptions for his restaurant are slightly more favorable than for Gino's. Phil needs to determine if the problem is real, i.e., are his prices really too high? Or is the problem one of customer misperceptions, i.e., are his prices perceived to be too high when in fact they are not? Once this is determined, he must develop a plan to improve customer perceptions of the pricing of his menu items. It may involve actually changing prices or it may require changing portion sizes or some other approach. But improvement in pricing perceptions could become a significant competitive advantage for Samouel's restaurant.

Bivariate Hypotheses Testing

Business researchers often test hypotheses that one group differs from another group in terms of attitudes, behavior, or some other characteristic. For example, Phil Samouel might like to know if there are any differences in the perceptions of older and younger patrons of his restaurant. If there are differences, he could develop separate marketing strategies to appeal to each segment. Where more than one group is involved, bivariate statistical tests must be used. In statistical terminology, the null hypothesis is there are no significant differences between the two groups. In the following section, we describe three bivariate hypothesis tests: Chi-square, which tests differences between groups using nominal and ordinal data, and the t-test and ANOVA, which test differences in group means based on interval and ratio data.

Cross-Tabulation Using Chi-Square Analysis   One of the simplest methods for describing sets of relationships is **cross-tabulation.** A cross-tabulation is a frequency distribution of responses on two or more sets of variables. This means we tabulate the responses for each of the groups and compare them. Chi-square analysis enables us to test whether there are any statistical differences between the groups. The following are examples of questions that could be answered using cross-tabulations and testing with Chi-square analysis:

- Are gender and work type (full-time vs. part-time) at Samouel's restaurant related?
- Do restaurant selection factor rankings (most important, second most important, third in importance, etc.) differ between males and females?
- Does frequency of patronage (very frequent, somewhat frequent, and occasional) differ between Samouel's and Gino's restaurants?
- Is usage (heavy, moderate, and low) of the Internet related to educational levels (elementary, middle, high school, some college, college degree, postgraduate work)?
- Is brand awareness (unaware, aware) related to the geographic area in which individuals live (North America, Europe, Asia, Africa, etc.)?

Business researchers can use the Chi-square test to determine whether responses observed in a survey follow the expected pattern. For example, Phil Samouel might believe there is no difference in the percentages of male and female customers with regard to their rankings of atmosphere as a restaurant selection factor. Similarly, he may think there is no difference in the percentage of his customers that rank food quality as the most important restaurant selection factor and the percentage of Gino's customers that give the same ranking. Thus, the null hypotheses would be: (1) the rankings of the restaurant selection factor atmosphere are the same for men and women and (2) the proportion of Gino's customers that rank food quality as most important is the same as for Samouel's customers. Hypotheses such as these can be tested using the Chi-square statistic. Phil would want to know the answer to these questions, because if there are differences he could use this information in developing his business plan.

The **chi-square statistic** is used to test the statistical significance between the frequency distributions of two or more groups. Categorical data from questions about gender, education, or other nominal variables can be examined. The chi-square statistic compares the observed frequencies (sometimes referred to as *actual*) of the responses with the expected frequencies. The observed frequencies are the data from our survey and the expected frequencies are what we think the population distribution should be. Our thinking (expected frequencies) here is derived from previous research or theory. The statistic tests whether or not the observed data is distributed the way we would expect it to be. It tests the "goodness of fit" of the observed distribution with the expected distribution. For example, Phil thinks that male and female employees of his restaurant differ in their work type (full-time vs. part-time). Exhibit 10-3 shows the observed and expected counts for male and female employees of Samouel's restaurant cross-tabulated with work type. Looking at the observed count in the column of females we see that the survey found there were thirteen female employees working full-time. If we compare this to the expected count of 13.5 we see there is little difference between observed and expected. Indeed, there is little difference for both males and females, and when we look at the Pearson Chi-square test in the lower portion of the exhibit, we see

EXHIBIT 10-3	OBSERVED AND EXPECTED COUNTS FOR MALE AND FEMALE EMPLOYEES OF SAMOUEL'S RESTAURANT AND WORK TYPE

X_{18}—Work Type * X_{19}—Gender Crosstabulation

			X_{19}—Gender		Total
			Males	Females	
X_{18}—Work Type	Full-Time	Observed Count	24	13	37
		Expected Count	23.5	13.5	37.0
	Part-Time	Observed Count	16	10	26
		Expected Count	16.5	9.5	26.0
Total		Observed Count	40	23	63
		Expected Count	40.0	23.0	63.0

Chi-Square Tests

	Value	df	Asymp. Sig. (2-sided)
Pearson Chi-Square	.073*	1	.787
N of Valid Cases	63		

* 0 cells (.0%) have expected count less than 5. The minimum expected count is 9.49.

that indeed there are no statistically significant differences in the work types of males and females. Therefore, Phil's conjecture is not supported.

When we conduct a Chi-square analysis, we set up a contingency table with a number of cells like that shown in Exhibit 10-3. A cell refers to the intersection of a row and a column that represents a specific combination of two variables. For example, a cell in the example in Exhibit 10-3 would be the number of females that work full-time (N = 13). Another cell would be the number of males that work part-time (N = 16). A 2 × 2 contingency table would have four cells. Proper use of Chi-square requires that each expected cell frequency have a sample size of at least 5. If this sample size minimum cannot be met, the researcher can either take a larger sample or combine individual response categories so the minimum size is met.

The Chi-square statistic should be estimated only on counts of data. When the data are in percentage form, we must first convert them to absolute counts or numbers. Additionally, we assume the observations are drawn independently. This means one group of respondents does not in any way influence the other group's responses. That is, in the example in Exhibit 10-3, women's responses to the question "Are you a full-time or part-time employee of Samouel's restaurant?" in no way influence men's responses to the same question.

Testing Differences in Frequencies Using Chi Square   As in all hypothesis testing, we begin by formulating the null hypothesis and selecting the appropriate level of statistical significance for our research problem. In the previous example, the null hypothesis is that male and female employees will not differ in their work type (full-time vs. part-time). This time we will test a hypothesis for the survey of customers. Phil develops his expected frequencies based on comments he has heard from customers in his restaurant. He has not talked with Gino's customers, so he cannot formulate expected frequencies for them (unless he had information from a published study, and he does not). The null hypothesis is no difference between male and female customers in their rankings of atmosphere as important in selecting a restaurant to dine at. We will assume the acceptable level of statistical significance is .05. Results for the test of this hypothesis are shown in Exhibit 10-4.

The first table in Exhibit 10-4 shows the number of responses for males and females for each of the categories of X_{14}—Atmosphere Ranking. These numbers are referred to as the observed counts from the sample data. Also shown in the table are the expected frequencies (counts) under the null hypothesis of no difference. For example, if we look under the Count (observed) column for Males, we see that in the sample survey we observed that sixteen males ranked atmosphere as slightly important. In contrast, we expected to have 11.9 males in these cells. How do we get the expected counts? The expected counts (num-

---

RESEARCH IN ACTION

USING SPSS TO CALCULATE CHI-SQUARE

Phil wants to use the SPSS Chi-square software to compare male and female employees and work type (full-time vs. part-time). To run the Chi-square analysis, the click-through sequence is: ANALYZE → DESCRIPTIVE STATISTICS → CROSSTABS. Click on X_{18}—Work Type for the row variable and on X_{19}—Gender for the column variable. Click on the Statistics button and the Chi-square box in the top left corner of the dialog box, and then Continue. Next click on the Cells button and on Observed (this may be the default) and Expected frequencies. Then click Continue and OK to run the program. The result will be the same as in Exhibit 10-3.

| EXHIBIT 10-4 | CHI-SQUARE TEST OF HYPOTHESIS |

X_{14}—Atmosphere Ranking * X_{22}—Gender Crosstabulation

			X_{22}—Gender		Total
			Males	Females	
X_{14}—Atmosphere Ranking	Slightly Important	Count (Observed)	16	6	22
		Expected Count	11.9	10.1	22.0
	Somewhat Important	Count	30	16	46
		Expected Count	24.8	21.2	46.0
	Very Important	Count	8	24	32
		Expected Count	17.3	14.7	32.0
Total		Count	54	46	100
		Expected Count	54.0	46.0	100.0

Chi-Square Tests

	Value	df	Asymp. Sig. (2-sided)
Pearson Chi-Square	16.270*	2	.000
N of Valid Cases	100		

* 0 cells (.0%) have expected count less than 5. The minimum expected count is 10.12.

RESEARCH IN ACTION
USING SPSS TO TEST A BIVARIATE HYPOTHESIS WITH CHI-SQUARE—BASED ON SAMOUEL'S CUSTOMERS

Phil is only able to formulate expected frequencies for his customers, so we must separate them from Gino's customers for an analysis of gender and importance of atmosphere. To do so, we go to the Data pull-down menu and first click on Select Cases, then "If condition satisfied," and then "If." Next highlight variable X_{25} and click on the Arrow box to move it into the box. Click on the equal sign (=) in the template below and then zero (0 = Samouel's customers). Finally click Continue and then OK to select only Samouel's customers.

To run the Chi-square analysis, the click-through sequence is: ANALYZE → DESCRIPTIVE STATISTICS → CROSSTABS. Click on X_{14}—Atmosphere Ranking for the row variable and on X_{22}—Gender for the column variable. Click on the Statistics button and the Chi-square box, and then Continue. Next click on the Cells button and on Observed and Expected frequencies. Then click Continue and OK to run the program. The result will be the same as in Exhibit 10-4.

ber) in a cell are calculated by using the total sample percentages and the sample sizes. For example, look in the far right column and you will see that 22 percent of the total sample ranked atmosphere as slightly important. Now look at the sample sizes (bottom of table) and there were fifty-four males and forty-six females. When you calculate 22 percent of fifty-four (number of males) you get 11.9 (number of expected males). Similarly, when you calculate 22 percent of forty-six (number of females) you get 10.1 (number of expected females). All of the expected counts are calculated in a similar manner.

The second table in Exhibit 10-4 shows the Chi-square value (16.270), which is significant at the .000 level. We therefore can reject the null hypothesis that there is no difference between the rankings of men and women for the restaurant selection factor

Atmosphere. For example, we expected there would be approximately fifteen females and seventeen males that rank atmosphere as very important. But, in fact, there were eight males (expected = 17.3) and twenty-four females (expected = 14.7) who ranked atmosphere as very important. Thus, we easily conclude that women rank atmosphere as much more important than men do in selecting which restaurant to dine in.

TESTING DIFFERENCES IN GROUP MEANS

One of the most frequently examined questions in business research is whether the means of two groups of respondents on some attitude or behavior are significantly different. For example, in a sample survey we might examine any of the following questions:

- Do the coffee consumption patterns (measured using the mean number of cups consumed daily) of males and females differ?
- Does the number of hours an individual spends on the Internet each week differ by income level? … by gender? … by education?
- Do younger workers exhibit higher job satisfaction than do older workers?
- Do big five accounting firms have a more favorable image than do regional accounting firms?

When we examine questions like the above, we first develop the null and alternative hypotheses. Then we select the significance level for testing the null hypothesis. Finally, we select the appropriate statistical test and apply it to our sample data. In this section we cover two statistical tests that can be used to examine questions that compare the means of two groups.

INDEPENDENT AND RELATED SAMPLES

Business researchers often find it useful to compare the means of two groups. When comparing group means, two situations are possible. The first situation is when the means are from **independent samples.** The second situation is when the samples are related. An example of the first situation, independent samples, might be when the researcher interviews a sample of females and males. If the researcher is comparing the average number of Cokes consumed per day by females with the average number of Cokes consumed by males, this is considered an independent samples situation. An example of the second situation, **related samples,** is when the researcher collects data from a sample of females only and compares the average number of times a week they eat at Burger King® with the average number of times a week they eat at McDonald's®. The following paragraph presents a brief overview of related sample testing. But the remainder of our discussion of hypothesis testing assumes independent samples.

The researcher must examine the information cautiously when confronted with a related-samples problem. While the questions are independent, the respondents are the same so the researcher does not have independent samples. Instead you are dealing with what is referred to as paired samples, and you must use a paired samples t-test. The SPSS software has options for both related-samples and independent-samples t-tests, so choose the appropriate one for each situation.

COMPARE TWO MEANS WITH THE T-TEST

The t-test can be used to test a hypothesis stating that the means for the variables associated with two independent samples or groups will be the same. Both univariate and bivariate t-tests require interval or ratio data. But with a bivariate t-test, we assume the sample populations have normal distributions and the variances are equal. The t-test assesses whether the observed differences between two sample means occurred by chance, or if there is a true difference. Although a normal distribution is assumed with the t-test, it is quite robust to departures from normality.

The t-test is appropriate in situations where the sample size is small (n = 30 or less) and the population standard deviation is unknown. The t-test uses the t-distribution, also called the student's t-distribution, to test hypotheses. The t-distribution is a symmetrical, bell-shaped distribution with a mean of zero and a standard deviation of 1. The Z-distribution is appropriate in situations where the sample size (n) is larger than thirty. But the t-distribution often is used for sample sizes larger than thirty because the two distributions are almost identical with larger sample sizes.

EXAMPLE OF A T-TEST OF DIFFERENCE IN TWO MEANS

Phil Samouel wants to find out if there are differences in the level of satisfaction between his customers and Gino's customers. The null hypothesis is no differences in the average level of satisfaction of the customers of the two restaurants. This hypothesis was tested using a t-test and the results are shown in Exhibit 10-5. The independent samples test was used because we are comparing Samouel's customers to Gino's customers.

The top table in Exhibit 10-5 contains the Group Statistics. The mean satisfaction level for Samouel's customers was considerably lower at 4.78, compared to 5.96 for Gino's customers. The standard deviation for Samouel's was somewhat larger (1.16) than for Gino's (.974). To determine if the mean satisfaction levels are significantly different, we look at the information in the Independent Samples Test table. Information in the column labeled Sig. (2-tailed) shows the means are significantly different (< .05) for assumptions of either equal or unequal variances. Thus, Samouel's customers are significantly less satisfied than Gino's customers, so Phil Samouel definitely needs to develop strategies to improve the satisfaction level of his customers.

EXHIBIT 10-5	TESTING DIFFERENCES IN TWO MEANS USING THE T-TEST

Group Statistics

	X_{25}—Competitor	N	Mean	Std. Deviation
X_{17}—Satisfaction	Samouel's	100	4.78	1.16
	Gino's	100	5.96	.974

Independent Samples Test

	t-test for Equality of Means			
	t	df	Sig. (2-tailed)	Mean Difference
X_{17}—Satisfaction				
Equal variances assumed	−7.793	198	.000	−1.18
Equal variances not assumed	−7.793	192.232	.000	−1.18

ANALYSIS OF VARIANCE (ANOVA)

ANOVA is used to assess the statistical differences between the means of two or more groups. For example, assume Samouel's customer survey reveals that satisfaction of very frequent patrons is 5.97, somewhat frequent patrons is 4.62, and occasional patrons is 4.04. Phil Samouel would want to know whether this observed difference is statistically significant. Knowing the answer to questions such as this would be quite useful for managers and business researchers, and particularly to Phil Samouel. ANOVA can test for statistical differences between the three satisfaction means, whereas the t-test could only compare two means. The null hypothesis is the mean satisfaction levels of very frequent, somewhat frequent, and occasional patrons are the same. The results of testing this hypothesis are shown in Exhibit 10-6. Note that the ANOVA test indicates a highly significant difference (.000) between the group means so we must reject the null hypothesis.

The term ANOVA stands for Analysis of Variance. It is a test of means for two or more populations. The null hypothesis is the means are equal. We discuss **one-way ANOVA** in this section. The term one-way is used since there is only one independent variable. ANOVA also can examine research problems that involve several independent variables. When several independent variables are included it is called N-way ANOVA. The independent variables in an ANOVA must be categorical (nonmetric). In ANOVA, we refer to the categorical independent variables as factors. Each factor has two or more levels. Each level is referred to as a treatment. For example, if we are examining the preference of a sample of individuals for Diet Coke, the dependent variable might be a preference measure using a 7-point scale with 7 = Very Strong Preference and 1 = No Preference at All. Likewise, the independent variable (factor) might be consumption measured using heavy, medium, and light. Since we have only one independent variable this is a one-way ANOVA. If we added a second independent variable, such as brand loyalty (measured using highly loyal vs. not loyal at all), this would be N-way ANOVA.

In our preceding example in which we wish to compare the satisfaction of three groups of patrons of Samouel's restaurant, a t-test cannot be used. ANOVA, however, can be used with

EXHIBIT 10-6	ANALYSIS OF VARIANCE TESTING MEAN DIFFERENCES IN SATISFACTION LEVELS OF SAMOUEL'S CUSTOMERS BASED ON FREQUENCY OF PATRONAGE

X_{17} Satisfaction

X_{25}—Competitior	X_{20}—Frequency of Patronage	Mean	N	Std. Deviation
Samouel's	Occasional Patron	4.04	47	.69
	Frequent Patron	4.62	21	.80
	Very Frequent Patron	5.97	32	.93
	Total	4.78	100	1.16

ANOVA Table

X_{25}—Competitor		Source		Sum of Squares	df	Mean Square	F	Sig.
Samouel's	X_{17}—Satisfaction* X_{20}—Frequency of Patronage	Between Groups	(Combined)	71.324	2	35.662	55.942	.000
		Within Groups		61.836	97	.637		
		Total		133.160	99			

three or more groups as long as the dependent variable is measured either as interval or ratio. In contrast, the independent variable(s), in this case the three groups of Samouel's patrons based on frequency, must be categorical. Both of these conditions are met so ANOVA can be used. As with other **bivariate tests,** the null hypothesis would be all the group means are equal. The null hypothesis, therefore, is that all three groups of Samouel's patrons (groups based on frequency of patronage) will express the same level of satisfaction with the restaurant.

The F-test assesses the differences between the group means when we use ANOVA. To do so, the total variance is partitioned into two forms of variation and they are compared. The first is the variation within the groups and the second is the variation between the groups. The F-distribution is the ratio of these two forms of variance and can be calculated as follows:

F = Variance between groups (VB) / Variance within groups (VW)

When the variance between the groups relative to within the groups is larger, then the F-ratio is larger. Larger F-ratios indicate significant differences between the groups and a high likelihood the null hypothesis will be rejected.

Unfortunately, ANOVA only enables the researcher to conclude that statistical differences are present somewhere between the group means. It does not identify where the differences are. In our example of satisfaction levels of Samouel's customers, we could conclude that differences in satisfaction levels based on frequency of patronage are statistically significant, but we would not know if the differences are between very frequent versus somewhat frequent patrons, somewhat frequent versus occasional, or occasional versus very frequent. We would only able to say there are significant differences somewhere between the groups. For this reason, business researchers must use **follow-up tests** to determine where the differences lie.

ANOVA USING FOLLOW-UP TESTS

Several follow-up tests have been developed to identify the location of significant differences. Many are available in statistical software packages such as SPSS or SAS. All of the follow-up tests involve simultaneous assessment of confidence interval estimates of differences between several means. Discussion of these techniques is well beyond the scope of this book, but the techniques differ in the extent to which they are able to control for the error rate. The SPSS software has fourteen tests that assume equal variances and four where equal variance is not assumed. In our example we will use the Scheffe procedure because it is the most conservative method of assessing significant differences between group means. But the Tukey and Duncan tests are widely utilized in the business research literature.

Our research question has two parts. First, we must determine if significant differences in satisfaction exist between any of the three customer groups defined by frequency of patronage. Second, if differences are identified we must determine between which groups the differences are statistically significant. We will do this using univariate ANOVA and the Scheffe follow-up test. The null hypothesis is the satisfaction means of the three customer groups defined by frequency of patronage will be the same. The results for the calculation of the Scheffe test for these hypotheses are shown in Exhibit 10-7.

The Descriptive Statistics table in Exhibit 10-7 shows the number of patrons in each of the frequency groups and the mean level of satisfaction by frequency of patronage. Note that in all cases higher frequency of patronage is associated with higher satisfaction. In the N column at the right of the table we see that Gino's has three or more very frequent and somewhat frequent customers than does Samouel's. Moreover, overall satisfaction with Samouel's restaurant is not as high (4.78) as it is for Gino's (5.96). The task for Phil Samouel, therefore, is to analyze the survey data and develop a strategy to improve customer satisfaction levels, attract new customers, and increase the frequency of dining at his restaurant.

Information in the table labeled "Tests of Between-Subjects Effects" (Exhibit 10-7) reveals that satisfaction levels do differ significantly between the groups identified by their frequency of patronage. You determine this by looking under the *Sig.* column for variable X_{20} (located in the Source column). Note the level of significance for Samouel's is .000 and for Gino's is .000, so satisfaction levels for customers of both restaurants vary significantly based on frequency of patronage. The null hypothesis of no differences is therefore rejected.

RESEARCH IN ACTION
USING SPSS TO RUN FOLLOW-UP TESTS IN ANOVA

When we run the Scheffe test to compare Samouel's and Gino's first go to the Data pull-down menu, click on split sample, then move X_{25} into the box and click on Compare Groups, and then OK. This will enable you to look at the customers of each of the restaurants separately.

The SPSS click-through sequence is: ANALYZE → GENERAL LINEAR MODEL → UNIVARIATE. Highlight the dependent variable X_{17}—Satisfaction by clicking on it and move it to the Dependent variable box. Next, highlight X_{20}—Frequency of Patronage and move it to the box labeled "Fixed Factors." Click on the Post Hoc box and highlight X_{20} in the Factor(s) box and then click on the Arrow box to move this variable to the box for Post Hoc Tests. Look to the lower left side of the screen and click on Scheffe test and then Continue. Next click on the options box, click Descriptive Statistics on the left side, and then Continue. Now click OK to execute the program. The results are shown in Exhibit 10-7.

EXHIBIT 10-7	THE SCHEFFE TEST FOR DIFFERENCES IN GROUP MEANS

Dependent Variable: X_{17}—Satisfaction

X_{25}—Competitior	X_{20}—Frequency of Patronage	Mean	N
Samouel's	Occasional Patron	4.04	47
	Frequent Patron	4.62	21
	Very Frequent Patron	5.97	32
	Total	4.78	100
Gino's	Occasional patron	4.78	9
	Somewhat Frequent Patron	5.69	29
	Very Frequent Patron	6.26	62
	Total	5.96	100

Tests of Between-Subjects Effects
Dependent Variable: X_{17}—Satisfaction

X_{25}—Competitor	Source	Type III Sum of Squares	df	Mean Square	F	Sig.
Samouel's	Corrected model	71.324*	2	35.662	55.942	.000
	Intercept	2137.359	1	2137.359	3352.800	.000
	X_{20}	71.324	2	35.662	55.942	.000
	Error	61.836	97	.637		
	Total	2418.000	100			
	Corrected total	133.160	99			
Gino's	Corrected model	20.207†	2	10.103	13.309	.000
	Intercept	1729.763	1	1729.763	2278.680	.000
	X_{20}	20.207	2	10.103	13.309	.000
	Error	73.633	97	.759		
	Total	3646.000	100			
	Corrected Total	93.840	99			

* R Squared = .536 (Adjusted R Squared = .526) (Samouel's)
† R Squared = .215 (Adjusted R Squared = .199) (Gino's)

To determine which group means are significantly different go to the "Multiple Comparisons" table shown in Exhibit 10-8. The far right column labeled Sig. shows the level of significance. For Samouel's and Gino's both, there are statistically significant differences between all the groups. This means the "Very Frequent," "Somewhat Frequent," and "Occasional" patrons differ significantly in their satisfaction levels. If there were any comparisons in which the group means were not significantly different, it would have been shown in the *Sig.* column of numbers.

To determine the nature of the differences we can examine the means shown earlier in the Descriptive Statistics table in Exhibit 10-7. For Samouel's, the mean satisfaction level of the "Very Frequent" patrons is 5.97, for the "Somewhat Frequent" patron the mean is 4.62, and for the "Occasional" patrons it is 4.04. Thus, as would be expected, the more frequent patrons are significantly more satisfied. A similar finding is true for Gino's. The mean satisfaction level of the "Very Frequent" patrons is 6.26, for the "Somewhat Frequent" patrons

EXHIBIT 10-8	COMPARISONS OF INDIVIDUAL GROUP MEANS FOR SIGNIFICANT DIFFERENCES

Multiple Comparisons
Dependent Variable X_{17}—Satisfaction

X_{25}—Competitor	(I) X_{20}—Frequency of Patronage	(J) X_{20}—Frequency of Patronage	Mean Difference (I–J)	Sig.
Samouel's	Occasional Patron	Somewhat Frequent Patron	−.58*	.026
		Very Frequent Patron	−1.93*	.000
	Somewhat Frequent Patron	Occasional Patron	.58*	.026
		Very Frequent Patron	−1.35*	.000
	Very Frequent Patron	Occasional Patron	1.93*	.000
		Somewhat Frequent Patron	1.35*	.000
Gino's	Occasional Patron	Somewhat Frequent Patron	−.91*	.027
		Very Frequent Patron	−1.48*	.000
	Somewhat Frequent Patron	Occasional Patron	.91*	.027
		Very Frequent Patron	−.57*	.018
	Very Frequent Patron	Occasional Patron	1.48*	.000
		Somewhat Frequent Patron	.57*	.018

* The mean difference is significant at the .05 level.

the mean is 5.69, and for the "Occasional" patrons the mean is 4.78. As has been noted elsewhere, Phil must be concerned that Gino's customers patronize his restaurant more often. A business plan must be devised to increase frequency of patronage as well as other performance indicators.

FACTORIAL DESIGN: TWO-WAY ANOVA

One-way ANOVA designs involve a single nonmetric independent variable and a single metric dependent variable. A factorial design examines the effect (if any) of two or more nonmetric independent variables on a single metric dependent variable. With one-way ANOVA the total variance is partitioned into the between-group variance and the within-group variance. But in factorial designs, the between-group variance itself is partitioned into (1) variation due to each of the independent variables (factors) and (2) variation due to the interaction of the two variables— that is, their combined effects on the dependent variable beyond the separate influence of each. Therefore, three null hypotheses are tested simultaneously by a **two-way ANOVA** factorial design: (1) the effect of variable one on the dependent variable; (2) the effect of variable two on the dependent variable; and (3) the combined (joint) effect of variables one and two on the dependent variable. The effects of the two independent variables are referred to as main effects, and their combined effect is referred to as the interaction effect.

EXAMPLE OF TWO-WAY ANOVA

Phil Samouel has observed that the frequency of patronage of his male and female customers appears to be different. If, in fact, the patronage frequency is statistically different he would like to better understand why and determine how he could use that information to grow his business. He also would like to know how gender of customers and frequency of patronage are related to satisfaction. The null hypotheses are: (1) no differences in mean satisfaction levels based on frequency of patronage; (2) no differences in mean satisfaction levels based on gender; and (3) no differences in mean satisfaction levels based on the combined effects of frequency of patronage and gender. Phil is not familiar with Gino's customer patronage patterns so he has no basis for examining hypotheses except for his customers. The metric dependent variable for these hypotheses is X_{17}—Satisfaction and the non-metric independent variables are X_{20}—Frequency of Patronage and X_{22}—Gender. The results for the test of the hypotheses are reported in Exhibits 10-9 to 10-11.

The first table in Exhibit 10-9 labeled Tests of Between-Subjects Effects shows the results of the ANOVA program. The null hypotheses were that there would be no difference between the mean scores for X_{17}—Satisfaction for customers with different patronage rates (X_{20}), no difference in mean scores on X_{17}—Satisfaction between females and males (X_{22}), and no interaction effect. The purpose of the N-Way ANOVA analysis is first to see if statistically significant differences exist, and, if they do, between which groups.

To assess the mean differences for each independent variable comparison, an F-ratio is used. As discussed earlier, the approach used in ANOVA compares the variance from the *between* groups grand mean to the variance *within* the groups. In this case, the groups are the three groups of customers who exhibit different patronage rates and the two gender groups. When the F-ratio is large, we are more likely to have larger differences between the means of the various groups examined.

The first main effect we examine is the impact of variable X_{20}—Frequency of Patronage on variable X_{17}—Satisfaction. The F-ratio for X_{20}—Frequency of Patronage for Samouel's customers is 39.639, which is statistically significant at the .000 level (see Exhibit 10-9). From the Descriptive Statistics table in Exhibit 10-10 below we can see that, for Samouel's restaurant satisfaction is higher for somewhat frequent (mean = 4.62) and very frequent customers (5.97) than it is for the occasional patron (4.04). Thus, we reject the null hypothesis and conclude satisfaction does vary by frequency of patronage of Samouel's restaurant. Moreover, as would be expected, the more frequent customers are significantly more satisfied than the less frequent patrons.

EXHIBIT 10-9 **TESTS OF BETWEEN-SUBJECTS EFFECTS**

Dependent Variable: X_{17}—Satisfaction

Source	Type III Sum of Squares	df	Mean Square	F	Sig.
Corrected Model	86.828*	5	17.366	35.232	.000
Intercept	1848.007	1	1848.007	3749.330	.000
X_{20}	39.076	2	19.538	39.639	.000
X_{22}	12.620	1	12.620	25.604	.000
$X_{20} * X_{22}$	2.377	2	1.189	2.412	.095
Error	46.332	94	.493		
Total	2418.000	100			
Corrected Total	133.160	99			

*R Squared = .652 (Adjusted R Squared = .634)

EXHIBIT 10-10	MEANS AND STANDARD DEVIATIONS FOR CUSTOMER SATISFACTION BY GENDER AND FREQUENCY OF PATRONAGE

Descriptive Statistics

Dependent Variable: X_{17}—Satisfaction

X_{20}—Frequency of Patronage	X_{22}—Gender	Mean	Std. Deviation	N
Occasional Patron	Male	4.38	.805	21
	Female	3.77	.430	26
	Total	4.04	.690	47
Somewhat Frequent Patron	Male	4.89	.782	9
	Female	4.42	.793	12
	Total	4.62	.805	21
Very Frequent Patron	Male	6.29	.464	24
	Female	5.00	1.309	8
	Total	5.97	.933	32
Total	Male	5.31	1.113	54
	Female	4.15	.868	46
	Total	4.78	1.160	100

RESEARCH IN ACTION
USING SPSS TO EXECUTE A TWO-WAY ANOVA

Phil has observed a pattern only for his customers so we must separate them from Gino's customers for this analysis. To do so we go to the Data pull down menu and click on "If condition satisfied," then on If, highlight variable X_{25} and click on the Arrow box to move it to box. Next click on the equal sign (=) below and then zero (0). Finally click on Continue and then OK; select only Samouel's customers for this analysis.

The click through sequence is: ANALYZE → GENERAL LINEAR MODEL → UNIVARIATE. Highlight the dependent variable X_{17}—Satisfaction by clicking on it and move it to the Dependent variable box. Next, highlight X_{20}—Frequency of Usage and X_{22}—Gender, and move them to the box labeled "Fixed Factors." Now click on the Post Hoc box and highlight X_{20} in the Factor(s) box and then click on the Arrow box to move this variable to the box for Post Hoc Tests. We do not move X_{22} because it has only two groups and not three. Look to the lower left side of the screen and click on Scheffe test and then Continue. Now go to the Options box and click on Descriptive statistics and then Continue. Finally, click on OK since we do not need to specify anything else for this test. The results are shown in Exhibit 10-9.

The second main effects comparison was whether there is a difference in satisfaction based on X_{22}—Gender. The F-ratio for gender is 25.604 and statistically significant (.000) (See Exhibit 10-9). We therefore reject the null hypothesis of no differences and conclude that satisfaction of Samouel's customers differs based on gender. Specifically, for Samouel's Greek Cuisine the females are significantly less satisfied than males (female mean satisfaction levels are consistently lower than those for males).

The third hypothesis was no differences based on the combined effect of frequency of patronage and gender. The interaction between patronage frequency and gender is non-significant (.095), meaning that the difference in satisfaction when both independent variables are considered together is very small. The null hypothesis of no difference is therefore not rejected for the interaction effect.

To better understand this, let's look first at the information in the Multiple Comparisons table shown in Exhibit 10-11. There are significant differences between all of the groups of patrons—"Occasional," "Somewhat Frequent," and "Very Frequent." Thus, higher frequency of patronage does indicate a higher level of satisfaction and the significant differences exist for all the group comparisons.

MANOVA

MANOVA (Multivariate Analysis of Variance) is similar to ANOVA. The difference is that instead of one metric dependent variable the technique can examine two or more. The objective is the same since both techniques assess differences in groups (categorical variables) as they impact metric dependent variables. While ANOVA examines difference in a single metric-dependent variable, MANOVA examines group differences across multiple metric dependent variables at the same time. With ANOVA the null hypothesis is the means of the single dependent variable are the same across the groups. In MANOVA the null hypothesis is the means of the multiple dependent variables are the same across the groups.

As an example, our customer survey has three relationship outcome variables—satisfaction, recommend to friend, and likelihood of returning in the future. All of these variables are measured metrically. An appropriate MANOVA would be to examine the relationship between gender (nonmetric) and the three outcome variables (metric). Similarly, another appropriate MANOVA application to our customer survey would be to examine the relationship between frequency of patronage (nonmetric) and the three outcome variables. MANOVA is not included in the student version of the SPSS software package, so we will not cover it in this text.

EXHIBIT 10-11 **MULTIPLE COMPARISONS**

Dependent Variable: X_{17}—Satisfaction

Scheffe

(I) X_{20}—Frequency of Patronage	(J) X_{20}— Frequency of Patronage	Mean Difference (I-J)	Sig.
Occasional Patron	Somewhat Frequent Patron	−.58*	.010
	Very Frequent Patron	−1.93*	.000
Somewhat Frequent Patron	Occasional Patron	.58*	.010
	Very Frequent Patron	−1.35*	.000
Very Frequent Patron	Occasional Patron	1.93*	.000
	Somewhat Frequent Patron	1.35*	.000

Based on observed means.
* The mean difference is significant at the .05 level.

SUMMARY

Discuss Hypothesis Testing and Why We Use It

Business researchers often have some preliminary ideas regarding data relationships based on their research objectives. These ideas are derived from previous research or theory, and typically are called hypotheses. In statistics a hypothesis is an unproven supposition or proposition that tentatively explains certain facts or phenomena. A hypothesis also may be thought of as an assumption about the nature of a particular situation. Statistical techniques enable us to determine whether our theoretical hypotheses are confirmed by the empirical evidence.

Explain the Concept of Statistical Significance

There always is a risk the inference a researcher draws about a population may be incorrect. Thus, in business research, error can never be completely avoided and the researcher performs statistical tests to decide whether to accept or reject the null hypothesis. The probability of making an error is termed the level of significance. The level of significance is equivalent to the amount of risk the researcher is willing to accept regarding the accuracy of the test. Researchers typically accept a level of significance of either .05 or 01, depending on the research objectives.

Understand How to Choose the Appropriate Statistical Technique

The choice of a particular technique depends on (1) the number of variables and (2) the scale of measurement. Univariate statistics can assess only a single variable. Bivariate statistics can assess two variables. Multivariate statistics can examine many variables simultaneously, and can handle both multiple dependent and independent variables. The appropriate statistic also varies depending upon whether your data is measured nominally, ordinally, intervally, or ratio.

Explain the Difference between Sample Statistics and Population Parameters

The purpose of inferential statistics is to develop estimates about a population using a sample from that population. A sample is a small subset of all the elements within the population. Sample statistics refers to measures obtained directly from the sample or calculated from the data in the sample. A population is a summary characteristic of the entire population. Generally, the actual population parameters are unknown since the cost to perform a census of the population is prohibitively high. Sample statistics are useful in making inferences regarding the population's parameters.

Explain the Difference between the T-test, ANOVA and Chi-square

Business researchers frequently want to test the hypothesis that one group differs from another group in terms of attitudes, behavior, or some other characteristic. Where more than one group is involved, bivariate tests must be used. In statistical terminology, the null hypothesis is there are no significant differences between the two groups. Three bivariate hypothesis tests were discussed in this chapter. The first, Chi-square, tests differences between groups using data that is measured on either a nominal and ordinal scale. The t-test and ANOVA are used to test differences in group means when data is measured with either an interval or ratio scale. Moreover, the t-test is appropriate to test difference in only two groups, while ANOVA can test differences in three or more groups.

KEY TERMS

alternative hypothesis	MANOVA	sample statistics
ANOVA	nonparametric	scale
bivariate test	null hypothesis	t-test
Chi-square	one-way ANOVA	two-way ANOVA
cross-tabulation	parametric	Type I error
follow-up test	population parameters	Type II error
independent samples	related samples	univariate test

ETHICAL DILEMMA

Dan Henderson, the CEO for a chain of department stores, believes the company needs to create a customer loyalty program designed to reward customers who spend more than $200 per shopping trip. Therefore, he asks his marketing analysts to create a program that can help the company identify and profile its most profitable customers. When the report is completed, the data indicates that the more affluent shoppers who spend more than $200 per shopping trip represent only a small part of the company's overall sales because they only shop 3–4 times a year and they tend to buy only lower margin designer clothing. Instead, the analysts report that the most profitable store customers tend to be over forty years old from average income households and shop at least twice a month spending an average of $100 per trip on everything from cosmetics to housewares to high margin private label clothing. After reviewing the report, Dan decides he still wants the customer loyalty program to reward the high-dollar purchasing customers justifying the decision by claiming that they are responsible for the store's upscale image which appeals to the regular store customer. What do you think about Dan's decision?

REVIEW QUESTIONS

1. What is hypothesis testing and why do we use it?
2. What is the difference between sample statistics and population parameters?
3. Compare and contrast univariate, bivariate, and multivariate analysis. When and why would we use each type of statistical analysis?
4. What are the differences between the t-test, ANOVA, and Chi-square?
5. Why do we use follow-up tests in ANOVA?
6. What is the difference in one-way and two-way ANOVA?

DISCUSSION AND APPLICATION ACTIVITIES

1. Give an example of a situation in which multivariate statistical techniques would be needed.

2. Why have computer software packages increased the use of multivariate statistical techniques?

3. A business researcher uses two-way ANOVA in a report for a client. The researcher does not check the assumptions of using the technique. Is this a problem?

4. SPSS Application: Use the customer survey database and compare the satisfaction, likelihood to recommend, and likelihood to return for Samouel's Greek Cuisine and Gino's Fine Dining using the t-test. Are they statistically different and, if so, how would you interpret the findings?

INTERNET EXERCISES

1. Go to one of the following Web sites. Participate in a survey at one of the sites and prepare a report on what you learned.

   a. www.prusec.com/quiz.htm

   b. www.dssresearch.com/mainsite/surveys.htm

   c. www.utne.com/lens/bms/9bmseq.html

   d. www.cc.gatech.edu/gvu/user_surveys

   e. www.survey.net

2. The Federal Reserve Bank of St. Louis has a database called FRED (Federal Reserve Economic Data). Go to their Web site, http://research.stlouisfed.org/fred/abotfred.html and report what you found. Identify some research questions that can be examined with the statistical techniques covered in this chapter.

3. Want more information on the fundamentals of statistical analysis and definitions of concepts and terms? Go to the Platonic Realms Interactive Mathematics Encyclopedia at www.mathacademy.com/pr/index.asp. Click on the Platonic Realms logo and then on Encyclopedia. Prepare a report summarizing the value of this Web site.

CHAPTER 11

Correlation and Regression

Learning Objectives

1. Describe the nature of relationships between variables.

2. Explain the concepts of correlation and regression analysis.

3. Clarify the difference between bivariate and multiple regression analysis.

4. Understand how multicollinearity can influence regression models.

5. Understand when and how to use stepwise multiple regression.

INTRODUCTION

Many business questions are concerned with the **relationship** between two or more variables. Questions such as "Are sales related to advertising?", "Is product quality related to customer loyalty?", "Is educational level associated with the purchase of a particular stock?", or "How much safety training is required to reduce accidents?" can be answered by using statistics to examine relationships between variables. This chapter explains how you can use statistics to examine questions like this.

TYPES OF RELATIONSHIPS BETWEEN VARIABLES

When variables have a consistent and systematic linkage between them, a relationship is present. Statistics are used to determine whether there is a statistical linkage or association between the variables. If there is a statistical association, it is important to understand the relationship is not necessarily causal. That is, one variable cannot be said to cause the other one. **Correlation** and regression are associative techniques that help us to determine if there is a consistent and systematic relationship between two or more variables. There are four basic concepts we need to understand about relationships between variables: presence, nature of relationships, direction, and **strength of association.** We will describe each of these concepts.

PRESENCE

Relationship presence assesses whether a systematic relationship exists between two or more variables. We rely on the concept of **statistical significance** to measure whether or not a relationship is present. If statistical significance is found between the variables we say that a relationship is present. That is, we say knowledge about the behavior of one or more variables enables us to predict the behavior of another variable. For example, if we found a statistically significant relationship between customer perceptions of the employees of Gino's Ristorante and their satisfaction with the restaurant, we would say a relationship is present and that perceptions of the employees will tell us what the perceptions of satisfaction are likely to be. We previously introduced the concept of a null hypothesis. With associative analysis, the null hypothesis is no association is present between the variables.

NATURE OF RELATIONSHIPS

A second important concept is how variables are related to one other. We typically say the relationship between variables is either linear or nonlinear. A **linear relationship** is a "straight-line association" between two or more variables. A **nonlinear relationship,** often referred to as curvilinear, is one in which the relationship is best described by a curve instead of a straight line. With a linear relationship, the strength and nature of the relationship between the variables remains the same over the range of the variables. But with a nonlinear relationship the strength and nature changes over the range of both variables (e.g., Y's relationship with X first gets weaker as X increases, but then gets stronger as the value of X continues to increase).

Linear relationships between variables are much easier to work with than are curvilinear ones. If we know the value of variable X, we can use the formula for a straight line (Y = a + bX) to determine the value of Y. But, when variables have a curvilinear relationship, the formula that best describes that linkage will be much more complex. Curvilinear relationships are beyond the scope of this book and most business researchers work with relationships that they believe are linear. In fact, most of the statistics covered in this book are based on the assumption that a linear relationship is an efficient way to describe the association between the variables being examined.

DIRECTION

If a relationship is present between the variables we also need to know the direction. The direction of a relationship can be either positive or negative. In our restaurant example, a positive relationship exists if customers who rate employees favorably also are highly satisfied. Similarly, a negative relationship exists if customers who perceive that prices are higher exhibit lower satisfaction ratings. A negative relationship between two variables is denoted with a minus (–) sign while a positive relationship has a plus (+) sign.

STRENGTH OF ASSOCIATION

Depending on the type of relationship being examined, we generally categorize the strength of association as slight, small but definite, moderate, high, or very strong. A slight, almost negligible situation is one in which a consistent and systematic relationship is not present between the variables. When a relationship is present, the business researcher must determine the strength of the association. A very strong association means there is a very high probability the variables have a relationship. A moderate association means there is likely to be a consistent and systematic relationship.

COVARIATION AND VARIABLE RELATIONSHIPS

Business researchers often want to know whether two or more variables are linked together. Variables are linked together if they exhibit **covariation.** Covariation is when one variable consistently and systematically changes relative to another variable. The **correlation coefficient** is used to assess this linkage. Large coefficients indicate high covariation and a strong relationship. Small coefficients indicate little covariation and a weak relationship. Thus, a correlation coefficient measures the degree of covariation between two variables. For example, if we know that purchases over the Internet are related to age, then we want to know the extent to which younger persons make more purchases on the Internet, and ultimately which kinds of products they purchase most often and why. Thus, when two variables change together on a reliable or consistent basis (i.e., covary), that information helps us to make predictions for use in developing sound business strategies.

One of the first issues we need to determine is whether the correlation coefficient is statistically significant. Regardless of its absolute size, a correlation coefficient has no meaning unless it is statistically significant. Most popular software programs tell you if a correlation is statistically significant. The SPSS program reports significance as the probability of rejecting the null hypothesis when is it true. Typical guidelines say that to be considered statistically significant the probability must be at least $< .05$. This means to reject the null hypothesis there must be fewer than five chances in one hundred you will be wrong if you reject the null hypothesis. In some business situations, a level of $< .10$ is considered acceptable. But to accept this probability level brings about more risk, and the analyst must decide if the situation warrants the higher level of risk.

Once we have determined the relationship is statistically significant, we then must decide what strength of association is acceptable. The size of the correlation coefficient is used to quantitatively describe the strength of the association between two or more variables. Rules of thumb have been proposed to characterize the strength of the association between variables, based on the absolute size of the correlation coefficient. As Exhibit 11-1 suggests, correlation coefficients between $\pm.91$ and ±1.00 are considered "very strong." That is, covariance definitely is shared between the two variables being examined. In contrast, if the correlation coefficient is between $\pm.00$ and $\pm.20$, even though the coefficient is greater than zero in the sample, there is a good chance that the null hypothesis won't be rejected (unless you are using a large sample). These levels are only suggestions and other guidelines regarding the strength of the relationship are possible.

Scatter diagrams are an easy way to visually display the covariation between two variables. A scatter diagram, sometimes referred to as a scattergram, is a plot of the values of two variables for all the observations in the sample. It is customary to plot the dependent variable on the vertical axis and the independent variable on the horizontal axis. Exhibits 11-2a–c are examples of possible relationships between two variables that might be plotted on a scatter diagram. In Exhibit 11-2a, there is no apparent relationship or association between the variables. That is, there is no predictable or identifiable pattern to the points. Knowing the values of Y or X would not tell you very much (probably nothing at all) about the possible values of the other variable. Exhibit 11-2a suggests there is no consistent and systematic relationship between Y and X, and thus very little or no covariation shared by the two variables. If the amount of covariation shared by these two variables were measured, it would be very close to zero.

In Exhibit 11-2b, the pattern of the two variables shows a very different picture. There is a distinct pattern to the points on the scatter diagram that is easily described as a straight line. We refer to this relationship as positive, because increases in the value of X are associated with increases in the value of Y. Similarly, if the values of X decrease, the values of Y will decrease as well. If we measured the covariation between the values of Y and X, it would be relatively high. Thus, changes in the value of X are consistently and systematically related to changes in the value of Y.

EXHIBIT 11-1 **RULES OF THUMB ABOUT CORRELATION COEFFICIENT SIZE***

Coefficient Range	Strength of Association
$\pm.91 - \pm1.00$	Very Strong
$\pm.71 - \pm.90$	High
$\pm.41 - \pm.70$	Moderate
$\pm.21 - \pm.40$	Small but definite relationship
$\pm.01 - \pm.20$	Slight, almost negligible

* Assumes correlation coefficient is statistically significant.

| EXHIBIT 11-2 | SCATTER DIAGRAMS ILLUSTRATING VARIOUS RELATIONSHIPS |

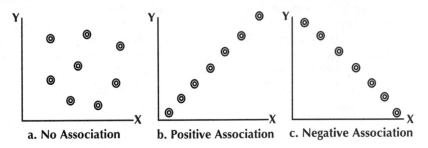

a. No Association   b. Positive Association   c. Negative Association

Exhibit 11-2c shows a similar type of pattern between the values of Y and X, but the direction of the relationship is opposite that in Exhibit 11-2b. There is a linear pattern, but now when the value of X increases the values of Y decrease. That is, the values of X and Y change in the opposite direction. This type of relationship is described as a negative relationship. There is a large amount of covariation between the two variables because Y and X consistently change together. The difference is they move in the opposite direction from Exhibit 11-2b. Covariation refers to the amount of shared movement between two variables, not the direction of the relationship.

CORRELATION ANALYSIS

Scatter diagrams enable us to visually demonstrate the relationship between two variables and the extent to which they covary. For example, a scatter diagram can tell us that as age increases the average consumption of aspirin increases too, or that on a hot day we consume more water. But even though a visual display of data is very useful, as we learned in Chapter 6 some situations may need a quantitative measure of the covariation between two variables to fully understand the relationship.

The **Pearson correlation** measures the linear association between two metric variables. The number representing the Pearson correlation is referred to as a correlation coefficient. It ranges from −1.00 to +1.00, with zero representing absolutely no association between the two metric variables. While −1.00 or +1.00 is possible and represents a perfect association between two variables, it very seldom occurs. The larger the correlation coefficient, the stronger the linkage or level of association. Correlation coefficients can be either positive or negative, depending upon the direction of the relationship between the variables. If there is a positive correlation coefficient between X and Y, then increases in the value of X are associated with increases in the value of Y, and vice versa.

The correlation coefficient assesses the association between two variables. The null hypothesis states there is no association between two variables and that the correlation coefficient is zero (or very small). For example, we may hypothesize that there is no relationship between preference for McDonald's® french fries and income levels. If you take measures of the two variables (consumption of McDonald's® french fries and income) from a sample of the population and calculate the correlation coefficient for that sample to be .36, the question is "What is the probability that you would get a correlation coefficient of .36 in your sample if the correlation coefficient in the population is actually zero?" That is, if you calculate a large correlation coefficient between two variables in your sample—

consumption of McDonald's® french fries and income—(and your sample was properly selected from the population of interest), then the chances the population correlation coefficient is really zero are small. If the correlation coefficient is statistically significant, you can reject the null hypothesis and conclude with some degree of confidence the two variables you are examining share some association in the population. In other words, consumption of McDonald's® french fries is related to income.

In addition to examining the correlation coefficient, we often square the correlation coefficient to get the **coefficient of determination,** or r^2. The coefficient of determination ranges from 0.00 to 1.0 and represents the amount of variation explained or accounted for in one variable by one or more other variables.[1] If a correlation coefficient is .543, then the R^2 would be .294, meaning that approximately 29.4 percent of the variation in one variable is associated with the other variable. As with the correlation coefficient, the larger the coefficient of determination, the stronger the relationship between the variables being examined.

When we use the Pearson correlation coefficient we must make several assumptions about the nature of the data. First, the two variables are assumed to have been measured using interval or ratio-scaled measures (i.e., metric). Other types of correlation coefficients can be used if they are nominal or ordinal measures. Later in the chapter we discuss the Spearman correlation coefficient for use with ordinal data. Another assumption of the Pearson correlation coefficient is the relationship we are examining is linear. That is, a straight line is an accurate description of the relationship between the two metric variables.

A third assumption of the Pearson correlation coefficient is the variables you are examining are from a normally distributed population. A normal distribution is a common assumption for many statistical techniques used by business researchers. But it often is difficult to determine whether sample data is normally distributed. Since correlation is considered a reasonably robust statistic when the distribution varies from normal, this assumption frequently is taken for granted. In a later section of this chapter we show you how to determine whether sample data has a normal distribution.

EXAMPLE OF BIVARIATE PEARSON CORRELATION

Phil Samouel collected information in his employee survey on employee cooperation and teamwork as well as likelihood of searching for a job. Since a stable workforce would be good for his restaurant, he wants to use his survey findings to better understand what can be done to retain good employees. One of the things he is considering implementing is a new training program for employees. He would therefore like to know if the relationship between the perceived cooperation among his employees and likelihood to search for a new job is significant and positive. If there is a relationship, he can use this information in developing a training program to ensure that his employees cooperate more in preparing meals and serving customers.

The null hypothesis is no relationship exists between perceived cooperation among Samouel's employees and likelihood of searching for a new job. Recall from the employee survey description in Appendix 1-B that information was collected on intention to search for another job (X_{16}) and perceived cooperation among members of a work group (X_4). To test this hypothesis, we must calculate the correlation between these two variables. This has been done and is reported in Exhibit 11-3.

EXHIBIT 11-3	BIVARIATE CORRELATION BETWEEN WORK GROUP COOPERATION AND INTENTION TO SEARCH FOR ANOTHER JOB

Descriptive Statistics

	Mean	Std. Deviation	N
X_4—Work Group Cooperation	3.89	1.345	63
X_{16}—Intention to Search	4.27	1.807	63

Correlations

		X_4—Work Group Cooperation	X_{16}—Intention to Search
X_4—Work Group Cooperation	Pearson Correlation	1.000	−.585[†]
	Sig. (2-tailed)	.	.000
	N	63	63
X_{16}—Intention to Search	Pearson Correlation	−.585[†]	1.000
	Sig. (2-tailed)	.000	.
	N	63	63

[†] Correlation is significant at the 0.01 level (2-tailed).

The Correlations table in Exhibit 11-3 shows us how the two variables are related. Stated another way, it tells us if the two variables covary. To interpret the table, look at the column and row where the variables intersect. For example, the far right column in the table is variable X_{16}—Intention to Search and the number at the top of the column is −.585. This indicates the correlation between variable X_4—Work Group Cooperation and X_{16}—Intention to Search is −.585, and the significance level is .001 (this number is right below −.585 and in the row labeled Sig. [2-tailed], which is the t-test that shows the correlation is significant). The numbers in the row labeled N represent the number of respondents used to compute the correlation; i.e., the sample size of sixty-three Samouel's employees.

The results reported in Exhibit 11-3 have confirmed that perceived work group cooperation is significantly correlated with intention to search for another job. This means we can reject the null hypothesis of no relationship between these two variables. Moreover, the correlation is negative and moderately strong, so we can conclude that employees who

RESEARCH IN ACTION

USING SPSS TO CALCULATE A BIVARIATE PEARSON CORRELATION

The SPSS click-through sequence to execute the Pearson bivariate correlation is: ANALYZE → CORRELATE → BIVARIATE, which leads to a dialog box where you select the variables. Highlight X_{16} and X_4 and move them into the Variables box. We will use the three default options: Pearson correlation, two-tailed test of significance, and flag significant variables. Next go to the Options box and click on Means and Standard Deviations and then Continue. Finally, click OK at the top right of the dialog box to run the program. The results will be the same as those in Exhibit 11-3.

believe there is less work group cooperation exhibit a higher intention to search for another job. To ensure a more stable workforce, Phil needs to implement the employee training he is considering so that he can improve cooperation within employee work groups.

PRACTICAL SIGNIFICANCE OF THE CORRELATION COEFFICIENT

If the correlation coefficient is strong and statistically significant, you can conclude there is a relationship between the variables. In our example, Phil Samouel can be reasonably confident the variables work group cooperation and intention to search are related because the correlation is –.585 and highly significant (.000). But if the correlation coefficient is small there are two possibilities. One, either a consistent, systematic relationship does not exist between the variables or, two, the association exists but it is not linear and other types of relationships must be considered.

Even if the correlation coefficient is statistically significant, this does not mean it is practically significant. We also must ask whether the numbers we calculated are meaningful. In calculating the statistical significance of a correlation coefficient the sample size is a major influence. With large sample sizes it is possible to have a statistically significant correlation coefficient that is really too small to be of any practical use. For example, if the correlation coefficient between work group cooperation and intention to search was .20 (significant at .05 level), the coefficient of determination would be .04. Is this coefficient of determination of **practical significance**? Is the value of knowing that you have explained 4 percent of the variation worth the cost of collecting and analyzing the data? It depends upon the research objectives. So you must always look at both types of significance (statistical and practical) before you develop your conclusions, particularly when examining more complex issues.

RESEARCH IN ACTION
USING EXCEL TO COMPUTE THE CORRELATION

We can use Excel to compute the correlation. First click on a blank cell anywhere on the spreadsheet. The Excel click-through sequence for correlation is: Insert → Function → Or select a category → All. After the sequence is completed, scroll down the list of functions in the large text box and highlight CORREL, which stands for correlation. Select OK and the "Function Arguments" box will appear. There will be two text boxes that are labeled "Array 1" and "Array 2." List the two columns you wish to compare in these two text boxes. To compare column "D" with column "E," for example, you would key in D1:D63 (the sample size) in the "Array 1" text box, and E1:E63 in the "Array 2" text box. The D1 means start with the first observation and the D63 means end with observation 63 (the sample size). Next select OK and the computer will calculate the correlation. The answer will appear in the blank cell selected.

To calculate the correlation between variables X_{15}—Proud and X_{16}—Intention to Search from the Samouel's restaurant employee survey, click on any open cell on the spreadsheet. Follow the above sequence of steps and select CORREL. When you see the two Array boxes type P1:P63 in Array 1 and Q1:Q63 in the Array 2 box. The P is used because this is the column that has the data for the X_{15}—Proud variable. The Q is used because that is the column that has the data for the X_{16}—Intention to Search variable. The 1 means start with the first observation and the 63 means stop with the last observation (i.e., include the total sample). Then click on OK and the result will appear in the open cell you selected. The result is a negative correlation of –0.598.

MEASUREMENT SCALES AND CORRELATION

Business researchers often find the answers to their questions can only be measured with ordinal or nominal scales. For example, if we want to see if gender is related to soft drink consumption, we have a problem because gender is a nominal variable. If we used the Pearson correlation coefficient to examine soft drink consumption of males and females, and assumed the measure has interval or ratio-scale properties, our results would be misleading. For example, using a 2-point scale (non-metric) instead of a 5-point scale (metric) substantially reduces the amount of information available and may result in an understatement of the true correlation coefficient in the population.

When scales used to collect data are nominal or ordinal (non-metric) what can the analyst do? One option is to use the Spearman rank order correlation coefficient rather than the Pearson product-moment correlation. The Spearman correlation coefficient typically results in a lower coefficient, but is considered a more conservative statistic.

EXAMPLE OF SPEARMAN RANK ORDER CORRELATION

The survey of restaurant customers collected data on four restaurant selection factors. Customers were asked to rank the following four factors in terms of their importance in selecting a restaurant where they want to dine—food quality, atmosphere, prices and employees. The survey variables were X_{13} to X_{16} and they were measured ordinally. Phil Samouel would like to know whether "food quality" rankings are related to "atmosphere" rankings. An answer to this question will help Phil to know whether to emphasize food quality or atmosphere in his advertising. This is ordinal (ranking) data so the Pearson correlation cannot be used. The **Spearman Rank Order Correlation,** or Spearman rho is the appropriate correlation to calculate. The null hypothesis is there is no difference in the rankings of the two restaurant selection factors.

Information in the Correlations table in Exhibit 11-4 shows that the correlation between variables X_{13}—Food Quality and X_{14}—Atmosphere is $-.801$, and the significance

EXHIBIT 11-4	CORRELATION OF FOOD QUALITY AND ATMOSPHERE USING SPEARMAN RHO CORRELATIONS			

			X_{13}—Food Quality Ranking	X_{14}—Atmosphere Ranking
Spearman's rho	X_{13}—Food Quality Ranking	Correlation Coefficient	1.000	−.801*
		Sig. (2-tailed)	.	.000
		N	200	200
	X_{14}—Atmosphere Ranking	Correlation Coefficient	−.801*	1.000
		Sig. (2-tailed)	.000	.
		N	200	200

* Correlation is significant at the .01 level (2-tailed).

level is .000. This demonstrates there is a significant, negative relationship between the two restaurant selection factors. The negative correlation means that customers who rank food quality high in importance as a selection factor will rank atmosphere as significantly less important. The restaurant customers rank food quality as very important much more often than atmosphere, as shown visually in the bar charts in Exhibit 11-5.

Phil now knows that customers rank food quality as relatively more important than atmosphere. But he does not know the rankings of the selection factors in general. Variables X_{13} to X_{16} are ordinal data. Therefore, we cannot compare them by calculating the means. Instead, we must use the median to compare the rankings of the four restaurant selection factors. This will enable us to better understand the relationships.

The rankings are shown in Exhibit 11-6. Recall the four selection factors were ranked from 1 to 4, with 4 = most important. Thus, the variable with the largest median is ranked the highest and is the most important, and the variable with the lowest median is the least important. Food quality (X_{13}) is ranked as the most important (median = 4) while X_{15}— Prices is the least important (median = 1). Moreover, note the minimum for variables X_{13} and X_{14} is 2 and for X_{15} and X_{16} is 1. Thus, based on the median rankings, customers of these two restaurants are interested in food quality first and atmosphere second. Moreover, by comparing the medians we can see that employees and prices are the least important selection factors. This does not mean they are unimportant and can be ignored by Phil, but rather that, relatively speaking, food quality and atmosphere are more important. In developing an action plan to compete with Gino's, Phil needs to focus initially on his food, then

---

RESEARCH IN ACTION

USING SPSS TO CALCULATE SPEARMAN RHO CORRELATION

The SPSS click-through sequence is: ANALYZE → CORRELATE → BIVARIATE. Highlight variables X_{13} and X_{14} and move them to the Variables box. The Pearson correlation is the default along with the Two-tailed test of significance and Flag significant correlations. "Unclick" the Pearson Correlation and click on Spearman. Then click on OK at the top right of the dialog box to run the program. The results will be the same as these shown in Exhibit 11-4.

EXHIBIT 11-5 BAR CHARTS OF RANKINGS FOR FOOD QUALITY AND ATMOSPHERE

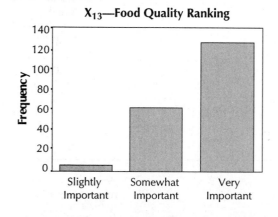

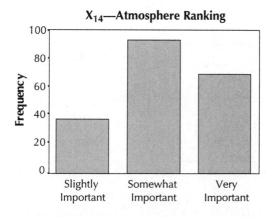

EXHIBIT 11-6	CUSTOMER RANKINGS OF RESTAURANT SELECTION FACTORS

Statistics

		X_{13}—Food Quality Ranking	X_{14}—Atmosphere Ranking	X_{15}—Prices Ranking	X_{16}—Employees Ranking
N	Valid	200	200	200	200
	Missing	0	0	0	0
Median		4.00	3.00	1.00	2.00
Minimum		2	2	1	1
Maximum		4	4	3	4

on atmosphere and to some extent on his employees (some customers ranked employees most important, as shown by the maximum value of 4).

STATISTICAL TECHNIQUES AND DATA ANALYSIS

Most business problems involve many variables. Managers look at multiple performance dimensions when they evaluate their employees. Consumers evaluate many characteristics of products in deciding which to purchase. Multiple factors influence the stocks a broker recommends. Restaurant patrons consider many factors in deciding where to dine. As the world becomes more complex, more factors influence the decisions managers make. Thus, business researchers must increasingly rely on more sophisticated methods of data analysis.

Our discussion to this point has dealt with univariate and bivariate analysis. Univariate analysis involves statistically testing a single variable, while bivariate analysis involves two variables. When business problems involve three or more variables they are inherently multidimensional and require the use of multivariate analysis. For example, managers trying to better understand their employees might examine job satisfaction, job commitment, work type (part-time vs. full-time), shift worked (day or night), age, and so on. Similarly, consumers comparing supermarkets might look at the freshness and variety of produce, store location, hours of operation, cleanliness, courtesy and helpfulness of employees, and so forth. Business researchers need multivariate statistical techniques to fully understand such complex problems.

Exhibit 11-7 displays a useful classification of statistical techniques. As you can see at the top, we divide the techniques into dependence and interdependence depending on the number of dependent variables. If there is a single dependent variable a technique is referred to as a dependence method. That is, we have both dependent and independent variables in our analysis. In contrast, when we do not have a dependent variable, we refer to the technique as an interdependence method. That is, all variables are analyzed together and our goal is to form groups or give meaning to a set of variables or respondents.

Using the classification, we can select the appropriate statistical technique. If we have a research problem that involves association or prediction using both dependent and independent variables, we should look at the dependence techniques on the left side of the diagram. The choice of a particular statistical technique depends on whether we have a metric or nonmetric

EXHIBIT 11-7   CLASSIFICATION OF STATISTICAL TECHNIQUES

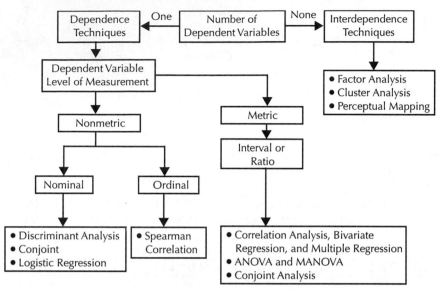

dependent variable. With a nonmetric, ordinally measured dependent we would use the Spearman correlation that we have already discussed. With a nonmetric, nominal dependent we use discriminant analysis, **conjoint** analysis, or **logistic regression.** On the other hand, if our dependent variable is metric, we can use correlation, regression, ANOVA or MANOVA, and conjoint (the statistical technique of conjoint analysis can be formulated to handle both metric and nonmetric variables). The various statistical techniques are defined in Exhibit 11-8.

REGRESSION ANALYSIS

Regression analysis is perhaps the most widely applied data analysis technique for measuring linear relationships between two or more variables. Correlation tells us if a relationship exists between two variables, as well as the overall strength of the relationship. Sometimes, however, these answers do not provide enough information for management to make the proper decision. For example, Phil Samouel may want to examine the relationship between several work environment measures and the commitment of his employees. Exhibit 11-9 shows the three supervision variables (X_3, X_6, and X_{10}) from the employee survey and one of the commitment variables (X_{14}—Effort). If Phil used **bivariate regression** he would have to run three regression models, one for each of the three supervision variables. But with **multiple regression** he could run only one regression model. That is, the metric dependent variable would be X_{14}—Effort and the three metric independent variables would be X_3, X_6, and X_{10} (all of these variables measure employee perceptions of supervision at Samouel's restaurant).

Managers often would like to be able to predict, for example, how much impact an advertising campaign will have on sales. The three typical methods to make these predictions are: (1) informed judgment; (2) extrapolation from past behavior; and (3) regression.

EXHIBIT 11-8	**DEFINITIONS OF STATISTICAL TECHNIQUES**

ANOVA	ANOVA stands for analysis of variance. It is used to examine statistical differences between the means of two or more groups. The dependent variable is metric and the independent variable(s) is nonmetric. One-way ANOVA has a single nonmetric independent variable and two-way ANOVA can have two or more nonmetric independent variables.
bivariate regression	This is a type of regression that has a single metric dependent variable and a single metric independent variable.
cluster analysis	This type of analysis enables researchers to place objects (e.g., customers, brands, products) into groups so that objects within the groups are similar to each other. At the same time, objects in any particular group are different from objects in all other groups.
correlation	Correlation examines the association between two metric variables. The strength of the association is measured by the correlation coefficient.
conjoint analysis	This technique enables researchers to determine the preferences individuals have for various products and services, and which product features are valued the most.
discriminant analysis	This enables the researcher to predict group membership using two or more metric independent variables. The group membership variable is a nonmetric dependent variable.
factor analysis	This technique is used to summarize the information from a large number of variables into a much smaller number of variables or factors. This technique is used to combine variables whereas cluster analysis is used to identify groups with similar characteristics.
logistic regression	Logistic regression is a special type of regression that can have a non-metric dependent variable.
multiple regression	This type of regression has a single metric dependent variable and several metric independent variables.
MANOVA	This is the same technique as ANOVA, but it can examine group differences across two or more metric dependent variables at the same time.
perceptual mapping	This approach uses information from other statistical techniques to map customer perceptions of products, brands, companies, and so forth.

EXHIBIT 11-9	**SELECTED VARIABLES FROM THE SAMOUEL'S EMPLOYEE SURVEY**

	Strongly Disagree						Strongly Agree
3. My supervisor gives credit and praise for work well done.	1	2	3	4	5	6	7
6. My supervisor recognizes my potential.	1	2	3	4	5	6	7
10. My supervisor is friendly and helpful.	1	2	3	4	5	6	7
14. I am willing to put in a great deal of effort beyond that normally expected to help Samouel's restaurant to be successful.	1	2	3	4	5	6	7

Informed judgment and extrapolation both assume that events and behaviors in the past will continue into the future. When these past events change, extrapolation and judgment cannot help the business researcher predict the future with an acceptable level of accuracy. In such cases, the business researcher needs a technique like regression analysis.

Our initial discussion will focus on bivariate linear regression. Bivariate regression analysis is a statistical technique that examines information about the relationship between one independent (predictor) variable and one dependent (criterion) variable and makes predictions. Values of the independent variable are examined and the behavior of the dependent variable is observed and compared using the formula for a straight line. The formula for linear regression is:

$Y = a + bX$
Where:
Y = the predicted variable
X = the variable used to predict Y
a = the intercept, or point where the line cuts the Y axis when X = 0
b = the slope, or the change in Y for any corresponding change in one unit of X

This is similar to the straight-line relationship we described underlying the correlation coefficient. When the scatter diagram is a straight line there is a high correlation between the two variables. Regression is directly related to correlation and, indeed, bivariate regression and correlation analysis are the same.

The task of the business researcher is to find the best method to fit a straight line to the data. The **least squares** method is a relatively simple mathematical method of ensuring the straight line that runs through the points on the scatter diagram is positioned so as to be the best possible. To do this, it minimizes the distances from the straight line to all the points on the scatter diagram. It measures these distances by looking at the errors in predicting Y from X. The least squares criterion minimizes the sum of the squared deviations between the actual values of Y and those predicted by the estimate of the regression line.

We must evaluate certain assumptions when we use regression analysis, just as with correlation. First, regression analysis assumes the relationship between two variables is linear. If the scatter diagram of the values of both variables looks like the plot in Exhibit 11-2b or 11-2c, this assumption would seem to be a good one. If the plot looks like 11-2a, regression analysis is not the appropriate choice.

Second, we refer to the two variables as independent and dependent but this does not mean we can say that one variable causes the behavior of the other. Regression analysis assesses the magnitude and type of association between two variables and makes predictions, but it is nothing more than a statistical tool. It often is a temptation to apply causation to the results of a regression analysis. But causation must come from theory, which is beyond the field of statistics. Consequently, even though two variables, such as sales and advertising, are logically related, regression analysis does not permit the business researcher to make cause-and-effect conclusions.

The remaining assumptions of simple regression are: (1) the variables are measured using interval or ratio scales and come from a normal population; and (2) the error terms are independent and distributed normally. We will cover these assumptions in more detail when we discuss multiple regression. One point we should make, however, is that nominal and ordinal scales can be included in a regression if they are converted to a dummy variable coding (discussed in the appendix to this chapter).

With bivariate regression analysis, we have one independent variable and one dependent variable. But business researchers often are interested in examining the combined influence of several independent variables on one dependent variable. For example, are purchasing patterns on the Internet related not only to age, but also to income, ethnicity, gender, geographic location, education level, and so forth? Similarly, Phil Samouel might want to know whether customer satisfaction with his restaurant is related only to perceptions of the restaurant's food quality (X_1), or is satisfaction also related to perceptions of menu variety (X_9), fun place to go (X_8), reasonable prices (X_{10}), and/or any of the other perceptions variables? Multiple regression enables us to measure these relationships without running several separate bivariate regressions. We first look at an example of bivariate or simple regression analysis and then move on to multiple regression.

EXAMPLE OF BIVARIATE REGRESSION

Phil Samouel regularly reads the American Restaurant Association trade publications to better understand the restaurant business and its trends. He consistently sees studies that report food quality as the most important variable used by customers in selecting and deciding to return to a particular restaurant again. He wants to know if having high quality food will help him to retain customers and grow his business. Bivariate regression analysis can provide information to help answer this question.

Phil's customer survey collected information on satisfaction (X_{17}). This variable was measured as 1 = Not Very Satisfied and 7 = Highly Satisfied. Variable X_1 was a measure of respondents' perceptions of the quality of food (1 = Strongly Disagree, 7 = Strongly Agree). The null hypothesis in this case is there is no relationship between X_{17}—Satisfaction and X_1—Excellent Food Quality. The alternative hypothesis is that X_{17} and X_1 are significantly related. This hypothesis can be tested using bivariate regression because we have a single metric dependent variable and a single metric independent variable.

The results for testing our hypothesis using bivariate regression analysis are shown in Exhibit 11-10. Note that we have separated the customer surveys into two groups—customers from Samouel's and customers from Gino's. This enables us to make comparisons between the results for the two restaurants. The Descriptive Statistics table displays the mean of Samouel's and Gino's for both the dependent variable X_{17} (Samouel's = 4.78; Gino's = 5.96) and the independent variable X_1 (Samouel's = 5.24; Gino's = 5.81). In the table labeled Model Summary we see that the R^2 for Samouel's regression model is .263 and for Gino's is .110. As you recall from our earlier discussion, R^2 shows the amount of variation in one variable that is accounted for by another variable. In this case, customer perceptions of Samouel's food quality account for 26.3 percent of the total variation in customer satisfaction with the restaurant, while for Gino's it is only 11.0 percent.

EXHIBIT 11-10 | **BIVARIATE REGRESSION OF SATISFACTION AND FOOD QUALITY DESCRIPTIVE STATISTICS**

X_{25}—Competitor		Mean
Samouel's	X_{17}—Satisfaction	4.78
	X_1—Excellent Food Quality	5.24
Gino's	X_{17}—Satisfaction	5.96
	X_1—Excellent Food Quality	5.81

Model Summary

X_{25}—Competitor	Model	R	R Square
Samouel's	1	.513*	.263
Gino's	1	.331*	.110

* Predictors: (Constant), X_1—Excellent Food Quality

```
RESEARCH IN ACTION
USING SPSS TO CALCULATE A BIVARIATE REGRESSION (SAMOUEL'S
AND GINO'S CUSTOMERS ARE CONSIDERED SEPARATELY)
```

The SPSS software can help us to test the null hypothesis of no relationship between customer satisfaction and food quality. Since we want to look at the customers from the two restaurants separately, we must first use the Data pull-down menu to split the sample into Samouel's and Gino's customers. To do so, go to the Data pull down menu, click on Compare groups, and then highlight variable X_{25}—Competitor and move it into the box labeled "Groups based on:" and then click OK. As noted earlier, we do this because Phil wants to compare his restaurant with Gino's.

To run the bivariate regression, the SPSS click-through sequence is: ANALYZE → REGRESSION → LINEAR: Click on X_{17}—Satisfaction and move it to the Dependent Variable box. Click on X_1—Excellent Food Quality and move it to the Independent Variables box. Use the default Enter in the box labeled "Method." Click on the Statistics button and use the defaults for Estimates and Model fit, then click on Descriptives. Finally, click Continue and OK to execute the program. The results will be the same as shown in Exhibits 11-10 and 11-11.

There are several other aspects of bivariate regression you need to know about. These include an understanding of the **F-ratio,** the regression and residual sums of squares, and the **regression coefficient.** Exhibit 11-11 contains this information for the bivariate regression of customer satisfaction and food quality. The ANOVA table shows the F-ratio for the regression models. This statistic assesses the statistical significance of the overall regression model. Under the Sum of Squares column, the variance in X_{17}—Customer Satisfaction that is associated with X_1—Excellent Quality Food is referred to as explained variance **(Regression Sum of Squares).** The remainder of the total variance in X_{17} that is not associated with X_1 is referred to as unexplained variance (referred to as **Residual Sum of Squares** in the table). The F-ratio is the result of comparing the amount of explained variance to the unexplained variance. Specifically, if you divide the mean square for the regression (35.001) by the mean square for the residual (1.002) you will get the F-ratio for Samouel's of 34.945. The larger the F-ratio, the more variance in the dependent variable is explained by the independent variable. In our bivariate regression example, the F-ratio for Samouel's (34.945) indicates the model is highly significant at the .000 level. The relationship for Gino's is relatively less significant (F-ratio = 12.095) but still very strong (.001).

The sum of squares also provides useful information in understanding regression. For Samouel's the regression sum of squares is 35.001 and the residual sum of squares is 98.159. For Gino's the regression sum of squares is 10.310 and the residual sum of squares is 83.530. Examination of the regression, residual and total sums of squares tells us that for both regression models there is a lot of unexplained (residual) variance in the dependent variable. Specifically, to determine the percentage of unexplained variance for a regression model, you simply divide the residual variance by the total variance. For Samouel's, you divide 98.159 (residual sum of squares) by 133.160 (**total sum of squares**) and you find out that 73.7 percent of the total variance is not explained by this bivariate regression model (98.159/133.160 = 73.7%). Moreover, if you divide 35.001 (regression sum of squares) by 133.160 (total sum of squares) and you find out that 26.3 percent of the total variance is explained by this bivariate regression model (35.001/133.160 = 26.3%). Note that dividing the regression sum of squares by the total sum of squares gives you the R^2 for this regression model (26.3%) as shown in Exhibit 11-10.

EXHIBIT 11-11 OTHER ASPECTS OF BIVARIATE REGRESSION

X_{25}—Competitor	Model		Sum of Squares	Mean Square	F	Sig.
Samouel's	1	Regression	35.001	35.001	34.945	.000*
		Residual	98.159	1.002		
		Total	133.160			
Gino's	1	Regression	10.310	10.310	12.095	.001*
		Residual	83.530	.852		
		Total	93.840			

*Predictors: (Constant), X_1—Excellent Quality Food

Coefficients*

X_{25}—Competitor	Model		Unstandardized Coefficients		Standardized Coefficients	t	Sig.
			B	Std. Error	Beta		
Samouel's	1	(Constant)	2.376	.419		5.671	.000
		X_1—Food Quality	.459	.078	.513	5.911	.000
Gino's	1	(Constant)	4.307	.484		8.897	.000
		X_1—Food Quality	.284	.082	.331	3.478	.001

*Dependent Variable: X_{17}—Satisfaction

Regression coefficients tell us how much of the variance in the dependent variable is explained by the independent variable. Let's look at the regression coefficient for X_1 for Samouel's restaurant that is shown in the Coefficients table in Exhibit 11-11. The column labeled **"Unstandardized Coefficients"** reveals the unstandardized regression coefficient for X_1 is .459. The column labeled Sig. indicates the statistical significance of the regression coefficient for X_1. The t-test tells us whether the regression coefficient is different enough from zero to be statistically significant. The t statistic is calculated by dividing the regression coefficient by its standard error (labeled Std. Error in the Coefficients table). If you divide .459 by .078, you will get a t-value of 5.911, which is significant at the .000 level (Note: Any differences in calculating the numbers are due to rounding errors).

The relationship between customer satisfaction and food quality for Samouel's is positive but only somewhat strong. The regression coefficient (b) for X_1 is interpreted as: "for every unit that X_1 increases, X_{17} will increase by .459 units." Recall Phil Samouel wanted to know: "Will excellent quality food improve customer satisfaction, and therefore the ability to attract and retain customers?" The answer is "Somewhat." The model was significant at the .000 level and the R^2 was .263, but is this practically significant? An R^2 of .263 suggests Phil should focus on improving his food quality, but continue looking for other areas to improve that also are related to customer satisfaction. He also must be concerned because Gino's food is rated as higher in quality with a mean value of 5.81 vs. 5.24 (see Exhibit 11-10). Finally, while the relationship between Gino's food quality and satisfaction is not as high as for Samouel's, there is still a significant relationship.

The Coefficients table contains both "Unstandardized Coefficients" (b) and **"Standardized Coefficients"** (betas). We need not be concerned with standardized coefficients in bivariate regression. But in multiple regression, when several independent variables are used, the scales measuring the several independent variables may not always be the same (e.g., using number of salespersons and advertising expenditures to predict sales). Standardization is a method of adjusting for different units of measure across variables. The term "Beta" refers to regression coefficients that have been standardized.

MULTIPLE REGRESSION ANALYSIS

Recall that in bivariate regression we used a single independent variable to predict a single dependent variable. With multiple regression analysis we enter several independent variables into the same type of regression equation and predict a single dependent variable. A separate regression coefficient then is calculated for each independent variable that describes its individual relationship with the dependent variable. These coefficients allow the researcher to evaluate the relative influence of several independent variables on the dependent variable. Multiple regression is a more realistic model because in the world we live in, predictions almost always depend upon multiple factors, not just one.

The relationship between each independent variable and the dependent measure is assumed to be linear as it was with bivariate regression. The task of the researcher is to find the best means of fitting a straight line to the data. The least squares method is a relatively simple mathematical technique that makes sure the straight line will best represent the relationship between the multiple independent variables and the single dependent variable. The logic of least squares is that no straight line can completely represent every dot in a regression scatter diagram. Even if there were a perfect correlation between the variables (and there never is) there will always be some differences between the actual scores (each dot) and the predicted scores using the estimated regression equation. In short, any estimated regression equation will produce some errors. The least squares method minimizes the errors in predicting the dependent variable from the independent variables. An F-test is then used to compare the variance explained by the regression to the unexplained variance (residual) and the result tells us if the overall relationship is statistically significant.

To understand the relationship between the multiple independent variables and the single dependent variable, we examine the regression coefficients for each independent variable. These coefficients describe the average amount of change in Y (dependent variable) given a unit change in the independent variable (X) you are examining. Additionally, a regression coefficient describes the relationship of each independent variable with the dependent variable. For example, assume the dependent variable is the number of bottles of water consumed in an afternoon. The two independent variables are temperature and distance walked. The regression coefficients for both of these independent variables are likely to be rather large because both are logically related to the number of bottles of water consumed.

Multiple regression is essentially the same as bivariate regression except you are working with more than one independent variable. With the addition of more than one independent variable, a couple of new issues must be considered. One issue is whether the independent variables are measured using the same or a different scale. If a different scale is used, we cannot make direct comparisons between the regression coefficients to determine the relative importance of each independent variable in predicting the dependent variable. For example, assume we want to predict annual sales revenue of the local Ford dealership using number of salespeople and advertising expenditures. These two variables are measured using different scale units. Salespeople are measured using the actual number and advertising expenditures are measured in dollars. When several independent variables are measured with different scales, it is not proper to directly compare the regression coefficients to see which independent variable most influences the dependent variable.

Since independent variables often are measured with different scale units, and business researchers typically want to identify which variables are relatively more important, we must have a way to overcome this problem. To do this, we use the standardized regression coefficient, referred to as a beta coefficient. This standardization process adjusts the regression coefficients to account for the different scales of measurement. Beta coefficients range from −1.00 to +1.00. When we use beta coefficients in multiple regression we can make direct comparisons between the independent variables to determine which have the most influence on the dependent variable. The larger the absolute value of a standardized beta coefficient the more relative importance it assumes in predicting the dependent variable.

Another issue we must be concerned about is that the several independent variables are statistically independent and uncorrelated with one another. If high correlations exist among the independent variables, **multicollinearity** is definitely a problem. As a researcher you must test for and remove multicollinearity if it is present. One way is to examine the correlation matrix for the independent variables and use only those that have low correlations. Another approach is to use internal checks built into most software programs that will signal multicollinearity is a problem and identify where such a problem exists. In the appendix to this chapter we show you how to use the internal checks in SPSS to do this.

STATISTICAL VERSUS PRACTICAL SIGNIFICANCE

When we discussed bivariate regression, we used the coefficient of determination to see if the variance in the dependent variable was consistently and systematically related to the independent variable. The same concept applies to multiple regression. The term multiple coefficient of determination indicates we are measuring the ability of the multiple independent variables to predict the single dependent variable. Just as in bivariate regression, the multiple coefficient of determination can be interpreted as the proportion of the variability in the dependent variable that can be explained by the several independent variables in the model.

The first step in examining the overall regression model is to see if it is statistically significant. We do this using the model F statistic. To be considered statistically significant, a rule of thumb is there must be $<.05$ probability the results are due to chance. Some business situations will accept a lower probability level of perhaps $<.10$, but most require a $<.05$ level and some expect $<.01$.

If the R^2 is statistically significant, we then evaluate the strength of the linear association between the dependent variable and the several independent variables. Multiple R^2, also called the multiple coefficient of determination, is a handy measure of the strength of the overall relationship. If you recall our discussion of R^2 from the section on correlation analysis, the coefficient of determination is a measure of the amount of variation in the dependent variable associated with the variation in the independent variable. In the case of multiple regression analysis, the R^2 shows the amount of variation in the dependent variable associated with all of the independent variables considered together (it also is referred to as a measure of the goodness of fit). Multiple R^2 ranges from 0 to +1 and represents the amount of the variation in the dependent variable explained by the independent variables combined. A large multiple R^2 indicates the estimated regression model works well while a small R^2 indicates it does not work well.

The larger the R^2 the more the dependent variable is associated with the independent variables we are using to predict it. For example, if the multiple R^2 between the number of bottles of water consumed in an afternoon (dependent variable), and the independent variables temperature and distance walked is .69, that would mean that we can account for, or "explain," 69 percent of the variation in bottled water consumption by using the variation in temperature and distance walked. A larger R^2 indicates a stronger relationship between the independent variables and the dependent measure. As before, the measure of the strength of the relationship between an individual independent variable and the dependent measure of interest is shown by the standardized regression coefficient (beta) for that variable. Thus, we would use the beta coefficient to tell us whether temperature or distance walked is a better predictor of bottled water consumption.

Just as we did with bivariate regression, it is necessary in multiple regression to test for the statistical significance of the standardized regression coefficients (betas) for each of the independent variables. We again must determine whether sampling error is influencing the regression results. The basic question is still the same: "What is the likelihood we would get a coefficient of this size for our sample if the true regression coefficient in the population were zero?" SPSS and most other statistical software calculate the t-test statistics for each regression coefficient so we can easily answer this question. If any of the standardized regression coefficients is not statistically significant, that particular independent variable is not a good predictor of the dependent variable. In other words, an insignificant beta means the relationship is due to sampling error and not a true relationship in the population. In short, the use of an independent variable that has an insignificant beta is meaningless and should be removed from the regression model. By removing insignificant independent variables and rerunning the regression model little information is lost and the model is more parsimonious.

In summary, to evaluate the results of a regression analysis do the following: (1) assess the statistical significance of the overall regression model using the F statistic; (2) if the F is significant, then evaluate the R^2 to see if it is large enough (see Exhibit 11-1); (3) examine each of the regression coefficients and their t statistics to identify which independent variables have statistically significant coefficients; and (4) rerun the regression with the significant independent variables and look at the beta coefficients to determine the relative influence of each of the independent variables. If you follow these steps you will have answers to the four basic questions about the relationships between your single dependent variable and your multiple independent variables: "Does a relationship exist?", "If there is a relationship, how strong is it?", "Is the relationship positive or negative?", and "If there is a relationship, what is the best way to describe it?"

EXAMPLE OF MULTIPLE REGRESSION

Phil Samouel would like to predict how satisfied his customers are based on their experiences while dining in his restaurant. As part of his customer survey, Phil collected information on customer perceptions regarding various characteristics of his restaurant. The first twelve variables in the database are the perceptions characteristics. They are metric variables and could be used as independent variables in a regression model. The perceptions are measured using a 7-point Likert-type rating scale with 7 = strongly agree (favorable) and 1 = strongly disagree (unfavorable). Variables X_{13} to X_{16} are nonmetric variables because they are ranking data, and it is not appropriate to use them in a regression equation. Variables X_{17}, X_{18}, and X_{19} are metric dependent variables measured on a 7-point Likert-type rating scale. These variables measure customers' reactions to their dining experience such as satisfaction and likelihood to return in the future. Variable X_{20}—Frequency of Usage is nonmetric as are X_{21}—Length of Time a Customer, X_{22}—Gender, and X_{25}—Restaurant Competitors = Gino's versus Samouel's. Thus, Phil's survey has collected information that could be used to develop a multiple regression predictive model that hopefully will be a much better predictor than his judgment or extrapolation from past information.

Several empirical studies have shown that food quality is the most important factor in selecting a restaurant. These same studies have shown that when restaurant customers mention food quality they are thinking of taste, proper temperature, good seasoning, variety, and so on. Thus, it is clear Phil Samouel will want to know whether in this situation perceptions of his food are related to satisfaction, as well as the other outcome variables like recommend to a friend and return to his restaurant in the future. A multiple regression model can answer these questions. For the initial regression model, we will examine the single dependent metric variable X_{18}—Likely to Return in Future, and the food independent variables X_1—Excellent Food Quality, X_4—Excellent Food Taste, and X_9—Wide Variety of Menu Items. These variables are shown in Exhibit 11-12 as they were used in the survey. To test the overall model, null hypothesis would be there is no relationship between X_{18} and X_1, X_4, and X_9. The alternative hypothesis would be X_1, X_4, and X_9 are significantly related to X_{18}—Likely to Return in Future. The Research in Action box on page 301 gives the click-through sequence for multiple regression.

The results of this initial multiple regression model are shown in Exhibit 11-13. For this example we have divided the sample into two groups—Samouel's customers and Gino's customers, so we can compare them. We show information for each of the multiple regression models. The Descriptive Statistics table shows the means of the variables in the regression analysis. Note the means for the independent variables X_1—Excellent Food Quality (5.24), X_4—Excellent Food Taste (5.16) and X_9—Wide Variety of Menu Items (5.45) for Samouel's are above the mid-point of the 7-point scale (4.0) and therefore represent positive perceptions of these attributes. The dependent variable X_{18}—Return in Future (Samouel's = 4.37) is lower but still slightly above the mid-point. What is of concern to Phil, however, is that Gino's customers are more likely to return to his restaurant in the future (mean = 5.55) and

EXHIBIT 11-12   SELECTED VARIABLES FROM SAMOUEL'S CUSTOMER SURVEY

	Strongly Disagree					Strongly Agree
1. Excellent Food Quality	1 2 3 4 5 6 7					
4. Excellent Food Taste	1 2 3 4 5 6 7					
9. Wide Variety of Menu Items	1 2 3 4 5 6 7					

	Definitely Will Not Return					Definitely Will Return
18. How likely are you to return to Samouel's restaurant in the future?	1 2 3 4 5 6 7					

on all three food variables Gino's has relatively more positive perceptions. This is information he must use to develop an action plan to improve his restaurant.

Information in the Model Summary table in Exhibits 11-13 and 11-14 indicates the R^2 for the regression of Samouel's restaurant is .262. This means that 26.2 percent of the variation in return in future (dependent variable) can be explained from the three independent variables. In general, R^2 always increases as independent variables are added to a multiple regression model. To avoid overestimating the impact of adding an independent variable to the model, some analysts prefer to use the adjusted R^2 (it recalculates the R^2 based on the number of predictor variables in the model and sample size). This makes it easy to compare the explanatory power of regression models with different numbers of independent variables and different sample sizes. The adjusted R^2 for the model is .239, which indicates only a slight overestimate with this model.

Information provided in the Coefficients table of Exhibit 11-14 tells us which of the independent variables are significant predictors of likely to return. In the significance column, we note that the beta coefficient for Samouel's food quality is significant (.028). Similarly, for Gino's, food quality is the only significant predictor (.024). Examining the Standardized Coefficients Beta column for Samouel's, we note X_1—Excellent Food Quality is most closely associated with return in future (Beta = .324) and the same situation is true for Gino's (Beta = .316). For both regression models Excellent Food Taste approaches significance but does not meet our criteria of <.05.

Caution should be exercised in examining the standardized Beta coefficients and their significance. We have concluded that only one independent variable in each regression model is statistically significant based on the reported significance levels. But levels of significance can vary if there is multicollinearity among the independents variables. Similarly,

EXHIBIT 11-13	MULTIPLE REGRESSION OF RETURN IN FUTURE AND FOOD INDEPENDENT VARIABLES

Descriptive Statistics

X_{25}—Competitor	Variable	Mean
Samouel's	X_{18}—Return in Future	4.37
	X_1—Excellent Food Quality	5.24
	X_4—Excellent Food Taste	5.16
	X_9—Wide Variety of Menu Items	5.45
Gino's	X_{18}—Return in Future	5.55
	X_1—Excellent Food Quality	5.81
	X_4—Excellent Food Taste	5.73
	X_9—Wide Variety of Menu Items	5.56

Model Summary†

X_{21}—Competitor	Model	R	R Square	Adjusted R Square
Samouel's	1	.512*	.262	.239
Gino's	1	.482*	.232	.208

*Predictors: (Constant), X_9—Wide Variety of Menu Items, X_1—Excellent Food Quality, X_9—Excellent Food Taste

---

RESEARCH IN ACTION

USING SPSS TO COMPUTE A MULTIPLE REGRESSION MODEL

For this example we will want to compare Samouel's customers' perceptions with those of Gino's, so go to the Data pull-down menu to split the sample. Scroll down and click on Split File, then on Compare Groups. Highlight variable X_{25} and move it into the box labeled "Groups based on": and then click OK. Now you can run the regression.

The SPSS click through sequence is ANALYZE → REGRESSION → LINEAR. Highlight X_{18} and move it to the dependent variables box. Highlight X_1, X_4, and X_9 and move them to the independent variables box. Use the default Enter in the Methods box. Click on the Statistics button and use the defaults for Estimates and Model Fit. Next click on Descriptives and then Continue. There are several other options you could select at the bottom of this dialog box but for now we will use the program defaults. Click on OK at the top right of the dialog box to run the regression. The results are the same as in Exhibit 11-13.

The remaining diagnostic information for the multiple regression models is shown in Exhibit 11-14. The regression model for Samouel's is statistically significant (F-ratio = 11.382; probability level = .000). The probability level of .000 means that the chances are .000 that the regression model results are due to random events instead of a true relationship. The Gino's multiple regression model also is significant at a very high level (.000). Thus, the food independent variables do predict whether a customer is likely to return in the future for both restaurants. We can therefore reject the null hypothesis of no relationship between the variables.

---

the signs indicating a negative or positive relationship between the independent and dependent variables can be reversed if there is multicollinearity among the independents variables. For this reason, when developing a multiple regression model, we always recommend that the simple correlations among the independent and dependent variables be examined closely to ensure the proper interpretation of the findings. We return to this topic later in the chapter because of its importance.

We interpret regression coefficients somewhat differently with multiple regression than we did with bivariate regression. In bivariate regression we interpret the unstandardized regression coefficient as the amount of change in the dependent variable for every one-unit change in the independent variable. But in multiple regression this interpretation must be modified somewhat. In our example above, if we use the beta coefficient for Samouel's X_1—Excellent Food Quality we would say the dependent variable would change .324 for every one-unit change in food quality, when all other independent variables are held constant. Thus, .324 is the estimated increase in likelihood to return in the future associated with a one-unit increase in food quality when food taste and variety of menu items are held constant. Note the signs of the coefficients are interpreted the same as with a correlation coefficient. Thus, with more positive perceptions of food quality, there is an increased likelihood to return in the future. This is consistent with the mean value of 5.24 for food quality that indicates Samouel's customers are relatively happy with his food. Similar findings were found for Gino's but it should be noted that Gino's food quality is perceived to be somewhat higher (5.81) than Samouel's.

This means we can reject both null hypotheses that the three food independent variables are not associated with X_{18}—Return in Future for Samouel's and Gino's restaurants. Using the beta coefficient for food quality, for example, we can conclude that every time X_1 increases by 1 unit, X_{18} will increase on average by .324 units for

EXHIBIT 11-14	OTHER INFORMATION FOR MULTIPLE REGRESSION MODELS

ANOVA[†]

X_{25}—Competitor	Model		Sum of Squares	df	Mean Square	F	Sig.
Samouel's	1	Regression	28.155	3	9.385	11.382	.000*
		Residual	79.155	96	.825		
		Total	107.310	99			
Gino's	1	Regression	22.019	3	7.340	9.688	.000*
		Residual	72.731	96	.758		
		Total	94.750	99			

*Predictors: (Constant), X_9—Wide Variety of Menu Items, X_1—Excellent Food Quality, X_4—Excellent Food Taste
[†]Dependent Variable: X_{18}—Return in Future

Coefficients*

			Unstandardized Coefficients		Standardized Coefficients	t	Sig.
X_{25}—Competitor	Model		B	Std. Error	Beta		
Samouel's	1	(Constant)	2.206	.443		4.985	.000
		X_1—Excellent Food Quality	.260	.116	.324	2.236	.028
		X_4—Excellent Food Taste	.242	.137	.291	1.770	.080
		X_9—Wide Variety of Menu Items	−8.191E-02	.123	−.094	−.668	.506
Gino's	1	(Constant)	2.877	.507		5.680	.000
		X_1—Excellent Food Quality	.272	.119	.316	2.295	.024
		X_4—Excellent Food Taste	.241	.132	.264	1.823	.071
		X_9—Wide Variety of Menu Items	−5.275E-02	.125	−.065	−.421	.675

*Dependent Variable: X_{18}—Return in Future

Samouel's and .316 units for Gino's, assuming the other variables are held constant. Thus, we can conclude that perceptions of food quality definitely are a predictor of likelihood to return in future.

Two other problems still remain, however. The first is the initial regression model for Samouel's explains only about 26.2 percent of the variation in X_{18} (Gino's explains 23.2 percent) so we need to consider other independent variables that might help us increase the predictive capability of our regression model, such as the other perceptions variables. Increasing the predictive capability of our regression by adding other independent variables will help Phil Samouel to develop a more effective business plan to compete with Gino. The second problem is Gino's customers are more likely to return in the future (5.55 vs. 4.37) to his restaurant so Phil's business plan must address this

---

One of our purposes in this chapter is to introduce you to the basic concepts of correlation and regression, and to help you interpret the statistics when you encounter them as output from a statistical analysis program. A lot of information is included in the SPSS tables we did not discuss. Managers typically do not use much of this information but statisticians may. With SPSS and other statistical software packages you will need to determine which information is useful for your analysis and which is not. This is more difficult as you consider additional kinds of analysis. We recommend you start out simple and then move to more sophisticated types of analysis. For example, the next problem you may wish to examine is changing the dependent variable from X_{18}—Return in Future to X_{19}—Recommend to Friend, or to X_{17}—Satisfaction, and run the same regression with the three food independent variables. You may also wish to again use return in future as the dependent variable and include all twelve perceptions variables as predictors. Recall that Appendix 1-C contains an overview of how to use SPSS.

---

issue as well. The research in Action box suggests other research questions that Phil could examine using SPSS.

MULTICOLLINEARITY AND MULTIPLE REGRESSION

In our discussion of multiple regression we have used the term independent variable to refer to any variable being used to predict or explain the value of the dependent variable. This does not mean the independent variables are independent in a statistical sense. Indeed, most independent variables in multiple regression are correlated. Multicollinearity in multiple regression analysis refers, therefore, to the correlation among the independent variables.

Multicollinearity can cause a number of problems with regression. For example, the F-test of the overall multiple regression model may indicate a statistically significant relationship. But when we examine the t-tests for the individual coefficients we may find none of them is significant. If this happens it is not possible to determine the individual effect of any particular independent variable on the dependent variable. In addition, in some cases of multicollinearity, the least squares estimates can have a sign opposite that of the coefficient being estimated. Thus, with a high degree of collinearity we cannot rely on the individual coefficients to interpret the results. Multicollinearity problems do not have an impact on the size of the R^2, or on your ability to predict values of the dependent variable. But they certainly can affect the statistical significance of the individual regression coefficients and therefore the accuracy of predictions.

So how do we know when multicollinearity is too high? A general rule of thumb adopted by statisticians is a sample correlation coefficient between two independent variables greater than +.70 or less than −.70 is evidence of potential problems with multicollinearity. Indeed, when there are several independent variables, all of which are intercorrelated, problems can arise sometimes when multicollinearity is lower than .70. When this situation exists you should remove one or more of the independent variables from the regression model and rerun it.

Statisticians have developed more precise tests than the above rule of thumb to determine whether multicollinearity is high enough to cause problems. We will examine them in the following paragraphs. They are referred to as the **Tolerance** and **VIF** tests.

EXHIBIT 11-15	COMPENSATION AND EFFORT VARIABLES FROM THE SAMOUEL'S EMPLOYEE SURVEY

	Strongly Disagree						Strongly Agree
1. I am paid fairly for the work I do.	1	2	3	4	5	6	7
9. My pay reflects the effort I put into doing my work.	1	2	3	4	5	6	7
12. The benefits I receive are reasonable.	1	2	3	4	5	6	7
14. I am willing to put in a great deal of effort beyond that normally expected to help Samouel's restaurant be successful.	1	2	3	4	5	6	7

EXAMPLE OF MULTICOLLINEARITY

Phil Samouel certainly needs to know whether multicollinearity is a problem with his regression models. An assessment of multicollinearity is necessary to ensure that he can interpret the relative importance of the individual independent variables in the regression models. Based on conversations with his consultant he wants to examine whether compensation issues are related to the effort put forth by his employees. He collected information related to this on his employee survey and we will use that to answer this question. To do so, we will use the single dependent metric variable X_{14}—Effort, and the three metric independent variables X_1—Paid Fairly, X_9—Pay Reflects Effort, and X_{12}—Benefits Reasonable. These variables are shown in Exhibit 11-15 as they appear on the employee questionnaire. The null hypothesis is there is no relationship between X_{14}—Effort and the three independent variables. We will test this hypothesis using multiple regression analysis.

The results from running the multiple regression model are shown in Exhibits 11-16 and 11-17. Information from the Model Summary table in Exhibit 11-16 indicates the R-Square for the model is .256. Looking at the ANOVA table we see that the model is highly significant

EXHIBIT 11-16	SUMMARY STATISTICS FOR EMPLOYEE REGRESSION MODEL

Model Summary

Model	R	R Square	Adjusted R Square	Std. Error of the Estimate
1	.506*	.256	.218	.92

*Predictors: (Constant), X_{12}—Benefits Reasonable, X_9—Pay Reflects Effort, X_1—Paid Fairly

ANOVA†

Model		Sum of Squares	df	Mean Square	F	Sig.
1	Regression	17.041	3	5.680	6.762	.001*
	Residual	49.563	59	.840		
	Total	66.603	62			

*Predictors: (Constant), X_{12}—Benefits Reasonable, X_9—Pay Reflects Effort, X_1—Paid Fairly
†Dependent Variable: X_{14}—Effort

(.001). The question now is which of the three independent variables are contributing to this regression model and how. To determine this we look at the coefficients table in Exhibit 11-17. Recall the standardized Beta coefficients tell us which independent variable contributes the most to explaining the relationship between the dependent and independent variables. Variable X_9—Pay Reflects Effort is highly significant (.001) and has a Beta of −.203. Neither of the other independent variable Betas is significant. Therefore in this regression model the only significant independent variable is X_9. But does that mean the other variables are not related to the dependent variable? We need to look further to answer this question.

At the far right hand side of Exhibit 11-17 is a column of numbers called collinearity statistics. Underneath this heading is a column labeled "VIF." VIF stands for **Variance Inflation Factor.** VIF measures how much the variance of the regression coefficients is inflated by multicollinearity problems. If VIF equals 0, there is no correlation between the independent measures. A VIF measure of 1 is an indication of some association between predictor variables, but generally not enough to cause problems. A maximum acceptable VIF value would be 5.0; anything higher would indicate a problem with multicollinearity. Looking at the information for the regression of X_{14}—Effort and the compensation independent variables, the VIF for variable X_1 is 4.894, for X_9 it is 1.701, and for X_{12} it is 4.456. This indicates the variances of the regression coefficients for two of the independent variables (X_1 and X_{12}) are somewhat inflated and multicollinearity may be a problem.

You can also examine the tolerance value to assess multicollinearity in regression (it is the opposite of VIF). Tolerance is the amount of variance in an independent variable that is not explained by the other independent variables. If the other variables explain a lot of the variance of a particular independent variable we have a problem with multicollinearity. Thus, small values for tolerance indicate problems of multicollinearity. The minimum cutoff value for tolerance is typically .10. That is, the tolerance value must be smaller than .10 to indicate a problem of multicollinearity. Since the tolerance value for X_9 is .588 and the VIF is 1.701 it clearly does not have a problem. But for the other two variables the tolerance numbers are .204 and .224 so we again conclude multicollinearity may be a problem with the independent variables in this regression model.

To better understand the multicollinearity issue, let's look at the bivariate correlations between the variables shown in Exhibit 11-18. The top of the table shows the correlations and the bottom half shows the level of significance. All three compensation variables are

---

EXHIBIT 11-17 **COEFFICIENTS FOR EMPLOYEE REGRESSION MODEL**

Coefficients*

Model		Unstandardized Coefficients		Standardized Coefficients	t	Sig.	Collinearity Statistics	
		B	Std. Error	Beta			Tolerance	VIF
1	(Constant)	3.089	.680		4.541	.000		
	X_1—Paid Fairly	.178	.281	.157	.633	.529	.204	4.894
	X_9—Pay Reflects Effort	.553	.157	.516	3.521	.001	.588	1.701
	X_{12}— Benefits Reasonable	−.256	.300	−.203	−.855	.396	.224	4.456

*Dependent Variable: X_{14}—Effort

| EXHIBIT 11-18 | BIVARIATE CORRELATIONS OF EFFORT AND COMPENSATION VARIABLES |

Pearson Correlations

	X_{14}—Effort	X_1—Paid Fairly	X_9—Pay Reflects Effort	X_{12}—Benefits Reasonable
X_{14}—Effort	1.000	.309	.496	.241
X_1—Paid Fairly	.309	1.000	.639	.880
X_9—Pay Reflects Effort	.496	.639	1.000	.592
X_{12}—Benefits Reasonable	.241	.880	.592	1.000

Significance (1-tailed)

X_{14}—Effort	.	.007	.000	.028
X_1—Paid Fairly	.007	.	.000	.000
X_9—Pay Reflects Effort	.000	.000	.	.000
X_{12}—Benefits Reasonable	.028	.000	.000	.

significantly correlated with the dependent variable effort. With regard to multicollinearity between the independent variables, the problems identified earlier by the VIF, and tolerance tests are evident. Variables X_1 and X_{12} are correlated .88, X_9 and X_1 are .639, and X_9 and X_{12} are .592. While two of the correlations are less than the recommended .7, the third (X_1 and X_{12}) correlated well above that level. Thus, clearly the multicollinearity has influenced this regression model. As a result, the model indicates that variables X_1 and X_{12} are not related to the dependent variable when in fact they are.

To fully understand the problem of multicollinearity in regression, you clearly have to examine the correlations between the independent variables ahead of time. If any are too high (> .70) then you should consider removing one of the highly correlated variables. How do you decide which independent variable to remove? One approach is to identify the independent variables that are most closely related to each other (highest correlation). Then keep the independent variable in your regression model that is most highly correlated with the dependent variable. Another approach is to run regression models with all combinations of variables and see which model has the largest R^2. Finally, common sense may determine which variable(s) are included.

STEPWISE MULTIPLE REGRESSION

Up to this point we have been using the Enter default in the SPSS regression software. When you use this option, all the independent variables you place in the regression are simultaneously used in an effort to predict the single dependent variable. There is another option, however, referred to as stepwise. It is a sequential approach in which the regression equation is estimated with a set of independent variables that are selectively added or deleted from the model. With backward stepwise regression, all of the independent variables initially are included in the regression analysis and then independent variables are removed one at a time. The first variable removed is the least significant and the regression model is recomputed. The process is repeated and each time the least significant and the one most highly correlated with another independent variable. The regression model is them recomputed.

The stepwise forward approach is the most often utilized, so we will focus on it. With this approach each independent variable is considered for inclusion in the regression prior to developing the equation. The first variable to be selected for inclusion in the regression is the one that contributes the most toward predicting the dependent variable. If none of the independents are significantly related to the dependent, no regression will be estimated. Following the inclusion of the first significant independent variable in the regression, all other independent variables are examined again and the variable that now contributes the most toward predicting the remaining unexplained variance in the dependent variable is included (assuming the new variable is not highly correlated with the already included ones). This process continues until only variables that are uncorrelated and have significant standardized Beta coefficients remain. The criteria for including an independent variable are beyond the scope of this text. For further explanation of the criteria for including an independent variable see Hair, J., et. al., 2003. *Multivariate Data Analysis: With Readings,* Prentice-Hall, 6th edition. If you choose to use a software package to compute a stepwise regression we recommend you use the default settings.

As was noted earlier, it is common to have multicollinearity among independent variables. To minimize or avoid problems caused by multicollinearity, you can use either the Tolerance or VIF diagnostic tests to remove independent variables that are a problem from the regression model. Both of these tests typically are included in the popular software packages, as well as the stepwise regression option. The Research in Action box gives the click-through sequence for stepwise regression.

EXAMPLE OF STEPWISE MULTIPLE REGRESSION

Phil Samouel would like to know whether his employees or his food attributes are most important in determining customer satisfaction (X_{17}). When we examine the perceptions variables we note that variable X_1 measures food quality, X_4 measures food taste, and X_9 is variety of menu items. Similarly, variables X_6, X_{11}, and X_{12} measure employee characteristics. We can use stepwise multiple regression to determine which of these variables is most important in predicting customer satisfaction. The results for a stepwise regression of these six metric independent variables and the single metric dependent variable satisfaction are shown in Exhibits 11-19 to 11-22. Remember that for this regression model we are looking only at the survey data for Samouel's restaurant.

Information provided in the Model Summary and ANOVA tables in Exhibit 11-19 shows that two statistically significant (.000) regression models were computed. The first variable to enter the regression was X_1—Excellent Food Quality and it produced an R^2 of .263. The second variable to enter the regression model was X_6—Friendly Employees and the R^2 then increased to .356. The other four variables could not add significantly to the predictive power of the stepwise regression equation so they were not brought into the model (the SPSS default criteria were used to exclude variables).

Information in the Coefficients table for the Tolerance and VIF measures (see Exhibit 11-22) tells us that multicollinearity is not a problem. To examine the relative importance of the two independent variables in predicting the dependent variable we examine the information for the second model when both variables have entered the regression. The standardized Betas are .449 and .312, so just as excellent food quality entered the equation

---

RESEARCH IN ACTION

USING SPSS TO RUN A STEPWISE REGRESSION MODEL USING SAMOUEL'S CUSTOMERS

The SPSS software has a stepwise regression option. Before executing the regression you must select Samouel's customers to analyze. To do so, go to the Data pull down menu and click on Select Cases. Next click on If condition satisfied and then on If. Now highlight variable X_{25}—Competitor and place it in the box. Click on the equals sign below and then place a zero after it (we use a zero because Samouel's is coded "0" and Gino's is a "1"). Now click Continue and OK to execute the selection of only Samouel's customers.

To run the stepwise regression model, the click through sequence is ANALYZE → REGRESSION → LINEAR. Highlight X_{17} and move it to the dependent variable box. Next highlight variables X_1, X_4, X_6, X_9, X_{11}, and X_{12} and move them to the independent variable box. "Enter" is the default in the Methods box. Click on this box and change it to "Stepwise." Click on the Statistics button and then on Estimate in the Regression Coefficients box. Now, click on Model Fit, Descriptives, and Collinearity Diagnostics, and then on Continue (If some of these boxes are already checked, leave them checked. For some versions of SPSS they are the default.) We will not use any of the options in the Plots, Save or Options boxes so click on OK to execute the program. The results will be the same as in Exhibits 11-19 to 11-22.

EXHIBIT 11-19 **STEPWISE REGRESSION BASED ON SAMOUEL'S CUSTOMER SURVEY**

Model Summary

Model	R	R Square	Adjusted R Square	Std. Error of the Estimate
1	.513*	.263	.255	1.00
2	.597†	.356	.343	.94

*Predictors: (Constant), X_1—Excellent Food Quality
†Predictors: (Constant), X_1—Excellent Food Quality, X_6—Friendly Employees

ANOVA‡

Model		Sum of Squares	df	Mean Square	F	Sig.
1	Regression	35.001	1	35.001	34.945	.000*
	Residual	98.159	98	1.002		
	Total	133.160	99			
2	Regression	47.421	2	23.711	26.825	.000†
	Residual	85.739	97	.884		
	Total	133.160	99			

*Predictors: (Constant), X_1—Excellent Food Quality
†Predictors: (Constant), X_1—Excellent Food Quality, X6—Friendly Employees
‡Dependent Variable: X_{17}—Satisfaction

EXHIBIT 11-20	**MEANS AND CORRELATIONS FOR SELECTED VARIABLES FROM SAMOUEL'S CUSTOMER SURVEY**

Descriptive Statistics

	Mean
X_{17}—Satisfaction	4.78
X_1—Excellent Food Quality	5.24
X_4—Excellent Food Taste	5.16
X_9—Wide Variety of Menu Items	5.45
X_6—Friendly Employees	2.89
X_{11}—Courteous Employees	1.96
X_{12}—Competent Employees	1.62

Pearson Correlations

	X_{17}—Satisfaction	X_1—Excellent Food Quality	X_4—Excellent Food Taste	X_9—Wide Variety of Menu Items	X_6—Friendly Employees	X_{11}—Courteous Employees	X_{12}—Competent Employees
X_{17}—Satisfaction	1.000	.513	.442	.328	.404	.183	.376
X_1—Excellent Food Quality	.513	1.000	.785	.688	.205	.081	.295
X_4—Excellent Food Taste	.442	.785	1.000	.769	.168	.015	.220
X_9—Wide Variety of Menu Items	.328	.688	.769	1.000	.139	.087	.180
X_6—Friendly Employees	.404	.205	.168	.139	1.000	.556	.709
X_{11}—Courteous Employees	.183	.081	.015	.087	.556	1.000	.598
X_{12}—Competent Employees	.376	.295	.220	.180	.709	.598	1.000

Significant Correlations (1-tailed)

	X_{17}—Satisfaction	X_1—Excellent Food Quality	X_4—Excellent Food Taste	X_9—Wide Variety of Menu Items	X_6—Friendly Employees	X_{11}—Courteous Employees	X_{12}—Competent Employees
X_{17}—Satisfaction	.	.000	.000	.000	.000	.034	.000
X_1—Excellent Food Quality	.000	.	.000	.000	.021	.213	.001
X_4—Excellent Food Taste	.000	.000	.	.000	.047	.439	.014
X_9—Wide Variety of Menu Items	.000	.000	.000	.	.083	.196	.037
X_6—Friendly Employees	.000	.021	.047	.083	.	.000	.000
X_{11}—Courteous Employees	.034	.213	.439	.196	.000	.	.000
X_{12}—Competent Employees	.000	.001	.014	.037	.000	.000	.

EXHIBIT 11-21 | **INDEPENDENT VARIABLES IN STEPWISE REGRESSION MODEL**

Variables Entered/Removed*

Model	Variables Entered	Variables Removed	Method
1	X_1—Excellent Food Quality	.	Stepwise (Criteria: Probability-of-F-to-enter <= .050, Probability-of-F-to-remove >= .100).
2	X_6—Friendly Employees	.	Stepwise (Criteria: Probability-of-F-to-enter <= .050, Probability-of-F-to-remove >= .100).

*Dependent Variable: X_{17}—Satisfaction

EXHIBIT 11-22 | **REGRESSION COEFFICIENTS FOR STEPWISE REGRESSION MODEL**

Coefficients*

Model		Unstandardized Coefficients		Standardized Coefficients	t	Sig.	Collinearity Statistics	
		B	Std. Error	Beta			Tolerance	VIF
1	(Constant)	2.376	.419		5.671	.000		
	X_1—Excellent Food Quality	.459	.078	.513	5.911	.000	1.000	1.000
2	(Constant)	1.716	.431		3.982	.000		
	X_1—Excellent Food Quality	.402	.074	.449	5.392	.000	.958	1.044
	X_6—Friendly Employees	.332	.088	.312	3.748	.000	.958	1.044

*Dependent Variable: X_{17}—Satisfaction

first it also is the strongest predictor variable. Both variables are reasonably strong predictors, and should both be considered in trying to understand what influences satisfaction at Samouel's restaurant.

SUMMARY

Describe the Nature of Relationships between Variables

There are four basic concepts we need to understand about relationships between variables: presence, type of relationship, direction, and strength of association. We will describe each of these concepts. Presence assesses whether a systematic relationship exists between two or more variables. We rely on the concept of statistical significance to measure whether or not a relationship is present. A second important concept is the type of relationship. We typically say there are two types of relationships—linear and nonlinear. A linear relationship is a "straight line association" between two or more variables. A non-linear relationship, often referred to as curvilinear, is one in which the relationship is best described by a curve instead of a straight line. If a relationship is present between the variables, we also need to know the direction. The direction of a relationship can be either positive or negative. Finally, when a relationship is present, the business researcher must determine the strength of the association. Depending on the type of relationship being examined, we generally categorize the strength of association as slight, small but definite, moderate, high, or very strong.

Explain the Concepts of Correlation and Regression Analysis

Correlation analysis calculates the association between two variables. The Pearson correlation measures the linear association between two metric variables. The number representing the Pearson correlation is referred to as a correlation coefficient. It ranges from -1.00 to $+1.00$, with zero representing absolutely no association between the two metric variables. While -1.00 or $+1.00$ is possible and represents a perfect association between two variables, it very seldom occurs. The larger the correlation coefficient, the stronger the linkage or level of association. Correlation coefficients can be either positive or negative, depending upon the direction of the relationship between the variables. If there is a positive correlation coefficient between X and Y, then increases in the value of X are associated with increases in the value of Y, and vice versa.

Managers often would like to be able to predict, for example, how much impact an advertising campaign will have on sales. The three typical methods to make these predictions are: (1) informed judgment; (2) extrapolation from past behavior; and (3) regression. Informed judgment and extrapolation both assume that events and behaviors in the past will continue into the future. When these past events change, extrapolation and judgment cannot help the business researcher predict the future with an acceptable level of accuracy. In such cases, the business researcher needs a technique like regression analysis.

Regression analysis is perhaps the most widely applied data analysis technique for measuring linear relationships between two or more variables. Correlation tells us if a relationship exists between two variables, as well as the overall strength of the relationship. Sometimes, however, these answers do not provide enough information for management to make the proper decision. For example, Phil Samouel may want to examine how both the atmosphere and food variables are related to satisfaction, instead of only one at a time. In such instances we use regression analysis because it enables us to use several independent variables to predict a single dependent variable.

Clarify the Difference between Bivariate and Multiple Regression Analysis

Bivariate regression has only two variables—a single metric dependent variable and a single metric independent variable. For both bivariate regression and multiple regression, data analysts typically refer to the coefficient of determination as R^2.

Understand How Multicollinearity Can Influence Regression Models

Multicollinearity can cause a number of problems with regression. For example, the F-test of the overall multiple regression model may indicate a statistically significant relationship. But when we examine the t-tests for the individual coefficients we may find none of them is significant. If this happens it is not possible to determine the individual effect of any particular independent variable on the dependent variable. Multicollinearity problems do not have an impact on the size of the R^2, or on your ability to predict values of the dependent variable. But they certainly can affect the statistical significance of the individual regression coefficients.

So how do we know when multicollinearity is too high? A general rule of thumb adopted by statisticians is a sample correlation coefficient between two independent variables greater than +.70 or less than −.70 is evidence of potential problems with multicollinearity. But statisticians have developed more precise tests than the above rule of thumb to determine whether multicollinearity is high enough to cause problems. The tests are referred to as the Tolerance and VIF tests. They can be examined using SPSS and other statistical software packages.

Understand When and How to Use Stepwise Multiple Regression

Stepwise multiple regression is a sequential approach in which the regression equation is estimated with a set of independent variables that are selectively added or deleted from the model. With stepwise regression, all of the independent variables initially are examined for inclusion in the regression analysis and then independent variables are added one at a time. The first variable included is the most significant. The process is repeated and each time the most significant variable is added until all uncorrelated variables with significant Beta coefficients are included. That is, only independent variables that help to predict the dependent variable and increase the R^2 are included in the final regression model. Some of the other independent variables may be related to the dependent variable but are not included in the final regression model because of multicollinearity with the other independent variables already in the regression model.

KEY TERMS

bivariate regression	multiple regression	Spearman rank order
conjoint	multicollinearity	correlation
correlation	nonlinear relationship	standardized coefficients
coefficient of	Pearson correlation	statistical significance
determination	practical significance	stepwise multiple
correlation coefficient	regression coefficient	regression
covariation	regression sum of squares	strength of association
F-ratio	residual sum of squares	tolerance
least squares	relationship presence	total sum of squares
linear relationship	relationship	unstandardized coefficients
logistic regression	scatter diagrams	

ETHICAL DILEMMA

A telephone company offering a variety of services hires a business research firm to determine the level of customer satisfaction for their local telephone, cellular and Internet services by target audience. Terry Brown, the firm's lead researcher uses Pearson's r to calculate the relationships in the survey data. When checking the results before preparing the first draft of the executive summary for the client, Terry's assistant notices that she includes the outliers in some calculations and not in others. (See Appendix 11-A.) Does the inconsistency affect the validity of the research? What should Terry's assistant do?

REVIEW QUESTIONS

1. What is the value of a correlation coefficient in measuring relationships between variables?
2. What is the difference between the statistical techniques ANOVA and MANOVA?
3. What diagnostic tests can be used to determine if multicollinearity is a problem in multiple regression?
4. Explain the relationship between explained and unexplained variance in multiple regression.

DISCUSSION AND APPLICATION ACTIVITIES

1. Why would the business researcher use multiple regression instead of bivariate regression?
2. Why might a business researcher use stepwise multiple regression instead of regular regression.
3. Why is it important to understand multicollinearity when running a stepwise multiple regression?
4. SPSS Application: Use X_{17}—Satisfaction as the dependent variable and X_1–X_{12} as independent variables. Split your sample by X_{25}—Competitor and run a multiple regression and determine the predictive capability for all twelve metric independent variables.
5. SPSS Application: Do the same as in question 6 but now select the stepwise option. Which independent variables are included in the final regression model? How does the R^2 differ from what you found in question 4.
6. SPSS Application: Calculate the median and modal responses for the restaurant selection factors (X_{13}—X_{16}). Compare the responses of male and female customers. Are the rankings the same? If not, how do they differ and how would Phil use this information in preparing his business plan.

INTERNET EXERCISES

1. Use the Google search engine. Type in the key words **multiple regression.** Prepare a brief report of what you found.
2. The Federal Reserve Bank of St. Louis has a database called FRED (Federal Reserve Economic Data). Go to their Web site http://research.stlouisfed.org/fred/abotfred.html and report what you found. Review the variables they provide information for and select a variable to be used as a dependent variable in a multiple regression model. Now look at the variables again and select several variables to use as the multiple independent variables to predict the dependent variable you chose. Prepare a brief report summarizing your logic in selecting the variables.
3. Go to the following Web site: http://ericae.net/pare/getvn.asp?v=8&n=2. It provides and overview of the four assumptions researchers should always test with multiple regression. Summarize this article in a report to be turned into your instructor.
4. Go to the following Web site: http://ebook.stat.ucla.edu/calculators/correlation.phtml. It is a correlation and regression calculator. In the first column input the following

numbers: 2,2,2,1,1,2, 3 and 2. Be sure to push the Enter key after you key in each number. In the second column input the following numbers: 2,1,2,2,1,3,3 and 2. Click on the Submit dialogue box to use your data in a correlation model. Prepare a brief report on the Web site and the correlation and regression results you got.

5. Go to the following Web site: www.surveysystem.com/correlation.htm. Prepare a brief report on the discussion of correlation.

NOTES

1. Technically, the r^2 symbol refers to the coefficient of determination in bivariate regression and the R^2 refers to the multiple coefficient of determination in multiple regression. In practice, analysts generally refer to both of these as the coefficient of determination and use the R^2 for both

Appendix 11-A: Special Topics in Multiple Regression Analysis

Learning Objectives

1. Explain the use of dummy variables in regression analysis.

2. Examine residuals and outliers as they relate to multiple regression analysis.

INTRODUCTION

Several more advanced topics on multiple regression analysis are covered in this appendix. They include **dummy variables,** examining regression assumptions, and identifying and dealing with outliers.

THE ROLE OF DUMMY VARIABLES IN REGRESSION

A dummy independent variable is a variable that has two (or more) distinct levels, which are coded 0 and 1. Dummy coded variables enable us to use independent variables not measured using interval or ratio scales to predict the dependent variable. For example, if you wanted to include the gender of customers of the two restaurants to understand satisfaction with the restaurant, it is obvious your measure for gender only includes two possible categories—male or female. In this case, we could use gender in a regression model by coding males as 0 and females as 1. Similarly, we might have purchasers versus non-purchasers and include them as an independent variable using a 1–0 coding. This represents a slight but acceptable violation of the assumption of metric scaling for the independent variables.

To use dummy variables we must choose one category of the variable to serve as a reference category and then add as many dummy variables as there are possible values of the variable, minus the reference category. Each category is coded as either 0 or 1. In the example above, if you choose the male category as the reference category, you would have one dummy variable for the female category. That dummy variable would be assigned the value of 1 for females and 0 for males. In the restaurant employee database, X_{19}—Gender is already coded as a dummy variable for gender, using males as the reference category (males are coded 0).

We can also use dummy coding with categorical independent variables that have more than two categories. Let's say you wanted to use an independent variable like occupation and you have physicians, attorneys and professors in your sample. To use dummy variables in your regression, you choose one category as a reference group (physicians), and add two dummy variables for the remaining categories. The variables would be coded as follows, using zero and one:

Category	X_1	X_2
Physician	0	0
Attorney	1	0
Professor	0	1

As you can tell from the list above, when the respondent is a physician, X_1 and X_2 will be zero (the reference category is always coded 0). For attorneys, the regression coefficient for X_1 represents the difference in the dependent variable compared to physicians. The regression coefficient associated with X_2 represents the difference in the dependent variable for professors compared to physicians.

EXAMPLE OF DUMMY VARIABLES

To enable him to prepare a better business plan, Phil wants to know more about his employees and what he can do to increase their productivity and commitment to working at his restaurant. In the employee survey he gathered data on employee commitment and job satisfaction as well as gender. The variables he collected data on are shown in Exhibit A-1 as they were used in the survey.

To investigate the relationship between job satisfaction and job commitment, as measured by being proud about working at Samouel's restaurant, we can use X_{15}—Proud as the dependent variable in a regression model, and the three job satisfaction variables X_2—Work I Want, X_5—Learning New Skills and X_7—Sense of Accomplishment as the metric independent variables. In addition to the job satisfaction variables, however, Phil wants to determine if the gender of his employees influences how proud they are about working at the restaurant. Therefore, we also include X_{19}—Gender (coded male = 0 and female = 1) in our regression model.

Results of the multiple regression analysis are shown in the Exhibits A-2 and A-3. The R^2 for the model is .393, as shown in the Model Summary table. Thus, approximately 39.3 percent of the total variation in X_{15} can be predicted by X_2—Work I Want, X_5—Learn New Skills, X_7—Accomplishment and X_{19}—Gender. The regression model is highly significant, with a probability level of .000, as revealed in the ANOVA table.

EXHIBIT A-1 | **SELECTED VARIABLES FROM THE SAMOUEL'S EMPLOYEE SURVEY**

	Strongly Disagree						Strongly Agree
Independent Variables (Job Satisfaction)	1	2	3	4	5	6	7
2. I am doing the kind of work I want.	1	2	3	4	5	6	7
5. My job allows me to learn new skills.	1	2	3	4	5	6	7
7. My work gives me a sense of accomplishment.	1	2	3	4	5	6	7
Dependent Variable							
15. I am proud to tell others that I work for Samouel's restaurant.	1	2	3	4	5	6	7
19. Your gender	0 = Male						
	1 = Female						

EXHIBIT A-2	REGRESSION MODEL OF SAMOUEL'S EMPLOYEES USING JOB SATISFACTION AS INDEPENDENT VARIABLES AND JOB COMMITMENT

Model Summary

Model	R	R Square	Adjusted R Square
1	.627	.393	.351

*Predictors: (Constant), X_{19}—Gender, X_7—Accomplishment, X_5—Learn New Skills, X_2—Work I Want

ANOVA

Model		Sum of Squares	df	Mean Square	F	Sig.
1	Regression	21.138	4	5.284	9.399	.000
	Residual	32.608	58	.562		
	Total	53.746	62			

*Predictors: (Constant), X_{19}—Gender, X_7—Accomplishment, X_5—Learn New Skills, X_2—Work I Want

†Dependent Variable: X_{15}—Proud

The Coefficients table in Exhibit A-3 reveals that X_{19}—Gender is a significant predictor of X_{15}—Proud with a beta coefficient of .445 (probability of .000). Work I Want (X_2) also is significant (.023) and has a beta coefficient of .325. Learn New Skills (X_5) and Sense of Accomplishment (X_7) are not significantly related to job commitment (X_{15}—Proud). Thus, Gender and Work I Want are independent variables that significantly explain Proud to Work for Samouel's.

To better understand these results, let's compare male and female employees' responses on the job satisfaction and commitment variables. The results of this comparison are in Exhibit A-4. As you can see, females are relatively more favorable (higher mean) on X_2, X_7 and X_{15}, but less favorable about X_5. However, the differences are significant only for variables X_5—Learn New Skills and X_{19}—Gender (See ANOVA table). Thus, females are significantly more favorable than males with regard to being proud to

EXHIBIT A-3	BETA COEFFICIENTS FOR JOB SATISFACTION AND COMMITMENT REGRESSION

Coefficients

Model		Unstandardized Coefficients		Standardized Coefficients	t	Sig.
1		B	Std. Error	Beta		
	(Constant)	2.716	.702		3.871	.000
	X_2—Work I Want	.348	.148	.325	2.344	.023
	X_5—Learn New Skills	9.943E-02	.109	.100	.911	.366
	X_7—Accomplishment	5.017E-02	.122	.055	.410	.683
	X_{19}—Gender	.853	.210	.445	4.056	.000

*Dependent Variable: X_{15}—Proud

work at Samouel's. This finding suggests that Phil needs to learn more about male and female employees and why they differ in their feelings about working at Samouel's restaurant. Indeed, he needs to go beyond these four variables and look at all aspects of working at the restaurant.

RESEARCH IN ACTION
USING SPSS TO EXAMINE DUMMY VARIABLES

The SPSS click through sequence to examine dummy variables is: ANALYZE → REGRESSION → LINEAR. Click on X_{15}—Proud and move it to the Dependent Variables box. Click on X_2, X_5, X_7, and X_{19} and move them to the Independent Variables box. The box labeled "Method" has ENTER as the default and we will use it. Click on the Statistics button and use the Estimates and Model fit defaults. Click on Descriptives then Continue and OK to run the regression. The results will be the same as shown in Exhibits A-2 and A-3.

EXHIBIT A-4 COMPARISON OF MALE AND FEMALE EMPLOYEE PERCEPTIONS

Residual Statistics*

		X_{19}—Gender	X_2—Work I Want	X_5—Learn New Skills	X_7—Accomplishment	X_{15}—Proud
Males	Mean		4.83	5.10	4.95	5.15
	N		40	40	40	40
Females	Mean		5.17	4.61	5.17	6.09
	N		23	23	23	23
Total	Mean		4.95	4.92	5.03	5.49
	N		63	63	63	63

ANOVA Table

			Sum of Squares	df	Mean Square	F	Sig.
X_2—Work I Want* X_{19}—Gender	Between Groups	Combined	1.778	1	1.778	2.406	.126
	Within groups		45.079	61	.739		
	Total		46.857	62			
X_5—Learn New Skills* X_{19}—Gender	Between Groups	Combined	3.525	1	3.525	4.210	.044
	Within Groups		51.078	61	.837		
	Total		54.603	62			
X_7—Accomplishment* X_{19}—Gender	Between Groups	Combined	.732	1	.732	.707	.404
	Within Groups		63.204	61	1.036		
	Total		63.937	62			
X_{15}—Proud* X_{19}—Gender	Between Groups	Combined	12.820	1	12.820	19.108	.000
	Within Groups		40.926	61	.671		
	Total		53.746	62			

RESEARCH IN ACTION
USING SPSS TO COMPARE GROUP MEANS

Using SPSS, it is simple to compare the responses of male and female employees. The SPSS click through sequence is: ANALYZE → COMPARE MEANS → MEANS. Click on X_{15}—Proud, and X_2, X_5, and X_7 and move them to the Dependent List box. Click on X_{19}—Gender and move it to the Independent List box. Click on the box labeled "Options" and then at the bottom left hand corner of the screen click on Anova and eta. Now click Continue and OK to run the program. The results are the same as in Exhibit A-4.

RESIDUALS ANALYSIS—ASSUMPTIONS AND OUTLIERS

When we run a regression model we develop an estimate of the explained variance (R^2) and the unexplained error (residuals). An analysis of the **residuals** helps us to determine whether the assumptions that have been made about the regression model are appropriate. Our assumptions are (1) the error variance is over all values of the independent variables; (2) the errors are uncorrelated with each of the independent variables; and (3) the errors are normally distributed. If our assumptions about the errors are not correct then our results may not be valid.

Residuals provide the best information about our errors. Thus, an analysis of the residuals is an important step in determining if our assumptions are correct. Most of residuals analysis is based upon an examination of graphical plots of the residuals. These plots typically involve plotting the residuals against values of the independent variable (most often used in bivariate regression), plotting the residuals against the predicted values of the dependent variable (most often used in multiple regression), a standardized residual plot, and a normal probability plot. For bivariate linear regression both the residual plot against the independent variable (X) and the residual plot against the dependent variable (Y) provide the same information. For multiple regression, the residual plot against the dependent variable is more widely used because there is more than one independent variable. Most statistical software packages provide plots of the regression residuals, such as the standardized regression residuals against the predicted dependent variable, a normal probability plot of the regression residuals, and a histogram of the dependent variable and the regression standardized residuals, so we will discuss them.

The plot of standardized residuals provides information on the assumption that the errors are normally distributed. To assess this, you look at a standardized residual plot and determine whether 95 percent of the standardized residuals are between −2 and +2. If they appear to be, and this is a judgment call, then we conclude that the errors are normally distributed.

The normal probability plot is another approach to determine if the errors are normally distributed. The normal scores are plotted on the horizontal axis and the corresponding standardized residuals on the vertical axis. If the standardized residuals are approximately normally distributed the plotted points should cluster around a 45-degree line passing through the origin. This kind of plot is referred to as a normal probability plot. Judgment is used to determine if the pattern of observed values deviates from the line enough to conclude that the standardized residuals are not from a standard normal probability distribution. If the points are grouped relatively close around the line we conclude our assumption of normality of residuals is reasonable. Generally speaking, the more closely the points are clustered around the 45-degree line, the stronger the evidence supporting the normality assumption. Any substantial deviations from the line suggest the residuals are not normally distributed.

Residuals analysis also can be used to identify respondents with data points that are outliers in determining the estimated regression model. Recall from our earlier discussion that an outlier is a data point (respondent) that is distinctly different from the values of the other respondents. An outlier is suspicious because it deviates from the pattern of the other respondents and therefore from our expectations. Outliers must be closely examined because they may represent erroneous data that needs to be corrected. Outliers also may indicate one of the regression model assumptions has not been met. But in some situations they are simply unusual values that occur by chance, as was true in the Bill Gates example in Chapter 9. In deciding how to deal with an outlier, we should first check to see whether it is a valid value for that respondent. If an error has been made in collecting the data or entering the data into the software file it should be corrected. But, in general, outliers should not be removed from your dataset unless clear evidence shows they are truly different from the population being studied and should not have been included in the original data set.

Standardized residuals can be used to identify outliers. If an observation (respondent) deviates substantially from the pattern of the rest of the data, the standardized residual for that observation will be large in absolute value. Most statistical software packages, including SPSS, identify respondents with standardized residuals that have large absolute values. In general, respondents with a standardized residual of less than −2 or greater than +2 are considered outliers. With normally distributed errors, standardized residuals should be outside these limits no more than 5 percent of the time.

EXAMPLES OF RESIDUALS AND OUTLIERS

By examining the error terms (residuals) we can diagnose potential problems caused by observations that do not meet the assumptions of regression. Residuals represent the difference between the observed (sample) values of the dependent variable and the predicted values of the dependent variable predicted by the regression model. That is, they represent the error term for the regression model (also referred to as the unexplained variation).

Recall that Phil Samouel is very interested in the relationship between the job satisfaction of his employees and their job commitment. The analyst he hired to conduct his survey data has pointed out, however, that even if the regression results are statistically significant they must be interpreted cautiously until the assumptions of the regression model are examined to see if there are any problems. We can conduct a residuals analysis to determine if any of the assumptions of the regression model have been violated (i.e., outliers, normally distributed errors, linearity, etc.).

The plot in Exhibit A-5 labeled "Histogram" shows the frequency distribution of the standardized residuals compared to a normal distribution curve. There are some residuals (e.g., those occurring at 2.25) that are beyond the right tail of the curve, but many of the residuals are fairly close. Also, some of the columns of residuals are above the curve and others are below it. One might conclude from examination of only this plot that there is a problem. But you need to look at all three plots, as well as information in the Collinearity and Casewise Diagnostics tables to make a final judgment. What we can conclude at this point, however, is the possibility exists that the observations to the far right are outliers.

Exhibit A-6 shows the second plot, labeled "Normal Probability Plot of Regression Standardized Residuals." It compares the observed standardized residuals against the expected standardized residuals from a normal distribution. If the observed residuals are normally distributed, they will be close to the 45° line shown on the plot. The residuals for our regression model are reasonably close to the line so the errors are normally distributed.

| EXHIBIT A-5 | HISTOGRAM OF EMPLOYEE SURVEY DEPENDENT VARIABLE X15—PROUD |

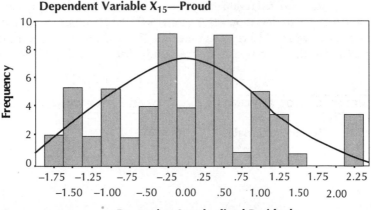

Dependent Variable X₁₅—Proud

Std. Dev = .97
Mean = 0.00
N = 63.00

| EXHIBIT A-6 | NORMAL PROBABILITY PLOT OF REGRESSION STANDARDIZED RESIDUALS |

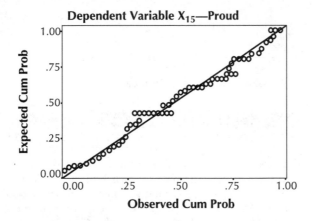

Dependent Variable X₁₅—Proud

Finally, the third plot (See Exhibit A-7) labeled "Scatterplot" compares the standardized predicted values of the dependent variable against the standardized residuals from the regression equation. To the far right hand side of the plot we see a couple of residuals by themselves (beyond 2), which suggests the possibility of outliers. Similarly, there are a couple of data points at the top of the graph beyond 2 standard deviations. But, overall, the scatterplot of residuals shows no large differences in the spread of the residuals as you look from left to right on the chart, and most of the points are within the −2 or +2 range. These findings again suggest a linear relationship with normally distributed error terms.

By examining the information shown in all three plots we conclude there are no significant data problems that would indicate the multiple regression assumptions have been seriously violated. This conclusion is reinforced by the fact that regression is considered a "robust" statistical technique where violations of the assumptions must be substantial before we encounter problems.

We still have further information to examine regarding outliers. To do so let's look at the table labeled "Residual Statistics" shown in Exhibit A-8. Across the top are columns labeled minimum, maximum, mean, standard deviation and N. Along the left side are rows labeled predicted value (for dependent variable = X_{15}), residual, standardized predicted value, and standardized residual. The standardization process produces values with a mean = 0 and a standard deviation = 1.00. Entries in the Minimum and Maximum columns for the standardized residual represent the number of standard deviations from the mean of 0. For example, the largest value of the standardized residual is 2.263 standard deviations

EXHIBIT A-7 **SCATTERPLOT OF EMPLOYEE SURVEY DEPENDENT VARIABLE X_{15}—PROUD**

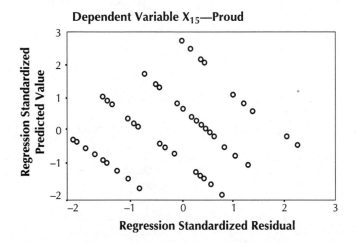

Dependent Variable X_{15}—Proud

RESEARCH IN ACTION

USING SPSS TO EXAMINE RESIDUALS AND OUTLIERS

SPSS includes several diagnostic tools to examine residuals. To run the regression that examines the residuals, first load the employee database. The click-through sequence is ANALYZE → REGRESSION → LINEAR. Highlight X_{15}—Proud and move it to the dependent variable box. Next highlight variables X_2, X_5, X_7, and X_{19} and move them to the independent variable box. Enter is the default in the Methods box and we will use it. Click on the Statistics button and Estimates and Model Fit will be the defaults (if they are not defaults in your version of SPSS, click them). Now, click on Collinearity Diagnostics and then go to the bottom left of the screen in the Residuals box and click on Casewise Diagnostics. The default is to identify outliers outside three standard deviations, but in this case we are going to be conservative and use two standard deviations. Click on Outliers outside and then place a 2 in the box for number of standard deviations. Next click on Continue.

This is the same sequence as earlier regression applications, but now we also must go to the Plots button to request some new information. To produce plots of the residuals to check on potential violations of the regression assumptions, click on ZPRED and move it to the Y box. Then click on ZRESID and move it to the X box. These two plots are for the Standardized Predicted Dependent Variable and Standardized Residuals. Next, click on Histogram and Normal Probability plot under the Standardized Residual Plots box on the lower left side of the screen. Examination of these plots and tables enables us to determine whether the hypothesized relationship between the dependent variable X_{15} and the independent variables X_2, X_5, X_7, and X_{19} is linear, and also whether the error terms in the regression model are normally distributed. Finally, click on Continue and then on OK to run the program. The results are the same as in Exhibits A-5 to A-7.

above its mean of 0. Recall that earlier we told you when you have a standardized residual of less than −2 or greater than +2 it is possible you have one or more outliers. That is because with normally distributed errors, standardized residuals should be outside these limits no more than 5 percent of the time. An even more rigorous test is to look for minimum and maximum values greater than 3.0, in which case residuals should be outside these limits no more than one percent of the time. That would mean that some of the predicted values and residuals are further than three standard deviations away from their means and in all likelihood there are outliers in the data. Since we have a standardized residual larger than +2, we can conclude that perhaps there are several outliers and we must individually examine them. As a point of clarification of information reported in the table, under the Mean column for Residual there is a number shown as −8.18E-16. This means we must add 15 zeros to the number (the decimal place is 16 spaces to the left) and it actually is −.000000000000000818, a number clearly too long to report in the table.

Exhibit A-8 also includes a table labeled "Casewise Diagnostics." It identifies the case numbers (respondents) and their ratings on variable X_{15}. Note that respondents 14, 51, and 53 all gave a rating of 7 on the 7-point scale (above the predicted maximum value of 6.95). The mean for all Samouel's employees was 5.49 and the standard deviation of the predicted value was .58 (see Residuals Statistics table in Exhibit A-8). Moreover, the predicted maximum value of X_{15} is more than two standard deviations from the mean (5.49 compared to 6.65 / Note that $2 \times .58 = 6.65$). Thus, these three respondents were more than two standard deviations above the mean and may represent outliers. To deal with this we could choose to either delete these respondents because they are so different, or we can retain them even though they obviously are very satisfied. To make a decision, we would examine their other responses to the survey and if they are very positive then we likely would retain them since their answers are consistent and we have little justification for removing them.

EXHIBIT A-8 RESIDUAL STATISTICS AND CASEWISE DIAGNOSTICS FOR EMPLOYEE SURVEY

Residuals Statistics*

	Minimum	Maximum	Mean	Std. Deviation	N
Predicted Value	4.41	6.95	5.49	.58	63
Residual	−1.35	1.70	−8.18E-16	.73	63
Std. Predicted Value	−1.858	2.500	.000	1.000	63
Std. Residual	−1.805	2.263	.000	.967	63

*Dependent Variable: X_{15}—Proud

Casewise Diagnostics*

Case Number	Std. Residual	X_{15}—Proud	Predicted Value	Residual
14	2.263	7	5.30	1.70
51	2.263	7	5.30	1.70
53	2.130	7	5.40	1.60

*Dependent Variable: X_{15}—Proud

SUMMARY

Explain the Use of Dummy Variables in Regression Analysis

A dummy independent variable is a variable that has two (or more) distinct levels, which are coded 0 and 1. Dummy coded variables enable us to use qualitative independent variables not measured using interval or ratio scales to predict the dependent variable. For example, if you wanted to include the gender of customers of the two restaurants to understand satisfaction with the restaurant, it is obvious your measure for gender only includes two possible categories—male or female. In this case, we could use gender in a regression model by coding males as 0 and females as 1. Similarly, we might have purchasers vs. non-purchasers and include them as an independent variable using a 1 – 0 coding. This represents a slight but acceptable violation of the assumption of metric scaling for the independent variables.

To use dummy variables we must choose one category of the variable to serve as a reference category and then add as many dummy variables as there are possible values of the variable, minus the reference category. Each category is coded as either 0 or 1. In the example above, if you choose the male category as the reference category, you would have one dummy variable for the female category. That dummy variable would be assigned the value of 1 for females and 0 for males. We can also use dummy coding with categorical independent variables that have more than two categories.

Examine Residuals and Outliers as They Relate to Multiple Regression Analysis

When we run a regression model we develop an estimate of the explained variance (R^2) and the unexplained (residuals). An analysis of the residuals helps us to determine whether the assumptions that have been made about the regression model are appropriate. Most of residuals analysis is based upon an examination of graphical plots of the residuals. These plots typically involve plotting the residuals against values of the independent variable (typically used in bivariate regression), plotting the residuals against the predicted values of the dependent variable (typically used in multiple regression), a standardized residual plot, and a normal probability plot. For bivariate linear regression both the residual plot against the independent variable (X) and the residual plot against the dependent variable (Y) provide the same information. For multiple regression, the residual plot against the dependent variable is more widely used because there are more than one independent variables. The SPSS software provides a plot of the standardized regression residuals against the predicted dependent variable, a normal probability plot of the regression residuals, and a histogram of the dependent variable and the regression standardized residuals.

In our discussion of multiple regression we have used the term independent variable to refer to any variable being used to predict or explain the value of the dependent variable. This does not mean the independent variables are independent in a statistical sense. Indeed, most independent variables in multiple regression are correlated. Multicollinearity in multiple regression analysis refers, therefore, to the correlation among the independent variables.

KEY TERMS

dummy variable   residual

CHAPTER 12

Reporting and Presenting Research

Learning Objectives

1. Convey the importance of effective communication to research success.

2. Describe the elements of a research proposal.

3. Provide an overview of effective research reports.

4. Summarize effective ways to deliver a research presentation.

INTRODUCTION

Good research is made useful by effectively communicating its purpose, methodology, results, and implications. The purpose of research is to answer specific research questions and thereby enable better decision making. Methodology is a detailed account of the research design and the way the project was implemented. The results and implications summarize the major findings and conclusions as they relate to the study's objectives.

Researchers use three formal communication approaches. These include the research proposal, the written research report, and the oral presentation. Occasionally, a project may skip one of the steps above; for example, the oral presentation. On other occasions, however, more than one presentation or report may be required. In any case, these three mechanisms provide opportunities to make the project's utility clear. Certainly there have been occasions when the research was correctly executed, but the results were ignored because they were presented poorly. If the research is to be useful in addressing the decision question that initiated it, careful attention must be given to these crucial communication opportunities.

This chapter describes proposals, reports, and presentations. The final form and content of these communication tools will vary depending upon the type of project and the extent of involvement required of the researcher. But the examples used here provide a basic framework from which to work. The different elements of each of the three communication tools are explained and illustrated using a project performed for Samouel's restaurant. In so doing, the characteristics of effective communication within each stage are described. Appendix 1-A includes the research proposal for Samouel's restaurant. Appendix 12-A is a sample report to Phil Samouel covering the primary research questions identified in the proposal.

WRITTEN AND ORAL COMMUNICATION

The primary role of the researcher is to place the decision maker in the best position to make an informed decision. The report and presentation should clearly highlight the key findings that will affect organizational decision making. Not all decision makers, however, process information in the same way. Therefore, the researcher must consider the level of sophistication of the **audience** in preparing both written and oral communications.

AUDIENCE SOPHISTICATION

The researcher must present the results as simply as possible without being misleading or seeming mysterious. Consider the following potential audiences: business professors, NASA scientists, brand managers for Proctor and Gamble®, and an entrepreneur (former car salesperson) wishing to start his or her own car dealership. The researcher would likely use different communication styles for each audience. However, the basic format of the communication devices would not change a great deal between these audiences.

NASA scientists and professors, considered to be academic, would be assumed to be relatively sophisticated. For this academic audience, the researcher places more emphasis on technical aspects of the **research methods** and results, since an academician has greater interest and an ability to understand these things. Likewise, a NASA scientist probably is familiar with basic research techniques. But care must be taken to define key business terms that may be unfamiliar to a technical audience. Overall, a slightly higher level of sophistication can be used when communicating with these groups.

For both the brand managers and the local automobile entrepreneur, the report likely would place less emphasis on technical aspects. Details of any statistical tests, for example, would be placed in a technical appendix. Moreover, any statistical analysis would be reported in a more elementary way. This audience, however, is likely to be much more familiar with basic business terminology.

Remember, decision makers are less likely to act on results they do not understand. Thus, the researcher should gear written and oral communication to the level of the least sophisticated potential user in the audience. This is sometimes referred to as the **least common denominator principle.**

WRITTEN COMMUNICATION

"Just the facts, ma'am," is a slogan made popular by Sergeant Joe Friday, a fictional Los Angeles police detective. He was the primary character in the books, television shows, and films titled *Dragnet*. While the researcher may not need to be as dry as Sergeant Friday, "just the facts" is a good orientation for writing business research documents. The writer must remember that the primary purpose of the document is not to entertain or impress someone with literary eloquence. Rather, it is to assist in decision making. The "Research in Action" box below provides a manager's view of the typical internal research report.

RESEARCH IN ACTION

MBAS OVERDO IT AGAIN

Managers often struggle to get the most essential information from a research report. Consider the following managerial views:

> First line supervisors are intimidated by the blather and complicated, convoluted, thick reports circulated by the young MBAs on the staff." What this supervisor didn't know was that the president of the division had virtually confessed the same thing to me on a flight to Los Angeles. He had suggested the reports from some of his own staff people—the ones with the graduate degrees—were a little intimidating and sent him to the dictionary more than once. Not possessing a business degree himself, he felt a little out of his depth and was loath to talk directly to them about the reports and, perhaps, show his ignorance. They (the report authors with MBAs) had fallen prey to the seductive reasoning that the boss will be impressed that the authors had really done a lot of homework if they included sophisticated words in their reports and made them look physically impressive.

Research reports would be more useful if they simply addressed the following points:
1. Where are we now?
   - Describe the situation that gave rise to the research.
2. Where are we headed?
   - Stay on course and make sure everything in the report is fulfilling its purpose.
3. How do we propose to get there?
   - Describe the analytical results that help accomplish the report's purpose.
4. How will we know when we have arrived?
   - Make sure the "answers" (or end result) are easy to find and not hidden within the body of the text.

SOURCE: Hull, William W. 1995. Writing Reports for Top Management. *Supervision* 56 (February): 8–13.

Guidelines for Technical Writing

Research proposals and reports typically are considered technical writing. The following simple guidelines can greatly improve the writing quality of a technical report.

1. **Front-end Loading.** The writer should realize that the first few pages of the report are the most read pages. Therefore, the researcher should strive to pack the most content possible into the first few pages. Thus, the key findings, implications, and recommendations, if requested, should appear in the first pages of the document, usually referred to as an **executive summary.**

2. **KISS**—Keep It Short and Simple. One of the best guides to technical writing is to be short and to the point. Follow these guides:

   - Shorter sentences are better than longer sentences.
   - Shorter words are better than longer words.
   - Summarize information in tables and charts when possible.
   - Use few prepositions (of, for, to, in, from, etc.).
   - Use as little statistical jargon as possible.

3. **Have Empathy.** Remember readers have varying abilities to understand technical information. Not everyone can gain meaning from technical details within the document. Respect the reader's time by eliminating unnecessary information. Technical details can be included in an appendix where they will not distract the less sophisticated reader.

4. **Goal Orientation.** Remember the document has a clear goal or goals. It is designed to accomplish some important purpose for the business. All writing should be framed within the context of providing this information. The reader should be clear, therefore, about how the purpose is accomplished.

5. **Edit, Edit, Edit!** Eliminate paragraphs, sentences, and words that are not necessary to complete a thought that helps build a case for the project.

6. **Be Graceful in Ignorance.** Avoid topics for which the report cannot shed any light. Furthermore, any limitations or shortcomings of the study must be spelled out clearly. Not only is this the ethical approach, it is better for the researcher to disclose any problems with the study as opposed to having them discovered later by the decision maker.

7. **Organization.** Clearly organize the paper's sections. Use a lot of headings and subheadings. These aid the reader tremendously. Also, include a listing of charts, figures, and tables to assist the reader in finding information within the report with minimal loss of time. The headings and subheadings provide an outline for the **table of contents.**

RESEARCH PROPOSALS

Research proposals are written during Phase I (see Chapter 2, Exhibit 2-1, Formulation Phase)of the research process. Proposals help ensure effective communication between the researcher and the decision maker. They describe the reasons for the study, including listing and explaining the research questions, a detailed description of the study design and tools to be used (research design), and a summary of the potential results. Finally, the research proposal includes a clear statement of the time schedule and proposed budget for the project.

Appendix 1-A (Chapter 1) contains sample proposals. One of the proposals is the result of an interview between a professional business researcher and Phil Samouel, owner of Samouel's Greek Cuisine. The researcher used several of the creative problem-solving techniques to identify and refine the following research questions:

1. Are employees being managed to maximize their productivity as well as commitment to the success of the restaurant?

2. What are the best approaches to attract new customers and to keep and grow existing customers?

The interview process creates a common understanding of the business situation faced by Samouel's. It is very important, however, to commit this understanding to writing. By doing so, it is less likely the research will produce useless results. This is because the decision maker, in this case Phil Samouel, will review and sign the proposal describing the research and its deliverables before the project gets underway. In other words, the proposal documents that the researcher and decision maker are "on the same page." The key sections of the proposal are described in Exhibit 12-1.

THE WRITTEN RESEARCH REPORT

The written report is the tangible result of a research project. For ongoing research, reports often are generated automatically through the DSS (Decision Support System), as described in Chapter 3 (see chapter 3, Decision Support Systems). While the content of the reports would be much the same, this chapter focuses on reports written for one-time research projects. The format of all research reports is similar. In some ways, they simply build on the research proposal by describing what happened instead of what will happen.

An Outline of an Applied Business Research Report

Recall that business research can be described as either basic or applied. The content and style of the final report will vary slightly depending upon which type of research is being performed. We first describe the outline of an applied business project. This type of report commonly results from projects completed by a business research consultant for a decision maker, like Mr. Samouel. Later, we discuss how the sections of the report might vary between applied and basic research projects.

Title Page   The **title page** lists the title of the project, the principal decision maker for whom the research is being performed, the date and names, affiliations, and contact information of the primary investigator(s). Titles should be kept short but still descriptive of the research performed.

Executive Summary   Beyond any doubt, this is the most read portion of a research report. Remember, business people are busy, so they want the key information summarized in an easy-to-read and concise format. In fact, many decision makers read only this section. So, it is a stand-alone, very brief overview of the entire report that clearly emphasizes the most important findings. The contents of the executive summary include (1) a statement of the purpose and key research questions, (2) a brief description of the research design and related details, (3) a summary of statistical results of testing research questions and/or hypotheses, (4) a written interpretation of the findings framed as

| EXHIBIT 12-1 | THE SECTIONS AND CONTENT OF A RESEARCH PROPOSAL |

Section	Description
Background Information	Describes the relevant business situation and the scope of the study. This includes an overview of related background material and previous research. The scope includes a statement of how the results are to be interpreted. For example, does the decision maker want operating recommendations from the researcher, such as strategies to improve Samouel's restaurant operations, or just a summary of research results? Some decision makers only want the researcher to answer the specific research questions, leaving the overall substantive interpretation to the decision maker.
Problem Statement and Research Questions	Clearly defines the research problem. Lists and describes research questions to be addressed. If specific hypotheses can be derived, they should be listed and explained briefly.
Research Strategy and Methods	Describes how the study will be conducted. Referring back to the Basic Research Process illustrated in Chapter 2, this section describes the processes listed in Phases II and III (see Exhibit 2-1). That is, it describes the research design to be used, the variables that must be measured, the data collection approach, data sources (sample), how data will be collected, and the statistical techniques that will be used to analyze the data, thereby testing the research questions.
Final Report Outline	A basic outline of the final report is provided. It lists the key sections of the final report along with a brief description of the expected contents. This is where dummy (or pro-forma) tables can be used to illustrate the type of quantitative results the researcher expects to find.
Budget and Schedule	A breakdown of the expected costs of performing the research project, including the researcher's fee and conditions of billing. It lists a time frame within which the research is to be conducted. This statement also may contain a brief description of the qualifications of the researcher.
Qualifications	

answers to the research questions, and (5) if requested, a list of practical business implications derived from the research.

Executive summaries should be short. Two pages are acceptable, but a one-page executive summary is preferable. It's important that the primary and/or most interesting findings be formatted to attract attention. A good idea here is to list them in a neat, bullet-type fashion. The executive summary also is the opportunity to "sell" the report. It should try to convince the reader that the project accomplished its purpose, and it should entice them to read further into the report.

Table of Contents A table of contents makes the document more useful. It should list the headings and subheadings by page number. The location of all exhibits, tables, and figures also should be listed. These should be labeled by their titles.

Introduction The **introduction** is much the same as that written for the proposal. It describes the purpose of the study, in detail, including a list of research questions and hypotheses along with explanations of each. It also includes background material that describes in detail how the study came to be conducted, including a reference back to the original proposal. The introduction prepares the reader for the information to come.

Research Methods   This section, as in the proposal, describes the way the study was conducted. It includes a description of the sampling process and sample characteristics, and the procedures used to gather data, including a description of the measures. In addition, this section may sometimes include a summary overview of all variables by presenting basic frequencies and/or descriptive statistics for all variables. This section also may refer to appendices that are included at the end of the document. These appendices usually contain an actual copy of the data collection devices, such as a questionnaire and tables containing the frequencies and/or descriptive statistics. This is a good way to provide the user with data that may be interesting but does not specifically address a research question.

Results   In this section, the results of tests that address the research questions and/or hypotheses are presented. The choice of data analysis techniques is explained and details of the results are presented. Quantitative results are presented in tables and/or charts. Several examples of appropriate tables and charts for specific statistical approaches are

---

EXHIBIT 12-2 **FREQUENCY DISTRIBUTION FOR X_{16}—INTENTION TO SEARCH**

X_{16}—Intention to Search

	Frequency	Percent	Cumulative Percent
Extremely Likely	7	16.3	16.3
Very Likely	5	11.6	27.9
Somewhat Likely	11	25.6	53.5
Neither = 50-50 Chance	3	7.0	60.5
Somewhat Unlikely	8	18.6	79.1
Very Unlikely	6	14.0	93.1
Extremely Unlikely	3	7.0	100.0
Total	43	100.0	

EXHIBIT 12-3 **DISPLAYING REPORT RESULTS USING PIE CHARTS**

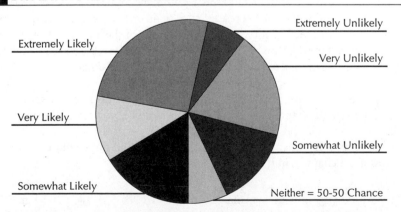

shown in this text. Managers generally appreciate results presented graphically. Exhibit 12-3 shows a frequency distribution for variable X_{16}. Exhibits 12-2 and 12-3 illustrate the use of two versatile charts to present different types of results.

The famous pie chart is particularly useful in showing tabulated frequencies for nominal or ordinal variables. The pie chart in Exhibit 12-2 displays the percentage of Samouel's restaurant employees and their likelihood of searching for another job. The size of the slice of pie is proportional to the number (percentage) of employees in each category. In this case, the chart graphically shows employees' likelihood of searching for another job. From the information provided in the frequency chart we can see a high likelihood of searching. Indeed, 53.5 percent of employees are at least somewhat likely to search for a new job (25.6 + 11.6 + 16.3 = 53.5%). This is something that needs to be addressed by Phil Samouel in developing a new business plan for his restaurant.

Exhibit 12-4 shows how bar charts can be used to display cross-tabulation results. The charts compare Intention to Search with Gender and Work Type. In the Likely to Search categories, males are much more likely to search, as are the part-time employees of Samouel's. This situation clearly deserves attention by Phil Samouel.

Pie and bar charts can be useful in depicting other results. For example, bar charts can be used to depict means or standardized regression weights. Both types of charts are easily constructed using computer software. Virtually all spreadsheet packages have a click-through sequence for creating pie and bar charts, as well as other types of charts. Finally, statistical packages like SAS and SPSS can be used to construct some charts.

Once again the researcher can make use of an appendix. The report itself should be kept as free of clutter as possible. While all statistical analyses should be documented, not all of it needs to be reported in the body of the report. Statistical results that cannot be presented in a simple straightforward fashion should be placed in an appendix.

The main emphasis in the results section is to report on the research questions and/or hypotheses. But the researcher may wish to include a section highlighting other results discovered during the study. Some may seem particularly relevant and worthy of highlighting and perhaps suggest ideas for a follow-up study. Such results should be considered exploratory since they do not address a current research question or hypothesis.

Recommendations and Conclusions   This section of the report begins by summarizing the results in everyday language. It is good practice to use bulleted text to highlight key results addressing specific research questions. Any logical implications that emerge from the results also are discussed. If requested, a list of recommendations is provided. Recommendations may include suggestions for further research that build on the current results. The recommendations and conclusions section also contains a discussion of the limitations of the research. No study is perfect, but the decision maker needs to be able to assess the confidence that can be placed in the results in light of a full accounting of the project's weaknesses.

Appendices   The appendix contains the questionnaire, descriptive statistics, and detailed statistical analyses. Another important component of the appendix is a reference list. A *reference list* provides a complete description of the sources cited in the report. There are several different styles for reference lists. You will notice quite a few reference lists following the chapters in this book.

EXHIBIT 12-4 | **DISPLAYING REPORT RESULTS USING BAR CHARTS**

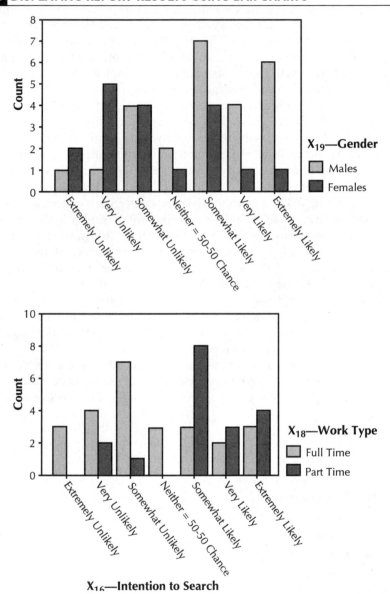

X_{16}—Intention to Search

An Outline of a Basic Research Report

Basic research is presented in much the same way as applied research. A basic research report has the same sections as an applied report. The Executive Summary is sometimes replaced, however, with an abstract. The abstract is shorter than an Executive Summary. Abstracts are 100–150 words and describe the general study purpose and give a hint of the study results.

A basic research report usually is more theoretically positioned. Therefore, a more thorough presentation of previous topical literature is presented. The hope is that this literature can be used to develop hypotheses, which generally are placed at the end of the literature review. Also, the term "Conceptual Background" often is used to title a special section focusing on how the research is conceptualized. That is, the relationships between the various elements that are being examined are displayed visually in a chart, and the text of the report describes and explains the relationships.

The research methods and results section differ little from an applied report. One exception in the style of reports is based on the intended audience. The primary audience for basic research is other researchers! Therefore, the writer typically is more technical and presents more detail about statistical and analytical issues. For example, a basic report usually includes tables with more detailed information, while an applied report will rely more on charts. Because the presumption is that the reader of a basic research report is more sophisticated, the casual reader will sometimes find basic research reports esoteric and difficult to read.

The Implications and Conclusions section will be similar to that of the applied report. However, it may focus more on theoretical results. That is, what are the implications for others who may study this same issue? Since it is a basic report, the implications will not pertain to any specific business, but rather to businesses or industries in general. For example, an implication may be that employees should be allowed input into their weekly work schedule. The desired result would be higher employee commitment. A basic research report also may provide more detail on future basic research. These studies are suggested as follow-ups to the present effort. In this way, basic researchers develop a theoretical body of knowledge about important topics.

Finally, the basic research report contains appendices and a reference list. There is less reliance on appendices to present statistical results, however, since much of this material will be included in the body of the report. A typical outline for a basic research report follows:

- Title page
- Abstract
- Introduction
- Conceptual background
- Research methods
- Results
- Implications and conclusions
- Reference list
- Appendices

Examples of basic business research reports can be found in any of the leading academic journals within each business discipline.

ORAL PRESENTATIONS

Decision makers often require the researcher to make a formal presentation when the report is finished. Researchers should enthusiastically welcome this opportunity. The presentation provides an opportunity to follow up on the report. Thus, the researcher can clarify any material that may be difficult to understand in writing. The report also is interactive. This means members of the audience may, and often do, ask questions. In answering these questions, the researcher has another chance to communicate important findings. Put simply, the presentation is the best opportunity to "sell" the research and gain the enthusiasm of the decision makers.

Consider the Audience

Just as in the written presentation, the researcher should consider the varying abilities of managers to understand the presentation content. It is usually a good idea to try to find out ahead of time which individuals may attend the presentation. Sometimes, the presentation may be delivered only to the decision maker who requested the research. More commonly, however, others will be involved. The decision maker may invite any employee who might be affected by decisions that will be made. This might include superiors and subordinates. In some situations, line personnel or employees with little technical experience may attend. It is not unusual to present before eight to twelve key employees in a boardroom type setting. Realize that each person may have different concerns. A line manager may be most concerned with how a decision might affect production schedules. An accountant is likely to be interested in the impact on company profits and expenses. A brand manager may be most interested in the effect the decisions will have on brand image. Communication is enhanced when the presenter can tailor the presentation to the audience.

Audiences almost always ask questions or raise issues during the presentation. In fact, it may be a bad sign if the audience fails to interact with the presenter. Have they fallen asleep? Questions and comments should be encouraged. It is good practice to try to anticipate questions and prepare a response before the presentation. Remember, researchers have an ethical obligation to make sure the research is useful. If the key players involved understand the research, it is more likely to be useful.

In preparing an oral presentation, it is a good idea to revisit the creativity phase of the business decision-making process (Chapter 3). Creative tools can be useful in designing effective presentation themes, identifying the assumptions and misconceptions of potential audience members, and developing lists of questions that may be asked. Creativity is especially needed in developing a title that is both catchy and informative.

Presentation Format

There are many useful approaches for delivering a business research presentation. Avoid a strictly oral (spoken) presentation. But even more important, do not read the report to the audience. Reading the report almost never makes a positive impact, and gives the appearance of a lack of familiarity with the project. It also may be insulting, since the material can be read by the audience. Presenters may use slides, transparencies, videos, flip charts, pre-prepared posters or even a Web-based presentation. Visual aids are helpful to both the presenter and the audience. They cue the audience to important pieces of information as well as helping to hold their attention. Moreover, they also serve as "cue cards" to the presenter by reminding them of the flow of the presentation and making sure important points are not forgotten.

Perhaps the most common presentation format today is the computer-based slide show. Several software packages can be used to construct these shows, including Corel's Presentations and Microsoft's PowerPoint. These software packages are similar and easy to use. They allow the presenter to prepare professional graphical aids, including charts such as those discussed above. It also is easy to make last-minute changes to presentations.

Presentation Do's and Don'ts

The following "top ten" list gives advice for preparing an effective presentation:[1]

1. **Prepare your own slides.** Presentation software is easy to use and anyone who does business research presentations should gain some competency with these important tools. Remember, as the presenter, you'll be blamed for any shortcomings in the visual aids. Do you want to trust this to someone else? Moreover, by preparing your own presentation, you maximize your familiarity with the material.

2. **Create an effective title.** Try to use the title to communicate. You would like it to be short but insightful. This applies to both the overall presentation title and to the titles of the various slides. Suppose a researcher is presenting results about the effectiveness of salaried versus commission-based salespeople on customer satisfaction. The slide could be entitled "Statistical Results" or "Commission Leads to Satisfaction." Which is more effective?

3. **Avoid clutter in your visuals.** Use a simple font such as Arial or Tahoma. If you want to be a little fancy, use bold, italicized, and shadowed Tahoma. Titles can be as large as 32–40 points. Lists of texts (bullets) are effective when they are 24–28 points. Avoid fonts smaller than 18 points for any important text. Limit the number of lines of text on any particular slide to six and the number of words to about thirty.

4. **Use simple backgrounds that produce high contrasts.** Elaborate backgrounds may be decorative, but they also can be distracting and sometimes inhibit read-ability. Use either a dark background with light letters or a white background with dark letters.

5. **Vary the slide layouts.** Slides do not always have to have clip-art on the right and text on the left. If there is no picture that pairs well with a slide's content, do not use any. Take advantage of the white space beside charts to drop in (add by using transition or animation) a meaningful word or phrase.

6. **Arrive early.** Presenters sometimes make presentations in a familiar room with familiar equipment. But more often, presentations are in an unfamiliar location with unfamiliar equipment. Particularly in these situations, arrive early enough to test the presentation. For example, different versions of the same software may not always work exactly the same. Animation or transitions may work differently or not at all. Allow enough time to make any last minute changes to ensure the presentation looks as it should.

7. **Use the time allowed.** Make good use of the entire time allowed for the presentation. Businesspeople normally allow between twenty and sixty minutes for a presentation. While it varies from person to person, a rule of thumb is that the presentation will last two to three times the number of slides. Plan on using the entire time while still allowing time for questions. Plan ahead for material that can be skipped should the presentation begin to run behind. Stay until all questions are answered.

8. **Use humor when possible.** Cartoons and funny phrases are usually acceptable. They help win the audience over and the break the monotony of what might otherwise be very dry material. The humor should always be in good taste. If there is any doubt over the appropriateness of a particular piece of humor, leave it out.

9. **Invite audience participation.** Ask questions of the audience. For example, if the research involves employee reactions to a new company policy, invite one of the key decision makers to guess at how a typical employee responded to a key question about the policy. This keeps their interest up and helps them become part of the presentation. Remember to always respond favorably to their answers to your questions. The wrong response could demean the audience.

10. **Do sweat the small stuff.** Presenters are part of the research package, so they must appear credible and professional. Pay attention to the details including your dress and mannerisms during the presentation. Dress appropriately and remember it is usually better to overdress than underdress. Like it or not, people will base their judgments of you and your work on your appearance. This may not always mean a business suit. If you are making a presentation to decision makers on a retreat in Tahiti, a suit may not make the best impression. However, anything less formal to the same decision makers in a London office building

---

RESEARCH IN ACTION
PRESENTATION ANXIETY? HAVE NO FEAR WITH THIS CURE-ALL

Giving an oral research presentation clearly is public speaking. Oral presentations absolutely frighten many people. Speaking about an innocuous topic or giving a classroom presentation is hard enough. A research presentation demonstrates the researcher's professional competence as well as the competence of any colleagues who also were involved in the research. Thus, there is considerable pressure to make a good presentation. If you are afraid, consider this advice:

1. You will make a mistake during the presentation! But even the best presenter will make mistakes. They are not fatal. Part of the apprehension may go away when you realize that mistakes are inevitable and that reasonable people expect them occasionally.

2. Study your material. One of the best ways to deal with nervousness is to be extremely familiar with the material. Discussing it becomes second nature at some point. It's as easy as dinnertime conversation. So make sure you know all the sordid details of the research. Find an audience to discuss the research with ahead of the presentation. Rehearsing the presentation relieves anxiety among some presenters, but having the confidence that you will be able to make some intelligent comment no matter what occurs is a good way of fighting presentation fear.

3. Practice your presentation out loud. Go into a room by yourself, perhaps stand in front of a mirror, and give your presentation. Try speaking at slower speeds, use pauses, and change the tone of your voice to avoid a monotone sound. When you cannot speak out loud, then mentally rehearse the presentation.

4. Take advantage of opportunities to do public speaking. At some point, you'll become quite comfortable standing in front of an audience of faces staring up at you.

5. Laugh. Use humor when (a) it is appropriate and (b) you have confidence that others will laugh with you. If you are unsure of a joke, don't use it. A punch line that doesn't deliver will only increase apprehension.

6. Be confident. The reason you are giving a presentation is because you probably know something the audience doesn't. Therefore, you have an advantage. You can tell them something worthwhile. Expect to give a good presentation and you usually will.

SOURCE: Kaye, Steve. 1998. "It's Showtime! How to Give Effective Presentations." *Supervision* 60 (March): 8–10.

would be very risky. Also, do not use distracting mannerisms and phrases. Try to limit the use of "you know," for example. If this is a concern, have someone else watch you do a presentation and count the number of times you use such phrases. You also may want to videotape yourself to identify distracting mannerisms. Usually, awareness of distractions is the best way to reduce them.

Some researchers are uncomfortable making presentations. Also, junior analysts or entry-level researchers seldom are called upon to make presentations. As the researcher advances, however, this changes. The "Research in Action" box gives advice to those who may be apprehensive about delivering presentations.

SUMMARY

Convey the Importance of Effective Communication to Research Success

Communication is essential to avoid wasting all the effort that went into the research. The research proposal, report, and presentation provide the means for the researcher to communicate the purpose, methodology, results, and implications of the research. If these are done poorly, it is less likely the research will ever be used to aid decision making. Therefore, these reporting vehicles "sell" the research project. This means they try to convince the users the information is useful and helpful.

Describe the Elements of a Research Proposal

The research proposal is used to maximize the chances the decision maker and researcher have the same understanding of the research purpose(s) and types of information it will produce prior to beginning the study. Proposals contain an introduction, a list of the research questions, a description of the research methods, a proposed outline of the final research report, including dummy tables, and a description of the time and financial resources required to complete the research project.

Provide an Overview of Effective Research Reports

There are many ways to increase the effectiveness of research reports. Executive summaries precede the body of a research report. They are, in effect, a mini report in themselves. They include the following sections: (1) a statement of the research purpose, (2) a brief description of the research design and implementation, (3) a summary of results derived from testing research questions and/or hypotheses, (4) a written interpretation of the findings framed as answers to the research questions, and (5) if requested, a list of practical business implications derived from the research. Given that this is often the only part of the report read in detail, great attention must be paid to make sure it communicates effectively. In preparing reports, the researcher must be sensitive to the audience. Do not overwhelm readers with technical jargon unless they have an everyday working knowledge of such terms. Finally, research reports are not a work of fiction and should present the facts in a concise way.

Summarize Effective Ways to Deliver a Research Presentation

Much like the report, effective communication in an oral presentation is essential. Careful consideration of the expected audience pays off by presenting the most important results and anticipating questions and objections. Ten suggestions are provided for aiding a presentation. Some of the more important ones include the strong suggestion to use visual aids of some type, invite audience participation, and to be creative in developing effective presentation titles and content.

KEY TERMS

audience	KISS	table of contents
executive summary	least common	title page
front-end loading	denominator principle	
introduction	research methods	

REVIEW QUESTIONS

1. List and briefly describe the three communication mechanisms used by business researchers. Is one mechanism better than the others?
2. List and briefly describe the elements of a research proposal.
3. What is an executive summary? Why is it so important? How long should it be?
4. What is the least common denominator principle and how would it apply when making a presentation to a group of military officers and enlisted people?
5. Explain the role of humor in a formal presentation.

DISCUSSION AND APPLICATION ACTIVITIES

1. Find an academic research report. Just about any article from *The Academy of Management, The Journal of Management, The Journal of Marketing, The Journal of Business Research,* or *The Journal of Retailing,* among others, will do. Read the abstract. Try rewriting it as if it were being presented to a group of line managers, none of which has a business or technical college degree.
2. The sample research report contained in the appendix of this chapter shows the results of examining only two research questions for the employee study. Develop a list of at least three more employee research questions and tell why they need to be examined. Similarly, the customer survey results examined only three research questions. Develop a list of at least three more customer research questions and tell why they need to be examined.
3. Use data analysis software and examine the research questions you developed in question 2. Prepare a brief report summarizing your findings and recommendations.
4. Using the SPSS customer data set accompanying this book, compute a cross tabulation of the selection factors prices (X_{15}) and employees (X_{16}) by restaurant (X_{25}). In other words, do Gino's and Samouel's customers rate prices and employees as equally

important? Present the results graphically using bar charts as shown in the chapter. Prepare the bar charts using a presentations software package.

5. Prepare a twenty-minute presentation for Phil Samouel to present the results shown in the sample research report in the appendix of this chapter. Assume he will be there along with his financial manager, floor manager, chef, and a member of the wait staff. Be sure to anticipate questions.

INTERNET ACTIVITIES

1. Access the Web site for this text (www.wiley.com/college/hair). Locate the "Presentation for Samouel's." Critique the presentation for possible areas of improvement.

2. Go to the following Web site: http://powerreporting.com/. Browse the Web site and prepare a brief report summarizing how a researcher might use this site.

3. Use a search engine of your choice. Use the key words "research reporting." Prepare a brief report summarizing what you found.

NOTES

1. Kaye, Steve. 1999. "It's Showtime! How to Give Effective Presentations." *Supervision* 60 (March), 8–10; Wareham, Hohn. 2001. "From the Podium." *Across the Board* 38 (March/April), 67–69.

Appendix 12-A: Research Report for Phil Samouel

RESTAURANT OPERATIONS AT SAMOUEL'S GREEK CUISINE: IMPROVING RELATIONS WITH EMPLOYEES AND CUSTOMERS

Research conducted for:
Phil Samouel
Owner, Samouel's Greek Cuisine

March 15, 2003

Research conducted by:
AdMark, International
3127 Tower Boulevard
Baton Rouge, LA 70803-6314
(225) 388-8614

Lead Researcher:
Joseph F. Hair, Ph.D.
Senior Analyst
jhair@admark.com

TABLE OF CONTENTS

EXECUTIVE SUMMARY

PURPOSE

The purpose of this project is to help find ways of increasing Samouel's profitability by improving customer satisfaction and enhancing employees' organizational commitment. Two separate research projects were undertaken. First, Samouel's employees were surveyed to assess key variables related to organizational commitment. Second, a survey of restaurant customers was conducted to measure key variables related to satisfaction and loyalty. The results of the surveys are highlighted as follows.

EMPLOYEES

- Younger employees, part-time employees, male employees, and those that have worked at Samouel's less than one year are more likely to search for another job.
- Supervisory approaches at Samouel's are perceived to be a strength.
- Work group functioning is poorly perceived and needs improvement.

CUSTOMERS

- Gino's customers report higher satisfaction (5.96) than do Samouel's customers (4.78).
- While perceptions of food quality are above the scale midpoint for Samouel's (5.24), they are better for Gino's (5.81).
- Gino's customers rate its employees significantly better than Samouel's customers rate its employees.
- Samouel's current customers' satisfaction is most affected by their ratings of perceived food quality, next attractive interior, and then by friendly employees.
- Gino's current customers' satisfaction is most affected by food quality and then ratings of employee friendliness.

Several recommendations emerge from these results. When implemented, these recommendations should make Samouel's more competitive with Gino's. Additionally, they will improve profitability by creating a more stable and satisfied customer and employee base. The key implications are:

- Place greater emphasis on industry experience as a hiring criterion.
- Provide additional training opportunities for employees.
- Hire an experienced executive chef to improve perceived food quality.
- Promote Samouel's as a "fun place to eat" with an excellent atmosphere.

INTRODUCTION

RESEARCH QUESTIONS

After extensive discussions with Phil Samouel and his employees, two researchable questions (RQ) were identified:

RQ$_1$: Are employees being managed to maximize their productivity as well as commitment to the success of the restaurant?

RQ$_2$: What are the ways to keep and grow the existing customer base and to attract new customers?

Each research question can be divided into more specific questions and hypotheses.

EMPLOYEE STUDY

Employee turnover is an issue at Samouel's, as it is in the restaurant industry in general. Industry statistics suggest that turnover rates are very high in the restaurant business, with rates of 50, 100, or even 150 percent not being unusual.[1] Basic research on the management of service employees documents the important roles of job satisfaction and organizational commitment in reducing turnover. Phil Samouel has tracked employee tenure and estimates that his turnover rate is almost 100 percent. This means each year he has to hire one new employee on average for every current worker. The result is increased costs due to hiring expenses and training. In addition, inexperienced employees sometimes are the source of poor service and thus, dissatisfied customers. Therefore, Phil Samouel would like to know which factors are related to organizational commitment and turnover intentions.

Phillip Samouel believes the age and experience of his employees might be related to turnover intentions and organizational commitment. Basic research in the restaurant industry[2] and in management suggests these factors are important.[3] He also believes gender might be important and management studies report women exhibit somewhat higher commitment than do men.[4] Thus, the employee study will explore differences based on gender and work status, such as part- versus full-time workers.[5] The belief here is that full-time employees will be more dedicated and generally display more positive work attitudes than part-time employees. Part-time employees are likely to have other priorities that diminish their commitment to Samouel's.

The supervisory staff at Samouel's could be influencing worker satisfaction and commitment. Employee perceptions of supervisory staff are important in understanding restaurant operations. Employees respond favorably to effective and empathetic supervisory treatment. Therefore, we expect that supervisory behavior will positively affect employee performance and organizational commitment (i.e., loyalty to the organization). Additionally, Phil Samouel wonders how effective monetary incentives are in improving employee outcomes. Tipping is a main source of income for his service employees. Previous research suggests that issues related to pay distribution are important in reducing turnover.

Numerous research hypotheses could be tested from the survey of Samouel's employees. In discussions with his consultant, Phil Samouel has decided to look first at their intentions to search for another job and their organizational commitment. This decision was based on feedback from employees and by trade publications that indicate highly committed employees will work harder and treat customers better, thus resulting in higher customer satisfaction and retention. The consultant recommended using X_{13} (Loyalty) as the initial measure of organizational commitment based on his previous projects. In reviewing the work environment measures, Phil and the consultant concluded that teamwork and cooperation among employees and supervisory approaches in the restaurant would be actionable areas where relatively quick improvement would be possible (within thirty to sixty days). Several items measuring these two areas were included in the survey. It was decided, therefore, to examine three hypotheses first, as shown following.

Employee Hypothesis 1 (EH1)

Employee work status, age, and gender are related to intentions to job search such that: part-time workers have higher search intentions than full-time workers, younger employees have higher search intentions, and men have higher search intentions than women.

Employee Hypothesis 2 (EH2)

Employee perceptions of supervisory style are positively related to organizational commitment.

Employee Hypothesis 3 (EH3)

Employee perceptions of work group functioning are positively related to organizational commitment.

Other hypotheses will be examined in a later report.

CUSTOMER ASSESSMENT PROJECT

Phil Samouel identified Gino's Italian Ristorante as his primary competitor. The two restaurants likely pull from the same market segment and customers often are choosing between them. Therefore, it is important to establish the competitive positioning of both restaurants. Phil expects that his customers are equally or more satisfied than are Gino's customers.

Phil believes that satisfaction is determined mostly by food quality and the service quality delivered by his employees. This belief is supported by basic research reported in trade and academic journals, as well as the experience of his consultant. Customers evaluate service industries in general based on two broad classes of attributes. Core attributes are those that most directly provide the primary benefit sought by customers. In the case of a restaurant, food-related attributes are a core attribute. Relational attributes are less tangible and deal with human–human and human–environment interactions. For restaurants, customer perceptions of the atmosphere and employee friendliness fall into this category.

Several articles in restaurant trade publications examine customer perceptions as they relate to satisfaction. The articles discuss the importance of food quality, including freshness and variety and restaurant cleanliness as two key factors shaping customer's service quality perceptions.[6] Thus, when customer perceptions of food, employees, and atmosphere improve, their satisfaction with the restaurant also should improve. Phil Samouel would like to know first whether customers rate Samouel's more favorably than they do Gino's. Second, he would like to know the controllable restaurant characteristics that determine customer satisfaction. This reasoning suggests the following hypotheses.

Customer Hypothesis 1 (CH1)

Samouel's customers report higher satisfaction than do Gino's customers.

Customer Hypothesis 2 (CH2)

Customer perceptions of restaurant employees are related positively to customer satisfaction.

Customer Hypothesis 3 (CH3)

Customer perceptions of restaurant atmosphere are related positively to customer satisfaction.

Customer Hypothesis 4 (CH4)

Customer perceptions of food quality are related positively to customer satisfaction.

RESEARCH METHODS: EMPLOYEE STUDY
Sample

Data were collected from a sample of Samouel's employees. Employees were asked to participate in a general study of restaurant employee attitudes. Each employee was interviewed away from the work premises and was paid $5 for participating. Employees were assured their responses were strictly confidential and that no interview would be identified with a specific employee. Sixty-three employees participated and completed an interview. A demographic profile of the sample demonstrated it is representative of all employees.

Measures

Measures from general social-psychological profiles were used to assess work environment and work outcome characteristics. Items were selected to represent organizational commitment and supervisor style, among other things. Seven-point Likert scales (Disagree = 1; Agree = 7) were used for most measures. Employees indicated their quitting intentions on a 7-point scale scored 7 = "High Intention to Search," and 1 = "Low Intention to Search." Various demographic characteristics also were included. (A copy of this questionnaire is found in Chapter 6 of this text).

RESEARCH METHODS: CUSTOMER STUDY
Sample

Data were collected that enable an examination of the relevant customer issues. Exit interviews were conducted as patrons departed Gino's Italian Ristorante and Samouel's Greek Cuisine. Interviews were conducted between 11:30 A.M. and 2:00 P.M., and 7 to 10 P.M., Monday through Saturday, for a period of ten days (the 10-day period was randomly selected from a 90-day realistic time-horizon for data collection). Customers were approached randomly and asked one rapport question and three screening questions. First, do you occasionally dine out in restaurants? Then, did you just eat at Samouel's/Gino's restaurant? Is your gross annual income $20,000 or more? And, have you completed a restaurant questionnaire for our company before? A yes for the first question and a no for the second prompted the request to participate in the survey. If the customer agreed, they were provided with a clipboard containing the study questionnaire, a comfortable place to complete it and $5 for their participation.

The goal was to obtain at least one hundred interviews from each restaurant. A total of 230 interviews were completed. However, thirty contained missing data sufficient enough to eliminate them from analyses. In all 447 customers were approached, yielding a 44.7 percent response rate (200 usable responses/447 attempts).

Measures

Measures for the study were derived following interviews with Mr. Samouel and by consulting previous industry research. Seven-point Likert scales (disagree to agree) were used to measure customer ratings of various evaluative criteria (e.g., food quality, clean facilities, etc.). See Appendix 1-B for a further description of the measures. (A copy of the questionnaire is provided in Chapter 7 of this text.)

RESULTS: EMPLOYEE STUDY
Intention to Search Results (EH1)

The first analyses involve profiling intentions to search for another job. The important variables were work type (part-time vs. full-time), age, gender, and how long an employee has worked for Samouel's. The bar charts in Exhibit A-1 show the results to be largely supportive of EH1. As can be seen, younger employees, part-time employees, and male employees who have been working at Samouel's less than a year are most likely to search for a new job. Now that it is clear who is likely to search, in a later report we will examine the reasons why and what might be done to reduce it.

Employee Commitment/Loyalty

The next set of analyses examines employee work environment and outcomes. The following variables were analyzed:

X_3—employee believes supervisor gives credit/praise for work well done

X_6—employee believes supervisor recognizes their potential

X_{10}—employee believes supervisor is friendly and helpful

X_4—employee perceives work group cooperates

X_8—employee believes work group functions as a team

X_{11}—employee perceives work group has skills and training needed

X_{13}—I have a sense of loyalty to Samouel's restaurant (represents organizational commitment)

Two hypotheses were examined. These were tested by examining the linear relationships between the dependent variable, loyalty, and the supervisory and work group variables.

| EXHIBIT A-I | EMPLOYEE INTENTIONS TO SEARCH |

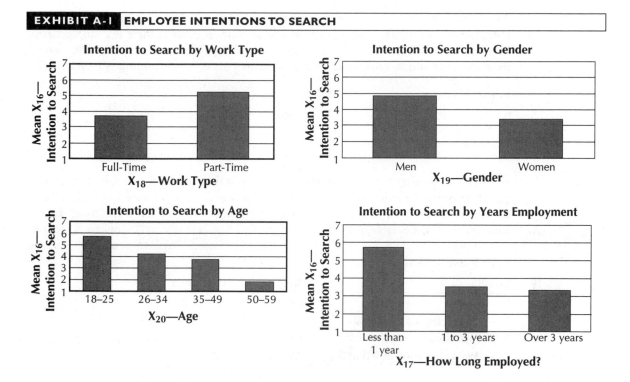

EH2

This hypothesis predicts that employee perceptions of supervisory style are positively related to organizational commitment. To test this hypothesis we use loyalty (X_{13}) as the dependent variable in a regression model and the supervisory variables (X_3, X_6 and X_{10}) as the independent variables. Multiple regression is used because there is a single dependent metric variable and three metric independent variables. Overall model results are shown as follows:

Model Summary

R	R Square	F	Sig.
.307	.094	2.045	.117

Predictors: X_{10}—Supervisor Friendly/Helpful, X_6 —Supervisor Recognizes Potential, X_3—Supervisor Praises

The regression model is not significant, as suggested by the F-value (df = 3, 59) of 2.045 and the corresponding p-value of .117. Therefore, EH2 is not supported. This indicates there is no relationship between supervisory style and loyalty to Samouel's restaurant. Phil must, therefore, look at other information for insights regarding loyalty.

EH3

This hypothesis predicts that employee perceptions of work group functioning are positively related to organizational commitment. To test this hypothesis we use loyalty (X_{13}) as the dependent variable in regression and the employee variables (X_4, X_8, and X_{11}) as the independent variables. Multiple regression is used again because there is a single metric (interval or ratio) dependent variable and three independent variables that can also be treated as at least interval. Overall results are shown in the Model Summary table.

Model Summary

R	R Square	F	Sig.
.637	.405	13.401	.000

Predictors: X_{11}—Work Group—Skills/Training, X8—Work Group—Team, X_4—Work Group Cooperation

The relationship between employee variables and loyalty is significant ($F = 13.401$, $p < .000$). Since the model predicts a significant portion of the variance in X_{13} (loyalty), a closer examination of the key predictor variables is needed. This is shown in the Descriptive Statistics table.

Descriptive Statistics

Variable	Mean	Std. Deviation
X_{13}—Loyalty	5.67	.97
X_4—Work Group Cooperation	3.89	1.39
X_8—Work Group—Team	3.41	1.21
X_{11}— Work Group—Skills/Training	3.57	1.12

Recall the variables were measured using a 7-point scale with 7 = strongly agree and 1 = strongly disagree. The descriptive statistics show that while loyalty seems relatively high (5.67 on a 7-point scale) the work group variables all seem relatively low. This indicates the employees may not work together as much as they should and may not believe they have the skills they need. This suggests that Phil Samouel needs to organize training sessions for his employees to improve their cooperative skills. The information in the following table shows that the Beta weights for the three variables are each significant ($p < .05$). While work group cooperation ($\beta = .579$) and work group skills/training are related positively to loyalty, work group—team is related negatively ($\beta = -.355$).

Coefficients

Variables	Standardized Coefficients	t	Sig.
	Beta		
X_4—Work Group Cooperation	.579	3.402	.001
X_8—Work Group—Team	−.355	−2.013	.049
X_{11}—Work Group—Skills/Training	.396	2.693	.009

Dependent Variable: X_{13}—Loyalty

Since the negative work group team to loyalty relationship is counterintuitive and inconsistent with the remaining work group variables, a closer examination of the relationships is called for. The Pearson correlation matrix between the four measures involved reveals the following:

Variables	X_{13}	X_4	X_8	X_{11}
X_{13}—Loyalty	1.00			
X_4—Work Group Cooperation	.57	1.00		
X_8—Work Group—Team	.38	.79	1.00	
X_{11}—Work Group—Skills/Training	.54	.68	.70	1.00

Work group—team (X_8) shows high correlations with both of the other independent variables. This, along with other detailed collinearity diagnostics, suggests that the regression coefficient for this variable may be unreliable. Further, the researcher recommends additional analysis using a data reduction technique such as factor analysis.

However, the results for both work group—cooperation and work group—skills/training support EH3, as do the correlations. Thus, a more cooperative and highly trained workforce is likely to produce higher employee loyalty.

RESULTS: CUSTOMER STUDY

Customer Research Question: Relative Satisfaction

The second research question examines issues related to customer satisfaction. CH1 tests the relative satisfaction of Samouel's and Gino's customers. An independent samples t-test comparing the satisfaction measure (X_{17}) of the two customer groups (X_{25}) was used to test this hypothesis. This test is appropriate because the independent or grouping variable is nominal (competitor = Samouel's vs. Gino's customers) and the dependent variable is interval (satisfaction). Results of this t-test follow.

Comparing Satisfaction of Samouel's and Gino's Customers: Independent Samples T-Test

	Competitor	N	Mean	Std. Deviation	t	Sig. (2-tailed)	Mean Difference
X_{17}—	Samouel's	100	4.78	1.16	−7.793	0.000	−1.18
Satisfaction	Gino's	100	5.96	0.97			

Gino's customers report higher satisfaction on the 7-point scale by an average of 1.18 (4.78 vs. 5.96). Although this difference is significant (p < .000), it does not support CH1 since it indicates higher customer satisfaction at Gino's. The hypothesis predicted the reverse. Further, relative to average satisfaction rates in the restaurant industry, neither of these is particularly high. Phil Samouel needs to correct this satisfaction deficit. The comparative performance analysis below may shed some light on this issue.

Comparative Performance

The comparative performance issue was examined by applying the independent samples t-test to the twelve attribute ratings (X_1–X_{12}) for the two restaurants. The means by restaurant are shown in the Independent Samples Test table.

As can be seen, Gino's is rated significantly higher than Samouel's on food quality (p < .001), generous portions (p < .003), excellent food taste (p < .001), good value for money (p < .005), and friendly employees (p < .000). Samouel's is rated higher than Gino's on attractive interior (p < .000), appears clean and neat (p < .002), and fun place to go (p < .000). Thus, Phil Samouel's problem with his employees, identified in the employee survey results, is also evident in the customer survey results. But his atmosphere is rated more favorably than Gino's, both in terms of the attractiveness and fun elements.

Independent Samples Test

	Competitor Means				
Attributes	**Samouel's**	**Gino's**	**t**	**Sig. (2-tailed)**	**Mean Difference**
X_1—Food Quality	5.24	5.81	−3.310	0.001	−0.57
X_2—Attractive Interior	4.94	4.46	3.843	0.000	0.48
X_3—Generous Portions	3.56	4.22	−3.004	0.003	−0.66
X_4—Excellent Food Taste	5.16	5.73	−3.457	0.001	−0.57
X_5—Good Value for Money	4.05	4.60	−2.865	0.005	−0.55
X_6—Friendly Employees	2.89	4.42	−10.925	0.000	−1.53
X_7—Appears Clean and Neat	4.36	3.86	3.079	0.002	0.50
X_8—Fun Place to Go	3.65	3.12	4.375	0.000	0.53
X_9—Wide Variety on Menu	5.45	5.56	−.648	0.518	−0.11
X_{10}—Reasonable Prices	4.14	3.97	1.286	0.200	−0.17
X_{11}—Courteous Employees	1.96	2.84	−7.404	0.000	−0.88
X_{12}—Competent Employees	1.62	2.75	−10.251	0.000	−1.13

WHAT DETERMINES CUSTOMER SATISFACTION FOR SAMOUEL'S?

Three hypotheses, CH2, CH3, and CH4, address this research question. The hypotheses suggest examining the relationship between satisfaction and customer perceptions of employee friendliness, interior atmosphere, and food quality, respectively. The hypotheses were tested with a single regression model using customer satisfaction (X_{17}) as the dependent variable and the three restaurant performance variables relating to the hypotheses (X_6, X_2, and X_1, respectively) as the independent variables. Regression is appropriate because both the dependent and independent variables can be treated as at least interval (i.e., metric). Also, to examine this question, it is possible to look at the two restaurants separately (Samouel's and Gino's customers evaluate only the restaurant they ate at so the regression model must be tested separately for each restaurant). It's possible that there are unique characteristics within each unique sample. In other words, Gino's customers may not react the same as Samouel's customers. The results are shown in the following table.

Satisfaction Regression Models for Samouel's and Gino's

X_{25}—Competitor	**R**	**R Square**	**F**	**Sig.**
Samouel's	.663	.440	25.155	.000
Gino's	.511	.261	11.321	.000

The regression model for Samouel's restaurant is highly significant (p < .000) and explains 44.0 percent of the total variance in customer satisfaction. The regression model for Gino's also is statistically significant (p < .000), but does not predict as much variance in customer satisfaction (R^2 is 17.9 percent less for Gino's; 44.0 − 26.1 = 17.9). Both predictive models are useful, however, in identifying which of the three independent variables is most strongly related to satisfaction. Other variables also may be related, but they will be examined in a later report. Hopefully, the other variables will increase the predictive level for satisfaction. But these initial regression predictive models are highly significant, predict satisfaction at a reasonable level, and therefore are helpful.

Since we found significant satisfaction predictive models, it is important to understand which independent variables are strong predictors. This information is in the table Important Predictors of Satisfaction. The cutoff point for a significant predictor in this analysis will be .10. Phil Samouel believes the higher risk (using < .10 instead of < .05) is acceptable in this situation. Also, it is consistent with the relatively small sample size of one hundred per restaurant. For Samouel's, all three attributes are positive predictors of satisfaction (p < .1). That is, more favorable perceptions of food quality, attractiveness of the interior, and employee friendliness are associated with higher levels of satisfaction. For Gino's, only two of the attributes are significant predictors (p < .1)—food quality and employee friendliness. Thus, CH2, CH3, and CH4 each are supported for Samouel's. Only CH2 and CH4 are supported for Gino's.

Important Predictors of Satisfaction
Coefficients

Attributes	Gino's Standardized Coefficients (Beta)	t	Sig.	Samouel's Standardized Coefficients (Beta)	t	Sig.
X_1—Food Quality (CH4)	.401	4.4964	.000	.367	4.531	.000
X_2—Attractive Interior (CH3)	.108	1.227	.223	.305	3.795	.000
X_6—Friendly Employees (CH2)	.385	4.3234	.000	.275	3.500	.001

Dependent Variable: X_{17}—Satisfaction

RECOMMENDATIONS AND CONCLUSIONS

The research described in this report addresses two general questions. They concern explanations of employee commitment as well as customer satisfaction. Results addressing these questions are summarized as follows.

EMPLOYEES

- Younger employees, part-time employees, male employees, and those that have worked at Samouel's less than one year are more likely to search for another job.

- Supervisory approaches at Samouel's are perceived as a strength.
- Work group functioning is poorly perceived and needs improvement.

CUSTOMERS

- Gino's customers report higher satisfaction (5.96) than do Samouel's customers (4.78).
- While perceptions of food quality are above the scale midpoint for Samouel's (5.24), they are better for Gino's (5.81).
- Gino's customers rate its employees significantly better than Samouel's customers rate its employees.
- Samouel's current customers' satisfaction is most affected by their ratings of perceived food quality, next by attractive interior, and then by friendly employees.
- Gino's current customers' satisfaction is most affected by food quality and then by ratings of employee friendliness.

RECOMMENDATIONS

Several recommendations follow directly from these results. They include:

1. Provide additional training opportunities for employees. Several local universities, as well as the American Restaurant Association, have service training programs for supervisors, wait staff, and kitchen staff. We recommend that each employee attend formal training sessions annually. This will give them better knowledge of industry standards and customer expectations. Moreover, reducing turnover is critical to Samouel's profitability. Samouel's should try to achieve a significantly lower turnover rate than the industry average within twelve months. Work group functioning influences turnover and can be dealt with quickly. Follow-up interviews with a few employees confirmed the need for this type of training.

2. Hire more workers over the age of twenty-five. The results clearly suggest that younger workers are more likely to quit. Employees over this age tend to be more stable. A more stable work force means reduced costs and probably greater customer satisfaction. Perhaps some consideration should be given to hiring retirees who wish to do some type of work.

3. Hire an experienced executive chef. Gino's customers report higher satisfaction than do Samouel's customers. This is a critical weakness. Gino's customers also rate the food quality higher than do Samouel's customers. Further, food quality is one of the key determinants of customer satisfaction. Therefore, Phil Samouel must improve food quality, particularly if he wishes to attract Gino's customers into Samouel's more often. The current kitchen staff does a good job of preparing the traditional Samouel's menu items. A new executive chef can improve food quality by adding menu variety, providing more formal training to kitchen employees, increasing the restaurant's

credibility, and improving food preparation and presentation. Improving food quality will not only create higher satisfaction among current customers, but since Gino's customers are most sensitive to this characteristic, it may attract some of that business.

4. Promote the importance of a clean, attractive, and fun atmosphere. Samouel's is rated as superior on atmosphere to Gino's. Persuasion can be accomplished either by changing beliefs or changing evaluations. If customers can be made to believe that a fun, clean atmosphere provides added value, they may become more sensitive to this characteristic. If so, Samouel's will benefit.

LIMITATIONS

Several limitations should be noted. First, the samples used in both studies have limitations. The employee sample consisted of only sixty-three Samouel's employees. How unique are Samouel's employees? A broader sample involving more employees from other restaurants of a similar service category may prove more insightful and allow for relevant benchmarking of Samouel's. In addition, the customer sample included only two restaurants. This allowed the research to focus on how Samouel's compared to its primary competitor. However, it did not allow us to understand how Samouel's might fit into the more general population of New York restaurant consumers.

Second, the questionnaires were limited for the sake of convenience. Longer questionnaires may allow for a better assessment of constructs such as employee performance, organizational commitment, customer satisfaction, and customer value perceptions.

FUTURE RESEARCH

Some findings suggest further studies. Why are part-time employees less committed and more likely to search? Perhaps this has something to do with Samouel's policies and treatment of part-time versus full-time employees. Also, do different compensation systems influence customer satisfaction? Customer price perceptions were not examined in great detail here. A future study might examine the trade-offs customers are willing to make. For example, how much more are they willing to pay for increased food quality or improved service quality? These studies may provide insights not available here. Alternatively, they may provide greater support for the above recommendations. Before pursuing other studies, we recommend that information from the current studies be more fully examined.

APPENDICES

Technical appendices would follow including a description of the questionnaire, all descriptive statistics, and specific details of analyses referred to in the report.

NOTES

1. Berta, Dina. 2000. Operators See Outside Volunteer Work as a Wise Way to Lower Turnover. *Nation's Restaurant News* 34 (December 18): 20–21. Also Prewitt, Milrod. 1999. Purdue Study: Low Benefits Boost Turnover, Increase Net Labor Costs. *Nation's Restaurant News* 33 (December 6): 1.

2. Sheridan, Margaret. 2000. Serving Notice. *Restaurants and Institutions,* 110 (March 15): 50.

3. Russ, Frederick A. and Kevin A. McNeilly. 1995. Links Among Satisfaction, Commitment and Turnover Intentions: The Moderating Effect of Experience, Gender and Performance. *The Journal of Business Research* 34 (Sep/Oct): 57–65.

4. Marsden, Peter V., Arne L. Kalleberg and Cynthia R. Cook. 1993. Gender Differences in Organizational Commitment. *Work and Occupations* 20 (August): 368–390.

5. Prewitt, 1999.

6. Klara, Robert. 1999. Fast and Fancy. *Restaurant Business* 98 (June 1): 19–21. Also Stern, Jane and Michael Stern. 2000. Familiarity Usually Breeds Regular Restaurant Customers. *Nation's Restaurant News* 34 (November 20): 24–26.

Advanced Topics in Business Research

CHAPTER
13

Other Multivariate Techniques

Learning Objectives

1. Explain the difference between dependence and interdependence techniques.

2. Understand how to use factor analysis to simplify data analysis.

3. Demonstrate the usefulness of cluster analysis.

4. Understand when and how to use discriminant analysis.

INTRODUCTION

Research projects sometimes include data reduction and/or simplification in their objectives. In such cases, we use statistical techniques that do not designate variables as either dependent or independent. Rather, they analyze only the dependent variables or only the independent variables. The two techniques appropriate in this situation are **factor analysis** and **cluster analysis.** The first technique we cover in this chapter is factor analysis. It is used for data summarization. The second technique discussed, cluster analysis, can be used to identify homogeneous subgroups of the total sample.

In previous chapters, we showed you how to assess predictive capability using regression analysis with a single metric dependent variable and one or more metric independent variables. We did not, however, examine how to assess predictive capability when there is a single nonmetric dependent variable and several metric independent variables. The appropriate statistical technique in this situation is **discriminant analysis.** This is the third technique we discuss in this chapter.

DEPENDENCE AND INTERDEPENDENCE TECHNIQUES

The statistical techniques multiple regression and discriminant analysis are referred to as dependence techniques. This is because the variables are divided into independent and dependent sets for analysis purposes. Sometimes we want to look at only one set of variables at a time to simplify or better understand them. In such cases we analyze only the independent variables or only the dependent variables, instead of both sets at the same time. When we use a statistical technique with only one set of variables at a time, it is referred to as an interdependence technique. Factor analysis and cluster analysis are **interdependence techniques.** The "Research in Action" box tells you how these and other multivariate statistical techniques are being used by many organizations to improve their decision making.

FACTOR ANALYSIS

Factor analysis is a multivariate statistical technique that can summarize the information from a large number of variables into a much smaller number of variables or **factors.** By identifying latent (not easily identifiable) relationships and combining variables into a few factors, factor analysis simplifies our understanding of the data. When you use factor analysis, the variables are not divided into dependent and independent categories. Instead, all variables are analyzed together to identify underlying patterns or factors. The technique can be used to factor analyze either independent or dependent variables considered separately.

Let's begin our discussion of factor analysis with an intuitive example. McDonald's® has over thirty thousand restaurants worldwide while Burger King® has only about twelve thousand. Burger King would like to close that gap and has set as a goal to open five hundred new restaurants each year worldwide. To do this they believe a survey to determine restaurant selection factors for McDonald's customers versus Burger King customers would help develop a marketing strategy to gain market share from McDonald's and attract customers to the new restaurants. Burger King surveyed one thousand current and potential fast food customers and asked them to rate Burger King and McDonald's on six

RESEARCH IN ACTION
GIVING CREDIT WHERE CREDIT IS DUE

Who decides whether you can afford to buy a new home or a car? These days, it's more likely to be a "what" than a "who"—a computer program based on mathematical figures that provides a score rating you as credit-worthy or a credit risk. More and more, lenders, merchants, and even many insurers consider a customer's credit score a critical tool for predicting whether they'll make money on that customer. The scores are based on complex and closely guarded mathematical assumptions developed by San Rafael, California based Fair, Isaac and Company, and calculated using multivariate statistical methods. In fact, Fair, Isaac and Company leads the industry so completely that credit scores are frequently referred to as FICO scores, after the company's initials.

What exactly is credit scoring? It's a three-digit number derived in part from a borrower's credit history. The FICO formula was developed by comparing past and current financial information provided by the country's three major credit bureaus—Equifax, Experian, and Trans Union—on a large sampling of consumers and then using that information to make predictions about future behavior. This information helps determine whether the borrower's tendencies match those of borrowers who default on debt, declare bankruptcy, or end up in other types of financial trouble.

The secret to an individual's FICO score isn't any single piece of information, but how the different variables interact. According to Fair, Isaac's Web site (www.fairisaac.com), the consumer's payment history and debt load account for 35 percent and 30 percent of the score, respectively. The other 35 percent is determined by how long the consumer has had credit, how actively the consumer is looking for new credit and the types of credit the consumer uses. On the FICO scale, the higher the score the better. A low score of 300 indicates that a consumer is a poor credit risk, while a high score of 850 represents a model borrower. According to the company, the median score is approximately 720.

So how do you find out what many lenders already know about your FICO rating? After receiving political and consumer pressure, Fair, Isaac recently launched www.myfico.com, a Web site that gives consumers access to their personal FICO scores. For a fee of $12.95, a consumer gets thirty days of online access to his FICO report. According to the company, more than one million consumers have paid for the service, which it operates as a joint venture with Equifax. In addition to their scores, consumers who buy the basic myfico.com service get a copy of their Equifax credit report and a general explanation of the factors that might be contributing to lower credit scores. Future upgrades to myfico.com include an online calculator that will let consumers see how seven key variables could affect their FICO score. For example, according to a prototype of the service, a consumer with a 707 score could raise it by as much as 20 points by paying down $750 on $2,230 in credit card balances.

The multivariate statistical methods being used by Fair, Isaac to develop their scoring models are being incorporated by many businesses as well as other organizations like the Internal Revenue Service, that uses them to identify which companies and individuals to audit. Keep in mind that in today's business environment, it's just as important to understand the relationship between variables as it is to gather the information in the first place. Thus, the importance of multivariate statistical methods that are used to understand relationships has increased dramatically in recent years.

SOURCE: www.fairisaac.com; Simon, Ruth. 2002. Numbers Game: Looking to Improve Your Credit Score? *The Wall Street Journal* March 19: A 1. *Morning Advocate.* 2001. September 30: 4I.

selection factors—taste, portion size, freshness, friendliness of employees, courtesy, and competence. The ratings of six customers who answered the survey are shown in Exhibit 13-1. Customers who gave lower ratings on friendliness also gave lower ratings on competence and courtesy. Likewise, when you examine the ratings of taste, portion size, and freshness you can see the ratings were quite high on all three variables. From a visual inspection of the ratings,

EXHIBIT 13-1	RATINGS OF FAST FOOD RESTAURANTS					
Respondent	Taste	Portion Size	Freshness	Friendly	Courteous	Competent
#1	9	8	7	4	3	4
#2	8	7	8	4	5	3
#3	7	8	9	3	4	3
#4	8	9	7	4	4	3
#5	7	8	7	3	3	3
#6	9	7	8	5	4	5

EXHIBIT 13-2	FACTOR ANALYSIS OF RESTAURANT SELECTION FACTORS

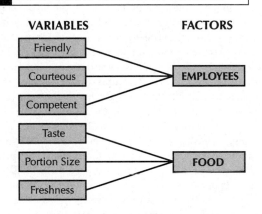

therefore, the six measures can be combined into two composite factors called food and employees (see Exhibit 13-2).

As is demonstrated by the above example, factor analysis enables us to examine the underlying relationships for a large number of variables and combine them into a smaller set of composite factors. Factor analysis is a statistical technique that develops linear combinations of variables that summarize the original variables based on their underlying patterns (latent relationships). For the above example, it was easy to visually see the relationships because we had only six respondents and six variables. But with larger numbers of variables and respondents we clearly would need a computer to use factor analysis.

Factor analysis is most useful with a large number of variables. But, in applying it, the researcher should have a minimum sample size of five times the number of variables analyzed. That is, if you are factor analyzing fifteen variables then your minimum suggested sample size is seventy-five.

Deriving Factors

A factor is a linear combination of the original variables. Factor analysis can derive as many factors as there are variables being analyzed. Using the example in Exhibit 13-2, a maximum of six factors can be derived. The first factor derived is the combination of variables that accounts for more of the variance in the data as a whole than any other linear combination of the original variables. The second factor accounts for the most residual (leftover or remaining) variance after the first factor is extracted. Each subsequent factor accounts for less variance than the earlier ones, but is still the best in terms of accounting for the largest amount of the residual variance. The researcher examines the factor solutions and decides when additional factors need not be derived because the added variance accounted for is so small.

To derive factors the analyst first must answer two questions: (1) What kind of factor model should be used? and (2) How should the initial factor solution be rotated to make it easier to interpret? There are two basic factor models. One is referred to as principal components analysis and the other is common factor analysis. Principal components analysis uses all of the variance in the data set while common factor analysis is based only on the **common variance.**

Factor Analysis Models   To help you understand the difference in the two factor analysis models, let's clarify what we mean by variance. Recall that variance describes the variability in the distribution of the data. In statistical analysis, each variable is assumed to have a total variance equal to one. The total variance can be divided into three types—common, unique, and error, as shown in Exhibit 13-3. The common variance is that portion of the total variance that is shared with all the original variables in the analysis. That is, the portion of the variance for which all the variables covary together. The **unique variance** is that portion of the total variance that is specific or unique to only one variable. **Error variance** is the portion of the variance that is the result of, for example, a measurement or data collection error. Principal components analysis uses all three kinds of variance to derive factor solutions. Common factor analysis uses only the common variance to derive factors.

Principal components analysis utilizes the entire variation in the set of variables being analyzed. The procedure reduces the original set of variables into a smaller set of composite variables, called principal components. Each principal component is formed by linearly combining the original variables. The objective is to explain as much of the original variance in the dataset as possible by a few principal components. As an example of principal-components analysis, let's consider the twelve perceptions variables from the Samouel's customer survey. If we were to run a principal components factor analysis program we would expect the twelve variables to be reduced into three, or perhaps four, components, which together explain 70 percent or more of the variance in the original variables. Each of the new components would represent a separate composite factor.

Common factor analysis utilizes only the common variance to derive a factor solution. The objective is to identify underlying (latent) dimensions referred to as common factors. If there are subsets of the original variables that are measuring the same underlying construct, the new common dimensions will be meaningful and interpretable. That is, we will be able to describe the original variables in terms of their common underlying dimensions. Common factor analysis frequently is used in the development of multi-item scales to see if the individual constructs are truly unidimensional (represent a single construct).

EXHIBIT 13-3   TYPES OF VARIANCE IN FACTOR ANALYSIS

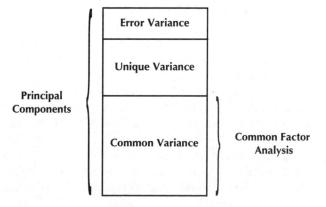

Principal components analysis (PCA) and common factor analysis (sometimes referred to as exploratory factor analysis—EFA) are both available in most popular statistical packages. If the business researcher knows that the unique and error variances are a relatively small portion of the total variance, and wants to reduce the original set of variables into a smaller set of composite variables, then principal components is typically used. In contrast, if little is known about the unique and error variance and the researcher wants to examine the original variables in terms of their common underlying dimensions, then common factor analysis is used.

The initial factors derived using PCA are made up mostly of common variance and a much smaller portion of unique and error variance. Also, principal components factor solutions tend to be more stable. For these reasons, principal components analysis is by far the most commonly used approach in business research so we will focus only on this method. There are several other analytical and computational differences between PCA and EFA that are beyond the scope of this text. For more information see Hair J., et.al., *Multivariate Data Analysis: With Readings,* 6th Edition, Prentice Hall, 2003.

Factor Analysis Rotation   The initial solution in a principal components analysis is unrotated. The unrotated solution produces factors that are independent (uncorrelated), but they are often difficult to interpret. For this reason, the researcher rotates the factors to get another view at their structure. There are two options for **factor rotation**—either an **orthogonal rotation** or an **oblique rotation.** When you choose an orthogonal solution the factors are rotated so they are independent of each other and the correlation between them is zero. An oblique solution permits the derived factors to be correlated with each other.

Factor rotation provides the researcher with different "views" of the same data. It is similar to the process you follow when you rotate a small object like a diamond in your hand to find the best viewing angle. That is, the one that allows you to understand it the best. In factor analysis, the term **simple structure** is used to describe factor analysis results in which each original variable has a high loading on only one factor and relatively low loadings on the other derived factors. A factor loading represents the correlation between an original variable and a derived factor. There is no guarantee that a given data set can produce simple structure. From a measurement perspective, however, results consistent with simple structure provide some evidence of convergent and discriminant validity. Simple structure makes it clear that an original variable is highly related to only one latent factor. One of the key reasons for factor rotation is to examine whether or not simple structure can be obtained.

Orthogonal and oblique rotated factors are illustrated in Exhibit 13-4. The vertical line represents unrotated factor two. The horizontal line is unrotated factor one. The unrotated factors are shown at a 90-degree angle, meaning they are uncorrelated. When we rotate factors we show them moving in a clockwise direction. The factors are rotated until they more closely intersect with the variables that load on them. When we rotate the axes together and keep the 90-degree angle, that is an orthogonal rotation (shown as a solid line). When we rotate each axis individually and let the two axes form an oblique angle (less than 90-degrees), that is an oblique rotation (shown as a dashed line). If our research objective is to have uncorrelated factors, then we would use an orthogonal rotation—for example, if we wanted to use factor scores in a subsequent regression model as we show you in Chapter 14. On the other hand, if we simply want to represent the factor structure that most closely portrays the relationship between the variables, then we would use an oblique rotation. In the real world, factors are almost always correlated, but to meet

EXHIBIT 13-4 **ORTHOGONAL AND OBLIQUE ROTATION OF FACTORS**

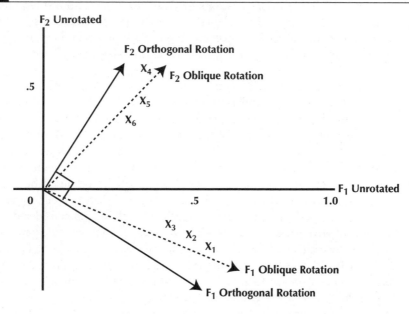

the statistical assumptions of our research problem we may choose to use an orthogonal rotation and represent the factors as uncorrelated.

An orthogonal rotation is by far the most commonly used approach in business research so we will focus only on this method. There are several different options for deriving an orthogonal solution, but we will use the Varimax option since it too is the most widely used. To summarize our decisions, we will use principal components factor analysis that is orthogonally rotated based on the Varimax procedure. For those who wish more information on factor models and rotation approaches see Hair J., et.al., *Multivariate Data Analysis: With Readings,* 6th Edition, Prentice Hall, 2003.

Number of Factors

Researchers use factor analysis in an attempt to summarize the information in many variables using only a few factors. Thus, a key issue involves how many factors are needed to effectively represent the variables. Our restaurant example derived only two factors, but most situations involve several factors. Deciding on how many factors to retain is a complex decision because most factor analysis problems can have more than one possible solution. That is, a three-factor and a four-factor solution may be very comparable and judgment is required to select the best one. We will discuss two of the most widely used methods to decide the number of factors to retain—the **latent root** and **percentage of variance** criteria. For an explanation of other approaches see Hair J., et.al., *Multivariate Data Analysis: With Readings,* 6th Edition, Prentice Hall, 2003. These two methods are used along with the ability to interpret and name the factors in deciding how many factors to retain.

The most widely used method to decide the number of factors is the latent root criterion. The latent root is a measure of the amount of variance a particular factor represents. This criterion states that with principal components analysis factors that have a latent root (also called an **eigenvalue**) of one or higher are retained. Factors with a latent root of less than one are considered insignificant and not retained. Each original variable has a variance of one. Therefore, if you factor analyze a set of twelve variables, the total variance is twelve. Since any single factor you retain must have a latent root of one or more, each factor you keep will represent at least 8.3 percent of the total variance (12/1 = 8.3%).

The latent root criterion is the default option in most statistical software programs. But the analyst needs to understand that it is calculated based on the unrotated solution. After rotation, some of the variance from earlier factors is shifted to later factors that then have a larger latent root. Thus, if the initial factor solution has four factors based on the latent root criterion the analyst will need to also request a five-factor solution to evaluate as well. This is because after rotation the 5th factor may have an eigenvalue of one or higher. Also, rotating more factors may facilitate interpretation of the factors.

A second criterion to use in deciding how many factors to retain is the percentage of the variance in the original data that is explained by all factors considered together. A factor analysis software package (such as SPSS or SAS) will tell you the percentage of variation explained by each factor, as well as the total variance explained by all factors. An illustration of the **factor loadings** and variance extracted is shown in Exhibit 13-5. It is a three-factor solution for our six fast food variables. In this example, the first two factors are definitely good. When added together they explain a total of 69.4 percent (38.7 + 30.7 = 69.4%) of the variability in the six original variables and their latent root is above 1.0. Since the third factor explains only 7.68 percent of the variance and has a latent root of only .45, it will not be retained. In fact, you would have to run the factor analysis again and either use the default criterion of retaining only factors with latent roots greater than 1.0, or request only two factors so you could eliminate the third factor.

Most analysts stop factoring when additional factors no longer make sense because the variance they explain often contains a large amount of error. The rule of thumb for this criterion is that a factor solution should account for a minimum of 60 percent of the total variance. But each situation may vary depending on the research objectives, and both less variance or more variance accounted for could be justified. In some situations, adding an

EXHIBIT 13-5 **EXAMPLE OF VARIMAX-ROTATED PRINCIPAL COMPONENTS FACTOR MATRIX**

Variables	Loadings			
	Factor 1	Factor 2	Factor 3	Communality
X_1 Friendly	0.93	0.19	0.09	0.91
X_2 Courteous	0.89	0.27	0.18	0.90
X_3 Competent	0.76	−0.21	0.27	0.70
X_4 Taste	0.11	0.76	0.31	0.69
X_5 Portion Size	0.03	0.67	0.44	0.65
X_6 Freshness	0.19	0.81	0.24	0.75
				Total
Sum of squares (eigenvalue)	2.32	1.83	0.45	4.60
Percentage of trace*	38.7	30.7	7.5	76.97

*Trace = 6.0 (number of variances analyzed)

additional factor to reach the 60 percent criterion cannot be justified because no variables load on the factor (i.e., loading >.30). Thus, the added factor is referred to as uninterpretable and the factor solution is unacceptable.

In most situations, the number of factors retained is based on the size of the latent root, the percentage of variance extracted, and the ability to logically name the resulting factors. Specifically, the business researcher retains only factors that meet the minimum latent root criterion of one, but the total variance accounted for by all the factors should be more than 60 percent and the rotated factors should be able to be assigned a logical name. In applying these three considerations, for example, the researcher most often would select the five-factor solution if all factors have a latent root of one or higher. But a four-factor solution may be chosen instead of a five-factor solution even if the fifth factor has a latent root of one. In such cases the four-factor solution must account for a minimum of 60 percent of the total variance and the logic for naming the factors must be more easily supportable and theoretically sound than with five factors. The ultimate goal is to derive a set of factors that are theoretically meaningful, relatively easy to interpret, and account for as much of the original variance as possible.

There is additional information in Exhibit 13-5 you will need to understand. The numbers in the columns under each factor (and beside each of the six variables) are referred to as factor loadings. The number at the bottom of each column of factor loadings is the sum of squared factor loadings, also referred to as an eigenvalue. To obtain this number, you simply square each factor loading for a particular factor and add them together. The sum of squared factor loadings indicates the relative importance of each factor in accounting for the variance in the set of variables being analyzed. Note the sum of squares for factors 1, 2, and 3 are 2.32, 1.83, and .45 respectively. The percentage of trace for each of the three factors also is shown at the bottom of the table. The trace is the total amount of variance in a factor analysis. In this case the trace is six (six variables = trace of 6). To get the percent of trace you divide a factor's sum of squared loadings by the trace. For example, for factor one, 2.32 divided by 6 equals 38.7 percent.

At the far right side of the factor matrix is the column of communalities. It represents the row sum of squared factor loadings. To get the **communality** you square each of the factor loadings for a variable (variable $X_1 = .93^2 + .19^2 + .09^2 = .91$) and add them together. The communality tells us how much of the variance in a particular variable is accounted for by the factor solution (all the factors combined). Large communalities indicate a large amount of the original variance in a particular variable has been accounted for by the factor solution. For example, a commonality of .91 for X_1—Friendly indicates the factor solution accounted for more variance in that variable than it did for variable X_5—Portion Size, which had a communality of only .65.

Interpreting Factors

To interpret a factor matrix we examine the factor loadings. Factor loadings are the correlations between each of the original variables and the newly extracted factors. Each factor loading is a measure of the relative importance of a particular variable in representing that factor. Similar to correlation coefficients, factor loadings can vary from +1.0 to −1.0. If variable X_1—Friendly is closely associated with Factor 1, the factor loading will be high. The factor analysis software will execute the statistical analysis and calculate factor loadings between each newly created factor and each of the original variables. An example of the results for this statistical analysis was provided in our example. In Exhibit 13-5, the three variables X_1, X_2, and X_3 have high loadings on Factor 1. Similarly, variables X_4, X_5, and X_6 have high loadings on Factor 2. A business researcher would use the pattern of loadings to name each of the factors. But before the pattern for these variables could be interpreted, the factor solution must be run again to request a two-factor solution.

What are the guidelines on which factor loadings should be used in naming a factor? The larger the absolute size of a factor loading, the more important it is in interpreting and naming a factor. Typical guidelines used by business researchers for important factor loadings are: +/ .30 are considered acceptable; +/ .50 are moderately important; +/ .70 are very important.

We next assign a name to the resulting factors. To do so, the researcher examines the variables that have the highest loadings on each factor. What we are looking for is a common underlying meaning among the variables that have high loadings on a given factor. We also prefer that there are no variables loading on a factor that are not related to the other variables with high loadings. In our example the three variables friendly (X_1), courteous (X_2), and competent (X_3) all loaded on the same factor, and we named this factor employees because the three variables are related to a customer's experience with the restaurant's employees. Similarly, the perceptions of taste (X_4), portion size (X_5), and freshness (X_6) have high loadings on the same factor, so we named factor 2 food because the three variables all deal with the restaurant's food. In this example, both of our factors were pure in that each variable had a high loading on one factor and a much lower loading on the other factors. Unfortunately, in practice we often find a variable will have comparable loadings on more than one factor. When this happens it does not mean the factor solution is wrong or that we cannot use it. We simply would prefer for a variable to load on only one factor because it is easier to interpret, assuming all the variables loading on a particular factor are in some way related. When variables load on more than one factor, however, it does complicate the naming of factors.

The process of naming factors is subjective. It combines logic and intuition with an assessment of the variables that have high loadings on each factor. Because of its subjective approach we must be cautious in developing names to represent factors to be sure the names do not misrepresent the underlying meaning of the factors.

Example of Factor Analysis

Phil Samouel would like to know if he could simplify his understanding of the perceptions of the two restaurants by reducing the number of variables to fewer than twelve. That is, can he represent the twelve original perceptions variables (X_1 to X_{12}) with a smaller number of meaningful factors. The null hypothesis is that the twelve perceptions variables cannot be represented by a smaller set of meaningful factors. The twelve perceptions variables as measured in the customer survey are shown in Exhibit 13-6.

Let's look first at the information in the Descriptive Statistics table shown in Exhibit 13-7. We can check the means and sample sizes to make sure the data was correctly analyzed. For example, if the sample size is not two hundred, then you may have analyzed the wrong data set, or some respondents may have been eliminated because of missing data.

Now look at the Rotated Component Matrix (also referred to as a **rotated factor matrix**) table shown in Exhibit 13-8. The names of the twelve variables analyzed (X_1–X_{12}) are shown in the left column. Note that the order of the variables is not from one to twelve, but rather the sequence is based on the sizes of the individual variable loadings on the factors. That is, the largest loadings are at the top of the column and they get smaller as you go to the bottom of the column of loadings. To make it easier to interpret the fac-

| **EXHIBIT 13-6** | **TWELVE PERCEPTIONS VARIABLES FROM RESTAURANT CUSTOMER SURVEY** |

Listed below is a set of characteristics that could be used to describe Samouel's Greek Cuisine/Gino's Ristorante. Using a scale from 1 to 7, with 7 being "Strongly Agree" and 1 being "Strongly Disagree." To what extent do you agree or disagree that Samouel's/Gino's has:

1. Excellent Food Quality	**Strongly Disagree**	**Strongly Agree**
	1 2 3 4 5 6 7	
2. Attractive Interior	**Strongly Disagree**	**Strongly Agree**
	1 2 3 4 5 6 7	
3. Generous Portions	**Strongly Disagree**	**Strongly Agree**
	1 2 3 4 5 6 7	
4. Excellent Food Taste	**Strongly Disagree**	**Strongly Agree**
	1 2 3 4 5 6 7	
5. Good Value for the Money	**Strongly Disagree**	**Strongly Agree**
	1 2 3 4 5 6 7	
6. Friendly Employees	**Strongly Disagree**	**Strongly Agree**
	1 2 3 4 5 6 7	
7. Appears Clean & Neat	**Strongly Disagree**	**Strongly Agree**
	1 2 3 4 5 6 7	
8. Fun Place to Go	**Strongly Disagree**	**Strongly Agree**
	1 2 3 4 5 6 7	
9. Wide Variety of Menu Items	**Strongly Disagree**	**Strongly Agree**
	1. 2 3 4 5 6 7	
10. Reasonable Prices	**Strongly Disagree**	**Strongly Agree**
	1 2 3 4 5 6 7	
11. Courteous Employees	**Strongly Disagree**	**Strongly Agree**
	1 2 3 4 5 6 7	
12. Competent Employees	**Strongly Disagree**	**Strongly Agree**
	1 2 3 4 5 6 7	

EXHIBIT 13-7 **DESCRIPTIVE STATISTICS FOR CUSTOMER SURVEY**

Variables	Mean	Analysis N
X_1—Excellent Food Quality	5.53	200
X_2—Attractive Interior	4.70	200
X_3—Generous Portions	3.89	200
X_4—Excellent Food Taste	5.45	200
X_5—Good Value for Money	4.33	200
X_6—Friendly Employees	3.66	200
X_7—Appears Clean and Neat	4.11	200
X_8—Fun Place to Go	3.39	200
X_9—Wide Variety of Menu Items	5.51	200
X_{10}—Reasonable Prices	4.06	200
X_{11}—Courteous Employees	2.40	200
X_{12}—Competent Employees	2.19	200

EXHIBIT 13-8 **ROTATED FACTOR SOLUTION FOR CUSTOMER SURVEY PERCEPTIONS**

	Components (Factors)			
Variables	1	2	3	4
X_4—Excellent Food Taste	.912			
X_9—Wide Variety of Menu Items	.901			
X_1—Excellent Food Quality	.883			
X_6—Friendly Employees		.892		
X_{11}—Courteous Employees		.850		
X_{12}—Competent Employees		.800		
X_8—Fun Place to Go			.869	
X_2—Attractive Interior			.854	
X_7—Appears Clean and Neat			.751	
X_3—Generous Portions				.896
X_5—Good Value for Money				.775
X_{10}—Reasonable Prices				.754

Extraction Method: Principal Component Analysis.   Rotation Method: Varimax.

Total Variance Explained

	Rotation Sums of Squared Loadings		
Component	Total	% of Variance	Cumulative %
1	2.543	21.188	21.188
2	2.251	18.758	39.946
3	2.100	17.498	57.444
4	2.060	17.170	74.614

tor solution, we do not show factor loadings under .30 in the factor matrix. This is called an **"easy read" matrix** because it does not show the smaller, less significant factor loadings. In the popular software packages, this is an option you should select. You should realize that the loadings for all the variables are still computed, they simply are not shown. It is easier to pick out any problems with simple structure once this option is selected.

To the right of the variable labels are columns of numbers representing the factor loadings for a four-factor solution. We only see three numbers for each of the factors. This is because all of the other factor loadings are under .30 and are not shown in this "easy read" factor matrix. As you recall, our preference is for a simple (pure) solution in which each original variable loads on only one factor and that is what happened in our example. But in many cases this does not happen. Instead, one or more variables will load on two factors.

Before trying to name the factors, let's decide if four factors are enough or if we need more. Our objective here is to have as few factors as possible, yet account for a reasonable amount of the information contained in the twelve original variables. We now look at the information shown in the Total Variance Explained table (see Exhibit 13–8) to do this. It shows that four factors accounted for 74.614 percent of the variance in the original twelve variables. This is more than the minimum amount of variance we should account for (60 percent), and we have reduced the number of original variables by about two-thirds—from twelve to four, so let's see if our factors seem logical.

To determine if our factors are logical and theoretically meaningful, look at the original variables that combine to make the new factors. Factor one is made up of X_4—Excellent Food Taste, X_9—Wide Variety of Menu Items, and X_1—Excellent Food Quality. Factor two is made up of X_6—Friendly Employees, X_{11}—Courteous Employees, and X_{12}—Competent Employees. Factor three is made up of X_8—Fun Place to Go, X_2—Attractive Interior, and X_7—Appears Clean and Neat, while factor four consists of X_3—Generous Portions, X_5—Good Value for the Money, and X_{10}—Reasonable Prices. To analyze the logic of the combinations we look at the variables with the highest loadings (largest absolute sizes). That is why only the loadings of .30 or higher are shown in Exhibit 13-8. Factor one is related to

RESEARCH IN ACTION
USING SPSS TO DEVELOP A FACTOR SOLUTION FOR THE CUSTOMER SURVEY

For this analysis, we use all two hundred respondents and do not split the sample. This is because we are looking for common patterns across all of the restaurant customers. The SPSS click through sequence is: Analyze → Data Reduction → Factor, which leads to a dialog box where you select variables X_1–X_{12}. After you move these variables into the Variables box, look at the alternatives below. Click first on the Descriptives box and then on the Univariate descriptives box. Unclick the Initial solution box because we will not examine it, and then click Continue. Next click on the Extraction box. We will use the default method of Principal components and the Extract default of Eigenvalues over 1, but you unclick the unrotated factor solution under Display and then click on Continue. Next go to the Rotation box where the default is None. Since we will rotate the initial factor solution you click on Varimax as your rotational choice (this removes the default of None) and then Continue. Finally, go to the Options box and click on Sorted by size, and then change the Suppress absolute values less than from .10 to .3, and click on Continue. The last two choices make the output easier to read because we eliminate information we will not use. We will not be calculating scores at this point so we can click on OK to run the program. The results should be the same as in Exhibits 13-7 and 13-8.

"Food," factor two is related to "Employees," and factor three is related to "Atmosphere." Factor four consists of the food portions and pricing variables. It is somewhat more complex to interpret, but still logical. We have labeled it a "Value" factor. The logic of this name is that customers who perceive the food portions to be somewhat larger also believe the prices are relatively more reasonable (positive correlation between the variables). Overall, customers believe the food portions are acceptable, but not necessarily good (mean = 3.89 on a 7-point scale). For the pricing variables the means are slightly higher but still not very favorable (Value for Money mean = 4.33 and Reasonable Prices mean = 4.06). Thus, there definitely is room for improvement in customers' perceived value for their money.

The factor analysis of the twelve perceptions variables has developed a four-factor solution. The four factors account for an acceptable amount of variance (above 60 percent) and display logic in the combinations of the original twelve variables. With this four-factor solution instead of having to think about twelve variables we can now think about only four variables—Food, Employees, Atmosphere, and Value.

There is one final topic to cover on the interpretation of a factor matrix. In our example, all of the factor loadings were positive. Since factor loadings are the same as correlation coefficients they can have either a positive (+) or a negative (−) sign. It is not unusual to have some variables with positive loadings and other variables with negative loadings on the same factor. If a variable has a loading with a negative sign it means it is negatively related to that factor. Since factors are orthogonally independent, a negative loading for a variable on the first factor does not have any relationship to the other factors in the solution.

The simplification and reduction of the original twelve perceptions variables to four factors could be an end in itself. In other words, we could conclude that by reducing the twelve variables to only four factors we had accomplished our research objective. In some instances, however, we may wish to use the new factors as independent variables in a regression or discriminant analysis. The new research objective, then, would be to see if the four factor variables could accurately predict a single dependent variable, such as satisfaction or likelihood to recommend the restaurant to a friend. We provide an example of such a situation in Chapter 14.

CLUSTER ANALYSIS

Cluster analysis is an interdependence multivariate technique. Cluster analysis enables us to combine objects (e.g., individuals, brands, stores) into groups so that objects within each of the groups are similar to each other and different from objects in all other groups. Cluster analysis combines objects so there will be high internal (within cluster) homogeneity as well as high external (between cluster) heterogeneity. That is, cluster analysis strives to identify natural groupings using several variables. But none of the variables is considered to be a dependent or independent variable. If it is successful, the objects within the clusters will be close together and the objects in different clusters will be far apart.

To better explain the process of cluster analysis, let's use an intuitive example. Sam's Clubs® is interested in identifying customers who, when shopping, are dominated or driven by low prices and bargains. To do so, they conduct a survey of individuals within a five-mile radius of ten of their stores. On the questionnaire they ask questions like "How often do you use coupons from the newspaper?", "How often do you use the Val-Pack coupons sent to you in the mail?", "How often do you shop at stores that advertise low prices?", and so on. They also collect demographic information such as age, income, education, and so on. After the data is collected, their statistical analyst cluster analyzes the questions relating to frequency of use of coupons and shopping based on sale offers and low prices. The cluster analysis identifies groups of individuals more highly motivated by coupon offers and low prices versus those who are not. Instead of using arbitrary approaches like the mean or median, cluster analysis identifies the natural groupings where individuals in each cluster are the most similar. By so doing, Sam's Clubs can identify one or more household segments that are most likely to shop at its stores for bargains. Once the price-driven segment is identified, Sam's Clubs advertising, products, and services can be tailored to appeal to them.

Exhibit 13-9 identifies three potential clusters or segments for Sam's Clubs. Cluster 1 contains households that seldom shop for bargains or use coupons, cluster 2 includes households that are occasional bargain hunters, and cluster 3 has households that frequently shop based on low prices and the use of coupons. Note that clusters 1 and 3 are very different (no overlap) while clusters 2 and 3 are somewhat similar (large overlap). By examining the characteristics associated with each of the clusters, Sam's management can decide which clusters to target and how best to reach them through their marketing communications. In this case, Sam's Clubs would definitely target cluster 3 and possibly cluster 2.

Cluster analysis is useful for the business researcher in many different situations. For example, a business that has collected survey data often is faced with a large number of observations where patterns are difficult to identify unless smaller, more homogeneous groups are identified. The researcher could use cluster analysis to identify groups like highly committed, loyal employees versus those who are not, good credit risks versus bad credit risks, highly satisfied versus dissatisfied employees, and so on. Cluster analysis can be used to perform this task on the basis of objective criteria instead of arbitrary ones.

EXHIBIT 13-9 **THREE CLUSTERS OF SHOPPER TYPES**

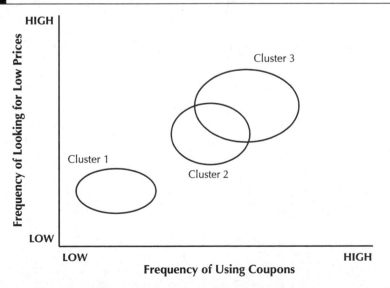

Deriving Clusters

Clusters can be developed from scatter plots. But this is a time-consuming, trial-and-error process that becomes tedious quickly as the sample size increases. Fortunately, software packages are available for this purpose and can be used to efficiently execute the clustering process. The mathematics underlying the various clustering procedures is beyond the scope of this book. But all the procedures are based on the concept of starting with some boundaries around an initial set of cluster seeds (individual respondents that are far apart) and adjusting the boundaries until the distances within cluster boundaries (within cluster variation) are as small as possible relative to the average distances between clusters. Exhibit 13-10 shows between- and within-cluster variation. The general approach for all cluster programs is similar, therefore, and involves measuring the similarity (or differences) between objects based on a distance measure.

Cluster analysis involves three separate phases. The first phase divides the total sample into smaller subgroups. The second phase verifies the groups are statistically different and theoretically meaningful. The third phase then profiles the clusters by describing the characteristics of each cluster in terms of demographics, psychographics, or other relevant characteristics.

Phase One

During this phase we must answer three questions. How do we measure the distances between the objects we are clustering? What procedure will be used to group similar objects into clusters? How many clusters will we derive? Unfortunately, there are many different answers to these questions, and, depending on the circumstances, more than one of them could be correct. We will therefore give you some general guidelines and refer you to other sources for the underlying details. Hair J., et.al., *Multivariate Data Analysis: With Readings,* 6th Edition, Prentice Hall, 2003.

The distances between the objects we are clustering can be measured in several ways. The most commonly used measure is **Euclidean distance.** Other options include squared Euclidean distances, the sum of the absolute differences, and Mahalanobis distance. Many

---

EXHIBIT 13-10 **BETWEEN- AND WITHIN-CLUSTER VARIATION**

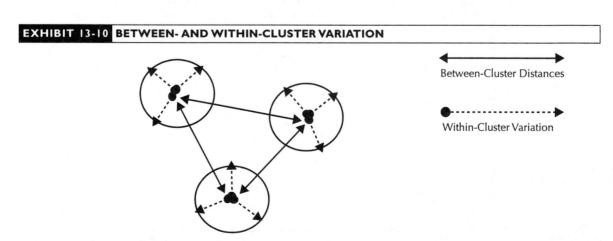

Between-Cluster Distances

Within-Cluster Variation

statisticians recommend Mahalanobis as the best measure, but few statistical packages include this option. Squared Euclidean distances have the fewest weaknesses of the remaining measures, so we recommend it as the best. Before running the cluster program we suggest you identify and remove outliers where appropriate since cluster procedures are very sensitive to outliers. We also recommend you standardize the variables included in the cluster analysis if they are measured on scales with different units of measurement. For example, if you are using two variables to develop clusters, with one variable being satisfaction measured on a 1–7-point scale and the other variable being amount purchased measured on a 1–100-point scale, you must standardize the data before doing the cluster analysis. Otherwise, amount purchased will be weighted more heavily because the range of possible responses is much larger.

A second question you must answer in phase one is what procedure will be used to group objects that are similar. Many approaches are available, but they all can be classified into two types: hierarchical and nonhierarchical. Both approaches attempt to maximize the differences (distances) between clusters relative to the variation within the clusters, as shown in Exhibit 13-10.

Hierarchical Clustering   A **hierarchical clustering** procedure develops a hierarchy or tree-like format. This can be done using either a build-up or a divisive approach. The **build-up** approach, also referred to as **agglomerative,** starts with all the objects (respondents) as separate clusters and combines them one at a time until there is a single cluster representing all the objects. The **divisive** approach starts with all objects as a single cluster and then takes away one object at a time until each object is a separate cluster. We will only discuss the agglomerative approach since it is the most widely used.

Exhibit 13-11 illustrates the build-up (agglomerative) approach for a sample of five objects. The illustration is referred to as a **dendogram,** or tree-graph. Note that objects four and five combine to form the first cluster (vertical lines indicate where two objects combine). Objects two and three combine next to form the second cluster. Then object one combines with the previously formed cluster of objects two and three. The final stage is when objects one, two, and three combine with objects four and five to form a single cluster.

The popular statistical software packages include many different options to calculate agglomerative clusters. Examples of these options include: between-groups linkage, within-groups linkage, nearest neighbor, furthest neighbor, centroid, median, and Ward's. Each of these options calculates the distances between clusters differently, has strengths and weaknesses, and often produces different results. An examination of each method is beyond the scope of this text. We refer you to Hair J., et.al., *Multivariate Data Analysis: With Readings,* 6th Edition, Prentice Hall, 2003. for additional explanation. The Ward's method is very popular and, more so than other methods, tends to result in clusters with approximately the same number of objects. We therefore recommend you use it

| EXHIBIT 13-11 | DENDOGRAM FOR HIERARCHICAL CLUSTER ANALYSIS |

first and then perhaps try the other approaches for comparison purposes. Hair J., et.al., *Multivariate Data Analysis: With Readings,* 6th Edition, Prentice Hall, 2003.

Nonhierarchical Clustering   **Nonhierarchical clustering** procedures, referred to as K-means clustering, do not involve the tree-like process of hierarchical clustering. Instead, one or more cluster seeds (initial starting points) are selected and objects within a prespecified distance from the cluster seeds are considered to be in a particular cluster. A cluster seed can be either a single object (respondent) that is chosen to be the center of a new cluster, or it can be several objects that together represent an initial seed point.

Several different procedures can be used to execute nonhierarchical clustering. They differ depending upon the number of cluster seeds initially selected, the sequence in which the cluster seeds are selected, and whether or not a single object can be reassigned to another cluster formed later once it has been assigned to an earlier formed cluster. Indeed, one advantage of some nonhierarchical clustering procedures is that objects can be removed from an early-formed cluster and reassigned to another cluster formed later in the sequence. This is not possible with hierarchical procedures. Reassignment of objects can be a disadvantage, however, since it requires more computing capability and, with large sample sizes, may not be possible on a PC. But the most significant disadvantage of nonhierarchical clustering is the lack of an objective, theoretically based method to identify initial cluster seeds. Because of this, hierarchical procedures are much more widely used and we will focus on them in the rest of our discussion.

A final question to be answered in phase one is, how many clusters should be retained? Sometimes the researcher may know ahead of time they want two, three, or some other number of clusters. Other times there may be theoretical considerations that suggest the appropriate number of clusters. Still other times the researcher may examine the extent to which error variances are reduced as one moves from fewer clusters to more clusters. Error variances are very large with one cluster, but drop substantially when you go to a two-cluster solution. As you move from two clusters to three, four, and so on, the error variances continue dropping, but not as quickly. Since a smaller number of clusters are easier to evaluate we recommend you run two, three, and four cluster solutions and select the one that is most logical and more closely meets your research objectives.

Phase Two

After you have determined the number of clusters to retain you must verify that the groups are, in fact, statistically different and theoretically meaningful. This process involves running statistical tests of the differences between the means of the clusters you have chosen. If one or more of the means of the variables used in the cluster analysis is statistically significant, then you would examine the logic of the differences in the group means for their underlying meaning. For example, recall that Sam's Clubs was interested in identifying individuals who would respond to coupons and low-price offers. If Sam's Clubs executes a two-cluster solution and examines the means, management would hope to find one cluster that frequently uses coupons and responds to low-price offers and another group that may be less responsive to such appeals. If the groups show this logic and are statistically different, then the two-group solution has been validated and we can name one group "Price Sensitive" and the other "Non-Price Sensitive," or something similar.

Phase Three

The third phase in cluster analysis examines the demographic and other characteristics of the individuals in each cluster and attempts to explain why the objects were grouped in the manner they were. For example, we would anticipate the "Price Sensitive" group identified above would perhaps have lower incomes or get more pleasure out of shopping for bargains. In contrast, the "Non-Price Sensitive" group would likely have higher incomes and get less pleasure out of shopping around for the best deal. This process is sometimes referred to as "profiling" clusters. Like the Sam's Club example, profiling other cluster analysis results may allow a business researcher to identify employees most likely to be promoted quickly, stocks most likely to exceed the Dow Jones Industrial average, or manufacturing units most likely to go on strike.

Example of Cluster Analysis

Phil Samouel is trying to decide whether or not to use different business approaches with different customers. From a business research perspective, this implies a research question asking whether there are different subgroups (segments) of restaurant customers who exhibit distinctly different restaurant perceptions. In discussing the problem with his consultant, he notes that variables X_1 to X_{12} are customers' perceptions of the restaurant and they are measured metrically. The task is to determine if there are subgroups or clusters of the two hundred respondents that are distinctly different. We could cluster using all twelve perceptions variables. But using a smaller number of variables will provide an example that is easier to understand. It also will focus on a single concept instead of several related, but different, concepts represented by the twelve perceptions variables (recall that in our factor analysis we identified four different factors/concepts).

In selecting which perceptions variables to analyze, we would look for variables that are logically related. We could also consider the results of our factor analysis in the previous section. Of the twelve variables, the three food variables (food taste, variety of menu items, and food quality) are related, as are the three employee variables (friendly, courteous, and competent). Let's work with the three employee variables—X_6, X_{11}, and X_{12}. The research objective then is to try to identify clusters of respondents that have distinctly different perceptions of the restaurant employees. The null hypothesis is that different clusters do not exist based on the customer survey perceptions variables for restaurant employees.

Example—Phase One   Phil's business consultant has recommended that the cluster analysis approach be Ward's method and measurement using squared Euclidean distances. These recommendations are based on his previous work that is similar to this research question. The next step is to decide the number of clusters to retain in the solution.

When perceptions of employees are examined as a single group, there typically is a lot of error associated with the group because you are combining a lot of variability together. As you separate the single group into two groups, the error is reduced substantially and continues to grow smaller as more groups (clusters) are identified. The reduction in error is measured by an error coefficient. Exhibit 13-12 shows the error coefficients associated with the clustering of the employee variables from the restaurant customer survey. The numbers in this column show how much error is reduced by going from one cluster to two clusters, from two clusters to three clusters, and so on. When you compare the coefficients for the one and two cluster solutions, you see a big drop (difference) in the error coefficient.

Each time you move up the column, the drop (difference) in the numbers gets smaller. In comparing the sizes of the coefficients, you are looking for the point where the difference between the coefficients gets substantially smaller. Small drops in the error coefficient do not justify going to a larger number if clusters.

As an example (see Exhibit 13-12), if the difference in the sizes of the error coefficients between a three-cluster solution and a four-cluster solution is small, your error has not been reduced very much. In our cluster analysis of employee perceptions variables, the change is rather small from three clusters = 251.618 to four clusters = 203.529, a difference of only 48.089 (251.618 − 203.529 = 48.089). The difference between the numbers as you go from three to four clusters is relatively small and a four-cluster solution is much more difficult to interpret. For this cluster solution, therefore, we definitely would choose three clusters over four.

Another option is to decide between two clusters and three clusters. When you move from two clusters to three, there is a drop in the error coefficient of 66.969 (318.587 − 251.618 = 66.969). Similarly, when two clusters are formed from one there is a drop of 356.143 (674.730 − 318.587 = 356.143). Certainly two clusters could be used because you reduce your error a huge amount by going from one to two clusters, and two clusters may be easier to understand than three. In this example, we could use either a two-cluster or a three-cluster solution. The decision to use a three-cluster solution would have to be based on what would be most useful for planning a new business strategy. That is, if there is business logic in using the three-group solution then the drop in error variance is sufficient to examine the three-group cluster solution.

Example—Phase Two   Phil and his business consultant have talked and agreed that, based on other studies and their judgment, they will initially examine a two-cluster solution. In phase two we must verify that the two groups are statistically different and theoretically meaningful.

Information from the Descriptives table of Exhibit 13-13 shows the sample sizes for each cluster (N) and the means of each variable for each cluster. For example, the sample size of cluster one is 101 and for cluster two it is 99. Moreover, the mean for X_6—Friendly Employees in cluster one is 4.61 whereas in cluster two the mean is 2.68. The means for courteous employees and competent employees have a similar pattern—they are higher in cluster one than in cluster two. To see if the differences between the group means are statistically significant, we go to the ANOVA table in Exhibit 13-13. The differences in the means of the clusters for all of the employee variables are highly significant (.000). Thus, we reject the null hypothesis of no differences.

EXHIBIT 13-12 **ERROR COEFFICIENTS FOR CLUSTER SOLUTIONS**

Error Coefficients	Error Reduction
Four Clusters = 203.529	3–4 Clusters = 48.089
Three Clusters = 251.618	2–3 Clusters = 66.969
Two Clusters = 318.587	1–2 Clusters = 356.143
One Cluster = 674.730	

RESEARCH IN ACTION

USING SPSS TO IDENTIFY CLUSTERS FOR
SELECTED CUSTOMER SURVEY PERCEPTIONS VARIABLES

For this example we analyze the total sample because we are looking for subgroups among all the restaurant customers. The SPSS click through sequence is: Analyze $\rightarrow$ Classify $\rightarrow$ Hierarchical Cluster. This will take you to a dialog box where you select and move variables X_6, X_{11}, and X_{12} into the Variables box. Now look at the other options below. We will use all the defaults shown on the dialog box as well as the defaults for the Statistics and Plots options below. Next click on the Method box and select Ward's under Cluster Method (it is the last one and you must scroll down). Squared Euclidean Distances is the default under Measure and we will use it. At this point we will not need the Save option so click on OK to run the program.

When the program finishes, look for a table called Agglomeration Schedule. There are lots of numbers in it, but we only use the numbers in the Coefficients column (middle of table). At the bottom of the agglomeration schedule table find the numbers in the Coefficients column. The number at the bottom will be the largest. As you move up the column the numbers (error coefficients) get smaller. For example, the bottom number is 674.730 and the one right above it is 318.587. The other numbers are shown in Exhibit 13-12.

We compare the means of the variables for each of the groups to understand the clusters. Respondents in cluster one perceive employees to be much more friendly (Gp. 1 mean = 4.61 vs. Gp. 2 = 2.68) as well as more courteous (Gp. 1 mean = 3.04 vs. Gp. 2 = 1.75) and more competent (Gp. 1 mean = 2.83 vs. Gp. 2 = 1.53). Thus, cluster one has much more favorable perceptions of the restaurant employees than does cluster two. But, interestingly, overall on a 7-point scale (7 = very favorable) employees have a lot of room for improvement (in many instances the means are well below the average of 3.5).

In phase two we were able to identify distinctly different clusters. Moreover, the cluster solutions are theoretically meaningful because we can say that group one has significantly more favorable perceptions of employees than does cluster two. Thus, we now can move on to phase three so Phil can make use of these findings in his business plan.

RESEARCH IN ACTION

USING THE SPSS ANOVA PROGRAM TO COMPARE GROUP MEANS

To do this we first must create a new variable that tells us to which cluster each of the two hundred respondents has been assigned. Use the SPSS sequence: Analyze $\rightarrow$ Classify $\rightarrow$ Hierarchical Cluster and click on the Save box. Your options are to create a new cluster membership variable for a single solution or for a range of solutions. Click on Single solution and place a 2 in the box. This will create a group membership variable for the two-group solution. The new variable is located at the far right hand side of your data set and is labeled clu2_1. You will see a 1 for respondents assigned to cluster one and a 2 for respondents assigned to cluster two.

We now must determine if the means on the employee variables are significantly different. To do so, we run a one-way ANOVA using the new cluster group membership variable. The null hypothesis is no differences in the group means. The click-through sequence is: Analyze $\rightarrow$ Compare Means $\rightarrow$ One-Way ANOVA. Next highlight and move variables X_6, X_{11}, and X_{12} to the Variables box. Then place the new cluster membership variable in the Factor box. This is the new variable in your data set labeled clu2_1. Click on the Options box and then on Descriptives. We use defaults for all other options, so click OK to run the program. The results are shown in Exhibit 13-13.

EXHIBIT 13-13 CHARACTERISTICS OF TWO-GROUP CLUSTER SOLUTION

Descriptives

Variables	Groups	N	Mean
X_6—Friendly Employees	1	101	4.61
	2	99	2.68
	Total	200	3.66
X_{11}—Courteous Employees	1	101	3.04
	2	99	1.75
	Total	200	2.40
X_{12}—Competent Employees	1	101	2.83
	2	99	1.53
	Total	200	2.19

ANOVA

Variables	Comparison	F	Sig.
X_6—Friendly Employees	Between Groups	300.528	.000
X_{11}—Courteous Employees	Between Groups	171.340	.000
X_{12}—Competent Employees	Between Groups	170.960	.000

Example—Phase Three Phase three of cluster analysis involves **profiling** the demographic characteristics of the clusters. You can run a one-way ANOVA between the two clusters to compare the demographic profiles.

The Descriptives table in Exhibit 13-14 displays the means of the demographic variables for each of the clusters, and the ANOVA table shows the statistical tests of differences. There are no statistical differences between the groups on gender (.895). There are, however, significant differences on age, income, and competitor. Recall that perceptions of cluster two were much less favorable than for cluster one. Thus, older, higher income customers perceive employees much less favorably than do younger, lower income customers. Similarly, cluster two is mostly Samouel's customers while cluster one is mostly Gino's customers (Samouel's coded = 0 and Gino's coded = 1). By interpreting the means of the cluster demographic variables, it appears the older group is in their forties or older (mean = 3.30) and has average annual incomes approaching $75,000 and higher (mean = 3.80). To make these interpretations you must examine how these variables were coded, as was shown in Appendix 1-B.

The two-group cluster solution could be the end of our analysis. Or we could go on to examine the three-group solution. But we also could use the clusters we identified in a subsequent type of analysis. In Chapter 14 we demonstrate how to use cluster analysis on a set of dependent variables and then combine its use with discriminant analysis, the topic of the next section of this chapter.

MULTIPLE DISCRIMINANT ANALYSIS

Recall from Chapter 11 that the selection of the appropriate statistical technique is based on several considerations, including the way your variables are measured. Business

---

The SPSS click-through sequence is: Analyze → Compare Means → One-Way ANOVA. Next you remove variables X_6, X_{11}, and X_{12} from the Variables box, move variables X_{22}, X_{23}, X_{24}, and X_{25} in, and leave the Cluster Membership variable in the Factor box. Click on the Options box and then on Descriptive. We use defaults for all other options so click the OK box to get the output. The results will be the same as seen in Exhibit 13-14.

---

researchers can easily find themselves confronted with a research problem that involves a nonmetric dependent variable and several metric independent variables. For example, the business researcher may wish to predict employees likely to search for another job versus those who are not likely to search, or similar nonmetric categories using relevant metric independent variables. Similarly, the researcher may wish to predict which customers are likely to purchase a particular product versus those who are unlikely to purchase, viewers versus non-viewers of a TV commercial, or satisfied versus dissatisfied employees. Discriminant analysis is a statistical procedure that can be used to predict which group an individual is likely to belong to using two or more metric independent variables.

As with factor analysis and cluster, we use an intuitive example to help you understand discriminant analysis. Recall our survey of one thousand McDonald's and Burger King customers discussed in the factor analysis section of this chapter. Burger King would like to know if their customers have different perceptions than McDonald's customers. Two of the perceptions variables measured on the survey were "fun place to go" and "food taste." The results of comparing the two customer groups could be plotted on a two-dimensional graph like that shown in Exhibit 13-15.

The scatter plot of the data from the survey shows two groups—one containing primarily Burger King customers and the other containing primarily McDonald's customers. The McDonald's plot is larger because they have more customers than Burger King. From this example, it appears that taste is more important to Burger King customers and less important to McDonald's customers. In contrast, fun place for kids is more important to McDonald's customers than Burger King customers. The two areas overlap but not by much. To have high predictive capability, there must be minimal overlap between the groups examined in a discriminant analysis. The plot indicates the customers of Burger King and McDonald's are fundamentally different in terms of what is important in selecting a restaurant. Thus, Burger King will have difficulty attracting McDonald's customers unless they become more similar to McDonald's.

Multiple discriminant analysis is the appropriate statistical technique for testing the null hypothesis that the means of the independent variables of the two or more groups are the same. The technique uses several metric independent variables to predict a single nonmetric dependent variable. The dependent variable can have two, three, four, or more categories. When you apply discriminant analysis, it examines group differences by finding a linear combination of the independent variables—the **discriminant function**—that identifies differences between the group means. Thus, discriminant analysis is a statistical tool that develops linear combinations of independent variables to predict group membership as defined by the dependent variable.

To explain the analytical approach used in discriminant analysis, we will use our survey of Burger King and McDonald's customers. The dependent variable, Z, is measured with a

| EXHIBIT 13-14 | DEMOGRAPHIC PROFILES OF TWO-CLUSTER SOLUTION |

Descriptives

Variables	Groups	N	Mean
X_{22}—Gender	1	101	.47
	2	99	.47
	Total	200	.47
X_{23}—Age	1	101	2.37
	2	99	3.30
	Total	200	2.83
X_{24}—Income	1	101	3.17
	2	99	3.80
	Total	200	3.48
X_{25}—Competitor	1	101	.80
	2	99	.19
	Total	200	.50

ANOVA

Variables	Comparison	F	Sig.
X_{22}—Gender	Between Groups	.018	.895
X_{23}—Age	Between Groups	38.034	.000
X_{24}—Income	Between Groups	13.913	.000
X_{25}—Competitor	Between Groups	117.356	.000

nominal scale (i.e., customers of Burger King versus McDonald's), and the independent variables—fun place for kids and food taste—are metric variables. The statistical objective is to predict whether an individual is a Burger King or McDonald's customer using the survey information. To do so, the researcher must find a linear combination of the independent variables that identifies statistically significant differences between the group means.

Discriminant scores (Z scores) are determined empirically by a linear function. That is, the computer analyzes the independent variables, develops a linear function, and uses it to predict in which group a survey respondent belongs. The Z score is calculated for each respondent using the following equation:

$$Z = W_1X_1 + W_2X_2 + \ldots W_nX_n$$

Where:

Z = discriminant score for each respondent
W_n = discriminant weight for the nth variable
X_n = respondent's value on the nth independent variable

Discriminant weights (W_n) are estimates of the predictive power of each independent variable. The discriminant analysis software package computes the weights so they are the optimal size for predicting the groups. Each independent variable has its own weight. The size of the weights is determined by the variance structure of the independent variables.

EXHIBIT 13-15	TWO-DIMENSIONAL DISCRIMINANT ANALYSIS PLOT OF RESTAURANT CUSTOMERS

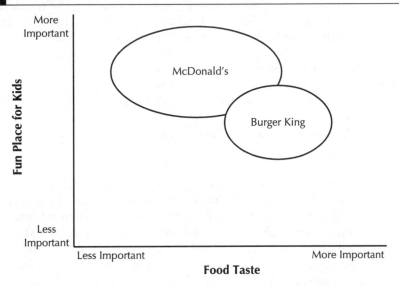

Independent variables that are good predictors are assigned larger weights. Variables that do not predict well are given small weights.

An illustration of a two-group discriminant analysis is shown in Exhibit 13-16. Assume you have two groups, A and B, and two variables, X_1 and X_2, for each respondent in the two groups. We could plot in the scatter diagram the association of variable X_1 with X_2 for each group. Group identity is shown by dots in group A and by stars in group B. The resulting ellipses enclose some specified proportion of the points for each group, such as 95 percent. If a straight line is drawn through the two points where the ellipses intersect and then projected to a new axis Z, we can say that the overlap between the univariate distributions of A′

EXHIBIT 13-16	SCATTER DIAGRAM AND PROJECTION OF TWO-GROUP DISCRIMINANT ANALYSIS

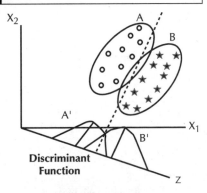

and B′ is smaller than would be obtained by any other line drawn through the ellipses representing the scatter plots. The new Z axis is the discriminant function that is a linear composite of the two independent variables.

The discriminant function in a discriminant analysis is very similar to a regression equation. Recall that a regression equation uses a weighted combination of values for selected metric independent variables to predict an object's value on a continuously scaled dependent variable (Y). With discriminant analysis, the discriminant function uses a weighted combination of the independent variable values to classify an object (typically a respondent) into one of the dependent variable groups. That is, it assigns the object a value that identifies it as being in one of the dependent variable groups. The discriminant function, therefore, is a weighted sum of values (Z) on individual independent variables.

How is the Z score used to identify group membership? The researcher must specify a cutoff score. Objects with discriminant scores larger than the cutoff score are assigned to one group, and objects with discriminant scores smaller than the cutoff score are assigned to the other dependent variable group. It there are two groups, there is only one cutoff score. But when there are three groups there must be two cutoff scores. If, for example, the cutoff score is .567, then any respondent with a Z score below that would be assigned to one group and any respondent with a Z score above would be assigned to the other group. Following the same procedure, each respondent in the analysis is classified into one dependent variable group or the other, depending upon its values on the individual independent variables and their weights.

Unless there is absolutely no overlap between the dependent variable groups, we are bound to make errors of classification. The larger the overlap, the more errors of classification are made. The concept of a cutoff score and discriminant function prediction is illustrated in Exhibit 13-17. In the top illustration (a) the discriminant function predicts good because there is very little overlap. In the bottom illustration (b) the discriminant function predicts poorly because there is a large amount of overlap. The cutoff score is in the middle and therefore the discriminant function has equal likelihood of predicting a respondent is in the wrong group. But if the cutoff score is moved to the right or left on the Z axis it changes the likelihood of predicting which group a respondent is placed in. For example, if the cutoff score is moved to the right the researcher could achieve 100 percent prediction accuracy for Group A and substantially lower prediction accuracy for Group B.

The business researcher must decide where to place the cutoff score based on the costs of misclassifying a particular respondent. If the costs of misclassification are equal, the cutoff score line is drawn in the middle. If they are unequal, then the cutoff score that results in the lowest cost of misclassification is chosen.

EXHIBIT 13-17 **DISCRIMINANT FUNCTION Z AXIS AND CUTOFF SCORES**

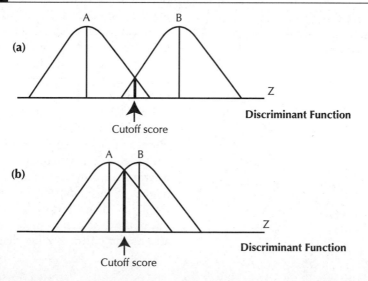

To clarify the nature of the discriminant function, let's again refer to our fast food example. But this time let's further assume that we have added a third variable—friendliness of employees. Assume the discriminant function estimates the weights are as shown in the equation below:

$$Z = W_1X_1 + W_2X_2 + W_3X_3$$
$$Z = .66X_1 + .37X_2 + .12X_3$$

The above results show that X_1—Taste is the most important variable in discriminating between customers of Burger King and McDonald's. The X_2—Atmosphere variable (fun place for kids) with a coefficient of .37 also has good predictive power. In contrast, the X_3—Friendly variable with a weight of .12 has little predictive power.

The first step in discriminant analysis is to determine if the function is statistically significant. With a large sample size, we could find a statistically significant function that does not predict well. Therefore, if we find a statistically significant function we must test it further to see if it will correctly classify objects (individuals) into groups. In our example, the objective is to correctly classify respondents into Burger King and McDonald's customer groups. The null hypothesis would be no differences in the groups and therefore no predictive power.

The results of using a discriminant function to predict group membership are displayed in a table referred to as a classification (prediction) matrix. Exhibit 13-18 is the **classification matrix** for our fast food example. It shows the estimated function correctly classified customers of Burger King 80 percent of the time and incorrectly classified them 20 percent. In contrast, the discriminant function correctly classified McDonald's customers 95 percent of the time and incorrectly classified them only 5 percent. Overall the predictive accuracy was 87.5 percent. This predictive accuracy is much higher than would be expected by chance (two groups = 50 percent).

The overall predictive accuracy of an estimated discriminant function is called the **hit ratio.** The hit ratio is the percentage of objects (respondents) correctly classified by the discriminant function. In our preceding example it was 87.5 percent, which is very high. But what is considered an acceptable or good hit ratio? Is predictive accuracy of 70 percent good? To answer this question you must determine the percentage of objects that could be correctly predicted by chance (without using a discriminant function). When you have two groups and the sample sizes are equal, the chance probability is 50 percent. Similarly, when you have three groups and the sample sizes are equal, the chance probability is 33 percent. This is because

EXHIBIT 13-18 **CLASSIFICATION MATRIX FOR BURGER KING AND MCDONALD'S CUSTOMERS**

		Predicted Group		
		Burger King	McDonald's	Total
Actual Group	**Burger King**	160 (80%)	40 (20%)	200
	McDonald's	10 (5%)	190 (95%)	200

Overall prediction accuracy (hit ratio) =
87.5% (160 + 190 = 350 / 400) N = 400

you could arbitrarily place all objects into one group without using a discriminant function and your predictive accuracy, for example, for the two-group situation is 50 percent.

When your group sample sizes are unequal the chance probability is based on the largest group. For example, if you have a sample size of one hundred with sixty objects in one group and forty in the other group, your chance probability is 60 percent. This is because you could place all objects in the group defined by the sample size of sixty and your predictive accuracy would be 60 percent.

To answer the question of what the classification accuracy should be relative to chance, we offer the following guidelines. The classification accuracy should be at least 25 percent larger than by chance. For example, if chance predictive accuracy is 50 percent we recommend 62.5 percent. Similarly, if chance predictive accuracy is 33 percent, we recommend 41.5 percent. In the final analysis, this decision must be based on the cost versus the value of the predicted information. If the costs associated with predicting at a 60 percent (chance predictive accuracy = 50 percent) are small relative to the value, then you should use discriminant analysis. If the costs are high then do not use it. For more information on this topic see Hair J., et.al., *Multivariate Data Analysis: With Readings,* 6th Edition, Prentice Hall, 2003.

Before we show you an example of discriminant analysis, several issues need to be clarified. First, we assume the sample sizes of the two or more groups are comparable in size. Second, the sample sizes of the groups should be at least five times the number of independent variables. That is, if your discriminant function has five independent variables then the smallest sample size of any single group should be twenty-five. Finally, the variance of the variables across the groups is assumed to be equal. In practice this last assumption is often violated, however, and fortunately the technique is robust and this does not create many problems.

EXAMPLE OF DISCRIMINANT ANALYSIS

Phil Samouel would like to know whether his customers perceive his restaurant differently from how Gino's customers perceive that restaurant. Discriminant analysis can be used to answer that question. The nonmetric dependent variable is X_{25}—Competitor. This variable is coded 0 = Samouel's customer interviews and 1 = Gino's customer interviews. The metric independent variables could be the twelve restaurant perceptions variables. But to simplify the research question let's look only at the three food variables (X_1, X_4, and X_9) and the three employee variables (X_6, X_{11}, and X_{12}). The null hypothesis is no differences in customer perceptions of the two restaurants on the food and employee variables.

The objective is to determine if perceptions of Samouel's customers, as measured by the six perceptions variables, are different from those of Gino's customers. That is, "Can the food and employee perceptions variables predict whether respondents are customers of a particular restaurant?" Wilks' Lambda is a statistic that evaluates whether the discriminant function has identified a statistical difference between the two or more groups. For our example the Wilks' Lambda is highly significant (.000), as shown in Exhibit 13-19. When this statistic is significant, we next look at the Classification Results information (also in Exhibit 13-19). Looking at the bottom of this table, we see that the overall predictive ability of the discriminant function is 83.0 percent. Without the discriminant function we could only predict with 50 percent accuracy (our sample sizes are Samouel's = 100 and Gino's = 100, so if we said all respondents were Samouel's we would predict with 50 percent accuracy). Therefore, this is an

---

RESEARCH IN ACTION

**USING SPSS TO EXECUTE A DISCRIMINANT
ANALYSIS USING THE CUSTOMER SURVEYS**

Using SPSS, the click-through sequence to execute a discriminant analysis is: Analyze → Classify → Discriminant. This takes you to a dialog box where you select the variables. First highlight variable X_{25} and move it to the Grouping Variable box at the top. Now click on the Define Range box just below it so you can specify the minimum and maximum numbers for the grouping variable. For our example, the minimum is 0 = Samouel's and the maximum is 1 = Gino's. Place these numbers in the box and click Continue. Next highlight and move variables X_1, X_4, X_6, X_9, X_{11}, and X_{12} into the Independents box. Now go to the Statistics box at the bottom and click on Means, univariate ANOVAS and Continue. Enter is the Method default and we will use it. Click on Classify and use the default—All Group Equal (recall that Phil interviewed one hundred of his customers and one hundred of Gino's customers). If you did not know whether your group sizes are equal then you should check the Compute from Group Sizes option. Now click on Summary Table and Continue. None of the options under Save are used so click on OK to run the discriminant analysis. The results will be the same as in Exhibits 13-19 to 13-22.

---

excellent hit ratio (predictive capability). Based on these findings we can reject the null hypothesis that the group means are the same on the food and employees variables.

You can note further the discriminant function is slightly more accurate in predicting Gino's customers (86 percent) than it is Samouel's (80 percent). The way to interpret this table is the discriminant function accurately predicted Samouel's customers 80 percent of the time and 20 percent of the time said a Samouel's customer was a Gino's customer. Similarly, 86 percent of the time the discriminant function accurately predicted a Gino's customer and 14 percent of the time it said a Gino's customer was a Samouel's customer.

Since we were able to develop a highly predictive discriminant function, we are now interested in finding out which independent variables have the most predictive power. To do this we examine the information in Exhibits 13-20 and 13-21. First, information from the exhibit labeled Tests of Equality of Group Means shows which perceptions variables are significantly

---

EXHIBIT 13-19 **DISCRIMINANT ANALYSIS OF CUSTOMER SURVEYS**

Wilks' Lambda

Test of Function(s)	Wilks' Lambda	Sig.
1	.541	.000

Classification Results*

		X_{25}—Competitor	Samouel's	Gino's	Total
			Predicted Group Membership		**Total**
Original Group	**Count**	Samouel's	80	20	100
		Gino's	14	86	100
	%	Samouel's	80.0	20.0	100.0
		Gino's	14.0	86.0	100.0

*83.0% of original grouped cases correctly classified.

EXHIBIT 13-20	TESTS OF EQUALITY OF GROUP MEANS

Variables	F	Sig.
X_1—Excellent Food Quality	10.954	.001
X_4—Excellent Food Taste	11.951	.001
X_6—Friendly Employees	119.366	.000
X_9—Wide Variety of Menu Items	.420	.518
X_{11}—Courteous Employees	54.821	.000
X_{12}—Competent Employees	105.073	.000

different on a univariate basis. We see that all of the variables except X_9—Wide Variety of Menu Items are highly statistically significant and likely to be good predictors. Variable X_9 is not significant and therefore unlikely to be a good predictor. Thus, the perceptions of the two restaurants are very different on a univariate basis, with the exception of one variable.

We now want to examine the independent variables from a multivariate perspective. To do so we can look either at the Standardized Canonical Discriminant Function Coefficients or the Structure Matrix correlations. Business researchers typically use the Structure Matrix correlations because they are considered more accurate so we will use them too (see Exhibit 13-21). We must first identify the numbers (correlations) in the Function column that are considered significant. Just as with factor analysis, the numbers represent the correlation between the individual variables and the linear combination of all the independent variables. The cutoff level is determined in a manner similar to a factor loading. All variables .30 or higher are considered to be helpful in predicting group membership.

The order of the loadings in Exhibit 13-21 is from largest to smallest (not the order they were listed in the database). Similar to the univariate results, the variable with the smallest loading (X_9) is the one that was not significant on a univariate basis. The question at this point is whether to consider variables X_1 and X_4 as significant predictors. According to our rule of thumb they are not considered helpful because they have loadings smaller than .30. But on a univariate basis they were highly significant (.001) so we may be experiencing a problem with multicollinearity. Another way to assess this would be to run a stepwise discriminant analysis to determine if they enter the equation and improve predictive accuracy. We also could run the

EXHIBIT 13-21	STRUCTURE MATRIX FOR RESTAURANT PERCEPTIONS VARIABLES

Variables*	Function
	1
X_6—Friendly Employees	.843
X_{12}—Competent Employees	.791
X_{11}—Courteous Employees	.571
X_4—Excellent Food Taste	.267
X_1—Excellent Food Quality	.255
X_9—Wide Variety of Menu Items	.050

*Variables ordered by absolute size of correlation with function

discriminant analysis without these variables and see if the predictive capability of the function is lower. What we can conclude at this point is that perceptions of employees are very important in differentiating between the two restaurants, while perceptions of food are relatively less important and menu variety is not important at all. Phil Samouel definitely must develop a plan to make improvements in the employee area of his business.

As noted earlier, the predictive outcome of the discriminant function was moderately high, with a hit ratio of 83.0 percent. Interpretation of the discriminant function is based on the group means in the Group Statistics table (see Exhibit 13-22). Using our rule of thumb for significant loadings (.30), we note that variables X_6, X_{11}, and X_{12} are all significant predictors. For all three variables the perceptions of Gino's are more favorable than they are for Samouel's (larger means indicate more favorable perceptions). This suggests that Gino's either hires much better employees or trains them better than Phil Samouel does. Thus, perceptions of employees are significantly different between the two restaurants and are good predictors of which respondents eat at a particular restaurant. But the findings suggest Phil Samouel must evaluate his employees and devise a method to improve their performance. This could be particularly good since, although Gino's is rated better on employees, the restaurant still is not rated very favorably (two of three variables are considerable below the midpoint of the scale).

One final approach to examining group differences is the **centroid**. In discriminant analysis a Z score is calculated for each respondent. The centroid is the mean of all the respondent Z scores in a particular group. A two-group discriminant analysis has two centroids and a three-group has three centroids. The centroids for our restaurant example are shown in Exhibit 13-22. Note that the Samouel's centroid is −.916 while the Gino's centroid is .916. This is an overall summary measure that indicates that Gino's is much more favorably perceived than is Samouel's.

EXHIBIT 13-22 MEANS OF INDEPENDENT VARIABLES FOR RESTAURANTS

Variables	Mean	
	Samouel's	**Gino's**
X_1—Excellent Food Quality*	5.24	5.81
X_4—Excellent Food Taste*	5.16	5.73
X_6—Friendly Employees*	2.89	4.42
X_9—Wide Variety of Menu Items	5.45	5.56
X_{11}—Courteous Employees*	1.96	2.84
X_{12}—Competent Employees*	1.62	2.75

*Significant < .05 on a univariate basis

Functions at Group Centeriods

	Function
	1
X_{25}—Competitor	
Samouel's	−.916
Gino's	.916

Canonical discriminant functions evaluated at group means

STEPWISE DISCRIMINANT ANALYSIS

As with multiple regression analysis, discriminant analysis can be applied using a stepwise approach to select significant independent variables. We can input the entire set of independent variables in the discriminant function. Then we can let the discriminant function select a smaller set of independent variables that hopefully discriminates well between the groups. The smaller set of independent variables is possible because of intercorrelations or redundancies among the independent variables. But, as in regression analysis, we must be cautious about multicollinearity. The popular statistical software programs have an option for the stepwise approach.

SUMMARY

Explain the Difference between Dependence and Interdependence Techniques

There are two broad types of multivariate statistical techniques. One type is referred to as **dependence techniques.** These techniques are used when one (or more) of the variables is identified as the dependent variable and the other variables are independent variables. Interdependence techniques are those where you analyze only one set of variables and do not identify any of them as independent or dependent. In this book we have discussed three dependence techniques—multiple regression, ANOVA, and discriminant analysis. Two interdependence techniques were covered—factor analysis and cluster analysis.

Understand How to Use Factor Analysis to Simplify Data Analysis

Factor analysis is an interdependence technique. It is most often used to summarize and reduce the independent variables. But you also can use it to simplify the dependent set of variables. Factor analysis examines the underlying correlations between the variables and finds the ones that are similar. It then combines the large set of variables using a linear approach into a smaller set of factors that have common relationships.

Demonstrate the Usefulness of Cluster Analysis

Cluster analysis also is an interdependence multivariate technique. Cluster analysis enables us to combine objects (e.g., customers, brands, products) into groups so that objects within each group are similar to one another and different from objects in all other groups. Cluster analysis combines objects so there will be high internal (within cluster) homogeneity as well as high external (between cluster) heterogeneity. That is, cluster analysis strives to identify natural groupings using several variables without designating any of the variables as a dependent variable. If it is successful, the objects within the clusters will be close together and the objects in different clusters will be far apart.

Understand When and How to Use Discriminant Analysis

Multiple discriminant analysis uses several metric independent variables to predict a single nonmetric dependent variable. The dependent variable can have two, three, four, or more categories. From a statistical perspective, this involves assessing group differences based on finding a linear combination of independent variables—the discriminant function—that identifies differences between the group means. Thus, discriminant analysis is a statistical tool for determining linear combinations of independent variables that predict group membership defined by the dependent variable.

KEY TERMS

centroid	eigenvalue	interdependence
classification matrix	error variance	techniques
common variance	Euclidean distance	latent root criterion
communality	factor analysis	nonhierarchical clustering
cluster analysis	factor	orthogonal rotation
dendogram	factor loading	oblique rotation
dependence techniques	factor rotation	profiling
discriminant analysis	hierarchical clustering	percentage of variance
discriminant function	(build-up or	criterion
discriminant scores	agglomerative)	rotated factor component
(Z scores)	hierarchical clustering	matrix
discriminant weights	(divisive)	simple structure
"easy read" matrix	hit ratio	unique variance

ETHICAL DILEMMA

A state lottery commission conducted a cluster analysis to gain a better understanding of public attitudes in the state toward the lottery and gambling. The commission planned to use the data to design marketing programs aimed at increasing support and participation in the weekly lottery drawings. The research identified five distinct clusters of citizens. Not surprisingly the largest cluster (27 percent) was opposed to the lottery and had a low understanding of the economic impact the lottery had on the state. The smallest cluster (13 percent) was made up of people who loved the lottery. This group also had the best understanding of the lottery's impact on their state. The other three groups fell somewhere in between in both attitude and knowledge—qualified support (25 percent), neutral (22 percent), and non-gamblers who see some benefit to the state (13 percent).

Before the marketing team begins designing the communications strategy for each audience, the group considers issuing a news release to announce the research findings, focusing on the fact that a majority of citizens were in favor of the lottery in hopes of making a positive impression on the state's legislature. Only one of the lottery commissioners is uncomfortable with the plan because he feels they are overstating the results. What do you think? Is the marketing team misrepresenting the data to the public?

REVIEW QUESTIONS

1. What is the difference between dependence and interdependence techniques?
2. What is factor analysis and when would the business researcher use it?
3. How does the researcher decide how many factors to retain?
4. How does cluster analysis differ from factor analysis?

5. Explain the three phases of cluster analysis.

6. Why would researchers use discriminant analysis instead of regression analysis?

DISCUSSION AND APPLICATION ACTIVITIES

1. Describe a research problem that would benefit from a factor analysis. What are the variables and what would you hope to achieve?

2. How could the researcher use cluster analysis to improve the validity of a research problem? Give an example to clarify your answer.

3. Describe a research problem that would require the use of discriminant analysis. Why would discriminant analysis be used instead of regression?

4. SPSS Application. Run a factor analysis using the twelve perceptions variables from the employee survey database. Prepare a brief report on your findings.

5. SPSS Application. Run a cluster analysis using the three organizational commitment variables (X_{13}, X_{14}, and X_{15}) from the employee survey database. Prepare a brief report on your findings.

6. SPSS Application. Run a stepwise discriminant analysis using the twelve perceptions variables from the customer survey database. Prepare a brief report on your findings.

7. SPSS Application. Run a cluster analysis using the twelve perceptions variables from the customer survey database. Develop a three-cluster solution instead of the two-cluster solutions reported in the chapter. Prepare a brief report on your findings.

INTERNET EXERCISES

1. Use the keywords *multivariate* and *multivariate data analysis* with the search engines www.google.com and www.dogpile.com. Prepare a brief report on what you found and how the searches differed.

2. Use your favorite Internet search engine. Type in the key words *factor analysis, cluster analysis,* and then *discriminant analysis.* Prepare a brief report on the similarities and differences you found. Identify one interesting site and click through to it. Include a description of what you found.

3. Go to the New Mexico State University Web site at www.psych.nmsu.edu. Look under the "Psych. Dept Links" and click on MRC w/Ren & Stimpy. Go through the tutorial and prepare a brief report of your experience.

14 Advanced Analysis and Presentation Approaches

Learning Objectives

1. Understand how to use cluster analysis with discriminant analysis.

2. Understand how to use factor analysis with regression.

3. Explain the use of summated scores instead of factor scores.

4. Clarify the visual impact of importance-performance analysis.

Introduction

In the previous chapters we have introduced you to several statistical techniques. Through their application to the restaurant employee and customer survey databases we have demonstrated their value in better understanding business problems when the techniques are used by themselves. In this chapter we first illustrate how two or more multivariate techniques can be used together to further analyze your data, and ultimately to better represent the underlying relationships. We then explain how and why researchers might want to use summated scores. Lastly, we demonstrate how **perceptual mapping** can be used to more effectively communicate your results.

Cluster Analysis and Discriminant

When business researchers use cluster analysis, one of the primary research objectives is to identify subgroups that are homogeneous. In Chapter 13 we provided an illustration of cluster analysis using the three employee independent variables from the customer survey (friendly, courteous, and competent) in which groups were identified, validated, and profiled. In this example, we demonstrate how we can use cluster analysis on a set of dependent variables.

Recall that the cluster variables must be logically and/or theoretically related. Looking at the five dependent relationship variables X_{17} to X_{21} from the customer survey (shown in Exhibit 14-1), the first three variables (X_{17}—Customer Satisfaction, X_{18}—Likelihood to Return in Future, and X_{19}—Recommend to Friend) represent satisfaction variables that are

---

EXHIBIT 14-1   RELATIONSHIP VARIABLES USED IN THE CUSTOMER SURVEY

17. How satisfied are you with
    Samouel's restaurant?

Not Satisfied **at All**						**Very** **Satisfied**
1	2	3	4	5	6	7

18. How likely are you to return to
    Samouel's restaurant in the future?

Definitely Will **Not Return**						**Definitely Will** **Return**
1	2	3	4	5	6	7

19. How likely are you to recommend
    Samouel's restaurant to a friend?

Definitely Will **Not Recommend**						**Definitely Will** **Recommend**
1	2	3	4	5	6	7

20. How often do you patronize
    Samouel's restaurant?

1 = Occasionally (Less than once a month)
2 = Frequently (1–3 times a month)
3 = Very Frequently (4 or more times a month)

21. How long have you been a
    customer of Samouel's restaurant?

1 = Less than one year
2 = One year to three years
3 = More than three years

well established in the literature. We could choose to cluster using these three variables. The question remaining, however, is how to deal with the other two relationship measures? Variables X_{20}—Frequency of Patronage and X_{21}—Length of Time a Customer are logically, but not theoretically, related to variables X_{17}–X_{19}. First, they are more behavioral measures of satisfaction as opposed to perceptions variables. Second, variables X_{20} and X_{21} are measured on a 3-point nonmetric scale instead of a 7-point metric scale. For these reasons, the cluster analysis will be based only on the three dependent variables X_{17}–X_{19}. The remaining two variables X_{20} and X_{21} will be used to validate the clusters identified with the other relationship variables.

RESEARCH QUESTION ONE: "CAN CLUSTERS BE IDENTIFIED?"

The first research question for this example is: "Can clusters be identified using the three metric dependent satisfaction variables?" If we can validate and logically profile the clusters, we will then examine whether the perceptions variables can be used to predict group membership in the newly formed clusters. The task then is to try to identify clusters of customers that have distinctly different perceptions on the satisfaction variables $(X_{17}–X_{19})$. The null hypothesis is that different clusters do not exist based on the customer survey satisfaction variables.

Phil's business consultant has recommended that the cluster analysis approach be Ward's method using squared Euclidean distances as the measurement criteria. These recommendations are based on his previous work that is similar to this research question. The next step is to decide the number of clusters to retain in the solution.

When customer perceptions are combined into a single cluster there typically is a lot of error associated with the cluster. As you separate the single cluster into two clusters, the error is reduced substantially and continues to grow smaller as more groups (clusters) are identified. The reduction in error is measured by an error coefficient. Exhibit 14-2 shows the error coefficients associated with the clustering of the dependent satisfaction variables from the customer survey. The numbers in the left column show the amount of error associated with a particular cluster solution. The numbers in the right column show how much error is reduced by going from one cluster to two clusters, from two clusters to three clusters, and so on. Note that by going from a single cluster (all two hundred observations in a single cluster) to the two-cluster solution, the error coefficient is reduced by 551.405, from 834.255 to 282.850 (834.255 − 282.850 = 551.405). When we move from a two-cluster to a three-cluster solution, the reduction is

EXHIBIT 14-2	ERROR COEFFICIENTS AND ERROR REDUCTION FOR SATISFACTION VARIABLES CLUSTER SOLUTION

Error Coefficients	Error Reduction
Four Clusters = 140.865	3–4 Clusters = 42.013
Three Clusters = 182.878	2–3 Clusters = 99.972
Two Clusters = 282.850	1–2 Clusters = 551.405
One Cluster = 834.255	

99.972 (282.850 − 182.878 = 99.972), and from three clusters to four clusters the reduction is only 42.013.

The decision now is whether to use a two-, three-, or four-cluster solution. All cluster solutions will exhibit a substantial drop in the error coefficient from one to two clusters. If there were other considerations such as previous research, theory, or business logic, then the researcher may choose to use a three- or four-cluster solution. Five- or more cluster solutions are used very seldom because they are very difficult to interpret. Indeed, four-cluster solutions are used infrequently as well. The decision most often is between a two-group and a three-group cluster solution. In our example, the reduction in error going from a three-group to a four-group solution is less than half as much as going from a two-group to a three-group solution. Because of the smaller reduction in error and the complexity of interpreting the four-group solution, Phil's business consultant has decided to consider only the two-group and three-group solutions.

When we are selecting the number of clusters to retain, in addition to looking at the reduction in error, we also look at the pattern of the means for the clusters. Specifically, we compare the means of each of the variables used in the cluster analysis across all the groups. Exhibits 14-3 and 14-4 show the means and mean plots for the two-cluster and three-cluster solutions.

Review of the means and means plots can help us to decide the number of clusters to retain. Looking at the two-cluster solution, it is clear that group 1 evaluates the restaurants substantially lower than group 2 on all three satisfaction variables. In the three-cluster solution, group 1 has not changed (N = 80) and this group again consistently evaluates the restaurants the lowest of all groups. Group 2 from the two-cluster solution (N = 120) is now split into two additional groups in the three-cluster solution. The new group 2 now has an N = 75 and the new group 3 has an N = 45 (75 + 45 = 120). In the three-cluster solution the new group 2 evaluates the restaurants highest on all three satisfaction variables and the new group 3 that is in the middle. At this point, we must decide whether to select a two-cluster or three-cluster solution. The three-cluster solution demonstrates a consistent pattern of differences among the clusters, and would appear to offer an opportunity to better understand group differences. But Phil's business consultant has recommended the two-cluster solution be examined first because of the simplicity in understanding the group differences. The consultant also believes that it will be quicker and easier to develop a business strategy to more effectively compete with Gino's.

RESEARCH IN ACTION
USING SPSS TO CLUSTER CUSTOMER SURVEY SATISFACTION VARIABLES

The objective is to identify the clusters that can be developed using variables X_{17} to X_{19}. The SPSS click-through sequence is: Analyze → Classify → Hierarchical Cluster, which leads to a dialog box where you select variables X_{17}, X_{18}, and X_{19}. After you move these variables into the Variables box, look at the other options below. Keep all the defaults that are shown on the dialog box. You also should use the defaults for the Statistics and Plots options below. Click on the Method box and select Ward's under Cluster Method (it is the last one so you must scroll down), but use the default of squared Euclidean distances under Measure. We do not do anything with the Save option at this point so we can click on OK at the top of the dialog box to execute the cluster analysis. The results will be the same as those in Exhibit 14-2.

EXHIBIT 14-3 **MEANS AND MEAN PLOTS FOR TWO-CLUSTER SOLUTION**

Variables	Groups	N	Mean
	1	80	4.14
X_{17}—Satisfaction	2	120	6.19
	Total	200	5.37
	1	80	3.83
X_{18}—Return in Future	2	120	5.72
	Total	200	4.96
	1	80	3.61
X_{19}—Recommend to Friend	2	120	5.53
	Total	200	4.76

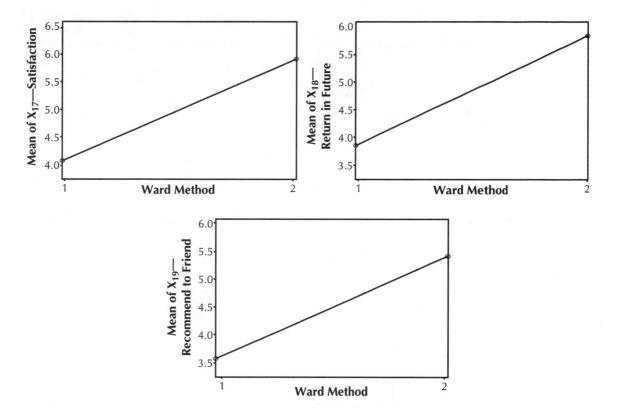

We now examine the means of the two-cluster solution to profile the differences in the groups. The means of group 2 are consistently higher across all three satisfaction variables. Indeed, all three variable means for group 2 are 5.53 or above, and this is very favorable considering we used a 7-point scale (7 = highly favorable). In contrast, the means of group 1 range from a low of 3.61 (X_{19}) to a high of 4.14 (X_{17}). Thus, while group one is not unfavorable, the satisfaction perceptions are consistently relatively less favorable than those of group 2. In addition, when the between-group differences are examined for significant differences (as shown in Exhibit 14-5), we note that for all three variables, the differences are highly significant

EXHIBIT 14-4	MEANS AND MEAN PLOTS FOR THREE-CLUSTER SOLUTION

Variables	Groups	N	Mean
	1	80	4.14
X_{17}—Satisfaction	2	75	6.53
	3	45	5.62
	Total	200	5.37
	1	80	3.83
X_{18}—Return in Future	2	75	6.20
	3	45	4.91
	Total	200	4.96
	1	80	3.61
X_{19}—Recommend to Friend	2	75	5.92
	3	45	4.89
	Total	200	4.76

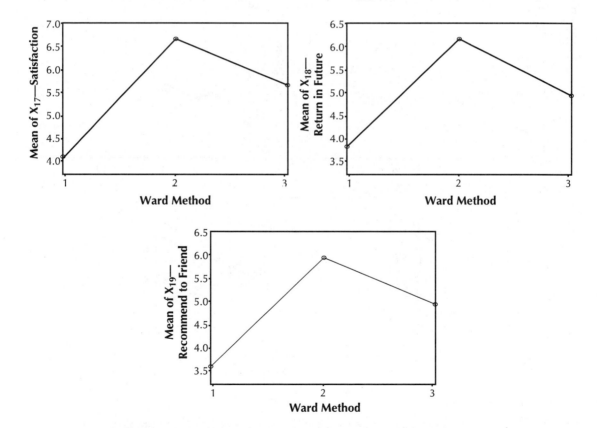

(.000). Group 2 can be identified, therefore, as the highly satisfied cluster, while group 1 is only moderately satisfied.

RESEARCH QUESTION TWO: "ARE THE CLUSTERS VALID?"

Now let's assess the predictive validity of the clusters. That is, can we compare the results of the two-group cluster with another variable to validate our cluster solution. To do this

EXHIBIT 14-5 | **ANOVA RESULTS FOR TWO-CLUSTER SOLUTION OF SATISFACTION VARIABLES**

Variables	F	Sig.
X_{17}—Satisfaction Between Groups	426.270	.000
X_{18}—Return in Future Between Groups	340.375	.000
X_{19}—Recommend to Friend Between Groups	394.646	.000

we select one or more variables that have a theoretically based relationship with the three satisfaction variables. The two variables that fit this criterion are X_{20}—Frequency of Patronage and X_{21}—Length of Time a Customer. Results in the tables in Exhibit 14-6 show the two variables are highly significantly different between the two groups. Moreover, the means for both validation variables are significantly smaller for group one than group two. It is logical that the group with the more favorable satisfaction variables (group 2) would be more frequent patrons and customers for a longer period of time. We have therefore established predictive validity for the two-group cluster solution based on the three metric dependent satisfaction variables.

RESEARCH QUESTION THREE: "DO THE PERCEPTIONS VARIABLES PREDICT THE CLUSTERS?"

Now let's turn to the third research question. Can the perceptions variables be used to predict group membership in the newly formed clusters? To examine this question we use multiple discriminant analysis. The non-metric dependent variable is the group membership variable created by the two-group cluster solution, and the metric independent variables are the perceptions variables.

Phil Samouel would like to know how and why the two clusters of customers view the restaurants differently. This knowledge will help him to prepare a better business plan to

EXHIBIT 14-6 | **VALIDATION STATISTICS FOR TWO-GROUP SATISFACTION CLUSTERS**

Descriptives

Variables	Groups	N	Mean
X_{20}—Frequency of Patronage	1	80	1.53
	2	120	2.63
	Total	200	2.19
X_{21}—How Long a Customer	1	80	1.40
	2	120	2.63
	Total	200	2.14

ANOVA

Variables		F	Sig.
X_{20}—Frequency of Patronage	Between Groups	139.289	.000
X_{21}—How Long a Customer	Between Groups	178.330	.000

RESEARCH IN ACTION

USING SPSS TO IDENTIFY CLUSTER MEMBERSHIP AND THEN COMPARE CLUSTER MEANS

Now that we have determined a two-group solution is best (based on reduction of the error coefficient), we need to profile the groups to assess their logic. We must first create a new variable that identifies group membership for the respondents in the newly formed clusters. We do this by running the cluster program again and using the Save option. Keep all the same options as before but go to the Save option, click on Single solution, and place a 2 in the box to request a new group identification variable for the two-group solution. This new variable will be created at the end of your customer dataset and its label is clu2_1.

We next must compare the means of the two clusters we have developed using the three relationship variables X_{17}–X_{19}. To do so, the SPSS click-through sequence is: ANALYZE → COMPARE MEANS → One-Way ANOVA. When you get to the dialog box, click on variables X_{17}–X_{19} to move them into the Dependent List box. Then move the newly created two-cluster identifying variable (clu2_1) into the Factor box and click Continue. For the Options click on Descriptives and Means plot and then Continue. Now click OK to run the program. The results are the same as in Exhibits 14-3 and 14-4.

compete with Gino's. Discriminant analysis can be used to answer these questions. The nonmetric dependent variable is the newly created two-cluster identification variable. That is, the variable identifies whether a respondent belongs in the moderately favorable or highly favorable group. This variable is coded 1 = group 1 (less favorable customers) and 2 = group 2 (more favorable customers). The metric independent variables could be the twelve restaurant perceptions variables. But to simplify the research question let's look only at the three food variables (X_1, X_4, and X_9) and the three employee variables (X_6, X_{11}, and X_{12}). The null hypothesis is no differences in customer perceptions of the two satisfaction clusters based on the food and employee variables.

The objective is to determine if the six perceptions variables are significantly different between the two satisfaction clusters. That is: "Can the food and employee perceptions variables predict whether respondents are members of the highly satisfied cluster versus the moderately satisfied cluster?" **Wilks' Lambda** is a statistic that evaluates whether the discriminant function has identified a statistical difference between the two or more groups. For our example the Wilks' Lambda is highly significant (.000), as shown in Exhibit 14-7. When this statistic is significant, we next look at the Classification Results information (also shown in Exhibit 14-7). Looking at the bottom of the table, we see that the overall predictive ability of the discriminant function is 79.0 percent. Without the discriminant function we could only predict with 60 percent accuracy (our sample sizes are highly satisfied group = 120 and moderately satisfied = 80, so if we said all respondents were predicted to be in the highly satisfied cluster we would predict with 60 percent accuracy; 120/200 = 60%). Therefore, 79 percent is an acceptable hit ratio (predictive capability). Based on these findings we can reject the null hypothesis that the food and employee variables cannot be used to predict cluster membership.

The information in the Structure Matrix table in Exhibit 14-8 enables us to determine which of the variables have predictive capability. The correlation between the derived discriminant function and the six independent variables is interpreted in a way similar to a factor loading. Therefore, we must agree upon the cutoff level for significant variables. In

EXHIBIT 14-7	PREDICTION OF CUSTOMER SATISFACTION CLUSTERS

Wilks' Lambda

Test of Function(s)	Wilks' Lambda	df	Sig.
1	.671	6	.000

Classification Results*

		Dependent Variables	Predicted Group Membership 1	2	Total
Original	Count	1	53	27	80
		2	15	105	120
	%	1	66.3	33.8	100.0
		2	12.5	87.5	100.0

*79% of original grouped cases correctly classified (53 + 105 = 158/200 = 79%).

general, the minimum loading would be .30, as in factor analysis. Using a criterion of .30 as the minimum, we can conclude that five of the six perceptions variables exhibit a minimum level of predictive capability for group membership in one of the two satisfaction clusters. The significant variables, in the order of their predictive capability, are X_6, X_{12}, X_1, X_4, and X_{11}.

The final task for this research question is to interpret the cluster means on the independent variables. The information in Exhibit 14-9 shows the group (cluster) means for the six perceptions variables. Recall that Group 1 was significantly less favorable than Group 2 on the satisfaction variables X_{19}, X_{20}, and X_{21}. Comparing the means for the two groups, we note that, for the independent variables that are significant predictors, in all cases the Group 1 means are lower than the Group 2 means. This suggests that favorable perceptions on these food and employee variables will lead to a higher likelihood of patronizing and being satisfied with a restaurant.

FACTOR ANALYSIS AND MULTIPLE REGRESSION

EXHIBIT 14-8	STRUCTURE MATRIX FOR TWO-CLUSTER SOLUTION

Variable	Function 1
X_6—Friendly Employees	.777
X_{12}—Competent Employees	.752
X_1—Excellent Food Quality	.510
X_4—Excellent Food Taste	.387
X_{11}—Courteous Employees	.384
X_9—Wide Variety of Menu Items	.189

Variables ordered by absolute size of correlation.

Recall from the factor analysis chapter that identifying factors can be the end of the research project. But in some instances we may want to use the results of a factor analysis with another multivariate technique, such as multiple regression. It is typical to do this when we have a large number of variables that have multicollinearity. Then we can combine the larger number of variables into a smaller set of variables that are orthogonally independent (exhibit no multicollinearity). We can demonstrate this with the example from Chapter

RESEARCH IN ACTION

USING THE SPSS DISCRIMINANT ANALYSIS SOFTWARE TO PREDICT THE SATISFACTION CLUSTERS

The task is to determine if the food and employee perceptions variables can predict the newly formed clusters based on the satisfaction variables. Another way of stating this is: "Can the six perceptions variables predict whether respondents are in the moderately favorable or highly favorable cluster?" The SPSS click-through sequence is: ANALYZE → CLASSIFY → DISCRIMINANT, which leads to a dialog box where you select the variables. The dependent, nonmetric variable is the newly created cluster variable (clu2_1). The first thing to do is move the cluster membership variable to the Grouping Variable box. Then click on the Define Range box just below it so you can enter the minimum and maximum numbers for the grouping variable. In this case the minimum is 1 = Cluster 1 and the maximum is 2 = Cluster 2, so just put these numbers in and click on Continue. Next you move the food and employee perceptions variables X_1, X_4, X_6, X_9, X_{11}, and X_{12} into the Independents box. Then click on the Statistics box at the bottom and check Means, univariate ANOVAS, and Continue. Enter is the Method default and we will use it. Now click on Classify and unclick the All Group Equal default and click on Compute from Group Sizes (we know the sample sizes are not equal so we check the Compute from Group Sizes option). You also should click Summary Table and then Continue. We do not use any options under Save so click on OK to run the program. The results should be the same as in Exhibit 14-7 to 14-9.

EXHIBIT 14-9 **GROUP MEANS FOR FOOD AND EMPLOYEE INDEPENDENT VARIABLES**

Group Statistics

Variable	Mean Group 1	Mean Group 2
X_1—Excellent Food Quality	5.01	5.87
X_4—Excellent Food Taste	5.06	5.70
X_6—Friendly Employees	2.93	4.14
X_9—Wide Variety of Menu Items	5.31	5.63
X_{11}—Courteous Employees	2.10	2.60
X_{12}—Competent Employees	1.64	2.55

13 where we combined the twelve perceptions variables into four factors—Food, Employees, Atmosphere, and Value. The factor matrix from Chapter 13 is shown in Exhibit 14-10.

If we do not use factor analysis, then we must examine customer perceptions using twelve separate characteristics. But if we use factor analysis we only have to consider four characteristics (factors). Moreover, we will eliminate the problem of multicollinearity. To use the four factors in a multiple regression, we first must calculate **factor scores.** Recall that factor scores are composite scores calculated for each respondent on each of the derived factors. The information in Exhibit 14-11 shows you what factor scores look like for the first five respondents in the customer survey. For each respondent, the original data from the twelve perceptions variables is replaced by four factor scores. The "Research in Action" box tells you how to use SPSS to calculate factor scores.

USING FACTOR SCORES IN A REGRESSION ANALYSIS

We can now use multiple regression analysis to determine if perceptions of the restaurants, as measured by the four factors, are related to satisfaction. In this example we want to compare the predictive capability of Samouel's and Gino's restaurants separately. Our single dependent metric variable is X_{17}—Satisfaction, and the independent variables are the factor scores

EXHIBIT 14-10 ROTATED FACTOR SOLUTION FOR TWELVE PERCEPTIONS VARIABLES ON THE CUSTOMER SURVEY

Variables	Components (Factors)			
	1	2	3	4
X_4—Excellent Food Taste	.912			
X_9—Wide Variety of Menu Items	.901			
X_1—Excellent Food Quality	.883			
X_6—Friendly Employees		.892		
X_{11}—Courteous Employees		.850		
X_{12}—Competent Employees		.800		
X_8—Fun Place to Go			.869	
X_2—Attractive Interior			.854	
X_7—Appears Clean and Neat			.751	
X_3—Generous Portions				.896
X_5—Good Value for Money				.775
X_{10}—Reasonable Prices				.754

Extraction Method: Principal Component Analysis.   Rotation Method: Varimax.

Total Variance Explained

Component	Rotation Sums of Squared Loadings		
	Total	% of Variance	Cumulative %
1	2.543	21.188	21.188
2	2.251	18.758	39.946
3	2.100	17.498	57.444
4	2.060	17.170	74.614

EXHIBIT 14-11 FACTOR SCORES FOR FIVE RESPONDENTS IN CUSTOMER SURVEY

Factors

Respondents	1	2	3	4
1	−.89212	1.24493	.84853	−.38169
2	−2.33246	−1.01861	.21274	.65610
3	−.55517	−1.14659	−.90178	−.91886
4	−.22994	−1.91237	.23862	−.20539
5	−.03014	.19599	1.30175	−.53036

RESEARCH IN ACTION
USING SPSS TO CALCULATE FACTOR SCORES

The SPSS program will calculate factor scores for us. For this analysis, we use all two hundred respondents and do not split the sample. This is because we are looking for common patterns across all of the restaurant customers. The SPSS click-through sequence is: Analyze → Data Reduction → Factor, which leads to a dialog box where you select variables X_1–X_{12}. After you move these variables into the Variables box, look at the alternatives below. Click first on the Descriptives box and then on the Univariate descriptives box. Unclick the Initial solution box because we will not examine it, and then click Continue. Next click on the Extraction box. We will use the default method of Principal components and the Extract default of Eigenvalues over 1, but you unclick the unrotated factor solution under Display and then click on Continue. Next go to the Rotation box where the default is None. Since we will rotate the initial factor solution, you click on Varimax as your rotational choice (this removes the default of None) and then Continue. Finally, go to the Options box and click on Sorted by size, and then change the Suppress absolute values less than from .10 to .3, and click on Continue. The last two choices make the output easier to read because we eliminate information we will not use. Looking at the bottom of the dialog box you see the Scores box which we did not use before. Click on this box and then click Save as Variables. When you do this there will be more options but just use the default—Regression. Now click Continue and then OK and you will calculate the factor scores. The result will be four factor scores for each of the two hundred respondents (each respondent has a score for each of the four factors). They will appear at the far right end of your original database and will be labeled fac1_1 (scores for factor 1), fac2_1 (scores for factor 2), and so on. An example of factor scores for the first five respondents in the customer database is shown in Exhibit 14-11.

---

for the four factors. We will therefore run two separate multiple regression models—one for Samouel's and another for Gino's.

The information in Exhibit 14-12 shows the descriptive statistics for the two multiple regression models. First note the satisfaction means of 4.78 and 5.96 for Samouel's and Gino's, respectively. Next, the factor score means for the four factors are shown beside each of the factors for each of the restaurants. As you can see, they are all smaller than 1 because factor scores are scaled to have a mean of zero and a standard deviation of 1.0.

EXHIBIT 14-12 **DESCRIPTIVE STATISTICS FOR MULTIPLE REGRESSION USING FACTOR SCORES**

X_{25}—Competitor	Variables	Mean	N
Samouel's	X_{17}—Satisfaction	4.78	100
	Food Factor	−.153	100
	Employees Factor	−.626	100
	Atmosphere Factor	.262	100
	Value Factor	−.076	100
Gino's	X_{17}—Satisfaction	5.96	100
	Food Factor	.153	100
	Employees Factor	.626	100
	Atmosphere Factor	−.262	100
	Value Factor	.076	100

Means displayed to 3 significant digits.

RESEARCH IN ACTION

USING SPSS WITH FACTOR SCORES IN A MULTIPLE REGRESSION ANALYSIS

To compare Samouel's customers' perceptions to those of Gino's, go to the Data pull-down menu to split the sample. Scroll down and click on Split File, then on Compare Groups. Highlight variable X_{25} and move it into the box labeled "Groups based on:" and then click OK.

Now you can run the regression models and compare the two restaurants. The SPSS click through sequence is: ANALYZE → REGRESSION → LINEAR. Highlight X_{17} and move it to the Dependent variables box. Highlight the newly created factor scores and move them to the Independent variables box. Use the default Enter in the Methods box. Click on the Statistics button and use the defaults for Estimates and Model Fit. Next click on Descriptives and then Continue. There are several other options you could select at the bottom of the dialog box but for now we will use the program defaults. Click on OK to run the regression. The results are the same as shown in Exhibits 14-12 to 14-14.

Looking next at the Model Summary table in Exhibit 14-13, we see the R-Square is .365 for Samouel's and .300 for Gino's. Both of these R-squares are statistically significant at a level of .000, as shown in the ANOVA table of Exhibit 14-13. This means that 36.5 percent of the variation in satisfaction for Samouel's restaurant can be explained from the four independent variables—the factor scores. Similarly, 30.0 percent of the variation in satisfaction for Samouel's restaurant can be explained from the four independent variables—the factor scores.

We examine the standardized coefficients (Betas) in Exhibit 14-14 to determine which of the factor score variables are significant predictors of satisfaction. First, the results reveal that Factor One—Food and Factor Two—Employees are significant predictors of satisfaction for both Samouel's and Gino's. The results show a positive beta coefficient, meaning a positive relationship, and a significant t-test result for each variable for each restaurant. Thus, the regression models suggest that food and employee perceptions are both strong predictors of

---

EXHIBIT 14-13 **MULTIPLE REGRESSION USING FACTOR SCORES**

Model Summary

X_{25}—Competitor	Model	R	R Square	Adjusted R Square	Std. Error of the Estimate
Samouel's	1	.604	.365	.338	.944
Gino's	1	.548	.300	.270	.832

ANOVA

X_{25}—Competitor	Model		Sum of Squares	df	Mean Square	F	Sig.
Samouel's	1	Regression	48.583	4	12.146	13.643	.000
		Residual	84.577	95	.890		
		Total	133.160	99			
Gino's	1	Regression	28.130	4	7.032	10.167	.000
		Residual	65.710	95	.692		
		Total	93.840	99			

Predictors: (Constant), Food Factor, Employees Factor, Atmosphere Factor, Value Factor

EXHIBIT 14-14	REGRESSION COEFFICIENTS FOR REGRESSION MODELS

X_{25}—Competitor	Model		Standardized Coefficients Beta	t	Sig.
Samouel's	1	(Constant)	39.221	.000	
		Food Factor	.433	5.155	.000
		Employees Factor	.319	3.736	.000
		Atmosphere Factor	.137	1.564	.121
		Value Factor	.162	1.951	.054
Gino's	1	(Constant)		45.521	.000
		Food Factor	.421	4.673	.000
		Employees Factor	.480	5.305	.000
		Atmosphere Factor	.028	.318	.752
		Value Factor	.091	1.052	.296

Dependent Variable: X_{17}—Satisfaction

satisfaction, with food being slightly better than employees for Samouel's ($\beta = .433$ versus $\beta = .319$, respectively) and employees being slightly better than food for Gino's ($\beta = .480$ versus $\beta = .421$, respectively). This conclusion is based on the relative magnitude of the beta for each of the factors. In contrast, factors three and four are not significant predictors (using a β of .05), although value for Samouel's is very close to significance (sig. = .054) and certainly should be considered by Phil in preparing his business plan.

In this section of the chapter we demonstrated how you can use one multivariate technique—factor analysis—with another technique—regression—to better understand your data. It is also possible, however, to use other multivariate techniques in combination. For example, we also used cluster with discriminant analysis in the first example of this chapter. In the next section we show you how to calculate summated scores and use them in further statistical analysis.

SUMMATED SCORES

In the previous section we demonstrated how to use factor scores in a regression analysis. Factor scores are helpful because they eliminate multicollinearity from the independent variables. But one problem in using them is that instead of being scaled like the original variables, they are standardized with a mean of zero and a standard deviation of one (see Exhibit 14-12). This makes it more difficult to compare groups and understand their differences.

To overcome this problem, the researcher can calculate summated scores to represent the factor analysis constructs. For example, in the previous section we developed four factors from the twelve perceptions variables on the customer survey. Each factor was made up of three variables. Instead of using factor scores to represent the four factors we can calculate summated scores in which the means will be on the same 7-point scale as the original variables.

To calculate summated scores, we simply take the original scaled responses and add them together and calculate the mean. Recall that the factor solution for the twelve perceptions variables on the customer survey identified four factors—food, employees, atmosphere, and value. The food factor consisted of variables X_1, X_4, and X_9. To calculate

RESEARCH IN ACTION
USING SPSS TO CALCULATE SUMMATED SCORES

The SPSS program will calculate summated scores for you. For this analysis, we use all two hundred respondents. Go to the SPSS data editor and look for the Transform pull-down menu. The SPSS click-through sequence is: Transform → Compute which leads to a Compute Variable screen. In the Target Variable dialog box, type in a label for the new variable (summated score) you wish to create. In this case we will be calculating the summated score for the food factor, so let's call the new variable *food_s* for food summated. Next go to the Numeric Expression box by clicking in it. Now click on the parentheses sign () below to place it in the Numeric Expression box. Now move variables X_1, X_4, and X_9 inside the parentheses sign and place a plus sign between each one as follows: ($X_1 + X_4 + X_9$). The plus sign is placed there by clicking on it below the Numeric Expression box. Now place the divide by sign (/) outside the parentheses and a 3 to calculate the mean of the three variables in the parentheses. Click OK and a new summated score variable will be created at the right end of your data set. The numbers will be the same as those in Exhibit 14-17. The same process is followed for all four factors to create summated scores.

EXHIBIT 14-15 **RAW DATA FOR TWELVE PERCEPTIONS VARIABLES ON CUSTOMER SURVEY**

Perceptions Variables

ID	X_1	X_2	X_3	X_4	X_5	X_6	X_7	X_8	X_9	X_{10}	X_{11}	X_{12}
1	6	4	1	6	4	4	4	3	6	3	3	2
2	6	5	3	4	4	6	5	4	4	4	4	3
3	7	4	4	7	6	4	4	3	7	4	3	4
4	3	4	5	3	3	2	5	4	3	5	2	1
5	5	4	5	5	5	5	3	3	5	4	3	2

a respondent's summated score for this factor, you would add the three variable responses together and calculate a mean. For example, the raw data for the first five respondents in the customer survey is shown in Exhibit 14-15. To calculate the summated score for respondent 1 it would be 6 + 6 + 6/3 = 6, and for respondent 2 it would be 6 + 4 + 6/3 = 5.33. The employee factor consisted of variables X_6, X_{11}, and X_{12}. To calculate the summated score for the employee factor with respondent 1 you would again add the three variable responses together and divide by three (4 + 3 + 2/3 = 3), and for respondent 2 it would be 4 + 4 + 3/3 = 3.67. This same process would be completed for all respondents on the four factors.

The calculation of summated scores for each respondent on each factor will give you four new variables. These variables will look as shown in Exhibit 14-16 for the first five respondents in the customer survey. The numbers under *food_s* are the summated scores for respondents 1–5 on factor one, and under *employ_s* are the summated scores for factor two, and under *atmos_s* for factor three, and under *value_s* for factor four. There are four new variables for each of the two hundred respondents in the customer survey. These new variables can be used in a follow-up analysis as metric independent

EXHIBIT 14-16	SUMMATED SCORES FOR FIVE CUSTOMER SURVEY RESPONDENTS

Respondent New Summated Scores Variables

ID	food_s	employ_s	atmos_s	value_s
1	6.00	3.00	3.67	2.67
2	5.33	3.67	4.67	3.67
3	7.00	3.67	3.67	4.67
4	3.00	1.67	4.33	4.33
5	5.00	3.33	3.33	4.67

variables to represent the four factors. Calculating summated scores can be a long and tedious process. The "Research in Action" box tells you how to use SPSS to calculate summated scores.

USING SUMMATED SCORES IN A MULTIPLE DISCRIMINANT ANALYSIS

Phil is interested in finding out if the summated scores for the factors can be used to predict the two satisfaction clusters identified in the cluster analysis earlier in this chapter. He believes this would be an effective way to simplify his understanding of the customer survey data. His consultant says he can use discriminant analysis with the dependent non-metric variable being the two clusters and the independent metric variables being the summated scores for the factors. The assessment of the discriminant function is reported in Exhibit 14-17. It is highly significant (.000) and the hit ratio is 79 percent. Thus, the summated scores can predict the satisfaction clusters.

Now let's find out which summated score factors are good predictors. This is reported in Exhibit 14-18. Note that three variables are significant predictors (loadings >.30). The employee, food, and value variables are all significant predictors. Moreover, by looking in

EXHIBIT 14-17	DISCRIMINANT ANALYSIS WITH SUMMATED SCORES

Test of Function(s)	Wilks' Lambda	Sig.
1	.716	.000

Classification Results

			Predicted Group Membership		
		Ward Method	1	2	Total
Original	Count	1	54	26	80
		2	16	104	120
	%	1	67.5	32.5	100.0
		2	13.3	86.7	100.0

*79.0% of original grouped cases correctly classified.

EXHIBIT 14-18	**SIGNIFICANT PREDICTORS IN DISCRIMINANT FUNCTION**

	Function
Variables	**1**
Employees Summated	.854
Food Summated	.444
Value Summated	.438
Atmosphere Summated	−.022

Correlations between discriminating variables and the discriminant function. Variables ordered by absolute size of correlation within function.

Exhibit 14-19 we see that for these three variables the means are all higher in the highly satisfied cluster. Thus, by improving perceptions on employees, food, and value Phil can be assured that his restaurant customers will be more highly satisfied and more likely to return in the future, as well as to recommend his restaurant to a friend.

In Exhibit 14-18 we have used summated scores with multiple discriminant analysis. It should be noted, however, that summated scores can be used as composite variables with almost any statistical technique. For example, the summated scores could be the metric independent variables in a multiple regression analysis. Summated scores are very useful to improve interpretation of research findings, but they do not eliminate multicollinearity, as does factor analysis.

PERCEPTUAL MAPPING

Perceptual mapping is a process that is used to develop maps that show the perceptions of respondents. The maps are visual representations of respondent's perceptions of a company, product, service, brand, or any other object in two dimensions. A perceptual map typically has vertical and horizontal axes that are labeled with descriptive adjectives. An excellent example of perceptual mapping of data is importance-performance analysis. We illustrate this approach in the following pages.

EXHIBIT 14-19	**CLUSTER MEANS FOR SUMMATED SCORE VARIABLES**

	Means	
	Cluster 1	**Cluster 2**
Variables	**Moderately Satisfied**	**Highly Satisfied**
Food Summated	5.1292	5.7333
Employees Summated	2.2200	3.0972
Atmosphere Summated	4.0792	4.0556
Value Summated	3.7375	4.3250

IMPORTANCE-PERFORMANCE CHARTS

One of the most widely used perceptual mapping procedure is referred to as an **importance-performance chart.** These charts have a vertical and horizontal axis and plot the values for these measures. The vertical axis plots the importance measures and the horizontal axis plots the performance measures. The quadrants (four squares divided by vertical and horizontal axes) are labeled as follows: top right quadrant = keep up the good work; top left quadrant = needs immediate attention; bottom right quadrant = overkill (too many resources allocated here); and the bottom left quadrant = no need for concern. Importance-performance charts are easy to interpret and can be very useful in developing action plans.

We can use our restaurant customer survey database to illustrate an importance-performance chart. The median values for the restaurant selection factors (X_{13}–X_{16}) shown in Exhibit 14-20 can be used to plot the importance rankings. For the performance measures we have chosen X_1—Excellent Food Quality, X_8—Fun Place to Go, X_{10}—Reasonable Prices, and X_{12}—Competent Employees. The means for these variables are shown in Exhibit 14-21. We plot the median rankings of the restaurant selection factors on the vertical axis and the means of the four perceptions variables on the horizontal axis. The plot is shown in Exhibit 14-22.

Exhibit 14-22 illustrates how to plot business research findings to facilitate interpretation. Note that Samouel's customers rank food quality highest (median = 4) and they also rate this as the highest performance characteristic (5.24). This spot is indicated by the symbol found at the point where 4 on the vertical axis intersects 5.24 on the horizontal axis. Gino's customers also rank food quality as most important. However, Gino's performs better than Samouel's on the food quality rating, as shown by the symbol for Gino's at the intersection of 4 and 5.81 on the vertical and horizontal axes, respectively. Gino's superior performance is noted by its positioning further to the right.

EXHIBIT 14-20 **RANKINGS OF RESTAURANT FACTORS**

X_{25}— Competitor			X_{13}— Food Quality Ranking	X_{14}— Atmosphere Ranking	X_{15}— Prices Ranking	X_{16}— Employees Ranking
Samouel's	N	Valid	100	100	100	100
		Missing	0	0	0	0
	Median		4.00	3.00	1.00	2.00
	Mode*		4	3	1	1
	Minimum		2	2	1	1
	Maximum		4	4	3	4
Gino's	N	Valid	100	100	100	100
		Missing	0	0	0	0
	Median		4.00	3.00	1.00	2.00
	Mode*		4	3	1	2
	Minimum		2	2	1	1
	Maximum		4	4	2	3

*Multiple modes exist. The smallest value is shown

In contrast, if we look at atmosphere, the selection factor ranked second in importance for both restaurants (with a 3), Samouel's (rating = 3.65) is performing better than Gino's (rating = 3.12), as shown by the Samouel's symbol being further to the right on the chart. By plotting the remaining importance and performance ratings for each restaurant, the other restaurant selection factors can be interpreted similarly. Gino's is

---

EXHIBIT 14-21 **MEANS OF SELECTED PERCEPTIONS VARIABLES ON CUSTOMER SURVEY**

X_{25}—Competitor			X_1—Excellent Food Quality	X_8—Fun Place to Go	X_{10}—Reasonable Prices	X_{12}—Competent Employees
Samouel's	N	Valid	100	100	100	100
		Missing	0	0	0	0
	Mean		5.24	3.65	4.14	1.62
	Minimum		3	1	2	1
	Maximum		7	6	6	3
Gino's	N	Valid	100	100	100	100
		Missing	0	0	0	0
	Mean		5.81	3.12	3.97	2.75
	Minimum		3	1	2	1
	Maximum		7	5	6	5

EXHIBIT 14-22 **ILLUSTRATION OF IMPORTANCE-PERFORMANCE CHART USING RESTAURANT CUSTOMER SURVEY DATABASE**

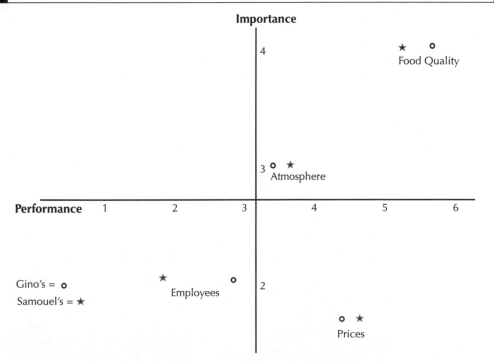

performing better on the employee rating and Samouel's is performing better on the price/value rating. Often times, a graphical portrayal like this is more easily interpreted by managers than are statistical printouts or tables containing only numbers. Managers can understand quickly their relative positioning by understanding the location of the symbols. Many spreadsheets and statistical packages facilitate the actual drawing of these charts by providing easy-to-use plotting features.

This is not the only way to prepare a perceptual map. There are many others. For example, factor analysis is used commonly. Factor scores, like the ones described before, are plotted along the dimensions representing the derived factors. Further, other statistical techniques, such as multidimensional scaling, can be used to develop perceptual maps. Detailed treatment of these techniques is beyond the scope of this basic business research text. However, the reader is encouraged to explore the statistical packages such as SPSS or SAS for more information about these procedures, as well as pursuing more information in some of the other sources cited earlier.

SUMMARY

Understand How to Use Cluster Analysis with Discriminant Analysis

Cluster analysis can be used with discriminant analysis to improve the business researcher's understanding of the data. Cluster analysis can be used to identify sub-groups of either the independent or dependent variables. It is most appropriate when the researcher does not know which respondents should be placed in a particular group and would otherwise have to use an arbitrary measure like the mean or median. For example, in developing the satisfaction dependent variable in this chapter we could have formed two satisfaction groups by placing all respondents with a mean score above 3.5 (middle of the 7-point scale) in one group and all those with a mean score below 3.5 in the other group. Cluster analysis enabled us to do that using a more objective approach. Then we were able to use discriminant analysis to predict group membership in the satisfaction clusters.

Understand How to Use Factor Analysis with Regression

Factor analysis was used to reduce the twelve customer perceptions variables to four new factor variables. Factor scores were calculated for each respondent on each of the four factors. The factor scores were then used to predict the single satisfaction variable X_{17}. This process enabled us to have a simpler regression model where there was no multicollinearity among the metric independent variables.

Explain the Use of Summated Scores Instead of Factor Scores

Factor scores are helpful because they eliminate multicollinearity from the independent variables. But one problem in using them is that instead of being scaled like the original variables, they are standardized with a mean of zero and a standard deviation of one. This makes it more difficult to compare groups and understand their differences. To overcome this problem, the researcher can calculate summated scores to represent the factor analysis constructs. These new variables can be used in a follow-up analysis as metric independent variables to represent the four factors.

Understand Perceptual Mapping

Perceptual mapping or maps can be produced from data generated in statistical analysis. The maps provide a visual representation of how companies, products, brands, or other objects are perceived relative to each other on key attributes such as quality of service, food taste, food preparation, etc. One of the most useful perceptual maps, importance-performance analysis, was illustrated in the chapter.

KEY TERMS

factor scores

importance-performance
    chart

perceptual mapping

summated scores

Wilks' lambda (λ)

ETHICAL DILEMMA

Monarch is a growing consumer products company with national sales. The company has a long-term relationship with The Data Group, a marketing research firm whose growth has been largely tied to Monarch's. When Barbara Newcomb is hired as Monarch's new president to help the company achieve the next level in growth, she schedules a meeting with Steve Harris, the president of The Data Group, to discuss increasing the level of sophistication of the marketing research being done for the company. During the meeting, Barbara specifically requests that The Data Group perform factor analysis for use in future analysis and multidimensional scaling to help her understand the differences in the actual versus perceived attributes of Monarch's products. Steve is comfortable that his firm is capable of handling the request for factor analysis but knows this is the first time a client has asked for MDS and that he will need to purchase new software and train his employees in order to meet her request. Monarch is the firm's largest client and he doesn't want to risk losing the business by disappointing their new president. What should Steve do?

REVIEW QUESTIONS

1. How can cluster analysis be used with dependent variables?
2. What criteria are used to determine the number of clusters to retain?
3. What are factor scores?
4. Why do we use factor scores in subsequent analysis?
5. What are summated scores?
6. Why do we use summated scores?
7. What is perceptual mapping?
8. What is importance-performance analysis?

DISCUSSION AND APPLICATION ACTIVITIES

1. Describe a research problem that could be better understood if two or more multivariate techniques were used to analyze the data. Which techniques would be used and why?

2. Why might the business researcher decide to use summated ratings instead of factor scores?

3. **SPSS Application.** Run a factor analysis using the twelve perceptions variables from the employee survey database. Calculate both factor scores and summated scores representing the factors. Prepare a brief report summarizing how the factor scores and summated scores differ.

4. **SPSS Application.** Run a cluster analysis using the three organizational commitment variables (X_{13}, X_{14}, and X_{15}) from the employee survey database. Select the three-cluster solution for the nonmetric dependent variable and the summated scores for the four factor solution as the metric independent variables in a discriminant analysis. Prepare a brief report on how you used cluster analysis, factor analysis, summated scores, and discriminant analysis together to better understand your research problem.

INTERNET EXERCISES

1. Go to the Data and Story Library Web site at http://lib.stat.cmu.edu/DASL. Familiarize yourself with the site by clicking first on "datafiles" and then on "stories." Now click on "Power Search" and type in the keyword *multivariate*. Browse through the topics and find two or three you think are interesting. Prepare a brief report on what you found.

2. Go to the Web site for BRINT at www.brint.com. Type statistics in the search dialog box at the bottom left side of the screen and click Go. Now click on Science:Math:Statistics on the left side of the screen under Related Topics and on the next screen under Related Topics click Education. Scroll through the Web pages listed. Find three links that sound interesting and browse them. Prepare a brief report on what you think of the BRINT portal and what you found on the links you visited.

Glossary

A

alternative hypothesis a statement that represents the opposite of the null hypothesis

ANOVA stands for analysis of variance; tests whether the means of two or more groups are statistically different on a single metric dependent variable

applied business research research motivated by an attempt to solve a particular problem faced by a particular organization

ATOCS an acronym standing for five characteristics of successful innovations (advantageous, trialability, observable, consistent, simplicity)

audience the individuals that are targeted with the message when written and oral presentations are prepared

B

balanced scale a scale in which the number of favorable and unfavorable response categories is equal

bar chart a chart that shows data in the form of bars that can be displayed either vertically or horizontally

basic business research research that is motivated by a desire to better understand some business-related phenomena as it applies to all of an industry or all of business in general

between-subjects design an experimental design in which each subject receives only one level of each experimental treatment (one combination with multiple experimental variables)

bivariate regression a type of regression that has a single metric dependent variable and a single metric independent variable

bivariate test a statistical test of significance using two variables

box and whiskers plot a visual display of the distribution's location, spread, shape, tail length, and outliers

branching question a question used to direct respondents to answer the right questions and to answer questions in the proper sequence

business ethics a field of study addressing the application of moral principles and/or ethical standards to human actions within the exchange process

business research process a basic three-phase roadmap providing directions for conducting a research project; it includes formulation, execution, and analytical phases

business research a truth-seeking function that gathers, analyzes, interprets, and reports information so that business decision makers become more effective

C

CAB process Creative–Analytical–Business decision-making process

categorical scale a nominally measured opinion scale that has two or more response categories

causal relationship a change in one event brings about a corresponding change in another event

causal research research that tests whether one event causes another

census contacts and collects information from all the elements in the population

central tendency measures the mean, median, and mode; they are measures used to describe the distribution of data

centroid the mean of all the respondent Z-scores in a particular group

Chi-square a statistical test used to assess differences between groups using nominal or ordinal data

classification (prediction) matrix a table that displays predicted group membership results from the discriminant analysis results

classification question a question placed at the end of a questionnaire to collect data, usually demographic data, to be used in classifying individuals for use in data analysis and profiling

close-ended question the respondent is given the option of choosing from a number of predetermined answers to a question

cluster analysis a multivariate statistical approach that combines objects (e.g., individuals, brands, stores) into groups so that objects within each of the groups are similar to each other and different from objects in all other groups

cluster sampling drawing a sample from randomly selected clusters or subpopulations of the target population; in stratified sampling all strata are sampled, but in cluster sampling individual clusters where sampling occurs are chosen randomly and not all clusters are sampled

coding assigning a number to a particular response so the answer can be entered into a database

coefficient of determination the square of the correlation coefficient; measures the amount of variation in one variable explained or accounted for by one or more other variables

coercion the use of forcing respondent participation by making the implications of nonparticipation unreasonable

common variance the portion of the total variance of a variable that is shared with all the other variables in the analysis; the portion of the variance that covaries among all the variables

communality represents the amount of variance in a single variable that is explained by the factors extracted in a factor analysis; can be found by summing the squared factor loadings across all extracted factors for the variable (across the row of the factor pattern)

computer dialogue a method of answering questions online through the use of a personal computer

concept a generic idea formed in an individual's mind, also referred to as a construct

concurrent validity scores on two simultaneous variables (scales) are examined to see if they are highly correlated

conjoint analysis a technique that enables researchers to determine the preferences individuals have for various products and services, and which product features are valued the most

constant sum scale asks a respondent to divide a constant sum over several categories to indicate, for example, the relative importance of the attributes

construct validity a type of validity that is assessed using either convergent validity methods to see if two scales are positively related or discriminant validity methods to see if two scales are negatively related

content analysis a method of obtaining data by observing and analyzing the content or message of written text

content validity a systematic but subjective assessment of a scale's ability to measure what it is supposed to measure, also referred to as face validity

context effect *see* position bias

convenience sampling selecting sample elements that are most readily available to participate in the study and who can provide the information required

correlation coefficient used to assess covariation between two or more variables

correlation examines the association between two metric variables;. the strength of the association is measured by the correlation coefficient

covariation when one variable consistently and systematically changes relative to another variable

creativity barriers natural behavioral and cognitive tendencies that make creativity challenging (such as group think, emotional inhibition, and expediency)

crisis management a decision-making situation occurs with little

notice and great potential for negative implications

criterion validity examines whether a scale (construct) performs as expected relative to other meaningful variables

cross-sectional studies a descriptive study providing a description of a sample at a given point in time

cross-tabulation a frequency distribution of responses on two or more variables

D

data editing inspecting data for completeness and consistency

data entry entering data into a database

data mining electronic application of mathematical algorithms that search through data warehouses looking for relationships among variables that may allow better decisions to be made

data preparation examining data for validity and correcting problems if possible

data transformation the process of changing the original form of data to a new form

data warehouse electronic inventory of organizational knowledge

data recorded information that intends to represent facts

debriefing a discussion taking place after an experimental session that involves revealing the true purpose of the experiment, the sponsor of the experiment, and, generally, a question and answer session

Decision Support System (DSS) software that allows a manager to interact with the MIS to examine potential outcomes related to common decisions

demand effect the degree to which an experimental task allows a subject to determine or guess a research hypothesis

dendogram a tree-graph that shows the history of how the grouping proceeded in a hierarchical cluster analysis

dependence techniques statistical tools in which variables are divided into independent and dependent sets and analyzed together to test dependence

dependent variable a measurement that depends upon, or is determined by, other study variables (independent variables)

depth interview a one-to-one discussion session between a trained interviewer and a respondent in which the respondent can usually provide unique insights on a specific topic

descriptive research research that describes something by measuring characteristics of events, objects, people or activities

descriptive theory seeks to describe the way things really are

discriminant analysis a statistical procedure that can be used to predict which group an individual is likely to belong to using two or more metric independent variables

discriminant function a linear combination of independent variables used to predict group membership; its form is $Z = W_1X_1 + W_2X_2 + ... W_nX_n$

discriminant scores (Z-scores) values calculated by inserting the appropriate values for an observation into the discriminant function and used to assign an observation to a group

discriminant weights estimates of the predictive power of each independent variable

dispersion measures describes the tendency for sample responses to depart from central tendency

disproportionately stratified sampling each strata in the sample has a sample size that is not proportionate to the size of that strata relative to the overall sample size; the sample size of the individual strata is based on some other criteria, such as the importance of a particular strata to the research findings

double-barreled question a question that includes two or more issues and makes interpretation difficult and often impossible

dummy tables tables that are used in a research proposal to show hypothetical research results of the same type that will result from the proposed study

dummy variable a variable that has two or more distinct levels that are coded 0 and 1; dummy-coded variables enable us to use independent variables not measured using interval or ratio scales to predict the dependent variable

E

"easy read" matrix a factor matrix that displays only factor loadings that reach some pre-specified minimum size, usually at least .30 or larger

eigenvalue represents the amount of variance in a data set that is represented by a single factor; it can be found by summing the squared factor loadings for a factor

electronic survey a self-completion survey approach in which data is collected via email, computer diskette, or the Internet

elements the individuals or objects being contacted in a sample

empirical test the evaluation of an idea by gathering and analyzing data

error variance the portion of the variance that is the result of a measurement or data collection error

ethical dilemmas situations in which a person is faced with a course of actions that have differing ethical implications

ethics checklist a list of questions that can be useful in guiding ethical decision making

ethnographic research a method of research involving observation of actual life experiences

Euclidean distance a commonly used measure representing the distances between objects in a cluster analysis

evaluative criteria characteristics used to judge the merits of different alternatives

executive summary a stand-alone, very brief overview of the entire research report that clearly emphasizes the most important findings

experiment a causal design in which a researcher controls a potential cause (experimental variable) and observes any corresponding change in hypothesized effects

expert system a component of the DSS that automates some decisions

exploratory research useful when the research questions are vague or when there is little theory available to guide predictions

F

face validity *see* content validity

factor analysis a multivariate statistical technique that can summarize the information from a large number of measured variables into a smaller number of latent variables, or factors

factor loading the correlation between a factor and an individual variable

factor rotation a different, but mathematically equivalent, representation of the linear combination that makes up a factor

factor scores composite scores that calculate a value for each factor for each respondent based upon factor analysis results

factor a mathematical, linear combination of the original variables of the form $F_1=\lambda_1 X_1+ \lambda_2 X_2+ \ldots+ \lambda_p X_p+e_1$

factorial design an experimental design that controls the levels of two or more experimental treatments at the same time

field experiment experiment in which the manipulation of the causal variable takes place in a natural setting, such as a relevant business context, which emphasizes external validity

focus groups relatively informal discussions among eight to twelve respondents led by a moderator who keeps the group focused on a primary topic

follow-up test a statistical test to identify significance between three or more group means

forced choice a scale that does not have a mid-point that can be considered neutral or no opinion

F-ratio a statistic that assesses the statistical significance of the overall regression model; it is the ratio of the explained variance to the unexplained (residual) variance

frequency distribution a table of numbers that displays the responses associated with each value of a variable

front-end loading placing as much as possible of the most important content in the first few pages of the report

functional fixedness a term that describes the fact that once one learns an effective rule or action, increased familiarity with the process makes it difficult to see other ways of doing the same thing, even if they are simpler

funnel approach the design of a questionnaire so that general questions are placed at the beginning and more specific questions at the end

G

GPS global positioning satellite system

graphic ratings scale measures concepts on a continuum in the form of a line with anchors that are numbered or named

H

hierarchical clustering (break-down or divisive) a clustering approach that begins with the initial assumption that every observation belongs to one cluster and then proceeds by separating the "furthest clusters" to result in two, then three, four, and more clusters; the process continues until all observations represent a separate cluster

hierarchical clustering (build-up or agglomerative) a clustering approach that begins with the initial assumption that every observation represents a separate cluster and then proceeds by combining the two closest observations (objects) to make a single new cluster, continuing the process until all observations are members of one cluster

histogram a vertical bar chart constructed from the information in a frequency distribution

hit ratio the proportion of observations classified correctly by discriminant analysis

human resources review committee a group that performs a review of research using human participants with an emphasis on checking research procedures to make sure all participants are treated ethically

hypothesis an unproven supposition or proposition that tentatively explains certain facts or phenomena

I

importance-performance chart a two dimensional perceptual map in which perceived importance is plotted on a vertical axis and performance measures are plotted on a horizontal axis

independent samples two samples of data that are independent, such as males and females

in-house research research conducted by employees of the decision-making organization

interaction the combined effect of multiple variables

interdependence techniques statistical tools in which the variables are not divided into independent and dependent sets; only independent or dependent variables are analyzed by themselves

interrogatories a creative decision-making tool that helps ensure a problem is not examined with tunnel vision; it involves describing the situation with multiple questions beginning with the words *what, where, why, when, who,* and *how*

interval scale a scale that uses numbers to rate objects or events so that the distances between the numbers are equal and the zero point is arbitrary (not fixed); it can be used to measure the magnitude of the differences between points on a scale

interview the researcher speaks directly to the respondent and asks questions and records answers

interviewer-assisted questionnaire a questionnaire in which an interviewer assists the respondent in answering the questions, typically by reading them and recording the answer

intranet an Internet-like network that links computers internally within an organization

introduction the portion of the report that describes the purpose of the report and lists the research questions and hypotheses

intuition-based decisions decisions that lack a readily apparent logical basis

issues things that, if altered, will close the gap between the actual and desired states

J

judgment sampling sometimes referred to as a purposive sample; it involves selecting elements in the sample for a specific purpose

K

KISS stands for "keep it short and simple"

kurtosis a measure of a distribution's peakedness or flatness

L

laboratory experiments the manipulation of the causal variable, which takes place in an artificial setting to emphasize internal validity

latent root criterion the number of factors extracted (computed) during a factor analysis is equal to the number of principal components with a latent root (eigenvalue) equal to or greater than 1.0

law-like generalizations expectations of what will happen under specified circumstances that allow predictions of reality

leading question a question that implies that a particular answer is correct or leads a respondent to choose a particular answer

least common denominator principle preparing written and oral communication designed for the level of the least-sophisticated potential user in the audience

least squares a mathematical technique that makes sure the straight line computed in a regression model is the one that will best represent the relationship between the independent and dependent variables

Likert scale a measure of attitudes or opinions using a single scale to assess how strongly individuals agree or disagree with a particular statement; other adjectives, such as favorable or unfavorable or positive or negative, can also be used with a Likert scale

linear relationship a straight line association between two or more variables

logistic regression logistic regression is a special type of regression that can have a nonmetric dependent variable

longitudinal studies a descriptive study providing a description of a sample over time using time series data, meaning the same sampling unit is measured multiple times

M

mail survey a survey delivered to a respondent via regular mail, fax, or overnight delivery

manipulation intentionally altering a causal (experimental) variable over different levels or conditions

manipulation check a follow-up question designed to assess whether a respondent understood the treatment in an experiment; for example, if a respondent is shown two advertisements, one of which is designed to be humorous and the other non-humorous, then the respondent is asked to indicate whether they interpreted the advertisements properly; i.e., the humorous ad was viewed as humorous and the non-humorous ad was viewed as non-humorous.

MANOVA similar to ANOVA, but it can examine group differences across two or more metric dependent variables at the same time

mean the arithmetic average of a set of values; one of the most commonly used measures of central tendency

measurement involves assigning numbers to a variable according to certain rules

median a measure of central tendency, it is the value that is in the middle of the distribution

metric scale interval and ratio scales are metric and considered quantitative

MIS Management (or Marketing) Information System, which generates reports using information fed into the computer through automatic or manual mechanisms

missing data survey data that is missing, typically because of data collection or data entry problems

mode the measure of central tendency that identifies the value that occurs most often in the sample distribution

monitoring assessing the extent to which a decision is accomplishing its stated objective

multicollinearity the correlation between the independent variables

multi-item scale a scale that consists of a number of closely related individual statements whose responses are combined into a composite score or summated rating used to measure a concept

multiple regression type of regression that has a single metric dependent variable and several metric independent variables

multi-stage cluster sampling a form of cluster sampling where primary clusters are first randomly selected, and then from the primary clusters a second set of clusters is randomly selected from which to collect data

N

networking systems of computers that are connected to each other through various servers

nominal scale the use of numbers as labels to identify and classify individuals, objects, or events on a scale

non-forced choice a scale that has a mid-point that can be considered neutral or no opinion

non-hierarchical clustering a clustering approach in which observations within a pre-specified distance from the cluster seeds are considered to be in a particular cluster; the observations can then be reassigned to different clusters in an effort to improve group distinctiveness

nonlinear relationship often referred to as curvilinear, it is best described by a curve instead of a straight line

nonmetric scales nominal and ordinal scales are non-metric and considered qualitative, sometimes referred to as comparative scales

nonparametric tests statistical tests used when the researcher cannot assume a normal distribution

non-probability sampling the inclusion or exclusion of elements in a sample is left to the judgment of the researcher; not every element in the population has a chance of being selected into the sample and the error associated with the sample is not known

normal distribution a symmetrical, bell-shaped curve that encloses almost all of the values of a variable

normative decision rule explains what someone should do when faced with a situation described by a theory

null hypothesis a statement that postulates no differences or relationships among variables

numerical scale a numerical scale uses numbers as response options instead of verbal descriptions

O

objective data measures are independent of any single person's opinion

oblique rotation a factor rotation technique that allows factors to be correlated with each other

observation a method of collecting data involving systematic observing and recording of behavior and activities of people, events, or objects

off-the-shelf data readily available information (including research results) compiled and sold by companies

one-shot research project research designed to address a single issue at a specific point in time

one-way ANOVA involves a single non-metric independent variable and a single metric dependent variable

ongoing research research that is performed constantly and not directed toward any specific issue

open-ended question places no constraints on respondents, who are free to answer in their own words

opportunity a situation (a particular point in time and/or space) that makes a potentially advantageous outcome possible through good decision making

ordinal scale the placement of objects or individuals in a predetermined category on a scale that is rank ordered by some criterion

organizational learning the internalization of both external and internal information to be used as an input for decision making

organizational memory the total data resulting from the organizational learning process

orthogonal rotation a factor rotation technique that produces factors that are independent of each other (the correlation between any two factors is zero)

outlier a data point for a respondent that is distinctly different from the values of the other respondents

outside research research conducted by someone not employed by the decision-making organization

P

paired comparison scale a scale that asks respondents to compare two attributes (objects) and select the preferred one

panel a method of collecting data by using the same group of respondents over a period of time

parametric tests statistical tests used when the researcher can assume a normal distribution

parsimony the theory that a simpler solution is superior to a complex solution

Pearson correlation a correlational measure that assumes interval or ratio (metric) data, a linear relationship, and a normal distribution

percentage of variance criterion a criterion used to determine the number of factors to extract; when applied, the number of factors is based on the total amount of variance accounted for by the factor solution, usually a minimum of 60 percent.

perceptual mapping an approach that uses information from other statistical techniques to map customer perceptions of products, brands, companies, and so forth

personal interview an interview that involves direct face-to-face contact with a respondent

pie chart a circle showing pie slices representing the proportions of responses to a question

population parameters variables or measures that describe the population

population the total of all the elements that share some common set of characteristics; also referred to as a group of knowledgeable people; *see* universe

position bias a situation where one question is positioned before another one on a questionnaire and tends to influence the response to the later question; may also be referred to as a context effect

practical significance a relationship between two or more variables that is meaningful, not just statistically significant

predictive validity assesses the ability of a scale (construct) measured at one point in time to predict another criterion at a future point in time

pretest evaluating the likely accuracy and consistency of responses to a questionnaire using a small sample of respondents with characteristics similar to the target population

primary data information collected for the purpose of completing the current research project

probability sampling based on the premise that each element of the target population has a known, but not necessarily equal, probability of being selected in a sample; if done properly, probability sampling ensures that the sample is representative and the error associated with the sample is known

profiling the act of describing groups identified by cluster analysis based on differences in easily identifiable characteristics, such as demographics

projective data data that results from an interview in which responses to an ambiguous stimulus are used to infer respondent characteristics

proportionately stratified sampling each strata in the sample has a sample size that is proportionate to the size of that strata relative to the overall sample size

push polls short phone calls used to spread negative, and often false, information about a candidate or issue under the guise of a poll

Q

qualitative data descriptions of things that are made without assigning numbers directly

quantitative data measurements in which numbers are used directly to represent the properties of something

questionnaire administration the method used to administer a questionnaire to respondents, such as telephone, personal interview, mail, Internet, and so on

questionnaire design the process of designing a questionnaire (survey instrument) to collect data in a survey

questionnaire a predetermined set of questions designed to capture data from respondents

quota sampling similar to stratified random sampling, but the selection of the elements from the strata is done on a convenience basis

R

range the spread of the responses; the distance between the largest and the smallest values of a sample frequency distribution

rank order scale an ordinal scale that asks respondents to rank order a set of objects or characteristics in terms of preference, similarity, importance, or similar adjectives

ratio scale a scale that has a unique (fixed) zero point and not only measures the magnitude of the differences between points on the scale, but also the proportional differences

regression coefficient a numerical value for the independent variable(s) that tells us how much of the variance in the dependent variable is explained by a particular independent variable, also referred to as a regression weight

regression sum of squares the explained variance in the regression equation

related samples data from the same group that compares two related variables, such as comparing the average number of Cokes® consumed each day by a group of females with the average number of cups of coffee consumed each day by the same group of females

relationship presence assesses whether a systematic relationship exists between two or more variables

relationship a situation when variables have a consistent and systematic linkage between them

reliability a survey instrument is reliable if its repeated application results in consistent scores

replicable research when another researcher can produce the same results as reported in the original research using the identical procedures employed by the original researcher

representative sample a sample that mirrors the characteristics of the population, thereby minimizing the error associated with sampling

research a discerning pursuit of the truth

research methods portion of the research report that describes the research methods used in conducting the research

research proposal a written document that describes the reasons for a research study, lists the research questions, provides an overview of the study design and tools, a summary of the potential results, and a proposed time schedule and budget

research questions questions that state general propositions about the phenomena being studied

residual sum of squares the unexplained variance in the regression equation

residual the unexplained or error variance in a regression model

respondents human participants in business research

rotated factor matrix the matrix of numbers in a factor analysis showing the rotated factor loadings

S

sample frame a comprehensive list of the elements from which the sample is drawn

sample statistics variables or measures computed from a sample

sample a small subset of the population that is used to derive conclusions about the characteristics of the population

sampling unit the elements or objects available for selection during the sampling process

sampling the process of contacting and collecting information from the sample

scale a tool used by researchers to measure individuals, objects, or events on variables that relate to the research problem

scatter diagrams also referred to as scattergrams, they are visual plots of the values of two variables for all the observations in the sample

science what is known about some definable subject

scientific method the method researchers use to gain knowledge about things

screening question a type of question used to ensure that respondents included in a study are those that meet the predetermined criteria of the target population

secondary data information collected previously for some other research purpose

self-completion questionnaire a questionnaire completed by a respondent without a researcher present

semantic differential scale several individual scales combined; uses bipolar end points labeled with adjectives and the intermediate points are numbered or have blanks to check

semi-structured interview the researcher uses a sequence of questions but is free to exercise his or her own initiative in asking follow-up questions in response to an interviewee's answer to a question

simple random sampling a style of sampling in which each element of the target population has an equal probability of being selected

simple structure the term used to refer to factor analysis results in which each variable loads highly on only one factor; this represents what is referred to as a pure factor solution

skewness measures the departure from a symmetrical or balanced distribution

snowball sampling also called a referral sample, it involves initially selecting respondents using probability methods and then using the initial respondents to help identify the other respondents in the target population

sorting a scale that asks respondents to indicate their beliefs or opinions by arranging objects (items) on the basis of perceived similarity or some other attribute

Spearman's rank order correlation coefficient a correlational measure that is appropriate with nominal and ordinal data and does not make assumptions about the distribution

standard deviation an index that describes the spread or variability of the sample distribution values from the mean; it is the square root of the variance

standardized coefficients regression coefficients that are standardized, referred to as beta weights

Statistical Package for the Social Sciences (SPSS) basic SPSS is an easy-to-use statistical software package that provides point and click access to statistical procedures like those discussed in this text

statistical significance a relationship between two or more variables that is true and not due to random events or error

stem and leaf displays a diagnostic tool closely related to histograms that show actual data values that can be inspected directly

stepwise multiple regression each independent variable is considered for inclusion in the regression model and the order in which they are entered is based on the one that contributes the most toward predicting the dependent variable; only variables that contribute significantly are entered into the regression model

stratified sampling the target population is partitioned into relatively homogeneous subgroups that are distinct and non-overlapping, called strata

strength of association the magnitude or extent to which two or more variables are related

structured interview an interview in which the interviewer follows a predetermined sequence of asking questions that typically are open-ended

subject a respondent who participates in an experiment

subjective data a measure that represents a person's (respondent or researcher) opinion

summated ratings scale a scale that measures attitudes and opinions of respondents and is obtained by summing the ratings of several individual Likert scales

summated scores the scores of several individual items (questions) are added together and the mean is calculated; they can be used instead of factor scores to represent several items combined

survey a procedure used to collect primary data from individuals

symptoms signals that some change may be needed to avoid further problems or to take advantage of some opportunity

systematic sampling a random sampling approach that involves randomly selecting an initial starting point and thereafter selecting every nth element in the sampling frame

T

table of contents lists the heading and subheadings of the research report by page number

target population the complete group of objects or elements relevant to the research project; they are relevant because they have the information the research project is designed to collect

telephone interview an interview that is completed over the phone, rather than face-to-face

test market an experiment that evaluates a new product or promotional campaign under real market conditions

theory a set of systematically related statements, including some law-like generalizations that can be tested empirically

theory-based decisions decisions based on theoretical rationale

title page the page listing the title of the research project, the principal decision maker the report is being prepared for, the date and names of contact individuals for the primary investigators

tolerance a measure of the multicollinearity among the independent variables; small values (<.10) indicate multicollinearity is a problem; the opposite of VIF

total sum of squares the total variance in a regression model

translational equivalence text can be translated from one language to another, then back to the original language with no distortion in meaning

t-test assesses whether the observed differences between two sample means are significant

two-way ANOVA involves two or more non-metric independent variables and a single metric dependent variable; also called a factorial design

Type I error occurs when the sample results lead to rejection of the null hypothesis when it is true

Type II error occurs when the sample results lead to not reject the null hypothesis when it is false

U

unbalanced scale a scale in which the number of favorable and unfa-

vorable response categories is not equal

unique variance the portion of the total variance in a variable that is specific or unique to that variable

univariate test statistical test of significance using one variable

universe a group of knowledgeable people; *see* population

unstandardized coefficients regression coefficients (weights) that are not standardized

unstructured interview an interview that is conducted without the use of an interview sequence; the researcher elicits information through a free and open discussion of the topic of interest

V

validity the extent to which a construct (scale) measures what it is supposed to measure

variance a measure of the variation or dispersion of the data

VIF stands for the variance inflation factor and it measures multicollinearity among the independent variables; the maximum acceptable VIF is 5.0 and any higher number indicates multicollinearity is a problem; the opposite of tolerance

W

Wilk's lambda (λ) the statistic that evaluates whether the discriminant function has identified a statistical difference between two or more groups

within-subjects design an experimental design in which each subject receives multiple combinations of experimental treatments

Index

NOTE: Page numbers in *italics* refer to **Exhibit** and **Research in Action** insets.

A

absolute zero points, 158
abstracts, 332–33
acceptable error, 218–19
accuracy. *see* validity
Acme Rent-A-Car, 17
advantageousness (of ideas), 95
advertising
    campaigns, 97, *137*
    content analysis, 128
    measuring effect of, *178,* 287,
      290–92
    sales, effect on, 51–52, 55, 290–93
    sales predictions from, 296–97,
      311
    targeting identified groups, 370
Agglomeration Schedule tables, *377*
AID (Automatic Interaction
  Detection), 15
aided questions, 198–99
alpha reliability coefficients, 172
alternative forms reliability, 170–71
alternative hypotheses, 253, 254–55,
  260–61, 266, 293, 299
American Business Information, *75,*
  134
analytical phase (business research
  process), 50–51, 76
analytical techniques. *see* cluster
  analysis; factor analysis
ANOVA (Analysis of Variance). *see
  also* factor analysis; statistical techniques
    assumptions, 270
    cluster analysis, 376–78, 397–98

customer assessment project,
  268–75
factor scores, 403
F-test, 269, 273, 294, *301*
hypothesis testing, 262, 268–75
metric scales, 256, 259
null hypotheses, 268–70, 272–75
one-way, 268–71, *379*
overview, 268–72, 276–77, 290–91
perception concept, *318*
regression analysis, 294–95, *302,*
  304–5, 307–8, 316–19
Scheffé test, 270–72
in SPSS, 269–70, *274, 377*
statistical significance, 270
tables, 269, 294–95, 304–5, 307–8,
  316–18, 376–78
two-way, 272–75
Appendices, 332, 334, 353. *see also*
  research proposals and reports
applied business research, 6–7, 51,
  127, 329–32. *see also* basic business
  research
arbitrary zero points, 156
assessments
    of concepts, 169–76
    demand effect, 111–12
    proposal outlining, *29–30*
    reliability, 169–74
    SWOT, 26
    validity, 169–70, 174–76
associative analysis, 280. *see also* correlation analysis; regression analysis
assumptions. *see also* hypotheses
    for ANOVA follow-up tests, 270
    in discriminant analysis, 384
    for estimating the mean, 219
    in factor analysis, 361, 362
    in the FICO credit measures, *359*

hypotheses as, 253
incorrect, 87–88, 98–99
of linear relationship as efficient,
  281
for parametric and nonparametric procedures, 259
for Pearson correlation coefficients, 284
for regression analysis, 292, 296,
  315, 324
for samples, 61
for self-completed questionnaires,
  132
testing, 319–22
in t-tests, 267
ATOCS (criteria evaluation), 95–96
attitudes/opinions of respondents,
  129, 148–49, 156, 158–66, 189
audience considerations, 326–27,
  334–35
Automatic Interaction Detection
  (AID), 15
average summated scores, *232*

B

balanced scales, 167–68. *see also*
  scales
bar charts, 43, *84,* 236–37, 288, *333,*
  346–47
Baruch College-Harris poll, *75*
basic business research. *see also*
  research proposals and reports
    designs, 57–65, 71–76, 77
    experiments, 65–71
    overview, 6–7
    process, 50–51, 76–77
    sampling, 208–20
behavioral learning theory, 52
beta coefficients, 296, 297–98,
  300–02, 305, 307, 312, 317, 348